To Shape a New World

TO SHAPE
A NEW WORLD

Essays on the Political Philosophy of

MARTIN LUTHER KING, JR.

EDITED BY TOMMIE SHELBY AND BRANDON M. TERRY

THE BELKNAP PRESS OF HARVARD UNIVERSITY PRESS

Cambridge, Massachusetts

London, England

2018

First printing

Library of Congress Cataloging-in-Publication Data

Names: Shelby, Tommie, 1967– editor. | Terry, Brandon M., editor.
Title: To shape a new world : essays on the political philosophy of
    Martin Luther King, Jr./edited by Tommie Shelby and
    Brandon M. Terry.
Description: Cambridge, Massachusetts : The Belknap Press of
    Harvard University Press, 2018. | Includes bibliographical
    references and index.
Identifiers: LCCN 2017034194 | ISBN 9780674980754 (alk. paper)
Subjects: LCSH: King, Martin Luther, Jr., 1929–1968—
    Knowledge—Political science. | King, Martin Luther, Jr.,
    1929–1968—Influence. | Political science—United States—
    Philosophy. | Racism—United States—Philosophy.
Classification: LCC E185.97.K5 T6 2018 | DDC 323.092—dc23
    LC record available at https://lccn.loc.gov/2017034194

For Ayana, Christopher, and Ella

But we do not have much time. The revolutionary spirit is already world-wide. If the anger of the peoples of the world at the injustice of things is to be channeled into a revolution of love and creativity, we must begin now to work, urgently, with all the peoples, to shape a new world.

—MARTIN LUTHER KING, JR., *The Trumpet of Conscience*

Contents

Introduction
Martin Luther King, Jr., and Political Philosophy
BRANDON M. TERRY AND TOMMIE SHELBY   I

PART I *Traditions*

1. The Du Bois–Washington Debate and the
   Idea of Dignity
   ROBERT GOODING-WILLIAMS   19

2. Moral Perfectionism
   PAUL C. TAYLOR   35

3. The Roots of Civil Disobedience in
   Republicanism and Slavery
   BERNARD R. BOXILL   58

4. Showdown for Nonviolence: The Theory and
   Practice of Nonviolent Politics
   KARUNA MANTENA   78

PART II *Ideals*

5. From Anger to Love: Self-Purification and
   Political Resistance
   MARTHA C. NUSSBAUM   105

6. The Prophetic Tension between Race
   Consciousness and the Ideal of Color-Blindness
   RONALD R. SUNDSTROM   127

7. Integration, Freedom, and the Affirmation of Life
   DANIELLE ALLEN   146

8. A Vindication of Voting Rights
   DERRICK DARBY   161

PART III *Justice*

9. Prisons of the Forgotten: Ghettos and
   Economic Injustice
   TOMMIE SHELBY   187

10. Gender Trouble: Manhood, Inclusion, and Justice
    SHATEMA THREADCRAFT AND BRANDON M. TERRY   205

11. Living "in the Red": Time, Debt, and Justice
    LAWRIE BALFOUR   236

12. The Costs of Violence: Militarism,
    Geopolitics, and Accountability
    LIONEL K. McPHERSON   253

PART IV *Conscience*

13. The Path of Conscientious Citizenship
    MICHELE MOODY-ADAMS   269

14. Requiem for a Dream: The Problem-Space
    of Black Power
    BRANDON M. TERRY   290

15. Hope and Despair: Past and Present
    CORNEL WEST   325

   Afterword
   Dignity as a Weapon of Love
   JONATHAN L. WALTON   339

   NOTES   351
   ACKNOWLEDGMENTS   419
   CONTRIBUTORS   421
   INDEX   425

To Shape a New World

Introduction

Martin Luther King, Jr., and Political Philosophy

BRANDON M. TERRY AND TOMMIE SHELBY

The fiftieth anniversary of the assassination of Martin Luther King, Jr., on April 4, 1968, will undoubtedly occasion many observances of his extraordinary life and enduring political legacy. This response is only befitting of King's profound sacrifices, as well as the sacrifices of those who traveled alongside him on what James Baldwin presciently and empathetically called his "dangerous road."[1] But even as we honor King's memory, it is imperative that we consider what his thought still has to teach us about how to build a more just and peaceful world and, more generally, about political morality, judgment, and practice.

Any attempt to interpret and critically engage King's political thought, however, confronts a paradox. On one hand, there is the inescapable fact that King may be the most globally celebrated political figure, as well as part of the most renowned social movement, to have emerged in the United States in the twentieth century.[2] In 1983, after occasionally rancorous debate, but only fifteen years after the civil rights leader's death, President Ronald Reagan signed into law a federal holiday commemorating King's birthday.[3] Twenty years later, at least 730 U.S. cities were home to a street bearing his name.[4] Perhaps the greatest testament to America's reverence for King is the monument to him that stands amid the presidential statues, war memorials, and national museums on Washington, DC's National Mall. There, near where King delivered "I Have a Dream"—arguably the most famous speech in American history—a sculpture dedicated to King's memory depicts him emerging from a massive "stone of hope" meant to evoke one of the most famous lines from that address: "With this faith, we will be able to hew out of the mountain of despair a stone of hope."[5]

But despite King's having been memorialized so widely and quoted so frequently, serious study and criticism of his writings, speeches, and sermons remain remarkably marginal and underdeveloped within philosophy, political theory, and the history of political thought—even in those subfields where one might expect his contributions to be essential reading. The latest edition of Michael Cummings's influential collection *American Political Thought* (2015) includes only "Letter from Birmingham Jail," giving King roughly the same amount of space as Orestes Brownson and Pat Buchanan. The *Oxford Handbook of Political Philosophy* (2012), meanwhile, mentions King only once, in a brief reference to his "dream," and the *Oxford Handbook of Political Theory* (2006) has no mention of him whatsoever.[6] In short, philosophers, historians of political thought, and political theorists (whom collectively we henceforth designate as "political philosophers") neglect King's well-considered and wide-ranging treatments of many important philosophical and political issues, including labor and welfare rights, economic inequality, poverty, love, just war theory, virtue ethics, political theology, violence, imperialism, nationalism, reparations, and social justice—not to mention his more familiar writings on citizenship, racial equality, voting rights, civil disobedience, and nonviolence.[7]

These dual phenomena of ritual celebration and intellectual marginalization are, we believe, connected, and their entanglement presents both an immediate obstacle and a significant risk to any scholarly venture that aims to examine King's political and philosophical arguments with rigor, clarity, and intellectual integrity. Such efforts must avoid crashing upon the shoals of the dominant narrative of the civil rights era, which portrays the movement only as a moment of intensive activism, legal struggle, and moral suasion focused on extending the existing rights and opportunities promised in America's founding documents to those African Americans living under the shadow of Jim Crow in the South.

This master narrative of the civil rights movement, with its heroic cast of characters, narrow geographic focus, and short timeframe (from 1954 to 1968), draws heavily on the formal qualities and figurative elements of romantic historical narratives.[8] In calling certain histories "romantic," we mean to indicate that their sense of what matters, their contentions about meaning and significance, and the world they purport to describe reveal thematic preoccupations similar to those of romance in literature. Although these elements of historical writing and discourse are often treated as "merely" stylistic, sustained attention to these qualities can help to bring to light the judgments about truth, ethics, and politics that subtly inform most renderings of the past and the lessons we are meant to draw from them. If, as Martha Nussbaum has argued, "style itself makes its claims," then we may see these "stylistic" questions of narrative form and genre as expressing "a sense of life and of value, a sense of what matters and what does not."[9]

In the domain of the civil rights movement, romantic narratives tend to organize the timeframe, geographic focus, and leading characters of civil rights history around the creation and culmination of presumed "national unity" from "racial division," as well as the story of "triumph" or "transcendence" over the evils of racial oppression. Consequently, they rely heavily on themes like a politically unified and heroic black community forged from disarray, a redeemed American citizenry overcoming its long racial divide to forge a more perfect American union, or progressive histories that mark discontinuities between racial orders in American history (for example, the break between the Jim Crow regime and the post–civil rights era) as sharp, transcendent, and culminating victories.[10] Invoking this sort of narrative, Cass Sunstein (approvingly) argues that the lesson to be drawn from the movement, which unfolds within the conceptual boundaries of the nation-state, national identity, and American federalism as the domain of "unity," is that the political and philosophical substance of the civil rights movement is "conservative and backward looking."[11] In other words, the defining meaning of the civil rights movement is understood as derivative of long-standing American ideals, enshrined within the founding documents, and thus most crucially realized via the impassioned insistence that America simply live up to its creed.[12]

From this vantage, what *appears* most innovative and valuable about the civil rights movement and the intellectual contributions of leaders like King is essentially *tactical* and *rhetorical*. This way of thinking trains our imagination and judgment to focus on those moments where the words of civil rights activists seem to most forcefully rearticulate a deep political consensus at the heart of American public culture while dramatizing how racial exclusions violate these commitments.

Indeed, despite the current proliferation of interdisciplinary studies of African American political thought by a handful of scholars, many political philosophers cleave to an old idea advanced by the Swedish social scientist Gunnar Myrdal in his enormously influential tome *An American Dilemma: The Negro Problem and Modern Democracy* (1944). This is the deeply misguided notion that black politics and political thought can be reduced largely to *strategic* thinking concerning how best to advance black interests by exploiting convictions and sentiments widely held among whites, and the *rhetorical* identification of black interests with the most deeply cherished American ideals and practices.[13]

In light of this inheritance and its operative narratives, we should not be surprised to find that King is uniquely vulnerable to having the richness and complexity of his thought ignored. His contributions, once shunted into this truncated realm of rhetoric and protest meant to unmask racial hypocrisy, seem ill-fitted for the disciplinary preoccupations of most political philosophers. Even more perniciously, the triumphalist themes of "overcoming" and "progress" characteristic of popular civil rights history seem to preemptively mark King as a figure entombed within a Jim Crow social order that our post-segregation (if not "post-racial") era has largely transcended.[14] It may seem, on this view, that the discrete Jim Crow context that gave rise to King's political thought and praxis limits the usefulness of his ideas in the present. Indeed, among the growing segment of scholars and activists who are intensely opposed to triumphalist or romantic narratives, King's legacy has suffered collateral damage. Given the significance of King's image to such narratives, many critics reflexively associate King himself, rather than the usurpers of his memory, with the historical erasure of local grassroots democracy, the marginalization of more "radical" forms of black politics, and morally objectionable class, gender, and sexual politics.[15] For these critics, King is easier to imagine as an *obstacle* than as a resource for critical thinking about injustice in our moment.

To paraphrase Wittgenstein, one might say that when it comes to King, contemporary political theory, philosophy, and social criticism are held captive by a picture. It is difficult to get outside that picture because it lies deep within our cultural common sense. The very vocabularies, narratives, concepts, and paradigms we have developed, ostensibly to understand someone like King, inexorably repeat back to us an image that conceals the scope and subtlety of his thought. The part of King's thinking that remains visible gets compressed into arguments or claims that, for most political philosophers, are already considered convictions. Thus, reading Martin Luther King seriously appears incapable of repaying the effort. As scholars of black political thought and African American philosophy, we find these interpretive obstacles, perhaps particularly acute in this case, to be familiar. We hope to demonstrate the wrongheadedness of this larger orientation while also presenting a valuable collection of original theoretical work on a historically significant but deeply underappreciated thinker.

Though he held a doctorate in systematic theology and spent a number of years studying the history of Western political thought and philosophy,

King was not an academic political philosopher.[16] In addition to being an activist and a Christian minister, he was, however, a serious public philosopher, writing numerous books and essays and delivering countless speeches for a general audience. Given the professionalization of political philosophy, there is a strong bias against treating public philosophers, even eminent world-historical figures like King, as worthy of sustained study. Academic political philosophers write largely for each other and rely almost exclusively on a tiny canon of nonacademic political thinkers—for example, Thomas Hobbes, John Locke, Jean-Jacques Rousseau, Karl Marx, and John Stuart Mill. There is a high bar to acceptance into this elite company, and few black public philosophers (with the exception, perhaps, of W. E. B. Du Bois and Frantz Fanon) are widely regarded as having cleared it. Public philosophers are generally seen as, at best, popularizers of the original ideas of more significant thinkers. The study of King has suffered because of this academic insularity and prejudice against political thinkers who seek a nonspecialist readership. So here, through our collective effort to critically engage King's writings, we aim to help correct this unjustified neglect—while also, we hope, appealing to nonspecialist readers ourselves.[17]

It is also important to acknowledge that King is often read through one of the most enduring and entrenched features of black political culture: the celebration of, and reverence for, virtuosic oratory performance and oracular wisdom.[18] Rooted in African American religious and artistic practice, these performances fuse style and substance and embody them in a charismatic rhetorical persona, which seems, to many, to confer authority and standing. A masterful orator and inspiring leader, King had an uncanny ability to turn a memorable and lyrical phrase, to conjure a vivid metaphor, to stir his listeners' emotions, and to move people to action across a wide range of audiences. These talents understandably continue to play a significant role in securing and shaping King's legacy.

Although poetic and prophetic performance can indeed impart vital philosophical insight, interpreting a public philosopher like King *solely* through this lens risks distortion and invites misuse. For instance, one can be tempted to invoke a phrase, abstracted from its context, to amplify an idea or advance a cause that King actually opposed. One might treat a quoted remark as if it were a standalone aphorism when in fact King used it as a premise in a wider argument. Or because a particular rhetorical presentation of an idea resonates powerfully, one might feel viscerally that it is grasped without, however, appreciating its full implications or philosophical grounding. We contend that King is a systematic thinker and thus it is imperative to dig beneath his soaring oratory and quotable phrases to find the complex reasons he provides to support his practical conclusions.[19]

This vision, more broadly, calls for analyses of black political thought that attend carefully to the details and nuances of arguments advanced by black thinkers and the often subtle philosophical differences between like-minded figures. This work demands the charitable reconstruction of theoretical claims to clarify and make explicit key insights and fruitful avenues for further research and reflection. To carry it out, we must avoid, or at least provisionally hold at bay, certain familiar tendencies in scholarly accounts of black political thought: treating political ideas solely as rationalizations for class and group interests or as effects of sociohistorical factors; regarding these ideas as worthy of study only because of their perceived social function; thinking of them as mere social or psychological phenomena to be empirically explained; and—particularly pernicious in the case of King—reducing these ideas to *mere* tactical moves to advance some agenda in a changing context.

The approach to black political thought that we favor also rejects hagiography. Black thinkers are due far more respect and attention than they typically receive from political philosophers. They should not, however, be uncritically celebrated or treated as oracles of near-divine wisdom. Criticism and disagreement are often appropriate, and necessary. Indeed, honest critical engagement (which eschews harsh polemics and *ad hominem* dismissals) is a way of showing genuine respect for black thinkers.[20] This is a conception of political philosophy shared by our contributors and our subject. It embraces historical specificity and close reading, considers and defends substantive principles, values, and goals, and builds upon the very ideas and theories put forth by the thinkers we sharply criticize. In doing so, it contributes to the rediscovery of rich and often overlooked traditions of political thought.

With regard to King in particular, our methodological starting point is an insistence on the careful study of King's writings, speeches, and sermons, particularly his five major published works: *Stride toward Freedom* (1958), *Strength to Love* (1963), *Why We Can't Wait* (1964), *Where Do We Go from Here: Chaos or Community?* (1967), and *The Trumpet of Conscience* (1968). There are also the seven published volumes of Clayborne Carson's indispensable and painstakingly edited *Collected Papers of Martin Luther King, Jr.*; the more popularly available collections in the Beacon Press King Legacy Series, including *"All Labor Has Dignity"* and *"In a Single Garment of Destiny": A Global Vision of Justice;* the classic edited collection of essays and speeches gathered in James Washington's *A Testament of Hope;* and the recent collection edited by Cornel West titled *The Radical King.*[21]

Relying on these works as a shared foundation, each contributor to this volume wrote an original essay on some dimension of King's thought. Some had written on King before, some had not. All had written extensively on justice, the history of political thought, democracy, and political ethics, often with a particular focus on black thinkers or racial justice. The contributors (including the editors) represent different schools of thought or approaches to the history of political thought and political theorizing. Given this pluralism, it is no surprise that we don't always agree in our interpretations of King, or on what is most valuable and enduring in his thought, or even where King might have gotten things wrong. The volume we have produced together aims to offer a unique addition to attempts to wrestle with King's legacy and to demonstrate how his thought might meaningfully inform pressing questions of politics and public philosophy in the present. The hope, fostered by years of our own reading and teaching of King's writings, is that he will be shown—even in, or perhaps *especially* in, disagreement—to be an important and challenging thinker whose ideas remain relevant and have surprising implications for public political debate.

Of course there remain significant methodological and interpretive difficulties that our contributors had to confront, a set of challenges that cannot be overcome simply by a call to return to "the text itself." These problems spill over into questions of pedagogy and curriculum in political theory, philosophy, and intellectual history. Another aim of this book, therefore, is to deepen a burgeoning methodological and pedagogical conversation that is unfolding in these fields concerning two broad sets of questions.

The first concerns the implications of describing black political thought (or African American philosophy or Afro-modern political thought) as a specific *genre* of political philosophy. In Robert Gooding-Williams's provocative formulation, this tradition "is bound together by certain genre-defining thematic preoccupations—for example, the political and social organization of white supremacy, the nature and effects of racial ideology, and the possibilities of black emancipation."[22] The category of genre, in its inherent recognition of multiplicity, has the distinct benefit of disclosing the otherwise obscured questions regarding what kinds of texts and types of communication should count as political philosophy and why. It also proffers the possible answer that these philosophical discourses may look radically different from more canonical works in political philosophy, in line with divergent themes and the results of formal experimentation. One difficulty in the study and pedagogy of black political thought is that it often takes forms—autobiography, sermon, open letter, pamphlet, novel, musical performance—that students of, say, social contract theory might find unfamiliar as objects of serious study. Thus, one question that informs the approaches in the book (on which there is no consensus among contributors) is whether the idea of an Afro-modern or black political thought "genre" helps reveal what is distinctive about these texts and fosters reading strategies attuned to this distinctiveness, or whether this categorization artificially obscures Afro-modern political theory's inextricable links with better-known traditions (for example, Marxism, conservatism, and liberalism).[23]

The second set of methodological-pedagogical questions concerns the relationship of political philosophy to history and historical imagination. If the account of the difficulties in studying King's political thought sketched above holds true, then it suggests that the most powerful engagements with his work will reveal ways to remove from center stage the romantic narrative of the civil rights movement and compel audiences to rethink their conventional picture of that era. A central piece of this decentering is likely to stem from a dialogue with the most recent developments in civil rights historiography. A steady stream of notable historical work aims to reconfigure our understanding of this era, and makes available new vantage points for understanding King and the civil rights movement.[24] This literature, moreover, seems particularly well placed to inform and be informed by both the philosophy of history and close readings of King and his contemporaries' writings—especially those that reflect on labor, poverty, war, imperialism, political ethics, violence, and black nationalism. Many of our contributors are in dialogue with new currents in civil rights historiography and aim to demonstrate what this sort of interdisciplinary engagement might disclose.

We articulate these pedagogical questions in part because one of the aspirations we have for this collection is that it will serve as an impetus for scholars and educators. We hope, in conjunction with the fiftieth anniversary of King's death, to turn to his enduringly significant corpus and read and teach these works *as* political philosophy. This volume not only provides useful and clarifying reconstructions of King's arguments, but also puts King in critical dialogue with leading scholars who are carefully thinking through the merits and implications of his positions with an eye to their import in the present. In clearing these pathways, we and our contributors hope to do justice to King's efforts to, as Vincent Harding put it, go beyond "telling the powerful stories of the experiences he shared almost daily with the magnificent band of women, men, and children who worked in the black-led Southern freedom movement," to insist on "constantly raising and reflecting on the basic questions" in his writing.[25]

In this spirit, the volume begins with a section entitled "Traditions," where contributors resituate King amid intellectual influences and intergenerational conversations that often go overlooked in studies of King. Because most of the existing scholarship on King, influenced by the important work by scholars of religion, covers his interest in prophetic African American Christianity, Social Gospel liberalism, and Christian personalism, we emphasize instead other important traditions. Approaching King's work from the angle of political philosophy, these contributors track elements of King's thought back to the Afro-modern tradition, perfectionism, republicanism, and other theorists and practitioners of nonviolence, such as Gandhi.

In Chapter 1, Robert Gooding-Williams probes King's political thought during what the leader of the Montgomery bus boycott described as the "first" phase of the civil rights revolution. Focusing on *Stride toward Freedom* and *Why We Can't Wait,* Gooding-Williams considers King's interpretation of the civil rights revolution from the perspective of the debate between W. E. B. Du Bois and Booker T. Washington, which arguably was the most influential intellectual exchange in the history of twentieth-century African American political philosophy. In particular, Gooding-Williams introduces the important and recurrent theme of *dignity,* in light of both King's critical engagement with Du Bois and Washington and King's own narration of the meaning and history of civil rights struggle.

In Chapter 2, Paul Taylor argues that one way to engage fruitfully with King's political thought is to situate him within the perfectionist tradition, which includes figures like Ralph Waldo Emerson and Stanley Cavell. Taylor's reading foregrounds the ethical depth of King's commitment to critical self-reflection and self-improvement, and highlights the philosophical depth of King's persistent sounding of tragic themes. Taylor argues that although we think of King as a "dreamer," his dream was always shadowed by thoughts of suffering, despair, death, and failure. Moreover, Taylor argues, King's spiritual and political hopes were always informed by the conviction that individuals and societies have to grow and change, in radical and perhaps revolutionary ways, in order to achieve justice.

Chapter 3, by Bernard Boxill, is resonant with Taylor's concern about the possibility of peoples and societies to enact these sorts of changes. Boxill, who has long been a model of the tradition of critical inquiry that we hope this volume helps promote, presented an important critique of King's theory of civil disobedience, with reference to theorists like John Rawls and Ronald Dworkin, in his classic work of African American philosophy, *Blacks and Social Justice*.[26] Boxill returns to that theme in Chapter 3, from a different point of departure: the long tradition of republican political thought that articulates its "nondomination" conception of freedom—the idea that each should obey only himself or herself—against the exemplary unfreedom of slavery. With republicanism undergoing a broad revival in political theory, Boxill asks us to consider King's defense of civil disobedience in this light, and reminds us yet again of the indispensability of African American political thought, including the reflection of black slaves, as an important touchstone for these debates, haunted as they are by the invocation and imagination of chattel slavery and its afterlives.

In Chapter 4, Karuna Mantena considers King's place in the theoretical and practical traditions of nonviolence—which, she reminds us, are more tightly linked conceptually than most political theorists are prepared to acknowledge. Mantena tracks King's evolution, underscoring how King was introduced to nonviolent political and ethical thought, and Gandhi in particular, through the efforts of a small coterie of African Americans in the mid-twentieth century, including activists in the orbit of the pacifist and civil rights activist group the Fellowship of Reconciliation (FOR), and black college theologians. Over time, Mantena argues, King was transformed from an eager student into a leading theorist, spokesperson, and practitioner of nonviolence, developing significant and enduring insights about nonviolent protest politics in democratic societies. Placing King in conversation with Gandhi, Mantena's reading draws out the "realist" and democratic elements in King's political thought, while offering a subtle reconstruction and sympathetic defense of his controversial insistence on discipline and voluntary suffering.

Several political ideals are closely associated with King—nonviolent resistance, an ethic of love, color-blindness, integration, dignity, and the unfettered right to vote. Part II features scholars explaining and defending some of these ideals as distilled from King's political philosophy. Yet they take their interpretations of King's conceptions of these ideals in surprising and illuminating directions and, importantly, show their relevance to our present. They also help us to understand his political philosophy as a coherent system of thought by connecting these more familiar ideals to King's less well-known values and political convictions.

In Chapter 5, Martha Nussbaum tackles the question of ideal emotional states for political action. King maintained that resistance to injustice should follow a practice of "self-purification," whereby one cultivates the necessary dispositions for effective and virtuous action and works oneself free of emotional states that are political liabilities. Nussbaum argues that, for King, anger is an emotion that must be controlled and perhaps extinguished in the process of self-purification because it is conceptually and practically linked to retribution, which is an unjustified response to injustice and wrongdoing. Refusing anger is an important component of a love ethic, which King recommends to those participating in struggles for social justice. A commitment to non-anger is also essential for nonviolent resistance. Instead of being a sign of weakness, passivity, or servility, refusing to give in to anger is a sign of moral strength, courage, and dignity.

It is well established that King did not advocate color-blind strategies to achieve civil rights goals. Nor did he propose color-blind policies to halt racial discrimination or to rectify the historical effects of racial domination. In Chapter 6, Ronald Sundstrom argues that King did, however, offer a vision of a just society that parallels an ideal of color-blindness. Sundstrom offers two reasons King did not support a color-blind practical political strategy; one reason is moral-psychological and the other is conceptual. Both reasons reveal the influence of Reinhold Niebuhr's Christian Realism on King's political thought. Drawing attention to these ideas sheds light on the structure of King's prophetic vision of a just society, which can, with caution, be seen as color-blind. Sundstrom outlines some implications of this analysis for thinking about character, embodiment, and pessimism.

King is widely recognized as one of the great defenders of racial integration. In Chapter 7, Danielle Allen takes up this commitment to integration through a close reading of King's essay "The Ethical Demands for Integration." She argues that King's defense of integration shows him to be an important innovator in the development of the republican conception of freedom as nondomination. On her account, King helps us to better understand the relationship between democracy and community and highlights the limits of the liberal conception of freedom as noninterference. Integration, she argues, is not mere desegregation through law but a matter of voluntarily and consciously sharing decision-making power. It is a way of life: a collective, inclusive, nonviolent, and creative endeavor on the part of citizens to realize political friendship, what King called "the Beloved Community."

One of the aims of the civil rights movement was to firmly establish equal voting rights for all citizens, a struggle that culminated in the confrontation at the Edmund Pettus Bridge in Selma, Alabama, and, ultimately, in the Voting Rights Act, signed into law in 1965. Derrick Darby, in Chapter 8, takes up King's defense of the right to vote as grounded in the value of dignity and explains the essential role of the franchise in securing legitimacy for a system of legal rights and duties. He finds that, for King, dignity has at least two related forms—conduct in accordance with certain public norms, and a capacity that gives each person intrinsic moral worth. On one reading, the denial of the right to vote is a failure to properly recognize the intrinsic moral worth of those who are denied the vote. But black Americans, acting collectively in a dignified manner, can call forth the recognition of the dignity that they are due. Darby argues that dignity (particularly in relation to voting rights) is best understood, not as justifying the right to vote, but as a status that a legal order can confer by granting the right to vote. Relying on this idea, he sheds new light on the moral significance of voter suppression tactics and efforts to resist them.

In Part III we consider in greater depth King's conception of justice. Here attention is given not only to race, poverty, gender, and war but also to history. The black freedom struggle, King maintained, must look backward and forward, and with determination, as it strives to realize justice. King, paraphrasing the Massachusetts abolitionist Theodore Parker, often claimed that "the arc of the moral universe is long, but it bends toward justice."[27] But what, exactly, does justice require? And whose responsibility is it to ensure that justice becomes a reality?

King believed that racial injustice and economic injustice have always been linked in America. In Chapter 9, Tommie Shelby takes up the race/class nexus by considering King's analysis of ghetto poverty. Like Jim Crow segregation, ghetto conditions are a threat to dignity. But they are also incompatible with economic fairness and nonexploitative capital-labor relations. Shelby discusses King's practical proposals for ending poverty in the United States and considers four principles of economic justice (each found in King's writings) that might justify these recommended remedies. He also asks what kind of egalitarian King was, and whether, as some commentators contend, he is best described as a socialist.

A regular refrain in King's later writings is that the three great modern evils are racism, poverty, and war. Patriarchy and sexism did not make the list. In Chapter 10, Shatema Threadcraft and Brandon M. Terry cast a critical eye on King's conception of manhood and the family and try to "think with King against King" to see how he might meet the challenge of incorporating gender justice. They offer criticism of many of King's prevailing ideas of masculinity, political agency, and economic justice, while working to reconstruct and restate those egalitarian or productively critical features of his thought. In particular, they focus on his critique of Black Power masculinity, his inclusive defense of civil disobedience, and his late turn to basic minimum income and activism around welfare as themes that might sustain a broader feminist vision of gender justice and inclusive political struggle.

It is seldom noticed that King called for compensation and atonement for the wrongs of slavery. Lawrie Balfour, in Chapter 11, digs into King's reasoning behind these overlooked claims of reparative justice. She finds that King had a more capacious view of moral debt than many who demand reparations for black people. A proper response to present-day inequality requires, King maintained, not only a serious reckoning with cumulative disadvantages traceable to the injustices of the past, but also a more expansive conception of collective responsibility that includes ending poverty for blacks and whites alike. She also examines how King used the genre of autobiography to highlight the repeated failures to seize opportunities to create a more democratic society, explain the source of current injustices, and identify appropriate means of redress.

In Chapter 12, Lionel McPherson extends his incisive work on questions of the ethics of war and political violence, considering King's position on the relationship between domestic justice and global justice. In discussing King's controversial remarks on war and peace in Vietnam, McPherson not only offers a comprehensive account of King's varied and occasionally conflicting positions on war broadly, but provides a sustained, powerful reflection on King's arguments about warfare, public expenditures, and moral priorities. Putting these contentions to work in a critique of the Obama administration's foreign policy and military endeavors, McPherson models the ways in which King's thought can speak trenchantly to present concerns about justice while challenging easy invocations of his legacy by public officials.[28]

In Part IV we turn to issues of conscience. Michele Moody-Adams, in Chapter 13, tackles the difficult question of how citizens might go about achieving some of the ideals articulated in Part III. She argues that over the course of his career, King defended a comprehensive vision of "conscientious citizenship." By this she means a way of living that aspires to create a community shaped by all-encompassing and unconditional love for humanity, and guided by the moral conviction that justice is "indivisible." King's most important theoretical and practical projects, including his commitments to black emancipation, nonviolent direct action, antimilitarism, and hope for economic justice—are, according to Moody-Adams, all united by a powerful vision of what it is to be a conscientious citizen.

In Chapter 14, Brandon M. Terry also wrestles with the contentious and tumultuous period toward the end of King's life. One of the problems with the influence of romantic narratives of civil rights history is that the significance of Black Power is largely characterized by the scale of its *threat* to civic unity and hope for racial reconciliation. Unsurprisingly, King looms large in such renderings as the heroic foil to, or tragic casualty of, the *enfants terribles* who—following their martyred idol, Malcolm X—ushered in what Christopher Lasch described as both "the politics of resentment and reparation" among blacks and the "revolt against liberalism" among whites.[29] Terry returns to the debates of the Black Power era to try to break through this picture, and to underscore the idiosyncrasy and import of King's intellectual interventions in this period, across the wide range of philosophical and political disputes among black intellectuals and activists. Using the familiar "violence/nonviolence" binary as an entry point, Terry aims to reveal, not only the complexity of Black Power thought, but the insights and shortcomings of King's critique as he ranged across themes of self-defense, masculinity, cultural nationalism, ghetto poverty, riots, and revolution.

The final chapter is by Cornel West, who has long attributed the inspiration for his "life vocation"—his scholarship in religion and political philosophy, labors as a public philosopher, and efforts as an organizer and activist—to the "grand example of Martin Luther King, Jr."[30] In his chapter, which offers a passionate rendering of King's confrontation with nihilism, West explores the interstices between King's concession that he is "personally the victim of deferred dreams, of blasted hopes," and his insistent ethical and existential demand that "we must never lose infinite hope."[31] Placing King alongside Du Bois in a tradition of critical reflection on the fragility of sources of resistance and redemption in black political and expressive culture, West treats King's thought and example as a touchstone for political and ethical judgment, and as an inspiring distillation of "costly hope." In doing so, he revisits debates among black intellectuals during the presidency of Barack Obama to pose profoundly important questions about patriotism, racial solidarity, sacrifice, and tradition.

West's contribution serves further to stress that this volume is imbued with a sense of urgency, given the crises of our political and intellectual moment. Not even a decade after the first African American president of the United States installed a bust of King in the Oval Office, our landscape has been dominated by insurgent social movements and urban riots, racist invective and ethno-nationalism, intractable inequality and civic distrust, and a loss of faith in political institutions and, possibly, in democracy itself. In a way reminiscent and resonant with the later years of King's life, we find ourselves and our students more frequently asking difficult and unsettling questions about what political morality and justice demand of us. On campus, battles over how or whether to forge community, and over the stance we should take toward those persons and ideas with which we have profound disagreements, are waged with passion and often contempt. So, too, are those controversies regarding the role of philosophical reflection on and in politics, and the place of academics and intellectuals within the muck and mire of public debate. Our suggestion is that now, perhaps especially, with all that is at stake, a turn to King and his efforts in public philosophy can provide us with a more robust ethical vocabulary, a smarter set of judgments, a more expansive political imagination, and a richer set of traditions to help navigate our own "dangerous road."

PART I   *Traditions*

The Du Bois–Washington Debate and the Idea of Dignity

ROBERT GOODING-WILLIAMS

In this essay I take up the charge of explaining how Martin Luther King, Jr., positioned his early political thought and activism with regard to a salient episode within the history of Afro-modern political thought: the debate between W. E. B. Du Bois and Booker T. Washington.[1] I explore how King adapted Du Bois's authoritative framing of that debate, giving particular emphasis both to Du Bois's analysis of what he called "the Negro problem" and to his typology of alternative political strategies for responding to this problem.

Specifically, I examine *Stride toward Freedom: The Montgomery Story* (1958) and *Why We Can't Wait* (1963), the two major statements of King's political thought belonging to what he described as the "first phase" of the "civil rights revolution."[2] In 1967 King held that with "Selma and the Voting Rights Act" the decade marking the initial chapter of the struggle for civil rights came to end. Dignity was the preeminent moral good animating the struggle during this period, he argues, whereas achieving the aim of economic equality would prove central to the period that followed.[3] Here, then, I focus not only on King's general engagement with Du Bois and Washington during the opening phase of the movement, but particularly on his use of these figures to explore the demands, achievement, and authority of human dignity.

King's treatment of Du Bois and Washington repeats Du Bois's framing of the debate—but with significant differences. Contrary to Du Bois, for example, King favorably invokes Washington to make the case *against* a politics that would "surrender" self-respect. And while King later takes

Washington to task for the "apparent resignation" of his philosophy, he inventively interprets that philosophy in terms of the temporality of human agency. In a related vein, King criticizes Du Bois for privileging the agency of the few at the expense of the many. To appreciate King in the perspective of Du Bois and Washington is in part, then, to appreciate his disagreements with these thinkers. For, like Du Bois himself—indeed, like all genuinely notable political theorists—King distinguishes himself as a moral and political thinker through his innovative appropriations of the intellectual legacies he inherits.

Du Bois on the Du Bois–Washington Debate

In chapter 3 of *The Souls of Black Folk* (1903), entitled "Of Mr. Booker T. Washington and Others," Du Bois elaborates his extraordinarily influential account of his turn-of-the-century debate with Booker T. Washington.[4] Du Bois's disagreement with Washington was a disagreement about the political strategies blacks should adopt to resist Jim Crow, the white supremacist regime that took hold of the southern United States between 1890 and 1910. Du Bois's framing of his debate with Washington had two components: his social theory of the Negro problem and his typology of the alternative political strategies that had historically shaped black political struggle.

Du Bois's Social Theory of the Negro Problem

For the early Du Bois, the Negro problem is, in essence, the problem of integrating the Negro into the mainstream of American society. The exclusion of the Negro from the mainstream is a function of two factors, one "external" and one "internal" to Negro life. The primary external factor is the injustice that is racial prejudice; the primary internal factor is the cultural deficiency of the Negro masses—their tendency to fall short of the standards of American civilization, a failing that Du Bois occasionally describes as cultural "backwardness." (Du Bois explains the masses' cultural deficiency in historical, not racialist, terms, beginning with slavery.) In *Souls of Black Folk*, Du Bois argues that the internal and external causes that explain the Negro's exclusion from the American mainstream mutually reinforce each other.

For Du Bois, then, addressing the Negro problem requires a political strategy that combats both the internal and the external causes of the problem.[5]

Du Bois's Typology of Alternative Political Strategies

Du Bois identifies three alternative political strategies by means of which an oppressed and "imprisoned" group can struggle against its oppression.[6]

One strategy expresses an attitude defined by feelings of hate, bitterness, revolt, and revenge. In "Of Mr. Booker T. Washington and Others," Du Bois mentions the violent slave rebellions of "Toussaint the Savior . . . Gabriel, Vesey, and Turner" as paradigmatic examples of the sort of political strategy that expresses these feelings.[7] In "Of the Training of Black Men," Du Bois explicitly worries that these feelings may soon take hold of the South's "brooding" and potentially "turbulent" black proletariat. In "Of the Faith of the Fathers," he attributes these feelings to northern Negroes and the northern black church.[8]

Du Bois attributes a second strategy, expressing an attitude of acquiescent submission and adjustment, to Booker T. Washington. In "Of the Faith of the Fathers," he also attributes that attitude to southern Negroes and the southern black church. The attitude defining the third strategy— self-respecting self-assertion—is the one that Du Bois himself embraces.[9]

Du Bois dismisses the first strategy, which is predicated on a rejection of the goal of integrating the Negro into the mainstream of American society, arguing that the aim of the emigrationist politics to which it tends—to escape the white race—is all but impossible to fulfill, if only because white supremacy is more and more a global phenomenon.[10] He likewise rejects the second strategy, in essence because it restricts itself to attacking the internal causes of the Negro problem. Presupposing his social theory of the Negro problem, Du Bois holds that solving that problem requires, *in addition* to the sort of self-help Washington promoted, a militant, self-respecting self-assertion directed against racial prejudice and racial injustice.[11]

Stride toward Freedom: The Montgomery Story

In this section, I proceed in two steps. First, I show that, broadly speaking, King adopts both Du Bois's framing of political options and his social-theoretical analysis of the Negro problem in *Stride toward Freedom*. Second, I analyze King's analysis of the moral costs of acquiescent submission and hatred. In this connection, I examine King's appeal to Washington—in the form of a remark that he twice attributes to Washington—to defend the thesis that hatred of the oppressor injures the dignity of persons resisting oppression.

King and Du Bois

In the final chapter of *Stride toward Freedom*, King's reliance on Du Bois's framing of political options and his analysis of the Negro problem is clear (although in that chapter King does not mention Du Bois by name).

According to King, the oppressed deal with their oppression in three characteristic ways: through "acquiescence: the oppressed resign themselves to their doom"; through violence, which "thrives on hatred"; and through nonviolent resistance.[12]

Echoing Du Bois, King (1) disavows the political strategies of acquiescent submission and hatred-inspired violence and (2) endorses a third, middle path that is militant, self-respecting, and self-assertive, but that avoids the nonresistance of the acquiescent and the violent resistance of the hater.

Although the phrase "the Negro problem" never appears in *Stride toward Freedom*, King's conceptualization of his political program is quite similar to Du Bois's. Its aim is not simply to end legally mandated segregation, but to integrate the Negro into the mainstream of American life—or, in King's own words, to achieve racial "reconciliation" through "genuine intergroup and interpersonal living."[13]

For King, as for Du Bois, external and internal factors alike explain the separation of the races. External factors include "all forms of racial injustice, including state and local laws and practices." Internal factors include "lagging" personal standards, such as uncleanliness, low morals, and a tendency to spend too much on drink. Like Du Bois, King argues that these factors reinforce one another. Initially, racial injustice causes lagging standards, but lagging standards, in turn, buttress "the arguments of the segregationist."[14]

Thus, for King as for Du Bois, nonviolent politics must "work on two fronts. On the one hand, we must continue to resist the system of segregation which is the basic cause of our lagging standards; on the other hand, we must work constructively to improve the standards themselves."[15]

King, Dignity, and Self-Respect

As we have seen, Du Bois's criticism of the politics of acquiescent submission has a practical dimension, for it evaluates that politics on the basis of its prospects for solving the Negro problem. Du Bois's criticism also has a moral dimension, in that it censures Washington for encouraging his people "voluntarily" to "surrender" their "manly self-respect."[16]

Du Bois's criticisms of the hate-animated politics of revolt and revenge tend to be practical, and not at all moral. Again, if the aim of that politics is to escape the white race, then it cannot succeed, for white supremacy has become a global phenomenon. Emigrationist politics is a futile flight from the Negro problem, not a realistic attempt to solve it. In a different vein, Du Bois also argues that a hate-animated politics, expressing the bitterness of an oppressed but increasingly tempestuous Negro proletariat, would likely disrupt social growth and progress in the South—and, therefore, stall the solution of the Negro problem. Finally, Du Bois notes that the bitterness that is characteristic of such a politics has shaped the spiritual life of the northern Negro church, thus isolating and alienating the northern church from the spirit of the black folk and thereby undermining its authority and potential efficacy as a source of political leadership that could help to solve the Negro problem.[17]

In his telling of the Montgomery story, King presents both moral and practical criticism of the politics of acquiescent submission and the politics of hatred and violence. But the moral criticism is paramount.

As we shall see, a part of the *content* of that criticism echoes Du Bois. More importantly, however, King (often quoting himself) portrays his *performance* of that criticism—that is, his delivery of the speech by means of which he presents that criticism to a captive audience at the Holt Street Baptist Church—as a critical episode belonging to the plot of the unfolding "story" and "drama" (King uses both terms) that he narrates in *Stride toward Freedom*.[18]

King's depiction of his performance of a moral criticism of both acquiescent submission and hatred is critical to the argument of *Stride toward Freedom* as a whole, the point of which is to establish that the *meaning* of the Montgomery story (the "bus struggle") was black Americans' achievement of a *new dignity*.[19] King's portrait of his performance of moral criticism advances that argument because it identifies hindrances that had to be overcome in order for that meaning to be realized. Let me explain.

Narrative Sentences and King's Narrative Perspective

In *Narration and Knowledge,* the philosopher Arthur Danto invents a character he dubs "the Ideal Chronicler." Danto's Ideal Chronicler "knows whatever happens the moment it happens, even in other minds. He is also to have the gift of instantaneous transcription: everything that happens across the whole forward rim of the Past is set down by him, as it happens, the *way* it happens. The resultant running account I shall term the Ideal Chronicle (hereafter referred to as I.C.). Once *E* [an event] is safely in the past, its full description is in the I.C."[20] The Ideal Chronicler is an ideal witness. But there is a class of descriptions, comprised of "narrative sentences," under which no event can be witnessed, even by an ideal witness. These descriptions, Danto argues, "are necessarily and systematically excluded from the I.C."[21]

Occurring most typically in historical writing, narrative sentences "refer to two time-separated events and describe the earlier with reference to the latter."[22] "The assassination of Archduke Franz Ferdinand triggered a diplomatic crisis that led to the beginning of World War I" is a narrative sentence, for it describes the assassination of the archduke with reference to the ensuing diplomatic crisis it caused. "Aristarchus anticipated in 270 B.C. the theory which Copernicus published in A.D. 1543" is a narrative sentence, for it describes Aristarchus's accomplishment in terms of Copernicus's accomplishment hundreds of years later.[23] Neither sentence could appear in the I.C., because the Ideal Chronicler, while possessing a perfect knowledge of what transpires, when it transpires, is blind to the future. Thus, he/she is incapable of grasping the *significance* that past events acquire when a historian, or a biographer, considers them in the perspective of subsequent events to which he or she attaches some importance.

In *Stride toward Freedom,* King writes both as a historian and as a biographer—more exactly, as an autobiographer. For the purposes of my analysis, it is significant that he concludes the historical and autobiographical chapter in which he lays out his moral criticism of acquiescent submission and hatred alike—chapter 4, "The Day of Days, December 5"—with two narrative sentences:

> That night we were starting a movement that would gain national recognition; whose echoes would ring in the ears of people of every nation; a movement that would astound the oppressor, and bring new hope to the oppressed. That night was Montgomery's moment in history.[24]

Describing the events of the night of December 5, 1955, in retrospect, King interprets those events (King's speech and his audience's response to that speech) as the *beginning* of a movement (the Montgomery "bus struggle"—which "is now history," King tells us at the opening of *Stride toward Freedom*'s final chapter).[25] That is, he interprets them with reference to the movement they initiated, while interpreting that movement with reference to its impact on the world. In effect, King's phrasing suggests that he grasps the events of that night as events of remarkable historical *moment,* because he grasps them as actions that gave rise to a movement that, in its turn, astonished and brought hope to people everywhere. The world-historical significance of the movement and the import of the actions that started it come into view in retrospect, through the use of narrative sentences—for only in retrospect is it possible for King to gauge the meaning of the movement and to explain its impact on the world.

But what, exactly, did the movement mean? In essence, King's answer is that the movement meant exactly what he intended it to mean when he spoke on the night of December 5.

What King Meant and What the Movement Meant

In his narrative of the moments that transpired fewer than fifteen minutes before he delivered his speech at Holt Street Baptist Church, King expresses a dilemma: "How could I make a speech that would be militant enough to keep my people aroused to positive action and yet moderate enough to keep this fervor within controllable Christian bounds?" Here, explicitly, we see King seeking a middle path between acquiescence and the hatred and bitterness he associates with violence: "I knew that many of the Negro people were victims of bitterness that could easily rise to flood proportions. What could I say to keep them courageous and prepared for positive action and yet devoid of hate and resentment?"[26]

As King recounts it, his speech presents an argument against acquiescent submission; an argument against hatred and bitterness; and a closing statement that expresses his hope as to how future historians will interpret the meaning of the movement that he and his listeners "were starting" "that night."[27]

The Argument against Acquiescence. In recounting the speech itself, King gives an encapsulated version of the argument against acquiescence, the substance of which he sketches when he recounts his thoughts before the speech.

In the encapsulated version, King quotes himself as proclaiming that "we had no alternative but to protest. . . . For many years, we have shown amazing patience. . . . But we come here tonight to be saved from that patience that makes us patient with anything less than freedom and justice."[28]

In the more substantive, expanded version of the argument, King explicates the elements of his thinking that remain implicit in the parts of his speech that he quotes, and thus explains *why* the black citizens of Montgomery needed to be "saved" from their patience: "I would seek to arouse the group to action," he tells us he decided, "by insisting that their self-respect was at stake and that if they accepted such injustices without protesting, they would betray their own sense of dignity and the eternal edicts of God Himself."[29]

As I read King, his argument rests on the following premises: (1) Each and every human being enjoys a God-given dignity, or worth, that is expressive of her personality.[30] (2) Through the course of her ordinary, day-to-day life, each person's dignity finds expression through a pre-reflectively, inwardly felt "sense of dignity," a sort of *incipient* self-respect. And (3) A human being oppressed by practices (like segregation) that insult her dignity counts as *appropriately* self-respecting just if she publicly demonstrates her pre-reflectively, inwardly felt sense of dignity through actions demanding that the agents responsible for those practices acknowledge her dignity.[31] From these premises, King validly argues that the black citizens of Montgomery cannot correctly be said appropriately to respect themselves if they fail to protest their oppression by demanding an acknowledgment of their dignity. They must save themselves from their patience, and so protest their oppression, he insists, for the sake of their self-respect.[32]

King's argument against acquiescent submission is moral criticism: such submission is not compatible with securing the moral good of (appropriate) self-respect. Here King echoes Du Bois's critique of Washington's politics as voluntarily surrendering the Negro's self-respect. In the Afro-modern, African American tradition of political thought, King's moral criticism of the politics of acquiescent submission also echoes Frederick Douglass. Recall, in this connection, Douglass's remarks after his famous fight with Edward Covey: "A man without force is without the essential dignity of humanity. Human nature is so constituted that it cannot *honor* a helpless man, although it can *pity* him; and even this it cannot do long, if the signs of power do not arise."[33] In effect, Douglass implies here that a slave who remains helpless in the face of domination will not manifest the dignity he must exhibit to motivate anyone with a human nature, he himself included, to accord him the honor—the respect—he deserves. Manifest dignity expresses the slave's struggle to resist the practice of treating him as animal property. It is "essential," not because one cannot be a human being without it, but because without it one cannot induce respect—either the respect of others or self-respect.[34]

The Argument against Hatred and Violence. Having laid the groundwork for militant action in his speech, King then presents the argument against hatred and bitterness as a cautionary warning: "We must hear the words of Jesus echoing across the centuries: 'Love your enemies. . . .' If we fail to do this our protest will end up as a meaningless drama on the stage of history, and its memory will be shrouded with the ugly garments of shame. In spite of the mistreatment that we have confronted we must not become bitter, and end up by hating our white brothers. As Booker T. Washington said, 'Let no man pull you so low as to make you hate him.' "[35] King gives a more textured version of the argument near the end of a lengthy discussion of his intellectual evolution (including important references to his encounters with Niebuhr, Nietzsche, Marx, and others) in chapter 6: "If I meet hate with hate, I become depersonalized, because creation is so designed that my personality can only be fulfilled in the context of community. Booker T. Washington was right: 'Let no man pull you so low as to make you hate him.' When he pulls you that low he brings you to the point of working against community; he drags you to the point of defying creation, and thereby becoming depersonalized."[36]

King's repeated use of Washington is striking—especially the suggestion that Washington anticipated an insight that King ultimately justifies with reference to his Brightman- and DeWolf-inspired personalism.[37] Although King twice puts Washington's words inside quotation marks, it is likely that he is paraphrasing a passage from Washington's *Up from Slavery*: "I would permit no man, no matter what his colour might be, to narrow and degrade my soul by making me hate him."[38] For King and Washington alike, hatred is morally shameful—again, King argues in the mode of moral criticism—for in permitting oneself to hate, one damages one's dignity.

Lending this point a religious twist, King maintains that to hate is to oppose oneself to the Holy Spirit's creation of community, and thus to put into jeopardy the possibility of preserving one's dignity intact. When one hates, one eschews the loving and "redemptive" goodwill (*agape*) that advances the creation of community and that one's dignity demands of him.[39] To give oneself over to hate, then, is to injure one's dignity by flouting and refusing to fulfill its demand to act with love and redemptive goodwill.[40] Dignity is an expression of human personality, and to refuse to fulfill that demand is to refuse to fulfill a demand that our personality places on us. (In *Stride toward Freedom*, King describes the risk of not fulfilling this demand as "depersonalization"; in *Why We Can't Wait* he describes it as the risk of losing one's "soul.")[41] The black citizens of Montgomery should militantly protest segregation, King believes, but if they hope to enact a drama that displays human dignity intact, rather than a morally shameful and nihilistic travesty of historically significant struggles for social justice, they must likewise repudiate hatred and violence.[42]

King's Closing Statement. King concludes his Holt Street Baptist Church speech by saying, "If you will protest courageously, and yet with dignity and Christian love, when the history books are written in future generations, the historians will have to pause and say, 'There lived a great people—a black people—who injected new meaning and dignity into the veins of civilization.' This is our challenge and our overwhelming responsibility."[43]

Compare these remarks to King's account of the meaning of the Montgomery bus struggle in the concluding chapter of *Stride toward Freedom*—the opening sentence of which is "The bus struggle in Montgomery, Alabama, is now history":[44]

> Once plagued with a tragic sense of inferiority resulting from the crippling effects of slavery and segregation, the Negro has now been driven to reevaluate himself. He has come to feel that he is somebody. His religion reveals to him that God loves all His children and that the important thing about a man is not "his specificity but his fundamentum"—not the texture of his hair or the color of his skin but his eternal worth to God.
>
> This growing self-respect has inspired the Negro with a new determination to struggle and sacrifice until first-class citizenship becomes a reality. *This is the true meaning of the Montgomery story. One can never understand the bus protest in Montgomery without understanding that there is a new Negro in the South, with a new sense of dignity and destiny.*[45]

Writing from the retrospective view of the historian, King argues that the meaning of the Montgomery story, which is the story of the bus struggle, is the new sense of dignity to which it gave rise among the Negroes who participated in it. King refers to a "new sense of dignity," because the Negro's God-given dignity is *now* attended by a "growing of self-respect"—that is, by the emergence of an *appropriate* self-respect, corresponding to each human being's "eternal worth to God," in contrast to the *incipient* self-respect that slavery and segregation tended to erode and replace with a "tragic" and "corroding sense of inferiority."[46] But this new sense of dignity—again, the meaning of the Montgomery story—is precisely the meaning that King, speaking in the Holt Street Baptist Church on the night of the "Day of Days," pictured future historians attributing to the bus struggle. In imagining that future historians will describe black protesters who protested *with dignity* as having "injected new meaning and dignity into the veins of civilization," King envisioned (1) black protestors as someday achieving the (appropriate) self-respect that one attains when, in demonstrating against oppression, one demands that others acknowledge one's dignity, and (2) future historians as describing that achievement as the achievement of a dignity that is itself *new* to the extent that, again, it is attended by a new sense of dignity—by the emergence of a self-respect not previously in evidence.

The meaning King wanted the bus struggle to have—again, the meaning he pictured future historians attributing to it—is the meaning that at least one future historian (and autobiographer), King himself, attributed to it. On King's account, in other words, there was a perfect correspondence between what he portrays himself as having initially intended and wanted the movement to mean and what it turns out to have meant in the retrospective perspective of *his narrative,* which assesses the movement in light of its actual achievements and impact across the world. King's retrospective narrative serves to vindicate his initial vision of the point of the movement, as well as his Du Bois–echoing argument for a politics that avoided both acquiescence and hatred—for, by his lights, the movement could not have given rise to a "new dignity" had the participants in the movement not taken King's "Day of Days" speech to heart and succeeded in avoiding the temptations of acquiescence and hatred.

By restricting his account of what the movement actually meant to what he presents himself as having initially intended it to mean, King collapses the perspectives of the actor and the historian or storyteller that the philosopher, Hannah Arendt, highlights in emphasizing the nonsovereignty of political action.[47] In effect, he invites his readers to reduce the meaning of the bus struggle to the high aims he entertained as a participant in that struggle. King's Montgomery story transforms the Montgomery phase of the civil rights revolution into a pleasing artifact, a self-contained and morally satisfying museum piece whose world-historical significance perfectly expresses its author's intentions. Indeed, in retrospect King's story comes into view as just the sort of celebratory, triumphalist narrative that some contemporary civil rights historians seek to displace by telling the tale of the "long civil rights movement."[48]

Why We Can't Wait

Here, again, I proceed in two steps. First, I consider the continuities between *Stride toward Freedom* and *Why We Can't Wait,* emphasizing the persistent centrality of the theme of dignity and highlighting King's indebtedness both to Du Bois's framing of black political options and his analysis of the "Negro problem." Second, I concentrate on King's criticisms of Du Bois and Washington. I give more space to King's criticism of Washington than to his criticism of Du Bois, because it resonates more deeply with what I take to be the most philosophically interesting line of thought sketched in *Why We Can't Wait:* namely, King's extended reflections on the relationship between human agency and time.

King's "Letter from Birmingham Jail" is the heart of *Why We Can't Wait,* and his critique there of "the white moderate" is the primary site of his reflections on the relationship between human agency and time. King's brief critique of Washington's "apparent resignation" is, I shall argue, of a piece with his critique of the white moderate. In the perspective of "Letter from Birmingham Jail," the primary hindrance to white Americans' acknowledgment of black Americans' dignity is an attitude toward time that disavows moral accountability. In King's view, the white moderate exemplifies this disavowal.

From Stride toward Freedom *to* Why We Can't Wait

In *Why We Can't Wait,* King's normative concerns continue to pivot around the concepts of dignity and self-respect, and he continues to tie dignity to human personality. In one place, however, he seems to identify dignity and equality and argues that dignity demands economic security: "Equality meant dignity and dignity demanded a job that was secure and a paycheck that lasted throughout the week."[49] Although King declines further to clarify his understanding of the relation between equality, dignity, and economic security in *Why We Can't Wait,* I read this remark as anticipating the argument of *Where Do We Go from Here* (1967)—that American society will properly be said to have acknowledged the dignity of black Americans only if, in addition to eliminating the caste stigma that was the target of the bus struggle, it secures their economic and political equality.[50]

King's ongoing fidelity to a Du Boisian framing of the options available to black politics is clearly evident in *Why We Can't Wait.* Here, however, he identifies the "force of bitterness and hatred," which "comes perilously close to advocating violence," with Black Nationalism and, specifically, with "Elijah Muhammad's Muslim movement."[51] Echoing *Stride toward Freedom*, King diagnoses the force of adjustment and "complacency" as expressing (1) feelings of inferiority ("drained of self-respect") and (2) the insensitivity of the black middle class to the problems of the black masses.[52] Yet again echoing *Stride toward Freedom*, he himself advocates a middle path between complacency and Black Nationalism, "the more excellent way of love and nonviolent protest."[53]

King's fidelity to Du Bois's view that the Negro problem is a function of both internal and external factors is also evident in *Why We Can't Wait*. He attributes the Negro's economic insecurity to color discrimination (an external factor) and the culture of poverty (an internal factor). Both obstacles must be overcome for the Negro to be "absorbed into the mainstream of American life." In addition to these two constraints, King equally emphasizes the impact of economic exploitation on the Negro, thus suggesting that the struggle for the acknowledgment of Negro dignity must operate on *three* (not just two) fronts.[54]

King's Criticisms of Du Bois and Washington

King's brief explicit criticisms of Du Bois and Washington indicate some important developments in his political thought.

In *Why We Can't Wait*, King criticizes Du Bois's conception of black politics, specifically his doctrine of the "talented tenth," arguing that it was a tactical doctrine designed for "an aristocratic elite who would themselves be benefited while leaving behind the 'untalented' 90 percent."[55] As an alternative to a politics ruled by the talented tenth, King advances a vision of the Negro "acting in concert with fellow Negroes to assert himself as a citizen . . . in the streets, on the buses, in the stores, the parks and other public facilities."[56] A few pages later, he adds, "In armies of violence, there is a caste of rank. In Birmingham, outside of the few generals and lieutenants who necessarily directed and coordinated operations, the regiments of the demonstrators marched in democratic phalanx."[57] By contrasting a hierarchical politics characterized by rule and military command—a politics where elites decide for and direct others—to a democratic politics where equals exercise agency in concert, King challenges a picture of black politics that held sway over African American political thought through much of the twentieth century, largely due to Du Bois's influence. King's terse criticism of this picture echoes the thought of several political theorists—e.g., Alexis de Tocqueville, Hannah Arendt, and Frederick Douglass—who have likewise questioned the ruler-centered conception of politics that Du Bois embraces.[58]

About Washington, King writes: "For decades the long and winding trails led to dead ends. Booker T. Washington, in the dark days that followed Reconstruction, advised them: 'Let down your buckets where you are.' Be content, he said in effect, with doing well what *the times* permit you to do at all. However, this path, they [Negroes] soon felt, had too little freedom *in its present* and too little promise *in its future.*"[59]

Characterizing what in the next paragraph he describes as the "apparent resignation" of Washington's philosophy, King's language highlights the relation of that philosophy to time.[60] On King's account, Washington argued that black politics should observe and respect the constraints that "the times" impose on it, and so presupposes that it is in the nature of time, or specific phases of time, to delimit the scope of human agency. Washington's Negro critics responded to this argument, King notes, by proposing that his understanding of human agency (of human "do[ing]" and action) assumes that time is more constraining than it really is, for it underestimates the full range of possibilities available to human agency in the *present moment* (it finds too little freedom in the present), and so too narrowly construes the extent to which human agency can change the world, the extent to which it can bring into being a *future* different from the past (it finds too little promise in the future).

King's comments on Washington's Negro critics appear in chapter 2 of *Why We Can't Wait.* "Letter from Birmingham Jail" is chapter 5. I suspect that King organized his book so that the former would anticipate the latter. Indeed, I conjecture that King penned "Letter from Birmingham Jail" before he wrote the remainder of *Why We Can't Wait,* and that thinking through the argument of "Letter from Birmingham Jail" led him to articulate his critique of Washington in terms that resonate with the reflections on time and human agency that animate his jailhouse missive, that crop up throughout *Why We Can't Wait,* and that doubtlessly informed his choice of his book's title.

Whether or not this hypothesis is true, my thesis regarding "Letter from Birmingham Jail" is that, in targeting the white moderate, it extends and deepens the argument that King attributes to Washington's Negro critics.

In characterizing the "white moderate," King quotes what he suggests is a typical letter from "a white brother" from Texas: "All Christians know that the colored people will receive equal rights eventually, but it is possible that you are in too great a religious hurry. It has taken Christianity almost two thousand years to accomplish what it has. The teachings of Christ take time to come to earth."[61] According to the white moderate, blacks can justifiably look forward to claiming equal rights, but they will be able to claim them only after they passively receive them. But they will receive them *eventually*—or ultimately, which is to say "in the end." But in the end of what?

The white moderate represents human history as a predictable sequence of events ruled by a "timetable"—a calendar that schedules events to occur at one or another time.[62] Negro equality, he suggests, is *not scheduled* to occur yet—it is scheduled to occur later, "in the end," which is, presumably, *at the end* of a determinate span of time marked by the timetable. The Negro will acquire his rights, the white moderate believes, when the teachings of Christ have taken the time they require to come to earth; or at least to the Jim Crow South; and there is no doubt in his mind that they will *finally* arrive on schedule. King errs, then, in not recognizing that he cannot "hurry along" the train of history—in not recognizing that nothing he can do can cause an event destined to occur at a later time to occur "now." Echoing Booker T. Washington (as King has interpreted him), the white moderate urges King and his followers to restrict their actions to what "the times" permit—or, in other words, to contemplate and respect the limits that the scheduled time of history imposes on the range of possibilities available to black political agency.

In setting the timetable for the Negro's freedom, the white moderate evinces a paternalistic attitude toward the Negro. Separating himself from "the very flow of time that will inevitably cure all ills," he purports to watch progress unfold, unavoidably and according to schedule, urging the Negro to do the same.[63] The Negro need not act to secure his rights, the white moderate insists, for time itself will deliver his rights to him. Rather than regard himself as an agent whose participation in political struggles can help shape the course of history, the Negro would do just as well to adopt the stance of a detached observer. What is best for the Negro, says the white moderate, is to adopt the posture of the white moderate himself.

In response to this line of argument, King writes: "Human progress never rolls in on wheels of inevitability; it comes through the tireless efforts of men willing to be coworkers with God, and without this hard work, time itself becomes an ally of the forces of social stagnation. We must use time creatively, in the knowledge that the time is always ripe to do right. Now is the time to make real the promise of democracy and transform our pending national elegy into a creative psalm of brotherhood. Now is the time to lift our national policy from the quicksand of racial injustice to the solid rock of human dignity."[64] Against the white moderate, and recalling the argument of Washington's Negro critics, King insists that the "now," the present moment, is replete with possibility—that it is eminently available to the agency of the resolute individual who would seize the time and act to bring into being a future "in which all men will respect the dignity and worth of human personality."[65] Demanding that he repudiate the posture of the detached observer who, declining to participate, sets himself apart from history in order to behold it, King entreats the white moderate to embrace the task of men willing to be God's co-workers.[66] In effect, he calls on the white moderate no longer to evade his duty to act and to commit himself, *now*, to doing the right thing.[67]

Conclusion

Although the two writings differ in genre, there is a philosophical affinity between *Stride toward Freedom* and "Letter from Birmingham Jail."

Stride toward Freedom presents itself as a backward-looking, narrative reconstruction of a struggle that is "now history." References to the past and the future abound in "Letter from Birmingham Jail," of course, but first and foremost it presents itself as belonging to a "present moment" that King and the clergymen his letter addresses both occupy. "Letter from Birmingham Jail" is an argument *for* acting at that moment and *against* waiting to act later. With respect to their temporal orientations, both *Stride toward Freedom* and "Letter from Birmingham Jail" may be compared to *Where Do We Go from Here,* the largely forward-looking text in which King distinguishes the first and the second phases of the civil rights revolution.[68]

The philosophical affinity between *Stride toward Freedom* and "Letter from Birmingham Jail" is thematic. King's preoccupation with the theme of moral accountability is central to both works. In *Stride toward Freedom,* this preoccupation is clearest when King argues against acquiescence in order to hold his audience accountable to the moral good of self-respect, and when he argues against hatred and violence in order to hold them accountable to the moral demands of dignity and personality. In "Letter from Birmingham Jail" it is clearest when he holds the white moderate accountable for failing to act to protect the dignity of his black fellow citizens.[69]

2

Moral Perfectionism

PAUL C. TAYLOR

To think seriously about Martin Luther King, Jr., as a political philosopher is to engage in multiple acts of heresy. Some of the orthodoxies that this way of thinking imperils begin with fixed and myopic ideas about the requirements of patriotism or of ethically permissible modes of dissent. Others begin with similarly fixed ideas about what a philosopher is, or about whether a philosopher can also be an activist, or a preacher, or even, as King would have said, a Negro.

One of these orthodoxies leads directly into the aspect of King's political thought that animates this chapter. It has become common to think of King's legacy as a matter of service, in the way the custodians of U.S. political culture have enshrined by making the King Day holiday a "day of service." There is a great deal to say about the politics and meaning of this holiday, and about the various and variously misaligned political imperatives that swirl around it. But for current purposes the key consideration is that reading King's political significance in this way effectively drains his legacy of political content. It reduces a challenging and expressly political vision to a superficial and "smoothly patriotic" ethic of abstract altruism.[1] Where the historical King aspired to transform the polis and its inhabitants, the King of "MLK Day" calls citizens, more or less as they stand, simply to serve the polis, more or less as it stands. The citizens might be more compassionate and more generous with their time, and their communities might have cleaner streets and parks and might operate their food banks more efficiently. But service still floats free of any sustained reflection on the ends one serves, or the implications of serving just these ends and not others.

The King Day orthodoxy is tenable only if one ignores the powerful resources that King himself mobilized for thinking through the work of political life and action. King insisted not just on service, but also on thinking carefully and courageously about whom to serve, and why, and how. More to the point, he argued that careful reflection on the burdens of political life may require transformation—transformation of society and of the self, as well as of our ends and of the means we use to pursue them. And he insisted further on a thought that gives the lie to the easy righteousness of the post–civil rights ethical consensus. Our earthly pursuits carry no guarantees: our judgments might be erroneous and our actions might never bear fruit, and this fact exacts a heavy existential and psychological toll on those who sincerely mean to take up the burdens of social ethics.

In what follows I develop these thoughts about transformational and experimental striving by describing King as a kind of moral perfectionist. To describe him in this way is to foreground his determination to deepen the ethical and experiential dimensions of democratic life. The ethical depth appears in his commitment to self-exploration, self-questioning, and self-improvement. The experiential depth appears in his persistent sounding of tragic themes.

I work out this picture of the perfectionist King in four steps. First, I make a quick pass at the familiar touchstones of the philosophical approach with which King is most often identified, the personalist tradition. I do this in part to give as much assurance as I can that my reading of him is consistent with more common approaches, but also to begin to explain why I prefer the language of perfectionism to the language of personalism. The remaining steps are then to explain what I mean by moral perfectionism, to locate this view in some of King's writings, and to address some concerns that this approach might raise.

Personalism

I take instruction on the idea of personalism from Kipton Jensen, a philosopher at Martin King's alma mater, Morehouse College.[2] Jensen argues that the Morehouse of King's day had an abiding commitment to a kind of personalism, and that it bequeathed this commitment, or the beginnings of a commitment, to its most famous graduate. I take no position on the probity of Jensen's argument in its application to Morehouse. What interests me is his clarity on the question of what personalism means.

Personalism's core idea, he reports, is that "there is no higher principle than the person. . . . Abstract laws, the state, property, and other institutions are all to be judged in the light of their effect on persons."[3] Morehouse's "pedagogical" personalism "stressed the sacred or otherwise inviolable dignity of persons . . . [and] promoted an educational process that activated the potential of individuals within and across diverse communities."[4] The emphasis on activating individual potential is crucial here, and comes through even more clearly in the thought of Howard Thurman, who says things like this: "The most important thing in life for any man at any time is the development of his own best self, the incentive to actualize his own potentials."[5]

There is much more to say about the personalist tradition, but saying just this much leaves us with a view that is legible to readers of Anglophone political philosophy. So far it appears that the tradition insists on the dignity of individuals, puts individuals at the center of sociopolitical life, and understands individuals not just as abstract centers of value but as distinct personalities in need of self-directed actualization. If this is a minimally acceptable account of what's at stake for personalism in the terrestrial sphere, then we can pivot from religious ethics to political theory and continue to press the argument in language that can register for people to whom the theological and metaphysical overtones of the view will ring hollow.

Making the turn to political theory sets the stage for the reading I propose to give. King is widely regarded as a personalist, and in fact regarded himself in this way. Personalism—or, as he sometimes put it, personal idealism—constituted his "basic philosophical position."[6] I would like my reading to do justice to King's personalist commitments, while distilling from his mix of metaphysical, theological, and ethical commitments a more straightforward approach to political life.

Taking this approach does raise the question of why personalism is not enough. What is the value of pivoting to political theory? Who needs the more straightforward approach I just called for?

I have three answers to these questions, only two of which strike me as adequate responses on their own. The first, inadequate response is a confession: I've never quite known what to do with personalism, in part because of the tendency of its adherents, including King, to define it in terms that are utterly unhelpful outside of theological contexts. King defines personalism as "the theory that the clue to the meaning of ultimate reality is found in personality."[7] I don't know what to do with locutions like this, especially because the reference to "ultimate reality" seems to make more sense against the backdrop of certain theological commitments than in the secular wild, at some distance from the thought that a personal, loving God orders the universe. Here in the wild it registers mostly as a blank check for a more technical vocabulary that must be available in some distant branch of intellectual activity. The best I can do is to cash the check by appealing to ethical and political traditions I know, like the ones I'll explore below. I present all this as a confession because it is surely a limitation of my own training, and perhaps an indication of the narrowness of my ethical vision, that this language registers to me mainly as a launching pad for a journey to another discursive space. This is why I say that the confession by itself is not reason enough to take the journey.

But the confession doesn't stand by itself. My second response to skepticism about turning away from personalism and toward political theory invokes certain realities of the professional academy. I am writing from, and at least partly to, intellectual communities in which social inquiry is specialized and conducted in specialized vocabularies. It just is a fact of these communities, and a consequence of the divergent paths that different forms of specialization mark out for different people, that many of the people who talk about personalism effectively inhabit a world that is different from the one that this essay and I both inhabit. So it is incumbent upon me to translate whatever I find of use in the technical language of personalism into a vocabulary that people like me can use. It might be better if I were trained more broadly, and if more of the people who share my training were fluent across the epistemic and institutional borders I'm marking now. But many of us are not, which means that my confession of incomprehension is a placeholder for a wider institutional failure of translation, or a marker of my membership in an intellectual community that needs this translation (fully recognizing that there are communities that don't). The translation I mean to offer is, then, if I get it right, of some value, perhaps even as a pathway for secular political philosophers to converse with religious ethicists.

My final response to concerns about the turn from personalism to perfectionism is that making this turn draws out something that is distinctive to King's version of "personal idealism." If the vocabulary of personalism were a live option for me, I might be tempted to say with Burrow that King's specific contribution to the tradition was the conspicuously political edge he gave to it by "translating it into social action."[8] But I prefer to leave that thought to the people who have something at stake in working it out in just those words. What's more vital for me is teasing out the political-theoretic import of the shift to social action. I want to understand how this shift bears on the work of democratic living, and how, in doing so, it positions King as someone through whom and with whom our political thinkers might continue to reflect and converse.

Perfectionism

I proposed above to read King's political philosophy through a focus on three key ethical commitments from the personalist tradition. This tradition (1) insists on the dignity of individuals, (2) puts individuals at the center of sociopolitical life, and (3) understands individuals not just as abstract centers of value but also as distinct personalities in need of self-directed actualization. This sounds to me a great deal like a kind of moral perfectionism, though it won't be clear what this means without some further explanation of the sort of perfectionism I have in mind.

I am concerned here with something like what Chris Lebron has called "moral-agency perfectionism."[9] The key to Lebron's version of perfectionism is that "there are better and worse ways to be, better and worse characters to have," for democratic citizens, and that the resources for distinguishing better and worse are ready at hand in our shared democratic culture.[10] This is as opposed not just to the neutralism that some theorists think political liberalism requires, but also to other modes of perfectionism that distinguish better and worse pursuits or goods by appeal to standards external or in opposition to the society as it stands. For a moral-agency perfectionist in Lebron's mold, a flourishing democracy, especially in settings defined by ongoing contests over modern racial injustice, depends on citizens calling each other to the better angels of their natures. This means reminding citizens of—"nudging them toward," Lebron says—the principles and norms that they already reflectively endorse. Supporting democratic arrangements in the context of modern liberal democratic racial states means working "to reliably connect our principles with our actions and dispositions" by activating our capacity for shame and the attendant desire to live up to the ethical standards we already endorse.[11] According to the moral-agency perfectionist, "public reason . . . must reach down into the self and elevate it to the level of moral excellence" that society demands.[12]

Lebron's account comes very close to the view I find in King, but needs supplementation to capture what's most vital. This vital element is the feature that has made Stanley Cavell's account of perfectionism so distinctive and influential: its dynamic *Emersonian* sensibility. (To say this is not yet to say that Emerson influenced King. It is simply to use in this context a slightly better-known quantity, Emerson, to illuminate a lesser-known one—King and his as of yet at least partly unspecified political philosophy.) Some of what is at stake in Cavell's invocation of perfectionism is reflected in the mid- to late-twentieth-century recuperation of virtue theory and virtue ethics. Like Elizabeth Anscombe, Alasdair MacIntyre, Bernard Williams, and the many who followed them, though using different resources, Cavell was keen to bring out what he described as "a dimension or tradition of the moral life" that the familiar traditions of utilitarianism and Kantianism failed to capture fully, where they credited it at all.[13] This dimension has in part to do with the importance of character, or, as Cavell puts it, "the state of one's soul." But it has most saliently to do with attending to the state of one's soul in light of an ideal of continual growth and self-transformation.

Richard Shusterman usefully summarizes Cavell's aims by making clear their distance from the Rawlsian picture of perfectionism.[14] As Shusterman puts it, "Rawls sees perfectionism as a fixed teleological principle 'directing society to arrange institutions and to define the duties and obligations of individuals so as to maximize the achievement of human excellence' in some particular set of valued domains."[15] Emersonian perfectionism, by contrast, "is no institutional principle promoting some fixed hierarchy of ends."[16] What is it instead? "It is rather an individual ethical injunction to strive to be better and to do so by being always open to exploring the claims of different ends. . . . Cavell advocates a dynamic self that is directed at self-improvement and (through this) at the improvement of society. Constantly in the making, the self should always be striving towards a higher 'unattained yet attainable self.' . . . but the process of striving is never completed: not because we never reach the next or higher self, but because in reaching it, we should always see yet a further, still higher self to reach for."[17]

The difference that the name "Emerson" marks, then, irrespective of whether one learns to credit this difference to Emerson himself or gets to it in some other way, involves turning away from a fixed teleological principle and toward a dynamic, persistently critical, continually revisable quest to improve both self and society. The focus on endless striving and self-transformation not only distinguishes Emersonian perfectionism from the static perfectionisms that Rawls repudiates; it also carries with it an important set of experiential and moral-psychological implications. Quoting once more from Shusterman:

Self-perfection, as "a process of moving to, and from, nexts," demands real courage. Not only must it overcome habit and anxious "resistance to internal change," but it must also face the unpleasant fact that we *need* radical improvement. For Cavell, this borders on self-loathing. "Emersonian Perfectionism requires that we become ashamed in a particular way of ourselves" so as to consecrate ourselves to our next selves and a better society. It involves "an expression of disgust with or a disdain for the present state of things so complete as to require not merely reform, but a call for a transformation of things, and before all a transformation of the self."[18]

A commitment to ongoing self-transformation requires courage, and it flirts with, and to some degree benefits from, self-loathing. A perpetual disdain for the current state of things can inspire the endless striving that perfectionism counsels, though it may also undermine the project of attending to the state of one's soul.

This embrace of shame and flirtation with self-loathing, combined with the commitment to the open-ended work of self-transformation, effectively dovetails with and deepens Lebron's perfectionism in ways that make it even more congenial to the cultivation of democratic citizens. As Lebron points out, one root of moral-agency perfectionism is the recognition that democracy is more than formal democratic institutions and practices—universal suffrage, routine elections, and the rest. But as Sheldon Wolin and many others have noted, the issue is not just that democracy is more than the sum of its current institutional forms; it is that the forms are always in danger of ossification or corruption, and therefore of losing the ability to support and defend the populace. Effective democratic citizenship, then, will require vigilance and creativity: vigilance in watching—*searching*—for signs that our institutions, practices, and personal habits have exhausted themselves; and creativity in seeking out and inventing new pathways for the expression of the democratic spirit. Democracies need their citizens to remain dissatisfied with things as they stand, and to remain open to the possibility that justice will require reconstructing both society and the self.[19]

It is important to be clear about the experiential stakes of the perfectionist commitment to ongoing criticism and transformation. To say that ethical striving is endless, that there is always another, wider circle to be drawn, is to say that there is no fixed endpoint at which to aim: it is to say, more to the point, that the prospect of error cannot be eliminated. There is no way to solve the equation, no proof to complete, no way to get social life completely right, once and for all. This, combined with the ethos of disdain and self-loathing, means that the transition from this self to the next may register as a failure, or, worse, that there is no guarantee of actualizing the potential of the current self. Taken to its logical conclusion, this dynamism is a tragic sensibility, combining the voluntaristic experimentalism of Emerson's circles with the tragic awareness that error, failure, and defeat are always in play. In deference to this explicit expansion of the view in the direction of a tragic sensibility, I'll henceforth refer to this mode of moral perfectionism not as Emersonian but as tragic.

If what I've said above is right, then we should be able to find in King's work his commitment to the key tenets of a tragic moral perfectionism. We should, in other words, find him focused on the following:

1. Character—insisting on the criticism and cultivation of character as core elements of democratic practice
2. Self-criticism—interrogating the self, perhaps to the point of self-loathing, as part of the work of ethical criticism and social activism
3. Shame (and the like)—mobilizing self-directed emotions as instruments for ethical self-criticism, especially as these highlight the gaps between professed commitments and actual practice
4. Experience—recognizing the lived dimension of perfectionist practice, with its reliance on conditions like shame, as well as its temptations to despair, disenchantment, and the like
5. Experimentation—insisting that the transformation of selves and societies is an open-ended and dynamic process with no guarantees of success.

The next two sections locate these commitments in King's work, first by looking at King's last sermon at Ebenezer Baptist Church, and then by examining the last book he published in his lifetime.

"Unfulfilled Dreams"

A month before King was murdered, he addressed his congregation on the theme of "Unfulfilled Dreams."[20] Whatever else it is, the sermon is an eloquent rehearsal of two perfectionist themes. It points out that our preferred outcomes are never assured and rarely even in view, and it takes seriously the existential burden of working through this fact in one's lived experience.

"Unfulfilled Dreams" is a remarkable text and performance, and it comes at a complicated moment in this most complicated of lives. Consequently, there would be great benefit in examining it from a variety of perspectives, using the tools of the literary critic, the rhetorician, or the historian, or of the scholar of performance or homiletics or the New Testament. I simply read the text as I would a straightforward essay on its topic, relying on the more or less plain meaning of the words, while acknowledging that there is much more to say about the work the words do in combination, and in the moment of delivery, and in their specific historical, discursive, and expressive contexts.

King begins the sermon in a way that will seem jarring to auditors and readers who know him only from the March on Washington oration. He directs the congregation to a text—1 Kings 8:17–19—where we find Solomon explaining that his father David had planned to build a temple to God but never succeeded. Solomon says this in the context of having fulfilled his father's dream, but King's focus is on David, whose experience reminds us, King says, "that life is a continual story of shattered dreams." A bit earlier he puts it this way: "One of the great agonies of life is that we are constantly trying to finish that which is unfinishable." He goes on in this vein, explicitly linking the human condition to David's plight: "The struggle is always there. It gets discouraging sometimes. . . . Some of us are trying to build a temple of peace. We speak out against war, we protest, but it seems that your head is going against a concrete wall. It seems to mean nothing. . . . You are left lonesome; you are left discouraged; you are left bewildered. Well, that is the story of life."[21] We struggle and fail, he says, and the failures are discouraging. But "that is the story of life."

At this point King might easily have gone on to embrace the consolations of optimism. He could have said that continued struggle in harmony with the divine plan would ensure success. Instead he says this: "The thing that makes me happy is that I can hear a voice crying through the vista of time, saying: 'It may not come today or it may not come tomorrow, but it is well that it is within thine heart. . . . It's well that you are trying.' "[22] The key is not that success is ensured; it is that one makes the effort.

So far we see the sermon sounding two perfectionist themes. One lesson is that life is an experiment, without the neat closure of guarantees or of clear pathways to our intended outcomes. But a related lesson is that the experiment is grueling, and imposes severe psycho-existential costs. Ethical life is hard; it is, literally, a struggle, and King speaks to this aspect of the project in a way that too often goes missing in studies of abstract principles and of less dynamic forms of perfectionism. We try, and the possibility of failure always dogs our trying, and this fact can tempt us to despair. Even worse, sometimes, like David, we die without seeing our plans come to fruition. But "that is the story of life." To pretend that there are guarantees, or that the experiences of despair and disappointment have no place in ethical life, is to fail to take the burdens of ethical life seriously.

This appeal to tragic experimentalism may seem inconsistent with one of the more familiar aspects of King's life and work. Even someone who knows nearly nothing about King would probably know that he said things like this: "The arc of the moral universe is long but it bends toward justice."[23] And this: "I've seen the promised land. I may not get there with you. But I want you to know . . . that we, as a people, will get to the promised land. . . . I'm not worried about anything."[24] How can one reconcile this King with a King who focuses on the trials of tragic, earthly striving and refuses the consolations of heavenly succor? I return to this below.

King's sermon also highlights the remaining perfectionist themes. To start, it insists on the importance of building the personal capacity—the character—to sustain one's earthly striving. We see this when he suggests that one of the obstacles to completing our temples, whatever they may be, is the unavoidable tension, in the universe and in human nature, between good and evil. Saint Paul captures the tension eloquently: "The good that I would, I do not: And the evil that I would not, that I do." This language would likely have had particular resonance for King at this moment in his life, after years of depression and anxiety, caused not just by the apparent failure to complete his "temple," but also by FBI threats to expose his extramarital affairs and publicly brand him a liar and hypocrite. But it resonates here for us because it explicitly raises the question of character.

King goes on in this vein in a way that not only stresses the centrality of character, but also accentuates and enacts the perfectionist commitment to ongoing self-criticism. After calling attention to the "civil war going on in [each person's] life," King points out that God did not condemn David for failing to complete the temple; rather, it was well that the dream of the temple was within David's heart. "In the final analysis," he explains, "God does not judge us by the separate incidents or the separate mistakes that we make, but by the total bent of our lives."[25] If the proper measure of our striving is not its final outcome, then one burden of ethical life has to involve focusing our moral energies not just on the end in view but also on the imperative of self-improvement. King closes this thought by offering himself as an exemplary case, reminding the congregation that he is a sinner like everyone else, but that he wants to be a good man, and that this sincere desire is, in its way, enough.[26]

Here we see King not only enacting the dialectic of self-criticism that tragic perfectionism requires, but also mobilizing something like self-loathing to do this work (how much like it, though, is a question to which I will return). He does this in a way that is particularly provocative, and that follows neatly from familiar Christian rhetoric: by distinguishing between lower and higher selves or aspects of the self, and refusing the lower and aspiring to the higher. "I'm a sinner," he says, "but I want to be a good man," which is to say something very much like what Lebron's project of mobilizing civic shame means for democratic citizens to say. *I've failed, by my own lights,* we're meant to say. *I can and will do better.*

Chaos or Community

Like "Unfulfilled Dreams," *Where Do We Go from Here: Chaos or Community?* reveals King's focus on the core perfectionist commitments—the centrality of character, the importance of self-criticism, the lived experience of despair and self-loathing, the attempt to leverage self-loathing into productive growth, and the importance of unending striving in a world of dynamic practices and corruptible institutions.[27] As a reflection on the state and the future of the mid-twentieth-century U.S. freedom movement, though, *Where Do We Go from Here* had a more expansive agenda than "Unfulfilled Dreams" did. As such, it is rather clearer about two implications of these commitments: the importance of the gap between professed commitments and actual practice, and of the evolving and dialectical nature of social and ethical experimentation.

We can see the commitment to moral evolution at work in a number of passages from *Where Do We Go from Here.* For example: "Nothing could be more tragic than for men to live in these revolutionary times and fail to achieve the new attitudes and the new mental outlooks that the new situation demands."[28] Or consider this appeal to Thoreau, which King recycled in a number of addresses and writings: "So much of modern life can be summarized in that suggestive phrase of Thoreau: 'Improved means to an unimproved end.' This is . . . the deep and haunting problem confronting modern man. Enlarged material powers spell enlarged peril if there is not proportionate growth of the soul."[29]

It was not uncommon for social critics in this era to worry about the gap between modern society's powers and its principles. It was especially common for heirs of the social gospel and liberal Christian traditions, and for participants in the currents of thought that informed these traditions. What's interesting about the way this sensibility registers in King is the way he brings it to bear on the black freedom movement, turning a key perfectionist commitment into movement strategy.

Remember that we entered the discussion of perfectionism not through Emerson and Cavell but through Lebron, for whom the tension between principles and practice took priority over the divide between moral truth and error. This tension was essential to King, too, in relation both to the way movement organizations like SCLC conducted their business and to the underlying philosophical commitments. But he read the tension dialectically, with the result that recommitting to one's principles also meant reinterpreting them.

One place where we see King's commitment to the tension between principle and practice is in the second chapter of *Where Do We Go from Here,* where he discusses the rise of the Black Power movement. He uses the chapter to recommend nonviolent direct action over actions built on violence, self-defense, or anticolonial self-assertion. After pointing out that resorting to violence would be extraordinarily impractical under the conditions that obtained in the United States at the time, he takes up a positive argument for nonviolent approaches. "Beyond the pragmatic invalidity of violence," he explains, there is the problem of "its inability to appeal to conscience."[30] Where violent methods "intensify the fears of the white majority, and leave them less ashamed of their prejudices toward Negroes," nonviolent direct action can make "an indifferent and unconcerned nation rise from lethargy and . . . struggle with a newly aroused conscience."[31]

King invokes resources like conscience and shame as a way of mobilizing existing commitments in the pursuit of justice. He was always clear that the revolution of values that he sought required a new commitment to our existing values, to closing the gap between our practices and our principles. But near the end of his life he was particularly clear that recommitting to our principles required, somewhat paradoxically, reinterpreting them. (It is not incidental to this reading that Hegel was one of King's favorite thinkers.)

We can see this dialectical approach at work throughout *Where Do We Go from Here.* In the first chapter we find King arguing that the recently concluded "first phase"[32] of the freedom movement showed that "the absence of brutality and unregenerate evil is not the presence of justice."[33] If this is right, if the absence of brutality does not equal the presence of justice, then a new phase is needed, during which we reinterpret the notion of justice so that it encompasses material and economic conditions. But here, once again, we find ourselves constrained by outdated ways of thinking. Our debates about political economy have gotten hung up, King claims, on the tension between capitalism and communism. His solution is tellingly Hegelian: "The good and just society is neither the thesis of capitalism nor the antithesis of Communism, but a socially conscious democracy which reconciles the truths of individualism and collectivism."[34]

Appeals to dialectical synthesis are so common in *Where Do We Go from Here* that one might read the book itself as an extended enactment of this mode of reflection. Each appeal has the same structure. *We thought the freedom movement was one thing: we thought it was a way of calling America to live up to its principles, or, for SNCC's erstwhile advocates of nonviolence, of building black political power, or, for fair-weather white friends, of eliminating the barbaric excesses of southern segregation. But issuing this call forced us to rethink the principles.* Justice requires more than integrating an America that remains otherwise unchanged, or making segregation more humane, or seizing power by any means. It even requires more than fighting simply against racial oppression. It requires that we understand the links between racism, militarism, and materialism, as King would point out more and more stridently near the end of his life. It requires, more broadly, that we accept not just that our principles, their authors, and their adherents are inadequate as they stand, but that our sense of this inadequacy must itself be subjected to critique and continually revised.

Objections and Replies

I could work through *Where Do We Go from Here* more carefully, in search of more evidence to support my reading. But two considerations encourage me to turn in another direction. First, I hope that what I've said so far is enough to give a sense of the book's ethical tone, enough, anyway, to count as a down payment on a more expansive reading. Second, and more important, to this point I've sped past some infelicities in my reading that might by now seem to require some attention.

There are three points in particular at which the reading I've proposed threatens to conflict with other approaches one might take, and with thoughts one might already have about King or about the ethical concepts I've put in play. First, the reading I've given generalizes rather hastily from two texts. Isn't this too slender an evidentiary basis for an account of King's overall orientation to the work of politics? Second, by sidestepping the unavoidably Christian roots of King's arguments, my reading of him might ignore convictions and commitments that are most crucial for and about him. And finally, I've appealed to self-loathing as a resource for personal growth and transformation, but this may be something of a stretch in light of King's emphasis on love and on fidelity to a personal, loving God. I'll close this chapter by addressing these concerns.

One might also worry that I've put shame too close to the center of King's thought. This might leave King, or my reading of him, vulnerable to contemporary criticisms of the turn to shame in political theory.[35] This might in turn leave me the burden of explaining more clearly why this aspect of King's thought deserves any more attention than his embrace of personalism. Unfortunately, following this thought out would take us too far afield of the main work of this chapter. Suffice it to say that while shame discourse does have its limits, the limits that concern people these days don't apply to King in any straightforward way.

What About the Other Texts?

First, let's consider the evidentiary basis for this perfectionist reading of King. It is true that I have hung this discussion largely on two texts, but the texts that appear here are points of entry or emblematic moments, highlighting themes that appear prominently in other parts of King's corpus. One might say that it is the virtue (or the vice) of the philosopher to focus on structured arguments rather than follow threads across multiple texts in multiple genres of expression. So where I found relatively self-contained arguments with their structures intact, I seized on them and worked through them. But we can find the elements of those arguments in other places. Consider, for example, this evocation of the ideal of growth and self-transformation from an address in 1960: "To suffer in a righteous cause is to grow to our humanity's full stature. If only to save ourselves from bitterness, we need the vision to see the ordeals of this generation as an opportunity to transfigure ourselves and American society."[36]

At this point the stage is set for a comprehensive engagement with King's corpus, and after that a contest of close readings. I discuss a few other pieces below, but I don't propose to do anything like the work that this sort of engagement would require. Perhaps a comprehensive study—not just of the sermons and writings for publication but also of the correspondence, meeting notes, and recorded oratorical performances—will show that on balance the moves I've shown King making play a minor part in the overall economy of his thinking. I don't think that's the case, but my aim has not been to anticipate and respond to this possibility. The burden of this piece is to assemble a plausible account of King's thought based on responsible readings of texts that have some claim to the status of representativeness. This reading is my hypothesis, and I trust that the division of specialized and professional scholarly labor is such that someone, somewhere, if the hypothesis is of sufficient interest, will comb through the historical record in order to confirm or disconfirm it.

What About the Voice?

My apparent indifference to King's theological commitments may be the most glaring issue. How can I give an account of Martin King's political philosophy without noting that the source of his normative judgments is his devotion to the Christian God? Can a reading that does this count as a reading *of King?*

One response to this worry would run through the strategy that animates Rawls's political liberalism, among other views: prioritize the right over the good, and subordinate metaphysics to ethics, at least provisionally, for public purposes. In this spirit one might say that what makes King an interesting political thinker is the degree to which his arguments about what's right, whatever their roots, can get traction with people in the public sphere, people for whom his faith claims, rooted in a comprehensive conception of the good, happen not to resonate. There is promise in this path, not least because it can actually be drawn out in a direction that King himself suggests, not least in his frequent description of Gandhi as a great Christian figure, despite the Mahatma's distance from Christocentric philosophical or theological commitments.

Unfortunately, prioritizing ethics over metaphysics may simply evade the deeper issue. The worry is really that perfectionism insists on a kind of ethical self-definition, and that this seems at odds with King's eager acknowledgments of an external source for his normative judgments. For King, one might say, *God tells us* how to identify the right, the good, and the virtuous. Perfectionist self-criticism can be a valuable resource, as it helps us tune out the noise of human affairs so that the divine voice can resonate clearly through the vistas of time. But it is merely a supplement to the real source of moral authority and motivation: it is a way of tuning in to an ethical signal, not of generating one. And if that's King's view, he must remain some distance from the perfectionist's willingness to call all values into question. He cannot say with William James that the highest ethical life consists in the breaking of rules that have grown too narrow for the actual case.

Another familiar move is available at this point, and turns us back, in a way, to the strategy of prioritizing ethics over ontology. We often distinguish what's living from what's dead in the thought of historical figures. Why not do that in this case? Why not simply say that King's value as a *political* thinker lies in the resources we can find in his work for thinking about the political without recourse to divine reassurance or backstops? For political purposes, for the purposes of political life in a pluralistic democracy, the politics is what matters, and the faith claims can drop away.

But distinguishing between the useful and the useless elements in King's thought in this way is an exercise in question begging. That distinction helps here only if one already accepts an essentially liberal framing, rooted in the idea of religious arguments as "conversation-stoppers" or some such. Jeffrey Stout and others have argued convincingly that it is not at all clear that appeals to religion always function in that way. It is particularly difficult to frame the issues in this way in relation to U.S. racial politics, where, for example, the abolitionist and civil rights movements were saturated with religious discourse and values, and got traction in the public sphere in part on account of this saturation. So the question still remains: How can one tell a story about King's political philosophy without giving the Godhead a starring role?

On one reading of this question, it threatens to become relatively uninteresting, or maddening. If it is just a question about whether I've gotten in touch with "the real" King, then addressing it would mean recasting the argument in very different theoretical and conceptual terms. This would mean taking up debates over the nature of interpretation, and over how and when we can distinguish the *real* author of a meaning-bearing cultural object from the counterfeit or stand-in that consumers of the object imagine or project. I don't care to go this route, not least because doing so would be like attempting to define something murky (the "real" King) in terms of something even murkier (the proper account of interpretation).

Here, as in many contexts, questions meant to distinguish some real thing from some counterfeit can work to obscure clearer, more interesting, and more precise questions that are worth keeping distinct. If the question is whether King would assent to the reading I'm giving, I have no way of knowing this. I think I have found him expressly endorsing elements of the view on offer here. But I don't know if he would embrace the perfectionist picture as a whole, or agree with me that the picture reveals something vital about his work and legacy. Still, this doesn't strike me as a deal breaker. One of the virtues of any robustly expressive activity—art, literature, therapeutic conversation, and so on—is that it can show its authors endorsing, or on the way to endorsing, thoughts that they had not previously entertained in any conscious way. Anyone who has written anything with any seriousness of purpose has likely had the experience of finding his or her thinking clarified by the act of writing. Just as we sometimes don't know what we mean until we start trying to say it, that is, until we externalize it and have it reflected back to us on a screen or a page, we might not know what we're committed to until the expression of commitment gets reflected back to us by other people, acting as critics. The reader or critic is the writer's therapist, in a way, and can carry the burden of telling the writer what he or she means. I assert the right to play this role with Dr. King, as I would with any other culture worker.

The appeal to therapy and art criticism points to a second version of the counterfeit question. Perhaps the question is the question one asks the critic: Is this reading faithful to the work? Has the critic teased out something that we can now see as essential, or at least as interestingly connected, to what makes this work what it is? Or, in the alternative, which may be more helpful right now: Is the critic doing violence to this work? Even if one can't with certainty locate the point beyond which a critical encounter descends into error, one can identify with confidence the encounters that overstep the line with seven-league boots. For example, if one reads Morrison's *The Bluest Eye* as a commentary on the frequency and destructiveness of meteor showers in Iceland, something has surely gone amiss.

So maybe this is the way to raise the counterfeit question. Does it do violence to King to read him without any sustained reference to his religious commitments? How do we square the perfectionist investment in ceaseless ethical transformation with the Christian commitment to a moral world bounded by the rules of a divine order? Two possibilities strike me as especially promising.

One possibility involves refusing the linkage between faith and metaphysics that has governed the discussion so far. The problem has been the tension between King's metaphysical commitments and the ethical posture that I find in his work. But what if his Christian commitments are not metaphysical but existential? That is, what if we read him through figures like Kierkegaard or Cornel West, figures for whom faith is not an epistemic condition, involving knowledge of or belief in supernatural states of affairs? What if, for King as for these figures, faith is about the psychological and existential effects of establishing a relationship with something larger than oneself, something somehow embodied or encapsulated in the divine?

We can see King embracing this existentialist approach in the sermon "Why Jesus Called a Man a Fool." The high point of the sermon for present purposes is the remarkably vulnerable moment near the end, when King describes the experience and resolution of what historian David Garrow calls a "crisis of confidence."[37] During the Montgomery boycott King received a death threat that, for whatever reason, affected him more deeply than usual. Unable to sleep, he got up and made coffee. He was "frustrated [and] bewildered," and these feelings grew progressively worse as the night wore on.[38] Finally, he says, "I couldn't take it any longer; I was weak."[39] And then, "It seemed at that moment that I could hear an inner voice saying to me, . . . 'Martin Luther, . . . stand up for righteousness, . . . stand up for justice, . . . stand up for truth. . . . And lo I will be with you, . . . even until the end of the world.' "[40]

Here we see what seems to be most vitally at stake in King's invocation of the inner voice. The voice is not a source of normative authority, nor does it affirm or underwrite the truth of ethical propositions. "Stand up for justice," it says. Not "here is what justice means . . ." It is, as King says earlier in the sermon, a response to the realization that "you can't make it by yourself in this world. . . . You need somebody to give you consolation in the darkest hours." Sometimes this consolation comes from our earthly companions; but at other times earthly comfort is not enough. "The problems of life will begin to overwhelm you; disappointments will begin to beat upon the door of your life like a tidal wave. And if you don't have a deep and patient faith, you aren't going to be able to make it." It is important to note that this faith is not cognitively or epistemically deep; the depth comes not from the firmness of belief but from the rich feeling of a personal experience.

I would have to say more about this sermon and about the resources I'm bringing to bear on it, to make this appeal to existential considerations appropriately compelling. But for reasons of space it is important to close out this line of thinking. Suffice it to say that reading King as a perfectionist will conflict with reading him as a Christian only if his religious commitments are doing a certain kind of work in his ethical life, a kind of work they seem not to do. If faith is the dispositive source of normative content—if, that is, the role of the inner voice is to make truth-claims about virtue and right (and, as we'll see in a moment, if those claims are static and completely clear)—then a tragic discipline of continual self-criticism and self-creation is probably not the right way to cash out King's ethical-political sensibility. But we see in the "Fool" sermon that the voice does not play this sort of role. The voice provides comfort, reassurance, and existential sustenance. It is "a balm in Gilead to heal the sin-sick soul," not a narration of the Divine Law.

I've been trying to defuse the tension between perfectionist ethics and Christian faith by shifting the terms of debate. One way to do this, as noted above, is to replace the idea of faith as a state of knowing with the idea of faith as an existential resource, and then to highlight King's reliance on the existential. A second approach might redescribe the relationship between perfectionist self-definition and external judgment, so that ongoing and dynamic self-criticism is not at odds with fidelity to external norms, but an essential element in acting on the norms.

Perfectionists needn't refuse all external sources of normative content. As social beings who engage in dialogue, humans are necessarily informed by external sources, even if, as is sometimes the case, we end up adopting primarily oppositional relationships to them. The perfectionist manages this piece of the human condition by emphasizing the irreducible role of reflection, deliberation, and discourse in translating norms into action, especially social action, and in endorsing norms across changing sociohistorical contexts. Rather than refusing any external sources for their ethical judgments, perfectionists simply accept the burden of working through the meaning of these sources for themselves, in ways that are never immune to change or error.

In this spirit, it is worth noting that King spent a considerable amount of time and energy arguing with other Christians, living and dead, in person and through the medium of writing, about what Christian norms required. He struggled for years with the specters of Rauschenbusch and Niebuhr, starting with his days in seminary, as he sought to understand the political dimensions of sin and ministry. Similarly, he criticized the U.S. Christian church establishments, black and white, for failing to see the connection between Christ's teachings and the issues of human rights, militarism, and poverty. (And he did this, of course, in the distant wake of the great abolitionist effort to relocate Christianity's center of moral gravity from the enslaver to the enslaved.) So in a way, what gives King's ethical-political perspective its claim on our attention is precisely not its roots in Christian teaching. Of all the Christians the world has seen, only one of them has been Martin King. King's view demands our attention because he transformed the generic Christian commitments—commitments that he by definition shared with millions upon millions of other people—into the distinctive career and perspectives that called forth this book. My suggestion is that a perfectionist ethic is at least one consequence of this transformational encounter with Christian orthodoxy.

Religious commitments are vital to King's work, of course. He says as much in, among other places, the "Fool" sermon: "All that I do in civil rights I do because I consider it a part of my ministry. I have no other ambitions in life but to achieve excellence in the Christian ministry."[41] My point here is that reading King as a perfectionist gives us a clearer sense of what achieving excellence meant to him. This reading does not evade or annul his Christian commitments, but clarifies his orientation to them. A full account of King's politics will require reference to these commitments. But if I'm right, it will also require fleshing out the perfectionist orientation that he brought to the commitments and that he used to translate his religious convictions into his distinctive political views.

The Arc of the Moral Universe

The problem of reconciling King's religious convictions with a perfectionist ethic is very much like the tension that, as I mentioned earlier, threatens to undermine my reading of King as an experimentalist. If King is an experimentalist—someone who refuses to backstop earthly striving with supernatural guarantees—then how are we to think of his own predilection for offering what look for all the world like guarantees? His familiar reworking of a line from Unitarian minister Theodore Parker may be the clearest point at which this worry gets traction: If one can confidently assert that the arc of the moral universe is long but also that "from what I see I am sure it bends towards justice," then how is that not a guarantee, or at least a way of pining for one?[42]

One approach to this question would require a lengthy excursion into Christian theodicy, and from there into knotty theological issues concerning the nature and efficacy of God's will and its relationship to human intentions and projects. This is not the place for any of that. I prefer simply to point out that whatever one says about all of those issues, one must also make room for the reflections that we find in "Unfulfilled Dreams" and elsewhere. One has to make room for the thought, for *King's* thought, that failure and frustration are central to "the story of life."

I'll put a down payment on the theology, or build a philosophical workaround, by insisting once again on the distinction between faith and belief. To say that the arc of the universe bends toward justice is, I'd say, an expression of faith, meant to affirm and shore up one's relationship to the God that underwrites all earthly striving. But faith is not knowledge, expressions of faith are not predictions, and to underwrite is not to guarantee success. In a different context I would at this point explore the thought that King is indulging here in an elliptical or enthymematic mode of homiletic expression that routinely attends pulpit oratory. *God will provide,* preachers say. They don't usually go on to add the thought that hangs unspoken in the air for anyone who's read Kierkegaard or suffered or noticed real loss: *unless He doesn't.* A great deal of vernacular religious discourse passes lightly over this essential caveat, which enables the sleight of hand that turns what sounded like a promise of earthly success into a bet on the eternal. King, to his credit, insists on the caveat, and wrestles with its meaning. *The arc will bend,* King says: *we will reach the promised land.* But King David thought he would build a great temple, and he did not succeed at that. The genius of the "Unfulfilled Dreams" sermon is that it makes this explicit. The Arc will bend *unless it doesn't,* in which case we, like King David, will have to grapple with that, and with the permanent possibility of disappointment and defeat.

Love and Loathing

The last of the obstacles to my reading of King is a possible tension between the perfectionist's reliance on self-loathing and the thoroughgoing love ethos that animates King's work and life. In fact, King's commitment to a love ethic might leave him with little use for the notion of loathing in any context. It will turn out that this potential conflict is more apparent than real.

The centrality of the love ethic for King is evident in any number of places, including a 1961 address to the Fellowship of the Concerned, an interracial group of racial progressives. Here King explains that a commitment to nonviolence rules out, not just the external violence that would injure another, but also the internal "violence of spirit" that countenances or implies injury to others. This internal nonviolence is an expression, he goes on to say, of the sense of love that the Greeks used the word *agape* to capture. "*Agape* is understanding, creative, redemptive, good will to all. . . . When one rises to love on this level, he loves men not because he likes them, not because their ways appeal to him, but he loves every man because God loves him. And he rises to the point of loving the person who does an evil deed while hating the deed that the person does."[43] Presumably this "love the sinner, hate the sin" argument must apply to the self, and thereby rule out any form of self-loathing.

Interestingly, King complicates this application of the love ethic to the self in terms that recall the internal "civil war" that we encountered in the "Unfulfilled Dreams" sermon. In the Fellowship of the Concerned address, the civil war becomes "a strange dichotomy," a "disturbing dualism within human nature."[44] The self is divided into higher and lower, torn between good and evil, and the lower self finds expression in actions that it is permissible to hate. To say this is very nearly to say that this hatred, this loathing, is directed at an aspect of the agent's character, and that the conflict between love and loathing is merely apparent, an artifact of the difference between perfectionist and Christocentric idioms of ethical discourse. For this reason, it may be useful to expand the vocabulary a bit, and, at least on occasion, to translate "loathing" into a broader notion of negative affect.

Reconciling King's love-oriented ethical practice with the idea of loathing in general takes us most of the way toward reconciling *agape* with the idea of *self*-loathing. Just as the love ethic entails self-love, the negative affect that attends the work of transforming character also has a self-directed aspect. We can also see this self-directed negative affect in "Unfulfilled Dreams," where King shares with the congregation his desire and determination "to be a good man."[45] Here we see the overt instruction to strive for self-improvement, arriving on the heels of a string of metaphors and literary references expressing Pauline dismay: "The good that I would, I do not: And the evil that I would not, that I do."

There are other moments like this in King's career, not least because he often recycled the civil war analogy in other settings. But limitations of space require that I leave the accumulation of examples (or counterexamples) to the division of scholarly labor that I mentioned above, and limit myself to one more word about the role that the *experience* of self-directed negative affect plays in the account on offer here. For the perfectionist, there is an experiential dimension at work in the appeal to self-loathing. The aim is not just to recommend an ethical practice of cultivating disdain for the lower self, and of using this disdain to motivate the work of self-transformation. The point is also that the appropriately sensitive ethical agent will have the experience of self-loathing, irrespective of whether he or she wishes it. The burden is to harness this experience so that it is productive rather than destructive, which means working through the experience with care (and in prayer, King might say).

Historian David Garrow clearly documents the phenomenological toll that the perfectionist's discipline took on King's life. After discussing King's consternation at his own inability to curtail his extramarital affairs, Garrow reports:

> King's intensely self-critical nature encompassed all aspects of his life, not just sex, and was often painfully visible to his family and closest friends. "He criticized himself more severely than anyone else ever did," Coretta remembered. "He was always the first one to say, 'Maybe I was wrong, maybe I made a mistake.' . . . He would go through this agonizing process of self-analysis many times."[46]

Conclusion

I have been keen to work out the perfectionist strands in King's thought and practice in part because this adds another layer of complexity to a figure that we seem determined to reduce to an empty signifier of generalized goodwill. If I'm right, we have to go beyond warding off this emptiness in the usual, still-essential ways. We can do more than juxtapose invocations of The Dreamer against appeals to "the radical King," with his longstanding focus on economic justice and his evolving interest in the links between racism, militarism, and imperialism. Alongside the Radical and the Dreamer we can also put the Perfectionist, and commit to reckoning with the depth of the challenge that King's perfectionism poses to democratic societies and citizens.

3

The Roots of Civil Disobedience in Republicanism and Slavery

BERNARD R. BOXILL

Martin Luther King, Jr., often expressed his esteem for the first claim in the long second sentence of the American Declaration of Independence: "We hold these truths to be self-evident, that all men are created equal."[1] And indeed, according to Adam Bedau, King "labored in the tradition" of all the claims in that famous sentence.[2] King further intimated a deep concordance between the theory summarized in the Declaration and his own theory of nonviolent direct action when he referred to the movement he led as the "Negro revolution," and claimed that its members had "written a Declaration of Independence."[3] But when he dismissed the Black Power movement as a "psychological reaction" to the slave masters' cruel agenda to make their slaves "perfect slave[s]" he implied that, unlike his own theory, it had no theoretical roots but was simply the reflexive valorization of qualities that opposed those the masters' agenda aimed at. Because that agenda aimed at making the slaves obedient, submissive, dependent, fearful, and convinced of their inferiority, the Black Power movement would defy white authority, glory in blackness, and declare independence from everything white.[4]

Regrettably, King's manner of criticizing the rival movement seems reminiscent of the habit of dismissing blacks' behavior as unthinking reactions to their predicament, as in the claim that black ghetto culture is an irrational response to poverty. Of course, human beings sometimes react unthinkingly—when suddenly confronted with danger, for instance. But when people have the time to think about a problem, they usually do *think* about it and try to find some way to resolve it, even though their thinking is not always effective, elegant, or morally correct. An interesting example of this kind of response to a prolonged and serious problem is the way some slaves responded to their predicament. These slaves did not simply surrender to its demands and become perfect slaves. They responded to it in the same way King responded to his predicament: by thinking long and hard about it, trying to find a way out of it, and trying to keep alive their hope and faith that they would succeed. Like King, some of them came up with a theory, considerably less worked-out than his, inspired by the Declaration of Independence. But this is also true of the Black Power movement. So we might say that, although King was right that this movement had "psychological roots" in the "soil" of slavery, so did his own movement and, as we shall see, both movements were to some extent anticipated by the work of philosopher slaves reworking the republican philosophy of the American revolutionary generation for their own salvation.

The American revolutionaries were widely reputed among their contemporaries to be more freedom loving than any other people. Only their great love of freedom, it was held, could have motivated them to risk ignominious deaths as traitors by rebelling against mighty Britain, which, corrupted by its own power, was trying to enslave them. On that view Patrick Henry's "Give me liberty or give me death" was therefore no vain boast but a true expression of the revolutionaries' love of liberty.

What accounted for the Americans' love of liberty? Many would have given most of the credit to the republican philosophy that the Americans studied closely, though the American environment was also widely believed to naturally encourage a love of liberty. Yet there were contemporaries, including sympathetic ones, who suspected that the revolutionaries' touted love of liberty, though genuine to a considerable degree, was also inflated by a love of certain other things, not always admirable, that in America happened to be associated with liberty. I will not examine this suspicion but focus on a different if related claim, namely that though the revolutionaries did love liberty, they did not pay special attention to the most important of the many different things that are called liberty, and that against all educated expectations the slaves, or at least some of them, inspired by the republican philosophy, but also educated by their enslavement, did identify, seek, and sometimes secure that most important of all the different things that are called liberty.

Slavery

It is a tautology that masters dominate their slaves. It is also a tautology that slaves must obey their masters. Apparently some philosophers disagree, perhaps because they think that domination simply means having the power to interfere with the interests of those you dominate. Because people do not always have to obey those who dominate them, these philosophers may think that it is not necessarily true that slaves must obey their masters. If so, they are mistaken. A considerable part of the ignominy of enslavement is that a slave has to obey his master; there need be no ignominy in simply having someone who has the power to interfere in your interests. Further that slaves must always obey their master best explains why slavery always involves cruelty. As Frederick Douglass, who should know, often repeated, cruelty is necessary for slavery's existence; take away the thumb-screw and the whip and there would be no slaves.[5]

Cruelty is necessary for slavery's existence because slaves must obey their masters. Or in other words, slavery is necessarily cruel because masters use cruelty to ensure that their slaves always obey them. Of course some people use the prospect of reward for obedience to get others to obey them. These people are not slave masters. Slave masters use cruelty to ensure that their slaves must always obey them. Specifically to ensure obedience, slave masters use punishment or the threat of punishment for disobedience, and the punishment they dispense usually takes the form of pain. This is not because they are all sadists, although many of them become sadists. It is partly because inflicting pain is in the circumstances cheaper than giving rewards, and masters often have slaves in order to make money, and partly because pain for disobedience better ensures obedience than reward for obedience. People can be unmoved by the prospect of reward if they feel that they have enough, but they are never unmoved by the prospect of great pain.

The fact that the people have to be rewarded or tortured to make them obey others suggests that they do not like to obey others; in other words they preferred to obey only themselves. The fact that slaves were tortured to induce them to obey their masters similarly suggests they did not like to obey their masters. This suggestion would be unwarranted if the masters were sadists, but as we have seen their cruelty can be accounted for without supposing that they were sadists. Consequently it remains that the slaves did not like to obey their masters. Further because it is implausible to suppose that the slaves disliked obeying their masters only because their masters had the power to threaten their disobedience with pain, it seems that the slaves did not like to obey any others, or in other words that they preferred to obey only themselves. We do not have to suppose that this preference was equally strong in all the slaves, or that it cannot be moderated by particular experiences; perhaps for example it was weaker in slaves who from birth witnessed slaves always obeying masters. But even if that possibility turned out to be true it would not follow that such slaves did not strongly prefer to obey only themselves. Slavery on mainland America was terribly cruel even when most slaves there were born into slavery. On the other hand it also does not follow that the slaves' preference to obey only themselves was ineradicable. Indeed masters strove and sometimes succeeded in eradicating it.

The masters' use of brutality to enforce obedience was based on the assumption that masters and slaves shared the same human nature. Masters desired not to always have to obey others, but knew that they would be inclined to obey if they were brutalized. They assumed that slaves would be the same in these regards. They also understood that the brutality that got their slaves to obey them would also get their slaves to desire retaliation, and that even more brutality would deter the slaves from acting on that desire. Consequently they beat their slaves to get them to obey, and then beat them again to deter them from retaliating for the first beating.

The strategy worked to some extent, but the abuse that deterred the slaves from retaliating also increased their resentment and their desire to retaliate. Slaves also naturally regarded their fear as an injury and a revelation of their own inadequacies, and this gave them further reason to resent and desire to retaliate against their masters, who by arousing their fear injured and shamed them. The masters were aware of this complication, knowing that this was how they would think if they were slaves, and were therefore never fully confident that brutalizing the slaves would altogether deter them from acting on their desire to retaliate. At least partly for this reason they opposed emancipation. They saw that it would leave the slaves' resentment intact, and even perhaps inflamed, given that resentment feeds and grows on the recollection of injuries and affronts that have not been avenged. At the same time, emancipation would make slaves less vulnerable to their former masters, diminishing the fear that had deterred them from retaliating. Thus, Thomas Jefferson feared that emancipation would lead to race wars and perhaps to the "extermination of the one or the other race."[6]

So the masters knew that although they had forced the slaves to suppress their desires to retaliate, that those desires remained, festered, and generated more desperate, more venomous, more furious, and more murderous desires. And it seems only fair to allow that the slaves were equally aware of the turmoil in their own souls. When all is going smoothly most people probably do not reflect on or are not even particularly aware of their own thoughts. When we want food and find it easily we may not even be clearly aware that we want food. But when we want food and cannot find it we become increasingly aware that we want food. I assume that this is true of most of our desires. We become most acutely aware of our desires and reflect on them when they are continually and repeatedly frustrated. I imagine that this is because frustrated desires are painful and people naturally take pain to be a reason to do something to avoid the pain or remove themselves from it. Now we are assuming that the slaves prefer not to have to obey others, desire to avoid the pain their masters are inflicting on them, and desire to retaliate against their masters, and we are also assuming that these three powerful desires are frustrated and therefore painful. Consequently it follows from what I have just said that slaves will become aware of and reflect closely on these three desires, as well of course on the desires those desires generate.

Of course, the obvious remedy for frustrated and therefore pain-generating desires is to satisfy one's desires, but in the case under consideration this remedy is unavailable. Consequently the slave will search for other remedies, and eventually he will come upon the remedy for ridding himself of the inevitably frustrated pain-causing desires, especially of course the root of all the trouble, namely the preference for obeying only himself. If the slave adopts this remedy and succeeds in prosecuting it to the end, he will become what the master wanted and was aiming at all along, an unthinking and therefore perfect slave.

But the slave will find that he cannot readily prosecute the remedy in question to the end, because human beings have a strong and persistent desire to obey only themselves. And his prolonged and painful acquaintance with that desire will inevitably lead him to wonder about its object and whether it is worth all the fuss and sacrifice. He will be tempted to believe that it is worthless, because then he would be able to devote himself to abolishing the desire for it with few misgivings. But on the other hand, his strong and persistent desire to not have to always obey his master will make it difficult for him to believe that its object is worthless, for human beings tend to invest the object of their strong desires with great value. Think of how people tend to sanctify the objects of their sexual passions—often against all available evidence.

Consequently it would be only natural for the slave to make the object of his desire to obey only himself not merely something he desires, but also a value. And having thus made freedom a value, ridding himself of his desire for it will become doubly difficult, despite the pain that it causes him. Ordinarily people tormented by such anxieties turn for counsel to their sages who store the accumulated wisdom of the culture. But the slaves had no such sages. Their elders were stolen from the wide variety of the different cultures in the vast African continent and their wisdoms clashed or were too disparate to be combined into coherent wisdom. So although Africa still influenced the slaves' thinking, for its music and therefore its sentiments lingered in America, they had to do the best they could remaking and perfecting for their own purposes a wisdom forged far from Africa and brought to the land of their enslavement.

The American Revolution

In the periods preceding and during the revolutionary period, Americans accused the British of taxing them without their consent, contended that this amounted to compelling their obedience and violating their freedom, and concluded that they were therefore obligated to fight the British to the death if necessary to recover their freedom. Their argument was inspired by a theory worked out by the English republicans and Whigs of the sixteenth and seventeenth centuries, including John Milton, James Harrington, Algernon Sidney, and John Locke. The American revolutionaries were extraordinarily vociferous and insistent about spelling it out. They made speeches, shouted slogans, and produced an endless stream of pamphlets and articles, all declaring and protesting their domination by the British and explaining why they were justified and indeed obligated to rebel and make war against the country that many of them considered their mother country. Providentially their loudest, most impassioned, and most insistent complaint was that their forced obedience to the British meant that they were slaves. John Dickinson, a prominent revolutionary, syllogized its argument: "Those who are taxed without their own consent, expressed by themselves or their representatives, are slaves. We are taxed without our own consent, expressed by ourselves or our representatives. We are therefore—SLAVES."[7] And a sentence from the "textbook" of their revolution, Algernon Sidney's *Discourses concerning Government,* confirmed the syllogism: "He is a slave," Sidney wrote, "who serves the best and gentlest man in the world, as well as he who serves the worst; and he does serve him if he must obey his commands, and depends upon his will."[8] And "We are slaves!" became the revolutionaries' mantra, with Jefferson, the future philosopher-president, leading the refrain.

Inevitably that refrain fixed the attention of black slaves on their masters' condition. After all, those slaves called themselves slaves too. At first they must have thought that their masters were lying or fooling when they called themselves slaves. After all, their masters' condition was different from theirs in every respect. Eventually, however, two considerations induced them to take their masters more seriously. First, the masters evidently hated the slaves' condition as much as they hated their own condition. Perhaps then the two conditions, however different, shared some factor that made them equally hateful. Second, the masters identified the factor that made their condition hateful. It was that they had to obey someone other than themselves. And the slaves found that it was the same factor that they found most hateful about their own condition. The only difference was that the revolutionaries had to obey King George, and their slaves had to obey the revolutionaries. Understanding this changed the black slaves fundamentally. Before that point life must have seemed a bad joke. Their self-reflection could only have led them to conclude that suicide, or self-mutilation, ridding themselves of their preference to obey only themselves, was their sole hope. For the preference seemed to guarantee misery: floggings for disobeying their masters, and frustrations when they obeyed their masters. And since it was the root cause of their desire to retaliate against their masters, it was also responsible for the frustration they endured when they suppressed that desire and for the floggings they suffered when they indulged it. Understanding how their masters reacted to their enslavement must have changed how the slaves viewed their own enslavement. They would have seen that having masters they had to obey was not an inherent part of nature that necessarily conflicted with their preference to obey themselves. They had thought that preference was evil and had considered ridding themselves of it; now seeing how their masters rejoiced in their own preference to obey only themselves, they would have been encouraged to think the corresponding preference in themselves was worth rejoicing in too, and that its object, not having to obey others, was among the greatest of all goods. Inevitably they adopted the philosophy of their masters and became republicans.

Because the Declaration of Independence distills the republican philosophy, no wonder W. E. B. Du Bois proclaimed "American Negroes" the "true[st] exponents of the pure human spirit of the Declaration of Independence."[9] And it's also no wonder that characteristic themes of the Declaration are plain in the works of David Walker, and present, if implicit, in the works of Henry Highland Garnet, Martin Delany, Frederick Douglass, Du Bois himself, King, and the Black Power movement.

Although the slaves had become republicans, few rebelled against their masters. Since the revolutionaries had rebelled against their masters they thought that their slaves could therefore not be republicans and consequently could not love liberty. The more perceptive and honest among them understood that they were far more favorably positioned for rebellion than their slaves. They had risked a lot in rebelling, but their chances of winning had been good if not overwhelming. They had the help of the French, and their master was far away on the other side of the vast Atlantic Ocean. Their slaves in contrast had no helpers as formidable as the French, and their masters were well armed and next to them in America. In their case rebellion would not be merely risky; it would be suicide. Still, most of the revolutionaries insisted that the slaves did not love liberty enough, or at least not as much as they did. Perhaps they thought that Patrick Henry's proclamation "Give me liberty or give me death" expressed their attitude that even a certain death was better than slavery. Actually they were wrong.

The republican principle that freedom is a great value implies that most losses should be endured to avoid slavery. But it does not imply that death is an acceptable way to avoid slavery. It cannot without contradicting itself. The slave has at least a chance to be free. The dead are not free, even if they are not enslaved, and do not have any chance to ever be free. If freedom is so great a value, having a chance to get it is better than having no chance at all. Patrick Henry contradicted himself if he meant his declaration to say that death was better than slavery. If he valued freedom so highly, he would have thought it worth waiting for, even in slavery.

But the Americans hung on to the idea that slaves did not love freedom. Sometimes they appealed to a classic argument of republican theory, namely, that freedom once lost can never be regained. Perhaps the Americans actually believed it. The supposition that they did believe it would explain their spleen at the small tax, quickly withdrawn, that the British imposed on them. In any case they even succeeded in persuading some prominent black thinkers, such as Martin Delany, that slaves come to love their enslavement. However, Delany denied the deadlier claim that slaves could therefore never regain their freedom.[10] Given the unpopularity of his call for blacks to emigrate to Africa and South America to regain their freedom there, he promptly proposed another plan for securing their freedom that did not require that they love their freedom, expecting that they would learn to love it once they regained it.

Jean-Jacques Rousseau gives the best argument for the republican claim that slaves cannot love freedom: "It is as true of freedom as it is of innocence and virtue, that one appreciates their worth only as long as one enjoys them oneself, and loses the taste for them as soon as they are lost. I know the delights of your Country, said Brasidas to a Satrap who was comparing the life of Sparta with that of Persepolis, but you cannot know the pleasures of mine."[11] But we need to spell it out. Brasidas knows and enjoys the Satrap's pleasures, but the Satrap cannot know or enjoy Brasidas's, because of the way Persepolis and Sparta, the hometowns of the Satrap and Brasidas, respectively, are governed. Persepolis was governed by the Darius, the emperor of the Persian Empire. Because the Satrap lives there, he must always obey Darius, and consequently he is Darius's slave, even though he has position and riches. Sparta, on the other hand, is a republic where no one rules anyone else. Because Brasidas lives there, he obeys only himself and consequently is free. Moreover, he must enjoy his freedom there more than he enjoys any other pleasures, because he has enjoyed these pleasures in Persepolis, but prefers to live in Sparta. The Satrap too should prefer to live in Sparta. He enjoys the pleasures of Persepolis, but Brasidas found those pleasures less enjoyable than the freedom in Sparta. But the Satrap prefers to remain in Persepolis. Therefore, he must not enjoy freedom. He does not love freedom according to Rousseau because he does not know it. This seems odd. He does not know freedom because he lives in Persepolis and there is no freedom there. But if he goes to Sparta, where there is freedom, it seems that he will quickly come to know it. But Rousseau denies this. The Satrap, he says, cannot know freedom by going to Sparta because freedom is a virtue and you cannot know a virtue simply by going to a city where citizens have that virtue. To know a virtue you have to understand what and why people are doing and feeling when they are exercising it, and such understanding can be achieved only as the result of a long and careful education. Consequently the Satrap cannot know freedom by simply going to Sparta. To know what freedom is, he would have to educate himself about it, like the Spartans do. But this he will not do, because he is already too captivated by the cheap and easy pleasures of Persepolis, which anyone can enjoy without any particular education. Consequently, he will never know what freedom is and thus will never enjoy it, or love it, because loving something implies enjoying it. The Satrap represents slaves—slaves will never enjoy or love freedom.

Slaves probably never will enjoy or love freedom—as Rousseau understands freedom. But that freedom is not the freedom that is the object of the slaves' simple desire not to have to always obey their masters. Neither does it seem to be the freedom that the Americans loved, which was also not having a master that they always had to obey.

But American revolutionaries did sometimes write as if they believed that the freedom they loved was Rousseauian or related to it. Of course, they knew that Americans were not deliberately educated like the Spartans to love freedom. But they seemed to believe that the carefully contrived circumstances in Sparta that secured its citizens' love of freedom were to some extent naturally duplicated in America. For example, one of their favorite themes was that the relative absence of luxury in America, along with the other circumstances of life there, prevented young Americans from developing a taste for the kinds of easy pleasures characteristic of Persepolis and left them with no choice but to pursue and eventually to love the arduous but ultimately more enjoyable pleasures of freedom. The American historian David Ramsay pushed that theme, claiming that "everything" in the American environment "contributed to nourish a spirit of liberty," and as if adding an argument to support his claim, noted, "Luxury had made but very little progress. . . . The large extent of territory gave each man an opportunity of fishing, fowling and hunting, without injury to his neighbour. Every inhabitant was or easily might be a freeholder. . . . His mind was equally free from all the restraints of superstition. No ecclesiastical establishments invaded the rights of conscience, or fettered the freeborn mind. At liberty to act and think, as his inclination prompted, he disdained the ideas of dependence and subjection."[12]

The disdain Ramsay speaks of seems to imply a disdain of domination, because dependence and subjection imply domination. And because disdaining something suggests a love of its opposite, Ramsay's claim seems to imply that early Americans loved not to be dominated. Consequently, it seems that early Americans loved republican freedom—if not Rousseau's version, then at least the contemporary version. But Ramsay's argument suggests a lot more than that. Take for example his claims about Americans' experience of having no restrains on their inclinations. This experience seems likely to have led to a hatred of restraints and consequently to the love of the opposite of having restrains, a love of negative freedom. In other words, the experiences that Ramsay described were likely to lead Americans to love many kinds of freedom. Further the early Americans were not only inclined to fish, fowl, and hunt, the inclinations Ramsay mentions; they were also inclined to steal the Native Americans' land, kill or drive them off, and then enslave blacks to work the land that they had stolen. If the Americans met with few restraints on these inclinations, and enslaving blacks is domination, it seems that Americans' love of negative freedom implied their love of dominating others.

But Americans were admired around the world for their love of freedom, which was usually rated as greater than that of any other people. Edmund Burke, for example, claimed that it was their "predominating feature" and "stronger . . . than in any other people of the earth."[13] But his "Speech on Conciliation with America" suggests that the world's impression of American freedom was inaccurate.[14] He began by noting that the "spirit of liberty" was more "high and haughty" in the southern states, where there was a "vast multitude of slaves," than in the northern states, adding that the association of slavery and a high and haughty love of liberty was universal.[15] In "any part of the world" where there was slavery, he observed, the free were "by far the most proud and jealous of their freedom."[16] And then he argued that this was because "freedom is to [the masters of slaves] not only an enjoyment, but a kind of rank and privilege," adding for good measure that the American love of liberty is also grossly inflated by the fact that in America liberty is so closely associated with wealth and leisure that when Americans think they love liberty, they are really mostly loving wealth and honor.[17] His comment "I cannot alter the nature of man" suggests that he was reluctant to blame the Americans for thus inflating their love of liberty, but he insisted he could not "commend the superior morality" of the Americans for loving what they called liberty, because it had "as much pride as virtue in it."[18]

In other words, although the slaves would have discovered with joy that their masters loved not having to obey others, just as they did, they also quickly discovered that the Americans loved many other kinds of freedom, some of which boded ill for their slaves. So instead of building castles in the sky, they set about understanding the most important of the freedoms that the Americans loved, the freedom that they loved most passionately, the freedom that they could have even in the state of unfreedom that the Americans' love of freedom would impose on them, something they would love, and that would help them prevail against the despair and doubt they feared could tempt them to abandon the long and difficult search for freedom in all its forms.

The Slaves' Freedom

You hand a gunman your wallet when he credibly threatens to kill you if you don't; a fugitive complies with an armed pursuer's command to stop or else be shot dead; soldiers surrender at gunpoint. In all these cases people obey someone other than themselves. But few if any would say that they were therefore slaves. And it would not matter if the scenarios were repeated many times. Even if the people continued to obey, most would continue to deny that they were therefore slaves. The result would be similar if someone offered the people in question a sizable reward for obeying him and they complied. The implication is that if obedience is necessary for slavery it is not sufficient. Although slaves must obey their masters, not everyone who obeys someone else is a slave. Why? The examples suggest that a plausible answer is that the people were acting rationally. It is rational to give up a wallet to avoid being killed and it is rational to obey someone else if he offers you a sizable reward for obeying, and I should add only if what you do does not cost you more than the reward and is permissible. But the rationality of obedience in these cases is a red herring. It suggests something about how the person acts that implies that he is not a slave though the rationality of his act does not itself show that he is not a slave. When we say that someone acts rationally when he gives up his wallet to save his life we mean that he weighed the costs and benefits of the alternatives open to him and decided that it was better to give up his wallet than to be killed. The rationality of the act suggests that he chose to do it. But it is the fact that he chose to do it not the fact that it was rational that suggests that he is not a slave. Conversely if he acted irrationally, giving up his wallet to avoid a small slap on the face, we might suspect that he was the gunman's slave, or at least that he was slavish, not precisely because he acted irrationally, but because his irrationality suggests that he acted in a panic. If he had deliberated but decided to do something foolish, perhaps because his deliberations depended on claims that turned out through no fault of his own to be false, we would not say that he was slavish, unless we had reason to suspect that fear had distorted his deliberations.

Now suppose the gunman commands you to hand over your life savings and credibly threatens to slap you if you disobey. If you obeyed him, most people would think that you were his slave. This is because your obedience would not be rational. The harm he threatens you with for disobeying him is not enough to make obeying him the rational thing to do. Consequently they would have to suppose that you obey him because you believe that his will that you do something is sufficient reason for you to do it. And that belief is the very definition of slavery.

These considerations suggest some distinctions in the condition we called slavery. All the people we routinely call slaves are unfree because they all have someone with the power to credibly threaten them with enough harm to ensure that they always obey his commands. This includes those who choose to obey him because considering his threat they decide that obedience is the most rational or the morally best thing to do. Strictly as we have seen their obedience does not necessarily mark them as slaves, but they are still unfree because they do things they would not do were it not for his threat. Still though these slaves are unfree, they seem less unfree than others. These others, the more unfree slaves, obey their masters when obedience is not the result of a choice on their part that obedience is the moral or rational thing to do. They obey either because they are overwhelmed by fear or because they take their master's desire that they do something to be a sufficient reason for them to do it. Let us call these slaves genuine slaves and call the other slaves, those who do what their master commands because they choose to do it, free in fact though slaves in form or, for short, more than half free.

I use the terms "free in fact" though "a slave in form" and "more than half free" after Douglass, who used them to describe a slave who "cannot be flogged."[19] For it turns out that such a slave is one who obeys only on the ground that he finds it rational or moral to obey. Further, he or she is most likely to keep the hope of freedom alive and thus motivate the search for it. Being more than half free was not easy. The masters hated more-than-half-free slaves. Because they obeyed only because they chose to do so, often after some deliberation, they slowed work down and reduced profits, and the constant threatening necessary to make them obey showed up the masters as bullies. Of course bullying was inseparable from slavery, and the masters were familiar with it and enjoyed its pleasures. But the typical master generally preferred to leave the bullying to his overseers. He wanted his bare command to be sufficient to guarantee obedience, because such obedience would better reveal his superiority. Thus he had powerful motives for getting rid of his more-than-half-free slaves. But he could not just kill them. Well, he could, of course, but greed usually dissuaded him. Slaves were valuable property. So he devised a remedy to make his more-than-half-free slaves more unfree. The remedy was "breaking," and its centerpiece—predictably—was frequent, severe, and unexpected flogging. Technically it was torture. It was applied not only after disobedience—flogging after disobedience was only punishment—but at any time whatsoever, randomly, whether the slave had been obedient or not, when he least expected it. Through mechanisms I cannot explore here the slave eventually lost his taste or ability to deliberate and choose, and consequently his preference to obey only himself, and the master's desire that he do something became sufficient to move him to do it. While this was going on, the master carefully tempted him with easy cheap pleasures like drunkenness, aiming in this way to distract him from the pleasures of thinking and consequently the pleasures of freedom, since the prospect of such pleasures might move him to deliberate and choose. Experience suggested that the remedy could break most stubborn slaves permanently in about a year, and the prognosis motivated some of the yet-unbroken and more perceptive slaves to find some strategy that would stop the remedy before its results became permanent.

Despite the limited means available, some of these slaves did find such a strategy, though it was crude, risky, dangerous, and depended on the slave being valuable and strong. Nevertheless it was sometimes doable. Its essential requirement was to stop the constant flogging, for it was this that made thinking impossible and thus eventually broke the slave. Of this Douglass was certain. He was under no illusion that human nature could withstand the constant pain of the process of breaking conducted over many months. It would eventually buckle and the slave would lose his desire or ability to think and choose and consequently to obey only himself. It was also essential that the slave not be killed in the process of stopping the flogging. The idea was not to get oneself killed but to make it possible to keep thinking for oneself. Life with any hope of liberty was better than death in which there could be no such hope. But how can the slave stop the flogging without also being killed? Douglass's answer was that he or she must physically resist the breaker's attempt to flog him. The purpose of such resistance was to make the attempt so troublesome, exhausting, and humiliating that the breaker would decide to give it up and to never try it again. The purpose of the resistance was not for the slave to kill the breaker or to have the breaker kill the slave. The slave must resist forcefully but nonthreateningly, that is, purely defensively, because such resistance would make it less likely that the breaker would think that he had to kill the slave in self-defense, and consequently also less likely that the slave would have to kill the breaker in self-defense. The strategy worked for Douglass. After careful preparation he forcefully but only defensively resisted the efforts of Covey—his appointed breaker—to flog him, and at the end of an exhausting and humiliating struggle Covey gave it up and never tried to flog Douglass again. As a result Douglass kept both his life and his desire and ability to think and to choose and consequently his preference to obey only himself.

Physically resisting the breaker was not strictly necessary in order to gain the status of a slave who cannot be flogged. Douglass reports that a slave said to his master, "You can shoot me but you can't whip me," and the slave "was neither whipped nor shot."[20] The master had understood the slave's ultimatum: Try to whip me and I will try my best to kill you. Whatever happens, you lose. If I kill you, obviously you lose. If you kill me, you lose too because I am a valuable slave and you cannot afford to kill me. And the master backed off because he could see that the slave had the resolve to make good on his ultimatum. That slave and Douglass both risked death in order to retain the preference to obey only themselves. Sometimes the risk was higher than the slave calculated. Denby, "among the most valuable" of his master's slaves, calculated that he would not be shot for defying a command to get out of a creek where he had fled to avoid a whipping.[21] He miscalculated. His overseer calculated that his bad example outweighed his value and shot him dead.[22] Douglass might also have miscalculated. He surmised that Covey failed to report his resistance to the authorities and thereby have him hanged because his reputation as a slave breaker and the income he earned from it would have vanished if people heard that a boy of seventeen had fought him to a draw. But he could not have banked on Covey thinking that way. Indeed the vagaries of slave life, the impossibility of knowing how the master or overseer might be thinking about the value of his slave on any particular day, meant that the slave employing Douglass's strategy could not really calculate his chances of success. To that extent he was doing more than merely risking his life. We all risk our lives every day after calculating the chances of success and finding them good enough. The slave employing Douglass's strategy had no idea of his chances of success. Literally he had to be prepared to die.

Clearly Douglass's strategy, so fraught with danger and risk, was not for everyone. Most slaves lacked the courage to attempt it, and some simply lacked the physical strength to make enough trouble to make it work. Not that it demanded that the slave be strong enough to stop the breaker from flogging her. Nelly was not strong enough to stop the overseer Sevier from flogging her, but before he succeeded she gave him enough trouble to dissuade any sane man from ever trying to flog her again. It does not follow that pure defiance without the strength to make plenty of trouble for the breaker would lead to success. He would keep beating her until she was broken. In addition to defiance the slave had to be capable of giving the breaker plenty of trouble.

Douglass reported his feelings after the fight as follows: "I felt as I had never felt before. It was a resurrection from the dark and pestiferous tomb of slavery, to the heaven of comparative freedom. . . . I had reached the point, at which I was *not afraid to die*. This spirit made me a freeman in *fact,* while I remained a slave in *form.* When a slave cannot be flogged he is more than half free."[23] It is worth spelling out his meaning. First, Douglass was not afraid to die. This follows from the fact that he could not know his chances for success when he challenged Covey. They could have been zero. He took a step that for all he knew guaranteed his death. Thus, he had to be prepared to die. Second, Douglass remained a slave in form. Anyone seeing him under Covey would have thought that he was a slave except for the fact that he was never whipped. But he worked hard, obeyed orders, and did not try to escape when Covey was watching. Third, Douglass was a freeman in fact. This is the most important of his claims. How could it be true? He followed orders and remained on the farm and consequently lacked both republican freedom and negative freedom. Douglass must have meant that these freedoms were the most important freedoms, the ones that made a person a "freeman" in fact.

For Douglass the most important of all freedoms, the one that made a person a freeman or freewoman in fact, was the preference to obey only himself, which meant retaining the ability and pleasure to think, deliberate, and choose for himself. It does not follow that he thought negative and republican freedom to be worthless. He was still very dissatisfied remaining on Covey's farm and obeying orders. He would risk his life to get negative and republican freedom. But he did not prefer to die if he could not have them. A slave still had a chance and a hope for both negative and republican freedom. Thus, Douglass was aware that he had not won all of his freedoms and consequently was a slave in form. But he believed he had retained the most important freedom and consequently was more than half free.

Douglass's risky strategy to achieve his more than half freedom impressed the slaves who witnessed or heard rumors of it, and the intellectuals who heard of it through his speeches and writings. Thus W. E. B. Du Bois developed more cautious versions of the strategy and credited it as a valuable aid to dignity and self-respect. Eventually in the middle of the twentieth century, Martin Luther King, Jr., stimulated by foreign influences, recovered the tradition and formed it into his theory of civil disobedience or nonviolent direct action.

King's Civil Disobedience

Even well into the twentieth century, especially in the southern states, black people lived in conditions that were not essentially different from the conditions that slaves in the revolutionary period and in Douglass's time lived in, at least according to the republican philosophy of the

American revolutionaries. The revolutionaries appealed to that philosophy to accuse the British of enslaving them because they were taxing them without their consent. But black people were taxed without their consent in the revolutionary period, in the time of Douglass, and in southern states in the mid-twentieth century; in King's words they did not have "the unhampered right to vote."[24] Consequently they were slaves. The American slaves regained their freedom by rebelling against their masters. The black slaves in 1776, in Douglass's time, and in the southern states in mid-twentieth-century America could not possibly regain their freedom in the same way. But Douglass showed that some of them could regain a part of their freedom, what we have called being more than half free—not as good as freedom itself of course, but good too, and a means for keeping the hope of achieving freedom alive. I'll argue that King's theory of nonviolent direct action, enacted in mid-twentieth-century America, was a similar way for black people to become more than half free and to keep alive the hope of achieving complete freedom.

I summarize it as follows: A manmade law is unjust if it does not "square" with the moral law or the laws of God or if it is "inflicted upon a minority which that minority had no part in enacting or creating because they did not have the unhampered right to vote." Segregation laws are unjust for both reasons. The minority had no part in enacting or creating them, because they did not have the unhampered right to vote. And they "give the segregator a false sense of superiority, and the segregated a false sense of inferiority," and thus do not square with the moral law or God's law. Segregation laws should therefore be disobeyed. But they should be disobeyed only in a certain way and with a certain attitude. They must be disobeyed, "*openly, lovingly* . . . and with a willingness to accept the penalty."[25]

The civil disobedient must have the right intention when he breaks an unjust law. He must think very carefully before he disobeys a law he thinks is unjust, both to determine whether the law really fails to square with the moral law or God's law and to determine that he has the right intention in disobeying the law, namely, "to arouse the conscience of the community over its injustice" by willingly accepting the penalty.[26]

So far King's theory of civil disobedience seems nonconsequentialist, in the sense that civil disobedience need not have good consequences to be justified, and indeed need not be likely to have good consequences to be justified. The civil disobedient disobeys a law conscience tells her is unjust, and she accepts the penalty in order to arouse the conscience of the community. But she may fail to arouse the conscience of the community, and she may know that the disobedience is unlikely to do so. And even if it does arouse the conscience of the community, nothing good may come of it. Conscience may incline the community to start reforms, but that inclination may be met and thwarted by inclinations stemming from material self-interest; or it may fail to get anywhere because the opposition against reform is just too powerful.

These considerations do not imply that civil disobedience cannot sometimes or often have good consequences, or that King thought that the civilly disobedient should not try to make their civil disobedience have good consequences. On the contrary, he thought of civil disobedience as an important means to the moral improvement of the society rather than as a means for the edification of the civilly disobedient. Further, although he believed that arousing the conscience of the community could contribute importantly to the moral improvement of society, he did not think that it was usually sufficient to do so. History, he tells us, shows that "privileged groups seldom give up their privileges voluntarily."[27] This implied that even if the morally persuasive aspects of civil disobedience aroused the consciences of many people in the community, it was not likely to arouse the consciences of the privileged and powerful people in the community. The lust of such people for more and more money and power, engendered by their privileged positions, prevented them from allowing their consciences to be aroused. Motivating them to contribute to the improvement of society required the use of stronger medicine than moral suasion. They had to be convinced that they might lose some of their privileges if they prevented reform. To that end King took care to arrange "direct action" to coincide with large shopping periods, to increase the economic costs to merchants and thus "pressure" them into negotiations.[28]

Thus, if King hoped that civil disobedience would arouse the conscience of the community and lead to good consequences, he was not banking on that consideration alone. He also believed that there was nothing wrong with "pressuring" the community to begin negotiations with the civil disobedient and to make concessions; and he believed that such pressuring was often necessary before meaningful changes would ever be made. Of course the negotiations in question might often involve some amount of moral suasion. But the obvious inference is that he hoped that nonviolent direct action would lead to reductions in segregation as merchants became informed that continued segregation might cost them in dollars and cents. Actually King went even further. Although he insisted that the civilly disobedient not commit violence in return for violence committed against them, he also insisted that they must be ready to engage in civil disobedience and as a result provoke violence if they must do so in the pursuit of justice. It is "immoral," he claimed, "to urge an individual to withdraw his efforts to gain his basic constitutional rights because the quest precipitates violence."[29]

Thus, King did not endorse the extreme view, associated with John Rawls, that civil disobedience is strictly a mode of address and cannot involve imposing economic costs on others, even when imposing these costs cannot be properly described as violence.[30] On King's view, civil disobedience can sometimes be strictly a mode of address, as when the civil disobedient intends only to arouse the conscience of the community. But it can also sometimes impose economic costs—though never violence—on others in order to move them to make necessary reforms. The explanation of this difference in the two theories is probably that Rawls designed a theory of civil disobedience to be used only in nearly just societies, whereas King designed a theory of civil disobedience to be used in the southern states of mid-twentieth-century America.

King's theory continues the transmutation of the republican philosophy already started by the slaves. The centerpiece of that philosophy was that injustice must be confronted, never evaded. It remains in King's theory, though it takes a different form. The revolutionaries confronted British injustice with violent revolution; King could not follow their example because it would be suicide and death is not freedom. His confrontation with American injustice had to take a different form, in which the agents of injustice were not killed or violently attacked. Instead, the laws they made were openly and defiantly disobeyed. Here, deliberately or not, King was following the teaching of the more-than-half-free slaves. They openly disobeyed their master's commands unless it was rational (or moral) that they obey. King's theory advises the civilly disobedient to refuse to obey the authorities unless it was rational that they obey. That is, it advises that if the police started killing them for refusing to obey unjust laws, then they should obey those laws. But up until that point they should stand firm and disobey. There was always a definite risk that the police would start killing them, but again, like the more-than-half-free slaves, they calculated that the risk was low enough to make it rational to continue disobeying the unjust law. Their calculation was based on the idea that the police would not kill them with the whole world watching. The slaves' calculation was that their masters would think them too valuable to kill.

Beyond that similarity, King's theory developed past the strategy of the more-than-half-free slaves. They risked their lives for their own more-than-half freedom. They did not seem to have supposed that their strategy would set an example for other slaves. Probably they knew that their example could not become widespread. First, because many slaves were broken; Douglass sometimes expressed contempt for such slaves, but he never blamed them. Probably he understood that they were broken before they could foresee the purpose and inevitable consequences of their torture. Second, the masters would never have allowed the defiance of the more-than-half-free slaves to become widespread. Those slaves were tolerable as long as they were a tiny minority. If their numbers rose, the master would have started losing money and at that point would have started killing. By the mid-twentieth century, circumstances had changed so that there could be many more more-than-half-free slaves before the masters started killing. This meant that King could put enough civilly disobedient people to work to hope that their defiance could have good effects on the wider community. As we have seen, he hoped these good effects would include pressuring the community into making reforms and arousing its conscience over its injustice. King appeared to be less than confident about the second of these possible consequences of civil disobedience, but perhaps he should have been positively skeptical, given his endorsement of the republican idea that people with power are always disposed to expand it. The same complaint may be aimed at Douglass, given his subtle vacillation about the cause of Covey's failure to report him to the authorities. He does suggest that the cause was Covey's interest in his reputation and income. But he describes it as only probable and admitted that he could not, years later, "fully explain" it.[31] Was he allowing that defiant disobedience could be morally persuasive, a possibility that King understood more clearly? If he was, we might see his philosophy of moderately violent defiance as a basis for King's philosophy of nonviolent disobedience.

4

Showdown for Nonviolence: The Theory and Practice of Nonviolent Politics

KARUNA MANTENA

Introduction: King in the History of Nonviolence

At the time of his assassination, at the age of thirty-nine, Martin Luther King, Jr., was the acknowledged leader of a national movement and the veteran of numerous nonviolent campaigns whose achievements included the passing of landmark civil rights legislation. By 1968 King had begun a new phase of political action, a turn to the North and the initiation of programs and protest against inequality, poverty, and war. In comparison, M. K. Gandhi at the same age was a little-known figure in India, just beginning to forge the tools of *satyagraha* in a series of campaigns on behalf of Indian migrants in South Africa. Gandhi was also on the cusp of a major turning point. In 1909, at the age of forty, he wrote *Hind Swaraj,* his most famous pamphlet and his first intervention in the debate on Indian independence. Ten years later Gandhi would employ *satyagraha* on a mass scale in the campaign that catapulted him to national leadership—the Non-Cooperation/Khilafat movement. The iconic Salt Satyagraha was still a decade away.

The contrast is striking: Gandhi's political career spanned five decades and two continents, during which he led countless campaigns. It was a career in which he would continuously experiment with, and refine, the theory and practice of nonviolence. Gandhi was also the self-styled inventor and greatest champion of nonviolent direct action. So thoroughly conjoined with nonviolence, Gandhi's life was to carry its message and fate.[1] King's own association with nonviolence was briefer, due to his tragically short life but also because he was, on his own account, a latecomer to nonviolence. Though his intellectual milieu had been ripe with admiration for Gandhi, it was his unexpected emergence as a leader of the Montgomery bus boycott that first turned King's eye to nonviolent politics. By the time of his assassination, however, King had become nonviolence's most powerful advocate. His identification with and commitment to nonviolence had so deepened that King, like Gandhi before him, saw his life as a referendum, a final test—a showdown—on the very possibility of nonviolent politics.[2]

This chapter charts King's journey from novice to spokesman. Its aim is to convey what was *important* and *original* in King's contribution to the theory and practice of nonviolent politics. I ask what nonviolence meant for King, how he understood its purpose for the movement, and how he shaped the practice of nonviolent protest. I hope to do so while keeping an eye to what is still alive for us today in this tradition of nonviolent politics.

In the study of nonviolence, Gandhi and King and the movements they led are treated as exemplary.[3] In particular the civil rights movement, a movement marked by the self-conscious adoption of Gandhian techniques, was pivotal in lending global notoriety to nonviolence. It is hard to imagine something called "nonviolence" expanding beyond India as it has—as the name for a distinct form of politics—without its flourishing under King. King seemed to fulfill Gandhi's own prediction, made famous in a 1936 meeting with Howard Thurman, that "it may be through the Negroes that the unadulterated message of non-violence will be delivered to the world."[4]

Less noticed, but as important for the future of nonviolence, was the *end* of the civil rights era. King's assassination marked the denouement not only of the movement but also of a distinct phase of nonviolence. Despite Gandhi's and King's iconic status, some of the defining characteristics of the nonviolence they championed have been rejected over time. In King's later years, radical activists acutely questioned the morality and utility of nonviolence. For advocates of Black Power, the critique was part of a rejection of the ideology of integration and interracial reconciliation with which King's nonviolence was so closely bound. For a radicalizing student movement, nonviolence was seen as too limited in scope and naive in intention to live up to the demands of social revolution. For both, this entailed abandoning some of the key concepts and tactics of nonviolent protest. Foremost was a rejection of the structure of moral appeal—the idea of persuading and "converting" opponents—that was at the core of classical nonviolent politics. This appeal, for Gandhi and King, was centrally linked to the staging of *suffering* and *discipline* in nonviolent protest. Such an orientation gave way as new cultures of protest came to celebrate what they considered to be more confrontational, transgressive, and authentic expressions of dissent and opposition.[5]

In that moment of intense reassessment, nonviolent theorists and activists began to draw a distinction between *principled* and *strategic* nonviolence.[6] That distinction, most influentially developed in the work of Gene Sharp, has now become paradigmatic; it is the core assumption of scholarly treatment as well as activist endorsement of nonviolence.[7] Gandhi and King are associated with a principled commitment to nonviolence, defined as a religious or absolute commitment to nonviolence/nonkilling. In contrast, today's advocates recommend nonviolence on ostensibly pragmatic or strategic grounds, as a set of useful tactics rather than a defining creed.

The problem with such a contrast is that it defines nonviolence as *either* discrete tactics and mobilization strategies *or* normative concepts and ideas. This leads contemporary activists to praise the political acumen of Gandhi's and King's campaigns while disavowing the very philosophy upon which their strategic thinking was based.[8] For Gandhi and King, the philosophy of nonviolence was not just the motivational grounds for adopting a tactic; it provided the reasoning for why and how nonviolent techniques would be politically effective.

To separate tactics from ideas is therefore to lose something essential about nonviolent politics. Tactics are where the philosophy of nonviolence comes alive, it is where the purpose and utility of nonviolence are clarified and demonstrated. In this essay I focus on how King linked the philosophy and the politics of nonviolence. He did so by developing a theory and a practice of nonviolence that were conceptually realist and intensely pragmatic, and that aimed at making visible the moral stakes of undoing racial domination. It was this combination that gave King's moral vision such political force.

Origins of African American Nonviolence

Stride toward Freedom, King's influential account of the Montgomery bus boycott, offered an origin story of African American nonviolence, of the movement's adoption of "the principle of love" and of King's realization of its power. In King's telling, the boycott spontaneously developed into an experiment in nonviolent noncooperation: "Christ furnished the spirit and motivation, while Gandhi furnished the method."[9] But King's "pilgrimage to nonviolence" was marked by moments of doubt. Gandhi appeared as a kind of revelation just as King came to question "the power of love in solving social problems."[10] At Crozer Theological Seminary King became alert to the tragic complexity of human motivation which seemed to limit the capacity of reason and love to actuate social change. This led King away from what he considered a sentimental and naive liberalism, associated with the social gospel, toward a more realist pacifist position. In this move King advertised his intellectual debt to Reinhold Niebuhr.[11]

King pinpoints a specific event—a lecture by Mordecai Johnson, then president of Howard—as the moment that excited his interest in Gandhi. The lecture was "so profound and electrifying" that when King left the meeting, he "bought a half dozen books on Gandhi's life and works."[12] He saw "for the first time that the Christian doctrine of love operating through the Gandhian method of nonviolence was one of the most potent weapons available to oppressed people in their struggle for freedom."[13] Until the Montgomery boycott, however, King had a "merely intellectual understanding and appreciation" of Gandhi's position.[14] It was the practical experience of the boycott that clarified for him the meaning and purpose of nonviolence. As King put it, these brewing intellectual dilemmas about social change "were now solved in the sphere of practical action."[15]

Doubts have been raised about the precision of this account. Indeed, biographers have differed on how to characterize King's nonviolence, and some question the depth of his knowledge of it as well as his commitment to it.[16] Taylor Branch, for instance, sometimes portrays nonviolence as merely window dressing for a national and global audience, an embellishment of basic Christian ideas to give the public effect of moral seriousness. Branch suggests that King acquiesced to being portrayed as a "Gandhian Negro" because it was useful for "public relations," but in private thought of Gandhian nonviolence as "'merely a Niebuhrian stratagem of power.'"[17]

This is a limited understanding of Gandhian nonviolence and what it meant to King as well as the conditions that made affiliation to Gandhi available and desirable. Take King's recollection of Johnson's speech on Gandhi. In Branch's view, King is concocting a genealogy—the reference is vague and maybe even apocryphal. But even as a passing reference, Johnson's speech speaks to the depth of interest in Gandhi and Gandhianism among African American intellectuals, especially theologians in the early half of the twentieth century. The interest was also a network of mutual contacts and connections. Johnson was one of many prominent theologians—such as Howard Thurman and Benjamin Mays (King's mentor at Morehouse)—who had traveled to India and had contact with Gandhi or the Gandhian movement. King came of age tied to people and institutions where Gandhi was a live reference.[18]

But the question of King's nonviolence, or more precisely his role in making nonviolence central to the movement, is still an open one. In comparison with leaders like Bayard Rustin, James Lawson, and James Farmer, King was a latecomer to nonviolence. He did not enter Montgomery already determined "to organize it in a socially effective situation."[19] Indeed, in the case of Montgomery the real catalyst for the self-conscious adoption of nonviolence was the arrival of Rustin and Glenn Smiley, field officers of the Fellowship of Reconciliation (FOR), a major international pacifist organization and disseminator of Gandhian nonviolence. Indeed, some of King's early writings on nonviolence, including parts of *Stride toward Freedom,* were strongly influenced by, even co-written with, Rustin and Smiley.[20]

Recent civil rights historiography also minimizes King's role, portraying him at times as an accidental leader. These accounts foreground already extant traditions of grassroots organizing and protest as both the real sources of the momentum of the early civil rights movement as well as the most consequential conduit of nonviolence.[21] In addition to Morehouse and Howard, institutions where nonviolence as philosophy and theology was cultivated, other key sources of African American nonviolence were labor organizing and antiwar activism.[22] Here again Rustin and FOR played a central role, in conjunction with labor leaders and union organizers like A. Philip Randolph and E. D. Nixon. In the case of Montgomery, where Nixon was a crucial initiator, one can also point to Rosa Parks's connection to the Highlander Folk School, where nonviolent methods were being taught from the 1940s onward.[23]

The student-led lunch counter sit-ins and freedom rides—the iconic protests of the civil rights era—were closely tied to earlier experimentation in nonviolence. An offshoot of FOR, the Congress of Racial Equality (CORE), was founded in 1942. CORE began to disseminate pamphlets on nonviolent direct action, and deployed these techniques against desegregation in and around Chicago.[24] CORE had already attempted interracial freedom rides in a campaign known as the Journey of Reconciliation as early as 1947. Likewise, the lunch counter sit-in movement that spawned the Student Nonviolent Coordinating Committee (SNCC) sprang from an engagement with nonviolent practice. The Nashville movement that gave SNCC its early leadership—James Bevel, Diane Nash, John Lewis, and Bernard Lafayette—was led in its nonviolent training by James Lawson, a student of Thurman's and himself recently returned from India.[25] From this perspective nonviolent protest was made possible by those already steeped in activist traditions, now catalyzed into mass action with students playing a crucial role. In this telling, the movement's nonviolence not only had an independent source and momentum, but in its early days kept outpacing King's adoption of it.

In the transition from novice to spokesman, King bridged these two traditions of African American nonviolence as he made nonviolence the overarching creed of the movement. The success of Montgomery, the student movements, and his 1959 trip to India all worked to cement King's commitment to nonviolence. His earlier intellectual admiration for Gandhian nonviolence made him extremely receptive to it and made him willing to recruit and learn from others like Rustin and Lawson how to best put nonviolence into practice. King's sense of the importance of practical organization and training in nonviolence would deepen over time. It would be key to the success of protests in Birmingham led by the Southern Christian Leadership Conference (SCLC) as well as the partially realized Poor Peoples' Campaign.

Unlike Gandhi, whose genius was always centrally linked to his organizational and tactical acumen, King's originality and power came more through the clarity of his moral and political vision. His own descriptions of nonviolent techniques were less interesting, drawing liberally and somewhat loosely from the existing texts of the movement—from Krishnalal Shridharani's *War without Violence* and Richard Gregg's *The Power of Non-Violence,* with Niebuhr's *Moral Man and Immoral Society* as an important theoretical base.[26] What was more striking was how King made sense of and defended nonviolence as the most effective method for social change in the context of an America in the throes of escalating racial crises. In so doing, King would lay bare both the place of the African American struggle in realizing a shared democratic life and, more broadly, the constraints and possibilities of nonviolence in and for democratic politics as such.

King's Arguments for Nonviolence

The political philosophy of nonviolence is often treated as an extension of a strict pacifism, grounded, for example, upon an absolute interdiction of violence.[27] From this premise, philosophical analyses tend to frame nonviolence as primarily a debate on when the use of force can and should be justified. Curiously, neither Gandhi nor King invested much time in elaborating the grounds or conditions or limits of nonviolence in these terms.

This is not, I think, because they were so "absolutist" in their commitment to nonviolence that such justifications seemed unnecessary. Rather, Gandhi and King were concerned with a different question and a different problem. They were animated by violence's *futility*—its dangerous and perverse consequences in politics. This, in turn, oriented them toward practical alternatives to violence.

Gandhi and King readily conceded the moral attractions of and legitimacy of violence, especially in circumstances of self-defense. Gandhi did so more cannily: first, by setting up a scale of moral values in which violence was always preferred to cowardice. Gandhi insisted that it was always better to fight than to run, though disciplined sacrifice would be the preferred option above all others.[28] But even in accepting violence to be at times a morally appropriate response, Gandhi would question the "self" in whose name self-defense stands. Gandhi suspected egoism in the assumed priority of the self as well as a tendency of the "I" of the self to bleed into an amorphous "we" and thereby extend the pretexts for violence.[29]

King endorsed Gandhi's preference for violence over cowardice, especially as a way to combat nonviolence's association with passivity and weakness.[30] But it was in response to defenders of militant self-defense that King most explicitly admitted the legitimacy of violence.[31] King took the right of self-defense to be an accepted moral universal that did not require explicit elaboration or defending.[32] The real issue was not whether violence could be morally just, but whether it could ever be a useful weapon for social change. This is what Gandhi and King denied: that a coherent, effective policy or strategy for change can emerge from the moral right of self-defense.

In autobiographical terms as well, Gandhi's and King's interest in nonviolence originated more directly from a need to devise creative methods to combat injustice and not from a critique of war per se. To be sure, their commitments to nonviolence would become expansive. In Gandhi's case, nonviolence encompassed an entire philosophy of living; in King's, it enabled a critical analysis of capitalism and war. But the prime attraction of nonviolence was that it offered a model of action that could effect social and political change in what seemed like a new and powerful way. In other words, for both Gandhi and King, nonviolence was first and foremost a philosophy of action, whose guiding conceptual concern was the "how" of social change.[33] And therefore the most prominent arguments for nonviolence concerned what it could achieve—morally and politically—as a distinct form of action.

King would offer a variety of arguments in this vein for nonviolent action, arguments that ranged from philosophical accounts of love and hate to very concrete questions of mobilization and organization. These arguments grew in breadth and depth; King hoped "that, as the Negro plunges deeper into the quest for freedom, he will plunge deeper into the philosophy of nonviolence."[34] Many of King's claims rehearsed familiar Gandhian propositions—that nonviolence can quell destructive cycles of hate; that it exposes and attacks systems of evil, not persons; that disciplined suffering can disarm and persuade opponents. But King endowed these claims with an original force and emphasis. This was due in part to their organic integration into Christian tropes and a redemptive theology. Moreover—and this is what I foreground—King connected nonviolence to the distinctive trajectory of African American political experience. This enabled King to detail the case for nonviolence as a uniquely viable strategy, given the history of black political struggle in America and the existing configurations of racial conflict and domination. Though he did not produce anything like a philosophical treatise on nonviolence, out of this engaged and specific adoption King offered genuine conceptual innovation and clarity in the theory and practice of nonviolent politics.

King portrayed the postwar world of race relations as reaching a head, a crisis that came to the surface of American political life as the "Negro revolution" took shape. For King, the oppressed had three options: passive submission to an unjust order, violent retaliation, or nonviolence. The third option was morally and practically superior, for it was the only one that could successfully navigate the poles of inaction and reaction. For clarity, I distinguish three kinds arguments for nonviolence: moral, strategic, and tactical. In a very real sense nonviolent action as proposed by Gandhi and King incorporated all three elements; indeed, the imbrication of the moral and the practical/political is one of the most original and striking features of nonviolent politics. What I delineate below, then, are not three discrete forms of action as much as three faces of nonviolent action.

King's moral argument contended that nonviolent action provides the means by which a disempowered, oppressed people could regain dignity and self-respect. In choosing to act, a once-subject people conquered fear and apathy; in King's terms, they overcame "stagnant passivity and deadening complacency."[35] Action undermined ingrained habits of deference and submission, that "tragic sense of inferiority, resulting from the crippling effects of slavery and segregation."[36] Thereby it became the vehicle for the recovery of moral and political agency. Nonviolent direct action provoked a radical reevaluation of the self: "the Negro . . . has come to feel that he *is* somebody."[37] Thus, even before "it stirs [the opponent's] conscience," the moral work of nonviolent action "first does something to the hearts and souls of those committed to it."[38] This was for King the greatest achievement of the civil rights movement.

The Montgomery story, as narrated in *Stride toward Freedom,* is a story of the recovery of agency and dignity through mass nonviolent action. On the eve of the bus boycott, King's speech at Holt Street Baptist Church made action a moral demand, a duty to oneself and to God. King declared "that their self-respect was at stake," and argued that to accept injustices without protesting would be to "betray their own sense of dignity and the eternal edicts of God Himself."[39] The following day's boycott was met with almost total compliance. This unexpected and extraordinary success, for King, "broke the spell" of inaction.[40] That the community could be roused to sacrifice and solidarity and remain resilient in the face of pressure was "demonstrating to the Negro, North and South, that many of the stereotypes he has held about himself and other Negroes are not valid."[41] The moral-psychological transformation enabled by action was so profound that King would insist that protest involve the prime actors affected by injustice and domination. This is in part why "the Negro . . . must assume the primary responsibility"[42] for securing integration, just as in the Poor People's Campaign, it was to be the poor that formed a visible column of the movement. In so doing, the oppressed and marginalized reconstitute themselves as agents (and not victims), simultaneously displaying and demanding self-respect and dignity.

King often spoke of nonviolence as "dignified social action."[43] Dignity in King's use would be a capacious concept.[44] Like the Gandhian ideal of *swaraj,* regaining dignity through action implied an inwardly generated capacity or experience of moral freedom. Quoting Tolstoy, King recognized this form of freedom as ontologically tied to the very nature of man.[45] Dignity like *swaraj* implied a kind of self-mastery or discipline, and King would often yoke the terms "dignity" and "discipline" together in characterizing the unique comportment of nonviolent protest.[46] Ultimately, not only was dignity recovered in action—nonviolence worked through its display and dramatization.

Nonviolent action, for King, embodied the spirit of *agape,* a disinterested and stern love that signaled goodwill. This took the form of acting "with wise restraint and love and with proper discipline and dignity," especially in the face of the resistance and resentment that direct action invariably aroused.[47] At its most noble and courageous, dignity was demonstrated in the willingness to suffer violence without retaliation. Discipline and dignity would also serve strategic and tactical purposes. As I argue below, they are key to nonviolence's political efficacy. Here I conclude by noting a further inner, moral dimension of nonviolent action that King would emphasize. Nonviolent action worked to "channelize" bitterness and mitigate despair.[48] Two hurdles stemming from the moral psychology of oppression were fear and apathy; another was the ever-present temptation of violent retaliation and revenge. For King, nonviolence had the unique ability to navigate a course between and beyond "acquiescence and violence."[49] King would return to the sublimating effects of nonviolent protest as a way to cope with the widespread anger, resentment, and despair that marked the urban rebellions of the late 1960s, beginning with the riots in the Watts neighborhood of Los Angeles in 1965.[50]

King's concerns about dignity and action were mirrored by his Black Power critics. This explains in part why he was sympathetic to many of their animating concerns. What King and Gandhi share with Frantz Fanon and theorists of Black Power is an emphasis on the existential or phenomenological element of action, in which dignified, strong, courageous action was the necessary means of both properly channeling inner rage and achieving agency, freedom, and self-respect.[51] Of course, many Black Power advocates differed from King insofar as they claimed that action needed to be violent—or at least, dramatically aggressive—to effect the kind of moral transformation that would fully purge corroding anger, fear, inferiority. This difference lent it itself to divergent accounts of what dignified action consisted in. Black Power advocates were concerned that nonviolent displays of black suffering and self-restraint, especially when undertaken to appeal to the dominant white majority, were too apt to signal weakness, even humiliation. This clash over the inner meaning of dignity was also interwoven with controversies about its outward effects, that is, more broadly the political efficacy and promise of nonviolence. Here, the moral argument for nonviolence quickly shades into arguments about its strategic necessity and tactical superiority.

"The Hard Cold Facts of Racial Life": The Strategic Argument for Integration

King insisted that the choice of nonviolence was both moral *and* practical. Political arguments for nonviolence take two forms. One set of arguments focuses on what I term the *tactical* advantages of nonviolence. Nonviolence is taken to be a creative form of protest, uniquely poised to confuse, shame, disarm, and outmaneuver opponents. As his experience and confidence with the tactical program of nonviolence grew, King would offer a powerful account of how the performance of dignity, discipline, and suffering exposed and dramatized evil while awakening the moral conscience of "the decent majority." In the next section I detail King's understanding of this logic. Here, I turn to an interconnected political argument for nonviolence, a strategic argument about the broader purpose and goal of nonviolent politics.

Strategic arguments for nonviolence are claims about nonviolence's capacity to engender better—more just, more stable—political results than violence. To be sure, tactical arguments are also about results but in the more immediate sense of transforming day-to-day political interactions and trajectories. The strategic argument is focused on long-term goals, about how nonviolence is best suited to realize and shape distinct political ends. For instance, Tolstoy and Gandhi insisted that violence led to evermore militarized political orders that amplified and legitimated the state's inherently hierarchical and exploitative tendencies.[52] In King's case, the ends or goals of militant nonviolence were associated, at the abstract level, ·with the founding of the beloved or redemptive community and, more concretely, with the demands of "integration" in American democracy.

Integration, in King's use, is an expansive and demanding ideal; it was a "democratic dream" associated with the "total emancipation" of the individual, who can fully flourish only in conditions of free and reciprocal equality.[53] As a process, integration was the positive, creative, and constructive side of desegregation that would bring about "genuine intergroup and interpersonal living."[54] Here we see that King's understanding of freedom—in comparison to Tolstoy's and Gandhi's emphasis on self-mastery—was more social and solidaristic: as individuals we cannot realize true freedom on our own, it requires a shared democratic life.

Integration was also centrally linked to King's understanding of African American history as "bound up with the destiny of America."[55] It would "complete a process of democratization which our nation has too long developed too slowly."[56] African Americans thereby became pivotal agents for the realization of democracy and carried a peculiar burden to redeem the American dream. King would go so far as to suggest that this redemption might be global in scope, for the black struggle in America was uniquely positioned to effect a nonviolent revolution of American values, which, in turn, would "reform the structures of racist imperialism from within," and help actualize the freedom of Asian and African peoples.[57]

To critics, King's ideal of integration, especially when evoked alongside the language of love and reconciliation, appeared both lofty and naive. This was why, especially in his late writings, King's endorsement of integration often came yoked with a harsh, practical realism. Integration was the only option, given "the hard cold facts of racial life in the world today."[58] In response to black nationalism, which often combined an ideology of racial separatism with a defense of violence, King portrayed the choice of integration as a brutal necessity. Tactical violence, King claimed, was always self-defeating. He could see no positive social outcomes issuing from it. For black America, it was a choice not only futile in a romantic sense but potentially genocidal in implication. Any successful revolutionary war, especially Fanon's kind of national liberation struggle endorsed by some of King's radical critics, was premised on the availability of mass, popular support—the sympathy of the "nonresisting majority."[59] But nonviolent black struggle in America made apparent the fact of popular (white) backlash and savage retaliation. African Americans were an oppressed minority, and a campaign of organized, insurrectionary violence would yield enormous causalities in the face of "a well-armed, wealthy majority with a fanatical right wing that would delight in exterminating thousands of black men, women and children."[60]

The political reality of numbers had to be reckoned with, and it imposed severe limits on the strategies one could pursue. In the starkest terms it meant that an oppressed minority could not achieve liberation on its own and in isolation. Instead, what was needed was the cultivation of progressive alliances across the variety of social groups that constituted multiracial America. After gaining full voting rights, black Americans could become an important and consequential political constituency; they might even secure majorities in many cities on their own. But even this consolidation of black power would not readily translate into improvements in the lives of the majority of African Americans. Garnering enough power to shape the future direction of the country required a more ambitious program of political development. King thought that in spurning that possibility, the ideology of Black Power was defeatist in its aims. Full integration in America, for King, was about gaining equal and full participation in all its political and social institutions. Through the building of alliances, African Americans could effect a progressive realignment and "marshal moral power" and influence *beyond* their numbers.[61]

King rightly intuited that the political predicament of black struggle in America made it qualitatively different from the Gandhian example. It was a movement of a minority against a majority bent on "massive resistance" to its empowerment. And yet the political fate of the minority was thoroughly intertwined with that same recalcitrant majority.[62] "Integration," King realized, would be "more complicated than independence."[63] This difference became more obvious to King over time, especially as white backlash to the civil rights movement grew. Successful anticolonial or self-determination movements tended toward separation and autonomy from their former oppressors. In that context, nonviolent tactics of mass boycott and noncooperation were especially good at staging mass disaffection. In moments of crisis, disaffection scaled upward to a total rejection of the existing regime and calls for its complete overhaul, usually in the form of a transfer of power to a new set of political actors.

Gandhi was concerned that such a transfer be built upon constructive nonviolent action, upon broad programs of self-reliance that would build the institutional foundations of self-determination. But from the outside, the main lesson of Gandhian noncooperation, and of anticolonial movements more generally, was how mass resistance exposed the illegitimacy of colonial power through direct confrontation. As Jonathan Schell has so vividly argued, even violent campaigns in Algeria and Vietnam ultimately succeeded not through military superiority but as political victories that galvanized and legitimated popular resistance.[64] Crucially, in both scenarios, liberation could be attained without any meaningful reconciliation with one's former enemies.

In the context of black struggle in America, it was an uncomfortable but hard moral fact that integration was required to complete the project of liberation. There could not be any—in King's terms—theoretical, sociological, or temporal divide between the moment of liberation and the moment of integration.[65] African Americans' primary antagonist was neither a distant foreign power nor an aloof, elite state apparatus. Instead, they would be "living tomorrow with the very people against whom [they were] struggling today." And "where the oppressed and the oppressor are both 'at home,'" liberation meant finding a means of coexisting in peace, equality, and dignity.[66] Ultimately this implied "the mutual sharing of power."[67] But even beyond political empowerment, the promise of full liberation was tied to conditions of social equality. In a true democracy, social equality would entail fellow citizens' reciprocally confirming mutual respect and dignity. For King, only under conditions of true "intergroup and interpersonal living" and doing can the freedom that comes with knowing and fulfilling one's "total capacity" be realized.[68]

King's understanding of liberation through integration brings into focus an essential and overlooked feature of nonviolent politics, namely, that its logic might vary in different political contexts. The "American racial revolution," for King, "has been a revolution to 'get in' rather than to overthrow."[69] Because of this divergence from other anti-imperial struggles with which the movement shared a moral vocabulary and political energy, its nonviolence also had to take on a different character. This crucial lesson of the civil rights movement has not been fully recognized. What King made apparent was that nonviolent reconciliation was not just a Christian imperative but also a *democratic* one.

One of the classic rejoinders to nonviolence was that it would be effective only in broadly liberal regimes, such as the United States and the British in India. Recent studies of nonviolence, however, seem to call into question this long-standing presumption. They have shown that nonviolence has been increasingly effective in overthrowing nondemocratic regimes, no matter how authoritarian such regimes may be.[70] A more significant determinant of successful nonviolent movements seems to be to their majoritarian nature. This is what underlay Gandhi's famous declaration that African Americans would be the carriers of "the unadulterated message of non-violence" to the world.[71] Gandhi was here intimating that only minority movements could offer a pure demonstration of nonviolence. The Indian experiment with nonviolence, in contrast, was "adulterated" in the sense that its success may be attributed to the working of majoritarian, collective power rather than to nonviolence as such.

The civil rights movement requires us to think harder about how nonviolence works in the context of democratic politics, and to be especially attentive to how and why democracies can be, in their own way, acutely hostile to nonviolent protest. King's understanding of the challenges of liberatory reconciliation implicitly recognized the difficulty of getting a democratic public to think critically about itself. King's contribution to the theory and practice of nonviolence stems in large part from this insight. Democratic politics make nonviolent direct action both necessary and demanding.

Democracy and Nonviolent Persuasion: The Tactical Work of Suffering

The democratic hope of social equality—what King referred to as "the ethical demands for integration"—compelled and shaped the language of reconciliation that was at the controversial core of King's nonviolence. If the goal of black struggle was liberatory integration and reconciliation, then it was that much more urgent that nonviolent direct action orient itself toward mutual understanding and not simply the defeat, overthrow, or humiliation of the oppressor. Racial progress for King depended on finding a way to get every American to see themselves personally implicated in racial domination.[72] And nonviolence was the best means to *persuade* a reluctant populace to actively engage in acts of moral reevaluation. Indeed, nonviolence was, for King, "the ultimate form of persuasion. It is the method which seeks to implement the just law by appealing to the conscience of the great decent majority who through blindness, fear, pride, or irrationality have allowed their consciences to sleep."[73]

It was also this idea of interracial moral appeal and persuasion that drew derision from King's radical black nationalist critics, from Malcolm X to Stokely Carmichael. In rejecting the goal of integration, they disputed the need to reach out to and elicit support from the dominant white majority. Such an orientation toward one's oppressors was seen as naive at best but also as likely to perpetuate psychological and political dependence. King's response was to draw attention to the hard economic and political realities of racial life, with an agenda for how to overcome them. By breaking the southern stronghold on democratic politics and bringing the poor and disenfranchised into a general alliance, the black struggle could construct a radically redefined progressive coalition.[74] When SNCC and CORE turned away from the practical work of building interracial coalitions, King saw this as a sign of retreat, resignation, and disillusionment. Though they used the language of militancy, they were in effect giving up on the possibility of radical transformation through political means.[75]

The idea of persuasion that King had in mind was not as naive or simplistic as his radical critics supposed. Nonviolent politics are built upon the persuasive power of *direct action*. The emphasis on action was premised on the recognition that political persuasion is difficult and rare, and that, in particular, rational argumentation is not a reliable means of convincing opponents or solving disagreement. For King, "reason by itself is little more than an instrument to justify man's defensive ways of thinking."[76]

Nonviolence may be able to more readily breakthrough affective responses and defenses—prejudice, fear, and pride—that thwart the recognition and progress of justice. This view of nonviolent political action was built upon a conceptual realism that closely followed Niebuhr's account of the complexity of human nature and its implications for social change.[77]

King drew from Niebuhr two central ideas about impediments to radical change. First, people in power do not give up privilege easily, and therefore entrenched power had to be challenged by alternative power. And, second, those who benefit from racial privilege and white supremacy will "react with bitterness and resistance," reactions that are imbued with blinding anger, unspoken fears, and deep-seated resentments.[78]

In *Moral Man and Immoral Society*—the text that originally tempered King's youthful optimism about the social gospel—Niebuhr argued that individual moral progress and education rarely serve as the main engines of social change. Individuals may be capable of moral progress and genuine altruism; they can learn to reason from and in terms of another's needs and perspective. Niebuhr believed this was much more difficult, if not impossible, for social groups, especially groups in conflict. Conflict between groups in the context of racial, class, or imperial domination was decided by power and not by the direct play of morality or reason.[79] Niebuhr offered a striking and counterintuitive account of group egoism and identification. A paradoxical melding of altruism and selfishness allows individuals to subordinate self-interest to group goals and, at the same time, justify and cling to privilege more readily as selfless support of the group.[80] More generally, Niebuhr noted the prevalence of resentment and indignation in response to political criticism.[81] These are structural and psychological barriers to the kind of social change that would be required in order to end racial domination.

Both King and Niebuhr recognized that these barriers also undermined a pure realist account of entrenched power ousted by emergent power. Perhaps coercion is necessary for social change and justice. But the use of force also compounds rather than resolves already extant tendencies toward retrenchment and recalcitrance. Political change through force would therefore result in a brokered truce likely to be upset by lingering resentments.[82] This was King's fear of racial conflict descending into "bitterness" and "an endless reign of meaningless chaos."[83] Both Niebuhr and King saw nonviolent action has having the potential to break this bind or at least mitigate its destabilizing and demoralizing effects. Niebuhr argued that nonviolent action was a power that was "least dangerous" in effect.[84] For King, it was a power still tethered to morality and compassion.[85]

In King we find three interlinked ideas of how nonviolent action can break through psychological resistance to radical change: (1) by dramatizing and exposing evil, (2) by disarming and unbalancing the opponent, and (3) by shaming the opposition and awakening conscience. All were underscored by the work of suffering. Suffering, for King, was a "creative and powerful social force," an agent of moral and political education, that could "transform the social situation."[86] King quoted Gandhi on the work of suffering: "Suffering is the law of human beings; war is the law of the jungle. But suffering is infinitely more powerful than the law of the jungle for converting the opponent and opening his ears, which are otherwise shut, to the voice of reason. . . . If you want something really important to be done, you must not merely satisfy the reason, you must move the heart also. The appeal of reason is more to the head, but the penetration of the heart comes from suffering. It opens up the inner understanding in man."[87]

For King, unearned suffering had a redemptive quality—this was its moral and religious significance. In terms of the logic of nonviolent protest, suffering enabled moral education through the display and dramatization of dignity and discipline.[88] Though we often associate nonviolent suffering with the ability to endure physical violence and mental distress, I think it might be better conveyed by the idea of self-discipline in action, or what I term *nonviolent discipline*.

For Gandhi this was given by its very definition, for "self-suffering" was a translation of the Sanskrit term *tapas* or *tapasya*, which connotes practices of ascetic self-discipline. And though the Christian conception of suffering more readily evokes images of physical martyrdom, King was also keen to tie the performance of suffering to the concept of dignity. This becomes most clear in the implied contrast between shame and pity.[89] As I show below, the suffering that is revealed and performed in the organization and style of nonviolent protest is meant to render public the *dignity* of the protestor. This is very different in form and function from an understanding of suffering as the experience and exhibition of abject pain and misery. The latter is likely to provoke feelings of revulsion and pity—responses that are incompatible with the moral end of recovering self-respect and incapable of doing the tactical work of exposing evil, disarming opponents, and engaging moral conscience.

When King spoke of nonviolent direct action as a program to "dramatize evil" or "dramatize the issue," the term *dramatize* concerned the idea of amplifying the seriousness of the issue.[90] In particular, it should bring into sharp focus the *moral* seriousness of the situation, that what was at stake were clear-cut questions of justice. King's use of the term also highlights the performative or theatrical element of nonviolent protest, where dignity is staged as part of a drama that attempts to make visible and stark who stands on the side of justice.

In the "Letter from Birmingham City Jail," King defends the disruptive character of protest. Protest brings to the surface underlying tensions and bigotry, with the hope that such exposure will be the first step toward an honest reckoning with racial domination. Even though protest occasions the release of already existing tensions, King was well aware that protestors would be accused of being their primary cause. This is what was implicit in the white moderate's repeated concern about the "untimeliness" of black protest, the charge that King felt most compelled to dispute in the "Letter from Birmingham City Jail."[91] Observers and critics who are not already sympathetic to the cause will doubly scrutinize the methods used by protestors and civil disobedients. Indeed, this was the most obvious drawback of using violence or threatening violence in political action, even in a society, such as America, that celebrates ideals of armed self-defense. Initiating violence "provokes questions about the necessity for it," and the initiator is "inevitably blamed for its consequences."[92] Violence necessarily becomes embroiled in rancorous debate about when and whether any particular use of force was justified—a debate that King thought worked only to confuse and distract the public from engaging with the moral message of the movement.[93]

Niebuhr and King recognized these as the responses to expect from any contestation of the status quo. Accusations of criminality, hooliganism, outsider infiltration consistently emerge to discredit activists.[94] King and the civil rights movement were persistently suspected of, and persecuted for, being a cover for communist agitation. Moreover, there was always an implication of lurking criminality and primitive violence. The staging of nonviolent discipline was crucial for undermining these expectations, accusations, and reactions.[95] For Niebuhr, protest undertaken with discipline and in the spirit of goodwill—which is what was exemplified in nonviolent action—could temper the egoistic emotions of disgust and resentment, the moral psychology that renders questions of justice opaque. Even if opponents (or perpetrators of injustice) are not directly affected by nonviolence, the neutral public—the decent majority—can see through the haze to more reasonably and objectively assess the underlying conflict.[96]

For King, again, scrutiny of means was a central feature of the politics of protest—we might say of all politics as such—and it threatens to obfuscate and obscure the moral and political issues at stake. This was why the question of *means* was so crucial for King, as well as in the theory and practice of nonviolence more generally. Indeed, this gives a sense of the practical basis underlying one of the central maxims of nonviolent politics, namely, that means and ends are inseparable or, in Gandhi's terms, "convertible."[97] At its most imaginative and powerful, nonviolent protest would involve a perfect convergence of means and ends, with the message itself being clearly conveyed in the *form* of protest.

Here are some examples of how discipline came to be embedded in the nonviolent protest of the civil rights movement. Given that the black struggle in America was a minority struggle, generating large numbers was crucial for drawing public attention to racial domination and asserting political pressure against it. But large crowds would immediately evoke the most resonant fears of disorder and anarchy as well as anxieties of black revenge.[98] For King, these "guilt-ridden" fears had to be reckoned with and mitigated through the organization of protest.[99]

Though King was not himself a hands-on, detail-oriented organizer, he recognized its signal importance. He was keen to involve and encourage the work of those, like Rustin and Lawson, who had a talent for organization and nonviolent training. The March on Washington was a case in point. This was the great landmark of Rustin's vision and organizational genius. It fulfilled the projected March on Washington Movement that Rustin and his mentor, the labor leader A. Philip Randolph, had planned more than twenty years earlier.[100]

From the moment the march was announced, anxious rumors and warnings abounded about the inevitability of violence in the context of a mass gathering of black people.[101] If such violence were to occur, it would be amplified many times over, given the national spotlight, severely damaging the cause and derailing the passage of the civil rights legislation that motivated the demonstration. Rustin was therefore all the more determined to quell any hint of disorder or violence. One of his most creative and effective decisions was to employ out-of-uniform black police officers—trained in nonviolence—to provide internal security. Rustin did not want a single uniformed DC officer policing the march.[102] An underlying camaraderie and shared intention between protestors and security would ensure that minor altercations or logistical problems would not become the pretext for violence or escalation. In a similar vein, Rustin made sure that the logistical plans for transportation, traffic, and facilities were adequate to the scale of the event, even attending to the smallest details of hygiene and cleanliness. To his mind, the monument lawn was to be left as pristine as when the first demonstrators arrived.[103]

From the Montgomery boycott to Birmingham to the strike in Memphis, the key to disciplined protest was careful attention to internal organization and nonviolent training. Training workshops showed protesters what civility and discipline looked like, as the appropriate dispositions and responses were rehearsed in prayer meetings and workshops. Training often took the form of staging "sociodramas" that placed activists in expected situations of confrontation where they would practice responding to provocation with indifference and quiet defiance.[104] For the Birmingham campaign, volunteers had to sign a commitment card and a pledge in order to participate. The pledge contained a series of rules and prescriptions that volunteers were to reflect upon and adhere to, in order to be sure they knew what was entailed in "the dramatic act of presenting one's body in the marches."[105] They would be screened again in person; those who did not pass the test were given "noncombatant" duties to help the cause. In the demonstrations themselves, the rules were meant to help muster and exhibit discipline in the face of threats, intimidation, and outright violence. And training leaders were deployed as field marshals to ensure that the protests retained civility and their intended purpose.

Another, underrated element of tactical discipline was the work of collective prayers, songs, and silence during large-scale demonstrations and marches. These marches themselves were also to be slow and deliberate. Songs and prayers cultivated unity, solidarity, and emotional resolve among protestors, a point King would praise. But to onlookers they communicated something equally important, an inner calm and resiliency that is very different from what we now associate with the paradigm of disruptive protest. Again, the purpose of nonviolent direct action here is to cool the emotional temperature of protest. Nonviolence chooses to whisper rather than to scream, to draw people closer and cultivate the willingness to listen. Moreover, the larger the crowd, the more crucial the need to mitigate any sense of intimidation, coercion, and potential unrest—to muzzle the cacophony that can drown out the voice of reason and conscience. In Gandhi's and King's practice of nonviolence, songs, prayers, and silence all had this double moral and political function and were preferred to the shouting of slogans.

A second aim of nonviolent protest is what King, following Richard Gregg, spoke of as morally "unbalancing" opponents. Nonviolence "has a way of disarming the opponent, it exposes his moral defenses, it weakens his morale and at the same time it works on his conscience."[106] Gregg famously described this process as a kind of "moral jiu-jitsu."[107] By this he meant that nonviolence, like the martial art, yields rather than attacks, and the opponents find their own force is set against themselves. It was, in effect, a provocative defense, a negative counterattack. The adversary is left "bewildered and panicky" in the face of new and unexpected techniques.[108]

Theorists of nonviolence from Tolstoy to Gandhi to Gregg argued that the police and military are trained to deal with violence and therefore prefer it.[109] More cruelly, it gives them an excuse to brutalize populations they have become accustomed to treating in such a manner. If the opposition desires physical confrontation—as certainly seemed to be the case in the context of southern segregation—the nonviolent response was to let them attack and imprison demonstrators, but in a context where such action would backfire. Here nonviolent discipline and planning work to outmaneuver the opponent by fully anticipating and then upsetting their responses. The "jail, no bail" tactic is an illustrative case.[110] The power to arbitrarily incarcerate was one of the foremost material and symbolic weapons of racial domination across the South. But it would be rendered ineffective if behind every arbitrary arrest stood hundreds more waiting to be jailed.[111] Such dramatic gestures instantly exposed the futility of force when enough people lose their fear of it.

For his account of moral unbalancing, Gregg drew heavily on Gandhi's Salt Satyagraha of 1930. This campaign and the 1963 Birmingham campaign are the two most celebrated campaigns in the history of nonviolence. Both used the power of suffering to dramatic effect as protestors were subjected to brutal police responses, iconic images and accounts of which circulated widely. Jeering opponents and state agents stood exposed, revealed as the true "instigators and practitioners of violence."[112] Gregg was particularly interested in how soldiers themselves became physically undone by witnessing the stern resilience of Gandhian activists. The most direct analogy in King's experience of this kind of immediate unbalancing was an incident in Birmingham in which the police found themselves unable to fulfill an order to turn a high-pressure hose on a group marching to the city jail to hold a prayer meeting. When confronted, the protestors stopped and knelt in prayer, and then continued past the "shaken" policemen.[113] Moral unbalancing was tethered to King's admiration of suffering understood as relentless determination and courage.

Finally, a third, related, mechanism King invoked to overcome resistance was the idea of awakening moral conscience through the process of shaming. The kind of shaming that he endorsed and hoped to provoke was a form of critical self-evaluation, different from the passive logic of pity, which he rejected.[114] Though King did not fully elaborate this point, the contrast is instructive. Pity is an externalizing impulse. In pity one is moved by scenes of oppression without necessarily feeling implicated in them. Moreover, when people are made objects of pity, it diminishes their agency just as it empowers those who pity. The latter become potential saviors, whose benevolence can be withdrawn at any moment. Shaming, by contrast, works by directing attention inward. It forces observers to reckon with their own place in the racial order. In the context of protest, nonviolent suffering was not aimed at presenting the black body as abject and in pain, generating pity. Instead it staged black dignity—in the wake of brutality—to turn the viewers' gaze back upon themselves and their complicity in perpetuating injustice.

Violence against peaceful protestors could bring about an extreme form of shaming. King sometimes offered a stark image of the oppressor who becomes ashamed of his brutality; the white southerner is "forced to stand before the world and his God splattered with blood and reeking with the stench of his Negro brother."[115] More often it was metaphoric—an appeal to the conscience of the "decent majority." Though critics saw such an appeal as either futile or perverse in the face of widespread white resistance, King's appeal was not premised on an empirical assessment of white opinion. It was an interpolation, a constructive act. The decent majority, the majority of liberal opinion, was a public that King brought into being through the rhetorical framing of the civil rights movement. When he spoke to, named, and upbraided the white liberal, King was positing a figure of *identification* and *aspiration*. He described how people ought to think and act if they want to see themselves as being on the side of justice.

King's political reasoning, here, as well as in the logic of nonviolent persuasion more generally, is the reverse of what is often assumed. Belief in racial harmony or white sympathy did not precede the choice of nonviolence as a strategic and tactical necessity. It is precisely because King understood the harsh realities of racial domination—the severity of crisis and conflict, the ever-present potential for violence, and the absence of political community across racial lines—that moral appeal became all the more urgent. Moreover, the moral appeal at the heart of nonviolent persuasion is very different from gestures of moderation and compromise. Nonviolence frames critique and dissent in relation to demanding and expansive ideals, ideals that resonate in such a way that everyone can invest in them and evaluate their conduct by them.[116]

Conclusion

One of the great achievements of nonviolent direct action was what King called its *universality*. The "social organization of nonviolence" invited and encouraged participation from all classes, ages, and genders. "There is more power in socially organized masses on the march than there is in guns in the hands of a few desperate men."[117] New empirical findings seem to confirm this. Chenoweth and Stephan characterize this as nonviolence's "participation advantage"—there are far fewer barriers to participating in nonviolent protest than there are to joining an armed movement. And it is this participation advantage that makes nonviolence twice as effective as armed movements in overturning authoritarian regimes.[118] Contemporary advocates of nonviolence likewise emphasize nonviolence's utility as a tactic of mobilization, as a way to organize and display collective power. But for Gandhi and King there was something more at work in nonviolent action, beyond its ability to bring out large numbers of people.

Universality itself was in its own way a moral and political lesson in dignity. To make this point, both Gandhi and King often dramatically brought to the forefront of action those bodies assumed to be the weakest and most vulnerable—women, children, the elderly. More generally, questions of power, size, and pressure were subordinated to the goal of conveying the right message—such as making visible the moral and political stakes of domination—and finding the most effective means for doing so. The nonviolence of King and the civil rights movement was not simply a symbolic gesture or rhetorical framing. To do the difficult work of political persuasion, nonviolence had to shape how protests are organized and enacted. Hence the crucial importance of the staging of suffering, dignity, and discipline—to convert opponents into allies, and to do so more effectively than could be done by brute force, pure pressure, or outright confrontation. Suffering worked to persuade by disarming, exposing, and awakening opponents; this was its strategic reasoning and tactical logic.

Of course, there is no guarantee that nonviolent protest will always succeed in persuading recalcitrant and resisting opponents. But King's wager was that it was always better to be oriented to the potential persuasion of opponents than their certain alienation. This idea of persuasion is perhaps especially important to keep in focus in relation to the demands of democracy. The arc of the civil rights movement attests to the constraints of nonviolence within the context of democratic politics. The resistance to the movement showed how self-described democratic publics can be surprisingly hostile to nonviolent protest, especially when waged on behalf of minority interests. America's history of racial domination made for a specific and entrenched history of divisive conflict. But all societies are riven by some forms of acute division and antagonism, tendencies that can be exacerbated by democratic politics.

Democracy provides institutional channels to express dissent and effect political change. When these channels and institutions are seen to be legitimate, a status quo bias predominates and insurgent politics are readily branded as extreme and deemed suspect. Democratic politics are also driven by dynamics of passion and power. The open, competitive, and continual contest for power fuels resentments, antagonism, and polarization. Nonviolent politics may have an especially useful role to play in realizing a form of disruptive politics that can mitigate resentment and, at the same time, enable the building of large, creative, plural majorities. The instantiation of a shared democratic life—learning to treat and relate to one's enemies and opponents as fellow citizens—requires the adoption of strategies of critique, programs of change, and tactical action that go beyond condemnation, confrontation, and disorder. Disciplined nonviolent action creates a space for the necessary but hard work of political persuasion. In this respect, the core elements of classical nonviolent action, lost in the wake of King's assassination, are especially ripe for reexamination as part of the renewal of democratic politics.

PART II *Ideals*

5

From Anger to Love: Self-Purification and Political Resistance

MARTHA C. NUSSBAUM

> But when I say we should not resent, I do not say that we should acquiesce.
>
> —MOHANDAS GANDHI, "The *Satyagraha Ashram*," 1915

Anger and Revolutionary Justice

Martin Luther King, Jr., is renowned for his views about and his practice of nonviolent protest and resistance. It is also generally acknowledged that his normative ethical theory includes a commitment to "self-purification," that is, to internal attitudinal change, and that he believed that nonviolent protest that was not preceded by internal change was both undependable and spiritually inadequate. But his precise attitudes toward that internal change deserve deeper philosophical inspection, and it is the purpose of this chapter to provide that inspection.

In my recent book *Anger and Forgiveness: Resentment, Generosity, Justice* I argued that King follows closely the thought of Mohandas Gandhi about anger and resentment and advises a complete removal of those emotional attitudes, on the ground that a wish for payback is a conceptual part of them.[1] Instead, both thinkers recommend an attitude that may criticize and express outrage about bad deeds, but that always eschews retribution, and that, furthermore, always extends to the wrongdoer a generous type of love and a hope for a future of cooperation and constructive work. Since, however, my concern in that book was to provide an argument of my own about the foundations of revolutionary justice, I studied

King and Gandhi together (linking them, eventually, with the thought of Nelson Mandela), and thus did not provide a separate textual analysis of King's specific attitudes, though I did include many textual references. It is time to perform that further task.

First, it will be useful to summarize the argument of *Anger and Forgiveness*.

I begin from Aristotle's definition of anger, which in most respects commands virtually universal acceptance in the Western philosophical tradition, and also corresponds to the insights of Santideva in the Hindu tradition. The emotion of anger includes and rests upon the following thoughts:

1. The thought that something bad has been done by some agent, affecting adversely the interests of something or someone of deep concern to the self.
2. The thought that this damage was wrongfully inflicted.
3. The thought that it would be good for the doer to suffer in some way for what was done.
4. The thought that the specific nature of the damage is typically that of a "down-ranking" or diminution in relative status.

I relatively quickly approve of 1 and 2, which seem both clear and uncontroversial. Along with most subsequent philosophers who in other respects follow Aristotle, I argue that we ought to reject 4, since many cases of anger do not involve relative status: I can get angry at harms to others whom I love, or at damages to important principles. Still, I suggest that status-injury is often an important part of anger, and that we should hold onto that thought, especially because modern psychological studies of anger have shown it to be very common. Most subsequent philosophical analyses in the Western tradition, including that of the ancient Greek and Roman Stoics, define anger more generally in terms of wrongful injury.

I then turn to 3. I argue that, contrary to what many might initially suppose, this wish for retribution or payback is in fact, as Aristotle insists, a conceptual part of what we might call "garden-variety anger." Without that wish, the emotion is likely to be something else: compassionate grief, perhaps. This argument takes a long time, and uses many detailed examples. But it is important for our purposes to remember that 3 does not entail the thought that the wronged person should actively take revenge herself. She may simply want the law to do so, or some type of divine justice. (Gandhi makes a similar point in order to deflect objections when he insists that the wish for payback is a conceptual element in anger.) Or, even more subtly, she may simply want the offender's life to go very badly in the future, hoping, for example, that the second marriage of a betraying spouse will turn out to be a dismal failure. Most subtly of all, like Dante, she may simply wish that the offender will have the ill fate of being forever the type of bad person he or she is, and that this is itself punishment. I use many examples to make this further argument.

Thus, in my view, and in agreement with a large number of philosophers and psychologists, anger has two parts: a protest part and a payback part. The protest is an assertion that damage was wrongfully inflicted. And then the payback part says that some type of retribution is an appropriate response to the damage. These two parts can in principle come apart, although in real life they are very commonly linked.

I turn next to the defects of garden-variety anger, so understood. The primary defect is that the payback idea does not make sense. Ideas of proportional retribution are ubiquitous, and perhaps a part of our evolutionary heritage. Whatever the wrong that was done, whether murder, rape, or assault, it is extremely common to think that the universe will be off-kilter unless the offender suffers in some duly proportional way for what he or she has done. Ideas of proportional payback have been defended by subtle philosophers, such as Herbert Morris and other retributivists in the philosophy of law. More important, they are a part of basic human psychology: we just aren't satisfied unless and until the doer suffers. But however useful such ideas might have been in human prehistory, in motivating a "strike-back" tendency that might have preserved the group, they are simply irrational when examined in the clear light of day. Executing a murderer (or even imprisoning him for life) does not bring the dead to life or even fill the gap left by the death of a loved one. As Aeschylus notes, "When once a man's dark blood is spilled upon the ground, what can call it back again?" It may possibly be the case that a proportional type of punishment will sometimes prove useful, whether through incapacitation, or through specific or general deterrence, or through reform. But that is an empirical question, and people rarely treat it as such. It might turn out that payback is in some instances not a very useful deterrent, or that milder or lighter penalties deter better than harsher ones—all being possibilities that the ancient Greeks and Romans, who wisely rejected retributivism and based ideas of punishment on welfare-oriented deterrence, duly investigated. On the whole, however, it is very easy and natural to avoid such difficult empirical questions and to think that the problem of crime (or other injustice) can be solved if only we make the doer suffer in a way that counterbalances the wrong.

I then argue that there is one, and only one, case in which the payback idea makes perfect sense and is fully rational, rather than magical: when the wrongful act is (as Aristotle recommends) seen as entirely and fully about relative status. If the real problem is not the murder itself, but only the way it has lowered my relative status in the community, I really can achieve what I want by payback: by pushing the offender relatively down (humiliating him or her), I really do raise myself relatively up, and because we are assuming that in this case relative status is all I care about, I am a winner. However, I am a winner at the cost of adopting an exceedingly narrow and skewed picture of value. Many people and many societies (including prominently our own) do encourage many people to care overwhelmingly about relative status and to see everything that happens as a move in a zero-sum game of social rank. But that is an objectionably narrow way of looking at life.

In short, a person who is angry in response to an injury arrives, I claim, at a threefold fork in the road. Either she goes down the *road of status*, seeing the wrong as all about her relative status—in which case her payback wish makes sense but her value system is objectionable; or she goes down the *road of payback*, seeing the wrong as important because of the intrinsic value of the victim's life or whatever, and thinks that payback will somehow nullify or atone for the injury—in which case she has a sensible scheme of values, but her payback thought doesn't make sense. Or, if she is sensible and rational, she will see that there is a third course open to her, which is the best of all: she can decide to drop the payback idea and to focus on what would make sense and do good going forward. Such a person can and usually should continue to protest the wrong, but without the spirit of retribution.

I call this healthy segue from payback thoughts into constructive future-oriented work and hope the Transition (a technical term in my theory), and I argue that it often occurs, both in personal relationships and in political relationships. I illustrate it, in fact, by examining the sequence of emotions King constructs for his audience in the "I Have a Dream" speech. Initially encouraged to feel anger at the outrageous wrongs of racism, the audience is then encouraged to refuse the road of payback and to turn forward to constructive work and hope.

At this point I introduce a major exception to my thesis that anger always involves, conceptually, a thought of payback. There are many cases in which one gets standardly angry first, thinking about some type of payback, and then, in a cooler moment, heads for the Transition. But there are at least a few cases in which one is there already: the *entire* content of one's emotion is, "How outrageous! Something must be done about this." Let us call this emotion *Transition-Anger,* because it is anger, or quasi-anger, already heading down the third fork in the angry person's road. One might give it some ordinary-language name, such as Jean Hampton's "indignation," but I prefer to segment it cleanly from other cases, because I think a lot of cases we call "indignation" involve some thought of pay-back. Hampton gives the word a technical sense, but it is sometimes easy to forget that. So I prefer the clearly made-up term. Transition-Anger, in short, has the protest part of anger without the payback part. Transition-Anger does not focus on status; nor does it, even briefly, want the suffering of the offender as a type of payback for the injury. It never gets involved at all in that type of magical thinking. It focuses on social welfare from the start. Saying "Something should be done about this," it commits itself to a search for strategies, but it remains an open question whether the suffering of the offender will be among the most appealing.

I illustrate the idea of Transition-Anger by discussing the attitude that loving parents typically have to the wrongful acts of their young children: they are outraged, but they don't wish for payback. Instead, wanting good to ensue for the child, they search for constructive strategies to en-sure that this act is not repeated. Transition-Anger is typically predicated on love. When one does not care about a person or group, or does not want good to ensue for them, one is less likely to adopt this constructive forward-looking attitude and more likely to indulge in empty fantasies of payback.

I acknowledge that garden-variety of anger can often be instrumentally useful, and this in three ways. First, it can be a signal or wake-up call to oneself that something is badly amiss. However, given the strong connec-tion of anger to status-injury, this signal is often inaccurate. Second, and important for our purposes, anger may motivate people who might other-wise despair to get up and do something. This can be accomplished by Transition-Anger alone, as when loving parents do something about their child's bad behavior. But anger with the baggage of the payback wish may often motivate real people, initially, to engage with a protest movement. Their motives may be an unclear mixture of payback wish with construc-tive desire for change.

I must introduce one further bit of terminology. When an instance of anger is right about what has occurred, about its wrongfulness, and about its seriousness, then I call that anger "well-grounded." I do not grant that it is "justified," because if it is ordinary anger, it includes the payback wish, and that is never appropriate or well based. "Well-grounded" means, then, "right about everything except the payback idea."

Subsequent chapters in my book put these ideas to work and test them further in a number of distinct "spheres" of human activity: the sphere of intimate personal relations; a sphere that I call "the Middle Realm," meaning the realm of interactions that are neither intimate nor political, such as interactions in the workplace or in casual daily encounters (anger on the road, in air travel, in dealing with rude personnel of many sorts, and so forth); and, finally, anger in the political realm. In the intimate realm, I conclude that anger is very likely inevitable in many cases, given the profound vulnerability involved in trusting another person, but that heading for the Transition as soon as one can is the best course, in order to avoid getting caught up in a fruitless "blame game," which does nothing to solve the real problems, whether the problem is repairing a damaged relationship or moving beyond the breakup of one. In the Middle Realm I suggest that the Stoics are correct: one should realize that these things are very trivial in the larger scheme of things, and should totally avoid garden-variety anger, difficult though this is to do.

I then turn to the political realm. First, I examine the world of "everyday justice," arguing that a sensible approach to crime and wrongdoing will, first of all, focus above all on ex ante strategies, such as education, nutrition, employment, and care, and will not try to solve everything by waiting until crime has occurred and then using harsh punishment. The fact that many societies fail to take this sensible approach probably shows that there is a failure of love for fellow citizens: we'd never find loving parents neglecting the child until a wrongful act had occurred and then doling out harsh punishment. Furthermore, when crime does occur despite wise ex ante strategies, the approach to punishment ought to be based upon empirically informed ideas of future social welfare.

We now arrive at revolutionary justice, where the claims of anger might appear to be especially strong. Isn't anger noble when society is corrupt and brutal? When people are kept down, they all too often learn to acquiesce in their "fate." They form "adaptive preferences," defining their lot as acceptable and acquiescence as fitting. But if they acquiesce, change is unlikely. Awakening people to the injustice of society's treatment of them is a necessary first step toward social progress. And don't we expect that awakening to produce justified anger? If people believe they are being wrongfully abused and don't get angry, isn't there something wrong in their thinking somewhere? Don't they, for example, seem to have too low an opinion of their dignity and rights?

Anger might seem to have three valuable roles in a revolutionary transition. First, it is seen as a valuable signal (both to the oppressed themselves and to others) that the oppressed recognize the wrong done to them. It also seems to be a necessary motivation for them to protest and struggle against injustice and to communicate to the wider world the nature of their grievances. Finally, anger seems, quite simply, to be justified: outrage at terrible wrongs is right, and anger (including its retributive wish) thus expresses something true.

When the basic legal structure of society is sound, people can turn to the law for redress without getting involved in personal anger. But sometimes the legal structure is itself unjust and corrupt. What people need to do is not just to secure justice for this or that particular wrong, but, ultimately, to change the legal order. That task is different from the task of preserving daily justice, albeit continuous with it. It appears to require anger, even if daily justice does not. Or so one might suppose.

Retributive anger has deep roots in the Christian tradition: it dominates the book of Revelation, in which the despised Christians are encouraged to take pleasure in the future suffering of their oppressors. It has been endorsed by many revolutionary leaders, including Malcolm X, as we shall see.

On the other hand, if we examine successful struggles for revolutionary justice over the past hundred years, we see immediately that three of the most prominent—and stably successful—were conducted with a profound commitment to non-anger, though definitely not in a spirit of acquiescence. Gandhi's noncooperation campaign against the British Raj, the U.S. civil rights movement, and South Africa's struggle to overcome the apartheid system were all highly successful, and all repudiated anger as a matter of both theory and practice. To the extent that any of them admitted anger as acceptable, it was either our borderline species of "Transition-Anger," a sense of outrage and protest without any wish for ill to befall the offender, or else a brief episode of real anger, but leading quickly to the Transition.

Mohandas Gandhi, utterly repudiating anger, and usually successful in not feeling it, showed the world that non-anger is a posture not of weakness and servility but of strength and dignity.[2] He expressed outrage, but always in a forward-looking and non-angry spirit. King (at least so I contend in the book) followed Gandhi, espousing both non-anger (or at least a quick Transition to non-anger, or Transition-Anger) and nonviolence, apart from some exceptional circumstances in the area of self-defense.

Nelson Mandela urged the African National Congress to drop nonviolent tactics when they were not working and to use violence in a limited strategic way; but he never ceased to look at any situation he was in, even the worst, in a generous forward-looking spirit. Though a man evidently prone to anger, he was also impressively capable of moving rapidly beyond it, through an unusual freedom from status-anxiety and an equally remarkable generosity. We now know that his long struggle with anger during his twenty-seven years of imprisonment was informed by Stoic meditative practices.[3] Studying this record, I argued, can help us to see why the idea of "noble anger" as signal, motivator, and justified expression is a false guide in revolutionary situations, and why a generous frame of mind is both more appropriate and more effective.

Here are some key points in my argument. First, the non-angry protester is not passive. All three leaders represent protest as determined activity requiring considerable courage, not supine acquiescence. Second, forgoing the idea of payback is not only not supine but actually quite powerful, if what is wanted ultimately is to make things better for all. Payback gets in the way of constructive achievement. Third, protest at outrageous deeds is a good way of separating the deed from the doer, indicating ways in which people who have done harm may transcend those past actions and join in projects aimed at justice.

Questions for King's View

But because my analysis in the book mingles texts from Gandhi and from King, a more detailed analysis of King's views is needed. Here, then, are the questions I would like to pose to the corpus of King's speeches, books, and essays:

1. What does King think anger is? (How, if at all, does he define anger?) Does he make any distinction corresponding to my distinction between the protest part of anger and its payback part? Does he recognize the borderline case of what I call Transition-Anger?

2. Does King think that anger is ever fully justified (correct in all its parts)?

3. Does he think that anger can be instrumentally useful, and in what way or ways?

4. How does he propose to address the problem of anger in his followers?

5. Does he think that violence is ever justified, and, if so, when and why?
6. How does he reply to the criticism that nonviolence is passive and supine?
7. What is the new attitude that he proposes to substitute for anger?
8. Does King adopt a full-fledged Stoic position about emotions, as Gandhi seems to have done, suggesting a more or less total detachment from all emotion?

One general observation before we begin. King is very interested in clearly defining some aspects of his position. On some issues he defines a concept over and over, making very clear and explicit distinctions. In other areas, however, he is much less explicit and precise, perhaps because he is less worried about being misunderstood, or thinks that people will get the drift of his ideas rather easily. He defines love dozens of times, enumerating and defining three distinct species of love and making it clear that his form is *agape,* not *eros* or *philia,* and that *agape,* in his view, is not a sentimental or emotional attitude at all, is not even "affectionate," but is a deliberate activity of will.[4] It's easy to see why he is so explicit here, since the use of the term "love" creates ample possibilities of misunderstanding, which he had no doubt encountered. With violence as well, he is quite explicit, although his position appears to evolve in the direction of a more total embrace of nonviolence. With other matters that greatly interest me, he is less explicit, and we need to work to unearth his view. But the work is worth it, because King has nuanced and defensible positions.

King on Anger, Hate, and Payback

I now attempt to answer my first four questions. Gandhi is quite explicit on these issues: anger (or "resentment"; he uses the terms interchangeably) always includes, as a constituent part, a wish for payback, if only through divine justice. For this reason, it is never fully justified. There are indeed serious wrongs, and outraged protest at these wrongs is justified (the attitude that I have called "Transition-Anger"). But full-fledged anger, including the payback wish, is always harmful and pernicious. It has no good role even instrumentally, because it interferes with the job of reconciliation.

King, by contrast, addresses none of these questions head on. He never explicitly defines "anger" or "resentment." He does come close to defining "hate," which he (correctly in my view) does not equate with anger. Hate is traditionally distinguished from anger and defined as an ongoing negative attitude to a person, not connected to a particular wrongful act. Anger's target is a person, the perpetrator of the wrongful act; but its occasion is the act, and it targets the person *qua* perpetrator of the wrongful act. Hate has no such rationale, and no such limit. It is the binary opposite of love. Aristotle thinks that it involves a wish that the person not exist any more at all; though this is not persuasive to me, hate does seem to be a pervasive negative attitude to a person, just as love is a pervasive positive attitude. But what does King think?

Although he offers no explicit definition of hate, he treats hate as the polar opposite of love. But if we can assume that hate is the polar opposite of love, which his usage strongly suggests, hate is a determined attitude of will seeking another person's ill.

If King thinks that love of the relevant sort is not an emotion, does he think the same of hate? He does not say. But if it is will and not emotion, it would likely be closely linked to, and supported by, the negative emotional attitudes that interest us.

About hate, King is very clear: it is never an acceptable attitude. One thing he repeatedly emphasizes is that we must separate the doer from the deed: deeds may be condemned, but people should always be shown love and goodwill, and we must always expect that they can be redeemed. "To retaliate with hate and bitterness would do nothing but intensify the hate in the world."[5] "Let no man pull you so low as to hate him."[6] "To meet hate with retaliatory hate would do nothing but intensify the existence of evil in the universe."[7] The nonviolent resister "not only refuses to shoot his opponent but he also refuses to hate him."[8] "Along the way of life, someone must have sense enough and morality enough to cut off the chain of hate."[9]

One might believe this while still thinking that anger, with its payback wish intact, is an appropriate emotion in many cases. But it seems clear that King did not think this. In a 1959 essay he says that the struggle for integration will continue to encounter obstacles, and that these obstacles can be met in two very different ways: "One is the development of a wholesome social organization to resist with effective, firm measures any efforts to impede progress. The other is a confused, anger-motivated drive to strike back violently, to inflict damage. Primarily, it seeks to cause injury to retaliate for wrongful suffering. Secondarily, it seeks real progress. It is punitive—not radical or constructive."[10] This passage makes it quite clear, I think, that King condemns the retributive attitude that seeks to return pain for pain, and condemns it on my terms, as confused and adverse to real progress. It does not answer the question whether King thinks that this retributive desire is a conceptual part of anger. One might think that the expression "anger-motivated drive" gives a negative answer to that question: if retributivism is caused by anger, it can't be a part of anger. And King often speaks of anger in a way that suggests that it can survive the removal of the retributive wish. For example, in *The Trumpet of Conscience* he speaks of a "very legitimate anger" that might be expressed either in rioting or in nonviolent protest.[11]

Frequently King uses the metaphor of "channeling" to express what I would call the Transition: anger is changed from something potentially destructive to something productive and creative. Here is one representative passage: "I think we have come to the point where there is no longer a choice now between nonviolence and riots. It must be militant, massive nonviolence, or riots. The discontent is so deep, the anger so ingrained, the despair, the restlessness so wide, that something has to be brought into being to serve as a channel through which these deep emotional feelings, these deep angry feelings, can be funneled. There has to be an outlet, and I see this campaign as a way to transmute the inchoate rage of the ghetto into a constructive and creative channel."[12] The clear sense of this passage is that anger must be not just directed toward a new goal but also, in the process, changed. The word "transmuted" is linked to the more neutral words "channel" and "funneled." He does not explicitly say that the protest part remains while the retributive part is transmuted into work and hope, but I believe that is the most natural way to read what he is saying. At first, then, anger has retributive wishes, and therefore it might lead to rioting and violence; but it can and must be transmuted into a creative force—into something like my Transition-Anger.

What is clear, in any event, is that King condemns the retributive wish. Elsewhere, too, King condemns utterly the retaliatory mind-set. "May all who suffer oppression in this world," he writes in 1957, "reject the self-defeating method of retaliatory violence and choose the method that seeks to redeem."[13] Furthermore, he emphasizes that nonviolent resistance must avoid "not only . . . external physical violence but also internal violence of spirit."[14] Nonviolent resistance involves "a willingness to accept suffering without retaliation, to accept blows from the opponent without striking back."[15]

We shall see that King finds room for real people's angry emotions as instrumental motivations that may lead them into his movement—but they must be purified and "channelized" before they will prove really useful. The structured training that is central to the protest movement is his way of addressing not just the possibility of angry behavior but also, insofar as is practicable, the resistant angry attitudes that could destabilize nonviolent protest.[16]

Anger, then, may bring people to King's movement; once there, it must undergo purification or change. But notice, too, that people always have a choice of what to do with their anger. If they follow it into King's movement, rather than into the alternative he always mentions, rioting and the destruction of property, then it appears that their attitude is pretty close to Transition-Anger already, because they might have chosen other movements that would help them pursue retributive goals.

King's views about anger can be further illuminated by a contrast with those of Malcolm X, who urged people to reject King's nonviolent movement as a slavish compromise with white power. "You don't have a peaceful revolution. You don't have a turn-the-other-cheek revolution. There's no such thing as a nonviolent revolution. . . . Revolution is bloody, revolution is hostile, revolution knows no compromise, revolution overturns and destroys everything that gets in its way."[17] He strongly endorses the spirit of anger, including its retributive element, urging his followers to seize property by violence in retaliation for years of white domination. He uses vivid metaphors to pour contempt on both non-anger and nonviolence. In one passage, he compares King's movement to the Novocain a dentist gives you to stop you from attacking him when he is about to pull your tooth.[18] In other words, King anaesthetizes people, dulling their natural emotions.[19] And he also compares King's movement to a lot of cream poured into coffee, turning it cold and weak: "But if you pour too much cream in it, you won't even know you ever had coffee. It used to be hot, it becomes cool. It used to be strong, it becomes weak. It used to wake you up, now it puts you to sleep. That is what they did with the march on Washington. . . . And as they took it over, it lost its militancy. It ceased to be angry, it ceased to be hot, it ceased to be uncompromising. Why, it even ceased to be a march. It became a picnic, a circus. Nothing but a circus, with clowns and all . . . white clowns and black clowns."[20] To be revolutionary, anger has to remain "hot," meaning poised to engage in violent retributive aggression. King is portrayed as the "black clown" who is nothing but a dupe of white slave masters, eager to infiltrate and destroy the revolution.

King's constant response to this critique is that retribution is weak and confused, and creative nonviolence is strong: it protests the wrong and then moves to the future. I think he is really talking about what I have called the Transition, and he has a very effective reply to Malcolm X and other advocates of retributive anger.

King on Violence and Nonviolence

It seems clear to me that non-anger does not entail nonviolence. A person firmly committed to the idea that anger's wish for retribution is always inappropriate can nonetheless at times and in limited ways use violence as a strategy. The clearest case would be self-defense: one can use violence when the lives of oneself and others are wrongfully threatened, without wishing retributive punishment upon the assailant. One may even fight a war in that spirit. Of course motives are hard to sort out, and during a just war many people will in fact harbor retributive wishes toward the enemy, but it is perfectly possible to engage in such a war hoping for peace and reconciliation at the end of it. Many who fought in the Second World War had no desire to visit punishment upon the Germans; indeed, they saw them as victims of Hitlerism. But they had to engage with German troops in order to prevent disaster. Some very likely wanted to punish Hitler and other ringleaders: but one may want punishment for more than one reason, and if their reasons were those of general and specific deterrence and incapacitation, they could carry out even those punishments, and wish for them beforehand, in a non-angry spirit. Winston Churchill's famous "Blood, Toil, Tears and Sweat" speech asks not for retribution but for sacrifice in order to preserve Britain's way of life.[21] Many people fought the war in that spirit, without hate and even without retributive wishes.

Similarly, at times, during a resistance movement, nonviolent tactics may fail. At such times, a wise leader might with regret opt for a strategic use of violence. I have argued that Nelson Mandela was such a leader: he never wavered in his opposition to retributive thoughts and emotions, but he did counsel the strategic use of violence by the ANC at a certain juncture in the movement, when all else had failed. To test whether a leader's use of violence was thus narrow and strategic, one would want to see whether human lives were spared insofar as was possible (and violence confined to strategic or technical targets); and one would want to see whether the means were carefully calibrated to well-thought-out ends. I think the ANC's use of violence met this test on the whole. And when the victory was won, Mandela rapidly and wholeheartedly turned to reconciliation and friendship, eschewing retributive emotions and actions and persuading his comrades to follow him.

Gandhi disputed the claims I have just made, holding that non-anger entails nonviolence. It seems likely that he embraced a metaphysical view of the person according to which a correct inner disposition entailed nonviolent behavior, and in which violence required an incorrect inner disposition.[22] (His speculations on meat-eating and violence in the *Auto-biography* are just one sign of this idea.[23]) As Richard Sorabji shows, Gandhi did make a few exceptions, primarily in connection with killing dangerous animals: but the constraint was always that physical violence is admissible only when it is for the good of the recipient. This constraint, he believed, is never satisfied in human relations.[24] We should not reject Gandhi's views simply because they have their roots in metaphysical views that are not widely shared and that seem superstitious to many of us. But we must ask whether Gandhi is persuasive when he holds that a person of a generous and loving spirit will never endorse or participate in violence.

He is not persuasive. Gandhi's views about war are not sensible. His idea that the best way, and a fully adequate way, to approach Hitler was through nonviolence and love was simply absurd, and would have been profoundly damaging had anyone taken it seriously. He made two grave errors. First, he equated a violent response to Hitler with "Hitlerism," saying that "Hitlerism will never be defeated by counter-Hitlerism."[25] This is simply unconvincing: self-defense is not morally equivalent to aggression, nor is the defense of decent political institutions equivalent to their subversion. Second, he also held that Hitler would respond to a nonviolent and loving overture: "Human nature in its essence is one and therefore unfailingly responds to the advances of love."[26] This is absurd. Responding to an imagined objector who says that all nonviolence would accomplish is to offer Hitler an easy victory, Gandhi interestingly backs off from his own preposterous empirical prediction, and simply concludes that in any case Europe, behaving nonviolently, would be morally superior. "And in the end I expect it is the moral worth that will count. All else is dross."[27] It is fortunate indeed that Nehru, who had observed German fascism in action while accompanying his wife to a sanatorium in Switzerland, had no interest in Gandhi's proposal, and neither, of course, did the British, who were still there. Gandhi's equally ugly proposal not to resist the Japanese if they invaded India requires no comment.

So Gandhi did not show that non-anger entails nonviolence. Mandela, surely a generous and loving person if ever there was one, has the right idea, thinking of nonviolence and negotiation as preferred strategies, but strategies to be abandoned if over a long period of time they don't work.

What about King? The record is complicated. He is usually understood to have had an unequivocal Gandhian commitment to nonviolence. But in fact he often acknowledges that there is a morally legitimate role for violence—self-defense being the general rubric he uses.[28] Early in his career, he does not oppose all wars, nor even all personal defensive violence.

He does, however, argue that in the particular situation of the freedom movement, leaving a loophole for the appeal to self-defense would be too dangerous, giving lots of opportunities for self-serving blurring of boundaries and, ultimately, strengthening resentment's hand.[29] If people can easily appeal to self-defense in justification of vengeful acts, they will be less likely to make the inner transformation he requires of them. Nor would such a movement, unpredictable and prone to outbursts, attain the coherence and stability King saw as necessary to win the respect of the majority and achieve the movement's social goals.

As for pacifism, in 1960 he insists forthrightly that he is "no doctrinaire pacifist" but has "tried to embrace a realistic pacifism."[30] He even goes so far as to say that the pacifist position is "not . . . sinless" but simply "the lesser evil" in many circumstances.[31] However, already in 1959 he declares his unequivocal opposition to the use of nuclear weapons and to all aggressive forms of warfare: "I have unequivocally declared my hatred for this most colossal of all evils [nuclear war] and I have condemned any organizer of war, regardless of his rank or nationality."[32]

As time went on, and above all as the United States became more and more deeply enmeshed in Vietnam, King appears to adopt a more absolutist anti-war position. Already in his 1964 Nobel address he hardens his view, saying, "Civilization and violence are antithetical concepts."[33] And in a speech of 1969 he states unequivocally: "I'm committed to nonviolence absolutely. I'm just not going to kill anybody, whether it's in Vietnam or here."[34] His 1967 Christmas sermon makes it clear that this absolutism is not simply local, pertaining to Vietnam: "Every man is somebody because he is a child of God. And so when we say 'Thou shalt not kill,' we're really saying that human life is too sacred to be taken on the battlefields of the world."[35] It seems likely that the shift was occasioned by Vietnam, with its constant hideous spectacle of televised violence; but it was not simply about Vietnam.

Another thread in his argument is his repudiation, by 1961, of what he calls the communist doctrine "that the end justifies the means."[36] One might argue that it was precisely this doctrine that Mandela relied on in his own shift from nonviolence to the strategic use of violence. But the context does not reveal whether King understand his former approval of violence in self-defense to be a mistaken use of this doctrine.

Did he really shift his position? The Vietnam War was far from a just war in self-defense. I know of no text, early or late, in which King repudiates armed participation in World War II—as Gandhi emphatically did. King says repeatedly that if he had lived in Hitler's Germany, he would have "aided and comforted" his "Jewish brothers";[37] but he does not say that he would have taken up arms as required for self-defense. He also does not say, early or late, that it was wrong to do so. I conclude tentatively that his position did shift to a more absolutist one, but evidence is thin.

Answering the Objections to Non-Anger and Nonviolence

Philosophers and nonphilosophers alike have seen anger as appropriate in situations of oppression, and as linked to the vindication of self-respect. It is, then, not surprising that non-anger should have struck many onlookers as strange, unmanly, even revolting. Webb Miller, the UPI correspondent who reported the nonviolent protest action at the Dharasana Salt Works in 1930 (under the leadership of the poet Sarojini Naidu, because Gandhi was in jail), observed scores of marchers getting beaten down by the police, and reacted with perplexity, as he records in a later memoir: "Not one of the marchers even raised an arm to fend off the blows. They went down like tenpins. From where I stood I heard the sickening whacks of the clubs on unprotected skulls. . . . At times the spectacle of unresisting men being methodically bashed into a bloody pulp sickened me so much that I had to turn away. The western mind finds it difficult to grasp the idea of nonresistance. I felt an indefinable sense of helpless rage and loathing, almost as much against the men who were submitting unresistingly to being beaten as against the police wielding the clubs, and this despite the fact that when I came to India I sympathized with the Gandhi cause."[38]

The marchers were not simply acquiescing. They continued to march, and they chanted the slogan "Long live the revolution." And yet, as Miller says: there is something in the mind, and not only the Western mind, that resists accepting this way of reacting to brutal behavior. One might also ponder the statement made to the court by Gandhi's assassin, Nathuram Godse, who says that his deed was prompted by his abhorrence of Gandhi's nonviolence:

> I could never conceive that an armed resistance to an aggression is unjust. I would consider it a religious and moral duty to resist and if possible, to overpower such an enemy by use of force. (In the Ramayana) Rama killed Ravana in a tumultuous fight and relieved Sita. (In the Mahabharata) Krishna killed Kansa to end his wickedness; and Arjuna had to fight and slay quite a number of his friends and relations, including the revered Bhishma, because the

latter was on the side of the aggressor. It is my firm belief that in dubbing Rama, Krishna and Arjuna as guilty of violence, the Mahatma betrayed the total ignorance of the springs of human action. In more recent history, it was the heroic fight put up by Chhatrapati Shivaji that first checked and eventually destroyed the Muslim tyranny in India. It was absolutely essential for Shivaji to overpower and kill an aggressive Afzal Khan, failing which he would have lost his own life. In condemning history's towering warriors like Shivaji, Rana Pratap and Guru Govind Singh as misguided patriots, Gandhi has merely exposed his self-conceit.[39]

It is, I think, significant that Godse focuses his critique, as does Webb Miller, on the case of self-defense in response to violent aggression, a point on which Gandhi's views were indeed extreme and questionable, and King's equivocal. What do Gandhi and King have to say to people who think anger—and violence—the right response to oppressive behavior, and the only response consistent with self-respect? Here I shall treat the two men closely together, since I believe that their views are very close. King, influenced by Gandhi but also by his study of Christian thought, as well as by the provocation of Malcolm X, develops a view that expands on Gandhi's in creative and interesting ways.

First, they point out that the stance they recommend is anything but passive. Gandhi soon rejected "passive resistance" as a misleading English rendering of the ideas he had expressed in Gujarati. As Dennis Dalton documents in his important philosophical study, starting already in 1907 Gandhi repudiated the term "passive resistance," insisting that "passive resistance" could be weak and inactive, whereas his idea was one of active protest; he eventually chose *satyagraha*, "truth force," as a superior term.[40] Both he and King continually insist that what they recommend is a posture of thought and conduct that is highly active, even "dynamically aggressive," in that it involves resistance to unjust conditions and protest against them.[41] "But when I say we should not resent, I do not say that we should acquiesce," says Gandhi.[42] For King, similarly: "I have not said to my people 'get rid of your discontent.' But I have tried to say that this normal and healthy discontent can be channelized through the creative outlet of nonviolent direct action."[43] In short: "This is not a method for cowards; it *does* resist."[44]

Moreover, the new attitude is not just internally active, it issues in concrete actions with one's body, actions that require considerable courage.[45] King calls this "direct action": action in which, after "self-purification" (rejection of hatred), one's own body is used to make the case.[46] This action is a forceful and uncompromising demand for freedom.[47] The protester acts by marching, by breaking an unjust law in a deliberate demand for justice, by refusing to cooperate with unjust authority. The goal? In King's case, to force negotiation and move toward legal and social change.[48] For Gandhi it is no less than to overthrow a wrongful government and to "*compel* its submission to the people's will."[49] The idea of acquiescence in brutality is presumably what revolted Webb Miller, but he misunderstood: there is no acquiescence, but a courageous struggle for a radical end.[50] (The Miller in the Richard Attenborough film *Gandhi* (1982), played by Martin Sheen, does not misunderstand, but admires: and it is clear that his press coverage of the demonstration aroused admiration around the world, whatever the inner ambivalence recorded in the later memoir.)

Did Godse also misunderstand? Probably not: for, then and now, the Hindu Right is wedded to an aggressive conception of masculinity that is comfortable with the use of violence.[51] So too Malcolm X: Although his satirical treatment of King is grossly unfair, he probably did not misunderstand the profound difference between his valorization of retributive aggression and King's commitment to hope and love.

What is the new attitude with which King proposes to replace anger and hate? It is, of course, love. "At the center of nonviolence stands the principle of love."[52] The important move recommended by both Gandhi and King is to separate the deed from the doer.[53] Bad deeds may and should be denounced; people always deserve respect and sympathy. King emphasizes repeatedly that the ultimate goal is "to create a world where men and women can live together," and that goal requires *agape* as its foundation.[54] All must have a share in "the creation of the beloved community."[55] He returns again and again to the idea of a brotherhood based on love's goodwill between the former oppressors and the former oppressed. Thus, the "I Have a Dream" speech, which I have discussed as an example of the Transition, is also a sentiment map that turns the critical and once-angry protester toward a future of enormous beauty, and one that is shown as possible and shortly available, by being rooted in concrete features of the real American landscape, all of which are now seen as sites of freedom.[56] Belief in the possibility of such a future plays no small part in the Transition. King was really outstanding here, and Gandhi somewhat less so: because of his asceticism, he kept portraying the future as one of impoverished rural simplicity, which was not very inspiring to most people, and he was quite unrealistic in thinking about how to build a successful nation. Moreover, because of his ascetic skepticism about the arts and even beauty, he eschews powerful aesthetic means of arousing sentiments of love and hope. King, by contrast, mines biblical and other texts (for example, the plays of Shakespeare) for powerful images of beauty.[57] King's prophetic description of the future furthermore, repositions opponents as potential partners in building the beautiful future. So then the question naturally becomes, How can we secure their cooperation? How can we get them on our side, joining with us? And that thought makes *agape* not just virtuous but also profoundly practical. King doesn't just tell people they ought to try to cooperate, he encourages a cooperative frame of mind by depicting a compellingly beautiful goal that needs the cooperation of all in order to be realized.

Stoic Detachment?

Gandhi urged complete detachment from emotions, prominently focusing on erotic love and even sexual desire. King typically does not offer general prescriptions for the whole course of a person's life. Although a religious man, he did not advance in his political writings a comprehensive metaphysical and religious doctrine, as Gandhi did. He focused on emotions that could disrupt the political movement, arguing that demonstrations and marches are a way of channeling repressed emotions—"resentments and latent frustrations"—that might otherwise lead to violence.[58] "If his repressed emotions do not come out in these nonviolent ways, they will come out in ominous expressions of violence. This is not a threat; it is a fact of history. So I have not said to my people 'get rid of your discontent.' But I have tried to say that this normal and healthy discontent can be channelized through the creative outlet of nonviolent direct action."[59] I argued earlier that this does not mean keeping anger as it is: for the "channelizing" and "creative" process changes the goal and hence (at least in my philosophical terms) the identity of the emotion: at most, people have at this point what I call the borderline emotion of Transition-Anger, not garden-variety anger with its retributive wish. But my point here is that King has no interest in counseling a complete extirpation of emotion.

Beyond this, King does urge extirpation of hate, but I've said that he sees hate as a posture of will. Again and again he insists that the demand to love one's adversary does not require even liking the person or people: it just means bending one's moral will in a creative and constructive direction.

In trying to respond to likely criticisms of the Gandhi/King idea, we must confront the objection that it imposes on people an inhuman set of demands. We have begun to reply by showing that, and how, they made it possible for people to accept and internalize non-angry practices. But this worry is certainly heightened by Gandhi's views about emotional and sexual detachment. Gandhi was close to being a thoroughgoing Stoic. He repeatedly asserted that one cannot pursue *satyagraha*, or non-angry resistance, adequately without conducting a struggle against all the passions, prominently including erotic desire and emotion. Nor did he cultivate the type of personal love and friendship that would naturally give rise to deep grief and fear. If he is correct in insisting that Stoic detachment is necessary for non-anger, that would give us reason to think it an unworkable and also an unattractive goal.

First of all, we must ask whether Gandhi was making an instrumental claim (emotional and passional detachment is instrumentally necessary for successful *satyagraha*) or offering a stipulative definition (*satyagraha* consists in nonviolent and non-angry resistance carried out with a commitment to emotional and passional detachment). The answer is unclear. For himself, Gandhi most likely meant the latter, given the evidence of his systematic self-discipline. For his movement, however, he does not appear to endorse even the limited instrumental claims, given that he made no attempt to convince Nehru and other key leaders to renounce particular love and other forms of strong passion.[60] Perhaps his idea was simply that the *leader* of a successful nonviolent resistance movement must (whether instrumentally or conceptually) pursue Stoic detachment. Even this, however, might worry a modern reader: If the path of non-anger demands an implausible and in some ways unappealing detachment of its leaders, how attractive can it be, as a path to justice?

A further specific claim Gandhi advanced concerns fear. Gandhi clearly thinks that the success of nonviolent protest requires a total reworking of people's psychology. For example, he argues that anger is frequently rooted in fear. In Nehru's shrewd diagnosis, Gandhi's greatest gift to his followers was a new freedom from the "all-pervading fear" that British rule had inspired in Indians. That "black pall of fear was lifted from the people's shoulders"—how?[61] Nehru suggests that this massive "psychological change" (which he compares to a successful psychoanalysis) had its source in Gandhi's ability to show an exit route from the reign of terror, and to inspire people, simultaneously, with a sense of their own worth and the worth of their actions. This made possible a form of protest that was calm, dignified, and strategic, rather than furtive, desperate, and prone to retributive violence.[62]

It seems to me that King agrees with Gandhi up to a point about fear, since he obsessively insists on the importance of facing the future with hope and not giving way to despair. At least he repudiates and strongly discourages a type of fear that would nullify hope and undermine courageous action. This leaves some room for fear, but far less than is common in most people's lives. Concerning grief, he differs considerably from Gandhi, positively encouraging grief in his followers. In his famous eulogy for the little girls killed in the 1963 bombing of the 16th Street Baptist Church, he refers to the deaths as "tragic" and encourages strong emotion about them, not detachment. The appeal to grief is not unmixed: King reminds his audience that the death of martyrs is redemptive and that Christianity affirms that death is not the end. He insists that God can lift people "from fatigue of despair to the buoyancy of hope."[63] Still, this is a long way from the correct utterance of the hypothetical Stoic father, who, on being informed of the death of his child, says, "I was already aware that I had begotten a mortal."[64] It is not possible for a committed Christian to be a thoroughgoing Stoic, because it is evident that the correct attitude to the Passion of Christ includes strong emotions of grief, guilt, and hope, and also (as Augustine memorably demonstrates in *The City of God*) that the biblical text shows Christ himself experiencing such emotions.

As for erotic love and sexual desire, Gandhi's persistent obsessions, King is basically silent.[65] He wants to make sure people understand that the *agape* he is talking about is not the same as *eros* or *philia,* but he never disparages those attitudes or urges their removal. For Gandhi, sexual renunciation was a central personal goal. But he was also strategic in his public focus on that goal: he understood that the image of the ascetic *sannyasi* had deep roots in the minds of most of his followers, and was a good way to win their loyalty. (Narendra Modi takes the same path today, though his appalling way of mingling of asceticism with genocidal violence shows profound disrespect for Gandhi's life and work.) King not only did not advocate renunciation as a central ethical goal, he also had no strategic reason to do so. Gandhi clearly knew that the Christian tradition contains an ascetic strand.[66] But this strand is not appealing to the American people, nor does it play a central role in American religious practice, at least in Protestant churches. American evangelical preachers are, by and large, if male, a profoundly erotic lot in the way they present themselves and appeal to followers—as Sinclair Lewis's *Elmer Gantry,* only partly satire, indelibly shows.[67] Nor are African American churches an exception, so far as I am aware. Although bad conduct in sexual matters is certainly condemned, renunciation is not the spirit in which religious joy is pursued. One can see this clearly in the nature of the music that animates and energizes American evangelical traditions. So King would not have been wise strategically to portray himself as a Gandhian ascetic or to preach *brahmacharya* (sexual renunciation). Philosophical views cannot move people if they are translated insensitively from one culture to a completely different culture, and King was a savvy strategist. And then there is of course the man himself, whose erotic personality and widely known love affairs may well have played at least some role in his popular appeal.

Taking on anger means taking on a central plank in the normative platform of American masculinity. The preacher of non-anger and nonviolence risks being seen as weak and effeminate. So we might say that an American male leader exemplifying non-anger needs to attend carefully to his masculinity credentials. It would surely be fatal for such a leader to represent himself as forgoing passion. If he is an African American leader attempting to attract a multiracial following, he must certainly be attentive to white paranoia about the black man as sexual aggressor: so he must walk a careful line, and for the most part King succeeded brilliantly in representing himself as neither unmanly nor a predator. This fascinating topic needs more exploration than I can give it here, but fortunately others have explored it already.[68]

For a variety of reasons, then, Stoicism was neither a strategic course for King nor one to which his own views and inclinations led him.

To conclude: King is in some respects less philosophically explicit than Gandhi. In other ways, however, he fleshes out and further develops Gandhian ideas, but also contributes creative insights of his own. And in the two areas in which he departs from Gandhi—his qualifications about violence in self-defense and his refusal of a total Stoicism about emotions—he appears to me to have the more philosophically defensible position.

6

The Prophetic Tension between Race Consciousness and the Ideal of Color-Blindness

RONALD R. SUNDSTROM

Martin Luther King, Jr., did not leave behind many references to the term "color-blindness." There is little trace of that phrase in his published books and collected papers, although he made direct reference to it as a distant ideal in a 1965 interview with Alex Haley, during which he spoke of a future when the nation "is stricken gloriously and incurably color-blind."[1] There is also a record of a critic chastising him and then recommending that he publicly adopt the phrase, but it does not appear he replied or was moved by the demeaning comments of the critic (a certain Mrs. W. Brown).[2]

King, accordingly, did not adopt the idea of color-blindness as a leading concept in his civil rights advocacy. In this chapter, I review the evidence for this claim and argue that, in contrast, he explicitly supported color-conscious politics. In addition to the well-documented historical evidence that King supported color-conscious civil rights remedies, I discuss two reasons he took this position, one moral-psychological and the other conceptual, both of which indicate the influence of Reinhold Niebuhr's Christian Realism on King's thinking. First, King held that there are serious limits to human rational capacities that affect ethical decision making, particularly where group-based interests are involved. Although King offered prophetic ideals, he warned against trusting them alone, and advocated for practical realistic strategies to achieve those ideals. The second reason builds from the first, and invokes his view of the prophetic nature of society's most transcendent ideals. In King's view, we can't expect to realize the color-blind ideal in the world because of humanity's inherent flaws; we need such ideals to guide and motive our actions, but their full realization is possible only through the intervention of God's grace—just as a good Protestant would believe. This deserves emphasis for two reasons: although King did not explicitly support color-blindness as a practical idea, there is a significant overlap between his leading concepts and a transcendent version of the ideal of color-blindness. The ideals that he appealed to can be understood only by reference to the transcendent, which gives them their normative force. I conclude this chapter by sketching some implications of this analysis on three prominent topics in contemporary black political theory: character, embodiment, and pessimism.

August 1963

"Color-blindness" was, for much of its modern history, a phrase of art in jurisprudence regarding the U.S. Constitution.[3] It originates from Justice Marshall Harlan's dissent in the *Plessy v. Ferguson* decision and his declaration that the U.S. Constitution was color-blind.[4] Harlan's constitutional interpretation was subsequently employed by many civil rights advocates, as it was by the attorneys who led the NAACP's legal fights, and who were slow to warm to King's extralegal civil disobedience tactics.[5]

King is associated with the idea of color-blindness because of a line from his "I Have a Dream" speech, delivered at the 1963 March on Washington.[6] In that speech King proclaimed he had a dream that one day his children, and all black Americans, would be judged by the "content of their character" rather than the "color of their skin."[7] It was repetition of a formulation of his dream that he offered on other occasions, including in his 1960 speech "The Rising Tide of Racial Consciousness."[8] Did King champion color-blindness as an approach to racial and social justice? Did he believe in color-blindness as an ethical, social, and political ideal?

Well, *yes*, if we follow the historian Eric J. Sundquist, who in his book *King's Dream* associates the idea of color-blindness with King's clear and frequent supportive references to legal and political equality, including the equal provision and defense of the rights of African Americans.[9] Likewise, one may think, as I have, that King supports a robust version of color-blindness that goes beyond legal and political considerations and extends the ideal to the social and intimate spheres of life.[10] This is an easy move, given his many and powerful references to another arguably parallel ideal he frequently mentions, that of a "beloved community," which provides an additional reason to think that King's dream is color-blind. His idea of a "beloved community" is grounded on his theological belief in the fundamental unity of humanity as created in God's image—a humanity, every member of which, without racial (or any other) distinction, is a recipient of divine love.[11]

And yet, *no*, King did not support color-blindness if one thinks of it primarily as a practical means to achieve legal and political racial equality. As I will discuss below, King repeatedly and publicly supported "racial consciousness" and advocated for several explicitly color-conscious programs focused on reparative and distributive justice to achieve racial equality. Nor did King oppose racial solidarity to counter racial discrimination, advocate for justice, or celebrate traditions or achievements. For example, he would have emphatically disagreed with Chief Justice Roberts's claim in *Parents Involved in Community Schools v. Seattle School District No. 1* that "the way to stop discrimination on the basis of race is to stop discriminating on the basis of race," as if a quitting cold-turkey approach to color-blindness would work to the benefit of all in educational or residential desegregation or integration policies.[12]

Is there a conflict between King's ideal end and the means he advocated? The contrast is striking if the fullness of his dream is taken seriously. The conceptual tension, or contradiction, cannot be easily dismissed by considering color-consciousness as a means to a color-blind end, because the social and theological facets of his dream are not ordinary ends. Plus, it is fruitful to *not* dismiss this tension. It calls to mind the distance between King's prophetic ideals and our limitations, and consonant with his spirit, such a tension encourages humility. For that reason, I do not reconcile King's dream with his practical political strategy, but I do offer a bridge between them.

Gloriously and Incurably Color-Blind

There is a fascinating temporal proximity between King's dream that African Americans would be judged by the "content of their character" rather than the "color of their skin" and the legal idea of color-blindness that partially accounts for the two ideals' close association. The NAACP Legal Defense Fund filed a brief in *Anderson vs. Martin*, on August 26, 1963, arguing that the U.S. Constitution was color-blind, and two days later, on August 28, Martin Luther King, Jr., gave the "I Have A Dream Speech." In the words of James Lindgren, "Within days of each other, both the political and legal leaders of the civil rights movement had called on the nation to give up its centuries-old practice of judging people by race. It was during this period—marked by the 1963 March on Washington and the Civil Rights Act of the following year—that the color-blind ideal reached its high water mark."[13] Note that King was a *religious*—a Christian—leader as well as a political leader of the civil rights movement. It is important to keep this in mind, because his ontological-theological conception of personhood is key to understanding his view of whether we as individuals, or a society, ought to be conscious of or "blind" to ethnic and racial distinctions.

King agreed with advocates dating back to the abolitionists who argued that the U.S. Constitution is color-blind, that it grants rights, duties, and obligations to all men and women without racial distinction, and that it does not presume or condone a racial state or state-sponsored racism. Additionally, King also recognized a broader, more robust version of the ideal of color-blindness that in its abstractness applied to all spheres of this life. In exactly one instance he labeled this "glorious" ideal "color-blind." All the same, we cannot assume that King advocated for universal color-blindness. King did not encourage insensitivity to racial or ethnic categories in private, social, or public life or political affairs, or in national law in the real, nonideal world, and particularly not in the world in which King himself lived. That he did not has been well established by political theorists and historians.[14] The plentiful evidence of this stretches from his earliest pastoral and civil rights work in Montgomery, Alabama, to his call for a social and economic Bill of Rights for the poor and disadvantaged in his *Where Do We Go from Here: Chaos or Community?*[15] King emphatically called on the United States to tend to the injustices imposed upon black Americans and other victims of the nation's discriminatory domestic policies. He urged the nation to adopt reforms to address inequalities with respect to segregation and disparities in the funding of schools; to adopt a "jobs first" policy specific to hiring the unemployed and additional support through vocational training and job certification; to expand government-funded human services to help the ranks of unemployed blacks find jobs; to increase the democratic participation and political voice of recipients of social services, through welfare and tenant unions, as a means to enfranchise those populations with respect to community planning and self-advocacy; to reform discrimination in housing policy, including predatory renting and sale of property, and indeed to dismantle segregation in housing across the nation; to facilitate the social mobility of blacks locked in ghettos to grant them access, through fair housing protections and subsidies, to better funded and properly resourced urban neighborhoods and suburbs. He advocated in no uncertain terms, in his Nobel Prize Acceptance Speech and in the "World House" chapter of *Where Do We Go from Here,* for the work of an egalitarian-minded welfare state, attuned to the history and lingering harms of racial discrimination, that would attend to its domestic and international responsibilities with a cosmopolitan intent.[16]

Even if there is an abstract legal or moral ideal of color-blindness in King's writings, it would not be unreasonable to think that it was absent in his pastorally and theologically informed civil rights work. It is not a leading concept in his work as a practical ideal to apply to everyday human actions and public policy. Yet there are reverberations of it in his writings, sermons, and speeches. Eric J. Sundquist has labeled this set of ideas, especially the legal and political ones, as King's dream and an ideal of color-blind justice.[17] The core of this dream is King's goal of legal and political equality, and particularly the equal application of rights, duties, and protections of the U.S. Constitution to all citizens regardless of race.

This is the focus of King's sole recorded positive reference to color-blindness in his 1965 interview with Alex Haley, in a section where they were discussing the increase in black demonstrations for civil rights. Given its importance for understanding King's relation to the idea of color-blindness it is worth extensively quoting:

> If the Constitution were today applied equally and impartially to all of America's citizens, in every section of the country, in every court and code of law, there would be no need for any group of citizens to seek extra-legal redress.
>
> Our task has been a difficult one, and will continue to be, for privileged groups, historically, have not volunteered to give up their privileges. As Reinhold Niebuhr has written, individuals may see the moral light and voluntarily abandon their unjust posture, but groups tend to be more immoral, and more intransigent, than individuals. Our nonviolent direct-action program, therefore—which has proved its strength and effectiveness in more than a thousand American cities where some baptism of fire has taken place—will continue to dramatize and demonstrate against local injustices to the Negro until the last of those who impose those injustices are forced to negotiate; until, finally, the Negro wins the protections of the Constitution that have been denied to him; until society, at long last, *is stricken gloriously and incurably color-blind.*[18]

King's evocation of a world struck "gloriously and incurably color-blind" looks like an endorsement of the ideal of color-blindness and the appropriate label for his dream. It accords, as well, with the theological ideas that were his leading concepts: *agape* or the universal love of God, grace, redemption, preferential treatment for the poor, and human personhood.

Clearly for King, God's love and grace are extended to all regardless of ethnic, racial, and class distinctions, but even on the other side of the "mountaintop"—within sight of the promised land—color and class mattered quite a lot to the realization of love and justice (to counter our social immoral tendencies) on the way to real-world promised land of a just society.[19] Therefore King, in "The Rising Tide of Racial Consciousness," explicitly advocates for the idea of "racial consciousness" and paired it with the ideal of "racial equality."[20]

What do we make of his reference to the vision of a society struck, as King states, gloriously and incurably color-blind? It could be seen as an anomaly since it ignores all the practical color-conscious methods he supported in the civil rights movement and the policy ends he worked toward. It could be seen as a touch cynical; as in, "we will live in a color-blind world, when society is no longer racist," or "we will be post-feminist when the world is post-sexism," or "we will be post-racial, when we are post-racism." That position would be consistent with the political Left's distancing of King's legacy from the idea of color-blindness.

But such cynicism is not apparent in King's words, although he applied his version of Niebuhr-inspired Christian Realism to the dream. He went on to tell Haley, "I confess that I do not believe this day is around the corner. The concept of supremacy is so imbedded in the white society that it will take many years for color to cease to be a judgmental factor. *But it is certainly my hope and dream.* Indeed, it is the keystone of my faith in the future that we will someday achieve a thoroughly integrated society. I believe that before the turn of the century, if trends continue to move and develop as presently, we will have moved a long, long way toward such a society."[21]

Michael Eric Dyson has argued that it is a mistake to see King as an advocate of a color-blind society. Dyson is plainly wrong on this narrow point; in this interview King identified a color-blind society as synonymous with his hopes and his dream. Yet, Dyson is correct to note "what King understood as a culture blind to color is a universe away from contemporary refusals to take race into account in creating a just society."[22]

This is the tension: King's dream has color-blind aspects, but King most certainly did not advocate for color-blind practical politics.

The bridge between these positions that I offer is to point out that the color-blind features of King's dream are more complicated than what an instrumental analysis uncovers. Achievement of the legal, social, and political features of his dream would require practical color-conscious means; but beyond a means-ends relation between the two ideas, King's theological views also deeply inform what color-consciousness and color-blindness means in this approach. Take, for instance, his conception of personhood, from which his view of human dignity is derived. Simply assuming that color-blindness is implicit in King's view of personhood is to beg the question. King expressed an ontological-theological conception of personhood that was both embodied and transcendent. Insofar as persons are alive *in the flesh,* they are characterized by the beauty, abilities, and limitations of the body, and their lives are interdependent in their mutual efforts to flourish; their differences, however, are transcended as they approach God. This conception is sensitive to the contexts and circumstances of individuals in the world, the meaning and effects of their differences, and it is sensitive to race, specifically the manipulation of race to dominate and oppress black Americans. Such a conception of personhood views human life as individual, yet complementary and "ultimately identical" in its relation to the divine.[23]

This view led King to embrace a Christian liberal egalitarianism, deeply informed by transcendence and the identities and contexts of individual lives, with evangelical as well as cosmopolitan ambitions—to join in world fellowship and to realize justice across what he called the "world house."[24] Paired with his and the work of many others in the civil rights movement, King's ideas challenged the racist and exclusionary conceptions of "person," "human," and "citizen" that masqueraded as universals and undergirded the American racial state from post-reconstruction through the passage of the 1964 Civil Rights Act and beyond.[25] In league with the civil rights movement and in the tradition of black political thought, King expanded the meaning of those universals and the moral imagination of the nation and the world.[26]

To characterize King's view of race and racial justice in America as simply "color-blind," then, is to mischaracterize the complexity of his ideas. At times Sundquist makes this mistake in his otherwise impressive history of King's "I Have a Dream" speech. Sundquist notes that distance is put between King's ideal of racial equality and the idea of color-blindness by the American political Left, but he writes as if this distancing is unfaithful to King's ideas: "For those on the political Left, King's dream became associated less with colorblind 'equal opportunity,' what was once the core value of democratic liberalism, than with race-based (and sometimes class-based) programs designed to achieve diversity, usually defined as proportionately equal outcomes, the new core value of democratic liberalism."[27]

Sundquist assumes that "equal opportunity" or equal justice can be equally associated with color-blindness, which ignores the many color-conscious means, and in particular, policies, required to guarantee and enforce equal opportunity, or even the more demanding idea of fair equal opportunity; and King, as even Sundquist recognizes, supported color-consciousness as a way to understand national racial problems and organize resistance and to support color-conscious policies to realize justice.

The common, mistaken view is that King's comment that black Americans generally should be judged by the "content of their character" rather than the "color of their skin" expressed a version of color-blindness that can be ideologically paired with Justice Marshall Harlan's color-blind principle from his dissent in 1896 *Plessy v. Ferguson* decision. Harlan rejected the idea that the Constitution grants *legal* recognition of racial caste or the dominion of whites over citizens of other races. In his words, "citizens are equal before the law" and the "law regards man as man."[28] Concurrently, Harlan was perfectly content with the *social* recognition of racial castes, and of course with the political ramifications of that racial stratification; for example, after arguing for the legal equality of blacks and whites, Harlan went on to complain that whereas blacks were segregated on train cars, the Chinese were allowed to sit wherever they pleased, even though, he claimed, the Chinese were too alien to be admitted as citizens or to be granted civil rights.[29]

In contrast to Harlan's legally narrow and hypocritical view of color-blindness, King's view of common human fellowship was broader and sensitive to the history of race and its enduring effects in America. In thinking that King's racial sensitivity was closer to the idea of color-blindness, I had in a previous work called it "ambitious" because it held that race was a morally irrelevant or illegitimate social identity that should *ultimately* make no moral, social, political, or legal difference in a person's life.[30] Reading King's color-blindness as robust is consistent with his hope and dream that America "will someday achieve a thoroughly integrated society."[31] But arriving at such an ideal means being sensitive to the contexts that require color-consciousness for the sake of realizing an ideal and distant color-blind world. This view is reinforced by King's reference to the suggestive "dream of a land where men do not argue that the color of a man's skin determines the content of his character" at the end of his analysis and advocacy of color-consciousness in "The Rising Tide of Racial Consciousness" from 1960.

The ideal of color-blindness that King evokes overlaps with color-consciousness, wherein they share the same ends of equal citizenship and justice in a society marked by mutually beneficial cooperation. Color-blindness, however, ultimately impedes the realization of fairness because it refuses to understand and confront the legacy of racial oppression. The best way then, as Amy Gutmann has put it, to express the basic moral insight of color-blindness is through the application of liberal conceptions of color-consciousness.[32] Moral, political, and legal color-consciousness is justified for the sake of the proximate realization of the ideal of color-blindness, where the end of color-blindness is, of course, simply fairness. This point deserves emphasis: that color-consciousness, especially in the context of law and public policy, is an important means to rectify past racial wrongs, to police against current racism and discrimination, and to think forward into the future to guide and assist current and future citizens in the building of a just society.[33] King's robust conception of color-blindness, which he explicitly tied to race consciousness for the sake of the realization of love and justice in the "beloved community," made this exact point. It is embedded in the logic of "The Rising Tide of Racial Consciousness."[34]

The flaw of the ideal of color-blindness is that it prompts its proponents to focus on the implications and applications of the ideal as if it were accomplished already, resulting in protestations such as Chief Justice Roberts's "the way to stop discrimination on the basis of race is to stop discriminating on the basis of race." Roberts's absolutism on color-blindness is an insistence on the purity of legal ideals in application that evokes the absolutism of religious ideals, which King and Niebuhr rejected on grounds of human fallibility. Such absolutism rejects the complementarity of human life in favor of a conception that insists upon an unrealistic strict identity and unity.[35]

It is no surprise that reactions to such false universalisms adopt an opposite but equally strict realism, and criticize absolutist applications of legal ideals in a nonideal world as a "reification" and "deification" of them. This was the point of Derrick Bell's racial realism, which is forcefully expressed in the title of his influential book, *Faces at the Bottom of the Well: The Permanence of Racism.*[36] The apotheosis of legal, moral, and political ideals, such as color-blindness, enables them to be regarded as morally pure while preserving unjust conditions on the ground. Such idolizing of the ideal of color-blindness, with its blindness or insensitivity toward human suffering, has drained it of its appeal, especially among African Americans and Latinos.[37] All the same, there are dangers in rejecting normative and transcendent ideals in favor of wariness and realism. This can result in pessimism and cynicism toward narratives of progress and reasonable means to ameliorate injustice, and in a darker turn toward vengeful hatred against real and perceived opponents.[38]

For these reasons, King cannot easily be associated with racial realism, because the pessimism about the possibility of racial justice or the ceasing of anti-black racism associated with racial realism does not square with King's emphatic embrace of hope, redemption, and transcendence through the grace of God. But King was a realist of sorts—and he adopted elements of Niebuhr's Christian Realism, as seen even in his sole reference to color-blindness—indicating he was wary of human limitations and the idolizing of ideals.

The Content of Character

The meaning of King's dream that one day his children will live in a nation "where they will not be judged by the color of their skin but by the content of their character" and its place in an ideal nation "struck gloriously and incurably color-blind" deserves further exploration. The judgment King spoke of was not simply one of rational administrative procedure on the part of individuals or institutions. It involves not merely a utilitarian calculus or measuring a person's typical (and socially determined) character traits to the complete exclusion of their "color"; instead it is a process that involves the recognition of the sacredness of personhood, the limitations of human judgment, the conditions of human suffering and oppression, the virtue of charity, and the role of grace. Judging the content of a person's character is hardly the faceless, ahistorical, quantifiable, and meritocratic calculation that some have misconceived it to be.

Fundamental to King's view of character was his adoption of the social gospel and the broad philosophical-theological idea of personalism. The Christian social gospel movement emphasized the application of Christian ethics to large social problems and was often progressive. The proponents of the social gospel that influenced King were Walter Rauschenbusch and Howard Thurman; both Rauschenbusch and Thurman emphasized social responsibility to address social ills.[39] Thurman, moreover, was a black minister and theologian who directly tied the social gospel to the lives and civil rights struggles of African Americans, and promoted love as an ethical response to racial oppression in his influential book, *Jesus and the Disinherited*.[40]

The social gospel demands that Christians, and society as a whole, recognize, respect, and support human dignity, and actively work to stop, reverse, and address the suffering of, in Thurman's words, the dispossessed and disinherited. At the heart of this view is the ideal of an inviolable human dignity, which involves respecting the self-respect and personal dignity of individuals. Without "self-respect and personal dignity," according to Thurman, "man is no man."[41]

The centrality of self-respect and human dignity in this view is shared by, and likely was derived from, the broad school of thought labeled personalism; its many variants include a strong sense of essential and universal human dignity, promote anti-materialist conceptions of human personhood, are contentedly anthropocentric, and emphasize the central role of human subjectivity and fallibility in ethical decision making.[42] King's view of personalism was formed through his studies at Boston University with his professors Edgar S. Brightman and L. Howard DeWolf. "It was mainly under these teachers that I studied personalistic philosophy—the theory that the clue to the meaning of ultimate reality is found in personality. This personal idealism remains today my basic philosophic position. Personalism's insistence that only personality—finite and infinite—is ultimately real strengthened me in two convictions: it gave me metaphysical and philosophical grounding for the idea of a personal God, and it gave me a metaphysical basis for the dignity and worth of all human personality."[43]

The idea of personalism appears in his work throughout his life and frequently in relation to his repeated references to human dignity, as in *The Measure of Man* (1959), "The Rising Tide of Race Consciousness" (1960), "Letter from Birmingham Jail" (1963) (where it appears in his use of Martin Buber's formulation of "I-It" versus "I-thou" relationships in his distinction of just from unjust laws), "Nobel Prize Acceptance Speech" (1964), "Christmas Sermon on Peace" (1967), and *Where Do We Go from Here* (1967). Furthermore, King's view of the social gospel and the idea of personalism were filtered through his appreciative tangles with the work of Reinhold Niebuhr, whose Christian Realism, as communicated through his *Moral Man and Immoral Society* and *An Interpretation of Christian Ethics*, runs through much of King's writings.[44]

Essentially, Christian Realism holds that religion, and in particular Christianity, provides a necessary moral unity and transcendent explanation of life; it is "realist" insofar as it emphasizes the limitations of human emotions, capacities, and character. It rejects a transcendent view of the human person whereby "personality" can only be understood in terms of the person's relation to divinity and apart from their embodiment. It also rejects a solely materialist conception of the human person. Likewise, while recognizing the principal role of rationality in all aspects of human life (such as, and importantly, the ethical and political), it recognizes the *fleshy* and egoistic—particularly in social contexts—limitations of human reason.

King's utilization of this view is clear in his evocations of realism. He opens *The Measure of a Man* by juxtaposing two views: "There are those who look upon man as little more than an animal" versus "There are those who would lift man almost to the position of a god." In contrast to those views, he offers a third, realistic view that "avoids the extremes of pessimistic naturalism and an optimistic humanism." This view is essentially that of Niebuhr, whom he directly references.[45]

King recognized that humans are rooted in "nature" and subject to their physiology and psychology, but that they are also creatures of spirit, which, *with their rational capacity,* allows them to access the "realm of freedom."[46] It is very important to notice, especially for contemporary philosophers uncomfortable with theism, that King did not fully equate *spirit* with *reason,* or reduce it to some materialist conception of mind.[47] Those are not interchangeable for King; reason can fail to follow spirit. This is the point of the distinction between "finite personality" and "infinite personality" that King referred to in his reflections on his studies.[48] This view was explicitly stated in his 1953–1954 essay, "The Theology of Reinhold Niebuhr": "At one and the same time man is under the dominion of nature and also transcends nature. Man's self transcendence forbids him to identify meaning with causality in nature; his bodily and finite particularity equally forbids the loss of the self in a distinctionless absolute of mind or rationality. God as will and personality is, therefore, the only ground of individuality. As creature, man is made in the image of God."[49]

King's own Christian Realism contextualizes his references to the other conceptions of human dignity, such as his citation of Kant's second formulation of the categorical imperative, the "humanity formulation" in "The Ethical Demands for Integration." In that speech, in a section titled "The Worth of Persons," he cites the biblical idea of "*the image of God,*" the Declaration of Independence, Frederick Douglass, Kant's formulation, and Buber to convey his view of the "sacredness of human personality."[50]

He wrote, criticizing segregation: "It debases personality. Immanuel Kant said in one formulation of the *Categorical Imperative* that 'all men must be treated as *ends* and never as mere *means*.' The tragedy of segregation is that it treats men as means rather than ends, and thereby reduces them to things rather than persons. To use the words of Martin Buber, segregation substitutes an 'I-It' relationships for the 'I-thou' relationship."[51] That passage is worth noting, because philosophers are tempted to see King's conception of human dignity and personhood in entirely rationalistic or even materialistic terms, as if this and his other leading concepts (love, the beloved community, and his dream) could be folded neatly into contemporary variants of liberalism.

King also distanced himself from the full implications of Niebuhr's views, especially Niebuhr's ultimate rejection of pacifism and nonviolence, and, relatedly, his pessimism. King accepted to a degree Niebuhr's realism and the idea of the fallen-ness of humanity and their capacity for sin.[52] Sin, for King, was the negation of our fundamental being, and, following Paul Tillich, in "Letter from Birmingham City Jail" he defined it as separation from God. Separation of ourselves from God was made material, in King's analysis, by segregation because it is "an existential expression of man's tragic separation, an expression of his awful estrangement, his terrible sinfulness."[53] Yet King criticized Niebuhr for ultimately surrendering hope by not leaving enough room for transcendence in the form of grace. "It was at Boston University that I came to see that Niebuhr had overemphasized the corruption of human nature. His pessimism concerning human nature was not balanced by an optimism concerning divine nature. He was so involved in diagnosing man's sickness of sin that he overlooked the cure of grace."[54]

King absolutely agreed with Niebuhr on the powerful, essential role of religion to provide humanity with moral ideals, but Niebuhr seems to restrict transcendence to the role of expanding or powering the moral imagination. In his own analysis of Kant, which may inform our understanding of King's employment of Kant, Niebuhr stated:

> The dimension of depth in the consciousness of religion creates the tension between what is and what ought to be. It bends the bow from which every arrow of moral action flies. Every truly moral act seeks to establish what ought to be, because the agent feels obligated to the ideal, though historically unrealized, as being the order of life in its more essential reality. Thus the Christian believes that the ideal of love is real in the will and nature of God, even

though he knows of no place in history where the ideal has been realized in its pure form. And it is because it has this reality that he feels the pull of obligation. The sense of obligation in morals from which Kant tried to derive the whole structure of religion is really derived from the religion itself. The "pull" or "drive" of moral life is a part of the religious tension of life. Man seeks to realize in history what he conceives to be already the truest reality—that is, its final essence.[55]

Except that King, unlike Niebuhr, had a confidence that humanity, through the grace of God, could follow through on the arc of the arrow of moral action.[56] "The arc of the moral universe is long but it bends toward justice."[57]

How do personalism and Christian Realism bear on King's hope that blacks would be judged by the content of their character rather than the color of their skin? Notice, first, that King did not uncritically and incautiously accept the high ideals he intoned. From his study of Niebuhr, he appreciated the role of prophetic, "impossible" ideals that drive humanity across the arc of the moral universe, yet he remained a realist (but not a cynic) about them.[58] They were yet to be realized, society would frustrate them, so they were not to be naively applied. This position keeps an appreciative eye on the normative core of color-blindness, but justifies a skeptical stance toward it.

Character should be understood in light of the conception of good character that King received from his moral tradition and his theological and philosophical training, and not by the tainted light of market-based or American-exceptionalist conceptions of character. From the vantage of King's view, character is to be judged by the virtues of charity, compassion, and forgiveness, all guided by the example of God's grace. And from his experience as a black man and leader in the African American wing of the American Baptist Church, judgment also means bringing to bear a wealth of historical and sociological understanding. His analyses include constant criticisms of anti-black racism, and explanations of the enduring effects of slavery and the harms of segregation and their effects on the life-chances and the spirit of blacks, along with evocations of self-empowerment, improvement of personal standards, and the engendering of initiative. The development of character, for King, is to be understood through the history and practice of "color" in America, so to cleave color from character and to see in King the demotion of the history and effects of "color" is to do violence to his legacy.

This is how we should read King's dream: a long arduous road involving personal discernment, the admission of sin, conversion, and transformation by living the demand of *Imago Dei*. This is hardly a color-blind process. The beloved community cannot be achieved by being blind to the pain of the suffering of others. He ends "The Rising Tide of Racial Consciousness" with these words:

> We must work assiduously and with determined boldness to remove from the body politic this cancerous disease of discrimination which is preventing our democratic and Christian health from being realized. Then and only then will we be able to bring into full realization the dream of our American democracy—a dream yet unfulfilled. A dream of equality of opportunity, of privilege and property widely distributed; a dream of a land where men will not take necessities from the many to give luxuries to the few; a dream of a land where men [d]o not argue that the color of a man's skin determines the content of his character; a dream of a place where all our gifts and resources are held not for ourselves alone but as instruments of service for the rest of humanity; the dream of a country where every man will respect the dignity and worth of all human personality, and men will dare to live together as brothers—that is the dream. Whenever it is fulfilled we will emerge from the bleak and desolate midnight of man's inhumanity to man into the bright and glowing daybreak of freedom and justice for all of God's children.[59]

The fulfillment of the dream is not simply color-blind either. For King, God was omniscient and not blind; all have equal worth as persons but their histories, circumstances, and contexts matter. The beloved community ought to have its eyes open too.

Glowing Daybreak

In the sections above I attempted to bridge the tension or apparent contradiction between King's color-conscious social and political strategies and the color-blind aspects of his ideal of racial equality, and in doing so I stressed his theological influences and commitments. Those commitments provide an additional reason, on top of the historical record, to believe he did not support color-blind practical politics, and that his views were inconsistent with such politics. Moreover, his theological commitments ensure that his dream, insofar as it may be labeled as color-blind, was not naive or superficial. To conclude this analysis, I will sketch how his conception of color-consciousness and his dream interact with three prominent topics in contemporary black political theory: character, embodiment, and pessimism.

As Sundquist noted, the political Left has opposed the association of King's dream with the idea of color-blindness; and given my analysis above, it is correct to disassociate his views from the project of color-blindness as it has been carried out by the American political Right. The obtuse and willful ignoring of racial practices and the enduring practice and effects of racial discrimination are not consistent with King's legacy. There is much in King's critiques that aligns with those who focus on the ways anti-black institutional and personal racism produce the intergenerational and concentrated poverty and attendant social ills that afflict poor African Americans. Yet, in his evocations of "character," King likely would not have entirely shied away from values- and character-based criticisms of the poor, whether black or white; that is evident in his references to "personal standards," and "initiative" in, for example, his "The Ethical Demands for Integration."[60] Black liberals and conservatives have been criticized for citing King's legacy in "culture versus structure" debates, but King's words are flat-out precedents for their chastisements, and King's legacy as a whole supports their advocacy of moral traditions and the traditional institutions (family, community, church, public service) that inculcate, nurture, conserve, and transfer intergenerationally.

Secondly, in regard to embodiment and blackness specifically, King did not ignore the fact of blackness and its meaning and operation in America, just as he did not ignore the fact of embodiment. In a discussion rooted in W. E. B. Du Bois's idea of double-consciousness, Frantz Fanon's existential-phenomenological analysis of the "lived experience of the Black," and James Baldwin's critiques of American racism, the idea of the black body—how it is experienced and how it is perceived (by those who perceive and are perceived)—is the focal point of understanding the meaning of blackness and anti-black racism. The question is whether King's view of race, given his personalism, is consistent with this theoretical approach. King did think that humanity is more than body, more than mere flesh, but his ethical view was concrete and incarnational. It moved between God and the flesh—and because the flesh he was fighting to secure rights for was black, he certainly did not discount blackness. King's ethical view of the raced body is fairly represented in a trinitarian structure and reflects complementarity: God recognizes and is the foundation of human equal worth, individuals ought to act toward one another guided (as with the Holy Spirit) by the knowledge of our individual yet shared sacred personhood, and in doing so we encounter others in the flesh (as with God incarnate). King did not emphasize blackness in his theological ethics, as James Cone did in his, *A Black Theology of Liberation*, but King's view paves the way for a Cone-style innovation.[61]

It may seem that a singular focus on blackness in an incarnational encounter with the other is on thin ice theologically. For example, early in his theological education King explicitly promoted what he called the "bigness of God." He noted that the idea of God should not be limited by exclusively associating God with a denomination or a particular race.[62] This view is seemingly inconsistent with James Cone's prophetic-provocation that "God is Black."[63]

This leaves us wondering how King would have responded to the contemporary politics of embodiment, as best represented in the Black Lives Matter movement's "unapologetically Black" guiding principle: "We are unapologetically Black in our positioning. In affirming that Black Lives Matter, we need not qualify our position. To love and desire freedom and justice for ourselves is a necessary prerequisite for wanting the same for others."[64] This principle has essentially two parts; the first is an unashamed and unqualified declaration that black lives matter, and the second sets a necessary condition for the reciprocal recognition that all lives matter. We can be fairly confident that King of 1968 would have analyzed this in the same way he analyzed the Black Power movement, although I imagine he wouldn't have stuck to his strict reading of a nonracialized theology that he held as a divinity student; that was, after all, a rejection of the assumption of the whiteness of God.

He might have found its foregrounding of blackness and its backgrounding of the universal to be at odds with his view of personhood that "human worth lies in relatedness to God" rather than in "racial origin."[65] What is foregrounded, for King, is the universal in God as the foundation of being. Or he might have recognized that black-somebodiness denied leads to separation and, in turn, separation leads to further loss of black-somebodiness. This, in the language of recognition, is the denial of black subjectivity, which then makes intersubjectivity between whites and blacks inconceivable to the white gaze; the result is that the black is objectified and denied inclusion in the universal. To borrow Charles Taylor's phrasing, foregrounding the universal emphasizes "unity-through-identity" at the cost of suppressing "unity-across-difference."[66] The remedy to this misrecognition is to hold that God and the universal are in fact ontologically foregrounded but rhetorically backgrounded in the idea of reciprocity embedded in Black Lives Matter's principle of unapologetic blackness.

Another challenge with applying King's dream to contemporary black political theory lies in its prophetic nature. It contains elements of what Niebuhr called impossible ethical ideals, which, though "impossible" given human shortcomings, were ethically necessary as guides for humanity. The ideal of the beloved community and the role of love set too high a bar; they are not what John Rawls, for example, would identify as concordant with a reasonable utopia, constructing a vision of which is one of the aims of political philosophy. A reasonable utopia is a conception of a just democratic society that pushes the limits of the possible, given our historical conditions, circumstances, and tendencies and the fact of pluralism.[67]

The fact of reasonable pluralism means that although we can ask for it, we nevertheless cannot expect the sort of social conversion and redemption that King dreamed of. Love—especially *agape*—is too much to ask for, and it certainly cannot be required because it cannot be compelled. King's dream may be excessive in its intimate and social-affective and epistemological requirements, but as such it resonates with political philosophers who prioritize a radical or liberal politics of shame, conversion, and redemption.[68] Their view, whether they recognize it or not, is deeply eschatological, because it parallels the linear narrative of fall–apocalypse–redemption that characterizes Abrahamic religions: the fall, confession, redemption (aka revolution), and resurrection (aka rebirth as the new man or woman). In *Where Do We Go from Here,* King in fact laid out a parallel criticism of Frantz Fanon and some proponents of Black Power who focus on violence, rather than love and shame, as the driving force toward rebirth.[69] This is not the place to fully detail my objections, but such eschatological and perfectionist liberalisms are unreasonable and border on the illiberal—they flout, as John Gray has argued, our historical conditions and circumstances, social tendencies, and reasonable pluralism.[70] They are the death of reasonable utopias and the birth of new tyrannies.

To set up the dream and the color-blind ideal in a manner that requires attitudinal and affective confession and redemption is to invite disappointment and, eventually, cynicism. Indeed, contemporary black racial realists and their kin, racial pessimists, may resonate more with Niebuhr's pessimistic attachment to impossible ethical ideals: "In the task of that redemption the most effective agents will be men who have substituted some new illusions for the abandoned ones. The most important of these illusions is that the collective life of mankind can achieve perfect justice. It is a very valuable illusion for the moment; for justice cannot be approximated if the hope of its perfect realization does not generate a sublime madness in the soul. Nothing but such madness will do battle with malignant power and 'spiritual wickedness in high places.' The illusion is dangerous because it encourages terrible fanaticisms. It must therefore be brought under the control of reason. One can only hope that reason will not destroy it before its work is done."[71]

Niebuhr's judgment is double-edged, because it applies to faith and reason. His rejection of exceptionalism, and unchecked confidence in faith or reason, echoes other philosophers and public intellectuals, such as Walter Lippman and Max Horkheimer, who warned against the distortion of reason into instrumental and nationalistic purposes. Recall, though, that King was similarly wary about the fallibility of reason and rationalistic ethical and political theories. King, and Niebuhr for that matter, did not wish to leave us in pessimism and at the edge of despair. To paraphrase Niebuhr, one can only hope that reason will not destroy impossible ethical ideals before that work is done. That is the work of King's ethical and political theology of love, justice, and hope. It is the transcendent force in his prophetic and infinitely demanding call: "No, we are not satisfied, and we will not be satisfied until justice rolls down like waters and righteousness like a mighty stream."[72]

7

Integration, Freedom, and the Affirmation of Life

DANIELLE ALLEN

Much of Martin Luther King's intellectual production was delivered in the context of church conferences and other religious venues, as was the case with his essay "The Ethical Demands for Integration," presented in December 1962 in Nashville.[1] Consequently, his important contributions to political philosophy have been largely overlooked by the guardians of that historical tradition, and its attendant academic disciplines. My purpose in this chapter is to spell out how, in "Ethical Demands," King made a significant contribution to democratic theory and, in fact, laid the foundations for a correction to the forms of modern liberalism that have dominated the Anglo-American academy at least since the 1971 publication of John Rawls's *A Theory of Justice*. Most importantly, if implicitly, he sought to reunite the two bundles of rights that nineteenth- and twentieth-century liberalism had separated into the categories of negative and positive liberties—freedoms from interference, on the one hand, and freedoms to participate in shaping the collective life of a community, on the other. For liberals from Benjamin Constant through Isaiah Berlin to John Rawls, the negative liberties have been nonsacrificeable, but not so the positive liberties.[2] In this important essay, King makes the case that the positive liberties are also nonsacrificeable, with important ramifications not only for democratic theory but also for political economy.

As a political philosopher, King makes a meaningful contribution to republican theories in which "the security of freedom depends on (a) a republic imposing constitutional constraints that guard against arbitrary power and (b) institutional spaces that allow citizens contestatory power to ensure the proper functioning of a constitutional order."[3] As Melvin Rogers has pointed out, the standard account of the history of political thought in the nineteenth and twentieth centuries represents republicanism as receding beneath rising tides of utilitarianism and liberalism, but this account fails to register how African American political thinkers kept republicanism alive throughout the nineteenth century, innovating on it as the century proceeded.[4] King carried this innovation into the twentieth century, once again showing how democratic theory that starts from the minoritarian point of view forces corrections in some of the most fundamental assumptions of liberal theory.

Integration the Ultimate Goal: A Theory of Freedom

King's essay is characteristically subtle, blending the theological and the philosophical. He spells out a systematic theory of freedom, without ever quite saying so, through an argument about desegregation and integration. As he does, he makes both a secular Kantian and also a theological case for the justice of integration, for the necessary and nonsacrificeable place of integration in freedom, and for the compatibility of this political theory with the demands of morality and religion. To see the important features of his argument, we must begin by clarifying his definition of integration.

Most importantly, King draws a sharp distinction between desegregation and integration. Although both respond to segregation, they are different modes of response. Desegregation entails the end of "prohibitive systems" that deny "equal access to schools, parks, restaurants, libraries, and the like" (118).[5] Implicitly invoking Berlin's distinction between negative and positive liberties, King identifies desegregation as "eliminative and negative, for it simply removes these legal and social prohibitions" (118). Integration, in contrast, is positive and "creative." It is the "positive acceptance of desegregation and welcomed participation of Negroes into the total range of human activities. Integration is genuine intergroup, interpersonal doing" (118). Desegregation provides freedom from prohibition and interference. Integration, in contrast, provides the freedom to "do." Only integration, he writes, "unchains the spirit and the mind and provides for the highest degree of life-quality freedom" (121).

I'll return to the idea of "life-quality freedom" shortly, but here we should note the existential framework that King applies to his definition of freedom. He writes: "I cannot be free until I have had the opportunity to fulfill my total capacity untrammeled by any artificial hindrance or barrier" (121). Whereas liberals from Kant, Constant, and Berlin onward through Rawls focused on securing the negative liberties as a route to securing autonomy, the most prized form of human development, King seeks something else, "the fulfillment of total capacity."[6] The goal is not merely to establish laws for oneself but instead to complete oneself. And the relevant completion requires fulfillment in and through participation in human community. In a sense, King picks up W. E. B. Du Bois's famous argument that the final phase in the achievement of freedom would require that African Americans become co-creators in the kingdom of culture. Human beings don't set laws individually for themselves, as isolates. They are social creatures who, together, weave the fabric of human culture that establishes the horizons of possibility for any given generation and community. Full freedom, the fulfillment of total capacity, entails the absence of artificial hindrances or barriers to participation in that process. This is the job not of desegregation but of integration.

But what, in concrete terms, does King have in mind by invoking this ideal of integration as the necessary basis for full freedom? If we trace his argument a level down, from the abstract claims about freedom's two branches, to the specific propositions about how each kind of freedom—negative and eliminative, on the one hand, and positive and creative, on the other—can be realized, we may find ourselves still frustrated. Our powers to achieve this ideal—the action steps and specific tools that King proposes—will seem limited and insufficient.

The law can indeed achieve desegregation, King argues. Judicial decrees can regulate behavior and "restrain the heartless," thereby altering the habits "if not the hearts" of the people every day (124). But law cannot secure integration. The pursuit of integration takes us beyond the legal realm into the domain of the moral or ethical, hence the title of his essay, "The Ethical Demands of Integration." King writes, "the ultimate solution to the race problem lies in the willingness of men to obey the unenforceable. Desegregation will break down the legal barriers and bring men together physically, but something must touch the hearts and souls of men so that they will come together spiritually because it is natural and right" (124). For humankind to come together spiritually is necessary and right on the grounds of the argument that we are all made in God's image, and on the grounds of Kantian views about treating our fellow human beings as ends, not means. In other words, King argues for an overarching, deontological, but unenforceable duty that in our hearts we all grant "thouness" to other human beings.

This overarching duty then generates two further ethical demands: first, that we recognize and enable the equal capacities of all to deliberate, decide, and take responsibility, and second, that we contest the failure to fulfill those first two duties through techniques and discipline of nonviolence. The techniques of nonviolence constitute a mode of fighting that fully embodies the principles being fought for—an attribution of "thou-ness" to all and an acknowledgment of the capacity of all to deliberate, decide, and take responsibility.[7]

But, again, we can ask, what exactly does King have in mind, in concrete terms, by way of a potential transformation of a democratic social world when he spells out this set of unenforceable ethical demands? His is not an argument for new laws or regulatory frameworks, nor for changes to existing ones, such as zoning laws or school districting. How, precisely, does he propose to drive change? How far can an ethical framework take us?

King seeks a transformation of humankind. He sought "an end to fears, prejudice, pride, and irrationality, which are the barriers to a truly integrated society" (124). These are "dark and demonic responses" that can be eliminated only "as men are possessed by the invisible, inner law which etches on their hearts the conviction that all men are brothers and that love is mankind's most potent weapon for personal and social transformation." He continues, "True integration will be achieved by true neighbors who are willingly obedient to unenforceable obligations" (124). And here we come back to the heart of the matter. On its own, desegregation gives us a society where people are "physically desegregated and spiritually segregated, where elbows are together and hearts are apart. It gives us special togetherness and spiritual apartness. It leaves us with a stagnant equality of sameness rather than a constructive equality of oneness" (118).

In contrast, integration consists of a spiritual opening of the hearts of citizens to one another across preexisting divides. This can arise only when an unenforceable moral law has been awakened in the souls of all. To effect this, the single tool that King offers, other than his own pulpit, was the discipline of nonviolent resistance. With his moving rhetoric, personal commitment, and self-sacrifice as an activist, King captured the imagination of the citizenry of the United States, shifting its culture and its understanding of its most salient values. With his definition of integration, and the avenues of possibility for achieving an equality of oneness and spiritual awakening, he delivered to modern America a powerful fantasy about how to cure the problem of racial domination in American democracy, and any democracy. Law wasn't off the hook—it provided a necessary foundation to the work through policies of desegregation, but then it was on all those who sought integration, as all should, to do ethical work with ourselves and our fellow citizens, so as to transform our hearts.

The soaring existential power of the view, but also its frightening limits, are surely quickly apparent. In the next section I will take the time to spell those limits out. Thereafter I will return to the philosophical contribution that King made, offer an account of its value, and make a proposal for how to build on his contribution going forward.

Integration and the Problem of Math

In King's most famous speech, from August 1963, he conjured up his dream with an evocative image that is important for our work in this volume. "I have a dream," he exhorted, "that one day on the red hills of Georgia, the sons of former slaves and the sons of former slave owners will be able to sit down together at the table of brotherhood." We should pause to ask specifically what picture is conjured by this rhetoric. If we do ask that, we will discover the reigning paradigms that have governed the project of integration for the last half century. What picture does King's image bring to mind for you? Do you imagine a table of eight people where seven are white and one is black? Or do you imagine a table split fifty-fifty? Do you imagine a table where the sons of former slave owners all cluster at one end and the sons of former slaves cluster at the other, yet still, in a sense, all sit together? Or do you imagine a dinner table around which are seated, say, six, or eight, or ten, or even fifty or a hundred people, with seats alternating between black and white?

The latter images—of a table split fifty-fifty, with black and white intermingling, and with maximal dispersal of the representatives of each group—is probably the picture that more commonly comes to mind when people hear King's rhetoric. The symbolism of integration has often involved the idea that in an integrated world, people of different colors will be distributed evenly throughout a population, or an organization, or an institution, as if on a checkerboard. When Elizabeth Eckford, one of the Little Rock Nine who integrated Central High School in Little Rock, Arkansas, in 1957, prepared for her first day of school, she sewed herself a dress with a border consisting of black and white checks. During the fiftieth-anniversary celebrations of the events in Little Rock, this dress became a museum piece, included in a traveling exhibit. Its symbolism is impossible to miss.

Strikingly, King's imagined table of brotherhood, Eckford's vision as expressed through her dress, and popular ways of imagining integration too, always exceeded mathematical reality. In 1960, African Americans, then still the largest ethnic minority in the United States, constituted just under 10 percent of the American population. It was never possible for black and white to be, as in King's words, elbow-to-elbow, in the sense of evenly distributed throughout the population. To whatever degree the symbolism of integration inspired this mental image, it oriented people toward a mathematical fantasy. Demographic realities would have dictated that on the checkerboard of integration, there would have been one black square for every nine white squares. For mathematical reasons, historically there has never been any realistic chance of Americans of different races or ethnicities being genuinely elbow-to-elbow throughout the entire social fabric of the nation, yet the goal laid out for us was nonetheless full spiritual affinity or social "oneness." The gap between reality and the imagined utopia has strained the project of integration.

King's concretization of the abstract goal of integration took us in the direction of a fantasy that undermines our capacity to pursue an eminently worthy ideal. Yet the definition of integration as a provision to all people of the positive liberties of social and political participation is a compelling ideal. The question, then, is whether we can develop an alternative approach to its concretization that avoids the problematic fantasy of all of us living continuously elbow-to-elbow with people from different ethnic and social groups. We might find a different path forward if we back up and start again from King's idea of life-quality freedom and his idea of an unenforceable law of nondomination. These concepts are salutary contributions to ongoing debates in democratic theory and are worth recovering for contemporary projects of egalitarianism.

Life-Quality Freedom

The most interesting and important concept in King's essay is "life-quality freedom," which he introduces in the section of the essay titled "Social Leprosy." There he argues, contra Constant and Berlin (and contra Rawls *avant la lettre*), that just like the negative liberties, the positive liberties are nonsacrificeable.

On a conventional liberal view, freedom can be restricted to expand freedom or to ensure that all have the same basic liberties. For instance, property laws put limits on what I can do with your property precisely so that you too can enjoy a right to your own property. The issue of nonsacrificeability emerges when proposals develop to sacrifice liberties for some other kind of good. For instance, Rawls held that the rights to autonomy, association, and expression could not be sacrificed to promote general social welfare, but he could imagine cases in which the positive rights to political participation might indeed need to be set aside, even if only temporarily, for the sake of securing material goods.[8] Whereas liberals and republicans agree about the possibility of limiting or restricting liberties, when liberties conflict, in order to achieve equal liberty for all, they disagree on the relationship between liberties and other values, such as material well-being. The centuries-old slogan of the republican, but not the liberal, is "Give me liberty or give me death." King, in fighting for freedom and exposing himself to the threat, and eventual fact, of assassination, embodied that commitment to freedom's nonsacrificeability.

King also makes the case that intellectual clarity about the nonsacrificeable nature of positive liberties is a distinctive contribution made possible by experience of a minoritarian position within a democracy characterized by racial domination. He writes, "Only a Negro can understand the social leprosy that segregation inflicts upon him" (121). He continues with an account of the material consequences of experiences of domination, the experience, as Philip Pettit defines it, of being subject to the arbitrary will of others. It is worth quoting this passage at length: "Only a Negro can understand the social leprosy that segregation inflicts upon him. The suppressed fears and resentments, and the expressed anxieties and sensitivities make each day of life a turmoil. Every confrontation with the restrictions imposed is another emotional battle in a never-ending war. He is shackled in his waking moments to a tiptoe stance, never quite knowing what to expect next and in his subconscious he wrestles with this added demon" (121).

These experiences constitute "the withdrawing of life-quality from groups." He provides further definition thus: "Nothing can be more diabolical than a deliberate attempt to destroy in any man his will to be a man and to withhold from him that something that constitutes his true reserve." The language of a "true reserve" introduces the metaphor of capital. In blocking positive liberties, and the freedom "to do," practices of domination withhold goods, whose value can be characterized with the vocabulary of materiality. King extends the claim about the material significance of violations of positive freedom, arguing, "Integration demands that we recognize that a denial of freedom is a denial of life itself." In other words, the positive liberties have a material significance no less than that of food, air, and water, and the other elements of bare survival. Only integration, he argues, "provides of the highest degree of life-quality freedom" (121).

By affixing the phrase "life-quality" to a definition of positive freedom focused on the positive liberties, King identifies those positive liberties not only as basic goods of material significance but also as nonsacrificeable, just as the right to life, a core instance of a negative liberty, is nonsacrificeable. Importantly, economic theory has not, to date, found a way of incorporating the value of positive liberty into theories of utility or theories of political economy. Yet King points to the need for just such an innovation.

Interestingly, "life-quality" has, in the ensuing decades, become a measurable good in theories of distributive justice related to health, as in the use of "quality-adjusted life years." The concept, which merges quantity and quality of time to measure disease burdens, is employed in economic evaluations of how best to allocate scarce health resources. This supports the notion that King intuited that the phrase "quality-life freedom" could install his concept of freedom within the panoply of basic goods protected as nonsacrificeable by then-emergent theories of distributive justice. Yet King's own intuition—that positive liberties, understood as nonsacrificeable, could be installed at the heart of a theory of justice—has yet to be cashed out. Doing so would require not only revisions to utility theory and political economy but also an alternative strategy for converting King's unenforceable moral law into concrete social practices to replace his reliance on the pulpit, nonviolence, and a fantasy of black and white living elbow to elbow. I will reserve the issues of political economy for another occasion and here focus on the second question by revisiting what I have dubbed King's unenforceable law of nondomination.

The Unenforceable Law of Nondomination

The first thing to recognize about King's unenforceable moral law and its ethical demands is that it does indeed spell out the social requirements of practices of nondomination. King defined integration as the "welcomed participation of Negroes," or out-groups generally, "in the total range of human activities" (118). This is a requirement, in other words, for hospitality, for welcome provided to those who propose to join in a given social or cultural activity. The purpose of his three ethical demands—that we recognize "thou-ness"; that we enable and respect everyone's capacities to deliberate, choose, and take responsibility; and that we commit to nonviolence—is to provide a framework for the provision of such hospitality. This framework for hospitality constitutes an account of the requirements of nondomination.

The key feature of the demand that we recognize the "thou-ness" of others is that we not treat them as means, or as "things." We convey that we treat others as "things" when we do not concern ourselves with their well-being but concern ourselves only with how well they perform some function of instrumental value to us. Take, as an example, criminal justice policy. When we focus on prisoner re-entry by seeking above all to reduce recidivism, in order to minimize the damage of criminality to a broad community, we are failing to consider the question from the point of the well-being of the former inmate. We might also be concerned to reduce recidivism as a way to measure how well we are supporting and achieving the well-being of former prisoners. To live up to a standard of nondomination, any given policy question would need to be addressed to considerations of the well-being of all those affected by it. Use of this "well-being" requirement is the first element of social practices of nondomination.

The second element concerns recognition and enablement of the capacities of all to deliberate, choose, and take responsibility. Segregation blocks these capacities by imposing "restraint on my deliberation as to what I shall do, where I shall live, how much I shall earn, the kind of tasks I shall pursue." It has the consequence of forcing people to live in "some system that has largely made these a priori decisions for me." The result is that "I am reduced to an animal" (120). Importantly, desegregation without integration only partially removes this element of domination. Unless members of out-groups are positively welcomed into all decision-making contexts with social significance, they are continually required to live in "some system [that] has already made these a priori decisions for me." Without positive liberties, and active participation in cultural and political creation, "I have been made a party to a decision in which I played no part in making." When this occurs, "the very nature of [a person's] life is altered and his being cannot make the full circle of personhood because that which is basic to the character of life itself has been diminished" (121). Alongside the "well-being" requirement, then, King here presents an ethic of nondomination as establishing a second requirement for the inclusion of all in social decision making. The inclusion cannot be merely formal. If decision making is structured by social practices that ensure that for some participants the results are always like decisions made for them a priori by others, then nondomination has not been achieved. King does not further develop an argument for the institutional and organizational forms that are necessary to realize a principle of full inclusion in social and political decision making, but he points to an agenda of questions to ask and answer, one that scholars have recently been taking up.[9]

Finally, there is the ethical demand that the oppressed respond to instances of domination through nonviolence. Alongside the "well-being" and "inclusion" requirements, this is a third piece of the framework of nondomination. Here King builds on the Gandhian concept of "noninjury" to build a theory of action that rests on recognition of the sacredness, the "thou-ness" and need for freedom, of every human being. The discipline of nonviolence provides a mode of contesting oppression and domination without turning the oppressor into a "thing." Indeed, the commitment to nonviolence demands that the practitioner "respect the personhood of [the] opponent." Thus, King writes, "nonviolence exalts the personality of the *segregator* as well as the *segregated*" (125). This principle might help us clarify contemporary debates about micro-aggressions and how to counter them. Micro-aggressions—subtle, even unintended insults that put down members of a marginalized group on account of their group membership—are part of the fabric of social practices of domination. They are failures to recognize the "thou-ness" of others, and failures to frame interactions with others through an orientation toward their well-being. They also can often serve to degrade the opportunities of members of marginalized groups to participate effectively in joint decision making. In other words, micro-aggressions can, and often do, work against full participation. Regardless of whether a given micro-aggression is, in its essence, a failure to recognize the "thou-ness" of others, or a blockage to full participation by members of marginalized groups, micro-aggressions can become the targets of nonviolent resistance. But what does this mean? Not that one must necessarily stage a protest or occupy a building in response to a particular micro-aggression, but only that one must ensure that whatever response one pursues accords with exalting the personality of the person who has inflicted the insult. On King's principles for an ethics of nondomination, one would respond to a micro-aggressor not by seeking to insult or humiliate in turn but in some other way—for instance, in the mode of a teacher, a figure who corrects or improves for the good of the person so educated, as well as for her own good. King acknowledges that this particular burden falls heavier on those "who have been on the oppressed end of the old order" (124).

The unenforceable law of nondomination, then, imposes three requirements on citizens of a democracy aspiring to complete itself: that they direct their interactions and policy debates always to the question of one another's well-being, and not toward mutual instrumentalization; that they secure a panoply of decision-making practices and organizations that are fully inclusive in their operations; and that they challenge and fight with each other in accordance with the "noninjury" standard of nonviolent resistance.

As I have indicated above, for King the reign of this law and its three requirements in the hearts of Americans could be established only through preaching (prophetic rhetoric) or nonviolent protest.[10] He linked these methods to a lofty but also a mathematically impossible fantastical vision of black and white living continuously elbow-to-elbow, neighbor-to-neighbor, with physical proximity being converted through interaction into spiritual affinity. Neither his instruments of implementation nor his vision for social experience deliver the ideal that he so promisingly sketched. The remaining question, then, is whether we can expand the resources available for concretizing and operationalizing the practices of nondomination that King so eloquently identified as necessary for fully securing freedom.

From Oneness to Wholeness

In arguing that integration might permit American democracy to shift from pursuing "a stagnant equality of sameness" to "a constructive equality of oneness," King repeated an error that has plagued the liberal tradition since the time of Thomas Hobbes. As I have argued at length in *Talking to Strangers*, the social contract tradition installed a problematic ideal of unanimity at the heart of the liberal definition of political legitimacy. The error lies not only in the fact that unanimity typically is impossible to achieve but more importantly in the fact that the idea obscures the fact that every political decision brings winners and losers. Democracies must rely instead on theories of legitimacy that address the question of what makes political loss in a democracy both legitimate and endurable. I won't review here my argument about how the problem of loss in democratic politics can be worked into a theory of legitimacy, but I wish to invoke the replacement ideal that I argue for. The goal of democratic politics should be the achievement not of "oneness"—total agreement or consensus or spiritual affinity—but of wholeness, "the coherence and integrity of a consolidated but complex, intricate, and differentiated body."[11]

In *Talking to Strangers* I argue that a democracy might achieve "wholeness" via pursuit of an ethics of political friendship that, like King's ethical demands for integration, scaffolds practices of nondomination. Like King in "Ethical Demands," I focus in *Talking to Strangers* not on law but on the ethical realm, the topic of how each of us can transform our daily practices of interaction with others and thereby transform our world, advancing a project for the completion of democracy. Therefore, my argument, like King's, is open to criticisms that I fail to concretize adequately the institutional and organizational forms necessary to bring nondomination genuinely into being. Similarly, both our arguments have been criticized (although wrongly, I think) for an excessive reliance on a utopian fantasy of a prospective emergence of something like spiritual affinity.[12]

In fact, it is possible to close the gap between King's ethical argument (and mine too) and the creation of concrete practices of nondomination in the lived reality of democracies. Drawing on King's account of practices of nondomination as entailing an orientation toward well-being (and not instrumentalization), toward full inclusion in decision making, and toward noninjury, we can close that gap. His explicit focus on the positive liberties, and on the requirement for full participation in the social and political decisions that establish the constraints in which we can exercise our freedom, opens up a zone of action. Alongside our political institutions, civil society organizations—both commercial and noncommercial—crowd the landscape of any democracy's collective life. Some significant number of these make socially meaningful or impactful decisions that frame the horizons of possibility of our shared world. King's list of the ethical demands of integration could easily be directed toward achieving changes in organizational practice throughout that landscape. We could pursue a "constructive policy of wholeness" by pursuing organizational transformation throughout the landscape of civil society, guided by the three principles articulated by King.

Let me provide just a few examples from one civil society organization in which I happen to spend a great deal of my time, a distinguished university in the northeast.[13] Under the heading of "Inclusion and Belonging," the university is in fact embarked on a project of integration. All three of King's ethical demands apply to the endeavor.

For instance, the "well-being" principle might be applied to adjust that university's values statement. Currently that statement includes a plain instrumentalization of staff. It reads:

> [The] University aspires to provide education and scholarship of the highest quality—to advance the frontiers of knowledge and to prepare individuals for life, work, and leadership. Achieving these aims depends on the efforts of thousands of faculty, students, and staff across the University. Some of us make our contribution by engaging directly in teaching, learning, and research, others of us, by supporting and enabling those core activities in essential ways.[14]

In this formulation, no attention is given to the well-being of staff members. Yet such a blind spot is unnecessary. Without making any sacrifices to the mission of the university to educate, that formulation could be rewritten to shift from a framework of instrumentalization to one that attends to the well-being of all. Consider this possible revision:

> [The] University aspires to provide education and scholarship of the highest quality—to advance the frontiers of knowledge and to prepare individuals for and provide fulfilling experiences of life, work, and leadership. Achieving these aims depends on the efforts of thousands of academic personnel, students, and staff across the University. Some of us make our contribution by engaging directly in teaching, learning, and research, others of us, by supporting and enabling those core activities in essential ways, while also pursuing professional growth.

With a revision such as this, the organization would reform itself in accord with the first of King's ethical demands of integration.

The second ethical demand, which concerns the principle of full participation in decision making, also applies. While the university has successfully pursued diversification and inclusion in staff hiring at the lower rungs of the organization, senior leadership throughout the university continues to be almost exclusively nonintegrated. King's second principle, that all should have full participation in the decision making that shapes our collective lives, would highlight the need for organizational transformation in a direction that brings about "the welcomed participation of [members of marginalized groups] into the total range of human activities," including senior leadership within the university.

Finally, with regard to the principle of responding to oppression with noninjury, my earlier example of how to think about micro-aggressions pertains again here. The university might reasonably articulate a set of expectations for membership in the community as set out in the following list:

- The right to full and free expression.
- The responsibility to prove ourselves trustworthy to one another.
- The responsibility to deal with one another in good faith, to assume good faith in others, and to strive for mutual resilience in the face of disappointment.

- The right and responsibility to engage in cooperative and productive disagreement, with civility and respect for differences of opinion and lived experience and for each person's dignity—the preconditions for turning difficult conversations into opportunities for learning and shared development.
- The recognition that all members of our community—students, staff, and scholars—are connected to one another.

The fourth point, that difficult conversations should be turned into opportunities for learning and shared development, accords with the discipline of nonviolent resistance and the requirement that responses to acts of domination meet a standard of noninjury. Pedagogic modes of response are, of course, particularly valuable in this context.

In short, this expectation-setting language aspires to embed the principle of nonviolence in the organization's culture. But can it pull that off? The organization would need to learn how to motivate members of its community to treat even the experience of micro-aggressions as teaching moments while also equipping people with the skills necessary to convert an affront to their dignity into a foundation for their success as teachers. This is challenging. Simultaneously, the institution would have to acknowledge what King expresses in this essay, that this third burden falls more heavily, and therefore unfairly, on those whose groups have historically received the short end of the stick. He writes: "I cannot conclude without saying that integration places certain ethical demands upon those who have been on the oppressed end of the old order" (124).

This is precisely where King's trio of ethical demands helps bring to the surface the multiple ways democratic citizens ask things of each other and demand sacrifices, and pinpoints how even differentiated burdens can be rendered compatible with an egalitarian political project. If the third ethical demand falls harder on those who have been "on the oppressed end" historically, then the second ethical demand, to transition to fully inclusive decision making, falls harder on those who have had the upper hand in the old order. Yes, as King says, transitioning to modes of decision making in which all participate is the right thing to do, but this does not make it costless. To adjust King's words, we might say that we "cannot conclude without saying that integration places certain ethical demands upon those who have been on the privileged end of the old order."

As members of each group seek to shoulder their integration burdens—for the privileged of transitioning to fully inclusive decision making, and for the formerly oppressed of responding with noninjurious pedagogy to witting and unwitting efforts to continue practices of domination—each in fact also meets the standard of the first burden, of considering their fellow citizens, including those from whom they have historically been divided, as ends in themselves, not means; they address one another with reference to their well-being, not with the question of how others can be made to do for me.

In sum, democracies can achieve wholeness by ensuring that society is held together by a comprehensive network of decision-making organizations that consistently meet the ethical demands of integration articulated by King. We need to work, not on our hearts only, but even more immediately on a transformation of the practices and protocols of our organizations. As a matter of our organizational practices, without the need necessarily to achieve spiritual affinity neighbor-to-neighbor, we can weave a holistic fabric of nondomination for civil society, and achieve affirmation of freedom and affirmation of life. This path bypasses the dilemma of the mathematical fantasy.

8

A Vindication of Voting Rights

DERRICK DARBY

> Any democratic nation that cannot guarantee all of its citizens the elemental right to vote is suffering from a moral sickness that must be cured if it is to survive.
>
> —MARTIN LUTHER KING, JR.

A nation espouses fundamental values and decides how to realize them within a system of rights. Failing to guarantee rights that promote these values, such as the right to vote, can be costly. It can lead to societal instability and civil violence, putting at risk the basic institutions that order our lives.[1] It can result in some citizens perceiving that their lives do not matter and that they are not full members of the polity.[2] And as white resistance and ambivalence to black civil rights have taught us in the United States, it can also diminish a nation's moral authority at home and abroad.[3] America's democratic experiment has, in many ways, been about working out our fundamental values of freedom, equality, and dignity within a coherent system of rights.[4] At times we have moved closer to this aim—if not always with deliberate speed—and at others we have moved further away from making these values and rights a tangible reality for all citizens.[5] This chapter vindicates a legal system of rights that guarantees all citizens the right to vote by drawing on philosophical insights about dignity found in the writings of Martin Luther King, Jr.

An Expressive Commitment to Dignity

King presumes that respect for human dignity is part of America's founding tradition and is thus one of the fundamental values it espouses.[6] This important point, which I shall take as a given, informs his dignity-based internal critique of the nation when it does not guarantee the right to vote; this "moral sickness," as he describes it, constitutes an assault on the dignity of persons in multiple senses. King does not offer us a uniform conception of dignity. But neither does Immanuel Kant.[7] Indeed, as we shall see, King, like Kant, uses the concept in different ways. Sometimes King directs attention to the importance of dignified conduct, which calls for behavior in accordance with particular norms. At other times, dignity indicates that something, such as human nature, or someone, such as a creature with the capacity to make choices, has inherent worth. King combines these uses to argue that in their struggle against racial injustice black Americans have a moral obligation to comport themselves in a dignified manner, as they work to pressure society to treat them as creatures with inherent worth, and to vanquish injustices (such as vote denial) that prevent them from being regarded by others as persons of equally high social status or rank.

Kant, in addition to having much to say about the nature of persons, also makes explicit the connection between being a person and having rank and dignity. He writes: "The fact that the human being can have the 'I' in his representations raises him infinitely above all other living beings on earth. Because of this he is a *person*," says Kant, "and by virtue of the unity of consciousness through all changes that happen to him, one and the same person—i.e., through rank and dignity an entirely different being from things, such as irrational animals, with which one can do as one likes."[8] Here Kant is distinguishing between humans and animals, but European colonialism and New World slavery contributed to introducing distinctions of rank and dignity within the class of human beings based on racial categories.[9]

Although this link between dignity and rank is not as explicit in his thought, King intimates that dignity is the equalization of an honorific social status that obtains when sources of hierarchy-sustaining social relations such as racial segregation are expunged from civic and social life by the force of law.[10] And here his thought about dignity resonates with a contemporary conception of dignity as rank.[11] One virtue of this conception, which links dignity to an honorific social status rather than the inherent worth of all persons, is that it allows us to register the historical reality of hierarchical social relations that diminish dignity (such as slavery, segregation, voter suppression) while also capturing the content of our normative aspiration to arrange our social world to undo these relations through the force of law. Another virtue is that it affords us yet another way to articulate and vindicate the distinctive normative importance of voting rights.

Voter suppression is among the injustices, according to King, that can undermine a citizen's capacity to make choices, thereby assailing their dignity. Within its system of rights, law can play a vital role in addressing the indignity of this and other hierarchy-sustaining injustices. King counts the right to vote among the rights essential to promoting dignity, understood both as the inherent worth of a citizen's capacity to make deliberative choices and as an honorific social status. Failing to make this right a reliable reality—one that every citizen can count on regardless of their race, gender, or how little time or money they have—is a distinctive moral failure according to King. But what exactly is the nature of this failure? Is it a failure to enact a right somehow grounded in dignity as inherent worth? Is it a failure to establish a right that expresses the kind of nation we profess and aspire to be, namely one where dignity as equalization of social rank for persons deemed to have inherent worth is publicly affirmed?

The first alternative suggests that the connection between dignity and rights is what I shall call a *grounding relationship*. Simply put, the idea is this: that someone has dignity entails that they have, or should be recognized as having, certain rights within a system of rights. Failing to enact the appropriate legislation is a grounding failure. The second alternative suggests that the connection between dignity and rights is what I shall call an *expressive relationship*. Here the idea is this: the system of rights we enact expresses the content and scope of our commitment to dignity. Failing to enact the appropriate legislation within a system of rights is an expressive failure.[12] Discerning King's vindication of voting rights is a matter I shall resolve by attending to King as an astute political philosopher in addition to being a radical black Baptist preacher and civil rights activist whom we can no longer sanitize.[13]

My specific goals in this chapter are to develop King's account of the moral value of voting rights, and his vindication of a public system of rights that includes them, by drawing on the expressive relationship between dignity and rights. From reading his work it is clear that he also considers the grounding relationship. He takes dignity, when understood as "one's capacity to deliberate, decide and respond," to be a value from which the right to vote can be derived. Yet I will not resolve the question of whether one or the other is a better or truer interpretation of his understanding of the relationship between dignity and rights. Nor will I take up the vexing question of whether the two possibilities are exhaustive or incompatible with one another.

There are, however, at least two good reasons for featuring his less obvious expressive understanding of the relationship between dignity and voting rights: (1) the grounding relationship between dignity and rights has come under heavy attack,[14] and (2) the expressive relationship may afford us a better way to unify King's philosophical outlook on the morality of voting rights with his preaching and activism, which, in large part, all involve getting America to make value choices—and own up to and publicly express the value choices it has made—about the kind of nation it professes and aspires to be. In his various roles, as preacher, political activist, and political philosopher, King holds America morally accountable for bringing its legal system of rights in line with its professed value of categorical respect for human dignity.

The Struggle against Racial Injustice

King was there when President Lyndon B. Johnson signed the Voting Rights Act into law in 1965. LBJ reportedly told King—in so many words—to go home, after he witnessed the signing of the Voting Rights Act. As the president handed King one of the more than fifty pens used to sign the bill into law, he told King "his work was now done, that the time for protest was over."[15] Johnson was not happy with the disruptive voting rights movement. He was not happy with the bad press, with having to tame Alabama governor George Wallace, or with having to divert attention from his other domestic and foreign policy agendas, most notably the war in Vietnam, to help blacks overcome. To his credit, the president signed the bill. However, as King appreciated, it would be naive to assume that this was because Johnson or any other member of government "had somehow been infused with such blessings of goodwill."[16] This was hardly the case.

King espoused *mature realism,* a methodological approach to achieving racial justice under nonideal conditions, animated by the plausible insight that agents, whether individuals or governments, must sometimes be moved to action by appealing to their base interests, notwithstanding the possibilities of love as a political emotion.[17] "We must develop, from strength," as King puts it, "a situation in which the government finds it wise and prudent to collaborate with us."[18] Johnson was undoubtedly moved to action by the overwhelming "situation" created by brutal and shameful white resistance to black civil and political rights, the peaceful nonviolent movement that responded to it, the bad press America was getting at home and abroad, and the looming threat of a potentially more explosive Black Power movement waiting in the wings if the turn-the-other-cheek strategy failed.

Telling King to go home—with the hope that things could get back to normal—shows that Johnson clearly overestimated the significance of passing the civil rights and voting rights bills into law in the nation's exhausting struggle against racial injustice. To be sure, black Americans are not the only ones who have grown weary in this ongoing struggle, though they have historically been on the most brutal end of it, as was the case on Bloody Sunday in Selma, Alabama. White conservatives, moderates, and even white liberals sometimes show signs of fatigue when they ask: "When will things get back to normalcy?"[19] This question, which can stem from hopeful optimism or mean-spirited patronizing, usually arises following periods of racial progress. Indeed, as King observed, after civil and voting rights were secured—on paper if not in practice—many white Americans, including President Johnson, were eager for the marching to stop, for the protestors to return home, and for everyone to celebrate the new birth of democracy so that things could return to normalcy.[20] From their perspective, the comprehensive federal antidiscrimination legislation and statutory protection of voting rights during this historic era afforded blacks "tremendous gains in the struggle for dignity and decency."[21] What more could blacks demand as a matter of justice?

Well, as it turns out, they could demand much more. To appreciate King's answer to this question, and ultimately to understand why many people, including President Johnson, overestimated the significance of this historic legislation, and why King refused to go home, we must take up two closely related matters. First, we must ask, What is normalcy? Apparently, in the heat of the civil rights demonstrations, a Birmingham, Alabama, newspaper asked: "When are Negroes going to end these demonstrations and allow things to return to normalcy?"[22] Addressing this question, which undoubtedly comes up today whenever marchers gather to proclaim that black lives matter, was a recurrent concern for King. He consistently argues that there are two types of normalcy, one of which we should always reject outright and "never work to preserve." There is the kind that represents the racial status quo that has existed in America for most of its history, where blacks do not really enjoy the rights promised to them by laws on the books, such as ones that prohibit school segregation by race, neighborhood redlining and lending discrimination that restricts blacks to segregated dark ghettos, as well as ones that guarantee them equal protection, due process of law, and access to the ballot box. Status quo normalcy, or what King calls "negative normalcy," is also the kind in which black citizens and their children do not really enjoy fair equality of opportunity to participate in the full range of possibilities that America has to offer. And beyond these things, showing that his political morality was not limited to combating racial injustice, King also identifies class inequality, militarism, and environmental pollution with the kind of normalcy we must reject.[23]

Blacks, and indeed "every people who have ever struck for freedom," have rejected status quo normalcy in favor of the abnormal, or more emancipatory, "positive normalcy," says King.[24] But what exactly is this? Is it merely the absence of racial discrimination and the end of brutal violence against blacks marching for their rights? Surely it is not, though these are certainly components of it. To be sure, under more ideal conditions of positive normalcy we would not see acts of terrorist violence against blacks such as "the tragic and ungodly murder of four innocent girls" in Birmingham, Alabama, in 1963, or the brutal massacre of nine people, including the pastor, at the Emanuel African Methodist Episcopal Church in Charleston, South Carolina, in 2015. We would not see the kind of normalcy that prevented blacks from registering and voting in places like Mississippi, Louisiana, Georgia, and throughout Dixie before and after the Voting Acts Right became law. And we would not see the kind that now makes registering to vote and voting much too dependent on resources like time and money, which are so unevenly distributed across the population and which the black poor have a disproportionately lower share of. Yet these points only speak to what "positive normalcy" is not. They are compelling examples of what's wrong with the world we live in, but say little, at least in the way of truly inspiring us, about the world we wish to achieve. We want to become a country where persons are not treated in certain ways based on arbitrary factors like racial membership. But surely there are loftier, more aspirational things we can say about how persons *ought* to be treated. Indeed there are, and King—the political philosopher—obliges us.

He supplies substantive positive insights about what "positive normalcy" should look like, and more specifically about the broader normative ideals it aims to realize. There are the generic points he makes: it's about making the brotherhood of man a reality and bringing the nation closer in line with the truth of its creed, articulated by Thomas Jefferson, that all men are created equal; it is also about being a more just and righteous nation, and about creating a better world for our children. Fraternity, equality, and justice are familiar and much discussed ideals, often called upon to describe how persons ought to be treated in a more ideal society where positive normalcy prevails. However, for King positive normalcy is also and perhaps chiefly about recognizing the dignity of all citizens and publicly expressing respect for it within a legal system of rights. The value of dignity is where we find King's most fertile normative insight for assessing the problem with racial injustice generally and with the particular injustice of vote denial.

In an ideal world where there is positive normalcy, racial and other types of justice will indeed "roll down like waters." But in our nonideal—unjust and imperfect—world, what is the moral compass that can take us there, guiding our way, normatively? How do we move from negative to positive normalcy? What normative ideal can facilitate our journey from a racially unjust world to a racially just one? Here King tells us, "We will only reach out for that type of normalcy in which every man will respect the dignity and the worth of human personality."[25] And, he further adds, "We only reach out for that normalcy where *all* of God's children in this nation will be able to walk the earth with dignity and honor!"[26]

Dignity, for King, is the moral torch that lights the way to positive normalcy and racial justice in a nonideal world. And, as I shall discuss below, he takes it that a legal system of rights plays a vital role in facilitating this journey. Although some people may take issue with his interpretation of America's grand moral mission—following a tradition of black political thought that includes Frederick Douglass, Frances Ellen Watkins Harper, and others—King offers his own moral reading of America's famous founding declaration, highlighting its association with the value of dignity. "The Declaration of Independence," King tells us, "proclaimed to a world organized politically and spiritually around the concept of the inequality of man, that the liberty and dignity of human personality were inherent in man as a living being."[27] The American Civil War, Lincoln's Emancipation Proclamation, and eventually the Thirteenth, Fourteenth, and Fifteenth Reconstruction Amendments to the U.S. Constitution were all key moments in bending the arc of the moral universe, and America's system of rights, toward extending the blessings of liberty to blacks and toward realizing an upward equalization of rank.

This illuminating and historically sensitive conception of human dignity, which philosopher Jeremy Waldron thoughtfully develops in his work, takes dignity to be a matter of having rank or high status, akin to what is reserved for nobility in some societies, a status that both morals and law can aim to protect and vindicate. If, as King says, "mankind through the ages has been in a ceaseless struggle to give dignity and meaning to human life," then America's experiment in representative democracy has been an ongoing struggle to realize an upward equalization of high rank for all persons under the authority of its laws.[28] I will say more about how King understands dignity and its demands in the next section, after tying up a second loose end.

Earlier I said there were two closely related matters we needed to understand to appreciate why many people, including President Johnson, overestimated the significance of the Civil Rights Act and the Voting Rights Act, and why King refused to go home after the latter was signed. The first had to do with settling for negative normalcy. Preferring to be maladjusted to this, King rejects the call—often from well-meaning liberals who want to end the war for racial justice—to return to normalcy unless this means marching forward with the goals and policies needed for the next, and high-priced, phase in the struggle against racial injustice and for dignity. Thus, the second matter pertains to King's more radical stance on what this phase of struggle required.

Dignity's demands are multifaceted in the pursuit of racial justice. The initial phase in America's epic struggle for dignity during the civil rights movement was to treat blacks with decency. Although doing this was no easy matter, many white Americans believed that eliminating the last vestiges of de jure discrimination from society, and the brutality with which racial caste had been enforced and nonviolent peaceful protestors had been dishonored and debased by it, would—along with guaranteeing blacks the right to vote—suffice to restore balance to the scales of justice and realize the value of dignity. So, for many whites the great victories in Montgomery, Birmingham, and Selma that paved the way for the Civil Rights and Voting Rights Acts were taken to be the end of war. With these transformative legislative accomplishments, it was believed that America's legal system of rights was finally aligned with affirming human dignity. King did not see it this way, however. For him they were but successful battles in the first phase of a larger struggle for racial justice, a larger struggle to express the moral ideal of dignity within positive law and the lived experiences of blacks in America. Phase two—the battle for equality—required taking on poverty, exploitation, and racial disparities.[29] And this meant reforms to create quality education, decent jobs that provided living wages, eradication of slums and substandard housing, and improved health outcomes, among other things. In addition, it required making sure that formally guaranteed rights such as the right to vote became more than nominal rights within America's system of rights.

Hence, the historic civil rights era antidiscrimination legislation did indeed afford blacks gains in the struggle for racial justice, important ones at that, but it did not suffice for working out the nation's normative commitment to upward equalization of rank or equal dignity for all. According to King, dealing with poverty and racial disparities were also necessary components of achieving this more lofty and demanding aim.

King was not naive about the serious challenges these second-phase battles would encounter. For one thing, as he keenly appreciated, because pursuing economic justice was much more expensive, the indispensable political alliances with liberal whites would be severely tested. "When Negroes looked for the second phase, the realization of equality," King observes, "they found that many of their white allies had quietly disappeared."[30] There are various reasons we can give for this. For instance, we might surmise that blacks and whites have rather different views about what the fulfillment of equality required, and about the extent to which winning phase one of the war against racial injustice was sufficient for this. King was charitable, preferring to give white Americans the benefit of the doubt, and loath to assume that they were acting in bad faith. He presumed that the majority of them supported racial justice. However, he further surmised: "They believe that American society is essentially hospitable to fair play and to steady growth toward a middle-class Utopia embodying racial harmony."[31] And he thought they were just plain wrong about this.

King had much to say about white psychology to explain white apathy and stiffening white resistance in the second-phase battle for racial justice, though I will not take this up here.[32] He was well aware of how costly the struggle against poverty and racial disparities would be for blacks and whites. As he put it, "Negroes have not yet paid the full price for freedom. And whites have not yet faced the full cost of justice."[33] So, when asked to go home by President Johnson after the signing of the Voting Rights Act in 1965, King could not heed this request. America still had much more work to do. From King's perspective, treating blacks with decency is not the same as treating them with equality, and both are necessary components of racial justice and organizing America's legal system of rights toward an upward equalization of rank, or dignity for all.

Dignified Conduct and Dignified Creatures

Selma, Alabama, was ground zero in the struggle for the right to vote in 1965. At the time, as King saw things, it was also the epicenter of a larger battle for dignity. As he put it, "This yearning for the franchise is another flash of the same quest for human dignity piercing the American sky."[34] Dignity is, to be sure, a philosophically contested concept.[35] King does not offer us a theory of dignity, and I see no point in shaping his thoughts into a careful, comprehensive, and consistent package. There are, however, a few prominent features worth highlighting and connecting. Some of his many discussions of dignity can be situated within two broad categories—one about how we should act when pursuing justice (*dignified conduct*) and one about the kind of beings we are (*dignified creatures*). These categories, which will be familiar to readers of Kant, who also influenced King's thoughts about dignity, provide us with conceptual resources for understanding the normative demands of the struggle for voting rights in the overarching quest for an upward equalization of rank.

Amelia Boynton Robinson bled and nearly died on the Edmund Pettus Bridge on Bloody Sunday. She and other brave African Americans unsuccessfully attempted to march from Selma to Montgomery in 1965 to demand the right to vote. On that solemn day, they settled instead for giving blood offerings in their struggle against racial injustice. Unfortunately, the vicious beating Robinson suffered was not her first. In an earlier encounter with the notorious Sheriff Jim Clark, she was punched in the face, beaten, and dragged off to jail for trying to register people to vote. It is no small feat to maintain one's dignity under such gruesome circumstances, but Robinson managed to do so. King the pastor would have said "well done."

In sermons on "the evil system of segregation" King implored fellow Christians to be dignified in their righteous protest and struggle.[36] "As you press on for justice," King preaches, "be sure to move with dignity."[37] He would undoubtedly have said the same to those struggling against vote denial and could have identified Robinson as a model to emulate. But "move with dignity," "be dignified," "comport oneself with dignity" are things we can implore or ask persons to do. And presumably they can be unsuccessful at it, in which case they would be without dignity and would warrant rebuke. Had Robinson armed herself not with the method of nonviolence and the Christian of weapon of love but with a firearm and the method of fighting brutal violence with the same kind of violence, and defended herself accordingly, King would have strongly disapproved. This would not have been an example of moving with dignity. This conception of dignity, which plays an essential role in King's normative understanding of what is required of persons struggling against racial injustice, is rooted in the idea that having dignity is about acting in accordance with standards of dignified conduct, particularly when confronting injustice or oppression. According to King, the imperatives of Gandhian nonviolent protest and unconditional Christian love supply the content of these normative standards.

We might agree with King that victims of racial injustice or racial oppression should not stand for these indignities, and that they should protest. They should act from a sense of dignity, as Rosa Parks did in not giving up her seat on the racially segregated bus in Montgomery, Alabama. As King saw it, "Mrs. Parks's refusal to move back . . . was an individual expression of a timeless longing for human dignity and freedom. . . . She was planted there by her personal sense of dignity and self-respect."[38] Yet there is a worry about the kind of nonviolent protest King takes to be sufficient for dignified conduct.

Acting with dignity is necessary to help persons regain a sense of self-respect, which is often lost or damaged under circumstances of injustice such as enforced racial segregation in public spaces or being denied the right to vote. These injustices contribute to a deeply felt sense of personal degradation as an inferior human being. Although engaging in nonviolent protest of these injustices may be sufficient to move with dignity in the face of injustice, it may not be enough to supply the needed evidence that one is *actually* moving with dignity. Refusing to comply with an order to give up one's seat to a white person on a racially segregated bus is one thing. Responding to the use of brutal physical violence to frustrate an attempt to exercise one's formally recognized rights without lifting a finger is another thing. In this case, turning the other cheek can also be read as servility, particularly if it becomes a consistent unbroken pattern of activity. So at some point it may be necessary to fight back, in ways that cannot be mistaken as "fighting back," to supply evidence to the oppressor, and perhaps more importantly to oneself, that one really has the self-respect indicative of moving with dignity.

To be sure, a person taking the brutal blows of injustice without returning blows might only be pretending to be servile, ultimately to get the best of the oppressor or to help others see the oppressor's brutality and evil. But at some point his pretense must betray the protestor. "If only occasionally," as philosopher Bernard Boxill observes, "he must shed his mask. And this may not be easy. Not only does shedding the mask of servility take courage, but, if a person is powerless, it will not be easy for him to make others believe that he has been wearing a mask."[39] Nevertheless, he must be "driven to make the evidence of his self-respect unmistakable."[40] Annie Lee Cooper, the voting rights activist portrayed by Oprah Winfrey in the movie *Selma*, took about all that she could before punching Sheriff Clark in the eye. Although Cooper's protest here could not be mistaken for servility, King may have nevertheless reprimanded her for not moving with dignity. According to King, in a racially unjust society where negative, not positive, normalcy prevails, African Americans, who are on the receiving end of injustice, must do their part in bending the arc of the moral universe toward a more just society by engaging in dignified conduct as they struggle and protest.

Immanuel Kant believed that humanity has dignity and that this imposes both self-regarding and other-regarding duties. At the highest level of abstraction, his categorical imperative—the formula of humanity—famously tells us never to treat humanity, "insofar as it is capable of morality," as a mere means to an end. Doing so would be "assaulting its holiness."[41] According to Kant we must take care to comport ourselves in ways that do not have this consequence. Although this imperative is not negotiable, we can go in different directions when bringing it down to earth to put respect for the dignity of humanity into practice within our everyday lives. This will depend on what standards, values, or virtues we, or the communities to which we belong, espouse. Our conduct and character is judged according to this measure. We promote it in our everyday practices. We find ways to sanction those who fail to measure up.[42]

From Kant's perspective, incurring debts that one cannot pay, begging, whining, and kneeling down (even to pray) is incompatible with paying proper respect for our dignity. In addition, Kant tells us, letting others violate our rights with impunity must not be tolerated.[43] Our status as dignified beings, in this sense, is clearly precarious. Were we to bow and scrape before others or in veneration of religious objects, to let others tread with impunity on our rights, or do anything that assaults our holiness, we would forfeit the respect we can demand as beings capable of morality. The same can be said of anyone that failed to heed King's call to move with dignity in the struggles against racial discrimination, segregation, and vote denial. Had Robinson and others not embraced nonviolence and love, they would have forfeited respect they were owed.

I am not sure if Kant and King would have seen eye-to-eye on how to respond to violence under circumstances of injustice. I suspect that Kant might have been critical of the turn-the-other-cheek approach, particularly insofar as it could be mistaken for allowing others to tread on one's rights with impunity. However, even if they disagree on this matter, it is clear that both associate dignity with acting in accordance with certain standards of dignified conduct. Moreover, they both believe that individuals have certain self-regarding duties to show proper regard for the holiness of their humanity, irrespective of whatever treachery or injustice befalls them. Moving with dignity in the struggle against racial justice is such a duty for King. But this is only one element of the equation. The other one, which construes dignity as something that cannot be compromised on account of failing to abide by certain standards of conduct, draws upon another sense of dignity also familiar to readers of Kant.

In an unambiguous, and especially strong, condemnation of denying blacks the right to vote, King remarks: "The denial of the vote not only deprives the Negro of his constitutional rights—but what is even worse—it degrades him as a human being."[44] Here King's debt to Kant is unmistakable. However, elsewhere in an argument on why racial segregation is immoral, he explicitly invokes Kant's formula of humanity. For King, both vote denial and segregation are injustices that reduce blacks "to things rather than persons," and they do so by cutting off "one's capacity to deliberate, decide and respond."[45]

Hence, there is another conception of dignity, bound up with the inherent value of our humanity, according to which dignity cannot be lost, no matter how one acts or fails to act. From this standpoint, to say of a person, such as Robinson, that she has dignity can also be understood as an ascription of inherent value or worth. Of course, this raises the question: What is the source or basis of this value? Here we can say any number of things. We can say that she has the capacity to move with dignity, in which case this sense of dignity and the foregoing one would be joined. Under the influence of the Judeo-Christian tradition, as King was, we can say that the source of Robinson's inherent worth is her being created in the image of God. Or, as King puts it, "Every human being has etched in his personality the indelible stamp of the Creator."[46]

In addition, following King, we can adopt a secular formulation of the value of humanity rooted in our capacity to make deliberative choices. "When I cannot choose what I shall do or where I shall live," King tells us, "it means in fact that someone or some system has already made these decisions for me, and I am reduced to an animal."[47] Indeed, from early on in his thinking, King regarded man as a rational being, noting that it was one of the "supreme resources of man," distinguishing him from his animal ancestry.[48] This perspective resonates with the long-standing tradition of linking the worth or dignity of humanity to rational autonomy, which we not only find in philosophy but in law, especially in judicial reasoning about privacy, abortion, and gay marriage.

So, in this sense, dignity—understood as worth—marks the sacredness of humans. This worth commands respect irrespective of how human beings act, what kinds of lives they live, what they believe, and no matter their intellect, racial origin, or social position.[49] And this kind of dignity cannot be forfeited.[50] This conception, which is also essential to King's understanding of what the struggle against racial injustice demands, captures the familiar idea that dignity is rooted in the essential nature of certain beings.[51] Depending on how this nature is understood, some creatures have dignity and others do not.[52]

In step with Kant's view that human dignity imposes peculiar self-regarding duties on us, King's two conceptions of dignity can be joined to formulate such a duty. Individuals struggling against racial injustice have a self-regarding duty to comport themselves with dignity, as they work to move society to respect their inherent worth as creatures with the capacity for deliberative choice within its legal system of rights. In other words, they must move with dignity in struggling to be treated as required by their dignified natures. Understanding the distinction between dignified conduct and dignified creatures and how they are related disambiguates this statement.

Perhaps King would not have welcomed even these minimal efforts—falling far short of attributing to him a theory of dignity—to clarify his various uses of dignity and their relationship to one another. He certainly would have had little interest in this were it a mere philosophical exercise. But I suspect if it were done to illuminate what is morally required of us and of society in the war against racial injustice, as I aim to do in this chapter, he would have approved. Although King indulges our philosophical curiosity in having a loftier, indeed more aspirational, perspective on how persons ought to be treated, he is mainly concerned with describing how dignity is assailed under nonideal circumstances of negative normalcy. Moreover, he aims to say what is required to right this wrong, moving us closer to positive normalcy and a fuller achievement of racial justice. That individuals engaged in the struggle move with dignity is one requirement; another requirement is that the law do its part in righting the indignity of racial injustice.

The Indignity of Racial Injustice

In a sermon on being a good neighbor, King describes segregation and discrimination as "evil monsters," calling attention to the nation's struggle to conquer these monsters that have "[stripped] millions of Negro people of their sense of dignity."[53] His list of evil monsters is long. Elsewhere in another sermon on the death of evil upon the seashore, King also counts oppression, colonialism, and imperialism as evil monsters that have reigned around the world. But, as he notes, these gradually gave way to the force of human dignity with independence movements in Africa and Asia that broke the yoke of colonial subjection, political domination, economic exploitation, and humiliation.[54]

If stripping Negro people, or any people, of their sense of dignity is a hallmark of an evil monster, then denying people the right to vote, a form of political domination about which I will say more later, is surely on the long list of monsters. In a reflection on successful independence movements in Africa, King laments that the struggle against political domination of blacks in America had not kept pace. "Voting as a badge of full citizenship has always had a special meaning to the Negro. But in 1965, in the context of world-wide developments," King tells us, "the denial of the right to vote cuts painfully and deeply into [the Negro's] new sense of personal dignity." When other blacks were gaining liberation around the world, he found it appalling that in the United States, African Americans could not exercise one of the most fundamental of all privileges of democracy—the right to vote.[55] Thus, for King, voting is a public badge of citizenship as well as dignity, which can be stripped away by the indignity of vote denial. Indeed, he went farther: "There cannot be citizenship without the right to vote. A voteless citizen is no citizen. Men and women who can not vote are forcibly exiled from their national heritage."[56]

It is also clear that King considers substantive inequality and unequal protection of law to be evil monsters. He points out that blacks and whites have grossly unequal shares of income. In 1963 King observed that "the average income of Negroes is approximately $3,300 per family annually, against $5,800 for white citizens."[57] And he provided examples, such as bombings of black Christian churches, where law and government clearly do not afford blacks the same protection and justice under the law. "If a government building were bombed in Washington," King maintains, "the perpetrators would be shot down in the streets, but if violence . . . affects the life or property of a Negro, not all the agencies of government can find or convict the murderers."[58] Hip-hop artist J-Live, in his socially conscious rap single "I Am A Man (American Justice)"—which quotes Malcolm X and Huey P. Newton and also bears a title inspired by signs from the 1968 Memphis sanitation workers' strike that King addressed the day before he was assassinated—vividly captures the deeply felt assault on black dignity, today, when blacks are not afforded equal protection of law against police brutality, and are instead made to fear the ones charged with protecting and serving them and their communities. He raps: "When you're treated less than human by a beast/It doesn't matter if it's the whole beast or nothing but the beast/If it's systemic, pandemic/and you don't even have the decency to condemn it? Goddamn it!"

All of these racial injustices, which sustain unequal social relations, have the effect of damaging the souls of black and white folk. They give blacks "a false sense of inferiority" as human beings and they give whites "a false sense of superiority."[59] As King says in his famous letter from Birmingham Jail, referencing Martin Buber, injustices such as segregation substitute "an 'I-it' relationship for an 'I-thou' relationship and ends up relegating persons to the status of things."[60] For black folk terrorized by these monsters, their social status is degraded to a lower rank, which corrodes their personality by instilling in them a sense of inferiority. The imposition of inferiority by these evil monsters, King explains, represents "the slave chains of today."[61] Insofar as blacks and whites are equally human beings, created in the image of God, as King assumes, with the capacity to make deliberative choices, that is, insofar as they have dignity in the sense of worth, King presumes that they should relate to one another, and be publicly regarded, as equals of the same high rank in civil society. But the reality of racial injustice in America, which has historically sustained unequal social relations and where positive normalcy has yet to come about, leaves the nation far short of achieving the normative ideal of upward equalization of rank.[62] In other words, America has yet to create circumstances were blacks have equal dignity with whites in the sense of social status.

Treating persons as equals with the same high rank does not preclude individual differences in income, wealth, education, and differences along other substantive dimensions. I find no evidence that King thought that it did. Furthermore, his remarks on the need for, and worth of, the labor of low-wage nonprofessional workers suggests otherwise. He locates the dignity (worth) of their vital labor in the serving and building of humanity.[63] That said, the differences in these resources certainly should not be so great as to preclude persons from being able to relate to each other as equals, nor should they be such that persons identified by some visible marker of difference enjoy a disproportionately lower or higher share of either the good or the bad things that society has to offer. Both of these outcomes—too much inequality or a seemingly nonrandom distribution—could impact both personal and public perceptions of high rank.

The indignity of racial injustice has a personal and a public dimension. The capacity to deliberate, decide, and respond, or what I have been calling the capacity for deliberative choice, is what endows human beings with dignity as inherent worth according to King. It distinguishes them from other creatures. The personal dimension of segregation, discrimination, political domination based on race, and the other evil monsters, is that they assail blacks' personal sense of worth. They impact how individual blacks perceive themselves. They impose upon the Negro "manacles of self-abnegation," says King, preventing them from saying and truly believing "I am somebody. I am a person. I am a man with dignity and honor."[64] How others perceive us, on the other hand, is the public dimension of these monsters. And it is significant that King mentions honor here.[65] The relationship of honor to dignity calls attention to another use of dignity as social status in King's thought, which is vital for elucidating the public dimension of the indignity of racial injustice.

The old saying "clothes make the man," Kant observes, "holds to a certain extent even for intelligent people." And as powerful as it can be, even our understanding "cannot prevent the impression that a well-dressed person makes of obscure representations of a certain importance."[66] In 1651 the colonial laws of Massachusetts regulated what apparel and adornments people could wear. These sumptuary laws aimed to maintain a rigid hierarchy of persons regarded as ladies and gentlemen, a high social rank, and persons of modest means and pedigree, a low social rank. They restricted the wearing of what we now call "bling"—gold, silver, silk, lace, and the like—to persons and their relations whose wealth exceeded a certain value (making exceptions for public officials, military personal, the well-educated, and persons whose estates had diminished in value), and imposed fines on violators of these laws. Ladies and gentlemen were deemed persons of honor, who retained a sense of dignity tied to this status. The bling laws gave dignity as honor public force by setting out specific rights to give it content. Persons without such standing were, of course, no different from those with it; they were likewise dignified creatures with the capacity for deliberative choice, which gives all who possess it dignity as worth. The amount of bling one has or lacks has no bearing on dignity in this sense. But clearly these sumptuary laws aimed to do more than "make the man." They aimed to bestow a socially recognized sense of dignity on certain men and women.

It is very much an open question, then, whether someone is a person of honor. If one's honor is tied to inherent worth, then one can claim to be a person of honor, even in the absence of bling laws that publicly mark this social status. But if it is tied to the public recognition of one's standing as a person of honor, then a legal system of rights is indeed a way of settling the matter. In a society where the distribution of honor is ranked, as it was in colonial and antebellum America—a stratified social hierarchy situating persons on a scale from low to high rank—we can have various reasons for wanting to undo this hierarchy and level up rank. We could, for example, maintain, as King most certainly did, that all human beings by virtue of being dignified creatures should be afforded the same high rank in civil society. We could also say, as King also did, that because all human beings are created in the image of God and are loved by God, they are of equal high rank, and that positive law should mirror divine law, eradicating hierarchy and leveling up social rank. But whatever one's reasons, on this conception of dignity it is *not* constituted by the metaphysical nature of our beings. Instead it is rooted in concrete social practices such as legal systems of rights that create legally supported ways of acting and being treated. An obvious consequence of this perspective is that because dignity must be granted, it can also be withheld or withdrawn. It can be won or lost. It can require sacrifice and struggle. Our inherent worth is something we have, even when we are not recognized as having it, as in a racist society that regards blacks as subpersons or subhuman. But our high social rank, on the other hand, and the public recognition that constitutes it, is something that we must struggle to achieve and retain.

King's extensive writings are full of references to the struggle for human dignity. In his famous speech on the steps of the Selma state capitol after the historic march, he includes public respect for dignity as one of the hallmarks of a yet-to-be-achieved great society, which he describes as "a society of justice where none would prey upon the weakness of others, a society of plenty where greed and poverty would be done away, a society of brotherhood where every man will respect the dignity and worth of human personality."[67] The conception of dignity tied to the social conferral of honorific status affords us a fruitful way to make sense of King's talk about the struggle and fight for dignity.

In colonial Massachusetts, bling laws regulated apparel and adornments to shape how some individuals were perceived by others. Because it was important in that society for ladies and gentleman to be publicly regarded as such, there needed to be tangible ways of distinguishing their honorific status from the status of those with more modest means and pedigree. Their legal system of rights gave expression to this value of dignity as high rank. The evil monsters of racial segregation, discrimination, and vote denial essentially serve the same function as these bling laws. They publicly mark persons, within a socially stratified hierarchy, as having lower and higher ranks, with persons of high rank being conferred greater dignity. The public dimension of racial injustices, of the sort that King condemns, is that they diminish the social rank of blacks, denying them the same honorific status afforded to whites. Dignity as high social rank is thus denied to blacks under nonideal circumstances of negative normalcy.

My reading of King on dignity comes to this: Black Americans, as dignified creatures, have a self-regarding obligation to move with dignity, engaging in dignified conduct, in their ongoing struggle to be socially recognized as having dignified status. This is necessary for moving America toward positive normalcy and a fuller achievement of racial justice in ways that are feasible and not counterproductive. However, the law must also do its part to bend the arc of the moral universe toward these ends. After all, laws are instrumental in why the nation falls short of these ends, and why blacks occupy a degraded rank. Law does its work within a system of rights. Through this system, law can level the social rank of persons up or down, and it should be judged accordingly. As King argued in 1963, "Any law that uplifts human personality is just. Any law that degrades human personality is unjust." Moreover, what was true then is arguably still true today, "Now is the time to lift our national policy from the quicksand of racial injustice to the solid rock of human dignity."[68] But apart from this judgment about the justness of laws, we can also ask whether the system of rights contains rights that express the values the nation professes to hold dear. If it does not, this would give us grounds to condemn the nation for the contradiction between its existing practices and its professed ideals. I shall take up this final matter by attending to King's case for the distinctive normative importance of a legal system of rights that guarantees all citizens the right to vote.

Vindicating the Right to Vote

This chapter began by identifying consequences that can befall a nation that does not guarantee its citizens the right to vote: damage to its stability, national solidarity, and moral authority. On this last point, King noted on more than one occasion that if the United States allows states like Mississippi to deny voting rights to blacks, it cannot argue against undemocratic practices elsewhere in Asia, Africa, and Latin America.[69] But there are also dire consequences for the individuals or groups who are denied the right to vote. In an annotated draft copy of an article on voting rights and jobs, King writes: "When Negroes are denied a right to vote and have their voices heard in Southern politics, they are denied the equal protection of the law, for Southern [sheriffs] like all politicians protect the people who put them in office; they are denied education opportunities, adequate wages, the right to organize and bargain collectively; and they are left to the mercy of those in political control."[70] Here King appreciates the connection between political representation through voting and one's interests being represented. I want to dwell, however, on this last observation, about being at the mercy of others. This is a prominent theme in King's normative argument for the right to vote. And it puts an ethical concern with dignity front and center.

Were we to set the foregoing grave costs of vote denial to one side, we would still have moral reasons for denouncing a government's failure to guarantee the right to vote. Moreover, we would also have reason to rebuke legislation that makes access to the ballot box conditional upon possessing resources like money and time, which are unequally distributed across the population of eligible voters—a serious consequence of today's voter ID requirements.[71] These moral reasons may focus on the harmful consequences for the happiness or well-being of persons whose right to vote is either denied or made more burdensome. But we may also take moral issue with them, following King, by highlighting how they result in a harmful form of interpersonal relations in the political sphere, making some persons vulnerable to domination by those who enjoy the full exercise of the right to vote. He makes this point in a speech at the Lincoln Memorial in 1957. "So long as I do not firmly and irrevocably possess the right to vote I do not possess myself," King declared.[72] "I cannot make up my mind—it is made up for me. I cannot live as a democratic citizen, observing the laws I have helped to enact—I can only submit to the edict of others."[73] Here we find King taking nondomination to be a political ideal and applying this ideal to defend the rights of African Americans to participate in the democratic political process on full and equal terms.[74]

This argument is, in part, about the adverse consequences of vote denial. However, this reading of the argument assumes that having to submit to the edict of others is detrimental to our happiness or well-being. But this may not be the case. If we suppose that those to whom we must submit not only have our best interests at heart, but that they succeed in making laws that best promote our happiness and well-being, then our consequentialist reasons for objecting to vote denial dissipate. Even if these fanciful assumptions were true, King would still take normative issue with leaving persons vulnerable to the political will of others by denying them the right to vote or making its exercise unduly burdensome.

This is because his appeal to nondomination also has a deontological dimension. It is rooted in a prohibition against actions that violate a categorical moral imperative calling upon us to respect agents who have the capacity for "making up their mind" or the capacity for deliberative choice. With this argument the value of dignity—in two senses in which King uses it—looms large. And both senses—dignified creatures and dignified status—can be brought to bear in expounding the expressive relationship between the right to vote and dignity, which in turn illuminates the normative significance of a public practice of rights that includes the right to vote within a legal system of rights.

Here is the short form of the argument I shall unpack below: The right to vote is one of the rights in a legal system of rights that promotes the exercise of deliberative capacity in the political sphere as well as the leveling up of social rank. Both senses of dignity, as the source of our inherent value and the source of honorific social status, are thus advanced by the right to vote. The first is advanced because this right gives one a say in making laws to which one is subject. The second is advanced because when we have a say, others do not subject us to political domination.[75] Both enable us to look others in the eye as political equals and to be socially recognized as having the same political rank. If protecting our interest in being so regarded is valuable, not just personally but as a professed national aspiration of an egalitarian democracy, then a nation whose commitment to the right to vote realizes these things has a robust commitment to dignity, whereas one that does not lacks such a commitment.[76]

So, according to King, having a capacity for deliberative choice or to make up one's mind is a metaphysical source of the worth of dignified creatures. A public commitment to valuing dignity aims to respect or promote the worth of persons within a legal system of rights. Mindful of the grounding problem, we may have real doubts about whether this notion of dignity affords adequate guidance in generating specific rights, and whether it is "sufficiently robust to deliver the full range of human rights recognized in contemporary international human rights doctrine."[77] But thinking about dignity as the ground of rights, such that we are aiming to infer particular rights from it, is not the only way to proceed. We can also consider the actual practice of rights we have before us, and ask whether, how, and to what extent it is dignity-respecting or dignity-promoting. If it is fully dignity-respecting, then it conforms to the categorical imperative to respect the dignity (worth) of persons.

Dignity, for King, is also an honorific status we should confer upon those we deem to be dignified creatures with inherent worth. But in this case the dignity is not metaphysical, simply flowing from the nature of one's being; it is something social that is conferred by de jure and de facto social practices and institutions. A public commitment to valuing dignity aims to level up or universalize this honorific status to all dignified creatures. We do not have to go too far back in American history to find a time when many questioned whether blacks were dignified creatures with the metaphysical source of inherent worth. During this time, they allowed social practices and institutions that maintained a stratified social hierarchy where blacks occupied a low rank and whites a much higher one. Back then there were Americans such as Frederick Douglass who proclaimed and defended the inherent worth of blacks, and argued for the abolishment of chattel slavery and racial segregation to facilitate a leveling up of their social rank.

Political domination via vote denial has long been an injustice perpetrated against blacks in America. Many people, blacks and whites alike, have worked tirelessly to win blacks the right to vote, from getting the Fifteenth Amendment passed to winning the Voting Rights Act.[78] In doing so they recognized the power of a legal system of rights in bending the arc of the moral universe to justice, and in making respect for dignity part of the lived experience of persons whose dignity had long been denied and diminished. They appreciated that a legal system of rights with the right to vote can address the evil monster of political domination and thus promote dignity as a capacity for deliberative choice, and as recognition of an honorific status for those we deem to be dignified creatures. A public practice of rights that includes the right to vote advances and promotes the value of dignity: it respects our deliberative capacity to make up our minds in matters that concern us, and it levels up our rank by freeing us from the indignity of having to submit to the edict of others by following laws we had no part in enacting. This practice observes Kant's categorical imperative, which King embraced, to respect humanity as an end-in-itself.

Conclusion

The right to vote gives people a public basis for making claims against others and empowers them to demand respect.[79] It gives people a "furious" sense of their rights, as Waldron puts it, and generates "a willingness to stand up for them as part of what it means to stand up for what is best and most important in oneself."[80] And, more broadly, it publicly expresses a governmental commitment to dignity, and to bringing our practices in line with our professed ideals, which in turn promotes stability, belonging, and the moral authority of the state. Making this expressive commitment is something that King—as a preacher, political activist, and political philosopher—was tirelessly devoted to getting the nation to do. Martin Luther King, Jr., teaches us that we have much to gain by ensuring that everyone has the right to vote.

PART III *Justice*

9

Prisons of the Forgotten: Ghettos and Economic Injustice

TOMMIE SHELBY

According to Martin Luther King, Jr., two developments marked the end of the first phase of the civil rights movement (1955–1965) and the start of a new radical black freedom struggle. The first was the passage of the Voting Rights Act, which Lyndon B. Johnson signed into law on August 6, 1965. The second was the emergence of riots in black ghettos, particularly the violent and destructive uprising that began on August 11, 1965, in the neighborhood of Watts and that spread throughout South Central Los Angeles.[1] The black freedom movement, King insisted, must turn *North* (here understood to include all U.S. regions outside the South) to attack the problems of the ghetto.[2] As usual, King backed up his words with action. He moved with his family to a West Side ghetto in Chicago.[3]

The aims of the largely southern civil rights campaign were to end racist brutality, to abolish Jim Crow ordinances, to secure freedom of association, and to establish an effective right to vote. The Voting Rights Act brought to a close the struggle for minimally "decent" treatment for blacks. The new phase aimed to realize substantive equality. We must, King argued, move beyond ending humiliation to ending poverty, prohibiting labor exploitation, and creating greater economic fairness.[4] The two phases, in King's conception, are part of one long struggle, because racial injustice and economic injustice are "inseparable twins."[5]

This second phase, however, would be even more challenging than the first. Abolishing Jim Crow cost affluent whites little. It mainly involved desegregating public spaces and allowing blacks to vote and to be elected to public office. It was costly to working-class whites, for now they had to compete with blacks for jobs and promotions on fairer terms. But fully realizing economic justice *would* cost more-advantaged whites. Thus, many white citizens, from all social classes, are inclined to resist it.[6] Abolishing poverty, ending involuntary unemployment, building affordable housing, providing quality education for all, and controlling crime would require money, probably a lot of it, and so would be harder to achieve than desegregation.[7] King was right about the difficult road that lay ahead, for here we sit, more than fifty years later, without these goals accomplished.

This chapter considers King's account of the injustices ghettos represent and his proposals for how to rectify them. In particular, I highlight the strengths and the limits of King's conception of economic justice. To do so I explain how he understood the problems of the ghetto and outline the activism and policies he believed were necessary to remedy these problems. I then delve into the political morality, the specific ethical principles, that he took to justify his practical prescriptions. Next, I take up how King compared his vision of economic justice with two competing political ideologies—capitalism (classical liberalism) and communism (Marxism). Going beyond King's well-known commitment to ending poverty, I aim to better understand what kind of "egalitarian" or "radical" he was and to determine the degree to which he was committed to socialist principles. I close by considering the relevance of his theory for understanding and combating contemporary ghetto poverty.

Social Problems of the Ghetto

Because of the enormous influence of Daniel Patrick Moynihan's *The Negro Family: The Case for National Action* (often referred to simply as "the Moynihan Report"), most post–civil rights discussions of ghettos take up questions of black family life, if only to reject the infamous report's conclusions. Like Moynihan, King offered a historically informed account of what he regarded as the "disintegration" and "disorganization" of black families in ghettos.[8] He emphasized the destructive role of slavery, noting that black families might have been able to repair themselves if newly freed persons had not been "thrown off the plantations, penniless, homeless, still largely in the territory of their enemies and in the grip of fear, bewilderment and aimlessness."[9] After the Civil War, most blacks toiled away in poverty for generations. Those who migrated north were contained in ghettos, which increased the challenge of adjusting to city life and industrialization.

Women have dominated black families in ghettos, King conceded, because they have had more ready access to education and employment than black men. Black women's employment was largely restricted to domestic service, however, so their wages remained low. Lack of marketable skills and racial discrimination kept blacks, men and women, out of the higher-paying jobs and prevented some from gaining employment altogether. Demoralized, many black fathers suffered low self-esteem, undermined their children's ambition, and in frustration struck out violently against their wives and children. Such families are fragile and often dysfunctional. At the root of their difficulties is punishing poverty, lack of opportunity to develop marketable skills, and humiliating forms of economic exploitation.

Crime is a serious problem in ghetto neighborhoods.[10] While police harass and brutalize ghetto denizens, they make little effort to protect black residents from crime. Street crime is de facto permitted in ghetto areas (provided it doesn't threaten to spill over into white neighborhoods), and law-abiding residents live in fear of it. Because parents are forced to work so much (and often at night and at great distance from home), children are left playing unsupervised in the streets, where they are exposed to crime and vulnerable to the influence of unsavory characters.[11]

Housing in ghettos is inadequate—unhealthy, overcrowded, and dilapidated.[12] Yet rents are high for even these appalling accommodations, and housing discrimination restricts blacks' housing options. Real estate brokers and white residents will allow only a few token blacks (if any) to reside in white neighborhoods, where housing is more plentiful and of higher quality. When blacks do overcome barriers to entry, whites flee these neighborhoods.[13] Therefore blacks, with only a few exceptions, are forced to live in deeply disadvantaged and segregated neighborhoods—that is, ghettos.

King argued that ghetto social problems are rooted in economic disadvantage, particularly in unemployment, low wages, and restriction to menial labor.[14] The resulting poverty and economic insecurity undermine healthy family life and make it difficult to escape from decaying and dirty housing. Some of these economic disadvantages are caused by ongoing racial injustices (for example, racial discrimination in employment, schooling, and housing). Some are caused by past racial injustices (generations of black bondage under chattel slavery and subjugation under Jim Crow). But there are general economic disadvantages that harm people of all races, though blacks are hurt disproportionately. For instance, some unemployment and underemployment is due to automation and plant re-location.[15] Automation increases productivity but, in the absence of government action, creates massive unemployment, as employers seek to lower labor costs to raise their profits.[16] Only a full-employment economy (with the creation of public sector jobs if necessary) can offset the damage done to low-skilled workers through automation.[17]

Riots and Economic Injustice

For King, the Watts riot and similar urban uprisings were not just a challenge to his philosophy of nonviolent resistance. Riots signify economic injustice, and they serve as a lens for understanding the problems of the ghetto. As he tells us, "The explosion in Watts reminded us all that the northern ghettos are the prisons of forgotten men."[18] Ghettos are combustible—there, as he says, "rage replaces reason"—because their inhabitants have suffered many abuses over a long period yet their voices of protest are disregarded.[19] The rioters would rather strike out, even in potentially self-destructive ways, than continue to be ignored.

In *The Trumpet of Conscience* (1968), King identified five factors that explained ghetto riots: a "white backlash" that took the form of resistance to racial equality and hostility toward blacks who demand justice; discrimination across several social domains (housing, education, employment); high unemployment, especially among black youth; blacks' disproportionate conscription into an unjust war in Vietnam; and inadequate public services in black neighborhoods.[20] But it is clear he thought unfair obstacles to acquiring well-paying jobs were the most important factor. As paths to economic mobility are closed off, cynicism inevitably sets in. This should not surprise us, because hope cannot be sustained without visible signs of economic progress.[21] Riots (like other ghetto problems) are primarily caused, King insisted, by unemployment, underemployment, relegation to menial jobs, and employment discrimination. The ubiquitous harassment and disrespect by police officers makes blacks' sense of economic insecurity more acute. Hope turns to despair; festering resentment turns to rage.[22]

King was convinced that ghetto denizens understood the source of their plight. This is evident in the fact that the damage done by black rioters was overwhelmingly done to property. There was little violence aimed at physically harming white people, King insisted.[23] (The deaths and injuries that did occur were mainly due to aggressive military and police action in suppressing the riots.)[24] Looting and the destruction of property are, he claimed, forms of protest directed at symbols of wealth and objects of need.[25] Riots communicate a message: outrage over economic injustice.[26]

King, however, sharply criticized political violence and morally opposed rioting as a mode of resistance. Nor did he think it would be an effective strategy: "As I have walked among the desperate, rejected and angry young men I have told them that Molotov cocktails and rifles would not solve their problems."[27] This steadfast opposition to rioting is sometimes obscured when commentators invoke King's memorable phrase "the riot is the language of the unheard."[28]

Yet King did not think that when blacks riot in America's ghettos, the rioters alone deserve blame. He believed whites share responsibility for these explosions of black rage. The white majority doesn't hold government accountable for changing the conditions in disadvantaged black communities but instead directs all its resentment and hostility toward black ghetto dwellers. In fact, the crimes of white society, King argued, are even greater than the lawbreaking of ghetto denizens. Welfare laws, rights to due process, building code regulations, employment laws, and entitlement to educational opportunity are all violated when it comes to blacks. It is *this* long-standing and pervasive lawlessness, perpetrated by the broader public, that has created and perpetuates ghettos: "The slums are the handiwork of a vicious system of the white society; Negroes live in them, but they do not make them, any more than a prisoner makes a prison."[29] Ultimately, only social justice will quell the threat of riots.[30]

The task, then, is to abolish the ghetto. This is the next step in the black freedom struggle, and it will require, King maintained, an "economic reconstruction."[31] It necessitates "radical changes in the structure of our society."[32] The question is what practical measures—from policy to activism—must be undertaken to effect these changes. Let's consider King's proposals.

Practical Remedies

Ghettos won't disappear unless aggressive actions are taken to address racial inequality and discrimination.[33] Effective antidiscrimination measures are needed to deal with ongoing racial injustices. King also suggested that compensatory measures were required to "atone" for past injustices and to remove inherited obstacles to equal opportunity.[34] Blacks can't compete on fair terms in a market society unless these handicaps are repaired or offset: "It is obvious that if a man is entered at the starting line in a race three hundred years after another man, the first would have to perform some impossible feat in order to catch up with his fellow runner."[35] More-over, blacks can't escape poverty in the same way white European immi-grants did in earlier periods, because there are too few decent jobs for those with low skills and educational disadvantages.[36]

However, the unemployment problem at the heart of the ghetto can't be solved by race-conscious policies alone. What's needed is a full-employment economy that makes a place for those with few skills and little education but without exploiting these vulnerable workers or rele-gating them to only menial jobs. Indeed, the historic March on Washington (August 28, 1963) was a demand for freedom *and* jobs, for the equal pro-tection of basic liberties *and* economic justice. The principal organizers of the March were Bayard Rustin (a close adviser to King) and A. Philip Randolph, both leftwing organizers and labor movement activists. At the March, in his justly famous "I Have a Dream" speech, King not only con-demned racism and discrimination but also remarked, "The Negro lives on a lonely island of poverty in the midst of a vast ocean of material pros-perity."[37] And in light of this, he says, "we cannot be satisfied as long as the Negro's basic mobility is from a smaller ghetto to a larger one."[38]

In *Where Do We Go from Here* (1967), King made several concrete policy proposals for creating a full-employment economy that includes the ghetto poor.[39] He believed government should subsidize (or lower the tax rate for) private companies that hire and train workers with limited edu-cation. There should also be an expansion in public sector jobs in human services for disadvantaged communities, and these jobs should be reserved for workers who lack a college degree. Colleges should be open to, and develop a curriculum for, those who in the past have not been successful in school but want to try their hand at it again. And there must be special employment opportunities for the hardcore jobless—those who have dropped out the labor market altogether and have subsequently lost the necessary work habits—where employers are tolerant and patient while their employees cultivate the relevant discipline.

King lamented the lack of a minimum wage that guarantees a decent standard of living, where "decent" means something like material well-being consistent with dignity.[40] Thus, he argued for a guaranteed annual wage and an adequate hourly minimum wage.[41] What King had in mind is that the minimum wage should be set so a full-time worker would have yearly earnings above an appropriate poverty line. He also insisted that all who are "willing to work" should be guaranteed employment, in the public sector if necessary.[42] When employment cannot be secured for everyone who wants it, a decent income should be guaranteed to the unemployed and underemployed.[43]

In some of his later labor speeches and writings, King advocated moving away from antipoverty initiatives that focus exclusively on finding poor people jobs to ones that attack poverty by directly providing necessary income.[44] He asserted that, just as each citizen has a constitutional right to vote, each should be constitutionally entitled to adequate housing, a quality education, and the income necessary to acquire basic necessities.[45] King's militant antipoverty stance led him to advocate a "Bill of Rights for the Disadvantaged" and to denounce the inadequate funding for the War on Poverty.[46]

Even more radically, he asserted that guaranteed income should be aimed at reducing economic inequality and not just at eliminating absolute poverty.[47] Here he suggested guaranteed basic income should be some percentage of median income, not set solely to meet basic physical needs. The guaranteed income must "automatically increase as the total social income grows."[48] Otherwise, those who receive it would suffer a relative decline over time. This position suggests King's concern went beyond securing basic necessities for all—an instance of his staunch commitment to abolishing poverty. He was also concerned with everyone's *relative* standing in society, with substantive equality. In other words, his proposal would appear to rest on a moral objection to certain forms of inequality. But this, I confess, isn't entirely clear, because he described his worry as about "nullifying the gains of [economic] security and stability," which need not be about relative social position.[49]

To reduce racial discrimination in employment, King called not only for more marches and demonstrations, but also for organized and sustained economic boycotts of businesses that served black customers but didn't hire or promote blacks in significant numbers.[50] This "Operation Breadbasket" (a form of nonviolent direct action initially launched in Atlanta but later expanded, under the leadership of Jesse Jackson, to Chicago) could work in ghetto communities to effect a more just distribution of non-menial jobs and to increase black employment.[51] King did not believe Operation Breadbasket was a form of extortion. Given the injustices blacks face, it was a permissible form of political dissent: "Basic to the philosophy of nonviolence is a refusal to cooperate with evil. There is nothing quite so effective as a refusal to cooperate economically with the forces and institutions which perpetuate evil in our communities."[52] He thought this same method could be used to improve housing conditions in ghettos. Black residents could establish tenant unions or organize rent strikes to pressure landlords to make repairs and to offer fair rents. In this way, the methods forged to fight segregation in the South could be deployed to fight economic subjugation in northern ghettos.

Unlike many Black Power advocates, who were generally skeptical of the mostly white labor movement, King called for a civil rights–labor alliance.[53] The problems of labor are also black problems, because the vast majority of blacks are ordinary workers. Even as early as *Stride toward Freedom* (1958), King realized "the poor white was exploited just as much as the Negro."[54] The black freedom struggle and the labor movement have, he claimed, essentially the same concerns.[55] Blacks must therefore join the labor movement and attempt to influence its demands. Together with workers of other races, blacks can create just economic conditions in America and elsewhere.

For this to be a fruitful alliance, though, the labor movement had to change.[56] It must steadfastly oppose racial discrimination in employment and union membership, which the movement had not consistently done. It must welcome blacks into the skilled trades, making training available to all seeking promotion to higher-skilled positions rather than reserving the most desirable roles for whites. The movement must fight for all workers, not just those who belong to unions or labor organizations.[57] Organized labor will be weak if millions are poor, as this will bring down wages and workplace standards. The existence of an economically insecure workforce is profitable for business, as it pushes down wages.[58] So the civil rights–labor alliance must fight for economic security for all.

Principles of Economic Justice

As is well known, King was a Christian minister. So many of his political views were rooted, in part, in his theological commitments, particularly in his reading of the gospel texts. But he was also a public philosopher who defended his political stances by relying on secular arguments and empirical evidence. He was fully aware that he had an audience (including many black radicals) who did not share his religious convictions. And his arguments were not designed to convert them (or bring them back) to the Christian faith. Rather, in the spirit of public deliberation in a pluralist democracy, he sought to persuade his political opponents using principles they could accept even if they had different religious beliefs or professed no religion at all. I believe his arguments have merit and import for the problems of the ghetto today. I contend that underlying King's practical recommendations are a set of moral principles that justify his proposed economic policies and social movement goals.

One of King's most basic principles, one he invoked frequently, is that: *No one should be forced to live in poverty while others live in luxury.*[59] This principle is open to an antipoverty and an egalitarian reading. King thought that knowingly allowing some to live in poverty when one has enormous wealth exhibits callous indifference to the suffering of others and thus is morally wrong. But he also regarded this social circumstance as a threat to the "dignity" of the poor and thus an injustice. Let me explain.

Indifference to human suffering is obviously wrong. We needn't rely on egalitarian principles of economic justice to condemn it. Yet this kind of indifference, when it prevails among advantaged members of a society, constitutes a moral indictment of that society.[60] Such poverty is unnecessary, given the resources and technology available, and so is a sign of barbarity—equivalent, King believed, to allowing cannibalism in an otherwise civilized society.[61] Given that economic impoverishment is gratuitous suffering, the refusal of the affluent to share their wealth with the poor is not just selfish but reflects insufficient concern for their fellow human beings. It demonstrates that some value profit and property more than they do persons, both indefensible priorities.[62] It is therefore a serious moral vice (not to mention un-Christian).[63] King took the same position with respect to the global poor. He insisted that we, as inhabitants of rich countries, have the resources and scientific knowledge to eliminate poverty wherever it exists, at least with respect to food, shelter, clothing, and basic medical care. Wealthy nations, King maintained, have a moral obligation to institute a Marshall Plan for Africa, Asia, and South America.[64]

Focusing explicitly on the ghetto poor in the United States, King emphasized that black ghetto residents feel humiliated to be living in such squalor while just blocks away others, mostly white, live in luxury and engage in conspicuous consumption.[65] Although whites lack intimate knowledge of ghetto impoverishment, black ghetto dwellers are fully aware of the opulence just beyond their reach, and this knowledge makes them miserable.[66]

This is an important observation and, if correct, explains a lot. But to be fully convincing, King needs to help us understand why these feelings of misery are rooted in reasonable resentment rather than irrational envy. It is not obvious why the poor's claim to have their impoverishment ameliorated is stronger because some have great wealth. If dire threats to physical health and mental well-being can be removed without great sacrifice, then surely such actions should be taken. Perhaps all King had in mind is that opulence is a visible sign the society has the *capacity* to reduce poverty yet does not take appropriate action to address the problem. But is there more to his principle than this?

I believe there is. King thought persons who are poor can't maintain their *dignity*, that is, their sense of intrinsic worth and equal civic standing, in the presence of great wealth. Allowing one's fellow citizens to languish in poverty communicates to the poor that they lack inherent equal worth and is therefore an insult. In what is supposed to be a society of equals— where each has the same moral standing and no one has natural authority over anyone else—it is a public expression of contempt to act in a way that suggests others' urgent needs have less moral weight than one's own access to extravagant objects of desire. The poor naturally, and appropriately, see such attitudes as an attack on their status as equal citizens.

Moreover, workers cannot sustain self-esteem and morale if their market position suggests their abilities are practically worthless to others in society. Poverty stigmatizes the jobless in a society that measures worth in terms of how much money each has or can earn. Dignity can be restored or maintained only if each is widely recognized as entitled to either a job or basic income. A sense of equal standing will be secure for everyone only when no one's basic worth is measured in terms of their labor-market competitiveness. A widely recognized right to basic income establishes these conditions, for it publicly conveys that everyone is entitled to live a decent life even if the market won't reward their conscientious efforts with a living wage.[67]

King also relied on a second principle that: *Individuals should be equipped with adequate material means so they can take full advantage of their formal freedoms.* While mere formal liberties provide *some* protection from threats to dignity, they are of limited value to those who possess them if these persons are poor.[68] The same holds true of formal opportunities. Even with discriminatory barriers removed, one can't move to an integrated neighborhood without the money for rent or mortgage payments. Real freedom and opportunity must be accompanied by sufficient means to take advantage of them: "Negroes must not only have the right to go into any establishment open to the public, but they must also be absorbed into our economic system in such a manner that they can afford to exercise that right."[69]

This principle rests on a distinction King made between an *abstract* right and a *concrete* right. Mere legal recognition of equal citizenship, even when adequately enforced, is not sufficient for social justice (concrete emancipation), for it does not, taken alone, enable each to enjoy the privileges of equal citizenship. Abstract rights, though codified in law, still allow second-class citizenship. This all strikes me as correct. But King could have made more of the fact that the value of the rights of some is substantially greater because they have considerably more resources than others, which enables them to exercise these rights more effectively and across more social domains. To emphasize this *inequity,* a kind of civic unfairness, would be to connect equality—as a democratic value—with liberty and opportunity.

King comes closer to explicitly egalitarian concerns when discussing employment compensation. However, the principle he invokes is vague: *The fruits of labor should be shared equitably, with labor and capital on equal footing.*[70] The exact content and scope of this principle isn't specified. Nor is it clear what it means in practice. Without an account of what grounds property rights and the relative moral weight of such rights (which so far as I'm aware King did not provide), we don't have a usable standard for deciding what constitutes a fair wage or profit margin. We do know, relying on King's first two principles, that full-time workers should not be paid poverty-level wages. "Labor needs a wage-hour bill which puts a firm floor under wage scales."[71] But this is compatible with capital taking the lion's share of the benefits of economic cooperation, so it doesn't help us understand what the call for "equity" comes to. Indeed, as discussed earlier, King believed everyone was entitled to basic necessities whether or not they are employed or own capital.

Recall that King emphasized the importance of building and strengthening labor organizations. So one might conclude that fair employment compensation is whatever union representatives and management agree to when labor's right to organize is concrete and not merely abstract. Perhaps when capital exploits labor this amounts to taking advantage of workers' weak bargaining position and blocking their attempts to strengthen it. Yet King makes it clear that the power of labor organizations is needed because the owners of capital operate, not from goodwill or reciprocity, but solely from the motive of private economic gain.[72] He laments this single-minded focus on accruing profit. Increasing the bargaining power of unions is merely a concession to this political reality, an effective means to acquire equitable compensation for workers, given that capitalists are inclined to withhold it. So he must have thought there is some independent standard for workplace distributive justice. But it isn't evident what he took that standard to be.

We gain some insight into King's overall conception of distributive justice by considering a final principle: *Productivity gains should benefit all, not just the owners of capital.*[73] As things now stand, capitalism, given how it spurs technological innovation, creates unemployment and underemployment. Joblessness is often interpreted as laziness or lack of ability, when in fact it is a byproduct of our economic system and our increasing reliance on machines in production. The market demand for efficiency and low labor costs pushes many into joblessness or insecure employment and thus poverty.[74] The purchasing power of the average worker has not kept pace with gains in productivity. It is this situation that justifies organizing labor, so workers can bargain for a greater share of the benefits of economic cooperation. It justifies guaranteed basic income for those whose labor has become less useful as labor-saving technology has evolved. It also justifies creating public sector jobs when private sector employment is insufficient to meet the demand for opportunities to make a positive contribution to society. Finally, it justifies dramatically expanding leisure time for working people, as technology reduces the need for burdensome and unrewarding labor.[75]

King argued that while technology is the product of human labor, imagination, and ingenuity—and as such something we all can be proud of—within a capitalist economy it can be a tyrannical and frightening force in the lives of everyday working people. It must therefore be subordinated to democratic will and used to promote human welfare, not utilized solely for profit or war.[76] We should of course seek scientific discoveries, but the resulting technology must be tamed by moral principle and concern for the most vulnerable.

Beyond Communism and Capitalism

To the disappointment of his revolutionary black nationalist and leftwing critics, King never advocated the overthrow of liberal-capitalist regimes. He was still, I maintain, a radical when it comes to economic justice. To achieve economic justice, King believed, there must be a "revolution of values."[77] And this revolution must ultimately transcend the values of both capitalism and communism. "The good and just society is neither the thesis of capitalism nor the antithesis of Communism, but a socially conscious democracy which reconciles the truths of individualism and collectivism."[78]

King's opposition to communism is consistent throughout his writings. He insisted that communism is "antithetical" to Christianity and the faith's most "formidable rival."[79] King rejected historical materialism (Marx's theory of historical change) on the grounds that it denies the efficacy of moral thought and action in radical social change. The Marxist commitment to metaphysical materialism leaves no room for spirituality.[80] Historical materialism makes no place for God, whom King believed to be the sustainer of life and the foundation of value. Materialist philosophy treats religion as ideological delusion rooted in fear and ignorance. It treats humans as self-sufficient, when in fact they need God.[81] The Marxist conception of human beings and history made it impossible for King, as a Christian, to embrace its philosophy.

Yet King had secular objections to communism as well. For instance, he regarded Marxists as moral relativists.[82] Communism denies there are universal and absolute moral principles. King (like many secular philosophers) didn't accept moral relativism but instead regarded justice and peace as fundamental and transhistorical values of the highest importance. Communists also advocate revolutionary violence, or at least they hold that political violence is sometimes permissible, even outside the just-war context.[83] King rejected the idea that good ends can justify violence or deceit as means: "Means represent the-ideal-in-the-making and the-end-in-progress."[84]

Communists also oppose liberalism. They deny that liberty is a paramount value, treating individuals as mere instruments to revolutionary change. Communists value the state and the ideal of a classless society above the individual and above personal autonomy. Though communists believe the state will eventually become obsolete in the socialist utopia, in the meantime individuals are regarded as mere means to abolish capitalism with no claim to any liberties that might interfere with the success of the revolutionary project or slow progress toward a classless society. Regarding totalitarianism as an acceptable political expedient in revolutionary times, communists don't recognize basic political liberties as human rights.[85]

King maintained, with other liberal thinkers, that individuals have inherent and inalienable rights, including a claim to participate in collective self-governance as equals. Freedom, here understood as the capacity for rational deliberation and choice, is what makes us human and gives us dignity. Communists don't appreciate the moral significance of this fact about us. Echoing a principle familiar from Immanuel Kant, King insisted: "To deprive man of freedom is to relegate him to the status of a thing, rather than elevate him to the status of a person. Man must never be treated as a means to the end of the state, but always as an end within himself."[86]

Nonetheless, King praised Marx for being a champion of the poor, the exploited, and the dispossessed. He believed the communist movement was, notwithstanding its official pronouncements, ultimately rooted in an abiding concern for social justice and is itself a protest against injustice.[87] Communists oppose racism and seek to realize a classless society.[88] Despite the fundamental flaws in communism, King was adamantly against suppressing it through war.[89] We must defeat communism by ending the injustices it is a response to and is nourished by. Indeed, King insisted there is truth in its collectivist spirit. We should seek to unite its concern for community and the least advantaged with respect for individual rights and free enterprise.[90]

King criticized capitalism, maintaining that it created not only immense economic inequality but also "superfluous wealth" and degrading forms of poverty.[91] He condemned the fact that in America "one-tenth of 1 percent of the population controls almost 50 percent of the wealth."[92] The driving ethos of capitalism makes people indifferent to the suffering of others. Given market dynamics and the centrality of the profit motive, capitalism rewards a win-at-all-costs competitive spirit and narrowly self-interested ambition. It also encourages us to evaluate everything, including the worth of other people, in terms of commercial values.[93] But King seems to have thought capitalism could be reformed to avoid (most of) these consequences. "We can work within the framework of our democracy to make for a better distribution of wealth."[94]

Although King is a radical (particularly by today's standards) when it comes to economic justice, it would be misleading to describe him as a socialist.[95] Though he called for a fairer distribution of wealth, he didn't criticize private ownership of productive assets and natural resources as inherently unjust. Nor did he argue for the nationalization of finance or industry. He simply didn't think such private wealth should be concentrated in the hands of the few, which would give them inordinate and dangerous power over the lives of others.

King did invoke Psalm 24: "The earth is the Lord's and the fullness thereof."[96] But the point of doing so was to emphasize that we should use natural resources (and the technology constructed from these resources) in a way that would garner God's favor, which means not wasting them on the consumption of luxuries (at least not while poverty exists) and being compassionate and generous toward those in need. This would not, it seems, require public ownership of all natural resources, productive technology, and banks.

King called for higher wages and a regulated labor market to protect vulnerable workers. But he did not regard wage labor as inherently exploitative. Nor did he demand that all workers, irrespective of their skills, be paid the same hourly wage. Although in favor of greater workplace democracy and strong unions, King didn't call for nonprofit worker cooperatives either. To be sure, the profit motive, left unconstrained by considerations of justice and state regulation, is a corrupting influence. And valuing the accumulation of profit over securing the basic well-being of others, he maintained, is immoral. But King didn't condemn for-profit enterprises as such. Capitalist profit is legitimate, though, only if workers are not reduced to poverty and every family is guaranteed a "livable" income.[97] King is therefore best described as a liberal egalitarian or social democrat.[98] His vision embraced the best elements from capitalism and socialism. He favored a mixed economy—a combination of private and public ownership—within which wealth and income are equitably shared under democratic self-governance, labor rights are robust, and no one is forced to live without basic economic security.

King's Philosophy and Today's Ghettos

Deeply disadvantaged black neighborhoods are still with us. We have yet to abolish the ghetto as a sociospatial site of racial and economic injustice. Discrimination in employment and housing remain a problem. None of King's four principles of economic justice have been fully realized in the United States. There is still enormous poverty in the midst of great and visible opulence. Approximately 15 percent of Americans live below the federal poverty line, and more than a third of all black children. The black unemployment rate is roughly double the white unemployment rate (and has been for decades), and the jobless rate among the ghetto poor is even higher. The federal minimum wage does not ensure that a full-time worker can raise a family outside of poverty, particularly those workers living in northern metropolitan regions where the cost of living is high, which is where many among the ghetto poor reside. Labor organizations wield limited power because unionization rates are low and "Right to Work" laws make it harder for workers to bargain for fair compensation. Even though technological innovation and productive efficiency have soared since King's death, the real wages of the average worker have remained flat. Federal spending on the military remains high. And it would be an understatement to say that we have not transcended traditional bourgeois values.

The War on Poverty yielded to an attack on welfare as an entitlement. The Personal Responsibility and Work Opportunity Reconciliation Act (1996) abolished unconditional, means-tested income support for poor families. There are now five-year lifetime limits on receiving federal welfare support (though some states grant extensions), and this support is conditional on recipients meeting work requirements. Notwithstanding this contraction of the welfare state, there is no entitlement to a public sector job for hard-to-employ workers. Under these conditions, dignity is threatened and equal citizenship is, for many, an abstract right at best. The abolition of the ghetto remains a distant dream, more than fifty years after the Watts riot.

Though many of King's insights are still relevant today, some must be revised or extended to take account of developments since his death. Three such developments stand out and are far reaching: (1) shifts in the class structure of black America, (2) the dramatic increase in black single-mother families, and (3) changes in the criminal justice system.[99]

In King's day, the black professional class was tiny, and most middle-class blacks lived in the same communities as working-class and poor blacks. Since his assassination (and partly in response to it and the riots it led to), opportunities in higher education have increased (in part a result of affirmative action policies). Now there is a large and visible black professional class whose members occupy positions throughout the economy and government. These well-educated blacks earn high incomes and many have moved out of traditional black communities, leaving a greater concentration of poverty in their wake. Although some affluent blacks remain committed to the principles of economic justice King espoused, the economic interests of the black elite are not aligned with (and, in some ways, may be opposed to) those of the ghetto poor. Black solidarity is much more fragile and a civil rights–labor alliance more difficult to cultivate and maintain. A social movement to abolish the ghetto would probably look quite different, in terms of the demographics of its principal constituents, from the one King envisaged. For instance, it would likely have to include many Latinos and disadvantaged undocumented workers, and black elites would probably have to play a smaller leadership role.

Since the Moynihan Report, single motherhood has risen among all racial groups but is particularly high among blacks. King, like Moynihan, saw black single-mother families as dysfunctional, brought about through the economic marginalization of black men. He did not address questions of gender inequality with the same sophistication that he tackled racial and economic inequality, and he largely viewed the situation of black women and children through a patriarchal lens. He had not absorbed the insights of black feminists.[100]

I don't think single motherhood is inherently dysfunctional. Single-mother families are fragile largely because of weak labor protections, the standard length of a workday, and limited public support for those who give birth to or rear children. Women with children have little workplace power and so are rarely able to ensure that they can properly raise a family while remaining in good standing on their jobs. Because the typical working day for a full-time employee in America is long, it is difficult for a working mother to be available to supervise and care for her children when they are not at school. Because childcare isn't generally viewed as a valuable contribution to society (for example, raising the next generation of citizens and workers), the demanding work it involves isn't properly rewarded or recognized. Thus, women who want to be mothers but perhaps do not yet (if ever) want to be married are often economically disadvantaged and have difficulty maintaining a well-functioning household (unless they receive considerable support from extended family and friends). This is the situation of many women in ghettos. Rather than push such women into greater dependence on men, liberal-egalitarian policy could reduce the length of the standard workday, increase financial support for parents of young children, and offer publicly funded childcare services. When we consider the inescapable web of mutuality King emphasized, that "single garment of destiny" as he called it, we must take care not to neglect or subordinate matters of gender inequality.[101]

The War on Drugs, mandatory sentencing laws, and aggressive policing and prosecution (among other factors) have led to the mass incarceration of black people, particularly poor black people. The incarceration of a family member makes already disadvantaged black families even more economically insecure. There is not only the possible loss of income during the period of imprisonment. After release from prison, a former felon will find it even more difficult to find work in the licit economy, for it is not illegal to discriminate against those with criminal records. The measures King recommends to reduce unemployment and to guarantee income for those who can't find decent work would have to be extended to those with felony convictions. The black freedom movement would also have to include reforming the criminal justice system. For without dramatic changes in that domain, ghettos will persist.

In this chapter, I have recounted King's diagnosis of the ills of ghettos and his proposed remedies. I have offered a reconstruction of the political philosophy I believe undergirds his vision for the second phase of the black freedom struggle. This phase, still far from over, focuses on questions of economic justice, which he regarded as the root of the problems of the ghetto. Although King does not have all the answers, we can learn from his approach to ghetto poverty, and we can build on it to address the persistence of ghettos in the post–civil rights era. His political thought, I would insist, should be regarded as a *living* legacy.[102]

10

Gender Trouble: Manhood, Inclusion, and Justice

SHATEMA THREADCRAFT AND BRANDON M. TERRY

Feminist approaches to the interpretation and assessment of Martin Luther King, Jr.'s political philosophy have primarily been characterized by two stances: *qualified acceptance* and *respectful rejection*. The first, *qualified acceptance,* combines a trenchant critique of King's sexism with an attempt to extract and salvage other features of his work for feminist thought and praxis. In one sense, this tradition follows that of black women activists who were contemporaries of King and worked alongside him, despite their criticisms. Septima Clark, the heroic educator and organizer of the Citizenship School movement, for example, criticized the sexist leadership of King's Southern Christian Leadership Conference (SCLC), where she served on the board. Recalling meetings where women were routinely prevented from placing items on the agenda, or openly mocked, Clark lamented, "Those men didn't have any faith in women, none whatsoever. They just thought that women were sex symbols and had no contribution to make."[1] Despite her "great feeling that Dr. King didn't think much of women," Clark still "adored" King and "supported him in every way [she] could," although she thought that SCLC should do more to promote local leaders and rely less on King. Nonetheless, she insisted that King's political philosophy and the example of "his courage, his service to others, and his non-violence" remained worthy of devotion.[2] Further, Clark appears to suggest that the *internal* logic of King's thought and praxis would have soon led him toward a more consistent egalitarianism in line with the demands of gender justice.[3]

Among contemporary critics, bell hooks similarly indicts Martin Luther King and other civil rights leaders of the 1950s and 1960s for "following the example of white male patriarchs" and being "obsessively concerned with asserting their masculinity."[4] The misguided way that movement leaders and intellectuals entangled "integration" and "equality," she argues, encouraged an imitative ethos that, in positing white elites as the norm, intensified black support for patriarchy and diminished the political standing and participatory parity of black women.[5] Nevertheless, hooks insists on the profound philosophical import of King's core ideals of the "beloved community" and an ethos of love that informs contentious politics.[6] In a world ravaged by systemic oppression and brimming with value pluralism, hooks sees these ideals—and King's theorization of them—as performing a crucial role in theorizing justice, sustaining the commitment to resolve conflict, and inspiring the practical faith in transformation necessary to sustain and expand human sympathy and solidarity.[7]

In a recent interview with hooks, the philosopher George Yancy asks her, "What should we do in our daily lives to combat, in that phrase of yours, the power and influence of white supremacist capitalist patriarchy?" hooks's answer is illustrative of how for her, King—once disentangled from his sexism—remains arguably *the* central touchstone of political and moral judgment: "Rather than saying, 'What would Jesus do?' I always think, 'What does Martin Luther King want me to do today?' Then I decide what Martin Luther King wants me to do today is to go out into the world and in every way that I can, small and large, build a beloved community."[8] This tradition, while inspiring in its commitment to endorsing substantive ethical ideals, tackling difficult ethical questions that emerge from political struggle, and treating King's thought with charity and sympathy, nevertheless confronts a fatal problem. This approach tends to treat the ideas to be recovered as easily disentangled from sexism and androcentrism without adequately *self-reflexive* inquiry.

As Thomas McCarthy has persuasively argued, "general norms are always understood and justified with an eye to some range of standard situations and typical cases assumed to be appropriate, and that if that range shifts, then so too do the understandings and justifications of those norms, the conceptual interconnections and warranting reasons considered relevant to them."[9] In other words, the imagined subjects, scenarios, and societies that circulate through King's thought may not be so easily accommodating of women, and certainly cannot be *presumed* to be when these background presuppositions remain buried and unthematized. Indeed, when confronted with Susan Moller Okin's enduring and effective query of whether his thought "can sustain the inclusion of women in its subject matter, and if not, why not," a range of serious dilemmas emerge.[10] In particular, the *qualified acceptance* approach tends to fail to adequately consider the conceptual and political implications of King's recalcitrantly gendered division of labor, his close association of masculinity with productive labor, and his beliefs regarding the importance of normative family structures for moral-psychological development (including the capacity for love) and social stability.

The *respectful rejection* approach, by contrast, encourages us tacitly and explicitly to turn away from King as a source of political-philosophical wisdom and from his exemplarity as a touchstone for political judgment. These feminists are part of a broader, although not solely feminist, effort to recover, reconstruct, and duly champion the work of "local people" and previously unsung women and queer people of color within the civil rights movement.[11] A distinguishing feature of the feminist strand of this historiography and criticism is that the turn away from King is not simply explanatory or descriptive, but *normative*. Woven throughout their historical narratives and explicit political arguments is a critique of King's thought and praxis for its acquiescence to the gender hierarchies and norms from both a socially conservative black religious tradition and the mores of the broader middle-brow public. Superadded to this is a criticism of hierarchical and antidemocratic modes of political action, and charismatic leadership. These criticisms, while leavened with genuine respect for King's enormous personal sacrifices, are deemed fatal to his project and grounds for its disavowal.

Perhaps the leading exemplar of this approach is Barbara Ransby's brilliant biography of the life and work of Ella J. Baker. Baker, a legendary grassroots organizer, played a crucial role in the world-making political successes of the three most important black-led civil rights groups of the twentieth century, the National Association for the Advancement of Colored People (NAACP), the Student Nonviolent Coordinating Committee (SNCC), and SCLC.[12] Ransby recovers Baker in large part to champion her as an exemplar and proponent of a pro-feminist, nonhierarchical, and radically democratic form of political struggle, and to criticize, by comparison, a conception of politics she attributes to King.[13]

Building upon Baker's own critique and diagnosis of King and SCLC, Ransby argues that the organization's sexism was, in large part, influenced by patriarchal attitudes prevalent within a larger black church culture. "The role of women in the southern church," Baker argued, "was that of doing the things that the minister said he wanted to have done ... not one in which [women] were credited with having creativity and initiative and capacity to carry out things."[14] These attitudes, as Ransby points out, played a role in otherwise inexplicable decisions such as refusing to invite "Rosa Parks nor Joanne Gibson Robinson nor any of the women who had sacrificed so much to ensure the Montgomery boycott's success . . . to play a leadership role" in SCLC, or even allow them to speak at events like the 1963 March on Washington for Jobs and Freedom.[15]

Ransby quotes from King's 1954 memo of recommendations to his Dexter Avenue Baptist Church congregation—"Leadership never ascends from the pew to the pulpit, but . . . descends from the pulpit to the pew"— to underscore this critique, but the memo's broader context is perhaps more damning. King goes on to state that, at least within the church: "The pastor is to be respected and accepted as the central figure around which the policies and programs of the church revolve. He must never be considered a mere puppet for the whimsical and capricious mistreatment of those who wish to show their independence, and 'use their liberty for a cloak of maliciousness.' It is therefore indispensable to the progress of the church that the official board and membership cooperate fully with the leadership of the pastor."[16] This dictate suggests an implicit hermeneutics of suspicion that interprets criticism, disagreement, and even independent initiative within the church as rooted in objectionable vices and as incommensurate with collective "progress."[17] Wherever such a stance rises to absolute authority within a social movement with egalitarian and democratic aims, ethical abuses are sure to arise.

Crucial to the respectful rejection analysis, however, is the contention that the depth of sexism in SCLC was intimately tied, not just to the culture of black southern religion, but to an antidemocratic and authoritarian mode of political organization based on charismatic leadership. Baker, for instance, vehemently disagreed with SCLC's incessant promotion of King's celebrity, and what she saw as an overreliance on charisma and spectacular events for organizing. Erica Edwards, self-consciously building upon Baker, explains that charisma "names a phenomenon, a dynamic structure, a figural process of authoring and authorizing," that mixes "sacred and secular narrative impulses" to "situate authority or the right to rule, in one exceptional figure perceived to be gifted with a privileged connection to the divine." This phenomenon, moreover, is always dependent upon what she calls a charismatic scenario and aesthetic.[18]

In other words, the attribution and apprehension of "charisma" to someone like King relies upon certain public narratives, rituals, symbols, affective states, and bodily performances.[19] The edifice of African American political charisma, Edwards argues, entails constitutive forms of violence—the silencing of local people and mass action, antidemocratic and repressive forms of authority, and the reinforcement of patriarchal hierarchies and sexual norms by equating charisma with normative masculinity. In the name of democracy and equality, Baker wanted to tear down much of this scaffolding, depriving traditional forms of charisma of their stage, and divesting them of their political authority and aesthetic force.

"Instead of the leader as a person who was supposed to be a magic man," Baker argued, "you could develop individuals who were bound together by a concept that benefited the larger number of individuals and provided an opportunity for them to grow into being responsible for carrying out a program."[20] Behind this vision lay a set of expansive commitments to democracy as a broad ethical ideal and a set of egalitarian sociopolitical habits and practices.[21] This conception of democracy aims to attain respect for the dignity and self-interpretation of everyday people, empower citizens to defend themselves from the arbitrary domination and hegemony of elites, and facilitate the cultivation of both individual human excellence and cooperative social goods.

This conception of democracy has evaluative standards that apply both to the broader social order *and* within insurgent social movements. "Anytime you continue to carry on the same kind of organization that you say you are fighting against," Baker argued, "you can't prove to me that you have made any change in your thinking."[22] Black political organizing, on Baker and Ransby's account, should focus on local groups of citizens, helping them articulate their own needs and demands, building their capacity to democratically achieve their ends against elite resistance *over time,* and creating forums for political speech and action that are antihierarchical, inclusive, and consensus-oriented.[23] These efforts, they argue, are incompatible with King-inspired visions of charismatic and messianic leadership, which are criticized for disparaging local knowledge, short-circuiting deliberative discussions, and, ironically, intensifying everyday folks' sense of their own inadequacy by generating messiah and inferiority complexes. Worse yet, with charismatic authority, political initiatives are subject to the caprice and veto power of one individual, whose authority, in turn, is dependent upon the whims of media and culture industries for publicity and staging.[24]

While we both have been strongly influenced by the *respectful rejection* approach, it is important to acknowledge that it has faults as well. Though it readily acknowledges King's sacrifice, it leads far too easily to a broad dismissal of King's thought and to thin accounts of his praxis. Often it falls into this trap by allowing King's public image, a critique of a certain kind of claim to racial representation, and the staging of his charismatic authority, to overdetermine our judgments. To say nothing of other concerns with power and representation, King's judgments about how to run SCLC, for example, are inflated, as if they describe his judgments about how to run *any* social movement organization, when there is evidence (such as his refusal to try to exert power over SNCC, his donations of his own prize monies and SCLC funds to other organizations, his criticism of media elites for fixating on spokespersons and protest rather than community organizing) that his views are not dogmatic on these questions.[25] Even more importantly, this approach tends not to engage with, or take seriously, King's personal struggles and intellectual shifts regarding gendered questions of justice, politics and political economy—even though his work still falls short in many respects. Finally, work within this tradition tends to miss what the first approach gets right, and therefore loses an opportunity to retrieve crucial resources for a resurgent emancipatory politics, informed by King's political thought, and oriented toward gender justice. In light of the faults of both of these stances, a better approach, and one open to political theorists, is to "think with King against King."

In her influential reconstruction of Hannah Arendt's political thought, Seyla Benhabib enjoins political theorists to think "with Arendt against Arendt." By this challenge, she means to call not only for "a reinterpretation of Hannah Arendt's thought but a *revision* of it as well," one where we "leave behind the pieties of textual analyses and ask ourselves Arendtian questions and be ready to provide non-Arendtian answers."[26] Specifically, Benhabib is concerned to subvert Arendt's problematic sociology, reconstruct her ontological categories, and retrieve from her political theory "those gems that can still illuminate our struggles as contemporaries."[27]

It strikes us that this is a promising interpretive approach to take toward Martin Luther King's political philosophy as well. In thinking with King against King, especially where questions of gender, identity, and justice are concerned, one must similarly challenge King's sociological premises (such as his sociology of the family), reconstruct his social ontology (his ontology of gender, for instance), and rethematize his political-philosophical arguments (for basic minimum income and so on). We hope to show that, although difficult, this project allows us to constructively revise some of King's most incisive critical insights and his most persuasive (and radically egalitarian) political commitments. In particular, two themes are of indispensable significance: (1) King's deflationary critique of Black Power's masculinist politics and the egalitarian and inclusive dimensions of his defense of nonviolent, mass civil disobedience as a preferred mode of agonistic political action; and (2) his defense of a basic minimum income and anti-humiliation ethics in welfare politics as a crucial part of a theory of justice.

Real Men: Toward a Critique of Black Power and Black Protest Masculinity

Peter J. Ling takes an interesting approach to King's sexism and Ransby's implicit call to turn away from his work in favor of the work of others. Ling acknowledges the sexism and the role it played in King's dismissing the considerable expertise of seasoned activists like Baker, but he invites his readers to consider possible benefits of King's particular brand of masculinity. Ling goes so far as to suggest, *contra* many feminist critics, that King's need to prove and perform manhood and manliness within his philosophical commitments may have helped to advance the cause of civil rights in his most influential years. Ling argues that Baker (and Ransby by extension) "underestimated the value of the kind of formal leadership—a combination of prophetic ministry, media politics and summitry that Dr. King exerted between 1963 and 1965," and a "mode of masculinity [that] prompted him towards a program of dramatic protest that pushed civil rights to the top of America's legislative agenda."[28] This thesis deserves more scrutiny than it has received, especially given the respectful-rejection tradition's persuasive case for the costs of SCLC gender ideology. Here, however, we want to focus on where Ling's contention seems most promising—as a reading of King as a critic of, or comparative foil to, other modes of black protest masculinity that were on offer.

One of the most pressing challenges to King's political philosophy and praxis emerged from critics who mobilized a conception of dignity that competed with and dissented from King's ethical-political commitment to nonviolence. In *Stride toward Freedom*, King describes his speech at the mass meeting that inaugurated the boycott as seeking "to arouse the group to action by insisting that their self-respect was at stake and that if they accepted such injustices without protesting, they would betray their own sense of dignity and the eternal edicts of God Himself." Yet that evening, and throughout his career, King insisted that love and nonviolence should be the regulative ideals of such dignity-engendering protest. On his account, these ideals are not simply *compatible* or *commensurate* with carrying out the duty to defend one's dignity by refusing to acquiesce without protest to injustice, but instead constitute "the *only* morally and practically sound method open to oppressed people in their struggle for freedom."[29]

For a prominent group of militant black intellectuals and activists, however, the refusal to embrace, or even countenance, violence was *itself* an undignified stance. For these thinkers, this judgment stemmed partly from King's politics running afoul of the presumed ethical demands of "manhood" in their embrace of "feminine" ideals like love, or eschewal of the presumed masculine domain of violence. That this is such a prominent feature of African American political thought should be no surprise, for as Wendy Brown has argued, "*politics* has historically borne an explicitly masculine identity" and "been bound up with protean yet persistent notions and practices of manhood" that subtly manifest themselves in the vocabularies and presuppositions of political thought.[30] Indeed, with regard to "manhood" discourse, one of the most distinctive features of African American political thought compared to other traditions might be how broadly "manhood" is figured as an aspirational *telos* of black political strivings, and how jarringly explicit and forthright much of the tradition has been about the significance of "manhood" as an organizing thematic of black politics.

Frederick Douglass, undoubtedly the most influential African American intellectual and activist of the nineteenth century, plays a crucial role in the preeminence of this frame. "Not only our equality as a race is denied," Douglass complains, "but we are even denied our rank as men; we are enslaved, oppressed, and even those most favorably disposed towards us, are so from motives more of pity than respect." This diagnosis leads Douglass to laud the "noble work" that awaits African Americans, describing black politics in his era as an attempt to "prove our equal *manhood* . . . [and] redeem an entire race from the obloquy and scorn of the world."[31] One especially influential argument within this tradition links dignity to its purported realization through manhood, and links manhood to the will *and* capacity to deploy defensive violence.

Douglass, again, is illustrative here. In perhaps the most famous vignette in African American literature, Douglass narrates his life-risking fistfight with an infamously brutal "slave-breaker," William Covey, as the moment that "revived a sense of [his] own manhood": "I was a changed being after that fight. I was *nothing* before; *I was a man* now . . . A man without force is without the essential dignity of humanity. Human nature is so constituted, that it cannot *honor* a helpless man, though it can *pity* him, and even this it cannot do long if signs of power do not arise."[32] Elsewhere Douglass extrapolates this contention to a broader, collective praxis of self-defense in resistance to fugitive slave catchers. Juxtaposing "submission" and violent resistance, he argues that submission can be justified only where it is recognized as virtuous and can have "some moral effect in restraining crime and shaming aggression." Where this does not hold, a failure to risk life and take life will be "quoted against them, as marking them as an inferior race." In this context, Douglass declares, "every slave-hunter who meets a bloody death in his infernal business is an argument in favor of the manhood of our race."[33]

King's political career overlapped with the most dramatic resurgence and popular promotion of these arguments since the 1850s. Robert F. Williams, the militant proponent of organized self-defense and author of the manifesto *Negroes with Guns,* for example, argued in response to state-abetted racial terror, "We as men should stand up as men, and protect our women and children. I am a man and I will walk upright as a man should. I WILL NOT CRAWL."[34] The black nationalist icon Malcolm X, indicting King and others for falling short of this standard, declared, "We don't deserve to be recognized and respected as men as long as our women can be brutalized . . . and nothing being done about it, but we sit around singing 'We shall overcome.'"[35] On this account, a necessary element of the right to equal respect and recognition, as well as honorable manhood, becomes the capacity and will to achieve the patriarchal role of familial protector of women and children.[36] As is often the case in nationalist discourse, however, there is an easy slippage between family and nation, and this purported duty becomes inflated from a familial one to a racial one.[37] The argument amounts to the claim that racial stigma is reproduced, in part, through the humiliating "failure" of black men to live up to this charge in the face of ritual humiliations visited upon the race, thus refracting even the unique degradations suffered by black women through a "lack" of manhood.

In light of this history and the allure of contemporaneous black nationalist militancy, King did not have an easy time persuading African Americans that his politics of nonviolence and love had much to offer those looking for a route to "manhood." This was compounded by the fact that the gender composition of southern congregations skewed away from male adolescents and adults. King was the leader of a Baptist church, and his flock, like the flock across town in America's most segregated hour, was predominantly women and children. His authority over male adolescents, who would have been trying on manhood models at the time of his greatest influence, was tenuous. Moreover, as Ling argues, African American men were not particularly disposed to nonviolence's ritual asceticism and performances of self-denial. Instead, like most American men, they delighted in "the athleticism, financial success and physical power of Joe Louis and Jackie Robinson" and tended to confuse nonviolence with a "pacifism that seemed to require an 'unmanly' repudiation of the right to self-defense."[38] Black youth culture in our own day contains elements that reject King's idolization on these very grounds. Tupac Shakur, to take one illustrative example, raps in his "Words of Wisdom" (1991): "No Malcolm X in my history text, why's that?/'cause he tried to educate and liberate all blacks/Why is Martin Luther King in my book each week?/He told blacks if they get smacked, turn the other cheek."[39]

Thus, while King benefited from the resonance of the philosophy of nonviolence with Christian teachings to "turn the other cheek," he also confronted a long-standing black self-defense tradition that advocated the use of violence to protect family and community. Lance Hill, the leading historian of the civil rights era self-defense group The Deacons for Defense, self-consciously channels one of this tradition's central contentions: "Nonviolence required black men to passively endure humiliation and physical abuse—a bitter elixir for a group struggling to overcome the southern white stereotype of black men as servile and cowardly." Nonviolence, Hill continues, also "tested the limits of [black men's] forbearance," by demanding that they "forgo their right to defend family members who joined nonviolent protests."[40] Disturbed by these charges, and certainly aware of the cultural imprimatur of figures like Joe Louis and the countercultural allure of outlaw violence, King took considerable time contesting these challenges in ways that are worth evaluating in the present.[41] His *deflating* responses to the masculinist conflation of violent self-defense with manhood, and manhood with dignity, can be separated into two modes: (1) inversion and (2) dissociation.

Deflation as Inversion

King's writing reveals not only that he was under considerable pressure to demonstrate the "manliness" of nonviolence, but also that he often acquiesced to that pressure. However, it is important to acknowledge that King's concessions (or compulsions) toward inherited vocabularies and significations of manliness have, in some registers, a subversive quality—even if in other registers they reinforce objectionable forms of hierarchy.[42] King's subversion manifests itself both in his rhetorical inversions, associating masculinity with nonviolent praxis, and in his practical action, which entailed what Linda Zerilli has called a productive or creative moment of figuration, the "newly thinkable."[43]

King inverted militaristic language usually reserved for the instruments and organization of violence to redescribe nonviolence, repeatedly referring to his "nonviolent army" and to those "who enlisted in an army that marches under the banner of nonviolence."[44] Further, King tried to claim the mantle of "true" manhood from Malcolm X and defenders of violence by playing on the gendered distinctions between activity and passivity, subtly turning the tables on his antagonists who defended violence partly by availing themselves of this age-old association. Malcolm X, for example, when drawing his (in)famous distinction between the figures of the House Negro/Uncle Tom (representing the "feminine" spheres of domesticity and accommodation) and the Field Negro (representing the "masculine" domains of productivity and rebelliousness), went so far as to equate the nonviolent movement not only with the House Negro, but also with a passivity on par with anesthesia: "Just as the slavemaster of that day used Tom, the house Negro, to keep the field Negroes in check, the same old slavemaster today has Negroes who are nothing but modern Uncle Toms, twentieth-century Uncle Toms, to keep you and me in check, to keep us under control, keep us passive and peaceful and nonviolent. . . . It's like when you go to the dentist. . . . You're going to fight him when he starts pulling. So he squirts some stuff in your jaw called novocaine, to make you think they're not doing anything to you. So you sit there and because you've got all of that novocaine in your jaw, you suffer—peacefully."[45]

King sought to invert these associations, reframing militant bromides launched from the relative safety of northern ghettos as far more passive than the nonviolent movement's harrowing and deadly acts of protest, and again using military imagery to characterize the work of direct action:

> Many of these extremists misread the significance and the intent of nonviolence because they fail to perceive that militancy is also the father of the nonviolent army. Angry exhortation from street corners and stirring calls for the Negro to arm and go forth to do battle stimulate loud applause. But when the applause dies, the stirred and the stirring return to their homes and lie in their beds for still one more night with no progress in view. They cannot solve the problems they face because they have offered no challenge but only a call to arms, which they themselves are unwilling to lead, knowing that doom would be its reward. . . . The conservatives

who say, "Let us not move so fast," and the extremists who say, "Let us go out and whip the world," would tell you that they are as far apart as the poles. But there is a striking parallel: They accomplish nothing.[46]

It is important to note here that while King's efforts of inversion aspired to a kind of epistemic critique of what his fellow citizens thought they "knew" about masculinity, their most compelling quality is ultimately linked to the productive novelty of his *praxis*.[47] By actually *staging* and *performing* an enactment of manhood commensurate with nonviolence, King and his allies helped introduce and give ethical-aesthetic force to a divergent model of the dignity-manhood-violence relation. With the subjective certainty suggested by King's willingness to risk and ultimately lose his life to adhere to principle, this mode of action—when set alongside the inaction of nonviolent rhetoricians—helped clear the ground for partially dissociating violence and masculinity.

Deflation as Dissociation

King was acutely aware of the difficulty of what he was advocating, and of how it flew in the face not only of prevailing dispositions of African American manhood but of American manhood *writ large*—which he characterized as having accepted the "eye-for-an-eye philosophy" as its "highest measure." "We are a nation that worships the frontier tradition," King diagnosed, "and our heroes are those who champion justice through violent retaliation against injustice. It is not simple to adopt the credo that moral force has as much strength and virtue as the capacity to return a physical blow; or that to refrain from hitting back requires more will and bravery than the automatic reflexes of defense."[48] Undaunted by this broader cultural challenge, King tried to deflate its pretensions by dissociating these "lower" iterations of manhood from their claims to constitutive, higher-order virtue.

Locating part of the appeal of the rhetoric of violence in its relationship with an American "frontier tradition," King sought to disentangle it from this "heroic" veneer. Rightly linking this self-conception to the genocide of indigenous peoples, King reminds us that "our children are still taught to respect the violence which reduced a red-skinned people of an earlier culture into a few fragmented groups herded into impoverished reservations."[49] Not only does this disposition toward violence, King warns, contain the horrifying possibility of genocidal atrocities as its outer limit, but it also involves the further objectionable quality of being *imitative* of white supremacy. "One of the greatest paradoxes of the Black Power movement is that it talks unceasingly about not imitating the values of white society," King proclaims, "but in advocating violence it is imitating the worst, the most brutal and the most uncivilizing value of American life."[50]

Elsewhere King attempts to dissociate violence, manhood, and courage, arguing that the turn to violent conflict has its roots in *fear*. "We say that war is a consequence of hate," King admonishes, "but close scrutiny reveals this sequence: first fear, then hate, then war, and finally deeper hatred." The turn to stockpiling armaments is an attempt to "cast out fear," but ironically it tends only to produce "greater fear."[51] Underscoring the significance of fear in his political thought, King attempts to unmask the "aura of paramilitarism among the black militant groups" as speaking "more of fear than it does of confidence." Putting pressure on the link between fear, violence, and manhood, King objected that one's need for arms reveals a lingering *fear* of death, and that its function was essentially a phallic totem—"one's manhood must come from within him," King insisted, not from the barrel of the gun.[52]

More subtly, King pursued the work of dissociation through his introduction of a hierarchical account of the body where, in moments of crisis, a demonstration of proper manhood entailed control and mastering of one's emotions. Not only did nonviolent protest show a true willingness to put bodies on the line that was absent in militants who advocated violence but were "all talk," but King claimed for his mode of protest an even greater degree of "sophistication": a willingness to put "properly ordered" (Platonically ordered, even) bodies in control of animalistic emotions on the line for grand social ideals. This appeal to self-mastery, more expansive notions of protection, and the disciplining of disorderly affective states associated with unbridled masculinity (such as anger, hatred) and femininity (impulsivity), was narrated and defended, in part, as a higher-order vision of manhood. King's contrast here is evident: "It is always amusing to me when a Negro man says that he can't demonstrate with us because if someone hit him he would fight back. Here is a man whose children are being plagued by rats and roaches, whose wife is robbed daily at over-priced ghetto food stores, who himself is working for about two-thirds the pay of a white person doing a similar job . . . and in spite of all this daily suffering it takes someone spitting on him or calling him a nigger to make him want to fight. Conditions are such for Negroes in America that all Negroes ought to be fighting aggressively."[53]

King's usurpation of the mantle of the "real" fighter also takes aim at the broader cultural fascination and investment in pugilistic sport as the truest expression of manhood, and the iconography around black boxers. In an especially pernicious and politically circumscribed version of the charismatic leadership scenario theorized by Edwards, African Americans' excellence in sport often functioned through the culture industry as a cipher for black political hope, social strivings, and other, darker desires for revenge and counter-humiliation. King, in a bit of cultural psychoanalysis, recalled the story of a teenage black boy being put to death in a southern gas chamber in the 1930s. As he suffocated on poison gas, he offered a last prayer in his final minutes, repeating, "Save me, Joe Louis."

For King, this cry shows "the helplessness, the loneliness and the profound despair of Negroes in that period"—a "groping" in a barren terrain for "*someone* who might care for him, and [who] had power enough to rescue him." But whereas this hopeless boy put his last faith in "a Negro who was the world's most expert fighter," King argued that the civil rights movement helped blacks—of all genders, notably—discover their *own* fighting spirit, internally and in solidarity, replacing the "bizarre and naïve cry to Joe Louis" with "confidence" in their own nonviolent direct action. In the wake of this transformation, King reports that when the contemporaneous world heavyweight champion, Floyd Patterson, came to Birmingham—he came "not as a savoir," but to "give heart to the plain people who were engaged in another kind of bruising combat."[54]

Many Rivers to Cross: Inclusion and Agency

These appeals to constructs like "the plain people" or the "nonviolent army," particularly in the context of arguments about the paramilitary vanguard leadership of black men, contain egalitarian content that is worth teasing out and restating to draw out their power. These formulations, and King's accounts of nonviolent direct action elsewhere, suggest that courage, active resistance, an ethic of community protection, and dignity need not necessarily be gendered in exclusionary or hierarchical ways. That such a position is not inconsistent with the *core* of King's thought, suitably reconstructed, is born out in his argument that "a nonviolent army has a magnificent universal quality" and can transcend many of the exclusions that violence (or even politics, in some traditions) places on participation or standing: age, physical disability, and status or rank.[55]

The egalitarian dimension of King's description is best underscored via juxtaposition with Malcolm X's mockery of the aesthetic force of sit-in demonstrations *precisely* for their supposed lack of masculine virility. "It's not so good," Malcolm warns, "to refer to what you're going to do as a sit-in. That right there castrates you. . . . An old woman can sit. An old man can sit. A chump can sit, a coward can sit. . . . it's time for us today to start doing some standing and some fighting to back that up."[56]

The growing empirical literature on nonviolent resistance suggests that King's vision is not simply an ideal. As Erica Chenoweth and Maria Stephen argue, violent insurgency often requires demanding physical skills, facility with weapons, and isolation from family and society, whereas nonviolent resistance generally is more open to female or elderly populations.[57] While it must be admitted that "female operatives—such as female suicide bombers and guerillas—have sometimes been active in violent campaigns in Sri Lanka, Iraq, Pakistan, Palestine, El Salvador, and East Timor, they are nevertheless exceptions in most cases."[58] Timothy Garton Ash also underscores this point, arguing, "If violent action has traditionally been a man's business, women often come to the fore in non-violent action, and in opposition to further violence," which, it bears noting, in conflict and postconflict situations often involves rampant sexual assault.[59]

Instead of forthrightly arguing in this register, or describing his insights in this fashion, however, King and his colleagues expended an unsettling amount of energy trying to demonstrate that nonviolence did not actually involve unmanly submission to white domination. They were not above invoking their own phallic imagery to frame conflicts, as did King when speaking of a confrontation during the Birmingham campaign, presenting the power of nonviolence as nonviolent adherents met a group of police. In King's account of one Sunday demonstration, Bull Connor, the notoriously racist Birmingham commissioner of public safety, screamed to his police officers, "Dammit. Turn on the hoses." The marchers "stared back, unafraid and unmoving. Slowly the Negroes stood up and began to advance. Connor's men, as though hypnotized, fell back, their hoses sagging uselessly in their hands while several hundred Negroes marched past, and without further interference, held their prayer meeting as planned."[60]

More disturbingly, despite appealing to the "magnificent universal quality" of a nonviolent army, King's characterizations of women's political agency suggests that underneath the invocation of inclusion lay objectionable patterns of interpretation and evaluation based on androcentrism and sexism. This is perhaps clearest in the case of the Montgomery bus boycott, the event that is not only credited with kicking off the "classical" phase of the civil rights movement but that also rocketed the young Martin Luther King, Jr., to fame. Catalyzed by a woman, conceived by a woman, sustained by women—those among us who do not shy away from grandiose statements might claim that without women, there would be no King. But why were women so important? And how did gender structure King's recounting of the boycott? What can his recounting tell us about his understanding of women and agency and the role this plays in his broader political thought?

The reasons women were central to the protest are simple: They spent the most time on buses, they experienced far and away the worst treatment on buses, and therefore they had the most to gain from the amelioration of conditions therein. The boycott's success disproportionately improved the lives of working-class black women. Occupational segregation by sex, traditional gender roles, and cultural misogyny all structured transportation access and black women's experiences riding buses; taken together they account for why working-class black women rode the bus more often than black working-class males, and why their experiences on buses were often much worse than black males'.

There have been a number of explanations offered for the causes of the boycott—including King's reference to "suprarational" divine force—but one must emphasize the material causes of the protest.[61] When describing the conditions, interpreters have long emphasized the insults blacks faced and among these insults the physical and verbal abuse blacks experienced at the hands of drivers, white passengers, and police; often armed drivers and passengers simply behaved as police. From this vantage point one might see the boycott as a black battle for human dignity, as devoid of any significant intersections and notable as a struggle that eventually transcended class boundaries. However, when one stops to consider how access to transportation is structured by class, and how simply purchasing a car would allow the better-off among Montgomery's blacks to avoid the above-mentioned insults, it becomes clear that it is crucial to view the protest as, in large part, the culmination of a long struggle for human dignity waged by Montgomery's transit-dependent poor, a protest that gained much-needed support when the black (male) middle class and black spiritual elite joined the efforts. This is particularly evident if one expands ones notion of protest and resistance to include what Robin D. G. Kelley has called the "infrapolitics" of Alabama's black working class.[62]

Yet without attention to gender as well as class, the picture is still incomplete. Among the working class, as with the wider American society and in truth with most societies, men and women rarely perform the same jobs. Montgomery was no exception to this, and it had not only a racial problem, but a spatialized gendered occupational problem as well. One question contemporary spatial feminists have put to urban planners—a question worth considering in the context of the protest—is this: Are female-dominated job sites as well served by transportation routes as male-dominated job sites? As it happens, buses are often best suited to serving working-class women's employment-related transportation needs, unlike traditional hub-and -poke transit models designed to move people from the residential margins to the industrial and financial centers.[63] This was certainly the case in Montgomery, where half of black working-class women worked as domestics in white homes and therefore had to travel from black neighborhoods across town to white ones each day.[64]

Perhaps this explains why so many of Alabama's pre-Parks bus protests involved women. Kelley writes that in Birmingham in 1941–1942, "nearly twice as many black women were arrested as black men, most of them charged with either sitting in the white section or cursing."[65] Kelley also points out that "unlike the popular image of Rosa Parks's quiet resistance, black women's opposition tended to be profane and militant."[66] This resistance was often violently quelled, with women brutally assaulted and arrested. The gendered pattern Kelley observed in 1940s Birmingham would be repeated in 1950s Montgomery; Danielle McGuire reports thirty complaints in 1953 alone, noting that "most of these complaints came from working class black women who made up the bulk of Montgomery's City Lines' riders, over half of whom toiled as domestics."[67]

The historical record—including arrest records—shows that working-class black women were not immune from physical violence, nor horrific sexual harassment and humiliation. McGuire argues that the gender-specific abuses black women faced were important factors in the decision of Parks and with her a predominantly black female working-class ridership to sustain the year-long boycott: "African-American women constantly complained about the atrocious treatment they received on buses. . . . Bus drivers, [Jo Ann] Robinson recalled, disrespected black women by hurling nasty sexualized insults their way. Ferdie Walker, a black woman from Fort Worth, Texas, remembered bus drivers sexually harassing her as she waited on the corner. 'The bus was up high,' she recalled, 'and the street was down low. They'd drive up under there and then they'd expose themselves while I was standing there and it just scared me to death.'" In McGuire's analysis, "Verbal, physical and sexual abuse"—including epithets like "black niggers," "black bitches," "heifers," and "whores"—maintained racial hierarchy in an enclosed space where complete separation of whites and blacks was all but impossible."[68]

And yet while the above makes it clear that black women had more than adequate reason to leave the buses after the protest was called, McGuire also makes clear that they risked a great deal more than their male counterparts when they made the decision to leave the buses. They were constantly endangered on the sidewalks and roadways, threatened with what Montgomery activist E. D. Nixon called "a ritual of rape in which white men in the segregated South abducted and assaulted black women with alarming regularity and stunning uniformity."[69]

Finally, McGuire makes a particularly compelling case for the role of racialized sexual violence played in Parks's resolve to keep her seat, as her archival research uncovered Parks's hitherto unknown anti-sexual violence work on behalf of the NAACP and strongly suggests the importance of that work in Parks's decision to keep her seat that fateful day. Ten years prior to Montgomery, Parks was part of a group that formed the Alabama Committee for Equal Justice for Mrs. Recy Taylor, and was part of a larger group that spread the story of Taylor's gang rape by white men, "from the back roads of Alabama to the street corners of Harlem." McGuire writes, "By the spring of 1945, they had recruited supporters around the country and had organized what the *Chicago Defender* called the 'strongest campaign for equal justice to be seen in a decade.' "[70] She later notes: "Indeed, many of the African Americans who cut their political teeth defending black women like Recy Taylor who were raped by white men in Alabama in the 1940s brought their experiences and organizational insight into other struggles for dignity and justice in the 1950s and 1960s. Like E. D. Nixon and Rosa Parks in Montgomery, they often became pillars of the modern civil rights movement."[71] Ransby, it should be noted, does not fail to point out Ella Baker's role in forging the protest. As it happens, Parks attended one of Baker's leadership conferences designed to spark action among the grassroots. The Atlanta conference was Parks's first trip outside of Montgomery, and Ransby notes that it made a lasting impression on the civil rights icon.[72]

Again, women made the boycott, and this was no accident—the conditions leading up to the boycott are impossible to understand without gender analysis; gender relations, specifically inter- and intraracial gender hierarchy, were important factors in transit use and transit experiences. Yet in the end, McGuire says, though observers noted women's importance in the boycott itself, "when the boycott took off, no one called it a women's movement."[73] How does a movement so rooted in the experiences of working-class black women come to be told as a story about *blacks as such*, without intersections of gender or class, and what is King's role in this process?

Was gender significant in King's understanding of the boycott? No and yes. His failure to attend to much of the above in his analysis of the boycott makes him an unreliable witness to the event itself, yet examining his account of the boycott with particular attention to how he saw women within the protest event, how he described them—their appearance, their age, and most importantly their agency, or more often their lack thereof, is revealing. So too is attention to when and how he mobilized women to advance arguments.

Take King's description of Parks, which is particularly striking in light of McGuire's recovery of her early activism. Much has been written regarding the role of the "politics of respectability" and what it necessitated regarding skin tone and gender presentation in the figure of Parks, how the boycott coalesced around her case and not that of the darker-skinned and eventually pregnant single teen Claudette Colvin.[74] But how did King see Parks? And how did he, as one of the first to present an account of the boycott, help to construct the Parks we had to unlearn? To King, Parks is not only "an attractive Negro seamstress," she was also "tired from long hours on her feet."[75] Although he first dispels the myth that she is an NAACP "plant" by saying "she was planted there by her personal sense of dignity and self-respect," he goes on to undermine that characterization by presenting her as he does many other women in his texts—an issue to which we turn below—as less agential, as a "victim" in fact, "of both the forces of history and the forces of destiny. She had been tracked down by the Zeitgeist—the spirit of the time."[76]

The Zeitgeist, too, seemed to have a thing for light-skinned, attractive women. King felt Parks was "ideal for the role assigned to her by history. She was a charming person with a radiant personality, soft-spoken and calm in all situations. Her character was impeccable and her dedication deep-rooted. All of these traits made her one of the most respected people in the Negro community."[77] His account is striking when contrasted with that of another of the boycott's participant-observers. Founding Women's Political Council president Mary Fair Burks describes Parks as "the catalyst"—not a victim or someone carried aloft by history, destiny, or zeitgeist—but as an agent who made a decision:

> There is no doubt that Rosa Parks was the catalyst. Her quiet determination, her belief in principles, her sense of justice and injustice,

her certainty of right and wrong, her never failing dignity, her courage in the face of adversity—all these qualities made her the inevitable catalyst. . . . Rosa as a rule did not defy authority, but once she had determined on a course of action, she would not retreat. She might ignore you, go around you, but never retreat. I became convinced that she refused to give up her seat not only because she was tired, but because doing so would have violated her humanity and sense of dignity as well as her values regarding right and wrong, justice and injustice.[78]

Some of this divergence must be attributed to King's understanding of divine forces intervening in the boycott. However, he repeats this lack-of-agency attribution so often in his descriptions of women that it must motivate deeper concern.

Gender, in addition to class analysis, is useful in evaluating King's thinking regarding how each class responded to the injustice of the bus system and racial oppression in Montgomery more broadly. King described Montgomery's uneducated—presumably the city's working class—as quiescent, its middle-class as indifferent, and the boycott as the moment the two came together, awakened and emboldened. Robin Kelley's analysis of pre-1955 dissent on buses, together with his insistence that one must attend to what the political anthropologist James Scott refers to as infrapolitics in order to get an accurate picture of the political history of the oppressed, casts doubt on the first part of King's claim. Kelley quotes Scott as saying of "infrapolitics" that "the circumspect struggle waged daily by subordinate groups is, like infrared rays, beyond the visible end of the spectrum. That it should be invisible . . . is in large part by design—a tactical choice born out of a prudent awareness of the balance of power." Kelley insists that, "these daily acts"—petty theft, footdragging and destruction of property, but also folklore, jokes and songs may "have a cumulative effect on power relations."[79] Indeed this is true, but it is only in attending to the work of women that we are able to dispel the second part of King's statement.

While it is true that all but a few middle-class black men and most middle-class black female organizations shied away from direct challenge to Montgomery's racial hierarchy, there is a glaring omission that would have been right in front of King. Women, specifically the middle-class women of Dexter Avenue Baptist Church's Women's Political Council, mounted the first organized resistance to blacks' treatment on the city's buses.[80] Founded in 1946, with Mary Fair Burks as its first president, the organization protested blacks' treatment on the city's buses as part of their three-tiered approach, which included political action and education aimed at increasing voter registration. When Jo Ann Robinson took over as president in 1950, she focused the group's attention on bus integration and fair treatment. Both Burks and Robinson were professors, middle-class, and not dependent on public transit. Robinson's horrific treatment on a bus on a day when she did not have access to her car saw her calling for a boycott as early as 1949. In 1955, she mimeographed and distributed an estimated 30,000 to 52,500 leaflets to drum up support for the December 5 boycott.

That King and his advisors overlooked the work of a group of women so close to him in evaluating pre-Parks Montgomery activism fits with his other failures on the question of gender equity. Like W. E. B. Du Bois before him, King tended to give names and descriptive specificity to men's activism and to generalize and caricature women and their activism, often leaving them unnamed or assessing their physical attributes. Men's ages do not factor in his descriptions but women's very often do, and he demonstrated a preference for noting the good deeds of older women alongside the attractiveness of younger women.

Three instances come to mind regarding King's assessment of women and agency during the boycott, which necessitate reading him alongside female observers of the boycott to get more perspicacious descriptions of what happened. The first, most egregious concern is that the women who conceived the boycott are unnamed in his account. In detailing the origins of the boycott King says: "Later in the evening word got around to a few influential women of the community, mostly members of the Women's Political Council. After a series of telephone calls back and forth they agreed that the Negroes should boycott the buses. They immediately suggested the idea to Nixon and he readily concurred. In his usual courageous manner he agreed to spearhead the idea."[81] It would be left to feminist historians to recover these "influential women."

King's description above also provides clues to how quickly a boycott catalyzed by a woman and conceived by women became men's business, as here Nixon valiantly agrees to "lead" something women initiated. King seemed all too comfortable with this, later writing, "While our wives plied us with coffee, and joined the informal discussion, we laid plans and arrived at agreements on policy."[82] Robinson tells the story differently, reversing the pulpit-to-pew conception of leadership: "One minister read the circular, inquired about the announcements, and found that all the city's black congregations were quite intelligent on the matter and were planning to support the one-day boycott with or without their ministers' leadership. It was then that the ministers decided that it was time for them, the leaders, to catch up with the masses. . . . Had they not done so, they might have alienated themselves from their congregations and indeed lost members for the masses were ready and they were united!"[83]

King not only tends to leave unnamed women whose physical attributes presumably do not interest him, he also often portrays older women as helpless. King writes of a man who helped an "elderly" woman across a street: "In the course of the day police succeeded in making one arrest. A college student who was helping an elderly woman across the street was charged with 'intimidating passengers.' "[84] Jo Ann Robinson also gave an account of the event, and the differences are stark: "A 19 year old college student, Fred Daniel, full of joy, pranks and frivolity, took hold of the arm of his friend, Mrs. Percival, and playfully 'helped' her across the street. The motorcycle police were upon him in a flash. They accused him of hindering the passenger from getting on the bus and held him until a patrol car came to take him to jail, where he was booked for disorderly conduct."[85] In Robinson's account the woman appears without reference to her age, she is named, and she does not need help. King's account is also devoid of the emotional richness Robinson's provides. She presents man and woman as happy equals, finding subversive joy in protest politics.

King and Robinson also both tell the story of a black domestic who leaked news of the boycott to whites, and thus to the white press. King tells a story of an illiterate, helpless domestic: "A maid, who could not read very well came into possession of one of the unsigned appeals that had been distributed Friday afternoon. Apparently not knowing what the leaflet said, she gave it to her employer. As soon as the white employer received the notice she turned it over to the local newspaper and the *Montgomery Advertiser* made the contents of the leaflet a front-page story on Saturday morning."[86] Robinson, by contrast, attributed malice, literacy, and agency to the woman: "Domestic workers who worked late into the day toyed with the slips of paper carrying the important information of the protests. Most of them destroyed the evidence, buried the information in their memories, and went merrily on their way to work. However, one lone black woman, a domestic loyal to her 'white lady,' in spite of her concern over the plight of her black peers and without any sense of obligation to her people, carried the hand bill to her job and did not stop until the paper was safe in her 'white lady's' hands."[87]

Finally there is King's frequent willingness to explain southern black women's agency by reference to innate, organic, and untutored virtue.

Despite Jo Ann Robinson being a crucial force in initiating and sustaining the boycott, King's reference to the college professor is as an "attractive, fair-skinned and still youthful" woman who "came by her goodness naturally." In sharp contrast to the veritable philosophical bibliography narrated in his own "Pilgrimage to Nonviolence," he presents Robinson as someone who "did not need to learn nonviolence from any book."[88]

These modes of rhetoric give with one hand and take away with the other. The "universal quality" of nonviolence is celebrated, on one hand, and the leadership and agency of women devalued on the other. The masculinist conflation of dignity, manhood, and violence is deflated on one hand, while "real" manhood reasserts itself in another register. The question that remains for us, as inheritors of King, is how we should respond to this ambivalent legacy.

That King's work aimed not only to convince adherents that nonviolence was morally superior and strategically sound, but that the means of nonviolence have an intrinsic connection to important ends, are features worthy of serious consideration for feminists. King was attempting important reconstructive work, in separating manhood from violence, and attempting to provide black males an alternate path to "manhood" that did not require violence. This may be unavoidable, indeed laudable, in a nonideal context, where sexist ideology, androcentrism, and patriarchy deeply structure people's value judgments and identities, making it difficult to gain critical scaffolding without more immanent forms of criticism. What is necessary, however, is to think with King against King, and place these efforts in a continuum or process that has as its *self-conscious* telos, a restatement of those *positively* egalitarian and inclusive formulations in his work that emphasize the importance, for *anyone's* dignity, of resisting oppression and the defensibility of nonviolent forms of resistance. This restatement, moreover, would have to restate and distill these commitments' importance for fulfilling an ideal of participatory parity and principle of anti-marginalization, while also bringing under scrutiny those sexist practices that King and SCLC leaders did not see as incommensurate with their arguments for inclusivity. In particular, it would require uprooting King's ontology of gender and sociology of the family, and reconstructing arguments about equality to disavow androcentrism. In our conclusion, we will briefly sketch what this might look like in the domain of King's arguments about economic inequality.

Gender and Economic Justice in King's Thought

King, as many of the other essays in this volume attest, intervened powerfully in debates about economic inequality, poverty, and justice. His later work, in particular, weaves together many compelling arguments about the incompatibility of poverty with political and civic equality, the need for basic liberties to be buttressed with economic parity, and, above all, the significance of social relations for individual dignity.[89]

In addition to these concerns, moreover, King argues passionately about features of economic inequality that are neglected in mainstream political theory. He is deeply concerned about poverty engendering inescapable feelings of humiliation in an affluent society. Further, he expresses concern about the injuries and civic responsibilities that might be said to arise when a democratic government spends national wealth extravagantly on war or luxury, while many citizens languish in severe material deprivation.[90] Of particular moral urgency for King was the dilemma of the rapidly consolidating postindustrial black ghettos within the United States, and the unique forms of marginalization, stigma, poverty, and exploitation they entail.[91]

Less noted, however, is that King often addresses questions of poverty in ways thoroughly inflected by his conception of gender. Intertwined with these arguments about poverty as corrosive of dignity, poverty as engendering of humiliation, and ghetto poverty being uniquely galling, are claims about what economic inequality means for the achievement and consolidation of gender norms. The "castration" or "diminished manhood" frames for understanding injustice that King productively unsettles in the domain of violence, for instance, come roaring back in the realm of political economy.

The 1960s were a moment of intense anxiety among intellectuals and political elites about the coming socioeconomic consequences of "automation," the catch-all phrase they often invoked to explain the intensification of capital investments in robotics and machinery, the spread of early computing technology, and the concomitant increase in economic productivity.[92] Of particular interest, of course, was the effect these changes were likely to have on employment, with some pessimists predicting that automation would put the United States on a path toward full *un*employment rather than the full employment then championed by left-liberals.[93] Important currents of this discourse emphasized the link between automation and disparity in black and white unemployment rates, identifying racial discrimination and the comparable lack of education and skills among blacks (especially black migrants from the South) as problems.[94] In a 1963 speech to the American Association of Advertising Agencies, NAACP president Roy Wilkins echoed these themes, expressing his worry that while "the trained and talented Negro" had an unprecedented array of occupations and opportunities, automation was "threatening the unskilled and semi-skilled Negro with economic extinction . . . [and] permanent unemployment."[95]

The mid to late 1960s also were a time of extraordinary controversy about the relationship between changes in political economy and the dynamics of black family formation. Out-of-wedlock births, promiscuity, female-headed households, and welfare dependency had long been grist for black nationalist bromides, but it is indisputable that this particular moment of discursive intensity revolved around the infamous 1965 "Moynihan Report." Drafted by Daniel Patrick Moynihan, a sociologist serving in the Johnson administration as Assistant Undersecretary of Labor, the report argued that the dynamics of black family life and formation, forged in racial domination and exacerbated by industrial and postindustrial black male unemployment, were an existential threat to the quest for racial and economic equality. On Moynihan's account, which drew heavily from the African American sociologist E. Franklin Frazier's *The Negro Family in the United States* (1939), "centuries of injustice"—including slavery, Jim Crow, and contemporaneous discrimination—had brought about deep-seated structural distortions in the life of the Negro American," most perniciously a "matriarchal structure which, because it is too out of line with the rest of the American society, seriously retards the progress of the group as a whole, and imposes a crushing burden on the Negro male and, in consequence, on a great many Negro women as well."[96] In order to break the "tangle of pathology" characteristic of black poverty, social policy and activism should aim at "strengthening" conventional family structure by "restoring" men to their normative place as the family's chief wage earner and head of household, and rebuilding their subjective sense of manhood.

King first responded to the leaked Moynihan Report with enthusiasm, perhaps unsurprisingly given Frazier's broader influence on his thought and his own long-standing ideas about families. "I am particularly concerned with the Negro family," King remarked in the report's wake, citing both its "alarming conclusion that the Negro family in the urban ghetto is crumbling and disintegrating," and its contention "that the progress in civil rights can be negated by the dissolving of family structure and therefore social justice and tranquility can be delayed for generations."[97] King's analysis, which declared the black family as "fragile, deprived and often psychopathic," focused especially on male joblessness and masculine authority, arguing that "the ultimate way to diminish our problems of crime, family disorganization, illegitimacy and so forth will have to be found through a government program to help the frustrated Negro male find his true masculinity by placing him on his own two economic feet."[98] In addition to the material harm of poverty and the cultural harm of "emasculation," King thought that black male unemployment corroded the sense of love and solidarity within families, fostered intimate violence, coercively pushed black women into an exploitative labor market instead of allowing them to concentrate on child rearing, and subjected blacks to the arbitrary and humiliating domination of welfare bureaucrats.[99]

At times, and especially early in his career, King's proposed solution to this problem appeared to be increasing black men's access to jobs that paid a "family wage," and the expansion of welfare programs traditionally organized in accordance with this ideal. The social ideal of the family wage, as Nancy Fraser writes, presumes that people are organized in heterosexual nuclear families with a male head-of-household who works a job earning enough to support the family while women work uncompensated domestic labor, and is commensurate with welfare policies that distribute social resources to support homemaking as well as the indigent, unemployed, disabled, and elderly.[100] In some of King's arguments, it appears that only the *racial* stratification of this arrangement is objectionable. A mark of racial injustice, he argued, was that the "average Negro woman"—unlike many white women—"has always had to work to help keep her family in food and clothes."[101] Elsewhere he decried, in the voice of aggrieved black manhood, "our fathers and our men not being able to be men, not being able to support their families." Black men needed to struggle for the "right for our wives and our mothers not to have to get up early in the morning, and run over to the white ladies' kitchen and clean and wash their clothes . . . but to be able to stay at home and raise their children."[102] What this demonstrates is a connection between paid labor and masculinity that he did not see as essential to femininity. In fact, he implies that true femininity was connected to the performance of unpaid labor inside the home.

This view, however, relied upon a number of misguided sociological, ontological, and political claims. Operative in the background are the essentialist presuppositions that the natural and normative place of women is the "domestic" sphere of childrearing and housework, and that productive labor outside the home is the natural domain of men. Some of the most sustained (and under-studied) evidence that King's conception of gender and family supports these views come from an advice column he wrote for *Ebony* magazine in the late 1950s and two sermons he delivered on families, "The Crisis in the Modern Family" (1955) and "Secrets of Married Happiness" (1961).

By 1955 King was already decrying a crisis of "disintegration" in American family life, evidenced by escalating rates of divorce and patterns of juvenile delinquency he associated with "broken homes." The ideal family, in King's imagination, "should be an intimate group of people living together in an atmosphere of good will, where the joys and successes of one are the joys and successes of all, and where the problems and failures of one are the concern of all."[103] One of the keys for success in the marriage, King argues, is that family life is informed by an "understanding of the nature of man and the nature of a woman," as they "differ decidedly in taste, opinion and temperament." King's particular exposition of these "natures" is a textbook notion of masculinist gender stereotypes: "A man's world is largely one of action. He is never happy unless he can measure his success or failure in terms of conquest in the exterior world. On the other hand, despite all her success in the exterior world, a woman is never happy outside an emotional world. She is most at home in the world of love and maternity. Woman is subjective, realistic, concrete. Man is objective abstract and general."[104] This romantic, complementarity-based ideal of the family, King worried, was under threat from the residual social dislocations of World War II and the Korean War, shifts in political economy that required women to work outside of the home, the temptations of urbanization, and, crucially, a pernicious individualism. "Rugged individualism," he lamented, had "seeped into the family . . . so today every individual in the family asserts his or her rights with little regard for the thoughts of the family as a whole."[105]

This insistence on gender complementarity, and separation of "rights-talk" from the sphere of the family, serves as a useful backdrop for understanding the advice he parceled out to readers of *Ebony*. When responding to letters from women complaining about their husbands' "tyrannical" behavior, verbal humiliation, or alcoholism, King never counsels the involvement of law enforcement, likely reflecting his skepticism about intrafamily rights claims, as well as the undeveloped regime of domestic violence law and the prevalence of racist policing.[106] Instead, he invariably asks women to first ask whether *they* are doing anything that might "arouse" or "precipitate" such abusive behavior, and to pursue reconciliatory dialogue and pastoral counseling to rebuild the relationship and reform male deviance.[107] This deference to family integrity stems as much from his larger sense that "decay in the family is the first step toward the decay of the nation," as it does from his assertion that women (naturally) and children (God's will) find their greatest fulfillment in married households.[108]

We should reject nearly all of the above. The family wage is the product of a historical conflict between capitalists and white male workers regarding access to (black and white) women's labor power. In her classic piece "The Unhappy Marriage of Marxism and Feminism," Heidi Hartmann argues that in the late nineteenth- and early twentieth-century disputes between capitalists and organized labor, it was evident that capitalists wanted women in the paid labor force and male workers wanted women at home, serving them. Most organized labor, instead of fighting for gendered equality in the workforce, fought for male gender privilege. The family wage was a resolution to the fight over women's labor power, where a non-wage-earning wife became part of the standard of living for a male wage worker. As men fought for and received a family wage, it meant women commanded lower wages and needed the family, complete with a male wage earner, to survive. By shutting women out of jobs and intensifying sexist occupational segregation, the wage differentials ensured that women's work—that is, female-dominated occupations—were undervalued, less paid, and less esteemed.

Where King defends a vision of economic justice based on a family wage, it falls short of gender justice. That ideal, especially when buttressed by the views on family and gender above, leaves far too many women dependent upon men and marriage to avoid poverty, subjects them to forms of exploitation and arbitrary subjection in the home, contributes to sexist forms of income inequality and leisure time distribution, and denies women full participation and equal respect in a democratic society.[109] Worse yet, while King sees the family as the crucial space within which children are to develop a sense of justice and a capacity for love, it would appear that the acquisition of these virtues would be deformed and undermined by habits of sexism, androcentrism, and patriarchy.[110] An ideal of gender justice actually worth our assent would avoid installing new forms of dependency and domination, disentangle gender identity from access to paid labor, government assistance, and childrearing and household duties, and champion equal respect, dignity, and participation. Is there a King that does this work?

If we think with King against King on these questions, we can deploy other dimensions of his thought against these retrograde commitments. Crucially, by 1964 King himself begins to downplay family wage agitation in favor of a guaranteed annual income (GAI), a commitment that grows in importance toward the end of his life.[111] Having long insisted that poverty is a threat to human dignity, King came to believe that the best way to cut through the inefficiencies of welfare bureaucracy, blunt the force of labor discrimination, and avoid the negative consequences of automation would be to introduce a constitutional right of GAI to all citizens.[112] Most importantly, in perhaps King's most radical argument, he insists that the American economy had reached such a level of productivity and affluence, that continuing to allow the labor market under advanced capitalism to dominate the rules by which a society distributes income was arbitrary, obscene, and unjust. Other interests in human dignity, civic equality, individual flourishing, and political participation should take precedence in an age of affluence, and it was thus incumbent upon the government (which created the possibilities for such affluence) to ensure that all citizens had a reasonable and nonhumiliating standard of living.[113] This move from wages based on market valuations and meager, stigmatized welfare support, to income granted in recognition of one's dignity and capacities, is central to left feminism and points toward a radical revaluation of the values that distribute wealth and income. "If the society changes its concepts by placing the responsibility on its system, not on the individual," King prophesied, "and guarantees secure employment or a minimum income, dignity will come within reach of all."[114]

In addition to these claims, King thought that a *guaranteed* annual income served a crucial role in preventing humiliation and arbitrary domination. A "stable," "certain," and constitutional entitlement would help avoid some of the stigmatization of more narrowly means-targeted programs and protect GAI recipients from the capricious whims and reactionary power of welfare administrations. In 1967–1968, as King tried to organize for his ill-fated Poor People's Campaign, he sought out alliances with the National Welfare Rights Organization (NWRO), a prominent group made up largely of African American women that organized welfare recipients and their supporters to advocate for a family minimum, protect recipients from bureaucratic abuse, and inform eligible citizens of their entitlements.[115] Learning deeply from the struggle of the NWRO, King began to object to the "uncontrolled bureaucratic or political power" exercised by welfare officials, from arbitrary humiliation to politicians removing insurgent citizens from the welfare rolls to coerce acquiescence.[116]

Not only does this King show a deep concern with vulnerability to exploitation and humiliation by state officials commensurate with left feminism, but he also champions the development of welfare and tenants unions as a significant moment in the history of democracy. Invoking the work these unions were doing in the late 1960s to organize public housing residents and welfare recipients, King argues that they are responsible for securing not only new rights, but "new methods of participation in decision-making." He claims for them significance akin to that of labor unions, and demands that similar federal protections for collective bargaining be implemented so as to secure welfare recipients from "reprisals and intimidation."[117] Indeed, his conception of the alliance that would bring about genuine social democracy in the United States prominently featured these groups.[118] Although not articulated in an explicitly feminist register, King's celebration of this form of political agency points quietly to a growing appreciation of women's activism, and also gives further evidence that King's views on representation and charismatic leadership were more variegated than is usually claimed. It is precisely in the context of discussions about organizing the poor that King excoriated a group of journalists for focusing incessantly on "prominent personalities," militant rhetoric, and spectacle, while ignoring "very constructive but quiet programs of progress."[119] Moving from King's view of SCLC to his conception of the broader movement may clear much more egalitarian terrain for participatory parity across gender.

What still looms ominously over this discussion, however, is King's ontology of gender and his normative view of the family. Are there similarly redemptive countercurrents in King's thought? King undoubtedly is much weaker on this front, but there are glimmers of hope for a feminist reconstruction. Although King advances indefensible conceptions of femininity, he also forcefully rejects those extreme reactionary ideas that women's overriding end is childbearing, that a husband exercises rights of dominion over other members of the household, that marriage should subsume the individuality of women, and that men should not participate in childcare.[120] These moves, however, are gestural, occasional, and woefully inadequate, not part of a systematic and comprehensive vision. They point, nevertheless, to glaring contradictions within King's understandings of gender identity and ideal family structure, and show the way toward the rejection of the gendered division of labor, within the family and without, as well as a jettisoning of the ideology of complementarity, that a fully persuasive reconstruction would have to pursue.

In our contemporary moment, where King's iconography holds a peculiar place in debates about the means and ends of black activism, we hope that this effort of thinking with King against King helps clarify what is at stake within his complex legacy. In this approach, we take some measure of inspiration from the work of Martin's wife, Coretta Scott King. Self-consciously laying claims to her slain husband's legacy, she devoted a great deal of her post-assassination activism to the pursuit of guaranteed basic minimum income and guaranteed employment, and organizing for the NWRO.[121] Despite her sense of *philosophical* continuity with her husband, however, she saw fit to break *institutionally* and *politically* from the SCLC over the "disrespect" with which she was treated by the Baptist preachers who "thought that women should stay in the shadows."[122] Like Scott King, we recognize that Martin Luther King's views on gender norms, his ideal of the family, and his support of the family wage suffer from severe problems. Our hope is to have shown that many of his other commitments can be reconstructed to criticize those views and generate more emancipatory visions of society. It is crucial to subject King's gender ideology to unmasking critique, as we have tried to do, but it would be tragic to lose track of other elements of his thought, including his important deflation of Black Power and black protest masculinity, his defense of civil disobedience as an inclusive mode of politics, and his radical positions on economic justice. In a world where productivity grows increasingly unmoored from income, equality, and employment, and where conventional gender norms are undergoing profound changes, it seems especially right to turn to this epochal figure, and linger over his insights and his failures.

Living "in the Red": Time, Debt, and Justice

LAWRIE BALFOUR

> Whether we realize it or not, each of us lives eternally "in the red." We are everlasting debtors to known and unknown men and women.
> —MARTIN LUTHER KING, JR., *Where Do We Go from Here*

> Democracy, in its finest sense, is payment.
> —MARTIN LUTHER KING, JR., *Why We Can't Wait*

"In the Red"

We are indebted, Martin Luther King, Jr., contends, to the labor and ingenuity of people around the world and to the work of generations bound together in an economy that is moral as well as commercial. King's claim is familiar to anyone who has spent time with his words and political example. The entanglement of every nation and each individual life with every other is a keystone of his thinking, from the Montgomery movement until his death in 1968. If there is nothing surprising about King's intimation that such connectedness spans historical eras as well as national boundaries, however, his formulation does more than reaffirm human beings' mutual interdependence. It joins King's understanding of justice to a philosophy of history in which today's generation is doubly indebted to generations past and yet to come. King's account of what it means to be "in the red" is also doubled in another sense. Even as he insists on the universalism of *our* indebtedness, thereby drawing all of his readers into a shared sphere of responsibility, King makes particular note of the debts, still unpaid, for what another great orator called "the wealth piled by the bondsman's two hundred and fifty years of unrequited toil," for "every drop of blood drawn with the lash," and for the century of exploitation and violent suppression that followed the Civil War. Looking back at this bloody history, King departs from Lincoln when he concludes that "the practical cost of change for the nation up to this point has been cheap."[1] Looking ahead, he urges his readers to reckon with unpaid bills, domestic and global, at once, or risk losing everything we value.

Although King rejects any politics based narrowly on interest, financial metaphors and critiques of unjust economic arrangements pervade his political writings. Perhaps the most famous example is his 1963 "I Have a Dream" speech, in which he speaks of traveling to Washington "to cash a check," to demand the fulfillment of the "promissory note" embodied in the Declaration of Independence.[2] Economic language, if less pronounced, also emerges in his earlier work. In *Stride toward Freedom: The Montgomery Story* (1958), for example, King decries "an essentially unreconstructed economy" that has preserved the exploitation of African Americans from emancipation to King's own time.[3] And it persists through King's posthumously published "A Testament of Hope," where he prophesies that "justice so long deferred has accumulated interest and its cost for this society will be substantial in financial as well as human terms."[4] Crucially, King departs from pure economic logic, insofar as he insists on the distinction between just and unjust transactions. The view that African Americans must pay for their basic rights, he argues, is unjust. He notes that U.S. democracy has been marked by illegitimate demands for payment, from the slave era, when men and women were forced to purchase their own freedom, through the twentieth-century expectation that civil rights would be purchased out of "the funds of patience and passivity."[5] When he joins democracy to payment, then, King draws on the language of money and debt, not to reinforce conventional understandings of politics as a game of competing interests, but to make vivid a history of the United States' unmet obligations.

In this light, it is unsurprising that King's political thought has been enlisted on behalf of arguments for reparations for past and ongoing crimes related to slavery. As Alfred Brophy notes, *Why We Can't Wait* (1964) has been a generative source for reparations advocates, because King connects the crimes of slavery to a demand for "compensatory treatment" and to a Bill of Rights for the Disadvantaged.[6] And Ta-Nehisi Coates draws on film footage to suggest that King advanced an argument for reparations toward the end of his life.[7] There is little evidence that King would embrace Coates's more tendentious remark that "reparations is not one possible tool against white supremacy. It is the indispensable tool against white supremacy."[8] Yet King's choice of words lends robust support to arguments for black reparations:

> Few people consider the fact that, in addition to being enslaved for two centuries, the Negro was, during all those years, robbed of the wages of his toil. No amount of gold could provide an adequate compensation for the exploitation and humiliation of the Negro in America down through the centuries. Not all the wealth of this affluent society could meet the bill. Yet a price can be placed on unpaid wages. The ancient common law has always provided a remedy for the appropriation of the labor of one human being by another. This law should be made to apply for American Negroes. The payment should be in the form of a massive program by the government of special, compensatory measures which could be regarded as a settlement in accordance with the accepted practice of common law. Such measures would certainly be less expensive than any computation based on two centuries of unpaid wages and accumulated interest.[9]

Although the statement looks backward to the crimes of two centuries of slavery, and it is framed as a matter of compensation, King extends his argument outward beyond a narrow calculation of what is due. Not only does King forego the accounting of the full worth of unpaid wages and interest on the debt, but he also advocates a Bill of Rights for the Disadvantaged that includes "the forgotten white poor," who are collateral victims of an economy predicated on the exploitation of black labor for white profits. What is distinctive about this move is that it refuses as illegitimate any choice between addressing the specific historical claims of black Americans and the universal value of fighting poverty. King looks backward to understand the injustice of the present, and he looks forward by demanding that "special," compensatory action for African Americans serve as an avenue for benefiting poor whites as well.

King's recurrent use of the language of debt and payment, and his alignment of those concepts with a love-driven universalism, troubles categories that have structured debates about historic injustice. Even as he returns, repeatedly, to the question of what is owed to black Americans, he refuses any singular conception of "the Debt." Even as he develops a devastating critique of the profits white Americans have reaped through the exploitation of African Americans, even as he identifies post–Civil War labor conditions as a new form of slavery, and even as he maintains that whites are psychologically unprepared for genuine racial equality, King trains his focus on the broad structural harms of white supremacy and eschews any scheme for a simple wealth transfer from white to black Americans. According to Anthony Cook, King's conception of the "beloved community" entails "social atonement" for racialized exploitation and oppression throughout U.S. history. "Black reparations," writes Cook, "is a way of restoring the bonds of humanity shattered by the burden of false superiority and contrived inferiority."[10] In this sense, Preston Williams rightly observes that King's conception of justice means that his allies are "not to press unduly their rightful claim for reparations."[11] This paper mines that tension between King's refusal to act "unduly" and his sense that reparations claims are "rightful," through a reading of *Where Do We Go from Here,* the last of the three "political autobiographies" that King published during his lifetime.[12]

To read *Where Do We Go from Here* as an autobiography is to situate it within a longer history of African American literary self-making. The form—a book of six chapters and an appendix, which King wrote in relative seclusion in Jamaica over several weeks in early 1967—enables this master of the sermon, the public address, and the open letter to lay out his moral and political priorities in greater depth through the recounting of critical moments in his life. Yet King's book also stretches the boundaries of autobiography, insofar as it does not offer a conventional birth-to-the-present narrative and reveals very little in the way of personal information. Like the successive autobiographies composed by W. E. B. Du Bois, it is usefully read as "political allegory," a way of narrating the story of the movement for civil rights as an exemplary case through which to reflect on democratic ideals and the demands of global justice.[13] In lieu of exploring his own life as example, *Where Do We Go from Here* goes further than King's earlier books in making good on his claim at the opening of *Stride toward Freedom:* "While the nature of this account causes me to make frequent use of the pronoun 'I,' in every important part of the story it should be 'we.' "[14] The shifting grounds of King's collective subject— sometimes "the Negro," sometimes participants in the movement, sometimes *all* human beings—conjoin existing and aspirational forms of identity. The shifting contours of the movement, furthermore, produce revisions in King's thinking and writing. Attentive readers will recognize phrases and ideas from stand-alone speeches and sermons, newly woven into a larger whole. The effect is not mere repetition, nor does it only indicate the pressures of writing with limited time; rather it suggests a form of intertextual engagement whereby King's thought develops in conversation with itself and with the unfolding of history in which it participates.

Appearing in 1967, *Where Do We Go from Here* is a product of King's most difficult year, when he moved his family to Chicago and attempted to refocus national attention from the evil so theatrically displayed by southern bullies like Bull Connor, Jim Clark, and George Wallace to the less visible poison of northern segregation and the forms of violence effected by poverty and public disregard.[15] Its publication also followed the uprising in Watts, the obvious failure of legislative victories to effect change on the ground, the escalation of the war in Vietnam, and King's lonely decision to take a public stand in opposition to that war. Although carefully tuned to the political frequencies of its time, King's text is illuminating insofar as it reimagines but does not abandon key commitments that shape his thought from the 1950s forward. In his diagnosis and critique of Black Power, for example, King insists that revolutionary change must be based in love, reaffirms the centrality of nonviolence (although he distinguishes his opposition to armed self-defense as a political project from the justifiable self-defense of one's home), and reasserts the necessary relationship between integration and liberation. While these themes are familiar, the argument makes crucial pivots from earlier claims.

The remainder of this essay focuses on King's interpretation of his present, his narration of the past, and his vision of the future as they are laid out in *Where Do We Go from Here*, in order to grasp the threads that connect justice and indebtedness in his political thought. The next section considers how King answers his own question—Where are we?—by presenting the civil rights movement's most celebrated victories as a moment of loss. Confronted by the stunning disconnection between legislative accomplishment, on the one hand, and the immiseration of black communities, on the other, King attempts to come to terms with what that disconnection reveals about white opposition to racial equality. His response to the challenges of Black Power and the urban uprisings in Watts and elsewhere indicates that a full analysis of the present requires reckoning with the cumulative effects of the exploitation and devaluation of black Americans and the unmet material needs of all citizens. In the third section, I ask how King's retelling of U.S. history decenters the Declaration of Independence and the U.S. Constitution to highlight the economic roots of slavery and trace its effects. The historical elements of *Where Do We Go from Here* serve three ends. They disclose the missed opportunities for establishing a genuinely democratic society, they provide an explanation for the inequalities that structure King's own time, and they lay the grounds for redress demands. In the final section, I turn to King's vision of the future. The interpenetration of present and future is a recurrent feature of King's political thought, from his early critiques of "the myth of time" through his repeated insistence that "tomorrow is today." Still, when King reiterates those claims from the vantage of 1967, he must contend with two developments: the breakdown of an earlier confidence that he and his white audience shared the same discursive space and moral-political commitments, and his growing apprehension regarding America's wreaking of destruction around the world. In *Where Do We Go from Here,* King's emphasis on the cumulative debts of past injustice summons the possibility that it is *already* too late and that, by our procrastination, we (his audiences, then and now) are failing to fulfill obligations to future generations whose inheritance is in our hands.

Where Are We?

Strikingly, *Where Do We Go from Here* begins as an account of loss. Such a beginning is striking because the book opens in the President's Room in the U.S. Capitol on August 6, 1965, at the very moment Lyndon Johnson signed the Voting Rights Act in front of an interracial audience. King notes, "The legislation was designed to put the ballot effectively into Negro hands in the South after a century of denial by terror and evasion" (1).[16] Where the reader might expect King to pause in acknowledgment of a triumph to which he had contributed in signal ways, he moves briskly past the signing to contemplate its context. Very quickly he notes that the civil rights movement failed to bridge a fundamental chasm between white and black objectives. "For the vast majority of Americans, the past decade . . . had been a struggle to treat the Negro with a degree of decency, not of equality" (3). Long a fierce critic of white moderates and the thinness of American goodwill, King reiterates his concerns about the fatal conjunction of white sincerity with "a fantasy of self-deception and comfortable vanity" (5). He presses this analysis further in *Where Do We Go from Here,* disclosing the degree to which white sincerity is an obstacle to progress. The upshot is a legal revolution that masks the reality that the changes already realized have been cheaply bought and that undoing the work of white supremacy will require sacrifices on a scale not yet seen or imagined.

In fact, King argues that white and black Americans do not even share "a common language" for equality (8). Worse, whites presume themselves to be the custodians of political meaning, its definers (to borrow from Toni Morrison). And King's reflections on the white presumption that the Negro is not, after all, really ready for equality resonates with Morrison in another way. In her account of the "black noise" of the enslaved, their manhood requires white authorization, without which they become "watchdogs without teeth; steer bulls without horns; gelded workhorses whose neigh and whinny could not be translated into a language responsible humans spoke."[17] As a rejoinder to such discursive dehumanization, King's "we" shrinks noticeably. Shifting from the national or global "we" that King's readers have come to expect, he observes: "*We* have written a Declaration of Independence, itself an accomplishment, but the effort to transform the words into a life experience still lies ahead" (20, emphasis added). Across his writings, King refers to civil rights organizing as a "revolution," but the passage of the landmark legislation of the 1960s discloses that most white Americans, while deeply troubled by the overt brutality of the Jim Crow South, are engaged in a form of counterrevolution. When King contends that most "white America is not even psychologically ready to close the gap—essentially it seeks only to make it less painful and less obvious but in most respects to retain it" (8), he contrasts the righteousness of black demands against the obduracy of white "racial exhaustion." Darren Hutchinson's phrase captures the dominant temporal perspective against which King battles, in which even modest measures of progress are met with white insistence that enough—or too much—has been done on behalf of African Americans, and that it is past time to move on from questions of racial injustice.[18]

King goes further, noting that celebrations of the progress of the civil rights movement obscure the degree to which Americans marched backward, even as they locked arms in singing "We Shall Overcome." "When the Constitution was written," King writes, "a strange formula to determine taxes and representation declared that the Negro was 60 percent of a person. Today another curious formula seems to declare he is 50 percent of a person" (6). This shift is systematic, King continues, showing how black Americans enjoy 50 percent of most benefits of life in the United States and are at least twice as likely to be subject to such harms as poor schools, infant mortality, combat deaths, unemployment, and much more. These statistics are neither accidental nor indicative of innate inferiority; they are, he avers, the product of an economic system predicated on cheap labor and a culture of denial. Although King accounts for significant changes—especially the successful attack on open forms of racial discrimination in the South and the energizing of African American citizens, along with a minority of whites, to challenge the status quo—he also notes how the backward march is both abetted and disavowed by Americans who continue to call for African Americans to "wait" for justice.[19] The failed implementation of *Brown v. Board of Education* and a range of civil rights laws intimates that "legal structures have in practice proved to be neither structures nor law" (10). Challenging liberal tendencies to conceive of integration in "aesthetic terms" (93), King recasts his long-standing critique of tokenism in terms that anticipate the "diversity" agendas of today's colleges and universities. His famous emphasis on "the fierce urgency of *now*" (202), in other words, resets a ledger that has overvalued American democratic accomplishments and failed to reckon with the cumulative effects of American crimes.

To offer an alternative to stillborn legislative measures and white intransigence, King turns the reader's attention to the significance of one of the greatest challenges to his own leadership at the time: the emergence of the Black Power movement. King enlists the idea of Black Power, even as he criticizes it, as "a cry of disappointment." That cry is rightfully animated by complaint. It reflects the unpunished murders of civil rights workers, the devaluation of black life, the timidity of the federal government in enforcing its own mandates, the extent of northern discrimination and segregation, and the gap between praise for black nonviolence, on the one hand, and U.S. militarism, on the other (33ff). The diagnosis offered by Stokely Carmichael and other younger activists is on the mark, King allows, no matter how much he refuses their proposed cure. And far from being "racism in reverse" (49), calls for Black Power, King contends, reflect the belief that racial separation is the only plausible response to a nation in the grip of white supremacy.

Despite King's rejection of what he sees as "a nihilistic philosophy born out of the conviction that the Negro can't win" (45), his figuration of the present reveals both that black Americans have not *yet* begun to win a fraction of what they are owed by the polity and that they could, in fact, lose a great deal more (along with their white neighbors and the overseas victims of American attention). In his response to Black Power activists, King identifies three arenas in which African Americans must organize on their own behalf. The first is the political arena. King reiterates his long-held commitment to the use of bloc voting and creative, active citizenship. In the economic arena, King highlights nationalists' emphasis on the pooling of financial resources within black communities as a positive step. Without retreating from his call for sweeping federal action to alleviate poverty among all Americans—he cites A. Philip Randolph's Freedom

Budget as an example—King embraces the idea of using black consumer power to challenge economic injustice. Finally, and most emphatically, King affirms the importance of countering the "cultural homicide" enacted through centuries of *white* power (44). It is not necessary to celebrate blackness uncritically, he reasons, but "one must not overlook the positive value in calling the Negro to a new sense of manhood, to a deep feeling of racial pride and to an audacious appreciation of his heritage. The Negro must be grasped by a new realization of his dignity and worth" (42–43). King repudiates retaliatory politics and separatism as self-defeating, but he uses the provocation of Black Power to reinforce his commitment to nonviolence, to integrated solutions, and to the inextricable connection between love and power.

Any advocacy of violence represents for King a destructive reproduction of the past, but he also discerns in the "cry of disappointment" an acute assessment of the ongoing workings of the past in the present. Writing against the progressive trajectories of American public discourse and liberal histories, King understands that the past is not passed; the frustrations that give rise to Black Power reflect injuries that perdure. They represent a process of what Ian Haney-López calls cumulation "in the double-sense of something that is at once aggregative and combinative, heaping up advantage and disadvantage and thereby creating dynamics that transcend the sum of the parts."[20] Insofar as the present reveals the cumulative effects of earlier institutions and practices, furthermore, philosophical distinctions between backward- and forward-looking policies are of little value.

King also signals the deep connections between corrective and distributive justice in his analysis of the urban uprisings of the mid-1960s. Although steadfast in his criticism of the futility and destructiveness of violence, King nonetheless insists that "a riot is at bottom the language of the unheard" (119). What have white Americans failed to hear? In the Massey Lectures that King delivered about six months after the appearance of *Where Do We Go from Here*, he translates the language of the riots into a series of political criticisms. Americans have ignored "the reversion to savage white conduct," long-standing practices of discrimination, persistent unemployment, unequal conscription to fight for "democracy" in Vietnam, and the deterioration of urban life as a consequence of willful neglect and the government's failure to address the pressures of migration out of the South into northern ghettoes.[21] This combined revolt against an enduring history of racial oppression and present-day deprivation helps to account for the rioters' restraint from violence against persons—a restraint that is absent, by contrast, in "white hoodlumism in Northern streets"—and the symbolic significance of their destruction of property. "The focus on property in the 1967 riots is not accidental," King writes. "It is saying something":

> This rare opportunity for bloodletting was sublimated into arson, or turned into a kind of stormy carnival of free-merchandise distribution. Why did the rioters avoid personal attacks? The explanation cannot be fear of retribution, because the physical risks incurred in the attacks on property were no less than for personal assaults. The military forces were treating acts of petty larceny as equal to murder. . . . A curious proof of the symbolic aspect of the looting for some who took part in it is the fact that, after the riots, police received hundreds of calls from Negroes trying to return merchandise they had taken. These people wanted the experience of taking, of redressing the power imbalance that property represents. Possession, afterward, was secondary.[22]

Riots, to borrow from Juliet Hooker, might be said to constitute a form of "democratic repair." King's writings resist Hooker's intimation that there is no alternative language, insisting that nonviolent militancy speaks with a power that physical destruction cannot match; but her analysis resonates with King's understanding of the riot/uprising as a rejoinder to structural injustice.[23] That rejoinder, furthermore, dramatizes the lived experience of struggling to articulate a righteous demand to an obdurate audience without acting unduly.

To be sure, there are places where King focuses wholly on the present-day imperative of a juster distribution of opportunity and material resources; and in other instances, he affirms the value of corrective justice as a matter of measuring past injuries. For example, King appears to draw upon that distinction when he maintains that "the white liberal must affirm that absolute justice for the Negro simply means, in the Aristotelian sense, that the Negro must have 'his due'" (95). This claim cannot be isolated from the larger argument of the text, however, which undermines the idea that there is a just status quo ante to which it is possible to return or that receiving one's due can be disconnected from corrections to the broader maldistribution of resources. In this sense King's argument resonates with Margaret Urban Walker's conclusion that "corrective justice may be at least artificial and perhaps incoherent in addressing histories, acts, or forms of injustice that consist in the radical *denial* of moral standing or in relentless enforcement of *degraded* moral status of individuals, especially when these are systemic conditions and persist over extended periods of time."[24]

King's approach to the challenges of realizing justice in *his* time, which acknowledges the layered features of time itself, comes closer to Iris Marion Young's "social connection model" of political responsibility. The debts that have accrued over the centuries do not only demand an accounting of liability in the legal sense. At least as crucially, they call upon all citizens to take action. Coming to terms with "plural temporalities" of responsibility for the structural forms of injustice decried by King demands an investigation of the ways in which such injustice has been sedimented over generations.[25] It is precisely this analysis that King perceives his white fellow citizens evading in their unwillingness to translate legal and legislative change into a substantive commitment to equality. Despite his concern that white and black Americans do not share a "common language," he persists in modeling in his own work key features of what Young calls political responsibility: "enjoining one another to reorganize collective relationships, debating with one another about how to accomplish such reorganization, and holding one another to account for what we are doing and not doing to undermine structural injustice." To be sure, King departs from Young in one critical respect. Where she rejects "the language of blame, debt, or liability" as antipolitical, King retains the concept of "debt," with its distinctive merging of the temporal and the material.[26] But he does so without *ressentiment,* without the corrosive aspiration to get even with white Americans. When he argues that "a society that has done something special *against* the Negro for hundreds of years must now do something special *for* him," by contrast, he advances a conception of special redress in terms that are simultaneously particular and general, corrective and distributive, backward- and forward-looking.[27]

Unfinished Business of the Past

King's argument depends on a restaging of American history. And the imprint of other African American political thinkers, especially Du Bois, comes to the fore in the historical narrative that he lays out in *Where Do We Go from Here.* In King's Carnegie Hall tribute to Dr. Du Bois, delivered shortly before his own assassination, he singles out Du Bois's work as historian as his signal contribution and avers that white Americans owe him a "debt" for cutting through the "fog of ignorance" that has obscured the truthful telling of U.S. history.[28] Likewise, King's chapter "Racism and the White Backlash" begins with the assertion that "it is time for all of us to tell each other the truth about who and what have brought the Negro to the condition of deprivation against which he struggles today."[29] The truth, he continues, is that racial injustice mirrors white Americans' unwillingness to commit to the full realization of democratic principles from the period of the founding through King's own time. A truthful examination of that history, King writes, exposes a series of missed opportunities, offers an explanation for present-day conditions, and provides the grounds for reparative policies.

Where the "I Have a Dream" speech talks generally about the promissory note that the nation has yet to fulfill, and *Why We Can't Wait* specifies that debt through a political-economic history of slavery and emancipation, *Where Do We Go from Here* investigates the relationship between the birth of democracy and the rise of slavery, and charts Americans' subsequent failures to commit to the former by fully abolishing the latter. This interpretive move is critical insofar as it squarely situates American democratic principles within a history of bondage and conquest. Amid the "electrifying expressions of the rights of man" by Paine, Jefferson, and others, King notes, the Founders perpetuated the "ghastly blood traffic" (75); and the wealth embodied in African slaves and conquered land shaped "the social-political-legal structure of the nation" (76). The opportunity to put democratic ideals into practice was eclipsed by the economic allure of slavery and the profound role of racism, so that "slavery was not only ignored in defining democracy but its enlargement was tolerated in the interest of strengthening the nation" (75). Adding that this history is joined to "the physical extermination of the American Indian" (84f), moreover, King denies himself untroubled recourse to "the great wells of democracy" as historical example, philosophical resource, or rhetorical bridge to the majority of white Americans who are not prepared to hear him.[30]

As the chapter unfolds, furthermore, King tackles the widespread misperception of the meaning of emancipation by retelling it as a story of abandonment. The contours of the story are familiar to any reader of Du Bois or Frederick Douglass or Ida B. Wells or other African American political thinkers who have attempted to challenge the perceptions of a nation that believes it freed the slaves and thereby settled the question of multiracial democracy. That this project of recovering the missed opportunities of the past is so vital to King's argument indicates the limited impact of those earlier reconstructions on Americans historical imagination. Indeed, King asks, "What greater injustice could society perpetrate?"

In 1863, the Negro was given abstract freedom expressed in luminous rhetoric. But in an agrarian economy, he was given no land to make liberation concrete. After the war, the government granted white settlers, without cost, millions of acres in the West, thus providing America's new white peasants from Europe with an economic floor. But at the same time its oldest peasantry, the Negro, was denied everything but a legal status he could not use, could not consolidate, could not even defend. As Frederick Douglass came to say, "Emancipation granted the Negro freedom to hunger, freedom to winter amid the rains of heaven. Emancipation was freedom and famine at the same time."[31]

The implication is stunning: what followed the Civil War was morally *worse* than the crimes that precipitated it. Offering "abstract freedom" without any concrete commitment to its realization, King argues, is itself a crime.[32] While "the formerly enslaved navigated between a travestied emancipation and an illusory freedom,"[33] white ambivalence flourished, and the evasion of legal mandates persisted from the Civil War Amendments through the *Brown* decision.

Where Do We Go from Here thus troubles a key element of King's earlier speeches and writings: his aspiration to radically reinterpret the *American* dream by re-presenting white leaders whom he names as fellow extremists in the cause of love and justice.[34] When he scrutinizes white unwillingness to embrace racial equality from the vantage of 1967, King recalls Thomas Jefferson's legacy as author of the claim that "all men are created equal" in light of his commitments as a racial scientist (81–82). Similarly, King supplements his earlier praise for Lincoln's extremism in the antislavery cause with a reflection on a man whose "torments and vacillations were tenacious" (82). By situating these men within the history of what they did to participate in, condone, or extend the life of racial slavery, King lays bare the danger of a common rhetorical gesture, whereby the word "but" acknowledges the hero's weakness and insulates his greatness from critique (80). Like Du Bois before him, he recasts official stories of democratic greatness to reveal "a fatal spirit of temporizing" that has characterized white Americans' approach to questions of racial justice from the founding era forward.[35]

A second feature of King's retelling of the history of racial injustice is its explanatory power. To counter the premise that racial inequality can be accounted for by racial difference, King traces the lineage and effects of "the white man's problem" (71). In chapter 3, he identifies the economic roots of slavery and tracks how "the doctrine of white supremacy was imbedded in every textbook and preached in practically every pulpit. It became a structural part of the culture" (79). In the chapter that follows, "The Dilemma of Negro Americans," King addresses the consequences of that doctrine for black communities. One of the striking features of this argument is King's emphasis on the degree to which those communities have been damaged. "The central quality of the Negro's life is pain" (109), King asserts. While *Where Do We Go from Here* makes note of the long-standing work of black women and men against impossible odds and characterizes their political activities as revolutionary, this chapter employs some of the most troubling rhetorical tropes of contemporary social scientists and policymakers to account for the ways in which they have been injured. In a book that declares "that the Negro must rise up with an affirmation of his own Olympian manhood" (44), King also paints a portrait of a people who have been "maimed," "crippled," "tortured," and psychologically wounded. Although he thoroughly discredits any attempt to blame African Americans for their poverty, the terminology conjures images of a people damaged at the core.

As many commentators have noted, King's account of the injuries inflicted by the polity also evinces a deep gender conservatism. Chief among the stunting effects of slavery and generations of economic exploitation, he notes, is "family disorganization" (110). In passages that appear uncomfortably close to Daniel Patrick Moynihan's notorious *The Negro Family: The Case for National Action* (1965), even if that report is not named, King decries the rise of a "matriarchy" under slavery and identifies it as the precursor to the "fragile, deprived and often psychopathic" black family of his own time (114). King's language poses a challenge for twenty-first-century interpreters. On the one hand, his equation of patriarchal families and male breadwinning with cultural well-being suggests that the "somebodyness" he enjoins requires the subordination of black women. On the other hand, he attributes these features of black life to an unjust economic system and the pathologies of *white* culture in ways that can support democratic arguments today.

Taken together, the account of missed opportunities, and of the damage done by centuries of racial oppression, provides a platform from which King proposes specific policies that will counter the legacies of that history. The policies he advances are redistributive, but their force derives from an account of both the duty to correct the effects of historic injustice and the duty to ensure that every member of society has the wherewithal to live a dignified life. "No society," King declares, "can fully repress an ugly past when the ravages persist into the present. America owes a debt of justice which it has only begun to pay" (116). It owes that debt to the enslaved workers who created American wealth, to the black Americans of King's time who are confined to unlivable urban neighborhoods, and to *all* Americans who are indirect victims of white supremacy. At the heart of King's scheme for repayment is the "abolition of poverty" through a livable guaranteed income. King is adamant that his aspiration is universal; after all, the primary beneficiaries of such a program would be poor whites, who outnumber their black counterparts by a two-to-one ratio (170–175). Real freedom, King argues, requires not only a guaranteed income for all citizens but also investment in education, housing, and employment, and a radically expansive conception of rights (203–214). At first glance this argument appears to distance itself from the historical sensibility that informs the rest of the text and to suggest that universal solutions are preferable to race-conscious policies and programs. But King's appeal to the idea of *abolition* is not incidental. Explicitly or not, King's language aligns him with a tradition of race-conscious radical democrats, like Du Bois before him and Angela Davis more recently, whose conceptions of abolition democracy draw upon the lost promise of Reconstruction to reveal the role of capitalism in entrenching the power of white supremacy. It also resonates with many twenty-first-century proponents of reparations for whom "the past is a signifier for the yet-to-be-seen possibilities and potential of American democracy."[36] To be effective, furthermore, these policies must be global. For the history King retells is also one of colonial arrogance and neocolonial power. When he envisions a "massive, sustained Marshall Plan for Asia, Africa, and South America" (188), King is careful to distinguish the kind of support that wealthier nations (including the Soviet Union) have to offer from the pretension that these nations have anything to teach their newly independent neighbors.

Where Do We Go?

At the conclusion of *Stride toward Freedom*, King asks: "Since the problem in Montgomery is merely symptomatic of the larger national problem, where do we go not only in Montgomery but all over the South and the nation?"[37] Like many of his other early political writings, King's first book does not stop at the U.S. border. Instead, it acknowledges a relationship between domestic politics and anticolonial struggles and—after detailing actions that should be undertaken by the government at all levels, by churches, and by white and black citizens themselves—he extends the argument to the global context of war-making and to the fundamental choice between "nonviolence or nonexistence."[38] Returning to that question nearly a decade later, *Where Do We Go from Here* reveals two important developments in King's understanding of the future. Where the earlier book insists that "it is still not too late to act" and calls on African Americans to take up the rare opportunity to "become instruments of a great idea" (nonviolent social change), the future that King envisions in 1967 demands immediate and radical action in the shadow of mounting evidence that it *is* too late to avert disaster.[39] Second, King decenters the United States as the receptacle of his hope and looks to the "world house," pivoting from earlier appeals to his nation to act as the Good Samaritan and toward the conclusion that the Jericho Road must be transformed in its entirety.[40]

What has changed? *Where Do We Go from Here* suggests two answers: the intransigence of white Americans, who not only value order above justice, but disclose that they do not really value racial equality in a meaningful sense; and the wantonness of American savagery in Vietnam. In an important sense, the "problem-space" from within which King imagines the future in 1967 has fundamentally altered from the context in which he produced *Stride toward Freedom* and *Why We Can't Wait*.[41] The revelation that white and black Americans do not share a common political language alters the kinds of questions King can ask and the discursive resources available to him to make his critique intelligible. The function of the founders and other white leaders as exemplars shifts accordingly. In the light of his new understanding of the racial divide, King enlists these figures as models for interpreting the present, but not for emulation. If he continues to embrace the values articulated by the Declaration of Independence and the Preamble to the Constitution, he cannot presume that those values are shared by the inheritors of the deep racial "ambivalence" he traces to Washington, Jefferson, and Lincoln. While all three of King's political autobiographies conclude with a plea for world peace, furthermore, this last one develops more fully the critique of U.S. foreign policy expressed in King's April 1967 Riverside Church address condemning the Vietnam War.[42]

In effect, the last chapter of *Where Do We Go from Here* reveals the possibility of a post-American King, who is inspired by the revolutionary accomplishments of the colonized—although not blind to the crimes committed by many postcolonial governments—and who sees the United States as a world leader in its destructive belligerence.[43] King's text is palpably haunted by a future in which generations of dreams and sacrifice come to nothing. Or worse. King's contemplation of the forward thrust of time yields one of the most chilling lines of his corpus: "Over the bleached bones and jumbled residues of numerous civilizations are written the pathetic words: 'Too late'" (202). The book testifies to the extent of the wreckage already piled up. And where King once observed that time is neutral—available for constructive or destructive purposes—*Where Do We Go from Here* refigures it as "deaf to every plea." It "rushes on."

Reading King's text in the twenty-first century is disturbing. Have we learned to live with the "chaos" that King intimates will come from his contemporaries' disregard for the children, women, and men trapped in poverty with few services or any reliable means of security or exit? What is the distance between the grim realities King delineates and the hostility black citizens encounter from the state—or from their fellow citizens—when they dare to proclaim that Black Lives Matter? King's account of the debts not yet paid in 1967 does not touch on the costs of mass incarceration or the mounting tolls of Americans' persistence in "talking peace while preparing for war" (193) or the price that the consumption habits of the wealthy exact from the people most vulnerable to global climate change. How has the ledger been reset over the nearly fifty years since King's writing? Admittedly, King's theological commitments disallow the conclusion that it is already too late to pay down these debts. His 1967 "Christmas Sermon on Peace," for instance, reaffirms "the ultimate morality of the universe" and circles back to an invocation of the "dream" after narrating his encounter with the American "nightmare."[44] And it would be a gross distortion to deny King's insistence on the necessity of hope in a God-created world.

Still, the anguish that animates the book's last paragraph recasts King's relationship to time. Moving ahead while looking back, King speaks to the reader not as Moses, leading his people out of the wilderness, but as one of those people, "standing bare, naked, and dejected with a lost opportunity" (202). This autobiography registers the personal effects of the losses incurred in his own time and the crimes committed in his name as an American citizen. The challenge that *this* accounting poses is its insistence that we confront the myriad ways in which we are "too late" already and yet take that belatedness as a spur to action, in King's words, to love. By calling us backward, to a deep and careful examination of U.S. history and forward to an appreciation for our mounting debts to future generations, King pleads with his readers to alchemize tragedy into justice. And his final book reminds us that the beloved thinker and activist whose last speech assured his listeners that he had seen the "Promised Land" had just as surely glimpsed its alternative.

12

The Costs of Violence: Militarism, Geopolitics, and Accountability

LIONEL K. McPHERSON

At the award ceremony for the Nobel Peace Prize in December 2009, President Barack Obama offered these words of humility: "Compared to some of the giants of history who've received this prize—Schweitzer and King; Marshall and Mandela—my accomplishments are slight."[1] Obama was early in his first term as the first black president of the United States, after one abbreviated term as a U.S. senator. Presumably, no one would have thought to compare him to Martin Luther King, Jr., who had demonstrated a commitment to justice through guiding principles, concrete achievements, and personal sacrifice.

The Nobel Committee hoped Obama would steer the United States away from the unilateral militarism, torture, and indefinite imprisonment practiced by the previous administration. He used the occasion to elaborate a defense of political violence while encouraging humanity to "reach for the world that ought to be—that spark of the divine that still stirs within each of our souls." In drawing a "clear-eyed" contrast to King, Obama provided a foil for us to explore the underappreciated practical wisdom of King's nonviolence. Their deeply different visions can be compared against the background of U.S. foreign policy and war after the al-Qaeda terror attacks of September 11, 2001.

Obama, like his predecessor, George W. Bush, accepted a version of the doctrine that American military power is indispensable for promoting international stability and liberal values. "America's commitment to global security will never waver," he told the Nobel audience. Obama affirmed in a later speech, "America must always lead on the world stage. If we don't, no one else will. . . . I believe in American exceptionalism with every fiber of my being."[2] When declining to amass troops in Syria, he tempered his ideal of global leadership: "America is not the world's policeman. Terrible things happen across the globe, and it is beyond our means to right every wrong." The "essential truth" remains that Americans are "exceptional," he said, because "we" believe we should protect children elsewhere "when, with modest effort and risk," we can "thereby make our own children safer over the long run."[3] This amounts to basic prudence of no exceptional distinction.

Sometimes described as pragmatic, Obama combined his vision of a world without the threat of nuclear war with action to maintain an over-whelming nuclear arsenal. During a historic visit to Hiroshima, the Japanese city on which the United States dropped the first atomic bomb in 1945, he encouraged nations "to ponder a terrible force unleashed" and "to mourn the dead" while looking to the future. "But among those nations like my own that hold nuclear stockpiles," he said, "we must have the courage to escape the logic of fear, and pursue a world without them," which would require "our own moral awakening."[4] News the day before was that "the [Obama] administration has reduced the nuclear stockpile less than any other post-Cold War presidency" and sought "sweeping nuclear modernizations" at a "cost up to $1 trillion over the next three decades."[5] Undoubtedly, King would have asked why the country still prioritizes extraordinary spending on the prospect of war rather than on domestic priorities such as fighting "unemployment, housing discrimination and slum schools."[6]

Pragmatism for Obama as president did mean a preference for tactical violence rather than wider war. He described his authorized drone strike that killed Taliban leader Mullah Akhtar Mansour in 2016 as "an important milestone in our longstanding effort to bring peace and prosperity to Afghanistan."[7] Five years earlier, he claimed that the special forces assassination of inactive al-Qaeda founder Osama bin Laden "once again reminded [us] that America can do whatever we set our mind to"—"not just because of wealth or power, but because of who we are."[8] Yet, more than fifteen years after September 11, American involvement in the Middle East had become a contemporary, more complicated analog of the Vietnam War. One needn't be a pacifist to ask, "Does the world's most powerful nation have no other choice but to persist in pursuing a manifestly futile endeavor?"[9] The United States might have been helpfully guided by King's pragmatic skepticism about the utility of political violence. In fact, bin Laden strategically anticipated that national faith in the power of killing would draw the country into a military, economic, and political quagmire.[10]

"Where force is necessary, we have a moral and strategic interest in binding ourselves to certain rules of conduct," Obama assured the Nobel audience. The drone warfare program grew from roughly 50 drone strikes under the Bush administration to roughly 500 under Obama's. "I also believe we must be more transparent about both the basis of our counterterrorism actions and the manner in which they are carried out. We have to be able to explain them publicly," Obama declared late into his presidency.[11] The issues of legality and accountability are not merely matters of principle. Thus, for example, "The White House and Pentagon boast that the targeted killing program is precise and that civilian deaths are minimal. However, [secret government] documents ... show that between January 2012 and February 2013, [drone strikes] killed more than 200 people. Of those, only 35 were the intended targets."[12] Many Americans, if they do not particularly care about civilian casualties among other peoples, might at least have a better understanding of "why they hate us."

My discussion of U.S. foreign policy after the September 11 terror attacks is not for the purpose of assessing the merits of Bush or Obama as president. The purpose is to consider the costs of political violence to a military and economic power. I will focus on three themes: (1) the relation between belief in American exceptionalism and commitment to militarism; (2) the limits of political violence in addressing geopolitical conflict; and (3) the importance of accountability for the use of political violence. I take my emphasis on "costs" to illustrate why King's orientation toward non-violence is both morally and practically superior to the pragmatic militarism Obama represented.

King's Worldly Pragmatism

With the Vietnam War as his real-time case study, King emphasized that political violence has opportunity costs in addition to obvious moral costs. Wars kill, maim, and traumatize people as well as divert—and when unjust, waste—financial resources and human capital that could be spent improving lives. The pragmatic aspect of King's critique has faded as a misimpression of him as impractical idealist has become dominant. Obama helped to spread this misimpression through his Nobel speech: "I cannot be guided by [Gandhi's and King's] examples alone. I face the world as it is, and cannot stand idle in the face of threats to the American people. For make no mistake: Evil does exist in the world." King never counseled that political leaders do nothing to protect their people or others from murderous aggression, even when he did express a commitment to personal pacifism.

The grounded nature of King's thinking about Vietnam was out in the open. Whereas Obama confined him to "an idealized world" governed by love and religious faith, a 1967 *New York Times* editorial took the civil rights leader to task for engaging the domain of international politics. This "Dr. King's Error" editorial, notable for its condescension and myopia, warrants highlighting:

> The Rev. Dr. Martin Luther King Jr. has linked his personal opposition to the war in Vietnam with the cause of Negro equality in the United States. The war, he argues, should be stopped not only because it is a futile war waged for the wrong ends but also because it is a barrier to social progress. . . .
>
> Dr. King makes too facile a connection between the speeding up of the war in Vietnam and the slowing down of the war against poverty. . . . The nation could afford to make more funds available to combat poverty even while the war in Vietnam continues, but there is no certain[ty] that the coming of peace would automatically lead to a sharp increase in funds.[13]

Of course, King's critique did not rely on a strictly necessary connection. That the United States could have, apart from the war, spent more to fight poverty actually highlights the issue of national priorities.

Certain trends—namely, aversion to taxes and to social spending on the poor, combined with support for high military spending—were evident fifty years ago.[14] In his famous 1967 speech "Beyond Vietnam: A Time to Break Silence," King lamented, "Then came the build-up in Vietnam and I watched [President Lyndon B. Johnson's 'War on Poverty'] program broken and eviscerated as if it were some idle political plaything of a society gone mad on war, and I knew that America would never invest the necessary funds or energies in rehabilitation of its poor so long as adventures like Vietnam continued to draw men and skills and money like some demoniacal destructive suction tube."[15] President Dwight D. Eisenhower had already warned in 1961 about "the acquisition of unwarranted influence, whether sought or unsought, by the military-industrial complex," his enduring description of the "conjunction of an immense military establishment and a large arms industry" whose "total influence—economic, political, even spiritual—is felt in every city, every State house, every office of the Federal government."[16] Facts today have proven King and Eisenhower right.

In 2015, the United States had 10 percent, roughly 50 million, of the world's poorest adults (lowest decile).[17] At that point, 38 percent of its adults qualified as "middle class" (50 to 60 percent qualified in "most high-income countries"), while it had 46 percent of the world's millionaires and 48 percent of the world's "ultra high net worth individuals" (worth more than $50 million).[18] In 2012, the United States had a child poverty rate of 32 percent, which is 24 million children, to rank 36th out of 41 countries in "the developed world" (roughly 1.5 percent behind Romania and 2 percent ahead of Mexico).[19] Of the world's military expenditures in 2015, the United States accounted for 36 percent, or $596 billion, which was more than the next seven countries combined (China came in second, at an estimated $215 billion, with no other country above $100 billion).[20] That $596 billion was over 54 percent of U.S. discretionary spending in 2015, which dwarfed federal spending on education and housing.[21]

The commitment to overwhelming capacity for political violence has struggled for public rationalization. For example, the Navy abandoned its tagline "A global force for good" after a study of the American public found that "only 20 percent of respondents felt that the Navy's primary mission should be as a 'global force for good', while 70 percent said it should primarily be 'to protect and defend the United States.'"[22] Incongruously, Obama had proclaimed in his Nobel speech, "We lose ourselves when we compromise the very ideals that we fight to defend"[23]—a sentiment that grants reservations about the methods of "fighting" yet sympathizes with the previous administration's claim to seek "the expansion of freedom in all the world."[24] Perhaps lost in rhetoric, the audience applauded in anticipation that a president who campaigned on the straightforward vow to end the U.S. wars in Afghanistan and Iraq would earn the Peace Prize awarded to him.

The deference Obama paid to political violence belongs to a tradition of equating nonviolence with absolute pacifism, then dismissing pacifism as unrealistic and even irresponsible. A prominent philosopher charges, for instance, that "pacifism teaches people to make no distinction between the shedding of innocent blood and the shedding of any human blood."[25] But hyperbole cannot obscure a glaring challenge to nonpacifism as practiced by military powers: Why believe that any country would dedicate tens of billions of dollars a year to military expenditures in order to serve humanity?

Skepticism about such nonpacifism led King to condemn the United States (under President John F. Kennedy's administration) for making "little or no attempt to deal with the economic aspects of racist exploitation" and being "silent about . . . the billions of dollars in trade and the military alliances which are maintained [with apartheid South Africa] under the pretext of fighting Communism in Africa."[26] He argued that for the world's "colored people, it is an almost inescapable conclusion that their condition and their exploitation are somehow related to their color and the racism of the white Western world."[27] One also might conclude that "national security" is usually a cover for the pursuit of national self-interest backed by political violence.

At a minimum, the notion that pacifism teaches passivity or false moral equivalence is ill informed.[28] Consider King's 1959 "War Resisters League" address: "My study of Gandhi convinced me that true pacifism is not nonresistance to evil; but nonviolent resistance to evil. . . . I feel free to say that we who believe in nonviolence often have an unwarranted optimism concerning man and lean unconsciously toward self-righteousness. . . . We must see the pacifist position not as sinless but as the lesser evil in the circumstances. . . . We who advocate nonviolence would have a greater appeal if we did not claim to be free from the moral dilemmas that the nonpacifist confronts."[29] King indirectly put some distance between his pacifism, or its presentation, and Gandhi's. Also indirectly, he implied that nonpacifists often do not confront the moral question of whether the literal expense of war (including war preparedness) and consequent (re)ordering of national priorities are generally worth whatever good realistically might be done through war as compared to nonviolent alternatives.

Grappling with King's orientation toward nonviolence fosters an understanding of war's costs that is more pragmatic than faith in the constructive power of killing. He ventured into earnest idealism with statements such as "The greatest hope for world peace today may well be the realization on the part of people all over the world and the leaders of the nations of the world that war is futile."[30] But U.S. foreign policy after World War II demonstrates that a lot worse can be done than to refrain from war—as implied by the so-called "Obama Doctrine" of "Don't do stupid shit," which evidently wasn't applied to drone strikes. This lesson, however, dodges a serious worry. Prior to 1967, King's statements seem open to familiar skepticism about pacifism. The efficacy objection is standard: What good is nonviolent resistance when up against the reality of violence carried out by a regime or group (think ISIS or apartheid South Africa) that has low regard for human rights or common morality?

The Parting of King's Pacifism from Gandhi's

King was not an absolute pacifist, politically speaking, contrary to popular perception today. On my reading of the trajectory of his thought, he had no static answer to the efficacy objection to nonviolent resistance. He shifted from highly qualified moral toleration of political violence to virtually unqualified commitment to personal pacifism. The shift suggests he understood there could be rare occasions for political violence in the service of justice, whether or not he continued to doubt the notion of a "just war."[31] By the time King's life was cut short in 1968, he had clearly acknowledged a morally legitimate role for political violence. He left unresolved the uncomfortable question of how, in fairness, pacifists could remain committed to personally abstaining from political violence while accepting that fellow citizens could have just cause to participate in political violence when the stakes are high.

In "The Greatest Hope for World Peace" (1964), King answered a direct question about the limits of nonviolence. He first affirmed his personal pacifism: "I am committed to non-violence absolutely, not merely as a technique or a passing strategy but as a way of life. For this reason I don't think I would fight in self-defense. I don't think that I would use violence in self-defense." His response then got complicated: "Now on the question of whether war is ever justifiable . . . there was a period when I felt that war could serve a negative good—by that I mean I went through the feeling that war could at least serve as a force to block the surge of an evil force in history like Hitler." Maybe war was necessary under extraordinary circumstances. "But now," King continued, "I have come to the conclusion that because of the potential annihilation of the whole human race, there can be no justification for any large scale war."[32] Apparently he believed that war could be justifiable to stop mass aggression, provided there was no threat of the use of nuclear weapons in a world war, and that tactical violence also could be justifiable. In neither case would humanity as a whole be in jeopardy.

Yet King's qualified political pacifism in "World Peace" is unsuited for the nuclear age. As Obama alluded to in his Nobel speech, love would not have stopped Hitler; and Nazi Germany's defeat, which could not have come quickly enough, was far from certain. If an aggressor regime were to possess nuclear weapons, the refusal by other nuclear powers to intervene would be reminiscent of the failed appeasement of Nazi Germany. In fact, possibly the only just purpose of a nuclear arsenal is to draw a genuine "red line" when aggression could not be stopped through conventional warfare and would pose a critical threat to a nation. (Compare the Kennedy administration's deft handling of the Cuban missile crisis.) King sidestepped the question of how such a case might otherwise be handled. His suggestion that the world should wait for a feasible alternative to a potential nuclear war is unhelpful as a policy proposal: any rogue country with nuclear weapons would know that it could pursue aggression without fear of reprisal.

Even when conveying flexibility, King had tendency to cite high principle. "We must re-examine the assumptions of the pacifist position," he previously urged in "War Resisters League." This reexamination mostly reviewed core values of pacifism "as they apply to Montgomery and . . . the quest for peace": Nonviolence "is not a method for cowards" but "does resist." It "does not seek to defeat or humiliate the opponent, but to win his friendship and understanding." It is "directed against forces of evil rather than against persons who happen to be doing the evil." Its practitioners have "a willingness to accept suffering without retaliation." And it "avoids not only external physical violence but also internal violence of spirit."[33] The Montgomery bus boycott (including its focus on Rosa Parks) was a perfect case for effective nonviolent resistance. This does not demonstrate much about the efficacy of nonviolence when confronting an opponent ready to deploy lethal violence. Still, the Montgomery example supports the moderate conclusion that nonviolent resistance can be used effectively when just aims might be achievable without resorting to violence.

It is not obvious that this lesson would suffice for King, given the doctrinaire framework of his pacifism. He favorably acknowledged that adherents might forgo self-defense, even at the cost of immediate just aims: "Gandhi resisted evil with . . . love instead of hate. True pacifism is . . . a courageous confrontation of evil by the power of love, in the faith that it is better to be the recipient of violence than the inflicter of it, since the latter only multiplies the existence of violence and bitterness in the universe, while the former may develop a sense of shame in the opponent, and thereby bring a transformation and change of heart."[34] Of course, the power of love is constrained by the psychological and material investment that opponents often have in hate and fear.

What of purveyors of violence who show indifference to justice and scant capacity for shame? What is to be done when there are no signs of change of heart or direction? Politically successful adoption of a Gandhian framework would appear to depend on the nature of a specific political conflict and the opponent's brand of ruthlessness. Gandhi himself, a leading scholar writes, "was not prepared to ask hard questions about the circumstances in which *satyagraha* [nonviolence] might or might not work in the practical terms of daily power politics."[35] He overgeneralized from examples of successful nonviolent campaigns.

The "faith" that King, like Gandhi, expressed in nonviolence seems more suited to spiritual life than political reality. Gandhi's interpretation of "the principle of nonviolence," or *satyagraha,* leaves little room for compromise: "*Satyagraha* is a weapon of the strong; it admits of no violence under any circumstance whatever; and it ever insists upon truth."[36] (He came to view the term "passive resistance" as essentially inadequate due to its connection with the "burning of houses" and "fasting in prison" of the suffragette movement in England.[37]) For the person who practices *satyagraha,* worldly consequences of the use of violence are never eligible for weighing. But King always left room for practical maneuver. Recall that in "War Resisters League" he deviated from the lead message when questioning the limits of commitment to pacifism: the critical "assumption" he "re-examined" was absoluteness. He judged that pacifism generally is "the lesser evil in the circumstances," which need not mean any and all circumstances. There could be genuine "moral dilemmas" of violence.

Gandhi, though reluctant to grant the possibility of justifiable violence, allowed for some such dilemmas. A controversial passage dispels the notion that he was an absolute pacifist: "I do believe that where there is only a choice between cowardice and violence I would advise violence. Thus when my eldest son asked me . . . whether he should have run away and seen me killed or whether he should have used his physical force which he could and wanted to use, and defended me, I told him that it was his duty to defend me even by using violence." Despite the perception that he fostered, Gandhi did not totally renounce violence in political contexts, either: "Hence it was that I took part in the Boer War [in South Africa], the so-called Zulu rebellion and the late War. . . . I would rather have India resort to arms in order to defend her honour than that she should in a cowardly manner become or remain a helpless witness to her own dishonor."[38] He viewed violence as a means, typically vicious, and saw cowardice as simply a vice that could never have redeeming value.

Judging that "X is better than Y" is not equivalent to judging that "X is morally justifiable." As I read Gandhi, the distinction is important, perhaps to mark a spiritual orientation that is not necessarily manifested in personal or political practice. By contrast, as I read King, he differentiated his thinking from Gandhi's on the narrow question of whether the pursuit of just aims can raise genuine moral dilemmas: King accepted that certain types of political violence could be justifiable in certain circumstances. Ironically, King did not waver on commitment to personal pacifism as a matter of principle. Yet he believed that doctrinaire emphasis on a pacifist spiritual orientation conveyed an inclination toward "self-righteousness" in the political domain. I propose that instead of seeing King as inconsistent about expressing the nature of his pacifism, he is more plausibly seen as consciously reflecting on the political efficacy of nonviolent resistance.

Nelson Mandela famously reached a similar crossroads, which he described in his "I Am Prepared to Die" statement for his 1964 Rivonia trial. "After a long and anxious assessment of the South African situation," Mandela explained, "I, and some [African National Congress] colleagues, came to the conclusion that as violence in this country was inevitable, it would be unrealistic and wrong for African leaders to continue preaching peace and nonviolence at a time when the government met our peaceful demands with force."[39] He articulated in substance a fundamental principle of just war theory: "It was only when all else had failed, when all channels of peaceful protest had been barred to us, that the decision was made to embark on violent forms of political struggle."[40] As he implied, the violence was not intended to bring down the apartheid regime but to raise the stakes of protest domestically and internationally.

The African National Congress, like King, had been committed to nonviolence on moral grounds. But Mandela was explicit that responsible political leaders could ask only so much from persons joined in pursuit of racial freedom and justice. Success of the just cause, not spiritual virtue, was the higher priority; this could mean that very restrained use of violence becomes necessary and legitimate as a means. Gandhi maintained that true pacifism could not conflict with political efficacy: "For a *satyagrahi* there can be only one goal, viz., to lay down his life performing his duty whatever it may be. . . . A cause that has such worthy *satyagrahi* soldiers at its back can never be defeated."[41] In effect, Mandela renounced such a vision, particularly after the Sharpeville massacre of black South African protesters in March 1960.[42]

With 1967's "Beyond Vietnam: A Time to Break Silence," King went further than recognizing moral dilemmas of violence. His emphasis on opportunity costs did not sit comfortably with pacifism. The *New York Times* editorial "Dr. King's Error" managed to illustrate why. King lamented the money and effort spent on the Vietnam War that otherwise could have been spent fighting domestic poverty. The editorial's objection to connecting the two had some point: If the war in fact did not bear on the poverty program, how strong would King's opposition to the war be? His response would be obvious: the Vietnam War was both unwinnable and unjust. Why, then, should he speculate about the war's impact on the poverty program, speculation that seems almost morally irrelevant as compared to his central reasons for opposing the war? There is the appearance of an element of bad faith in King's opportunity-costs line of criticism, even if a practical connection existed between spending on the Vietnam War and spending on the War on Poverty program.

Bad faith is a weakness Gandhi was determined to avoid. He developed this sensibility during his formative years as a theorist and practitioner of nonviolence in South Africa (and before adopting the key word *satyagraha*): "All Passive Resisters do not understand the full value of the force. . . . Some again were only Passive Resisters so-called. They came without any conviction, often with mixed motives, less often with impure motives. . . . Thus it was that the struggle became prolonged; for the exercise of the purest-soul force, in its perfect form, brings about instantaneous relief."[43] Opportunity costs would have no bearing on principled opposition to violence, and contemplating them could prove a distraction from the pure path of *satyagraha*.

Nevertheless, King's calling attention to the waste of financial resources and human capital as an additional, compelling reason to oppose the Vietnam War cannot fairly be attributed to bad faith. To reiterate, he was wary of appealing to nonviolence "merely as a technique or a passing strategy"; his vision of nonviolence "as a way of life" would be integrated and holistic. A straightforward interpretation of his position is this: The commitment to shooting and bombing undermined the War on Poverty's moral urgency, which exacerbated the moral wrongness of an unjust war. As philosophers might say, the wrongness of an unjust war was morally overdetermined. King spelled out why he believed the Vietnam War failed at the level of just cause: "Our government felt then that the Vietnamese people were not 'ready' for independence. . . . With that tragic decision we rejected a revolutionary government seeking self-determination, and a government that had been established . . . by clearly indigenous forces that included some communists. For the peasants this new government meant real land reform, one of the most important needs in their lives."[44]

That the war was unwinnable by the United States also morally overdetermined the case against it. The critical moral reason for opposing the Vietnam War was that it was unjust.

Beyond Any Current War

The basic moral calculus of King's opposition to the Vietnam War is undeniable: If the war was unjust, it shouldn't be won; and if it was virtually unwinnable, it shouldn't (continue to) be fought. Pragmatically speaking, this does not require accepting that the war was unjust. The political problem was that the United States had committed to the war and would be extremely reluctant to concede defeat. Moreover, the United States had already ignored Senator George D. Aiken's "far-fetched proposal" that became famous through the paraphrase "Declare victory and go home." The actual proposal Aiken elaborated was serious and perceptive: "The United States could well declare unilaterally that this stage of the Vietnam war is over—that we have 'won' in the sense that our Armed Forces are in control of most of the field and no potential enemy is in a position to establish its authority over South Vietnam." This in turn "would herald the resumption of political warfare as the dominant theme in Vietnam."[45] Unfortunately, as with its later wars in Afghanistan and Iraq in the "global war on terrorism," the United States had raised such high expectations for its outcomes in Vietnam that accepting the limits of what U.S. military power could achieve and going home became almost unfeasible politically—regardless of the private skepticism of President Johnson.[46]

The general form of the problem for American antiwar activists, for a U.S. war-in-progress, is that the moral question of just cause is generally taken for granted as an article of faith across the mainstream political spectrum. Such faith is a prerequisite for belief in American exceptionalism, which now openly functions as a loyalty test for American political leaders. So the question of winnability becomes paramount, along with a popular imperative to "support the troops." But once the United States has started a major war, the article of faith among the foreign policy and military-industrial establishments shifts to conviction that the war must be winnable—if only political leaders had the wisdom and courage to commit ample resources to the long-term endeavor and were prepared to authorize the means to do what is necessary to win (deemed worth the accompanying increase in "collateral" casualties among civilians in places bombed, droned, or raided in order to bring "peace and prosperity").[47]

In my estimation, King in "Beyond Vietnam" understood well the general problem for American antiwar activists. Contrary to the *New York Times* editorial, he did not believe that money spent on the Vietnam War was money literally taken away from the War on Poverty program. The poverty program could have disproportionately benefited colored people, because they were (and still are) heavily overrepresented among America's poor.[48] Also, a shift in priorities from fighting in Vietnam would have translated into fewer men being shipped off to an unjust fate. This, too, could have disproportionately benefited colored people, who were overrepresented among combat deaths in Vietnam.[49] King had hoped that the War on Poverty program signaled a revision and reordering of American values. His hopes were dashed: "Perhaps the most tragic recognition of reality took place when it became clear to me that the war was doing far more than devastating the hopes of the poor at home. It was sending their sons and their brothers and their husbands to fight and to die in extraordinarily high proportions. . . . We were taking the black young men who had been crippled by our society and sending them 8,000 miles away to guarantee liberties in Southeast Asia which they had not found in Southwest Georgia and East Harlem."[50]

A radical call to reconsider U.S. national priorities—not a narrow appeal for immediate reallocation of resources to fight poverty—was King's main purpose in "Beyond Vietnam." He knew the time had probably passed for changing course (for the better) in Vietnam, which is why he wrote in a postmortem past tense. King was anticipating debate over the prospect of the next major war, not simply condemning a war that the United States was extremely unlikely to abandon without fighting to the verge of outright defeat. Nor did he truly imagine that the United States was dedicating so much money and so many of its men on a mission "to guarantee liberties in Southeast Asia"—except, perhaps, in the sense that "our nation has taken . . . the role . . . of those who make peaceful revolution impossible by refusing to give up the privileges and the pleasures that come from the immense profits of overseas investment."[51] King's broader, integrated perspective connecting Western military power to the global exploitation of colored peoples, a theme that is the focus of 1967's "Racism and the World House," indeed looked "beyond" the war in Vietnam. He was uncharacteristically despondent and pessimistic about what he saw.

By the time of his assassination, King had given up any appearance of commitment to absolute pacifism. 1967's "The Middle East Question" removes any doubt: "SCLC and Dr. King have repeatedly stated that the

Middle East problem embodies the related questions of security and development. *Israel's right to exist as a state in security is incontestable. At the same time the great powers have the obligation to recognize that the Arab world is in a state of imposed poverty and backwardness that must threaten peace and harmony."*[52] (This statement came a few months after Israel had won the Six-Day War against the neighboring states of Egypt, Jordan, and Syria.) In the domain of international politics, such "security" is not possible without the credible threat of the use of violence. King acknowledged that nonviolence has its limits. Then, again, were he looking today at the Israeli-Palestinian conflict, its gross imbalance of power, and its humanitarian catastrophe, he undoubtedly would be despondent and pessimistic about the prospect of a just and stable peace going forward in that region.

The pragmatism of King's vision for nonviolence does not have to offer a solution for all conflicts in order to accommodate urgent realities of international politics. Obama's caricature of that vision set the stage for the pragmatic militarism his administration pursued within the confines of the American foreign policy establishment. Affirmation of American exceptionalism continued to fuel the national faith that, as King observed, "we have some divine, messianic mission to police the whole world."[53] Rather than reimagine this faith, the Obama administration tried to apply it more prudently. Left intact was the conviction that overwhelming capacity for political violence must yield the weapons and tactics to achieve geopolitical goals—despite all evidence after September 11 that America's approach to war and counterterrorism has strategically backfired across the Middle East and into Africa and Europe.

At the very least, King's pragmatic skepticism about the utility of political violence points toward a more honest, thoughtful assessment of national priorities and realistic means for achieving them. Domestic transparency about human and material costs is a prerequisite. A president might learn that lack of accountability for the costs imposed far from home is strategically self-defeating: the cover of darkness enables blind faith in the value of "doing something" by killing, and killing some more.

PART IV   *Conscience*

13

The Path of Conscientious Citizenship

MICHELE MOODY-ADAMS

On April 4, 1967, exactly one year before he was assassinated, Martin Luther King delivered the most controversial, yet most theoretically illuminating, speech of his career: his Riverside Church speech "A Time to Break Silence" (sometimes referred to as "Beyond Vietnam").[1] One source of controversy—even for his close associates—was King's readiness to join the heated national debate about the morality of the Vietnam War while the struggle against racial segregation and oppression was entering a new and more challenging phase. King's advisers were concerned that a public declaration of his opposition to the war might endanger the movement's relationship with President Lyndon Johnson, whom they deemed a significant supporter of the African American struggle. King acknowledged this concern early in his remarks: "Peace and civil rights don't mix, they say. Aren't you hurting the cause of your people, they ask?"[2] But he was undeterred:

> Such questions mean that the inquirers have not really known me, my commitment or my calling. Indeed, their questions suggest that they do not know the world in which they live.
>
> In the light of such tragic misunderstanding, I deem it of signal importance to state clearly, and I trust concisely, why I believe that the path from Dexter Avenue Baptist Church—the church in Montgomery, Alabama, where I began my pastorate—leads clearly to this sanctuary tonight.[3]

I argue in this chapter that the "path" to which King refers—the path he had followed from the start of the Montgomery bus boycott, and the path he believed we are *all* obligated to follow—was the path of conscientious citizenship. As the speech "A Time to Break Silence" makes abundantly clear, King had always maintained that the conscientious citizen has an obligation to resist and redress injustice *both* "at home" and abroad. In "Letter from Birmingham City Jail," for instance, King was emphatic that "injustice anywhere is a threat to justice everywhere," and it was on the basis of his belief that "justice is indivisible" that he had rejected the charge that his support of nonviolent direct action in various southern communities amounted to a call for outside interference and agitation.[4] Further, as early as 1958, in *Stride toward Freedom*, King argued that the "racial crisis" that emerged in America during the 1950s and 1960s was part of a larger "world crisis," reflecting a broader resistance to colonialism and imperialism rooted in "a quest for freedom and human dignity."[5] Thus, although King's critics were deeply unsettled by his challenge to America's role in Vietnam, his "passionate plea to [his] beloved nation" expressed a lifelong commitment to conscientious citizenship.[6]

Yet King's plea in "A Time to Break Silence" was not just a call to end the war. In a critical passage of that essay, he calls for a "worldwide fellowship that lifts neighborly concern beyond one's tribe, race, class and nation" and embodies "all-embracing and unconditional love for all men."[7] My goal is to reconstruct the comprehensive vision of conscientious citizenship that underwrites this call. I contend that, for King, conscientious citizenship is a way of living that seeks to give substance to the idea that justice is indivisible, aspiring to an ideal that (adapting a notion from Josiah Royce) King called the "beloved community"—by which he meant a world that would allow reconciliation between the former oppressed and their former oppressors, and embody an all-embracing love for humanity.[8]

I will show in the first section that, for King, conscientious citizenship prescribes an absolute duty—within the bounds of broad respect for the rule of law—to resist and redress injustice within one's own society, as well as injustice that flows directly from that society's policies and practices toward nonmembers.[9] Conscientious citizenship requires us to resist and redress injustice whether or not we can claim to have been a victim of the relevant injustice, and to do so relying entirely on nonviolent resistance—even if this might require our own suffering and sacrifice. It is often thought that the philosophy of nonviolence was the theoretical core of King's thought, but I contend that one of King's most important (though least appreciated) achievements was to articulate the *value* of nonviolence as part of a larger view about the moral obligations of conscientious citizens to resist injustice in a manner that makes the beloved community possible. As he urged in "The Birth of a New Nation," upon returning from celebrating Ghanaian independence in 1957, "the aftermath of nonviolence is the beloved community" because the aftermath of nonviolence allows for redemption and reconciliation, rather than the perpetuation of hatred and bitterness.[10] In the second section I will extend the discussion of the concept of conscientious citizenship by considering several important challenges to its plausibility as an ideal.

In a passage from *The Trumpet of Conscience,* King seeks to confirm the plausibility of that ideal by celebrating what he took to be a noteworthy example of conscientious citizenship from the first phase of the civil rights movement: "The Negro freedom movement would have been historic and worthy even if it had only served the cause of civil rights. But its laurels are greater because it stimulated a broader social movement that elevated the moral level of the nation. . . . The Negro and white youth who in alliance fought bruising engagements with the status quo inspired each other with a sense of moral mission, and . . . gave the nation an example of self-sacrifice and dedication."[11] It is thus ironic that, in an essay published shortly after King's assassination, the political theorist Herbert Storing derided civil disobedience as the "theoretically and practically weak resort" of the "*subject* of law" who "cannot or will not take up the rights and duties of citizens." Storing also charged that King's defense of civil disobedience was "an unsuccessful attempt to combine, on the level of principle, revolution and conventional political action."[12] Yet as I show in the third section, the first phase of the civil rights movement (1956–1965) was quite successful at combining revolution and political action, and King was prescient in appreciating the significant role that civil disobedience could play in a modern constitutional democracy. King was surely right to characterize the first phase of the civil rights movement as a "genuine [revolution] . . . born from . . . the womb of intolerable conditions and unendurable situations."[13] Culminating in the Civil Rights Act of 1964 and the Voting Rights Act of 1965, it achieved a revolutionary expansion of American "political space" and a fundamental redrawing of the boundaries of the concept "equal citizen." Yet because it also called America back to the constitutional requirements set out in the so-called Reconstruction Amendments, the first phase of the movement showed that civil disobedience could be what John Rawls would eventually characterize as a "stabilizing device" in a constitutional democracy, bringing it back to (at least some) of its fundamental commitments.[14] In cities such as Montgomery, Birmingham, Selma, and Nashville, civil disobedience was a remarkably effective means of claiming and exercising the rights and duties of citizenship.

Yet even as King recognized and approved of the movement's potential to expand the political space in which African Americans could assert the rights and duties of citizenship in this transformative way, as I show in the fourth section, he often maintained that "the true meaning of the Montgomery story"—and indeed the true meaning of the African American struggle as a whole—was to be found in the emergence of a new collective self-understanding in the African American community.[15] That new self-understanding, King urged, was defined by a growing self-respect and an awareness of being "an equal element in a larger social compound" deserving of "first-class citizenship."[16] For King, this strongly suggested an important causal relationship between participation in certain kinds of social protest and the rise of political self-assertion and a sense of political efficacy. However, there is much disagreement about the importance of this connection and even about King's characterization of it. In the fourth section I discuss the content and broader implications of this disagreement.

Finally, I argue in the fifth section that while King clearly valued the "civil rights revolution" achieved by the "classic" phase of the civil rights movement, the focal point of his moral concern had always been the power of conscientious citizenship to produce a "true revolution of values."[17] His argument, in "A Time to Break Silence," about what that revolution would entail reflects his lifelong refusal to be governed by what he called "the apathy of conformist thought." It also confirms that King's commitment to the moral transformation of American society is a profound contribution to philosophical reflection on the obligations of conscientious citizenship.

"Justice Is Indivisible"

King certainly began as an "organic" intellectual, as Cornel West has argued, and some of his theoretical commitments were initially formulated to focus mainly on the challenges posed by the African American freedom struggle.[18] Moreover, in the 1950s and early 1960s, many of King's sermons, speeches, and theoretical writings emphasized his role as an organic intellectual, particularly his understanding of the need to bridge the gap between "theory" and the strategic and tactical demands of the first phase of the civil rights movement. This understanding framed his assertion in *Stride toward Freedom* that any successful emancipatory social movement must be grounded in "a philosophy that wins and holds the people's allegiance," and his claim that the philosophy of nonviolence was a main source of the cohesiveness of the first phase of the movement.[19] But as King maintained in such works as *Where Do We Go from Here* and *The Trumpet of Conscience,* the theoretical underpinnings of the civil rights movement were a serious contribution to broader debates about the requirements of justice. I contend that the essence of that contribution is captured in King's conception of conscientious citizenship, rooted in the idea that justice is indivisible.

To fully understand that conception, we must begin with the discussion in *Stride toward Freedom* in which King (implicitly) defines conscientious citizenship partly—though not exhaustively—in terms of a demand to conform to three moral principles.[20] According to the first of these principles, "Non-cooperation with evil is as much a moral obligation as is cooperation with good," and for King the obligation applies as fully to those who are victims of oppression as to those who are not.[21] But King believed, further, that noncooperation with evil must be guided by a second principle, according to which "nonviolence is an imperative in order to bring about ultimate community."[22] His commitment to nonviolence was partly rooted in the belief that it was the most reliable means for those who protest injustice to avoid becoming as evil as those who perpetrate it.

Yet he was also convinced that nonviolence was the most stable basis for moral reconciliation between the formerly oppressed and those who had oppressed them, and that reconciliation was critical to the possibility of the "beloved community"—in which it might be possible to realize an all-embracing love of humanity.[23] Still further, the effort to bring about the "beloved community" through nonviolent resistance must be shaped by a third principle: "Injustice anywhere is a threat to justice everywhere."[24] King appeals to this principle in one of his most famous replies to critics in "Letter from Birmingham City Jail," insisting that all Americans have both a right and duty to protest injustice in whatever regions of the country it might be found.

It is important, of course, to try to articulate the conception of justice underwriting King's conception of the beloved community. One challenge for his interpreters is that when King wrote or spoke from the rhetorical perspective of the organic intellectual, or as a prophetic and inspirational pastor, he did not always find it useful (or perhaps even possible) to fully articulate his fundamental commitments.[25] Nowhere is this more evident than in the well-known, but complex, passages from "Letter from Birmingham City Jail," in which King discusses the problem of distinguishing just from unjust laws. In these passages I take King to be appealing to

several different *criteria* of justice that are derived from a more fundamental *principle* of justice. For instance, one criterion is whether a law produces the "uplift" or "degradation" of human personality—and, of course,
King argues that humiliating segregation statutes degrade and distort
human personality. A second criterion is whether a law or code issued by
a majority makes demands of the minority that are not made of the majority enacting it. A third criterion asks us to consider whether a minority
has had a role in enacting or creating the laws to which it is subject. There
is no inconsistency here, for these criteria can be plausibly understood as
applications of a principle of equal liberty—a principle that, fully articulated, must surely include a requirement of equal political liberty.[26] Thus a
segregation statute is "unjust on its face," to adapt King's language, because
it violates an underlying principle of equal liberty. Other statutes can be
unjust in their application if applied in a fashion that violates the principle
of equal liberty, as when a law against parading without a permit is used, as
King writes, "to preserve segregation and to deny citizens the First Amendment privilege of peaceful assembly and peaceful protest."[27]

Yet we cannot understand King's comprehensive conception of justice
unless we also recognize the depth of his concern about economic inequality, and the disproportionate burden that he believed it placed upon
African Americans because of centuries of slavery, racial segregation, and
oppression. Some of King's admirers—and most of his hagiographers—
adopt an interpretation of King's legacy that focuses on his role in the fight
to outlaw segregation in public accommodations and to enforce the
right to vote for all Americans. But those struggles never constituted the
whole of the civil rights agenda, despite the tendency of popularized accounts of the civil rights movement to assume otherwise. Indeed, as Robert
Michael Franklin has argued, taken together King's contributions to the
debate about justice show that he believed that a just society would both
"protect the equal liberty of all citizens and provide a decent living standard for the most oppressed members of the community."[28] Moreover,
King's conception of "decent living standard" included an argument for a
guaranteed minimum income, and in such essays as the posthumously published "Showdown for Nonviolence," King argued for an "economic bill
of rights" that would also include such things as guaranteed jobs for all
who want to work.

Perhaps the most succinct account of King's comprehensive understanding of justice, as Franklin contends, appears in a critical passage
from *Where Do We Go from Here*, where King insists that "truth is found
neither in traditional capitalism nor in classical Communism. Each repre-

sents a partial truth. Capitalism fails to see the truth in collectivism. Communism fails to see the truth in individualism. Capitalism fails to realize that life is social. Communism fails to realize that life is personal. The good and just society is neither the thesis of capitalism nor the antithesis of Communism, but a socially conscious democracy which reconciles the truths of individualism and collectivism."[29] King went on to acknowledge that realizing this vision in the American context would require a "true revolution of values," and he argued that this revolution would "look uneasily on the glaring contrast of poverty and wealth," because "true compassion is more than flinging a coin to a beggar; it understands that an edifice which produces beggars needs restructuring."[30] As I will show in the last section of this chapter, in the last years of his life King became even more emphatic about his hope that, over time, the civil rights movement might nonviolently achieve the kind of moral revolution that could produce this restructuring of American institutions.

To summarize, then, King believed that any morally defensible response to injustice must conform to these three linked moral principles:

1. Noncooperation with evil is as much a moral obligation as cooperation with good.
2. Nonviolence is an imperative in order to bring about the beloved community.
3. Injustice anywhere threatens justice everywhere.

He also believed that, taken together, these principles constituted the best means of respecting human dignity, protecting equality and freedom, and expressing compassion in a way of life that acknowledges human interrelatedness while also respecting human individuality.

"Instruments of a Great Idea"

When we consider what these moral commitments entail, we see that King's conception of conscientious citizenship holds up a morally demanding—even morally arduous—ideal. This characteristic of King's general conception of conscientious citizenship, considered along with the implications of some of its specific demands, has raised four persistent questions. First, does King's conception embody an entirely unrealizable ideal? Second, if not, what does it really take for us to bring its realization within reach? Third, does the imperative of nonviolence constitute a flawed ideal, or perhaps make demands that are politically suspect from the point of view of those concerned to challenge racism, colonialism, and imperialism? Fourth, does the imperative of noncooperation with evil come perilously close to holding victims responsible for their own oppression?

King seems to have struggled with the "Is it realizable?" question for much of his early religious and intellectual life. He was profoundly skeptical of the power of discursive reason to help bring about social change, and in "Pilgrimage to Nonviolence" he wrote of the need for the "purifying power of faith"—especially in the form of Christian *agape*—to challenge the "distortions and rationalizations" of human reason.[31] For a time he apparently also "despaired of the power of love in solving social problems"—at least until he encountered the life and teachings of Mahatma Gandhi and then experienced the power of Gandhian *satyagraha* (understood as "truth-force" or "love force") at work in the Montgomery bus boycott. These experiences eventually confirmed his nascent sense that "the Christian doctrine of love operating through the Gandhian method of nonviolence was one of the most potent weapons available to oppressed people in their struggle for freedom."[32] In this way King eventually came to have a quite robust belief that the ideal of conscientious citizenship was humanly realizable, and he thought it important that he could find confirming evidence for his confidence in the courageous efforts of men and women who challenged segregation in the American South.

It is not clear whether King knew that Gandhi understood himself to be giving substance, in a modern political context, to the Socratic conception of conscientious citizenship. Gandhi had read an English translation of Plato's *Apology* in 1908 while serving a two-month prison sentence for his activism in South Africa, and he eventually translated the *Apology* into Gujarati as an affirmation of his belief that Socrates was a *satyagrahi* (a soldier of truth).[33] Of course, as we learn in "Letter from Birmingham City Jail," King also believed in the power of Socratic dialectic to help expose the rationalizations that preserve injustice, by generating what King called a "creative tension" within a society that could force it to confront and address the shame of that injustice. But King came to agree with Gandhi that to create the *kind* of "tension" capable of resisting and redressing injustice in the modern nation-state, it would often be necessary to assert the claims of justice through massive resistance in the form of nonviolent noncooperation.

But even if King's conception of conscientious citizenship can, thus, be held to embody a realizable ideal—as I think it does—it is clearly still a demanding ideal. Like Gandhi, King recognized that pursuit of the ideal required a special kind of strength: King often called it the "strength to love."[34] He also acknowledged that the strength to love combined several cognitive and dispositional elements, some of which took self-discipline and "self-purification" to develop and to sustain. Two of these elements are most important here. First, King thought that one had to be willing not only to endure sacrifice and suffering, but also to believe that undeserved suffering could be redemptive.[35] As he wrote in reflecting on Kwame Nkrumah's struggles in pursuit of Ghanaian independence, "there is no crown without a cross."[36] But second, and perhaps most fundamentally, King believed that one had to be able to willingly accept "unwanted and unfortunate circumstances" without relinquishing "infinite hope."[37] For much of his life King seemed to struggle with the question of the nature, sources, and possibility of infinite hope, and sometimes he seemed to think that it was accessible only to those who believed in the infinite goodness of a divine presence in the world. But he sometimes argued, as in "The Power of Nonviolence," that even nonreligious participants in the civil rights movement could retain the kind of hope that would support a commitment to the struggle, as long as they continued to believe that "something in the universe unfolds for justice."[38] Moreover, he was convinced that the outcome of modern freedom struggles in places such as India and Ghana provided reasons for the most secular among us to hold on to that belief that the universe is unfolding for justice.

So, let us assume that King can help us make sense of where the strength to act from disinterested love might come from (that is, how an "ordinary" person might find or develop disinterested love and the capacity to act from it), but we might still reasonably wonder whether the imperative of nonviolence embodies a fundamentally flawed ideal. For instance, Frantz Fanon famously objected that in the "colonial situation," the concept of nonviolence was typically introduced by colonial bourgeoisie hoping to "settle the colonial problem" through negotiations with colonized elites that excluded the supposedly "dangerous" (that is, potentially violent) colonized masses.[39] Yet it is important that during the American civil rights movement, the philosophy of nonviolence was never perceived or presented as an abstract, rarified ideal, but was disseminated through mass meetings that sought to transcend class and educational achievement. In fact, King was emphatic that in those meetings, "physicians, teachers, and lawyers sat or stood beside domestic workers and unskilled laborers" and that "the Ph.D.'s and the no 'D's' were bound together in a common venture."[40] We must recall his confidence, expressed in *Stride toward Freedom*, that the philosophy of nonviolence was in fact a principal source of the movement's cohesiveness.

In the context of the African American struggle, Stokely Carmichael was credited with an especially provocative formulation of the Black Power movement's principal objection to King's stance: "It made one fallacious assumption: In order for nonviolence to work, your opponent has to have a conscience. The United States has no conscience."[41] Yet, in an essay published after his return from a visit to India, King suggested that the truth of nonviolent resistance is far more complex than Carmichael's comment allows: "True nonviolent resistance is not unrealistic submission to evil power. It is rather a courageous confrontation of evil by the power of love, in the faith that it is better to be the recipient of violence than the inflictor of it, since the latter only multiplies the existence of violence in the universe, while the former may develop a sense of shame in the opponent, and thereby bring about a transformation and change of heart."[42] Of course, it is possible to produce a sense of shame only in those people who have not lost their capacity for shame, and that capacity surely depends on having what Carmichael refers to as "conscience." But King never denies that the nonviolent struggle against American racial segregation and oppression unavoidably involved confrontations with evil. Further, we must assume that some of the perpetrators of this evil were so consumed by hatred and bitterness that even if they had the capacity to feel shame, that capacity was either nonfunctional or could not be counted on to produce shame in response to the suffering of those people who were the objects of their hatred.

King eventually acknowledged that the skepticism embodied in the Black Power movement's stance on nonviolence was an understandable product of "despair and disappointment" in response to several ugly facts, including the frequency with which white brutality continued to go unpunished (even after Selma); the continuing economic precariousness of so many African Americans; the overrepresentation of poor and working-class African Americans in the ranks of those young men sent to fight in Vietnam; and the seemingly uncaring attitude of too many middle-class African Americans who seemed more consumed with protecting their position than with creating the beloved community.[43] But King nonetheless insisted, first, that the appeal to conscience had sometimes worked—perhaps especially in the period from the Montgomery bus boycott in 1956 to Selma in 1965. Second, he seemed to gradually acknowledge—as in the late essay "Showdown to Nonviolence"—that, going forward, nonviolent direct action might become less of a strategy to appeal to America's "conscience," and more of a critical effort to create multiracial alliances with the persistence to keep their shared socioeconomic interests in the center of

American political debate. That is, King seemed fully ready to acknowledge that there might be limits to the political effectiveness of the "classic" Socratic dialectic.

But what of King's claims about the scope of the obligation to refuse passive cooperation with evil? Could these claims possibly commit him to a way of thinking that "blames the victim"? King was certainly adamant that the failure to actively resist an evil to which one knows oneself to be subject is, essentially, to willingly accept and even "cooperate" with that evil.[44] Further, he believed that to cooperate with the oppressor is ultimately to provide the oppressor with "a convenient justification" for oppression, and that "to be true to one's conscience . . . a righteous man has no alternative but to refuse to cooperate with an evil system."[45] Some contemporary critics will surely object that this way of thinking about the obligation to resist injustice involves a slippery slope that too easily leads to a tendency to "blame the victim." I believe that King's account foreshadows a view defended by Iris Young that allows us to distinguish between the concept of moral blame for perpetrating the evils of racial oppression and the concept of responsibility to resist and redress the injustice of that oppression.[46] But I do not deny that King's conception of conscientious citizenship places a stringent demand on those who have been subject to racial oppression to affirm their "righteousness" by refusing to cooperate with the evils of racial oppression.

Yet King clearly believed, and I think correctly, that it would not have been possible to destroy the legal foundations of American racism if African Americans had not been willing to take on a large part of the responsibility for claiming the rights of first-class citizenship. In this regard King was echoing Frederick Douglass's insistence, in 1863, that emancipated "colored men" had a duty as American citizens to enlist in the Union Army, even though King is calling on the power of nonviolence, rather than the violence of war, to fight racial oppression.[47] King certainly understood that "the way of nonviolence" demanded a courageous willingness to suffer and sacrifice.[48] He also understood that, as with any population, not every African American could be expected to be ready to participate in acts of resistance. But he continued to hold the position, best articulated in *Stride toward Freedom,* that if a "creative minority" could stand ready to say "We will match your capacity to inflict suffering with our capacity to endure suffering," it might be possible to wear down opposition to segregation and produce a way of living with the capacity to outlive the "broken community" that tends to result from violence. King never stopped believing, that is, that it was critical for African Americans to understand that they had the opportunity to be "instruments of a great idea" and that such an opportunity comes along very rarely.[49]

"A Most Creative and Powerful Social Force"

It should be clear by now that the ideals, values, and principles that constituted King's conception of conscientious citizenship reflected his effort to combine theoretical resources from several important religious and philosophical traditions: most notably (1) the philosophical legacy of the Platonic Socrates; (2) Gandhi's understanding of the constructive political possibilities of noncooperation as *satyagraha* (or "firmness in the truth"); and (3) his Christian commitments to human dignity and equality, the virtues of faith, hope, and disinterested love, along with a belief in the possibility of redemptive suffering and the ideal of the "ultimate" or beloved community. Yet as King acknowledges in "Letter from Birmingham City Jail," one of the most salient characteristics of this conception is the fact that it is a powerful echo of Socrates's commitment to the examined life, and a modern affirmation of the political importance of Socrates's conscientious stance as a "stinging fly" on the neck of Athens. It is thus ironic that some critics of the civil rights movement—including Herbert Storing, as I note above—remained resistant to the idea that the movement was a clear commitment to the idea of conscientious citizenship.

This resistance may partly reflect an implicit recognition of the extraordinary difficulty of the task facing the civil rights movement in the period from 1956 to 1965. The Reconstruction Amendments (allegedly) meant to secure equal citizenship for African Americans had been effectively invalidated by the fiction, in the 1896 Supreme Court decision in *Plessy v. Ferguson,* that "separate but equal" citizenship was a constitutionally acceptable substitute; southern legal structures and extralegal brutalities and indignities cemented the power of that fiction; and powerful coalitions in the U.S. Congress continued to block every effort to legislatively reject that fiction.[50] So how could a movement drawing only on nonviolent resistance create a path toward the redefinition of what it meant to be an "equal citizen"? That is, how could civil disobedience effectively challenge the cruelties and indignities of racial segregation that had become such a powerful obstacle to African American freedom in the twentieth century? Still further, how could it mount such a challenge and—at the same time—count as "taking up" the rights and duties of equal citizenship, rather than acting simply as the subject of unjust laws?

To begin, it is important to recognize that the civil rights movement had to address two different but related problems associated with the legacy of *Plessy v. Ferguson*. First, it was necessary to expose the conceptual inconsistency embodied in the idea of separate-but-equal citizenship. To do this meant showing that in education, employment, housing, and even everyday encounters with critical "public accommodations," the social, legal, and economic practices that constituted racial separation in American life could do nothing but produce *profound* inequalities. Some of the inequalities were material in nature. For instance, if one is denied equal opportunity for certain kinds of employment, the inequality that results will surely be a material inequality. If one is unable to count on receiving equal protection from the local police force when one is the victim of a crime, the inequality that results is likely to be material. But as was implicit in central arguments in *Brown v. Board of Education* (1954), some of the most salient inequalities produced by racial segregation were not essentially (or at least not primarily) material inequalities. Rather, they were inequalities in the distribution of what we can call "psychosocial goods," such as social standing and self-respect. This is why King's account of the "stinging darts of segregation," in a powerful passage from "Letter from Birmingham City Jail," devotes so much attention to providing a complex catalogue of both material and psychosocial inequalities.[51]

But, second, it was necessary for the movement to find some way to prevent the average American (who, we must assume, might not have been directly perpetrating the worst evils of segregation) from effectively "averting their glance" from the effects of segregation. I have argued elsewhere that one of the most common, but vexing, sources of the failure to resist and redress injustice is the widespread human tendency to "affect ignorance" of wrongdoing and evil.[52] The success of the first phase of the civil rights movement surely depended on its capacity to make it difficult to avert one's glance from the evils of separate-but-equal citizenship, wherever one lived. As I note above, King doubted that ordinary discursive reason-giving and argument could be effective in these contexts—and rightly so. He also realized—as a matter of practical political wisdom—that not even his innovative amalgamation of Socratic dialectic, Gandhian nonviolent noncooperation, and Christian *agape* would have been sufficient, in itself, to keep the average nonblack American from turning away from disturbing evidence of the evils of segregation. This is why, as many commentators have noted, King came to rely so heavily on the willingness of the national (and eventually international) press to expose the cruelties and indignities of segregation.

But I want to challenge the idea that the movement's reliance on media attention to the evils of segregation was *merely* a political strategy. In an otherwise insightful and compelling account of the civil rights revolution, the constitutional scholar Bruce Ackerman dismissively describes King's approach as a "mix of high Gandhian principle and shrewd media politics."[53] But that approach was much more theoretically sophisticated than this comment allows. For it revealed King's appreciation of an unexpected complexity of moral argument and inquiry that has special importance for the work of social movements. What King understood is that moral progress in social and political institutions sometimes depends on expanding *perceptual* space—to dislodge prejudices and habits of belief that limit our ability to take a novel view of the world, our place in it, and our relationships to others. This is the sort of insight that plausibly led John Dewey to claim, in *Art as Experience,* that we must sometimes rely on art—as an expression of creative imagination—to bridge the barriers between us.[54] It is also the insight that often led King to make the (otherwise mysterious) claim that nonviolent civil disobedience (sometimes by virtue of the unearned suffering and sacrifice it required) is a "creative" force for social change.

Like Dewey, King realized that discursive reason-giving and argument are often ineffective at bridging the barriers that divide us, and that sometimes we must rely instead on the arresting, disarming, and perceptually disruptive power of images (in the broadest sense)—including disturbing images—to produce morally important transformations in the way human beings perceive the world and their place in it. This is the realization that shaped the New Deal Photography project (1935–1944) meant to document the hardships of rural poverty in Depression-era America in order to generate public support for the programs.[55] Moreover, even if such projects can also function as "shrewd" politics, and even if we want to label their appeal as "propagandistic," there is a moral difference between the cynical use of images to encourage exclusion, coercion, and violence and the nonviolent use of images to promote a more inclusive society.

Most important, there are good grounds to accept that King was sincere in his belief that unearned suffering was redemptive, and in his conviction that the image of unearned suffering was a morally legitimate way of trying to produce moral transformations in others. These beliefs are at the core of those Christian elements of his conception of conscientious citizenship, and as King's interpreters we must not let the cynicism of an aggressively secular age make us unable to suppose that a Baptist minister committed to social justice could be sincere in believing that his religious convictions provided a plausible support for that project. Indeed, as many of King's interpreters have argued, we have to understand that King's political thought was suffused with the principles of the social activist tradition of the Black American Church.[56] Perhaps most important, it is a significant virtue of King's life and work that he could recognize and celebrate those aspects of non-Christian religious traditions, and of secular moral views, that he took to be "saturated" with the power of socially constructive Christian values like forgiveness and disinterested human concern (*agape*).[57]

To be sure, the civil rights revolution that resulted from the first decade of the civil rights movement was not achieved solely—or even primarily—by those who were willing to answer the call of conscience in response to images of suffering. As sociologist Aldon Morris has shown, the first decade of the civil rights movement was extraordinary evidence of the capacity of African American communities to organize for social change.[58] The revolution they helped bring about required the courageous action of hundreds of thousands of people (sometimes in multiracial and multiethnic alliances) who participated in boycotts, marches, sit-ins, freedom rides, and efforts to integrate schools and colleges. These were organized and supported by groups such as the Montgomery Improvement Association, the Southern Christian Leadership Conference, the Student Nonviolent Coordinating Committee, and the NAACP. Leaders of these groups built on the lessons of the boycotts, sit-ins, and marches (and the brutality that often arose "in reply") to exert pressure on courts (especially the federal courts), the Congress, and the Executive Branch to finally give legal force to the pre-*Plessy* Reconstruction Amendments.

But the fact that they were calling for legal enforcement of nineteenth-century amendments should remind us that, for all that was revolutionary about the movement's success, there was *nothing new* in the idea that systematic racial segregation and exclusion were incompatible with the ideals of American political morality that were supposed to have been embodied in the Thirteenth, Fourteenth and Fifteenth Amendments to the U.S. Constitution. This is the truth that King conveys so powerfully in famous public addresses like the "I Have a Dream" speech and in the historic essay that we now call "Letter from Birmingham City Jail." When critics like Herbert Storing failed to appreciate that truth, what they failed to understand is that—in the words of John Rawls—"used with due restraint and sound judgment," civil disobedience can be an important "stabilizing device" in a constitutional democracy, calling it back to its fundamental "conditions of free cooperation."[59] What could be a more reasonable and conscientious exercise of rights and duties of citizenship than to draw on the "creative and powerful social force" of nonviolent resistance to reestablish the conditions of free cooperation in the experiment that we call American democracy?

"The True Meaning of the Struggle"

One source of King's confidence in the creative and powerful force of nonviolent resistance was his belief that it had helped African Americans better appreciate their capacity for political agency and ultimately develop a collective sense of genuine political efficacy. In *Stride toward Freedom* King urged that the "true meaning of the Montgomery story"—and by extension of the entire first phase of the civil rights movement—was to be found in the emergence of an African American self-understanding that involved both a consciousness of being "an equal element in a larger social compound" and a "new determination to struggle and sacrifice" in pursuit of first-class citizenship. "One can never understand the bus protest in Montgomery," he wrote, "without understanding that there is a new Negro in the South, with a new sense of dignity and destiny."[60]

Yet in the 1960s, early attempts by political theorists to analyze the structures and processes through which the movement worked often failed to appreciate the grounds of King's confidence. This failure was largely a function of the fact that these early analyses tended to focus mainly on the external, outward-facing characteristics of political protest, rather than on the possibility there might be "inward-facing" goods internal to the practice of political protest. Nor could they consider the possibility that some of the goods internal to participation in political protests might have both intrinsic value—a new sense of dignity and destiny—as well as instrumental value—a willingness to engage in political action to claim one's citizenship rights. Thus, in what became an influential early discussion, James Q. Wilson sought to understand the politics of protest by framing it as, essentially, "the problem of the powerless" who seek to enter into a process of political bargaining, but who have no genuine political resources to exchange and so rely on "negative inducements"—such as unfavorable publicity or economic boycotts.[61] Wilson, like many who drew on his analysis, was (not unexpectedly) pessimistic about the long-term merits of protest as a political strategy.[62] But these accounts relied on a way of framing the civil rights movement that failed to consider the possible longer-term value of some of the goods internal to it.[63]

But even more sympathetic critics differed with King over the "true meaning" of the first phase of the civil rights movement, as well as over the extent to which the external and internal revolutions it brought about were as momentous as King may have thought. In a provocative article entitled "From Protest to Politics: The Future of the Civil Rights Movement," Bayard Rustin made the (possibly surprising) claim that many of the gains of the "classic" era of the movement were "relatively peripheral both to the American socioeconomic order and to the fundamental conditions of life of the Negro people."[64] He went on to ask, for instance, "what is the value of winning access to public accommodations for those who lack money to use them." Rustin was especially concerned to challenge the reliance on "protest," urging that the time had come for the civil rights movement to "translate itself into a political movement."[65]

King explicitly acknowledged the ending of the first phase of the civil rights movement—though he marked the end by reference to the Voting Rights Act of 1965, rather than the Civil Rights Act of 1964. He also understood that because the African American struggle needed to turn more directly to the pursuit of substantive socioeconomic equality, it might well require new strategies and tactics. Thus, in *Where Do We Go from Here* he discussed the need for African Americans to amass political power, to focus their political energy on trying to change the institutions and practices that governed material well-being, and to recognize that in making these moves they would certainly encounter a "stiffening of white resistance" to their efforts. But as he stressed in late works such as *Trumpet of Conscience* and the tragically prophetic essay "Showdown for Nonviolence" (published in 1968, shortly after he was assassinated), what he would not relinquish was, first, the idea that nonviolent collective action might be at least part of a defensible strategy to pursue socioeconomic equality and, second, the idea that the right *kind* of collective action should seek to develop new allegiances—both multiracial and eventually international—organized around concerns that could unite the poor and economically insecure workers across familiar racial and ethnic lines. This stance was partly a reflection of his belief in the power of collective action to create a new sense of community across formerly divided groups. In "Showdown for Nonviolence," for instance, he wrote hopefully of the possibility of a "coalition of conscience" that might generate a new spirit of class and racial harmony.[66] But his continuing commitment to collective action also reflected his confidence in the power of nonviolent action to generate a new sense of political efficacy in its participants.

Disagreement about the true meaning of the civil rights struggle took on a very different character in the debate between King and leaders of the Black Power movement. Stokely Carmichael argued in "Toward Black Liberation" that instead of a "New Negro" imbued with a "new sense of dignity and destiny," the true posture of the civil rights movement "was that of the dependent, the suppliant. The theory was that without attempting to create any organized base of political strength itself, the civil rights movement could, by forming coalitions with various 'liberal' pressure organizations within the white community . . . influence national legislation and national social patterns."[67] Carmichael was adamant in his claims that the lessons of American history revealed the limitations of this stance. He insisted, for instance, that political alliances based on "appeals to conscience" were unreliable, because the organizations and institutions making up those alliances "have no consciences outside their special interests." The only path to African American liberation, for Carmichael, was the path of Black Power.

It is seldom noted that one of King's challenges in responding to Carmichael's interpretation of the civil rights movement was that—coming out of the context of the American South, which legally suppressed African American access to the ballot box—it was only with the passage of the Voting Rights Act in 1965 that it made strategic sense to foreground the importance of African American participation in "ordinary" political processes. Moreover, after the passage of the Voting Rights Act, King consistently emphasized the importance of developing African American political power and even challenged what he saw as continued African American reluctance to participate fully in political life. Of course, even as he began to emphasize "conventional" political participation, he continued to stress the value of multiracial political allegiances—including allegiances with organized labor—that he thought critical to furthering the African American struggle for socioeconomic equality. Still further, he simply did not believe that it would be possible for the successful pursuit of African American economic well-being to be built on a "separatist" foundation.[68]

But perhaps most important, King believed that even though the idea of Black Power provided a "gratifying slogan," it was rooted in a fundamental hopelessness that would not allow any movement built on that idea to last.[69] King always acknowledged that revolutions have often been built on the combination of hope and hate—even as he continued to assert the superiority of the Gandhian project of building revolution on the combination of hope and love. King also recognized that revolution is often born of despair. Yet he insisted that though born of despair, revolution "cannot long be sustained by despair." Indeed, for King, an important lesson of the civil rights struggle was to be found in the proof it provided of the transformative power of hope, more precisely the transformative power of what he called infinite hope.

King clearly had an extraordinary capacity to hold on to infinite hope. For instance, it seems to have underwritten his continued confidence that—even in spite of persistent political indifference toward economic inequality, the urban riots that responded to that indifference, and (apparent) white "backlash" to those riots—multiracial collective action might create a new "coalition of conscience" and "a new spirit of class and racial harmony" to produce real economic benefits for the poor and the underemployed.[70] The power of infinite hope also seems to have been a force in shaping ambitious plans for the Poor People's Campaign (which King would not live to really see). Further, it was surely infinite hope that sustained King's commitment to the possibility of the worldwide fellowship described in "A Time to Break Silence."

But King nonetheless understood that the African American capacity for hope had been greatly tested by the national failure to mount consistent and substantive responses to socioeconomic inequality. King revealed his own frustrations in a provocative passage from *Where Do We Go from Here:* "The daily life of the Negro is still lived in the basement of the Great Society. He is still at the bottom despite the few who have penetrated to slightly higher levels. Even where the door has been forced partially open, mobility for the Negro is still sharply restricted. There is often no bottom at which to start, and when there is, there is almost always no room at the top."[71] Like many other leaders in the African American community, King came to believe that America's war in Vietnam was a serious part of the problem.

"A True Revolution of Values"

Even before the path of conscientious citizenship led King to publicly condemn the Vietnam War, he had indicated in numerous contexts his conviction that the genuine pursuit of justice in America would require a "true revolution of values." King had long maintained, for instance, that no judicial decision or act of Congress could, alone, destroy America's deepseated racism; that the remedy for persistent poverty in America would require the fundamental rejection of American materialism; and that reliance on violence to resolve human conflicts would continue as long as love and power were construed as "polar opposites."[72] Moreover, even as early as 1961 King had argued that the best of "the American dream" would be broadly accessible only if America could learn to adopt a global perspective on the requirements of justice and on its role in realizing justice.[73]

But the speech "A Time to Break Silence" is important for the clarity with which King linked his call for a revolution in values with his belief in the indivisibility of justice. That speech is in a sense an extended argument for the claim that the problems of racism, persistent poverty, unbridled materialism, and militarism are inextricably linked together. In one instance of what King took to be the intertwining of different forms of injustice, he makes a compelling case for the view that while various poverty programs had offered "real promise" of hope for alleviating poverty, the war in Vietnam was drawing "men, skills and money" at such a rate that it was destroying the hopes of the poor. In another example, King decried the nation's readiness to send young black men and young white men to kill and die "in brutal solidarity," while remaining unwilling to allow many of those same young men to study together in the same schools.

However, "A Time to Break Silence" is no betrayal of King's fervent commitment to the moral imperative of compassion and nonviolence. In fact, it is a powerful expression of King's concern about the inconsistency of calling for young African Americans to reject violence as an outlet for their anger and despair without also challenging the violence being carried out in the war. Moreover, in taking the extraordinary (and, at the time, extremely controversial) step of asking Americans to try "to see the enemy's point of view, to hear his questions, to know his assessment of ourselves," King was urging his audience to reflect on what compassion might really come to.

An equally important characteristic of King's speech was the way in which it made explicit a notion that had always shaped his reflection: the notion that there is a fundamental link between conscientious citizenship and democratic accountability. At one point in the essay, King even encourages ministers of draft age to trade their (standard) ministerial exemption from fighting for status as conscientious objectors, because "every man of human convictions must decide on the protest that best suits his convictions, but we must all protest." Like all of King's discussions of the duties of conscientious citizenship, this argument should remind us of the wisdom of John Dewey, who insisted that democracy works only if we come to see it as "a way of life" rather than some external "mechanism" that demands nothing more than the habitual, unthinking performance of preexisting political duties.[74]

Of course, there is significant risk in actively accepting the obligations of conscientious citizenship as a way of life. This lesson has tragically unfolded, again and again, in the lives of virtually all the great theorists and practitioners of conscientious citizenship, from Socrates to Gandhi and King. But given the challenges that still confront us, we can only hope—as King would surely have wanted us to hope—that the spirit of conscientious citizenship remains alive and well.

14

Requiem for a Dream: The Problem-Space of Black Power

BRANDON M. TERRY

On June 5, 1966, the irascible civil rights activist and veteran James Meredith set out on his controversial "March Against Fear," pledging to walk from Memphis, Tennessee, to Jackson, Mississippi, to inspire militant confrontation with "the all-pervasive and overriding fear that dominates the day-to-day life of the Negro in the United States." Few leading civil rights activists or reporters expected anything of consequence to come from this trek, but Aubrey James Norwell, a self-appointed defender of white supremacist rule, could not countenance even this idiosyncratic provocation. On the campaign's second day, he ambushed Meredith, firing scores of shotgun pellets into the civil rights icon's flesh.[1]

Meredith survived, and in the shooting's wake Martin Luther King, Jr., and other civil rights leaders rushed to his hospital bedside, hoping to secure blessing to continue the march. This commitment, however, would require a compromise between organizations increasingly at odds over a range of issues, including Vietnam, riots, progressive coalitions, and black nationalism. A tense, foreboding meeting at the same Lorraine Motel where King would soon be assassinated ended with no such conciliation. A dispute over criticisms of the Lyndon Johnson administration and its proposed 1966 Civil Rights Bill led the National Association for the Advancement of Colored People (NAACP) and the National Urban League (NUL) to defect from the march to retain Johnson's favor, while Stokely Carmichael, the brash organizer recently elected the chairman of Student Nonviolent Coordinating Committee (SNCC), and Floyd McKissick, the radical lawyer who had become director of the Congress on Racial Equality (CORE) earlier that year, decided to forge ahead.[2]

Even this fragile compromise, however, quickly buckled as Mississippi's Highway 51 became an impromptu forum for passionate discussions between King and others over the ethics of racial solidarity, the legitimacy of interracial coalitions, armed self-defense, and other matters. These debates erupted into public view on June 16, as the Meredith March reached Greenwood, one of the principal sites for SNCC's voter registration and community organizing efforts. Carmichael later described his arrival as "like a homecoming," joking that organizing had landed him "in jail so much even the police chief knew [him]."[3] That Greenwood police would again that day subject their old foe to the familiar indignity of arbitrary arrest, therefore, was less notable than Carmichael's dramatic speech in response at a rally later that evening: "This is the 27th time I have been arrested—I ain't going to jail no more! . . . We want Black Power! . . . That's right. That's what we want, black power. We don't have to be ashamed of it . . . We have begged the president. We've begged the federal government—that's all we've been doing . . . It's time we stand up and take over. Every courthouse in Mississippi ought to be burned down tomorrow to get rid of the dirt and the mess."[4] As Carmichael's biographer Peniel Joseph writes, this speech, and the widely reported spectacle of an enthusiastic crowd repeating "Black Power" in response, "transformed the aesthetics of the black freedom struggle and forever altered the course of the modern civil rights movement."[5]

Carmichael's appropriation and weaponization of the phrase "Black Power," and the stunning coalescence of political ideas, cultural criticism, and social movement activity under its sign, plunged Carmichael, King, and a host of intellectuals, activists, state actors, and others into a period of frenzied argument, organizing, and combat.[6] Marked by the emergence of critical periodicals, like *The Black Scholar, The Black World* (formerly *Negro Digest*), *Ramparts,* and *NKOMBO,* and the founding of important organizations and collaborative political efforts like the Black Panther Party (BPP), the Black Arts Movement (BAM), the Detroit Revolutionary Union Movement (DRUM), US, and the National Black Political Convention, this ferment represents a vibrant period in the history of the black "counterpublic" sphere.[7]

Tragically, however, most renderings of this period obscure its political-philosophical import, or the creative and compelling role King played in these arguments, by failing to treat the thinkers of the civil rights and Black

Power eras as engaged in serious intellectual exchange, rather than as convenient foils in a hackneyed narrative. As scholars of "Black Power studies" have long lamented, there remains a pernicious influence of a "good sixties/bad sixties" dichotomy that structures prominent narratives of the era by contrasting "the heroic, nonviolent demonstrations against Jim Crow that flourished between the 1954 *Brown* decision and the 1965 Watts uprising, with the downward spiral of identity politics, open advocacy of armed rebellion, and sectarianism that followed the turn to Black Power."[8] This binary serves as the skeletal structure for further obscurantism, when fleshed out by characterizations that reduce the emergence and intellectual substance of Black Power *solely* to geographical, generational, emotional, or psychological criteria.[9] Suffering collateral damage is our grasp of the import of King's critical engagement with black nationalist and Black Power thought.

It must be admitted that occasionally King's own formulations have led to these unfortunate intellectual dead ends. King once derisively claimed that Black Power "did not spring full grown from the head of some philosophical Zeus," and criticized it as "a cry of disappointment . . . born from the wounds of despair."[10] The *prima facie* profundity of this objection, however, dissolves upon pressure. Even schools of thought we associate with a single, pathbreaking intellectual (such as Marxism) have multiple currents of influence and overlap that constitute them. Black Power's particular currents remain influential both in black political life and in contemporary political thought more broadly.[11]

Moreover, many indispensable works and traditions of political philosophy also emerge from "wounds of despair." A formative impetus for liberal political philosophy, at least in its social contract variant, was the traumatic experience of religious conflict in the English civil wars, and Marxism was born, in large part, from meditation on the sufferings of European laborers at a decisive stage of industrialization.[12] These moments of despair—of cultural crisis, intense political contention, and communicative breakdown—are, not infrequently, generative of semantic innovation and political-philosophical creativity.[13]

King himself, in his later work, narrates a train of disappointing abuses against blacks that continue despite the optimism behind the passage of civil rights legislation, the supposed avowal of federal authorities to enforce these laws, and the courageous, nonviolent politics of democratic sacrifice proffered by activists. The relevant question, therefore, is not *disappointment as such*, but whether these disappointments license a more general skepticism toward civil rights liberalism or American civic culture.

Such debates speak quite clearly to familiar criticisms of liberalism and liberal democracies from other traditions, particularly the Marxist and republican critique that the rule of law and civil rights need expansive economic equality and countervailing political power for fulfillment of the freedom they purport to inscribe, or the Hegelian and Schmittian contentions that the liberal fictions of social contract and cooperation, or the "universal" extension of rights, are qualified or undermined by thicker, and more fundamental, practices of recognition, group antagonism, and collective identification.[14]

A similar critique could be leveled against King's influential and totalizing characterization of Black Power as fatalistic and hopeless. Pessimism, it must be remembered, attaches to *particular* objects or concerns. Therefore, while we can certainly describe Black Power intellectuals as not especially sanguine about King's left-liberalism, moralism, or aspirations for racial reconciliation, they are often jarringly (and occasionally absurdly) optimistic about black folks' autonomous capacities for world-making collective action, cultural creativity, and self-redefinition.

The Problem-Space of Black Power

If the Black Power movement "remains an enigma," as Peniel Joseph has suggested, it seems that a great deal of the mystery flows from our failure to plumb these sorts of questions by carefully mapping the character of shifts in the "problem-spaces" of black political life. Drawing upon David Scott, I use "problem-space" to describe a "cognitively intelligible arrangement of concepts, ideas, images, meanings, and so on," but more importantly, a contingent *"context of argument and, therefore, one of intervention."*[15] Because Black Power is far less a unitary movement than an assemblage of resonant and overlapping activity in politics, cultural production, and creative expression under a sign that tracks particular questions, contentions, and concepts, this analytical approach is more likely to bear fruit than those that try, hopelessly, to "define" Black Power as such. The idea of a problem-space, as Scott expounds, helps us keep track of "an ensemble of questions and answers around which a horizon of identifiable stakes (conceptual as well as ideological-political stakes) hangs," including the very definition of what rises to the level of a *problem* and "the particular questions that seem worth asking and the kinds of answers that seem worth having."[16]

This angle of approach is also an advance over characterizations of Black Power debates as the repetition of a transhistorical "black nationalism" against a similarly timeless "integrationism." Such binary formulations do special violence to the complexities of King, whose thought moves dialectically between race and nation in its accounts of the wellsprings of political struggle, African American particularity, and the meaning and direction of history. For example, a central braid running through King's thought is the idea that African Americans are engaged in the struggle of a "creative minority," in Arnold Toynbee's conception, to draw insight from their ambivalent heritage on the margins of the great civic traditions of American democracy *and* their fragile, transnational identification and solidarity with oppressed, nonwhite peoples, to "give the new spiritual dynamic to Western civilization that it so desperately needs to survive."[17] This neo-Du Boisian idea provides the scaffolding for King's remarks elsewhere that "consciously or unconsciously, the American Negro has been caught up by the black *Zietgeist* . . . [and] feels a deepening sense of identification with his black African brothers, and with his brown and yellow brothers of Asia, South America, and the Caribbean," as well as his suggestion that African Americans are moving "*with them* . . . toward the promised land of racial justice."[18] This is *not*, it should be emphasized, a conception of black identity, or black peoplehood, that treats American citizenship or "inclusion" as the *singular* horizon of ethical or political significance.

In this vein, a more careful reconstruction of the "problem-space" of Black Power intellectuals, and of King's critical navigation of this space, requires not simply a return to key texts and speeches of the Black Power era, but a more granular mapping of political disagreement.[19] This approach sees reiterations of black nationalist claims about the encumbered selves forged by intergenerational belonging, linked fate, common oppression, and/or shared identity; political aspirations to institutional autonomy, "self-determination," and "self-defense"; and normative demands on racial loyalty, solidarity, primacy, and pride, as all articulated through the horizons of a unique historical moment. Thus, although Black Power is distinguished, in particular, by a revival of black nationalist ideas that can be traced back to Martin Delany and other advocates of black emigration from the United States in the nineteenth century, the *dynamism* of Black Power emerges from historically particular sources of urgency, crisis, and authority. Put differently, these ideas take on a particular form and direction when understood against a horizon inflected by successive urban riots, portentous changes in political economy, a resurgent and racially charged American conservatism, the intensification of global anticolonial revolt, and the machinations of Cold War geopolitics seemingly on the brink of nuclear annihilation.

A comprehensive cartography of Black Power contestation, I argue, would cover roughly eleven themes: (1) political violence, (2) the politics of "self-determination," (3) identity and culture, (4) the social theorization of the ghetto, (5) gender, sexuality, and the family, (6) the political agency of the poor, (7) theories of racism, (8) social justice in an age of emerging postindustrial capitalism, (9) mid–Cold War geopolitics, (10) the political critique of African American religion, and (11) philosophical reflections on hope and pessimism. Constraints of space here do not allow for a full elaboration on each of these domains, but I hope to use the more familiar theme of violence—especially as topics of integration and racial identity are covered elsewhere in this volume—as a generative point of entry toward a sketch of this larger terrain and King's movements therein.[20]

It is foolish, however, to proceed in any reflection on the debate over political violence in the Black Power era without immediately distinguishing between *forms* of political violence advocated or entertained by Black Power writers, and the divergent justifications or criticisms that might be marshaled accordingly. Black Power debates were primarily concerned with eliciting or preventing African Americans' potential commitment to three forms of violence: (1) armed self-defense, (2) rioting, and (3) revolutionary violence (including terrorism and other asymmetric violence, such as guerilla warfare). Analytically distinct, but in practice promiscuously mingled, is a fourth theme: (4) the ethics and strategy of *rhetorically* calling for the oppressed to use violence (which, of course, includes both *sincere* and *insincere* calls for violence).[21]

On Self-Defense

One of King's earliest militant critics was Robert F. Williams, the chairman of the Monroe, North Carolina, outpost of the NAACP in the 1950s, who later became an icon among Black Power advocates. A decorated veteran, Williams rejuvenated his moribund branch through the recruitment of working-class members and a commitment to local demonstrations.[22] A series of horrific injustices involving sex and the color line, however, catapulted Williams to national prominence. In one, a white man sexually assaulted a pregnant black woman in her home in front of her children and was acquitted by a baldly racist and sexist defense.

Incensed by these miscarriages of justice, and compelled by local black women to organize for protection, Williams released a statement declaring to the press that because "the federal government will not stop lynching, and since the so-called courts lynch our people legally, if it's necessary to stop lynching with lynching, then we must resort to that method."[23] These remarks led immediately to censure by the NAACP's national leadership and criticism from King.[24] King argued that Williams's public pronouncements structured the pathways of black political action along a false dichotomy. Williams, he charged, was an advocate "of violence as a tool of advancement, organized as in warfare, deliberately and consciously," and that he treated the choice confronting African Americans as one between "tak[ing] up arms," or becoming "cringing and submissive."[25]

In response, Williams defiantly pressed his case in print and in practice, achieving notoriety for his role in an outbreak of white mob violence occasioned by Freedom Ride demonstrations in Monroe. Leading armed resistance to what he later described as a "pogrom," Williams himself was forced to flee under the threat of felony charges or extrajuridical violence.[26] Disputing the legitimacy of these charges, and unable to secure safety via police protection or extradition, Williams ultimately fled to Cuba, living in asylum under Fidel Castro before moving to China as a guest of Mao Zedong. While in exile, Williams authored *Negroes with Guns* (1962), a canonical text for the emerging Black Power generation. Attempting to clarify and substantiate his more caustic public remarks, the book articulates influential arguments about the importance of armed self-defense for African American civil rights activism.

In his book Williams claims—as his "only difference with Dr. King"— that "flexibility in the freedom struggle" is necessary. In this formulation, "flexibility" entails supporting "passive resistance" and "non-violent tactics," but *only* where "feasible." This feasibility criterion turns on a distinction Williams draws between "civilized conditions where the law safeguards the citizens' right of peaceful demonstrations" and those where there is a "breakdown of the law." In the latter context, Williams proclaims, "the individual citizen has a right to protect his person, his family, his home and his property." This "accepted right of Americans," he argues, "is so simple and proper that it is self-evident.[27]

King, however, never denied either the existence of a natural or civil right to self-defense or the legitimacy of its exercise in some circumstances. In 1959 he conceded that a "pure nonviolence" that abjures even self-defense cannot be the foundation of black protest politics because it requires forms of discipline and courage that are implausibly "extraordinary" and cannot attract mass support. With no particular ambivalence, King also grants that "all societies, from the most primitive to the most cultured and civilized, accept [the right to exercise violence in self-defense] as moral and legal." In some cases, he allows, self-defense can even garner the support of other citizens and spectators, insofar as its judicious use re-flects "courage and self-respect."[28] When pitched in these terms, King ar-gued that a debate over self-defense was "unnecessary" and proceeded largely by way of a strawman.[29] King knew quite well what the historian Lance Hill has recently argued—that self-defense activities were already operating without publicity and as "apolitical auxiliaries to political organ-izations."[30] "The question," King insisted, "was not whether one should use his gun when his home was attacked, but whether it was tactically wise to use a gun while *participating in an organized demonstration.*"[31]

This leads us closer to the enduring import of the King-Williams contre-temps. The existence of a right, after all, does not determine with any degree of specificity the wisdom or judiciousness of its exercise, nor its proper role in public political life. Williams, however, supplements his sparer assertion of right with more robust claims about the *pragmatic utility* of armed self-defense as part of civil rights demonstrations, and the *ethical significance* of collective, armed self-defense as a constitutive practice of dignity and man-hood in an atmosphere of terror and domination.[32]

Williams's *pragmatic utility* argument about the need for nonviolent direct action to be supplemented by self-defense has three major elements. First, he argues that in an atmosphere of racist terror, organized and declared self-defense functions as justified *deterrence* against excessive brutality and heavy casualties, both in everyday life and when directed against protest demonstrations. Oppressors are "most vicious," Williams argues, "when they can practice violence with impunity."[33] Second, Williams suggests that *violent* racial conflict is uniquely apt to draw negative international atten-tion, especially from nonwhite nations in Africa, Asia, and Latin America, and that the risk to strategic geopolitical interests and diplomatic standing can compel the federal government to intervene in the South to enforce the rule of law against antiblack terror and dismantle Jim Crow segregation.[34] Third, Williams contends that the organization of declared, cooperative self-defense dramatically alters the prevailing interests and bases of power, and thus the decision-making calculus in negotiations between powerful white elites, state officials, and representatives of black communities. "When our people become fighters," Williams argues, "our leaders will be able to sit at the conference table as equals, not dependent on the whim and the gener-osity of the oppressors."[35]

One might think that the profound asymmetry of force would make a mockery of such "equality," but Williams suggests that oppression is *nec-essarily* entangled with moral weakness and cowardice, causing oppressors to lack the resolve to mount a full defense of their unjust prerogatives. This is exacerbated when the oppression is *racist,* because racists ascribe disproportionate value to the lives of their own group and are "not willing to exchange their superior lives for our inferior ones" when challenged.[36] This realignment of power underlying competing bargaining positions, Williams insists, is especially crucial as demands move from securing civil liberties and integrated public accommodations to matters of economic inequality and fair equality of opportunity, which he argues provoke more intense resistance. It seems that Williams thought this deterrence, far more than moral authority from nonviolence, was what would prefigure a genuine society of equals.

King, however, worries that rhetorical and performative demonstrations of a forthright willingness to organize collaborative self-defense, apart even from its actual exercise, can turn expected *deterrence* into *provocation.* By unleashing ever-escalating retaliations, such action may inject moral confusion and muddled judgments of responsibility into the popular reception of civil rights demonstrations.[37] Like Williams, King considered *fear* to be a constitutive element of anti-black racism, but did not think that white racism would collapse like a schoolyard bully in the face of violent defiance. Instead, following the sociologist E. Franklin Frazier, King often resorted to the language of psychopathology to describe antiblack racism, emphasizing its paranoid, irrational, and inflationary dimensions.[38] In particular, the fear of violent anti-white reprisal, King argues, can inspire preemptive violence and provide a legitimating veneer to racial oppression by framing the black struggle for social justice as a zero-sum struggle for spoils and security. King's hope, at this stage in his career, was to show through "adherence to nonviolence—which also means love in its strong and commanding sense"—that forgiveness and reconciliation are of paramount interest to all, and that whites, therefore, have "nothing to fear" in the way of economic, social, or political revenge, and indeed, have much to gain, materially and morally, from extending equal civic standing and recognition to blacks.[39]

King understands one of the *political* problems bequeathed by a history of racial domination to be the formation of an atmosphere of fear-fueled civic distrust that distorts political rhetoric and action, while corroding the ethos of sacrifice and cooperation that democratic society draws upon for its reproduction.[40] "The minute a program of violence is enunciated, even for self-defense," King warned, "the atmosphere is filled with talk of violence, and the words falling on unsophisticated ears may be interpreted as an invitation to aggression." Citizen-spectators are easily distracted from questions of justice with the back-and-forth of threats and violence relayed through hysterical media coverage.[41]

Williams's own short-lived movement is perhaps one of the best illustrations of this point. In *Negroes with Guns,* Williams treats the arrival of nonviolent Freedom Riders as the chief precipitating cause of the white mob violence that eventually led him to flee Monroe, and his efforts at self-defense as the saving grace of a black community that could have suffered a pogrom. Yet, on his own account, government officials, from the governor's office to the local police chief, used Williams's advocacy of armed self-defense as their chief *justification,* in public and private, for demurring to escalating mob violence and ignoring the pleas of nonviolent demonstrators for the protection of their constitutional rights.[42] Even federal officials followed this lead, treating Williams as a fugitive in interstate flight while abetting local authorities as they arrested and sentenced a number of black teenagers who fought alongside Williams.[43] And, as Williams demonstrates through the sections concerned with disputing his portrayal in the media, his power and standing to effectively contest these negative representations, even after the fact, was extremely limited. The atmosphere of hostility marshaled against Williams was so intense that he spent years in exile, only being able to return to the United States by bartering information about Mao with the Nixon administration.[44]

It is tempting to suggest that Williams's embattlement was as unique as his exile, but it is helpful to contrast a moment when King was similarly besieged alongside Freedom Riders. In 1961, as King led activists and community members gathered in worship at the First Baptist Church in Montgomery following a demonstration, a mob surrounded the building, setting fire to cars, assailing the church with debris and tear gas, and threatening to burn all inside. In the midst of mounting chaos, King delivered a speech that crystallizes his response to Williams. There, King does not outright reject the importance of armed deterrence against injustice, but insists that *lasting* justice, including the peaceful and permanent recognition of each other's rights, will be secured only by nondiscriminatory, federally enforced rule of law and an ethos of community—not a permanent state of tension between retaliatory and defensive counterviolence. "Violence," he writes, "brings only temporary victories . . . [and] never brings permanent peace . . . unborn generations will be the recipients of a long and desolate night of bitterness, and our chief legacy to them will be a never-ending reign of chaos."[45]

Thus, while Williams and his allies sought to, as James Boggs put it, "convict their attackers on the spot," King thought such action was unlikely to produce an enduring reconfiguration of the American constitutional order capable of reflexively protecting African American civil rights and unmasking states' rights discourse for its complicity with local terror.[46] Ironically, although historical accounts emphasize their purported "self-reliance," leaders of the Deacons for Defense—a Louisiana- and Mississippi-based self-defense collective—also imagined their resistance to white terror as precipitating intervention by state and federal officials and reestablishing the rule of law.[47] Implicit in their organizing is a judgment that the intensification and escalation of violence would elicit a prompt and even-handed response from the state, eager to reaffirm its monopoly on the legitimate use of violence and protect commercial interests. For King, however, this faith in violent self-defense transgressed both moral and practical considerations and belied Williams's experience. It is one thing to turn guns on anonymous Klansmen or vigilante citizens, but how would African Americans retain government or popular support with violence directed against the state itself (police, national guardsmen), with its "control [of] the instruments and techniques of violence" intervenes as the agent of domination?[48]

More fundamentally, King conceived of ethical political struggle as being, above all, animated by a conception of *love*. Most fully fleshed out in his sermons "On Being a Good Neighbor," "Love in Action," and "Loving Your Enemies," King's concept of loving resistance builds upon the Danish philosopher Søren Kierkegaard, and defends an ethics embodied in the parable of the Good Samaritan (Luke 10:25–37) and the "Great Commandment" Jesus issues in Mark 12:31—"Thou shalt love thy neighbor as thyself."[49] Distilled to its core, King's conception of love in contentious politics enjoins us to treat our opponents as *neighbors*. In other words, we are to see even our enemies as those whose needs, welfare, and capacities obligate us to equal and sympathetic consideration on the basis of our shared moral equality as human beings, and *not* allow particularity or enmity to blind us to these claims. One concrete manifestation of this view is that forms of resistance that "humiliate the opponent rather than win his friendship and understanding," or "annihilate rather than convert," make the mistake of denying others the capacities for moral learning and character transformation we assume in ourselves. Further, these humiliations judge, *a priori*, the life horizons of our opponents based on their worst transgressions and foreclose the possibility of more ideal forms of community.

King's early faith in the possibility of recalibrating the American social order toward achieving such community comes from three sources: (1) the faith that nonviolent direct action that purposely takes on a "season of suffering," marked by a spirit of love and forgiveness, will produce a positive transformation in the ethical self-conception and practices of American citizens; (2) a judgment that the founding charters of the United States and the public political culture they inform are not self-undermining, and thus are capable of bearing the demands of the rule of law against Jim Crow white supremacy; and lastly, (3) that the threat of public incidents of racial violence, injustice, and disorder would leave the international "image of the United States . . . irreparabl[y] scarred" in the midst of a Cold War battle with global communism, and spur anticommunist policymakers to realize that "our greatest defense against Communism is to take offensive action on behalf of justice and righteousness."[50]

The crucial question for King, therefore, is not a choice between moralism and realism, or nationalism and internationalism, but a problem of political judgment that explodes these dichotomies. This is none other than the question of whether defensive violence or even the *provocative rhetoric* of defensive violence in an atmosphere of racial distrust might allow fear to confuse political judgment, undermine geopolitical leverage, and prevent an identification of the civil rights cause with the achievement or failure of national honor. These "realist" considerations are, nonetheless, in pursuit of a grand moral ideal: a multiracial, democratic society characterized by civic friendship and full equality.

In his navigation of this problematic, King rejected the clearly false assertion that cooperative black self-defense was *necessary* to generate international condemnation against the United States' failure to secure civil rights, or to put pressure on those officials charged with shepherding "national security interests" in the midst of the Cold War. As early as 1954, before King and Williams were national figures, the State Department submitted an influential *amicus curiae* brief in favor of desegregation in *Brown v. Board of Education*, arguing that Jim Crow would undermine American grand strategy, especially the attempt to win the allegiance of newly decolonized nonwhite nations and thwart Communist propaganda efforts.[51] In taking this approach, however, King's tragic challenge became to somehow transform the anticommunist imperative, via immanent critique, into a more *radical* instantiation and implementation of democratic and left-liberal principles, while eluding the repression that such a project would inevitably invite. "Communism," King wrote, "is a judgment on *our* failure to make democracy real and to follow through on the revolutions that we initiated," by "declaring eternal opposition to poverty, racism and militarism."[52]

Further, while Williams was right to note that the ethical-aesthetic force of violence (and its threat) inevitably accounts for much of the attention granted to civil rights protest in publics at home and abroad, King was concerned to harness these spectacular forces in a way that confronts Americans as a crisis of national *honor*, rather than national *security*. By honor, I mean to describe, following K. Anthony Appiah's work in moral psychology, the peculiar mix of self-respect, recognition-respect, and social esteem that comes from living up to the principled codes and practices associated with, and widely acknowledged as the proper conduct commensurate to, one's social identity (in this case a *national* identity).[53] From the late 1950s through the mid-1960s, King gives special prominence to arguments and tactics meant to put pressure on honor subjectively and with regard to reputation, exhorting America (and Christianity) to "rise up and live out the true meaning of its creed" with integrity, and provoking internationally broadcast spectacles where, if fellow citizens and public officials fail to do so, they shall lose face and invite contempt. The oppressor, King writes, "will find . . . that he is glutted with his own barbarity" and "forced to stand before the world and his God splattered with the blood of his brother, he will call an end to his self-defeating massacre."[54]

A critical element of King's early formulations of nonviolent protest was the aspiration that such demonstrations, in their threat to *honor*, would provoke a widespread and ethically motivating sense of *shame*: the affective state that accompanies the awareness that we have fallen short of our integral ideals in an objectionable and irresponsible way.[55] Therefore, we should see King's interest in the *geopolitics* of protest as stemming partly from his desire to stage what amounts to an "othering" experience for the American public and its political leaders. The reflexive moment comes when the dishonor brought to national identity can be *seen* through the objectifying gaze of global spectators, and *felt* initially through a visceral apprehension of their horror and disgust. As King proclaimed in a 1963 speech: "Our declarations that we are making progress in race relations ring with pathetic emptiness in their [the Third World's] ears. . . . As the shame of Oxford, Mississippi, and Birmingham, Alabama, flashes around the globe, the world is becoming aware of our deficiencies."[56]

This form of appeal, however, assumes the "Third World's" moral agency and capacity to compel recognition. Black Power militants countered by acidly pointing out that the world was already experiencing America's "deficiencies" on an intensifying and intimate basis. In ways that King could not readily anticipate, geopolitics was shifting under his feet. The aftermath of the Cuban revolution and missile crisis, the Sino-Soviet split, Kennedy's assassination, and the deposing of Nikita Khrushchev as Soviet premier would soon push the Cold War toward a phase shift. While competition over "Third World" influence intensified, American policymakers steadily came to judge the Kennedy administration's emphasis on defeating Communism through the technocratic implements of modernization ideology (foreign aid, technical advice, and accelerated economic development) a project with too much risk and not enough progress. Under Johnson, the United States increased collaboration with authoritarian governments and pursued more direct forms of military intervention.[57]

More broadly, in the period from 1953 through 1968 alone, the United States attempted, with often-covert military or material contribution, to overthrow left-leaning governments in Iran, Guatemala, Cuba, the Dominican Republic, Brazil, the Congo, and South Vietnam, to say nothing of the support given to apartheid South Africa or the neocolonial rule exercised over Puerto Rico.[58] Citing these denials of reciprocity, self-determination, and acknowledgment abroad, Black Power militants insisted, with increasing vociferousness, that where the interests of nonwhites were concerned, American society was far better at deepening capacities for hypocrisy, bad faith, and arrogance than cultivating receptivity to shame.[59] If white Americans were not, as Carmichael and Hamilton put it, "capable of the shame which might become a revolutionary emotion," then the solidarities most worth forging, many concluded, would be "on the side of the Third World" against the claims of American peoplehood.[60] King's dialectical reconciliation between them would have to be disavowed.

On Riots

King offers compelling, if perhaps context-bound, responses to arguments about self-defense as deterrence and geopolitical leverage, but the ethical questions posed by the relationship between the threat of black retaliatory violence and the negotiating power of black political spokespersons present other, thornier dilemmas. King would confront this problem, in part, with the outbreak of waves of ghetto rioting and civic unrest across American cities from 1964 until King's assassination in 1968 unleashed the most widespread explosion of domestic violence in any day since the Civil War.[61]

King understood urban revolt to be a profound practical and theoretical challenge, calling it "a crisis for the nonviolent movement."[62] Contemporary accounts of the riots emphasized the critical influence of the collision of rising expectations set by the successes of civil rights activists in the South, with the intractability and manifest injustice of ghetto life.[63]

King himself conceded this argument, insisting that "as elation and expectations died, Negroes became more sharply aware that the goal of freedom was still distant and our immediate plight was substantially still an agony of deprivation."[64] Not only did this chasm between expectation and reality provide additional scaffolding for the worry that the mode of politics defended by King and SCLC had reached its exhaustion point, but this judgment also tended to implicate King himself in helping to bring about an increasingly volatile urban crisis, either by raising aspirations or by undermining the rule of law with civil disobedience.[65] More distressing yet, the riots and the ghetto conditions they helped publicize, raised suspicions that, beneath the civil rights movement's paeans to shared black interests or exhortations to racial solidarity, lay a set of narrower, bourgeois class interests that diverged from those of the poorest blacks.[66]

Identifying themselves with these intimations of dissent "from below," nearly all Black Power intellectuals proffered claims that ghetto riots marked a decisive break in African American politics. In their interpretive gloss, rioting signified a defection from principles (nonviolence, pro-integration, and Christian love ethics), actions (moral appeal, nonviolent direct action, and political alliances with Great Society Democrats), and constituencies (black middle class, white liberals and labor, and Cold Warriors) they identified with King and the "classical" phase of the civil rights movement.[67]

Pressed to justify these uprisings, some black militants defended the riots on pragmatic terms. Like Bertrand Russell's realist defense of civil disobedience as often being the only route by which "people are roused to inquire into questions which they had been willing to ignore," these arguments treat civil disorder as a way to puncture the fog of societal indifference and produce decisive ameliorative action on behalf of ghetto denizens.[68] Implicitly, these pragmatic claims tend to rely upon further "realist" or aesthetic contentions. The "realists," characterizing politics as a contest of interests and force, treat rioting as coercively undermining the political will to preserve racial hierarchy by raising the costs (life, property, stability, sacrificing other interests) of its reproduction.[69] Those who focus on the riot's "aesthetic" dimensions, contend that the spectacle of revolt produces sublime terror and awe, which compels whites to viscerally recognize both the fragility of the existing order, and fear the profligately destructive power of violence organized against it.[70] This awe, in turn, is said to provide necessary motivation to dismantle injustice. King, drawing on his long-standing and competing argument about the direction of the relationship of racism and opportunity-hoarding to fear, rightly predicted that rioting would instead "strengthen the right wing of the country" and its punitive attitudes toward blacks.[71]

Nonetheless, these arguments still present an important challenge to King, as they help flesh out the persistent objection that nonviolence's supposed ethical purity is compromised by its immanently *coercive* dimensions, or its parasitic relation to an implied *threat* of violence if its spokespersons are rebuked.[72] King, however, never denied that nonviolent direct action was coercive. In this, he was deeply influenced by Reinhold Niebuhr, who—in studying strikes, boycotts, and protests—thought that drawing an absolute distinction between violence and nonviolence on the grounds of "coercion" was an "impossibility."[73] Channeling the famed theologian, even the early King thought that while it remained indispensable to appeal, through persuasion, to others' moral or ethical sense, we would never "get by coercion totally because of man's capacity for evil," which makes "an element of coercion necessary."[74]

In describing his politics as "moral, non-violent coercion," King wants to acknowledge the ethical dilemmas of coercion *and* retain the Niebuhrian distinctions between the intentions, spirit, and likely consequences that attend to violent versus nonviolent resistance. His argument may be restated as follows: *When leveraged against oppression and resentment, leavened with a spirit of love and forgiveness, and articulated through a willingness to take on more suffering than one's opponent, nonviolent coercion may be justified.* Indeed, it is the mode of politics most effective for defending one's dignity in the face of oppression, while also remaining capable of creating a "mutual friendship based on complete equality" without the "aftermath of hatred and bitterness that usually follows a violent campaign."[75]

This acceptance of the necessity of *coercion* goes a long way toward explaining the rapid radicalization of King's thought and rhetoric over the course of his career. In the 1950s, while King defended the coercive power of the boycott, his justifications of nonviolent protest turned primarily on its capacity to elicit shame, spiritual conversion, and social transformation. By 1963 in Birmingham, however, faced with the "massive resistance" of segregationists, he began to accent the more baldly coercive and "realist" dimensions of nonviolent direct action. "The purpose of our direct-action program," he proclaimed, "is to create a situation so crisis-packed that it will inevitably open the door to negotiation."[76] By 1968, confronted with the intractability of ghetto poverty, the strength of reactionary conservatism, the crisis of Vietnam, and the visceral challenge of Black Power, King argued for a turn toward a program of "mass civil disobedience." This program was distinguished, not only by its aspiration to "national" scale or its disdain for party politics, but by its refusal to "count on government goodwill" or even the moral force of "a statement to the larger society." Instead, the need was to deploy "a force that interrupts [society's] functioning at some key point," to "compel unwilling authorities to yield to the mandates of justice"—including economic and reparative justice.[77]

Indeed, the later King's argument against the pragmatic defense of riots is that he imagined mass civil disobedience to be a *more effective mode of coercion and aesthetic performance.* "To dislocate the functioning of a city without destroying it can be more effective than a riot," King argues, "because it can be longer-lasting, costly to the larger society, but not wantonly destructive." To this he adds the contention that, in virtue of its scale and its moral authority, mass civil disobedience "is more difficult for the government to quell by superior force."[78] This invokes Niebuhr's argument that, in contrast to violence, the commitment to nonviolence "rob[s] the opponent of the moral conceit by which he identifies his interests with the peace and order of society," and frustrates attempts to place demonstrators in the "category of enemies of public order, of criminals and inciters."[79]

For King, this disruptive import of nonviolent coercion is accompanied by an *aesthetic* force, which he juxtaposes to that of the riot. On King's account, the aesthetic experience of witnessing the inarticulate insurgency of ghetto rioting induces "understandable" feelings of menace and fear, which, in their overwhelming impact upon the senses, provoke reactionary and racist responses. The exacerbation of fear, and the spectacle of chaotic rebellion, becomes grist for racist ideology, which charges that blacks lack the capacity for civil participation and justifies repression and rightlessness by treating black dissent as an existential threat to society.[80] By contrast, mass civil disobedience, in King's imagination, can achieve disruption and secure attention through a sublime demonstration of power and discipline that he contrasts positively to the riot's chaotic destruction: "If one hundred thousand Negroes [repeatedly] march in a major city to a strategic location, they will make municipal operations difficult to conduct; they will exceed the capacity of even the most reckless local government to use force against them . . . Without harming persons or property they can draw as much attention to their grievances as the outbreak at Watts . . . while retaining their dignity and discipline."[81] Elsewhere, he describes the need for "militant non-violence . . . that will be as attention-getting as a riot, that will not destroy life or property in the process."[82]

Tragically, King did not live long enough to give further exposition to these ideas, or test them out as planned in his Poor People's Campaign.[83]

King would have certainly had to more adequately theorize the government's ability, in part developed in response to his own successes, to suppress dissent and disrupt insurgency with tools other than spectacular force. He would have also needed to square the idea of a general protest against poverty with his prior assessment that his protest against "segregation" *writ large* in Albany, Georgia was too "vague."[84] Perhaps more fundamentally, however, given the proximity of mass nonviolent civil disobedience to revolutionary action, and its tendency to "coerce and destroy" (in Niebuhr's phrase), King would have had to more fully resolve the paradox of his politics becoming more radical precisely when avenues of formal political participation and social incorporation became more readily available to African Americans. How does one, as Sheldon Wolin asks, defend radical, coercive action as "appropriate or obligatory . . . when the political system retains some of the formal features of democracy"?[85] How can one possibly take on more *personal* suffering, than that caused by bringing a national government to a halt with mass civil disobedience? However King might have ultimately tried to resolve such dilemmas, it seems clear that we should see his growing radicalism as King finally coming to recognize the severity of the challenge Robert Williams posed in 1962 about the relationship of nonviolent direct action to economic injustice, and asking "can a program of nonviolence—even if it envisions massive civil disobedience—realistically expect to deal with such an enormous, entrenched evil?"[86]

One final, and overlooked, measure of King's creeping skepticism about the answer to this question toward the end of his life might be his increased reliance on the rhetorical tradition of the jeremiad, which blends the prophecy of impending decline or devastation of society, while holding out a final, fleeting opportunity for social and spiritual redemption.[87] In a posthumously published essay from 1968, for example, King declares that "we have come to the point where there is no longer a choice now between nonviolence and riots. . . . The discontent is so deep, the anger so ingrained, the despair, the restlessness so wide, that something has to be brought into being to serve as a channel." While declaring his *own* faithfulness to nonviolence, he contends, "if our nonviolent campaign doesn't generate some progress, people are just going to engage in more violent activity, and the discussion of guerrilla warfare will be more extensive."[88] While the redemptive dimension of these statements evoke King's love ethic and a magnanimous desire that we all avoid the dystopian future of racial warfare, the prophesying of impending catastrophe reveals the intimate connection between nonviolent direct action and insurrectionary violence. In the background of King's jeremiad rhetoric, where humans, not God, are the agents of apocalypse, is the contention that if his efforts are "rudely rebuked," the energies they elicit are "not transformed into resignation and passivity," but instead become "alternatives [which] could be intolerable."[89] The threat that nonviolent protest may exacerbate social discontent, or grant further legitimacy to violent resistance if unsuccessful, subtly introduces another coercive element into direct action and the bargaining that accompanies it, which troubles conventional distinctions between violence and nonviolence in practice.

Ghetto riots, however, produced more ambitious defenders than those who would rely chiefly on pragmatic-practical arguments. Embracing a more total mode of lawbreaking, with no investment in performing it "openly, lovingly, [or] with a willingness to accept the penalty," these militants radicalized arguments generated in defense of civil disobedience.[90] This wing of Black Power argued that the expanse and endurance of racial injustice in the United States—especially the existence of ghettoes—coupled with the deficits of democratic government, undermined the obligatory force of normative and civic duties to obey the law, defer to police, or respect the claims of private property rights and symbols of government authority.[91] Eldridge Cleaver, the Black Panther Party's minister of information, and arguably the most influential writer of the Black Power generation, judged the rioting in Watts and elsewhere as evidence "that in America the blacks are in total rebellion against the System."[92] For Cleaver, looting in the face of unrepaired historical injustice, contemporary material deprivation, and widespread resource and opportunity hoarding by whites, represents the "sanctity surrounding property . . . being called into question" and the "mystique of the deed of ownership . . . melting away."[93] Although in nearly every uprising, an episode of alleged police brutality was the catalyst, Cleaver sees police violence as inexorably linked to, and constitutive of, these other ills and the myopia of white liberalism. "Police brutality," he declares, "is only one facet of the crystal of terror and oppression. . . . Behind police brutality, there is social brutality, economic brutality, and political brutality."[94]

At their most radical, some Black Power advocates insisted that black ghetto conditions were so unjust, and the prospects for nonviolent amelioration so minimal, that even supposed natural duties against killing and other forms of lethal and interpersonal violence (such as rape, assault) were broadly suspended, at least where whites, traitorous "Uncle Toms," and other persons identified as agents of oppression or repression were concerned.[95] If anything, King's assassination pushed, at least for a critical moment, a handful of Black Power's most prominent figures toward this more extremist position. In the wake of the King riots, Cleaver released his "Credo for Rioters and Looters," a statement of this view as succinct as it is inflammatory: "Is it any wonder that we loot you—you who have looted the world? Who are you to judge? You have no say in the matter. In the councils of the oppressed, the oppressor has no vote. The oppressor has no right which the oppressed are bound to respect. America you will be cleansed by fire, by blood, by death."[96]

These exhortations bear the influence of themes creatively appropriated from the text Cleaver effusively praised as "the Black Bible," the psycho-analyst and revolutionary political theorist Frantz Fanon's *Wretched of the Earth* and translated to the postwar U.S. racial order.[97] They follow Fanon's argument that the "colonial world is a Manichean world" and his claim that the *violent* imposition of a binary opposition between colonizer and native, or white and nonwhite, becomes the fundamental axis of difference through which the normative order of the imperial West is refracted. Colonialism, for Fanon, is fundamentally a relation of extreme domination, whose determinant *purposes* are extractive, exploitative, and subordinating, and whose *essence* is violence—not just physical and psychological, but *symbolic* and *epistemic*.[98]

Through these notions of symbolic and epistemic violence, Fanon argues that discourses of ethics, epistemology, and aesthetics are, despite their ostensible universalism, structured by the metalanguages, habits, and affective dispositions of white supremacy and imperial expropriation.[99] In this way, for Fanonists, ethics becomes subordinate to politics, while domination serves to violently disintegrate reason, disfigure affect, and disrupt communicative intelligibility. Even the values and vocabularies of humanism, for Fanon, function *violently* in the colonial (or antiblack) world.[100] Within this order of domination, therefore, the idea that anticolonial struggle involves "a rational confrontation of viewpoints," "a discourse on the universal," or "moralist" praxis like nonviolence, is understood to be a profound mistake.[101] Or, as Malcolm X put the point, "when you and I begin to look at [an oppressor] and see the language he speaks, the language of a brute, the language of someone who has no sense of morality, who absolutely ignores law—when you and I learn how to speak his language, then we can communicate . . . If his language is with a shotgun, get a shotgun."[102]

Some Black Power advocates, following Malcolm's connection between these analyses of European colonialism and the racial order of the United States, pressed this argument into a defense of rioting. The bellicose H. "Rap" Brown, for example, who served briefly as SNCC chairman after

Carmichael, juxtaposed the spectacular, militarized, and moralized response to ghetto riots with the persistent failure to adequately secure equal protection under the law for African Americans. "They talk about violence in the country's streets!," Brown proclaimed, but "Each time a Black church is bombed or burned, that is violence in our streets! Where are the troops? . . . Each time Black human rights workers are refused protection by the government, that is anarchy! Each time a police officer shoots and kills a Black teenager, that is urban crime!"[103] In other words, in an anti-black racist society, even mundane judgments about what constitutes seemingly familiar and intuitive phenomena like "violence," "anarchy," and "crime" are overdetermined by racism. On this account, the impossibility of reciprocal recognition creates a normative order that cannot generate effective moral condemnation or sustain a hermeneutics capable of recognizing the import of black suffering or the ethical force of black dissent.

Redeploying Fanon's prescriptions to the terrain of U.S. "race riots," these figures insisted that violent action could set in motion a new dialectical movement in history, one that establishes the possibility of further development toward black self-consciousness and self-respect, and perhaps even a politics of liberation. The embrace of rage and riot represent, on this account, a shedding of the psychology of fear, deference, and internalized inferiority inculcated by domination. The *doyen* of the Black Arts Movement, Amiri Baraka, describes his experience of the 1967 Newark riots in precisely these terms, claiming, "For me, the rebellion was a cleansing fire. . . . I felt transformed, literally shot into the eye of the black hurricane of coming revolution . . . what must be consumed is all of my contradictions to revolution. My individualism and randomness, my Western, white addictions, my Negro intellectualism."[104]

In addition to this psychological "cleansing," these defenders of riot insisted that looting, destruction, and resistance to police repression represent an important attainment of what Fanon, invoking Hegel, called the experience of subjective certainty—"when the colonized subject states he is equal to the colonist," not in words, but by being "determined to fight to be more than the colonist . . . [and] take his place."[105] Translated to the terrain of the riot, there is an insinuation of egalitarianism to practices of looting and destruction. The riot's chaotic blend of the carnivalesque, the anarchic, and the defiant, appears, for a moment at least, to upend hierarchy, and allow the "wretched of the earth" to prefigure "a social fabric that has been changed inside out" by "the substitution of one 'species' of mankind by another."[106] Malcolm X makes similar claims for anger, defending it not only as an affective foundation for moral judgment, epistemic insight, and political motivation, but also as embodying an authentic assertion of self-respect and equal standing capable of compelling recognition. "When [people] get angry," Malcolm argued, "they realize the condition that they're in—that their suffering is unjust, immoral, illegal, and that anything they do to correct it or eliminate it, they're justified. When you and I develop that type of anger and speak in that voice, then we'll get some kind of respect and recognition."[107]

Although King, like his militant interlocutors, treated the crimes committed in the course of rioting as "derivative crimes . . . born of the greater crimes of white society," he drew quite divergent conclusions from this judgment. He shared the position that any exhortation to "abide by the law" loses a measure of legitimacy when elsewhere the laws protecting people's most basic interests—welfare rights, building codes, antidiscrimination law—are evaded by fellow citizens for the sake of profit and prejudice.[108] The only "absolute guarantors," King argues, to prevent a riot, are "social justice and progress."[109]

Perhaps surprisingly, King even offered qualified versions of two of Black Power's more controversial theses. One is that while looting and riotous destruction do contain, whatever else their flaws, a kernel of egalitarian content, namely, the desire for the "experience of taking," which involves fleetingly "redressing the power imbalance that property [distribution] represents," and an attack against available "symbols of exploitation."[110] The other is King's narrow concession that, perhaps in "a special psychological sense," violence may involve *some* measure of the "cleansing effect" attributed to it by Fanon, and represents an expression of legitimate, repressed rage that must find an outlet.[111] None of these judgments, however, result in King's *embrace* of riot.

King understands his commitment to natural law to entail recognition of "the sacredness of human life," and this divine gift compels acknowledgment and deference in the form of nonviolence toward persons. "Man is a child of God, made in His image, and therefore must be respected as such . . . when we truly believe in the sacredness of human personality, we won't exploit people, we won't trample over people with the iron feet of oppression, we won't kill anybody."[112] Only immediate self-defense seems to qualify this duty, but even here King suggests it is incumbent on us to try mightily to resolve conflict without resort to interpersonal violence (indeed, he finds solace in the fact that riots involved primarily property damage and not mass violence against white persons). Also, while King characterizes black anger as "legitimate," he argues that to express it spontaneously without regard to appropriate ends or duties is a profound mistake. As a matter of political efficacy, moral excellence, and therapeutic transformation, anger should not be indulged, but "controlled" and "released ... under discipline for maximum effect."[113]

Beyond the practical, theatrical demands of protest demonstrations, King worries that the emotive force of anger, when not subjected to higher ends and instead treated as its own authorizing power, can produce myopic forms of self-pity, indiscriminate racial paranoia, and a politics and culture of nihilism. Spiritually, this can aid the slippage of anger into *hatred,* a disposition or style of attention toward the world that "destroys a man's sense of values and his objectivity ... [causing] him to describe the beautiful as ugly and the ugly as beautiful, and to confuse the true with the false and the false with the true."[114] This style of attention to the world, or structure of feeling, corrodes the powers of judgment that we need to sustain a more just society and develop core human excellences. Worse yet, the indulgence of anger has, for King, ultimately anarchic political import—it will come to seek "disruption for disruption's sake."[115] This anarchic, cathartic impulse, which finds expression in the riot, must ultimately confront its own limitations in the repressive power of the state and other sources of social power arrayed against it. This inevitable defeat, knowledge of which is inscribed in the frantic conduct of the rioters themselves, simply deepens the cycle of repression and rage with an intensifying "sense of futility."[116]

These allegations of anarchism and nihilism struck decisively at the core ambivalence and paradox at the heart of Black Power's relationship to the urban riots of the 1960s. The spectacle of the riot, and its inherent inarticulacy and ripeness for interpretive mediation, provided an unprecedented opportunity for Black Power militants.[117] Against the backdrop of burning metropolises, Black Power acolytes could make prophetic pronouncements about the direction of black protest movements and rhetorically conjure a sense of power, authenticity, and constituency to wield in the public sphere. However, as King often pointed out with unmasking clarity, Black Power militants never exercised, and perhaps *could not have exercised,* the power to begin, lead, or control these uprisings themselves. This critique undermines the interpretive authority claimed by black radicals over the meaning of riots, and forces a confrontation with the anarchic, ephemeral, and relatively anonymous quality of the riot as event and the "rebellious ghetto" as imagined constituency. This criticism, pressed by King and others, backed Black Power militants into a difficult corner. In claiming the riots as warrant for, or sign of, their political ascendancy, Black Power militants who eschewed the more gleefully anarchic tendencies of the early Cleaver and defended a positive program of political action were forced to articulate how such energies (and the ostensible constituencies behind them) could be effectively disciplined and directed. One prominent "solution" to this dilemma was revolutionary theory.

On "Revolution"

In the history of African American political life, the late 1960s and the 1970s stand uniquely alongside the 1840s and 1850s as moments where the black counterpublic sphere was riven with sustained, serious meditation on arguments for armed revolutionary violence. A critical mass of influential Black Power figures, especially those affiliated with the Black Panther Party and the Revolutionary Action Movement, argued forthrightly in support of revolution, inviting sustained debate from other African American intellectuals and intensive repression from the state.[118] This turn toward more explicitly revolutionary formulations drew inspiration, not only from the long U.S. black nationalist tradition and the liberal revolutionary principles enshrined in the Declaration of Independence, but also the influence of revolutionary anti-imperialist movements and their innovative transformations of Marxist theory (especially in Cuba, China, and Algeria). Theoretically, the resurgence of Marxist thought in black political life, helped enable a shift away from the discourse of *inclusion* and *citizenship rights*, toward emphases on *oppression* and *domination*. Of special import after the 1964 Civil Rights Act and the 1965 Voting Rights Act, was the idea that the attainment of liberal rights protections is *not* equivalent to genuine emancipation, which would entail more radical economic and ideological transformations—perhaps only attained via revolution.[119]

Another crucial factor animating this shift was the felt need for more adequate metaphors to characterize those *structural* and *cultural* dimensions of the racial order. Black Power thinkers were critical of vocabularies of "prejudice," "discrimination," or "exclusion," which remained too closely tied to concepts of intention and animus to have the kind of explanatory utility they sought to explain the post-segregation racial order, and which seemed deficient for capturing the stakes of battles over cultural particularity and recognition.[120] Of particular import and allure, therefore, was the metaphorical rendering of the black condition as that of an *internally colonized people* whose destiny was incongruent with the civic affiliations and aspirations of American nationalism, and who were subject not to second-class citizenship, but *cultural degradation* and sociopolitical *domination*.[121]

On the Cultural Revolution of Values

Black Power discourse relied heavily upon Fanonist premises and the colonial metaphor. Its claims about "cultural imperialism" are best understood as weaker versions of Fanon's argument that colonialism aims to obliterate or foreclose the living reality of precolonial or subaltern cultural formations, and subjects the colonized to pervasive and psychologically traumatizing forms of physical and symbolic violence that are normalized in imperial culture.[122] This atmosphere of fear and repression, humiliation and deprivation, misrecognition and mythmaking, Fanon argues, produces psychic states of aggression, alienation, envy, and shame in the oppressed. These emotions, their expression blocked by violent colonial repression, are in turn sublimated and displaced elsewhere, through psychopathology (neuroses, inferiority complexes, fantasy, and so on), intracommunity violence, and expressive cultural forms like dance, music, or religion whose expenditures of energy are cathartic, yet politically impotent.[123]

Black Power advocates were surprisingly open to appropriating elements of these analyses, if not always Fanon's prescriptions from them. Carmichael argued that colonialism (internal or external) *requires* the destruction of culture, language, and values to ensure acquiescence to subordination.[124] Others, like Amiri Baraka, insisted on the improbable survival of a vibrant, life-affirming African American cultural forms (blues, jazz, dialect, religion, vernacular poetry), while nonetheless characterizing the broader society as broadly hostile to "Black culture" and incapable of sustaining black self-respect, dignity, and identity.[125]

Against this subjection, Carmichael and Baraka contended that Black Power needed a "cultural base," by which they meant a broadly shared, self-created ethos and identity, protected and furthered by independent institutions, which would provide the appropriate "value system" to the politics of the "Black nation" and terms for recognition from the broader society.[126] The *weak* version of this argument involves, primarily, a critique of white supremacist or ethnocentric evaluations of putatively "black" forms of cultural achievement or beauty, a critique of inferiorizing racial representations, and an insistence on preserving and cherishing with concerted practical effort, the cultural particularity and historical achievements of African Americans. *Stronger* versions of this argument, defended by Baraka, Ron Karenga, and others, attempt to render or reform African

American identity into something more essentially "African" and categorically oppositional to "the West."[127] Stronger versions of this thesis also suggest that emancipatory black politics *demands* racial unity. Such unity, they surmised, is dependent on the flourishing of a "Black culture," understood as an expressive totality where a wide range of behaviors and beliefs (endogamy, uplift service, cultivation of certain aesthetic tastes, and so on) are informed by value orientations, ideas of duty, and judgments held in common across generations.

King did not write at great length on these considerations, but it is clear that, especially by the end of his career, he defended a version of the weak cultural particularity thesis. Following Du Bois, Ralph Ellison, and Albert Murray, among others, King asserts a conception of *African American identity* that is "a true hybrid, a combination of two cultures . . . Africa and America," and a conception of *American* culture where "the language, the cultural patterns, the music, the material prosperity and even the food of America are an amalgam of black and white."[128] King agreed that internalizing a sense of shame in regard to putatively black cultural forms, physical features, and African or slave ancestry is a threat to one's self-respect, and championed the development of "a rugged sense of somebodyness" through which blacks can affirm self-worth and beauty.[129] Politically, this cultural project has import for King in at least two ways. The first is insofar as it helps sustain racial solidarity by promoting "group consciousness" and undermining ideological sources of distrust, aversion, alienation, and disrespect for other blacks that are an effect of socialization in a broadly anti-black cultural horizon.[130] The second, discussed briefly at the beginning of this essay, is the neo-Du Boisian notion that black folk culture, particularly African American Christianity, has resources that should be conserved in order to help overcome certain moral and spiritual ills, like consumerism, political pessimism, and cruelty.

Importantly, King never thought these commitments entailed stronger forms of nationalism, like a deep-rooted Pan-Africanism or black separatism, nor did he see a need to secure a strong cultural base for political unity. He criticized pan-Africanist cultural nationalists for fleeing the "ambivalence" of African American identity in search of an illusory wholeness in expressive cultural practices they associate with Africa. While King often invoked African Americans' connection to Africa, and suggested modes of transnational solidarity, his formulations placed less emphasis on the idiom of "racial" ancestry than resonant and shared features of racial oppression between colonialism and Jim Crow.[131] He lodged a similar objection against cultural separatism, characterizing it as an excessive reaction to the vulnerability that inheres in the fact that self-respect, self-esteem, and dignity are dependent upon others.[132] Even granting the force of Carmichael and Hamilton's critiques of power relations *within* political coalitions, one cannot deny, *a priori*, as unadulterated separatists do, that African Americans can find no egalitarian cooperation, common endeavor, or shared interests across racial lines because of cultural difference or the existence of a corporate "white" interest—especially in an age of intensifying automation and economic vulnerability across the color line.[133]

The fear of mutual dependence and ineliminable vulnerability, born of the wounds of racial domination, must be overcome by something other than the futile reliance on the totemic power of a mystical African past or the fantasy of pure independence. King saw authentic self-affirmation as emerging from *resistance* to assaults on dignity and the willingness to affirm our equal standing, while the long-term prospects for our dignity are entangled with the achievement of social justice and beloved community. Without the kind of political radicalism capable of bringing such a social order into being, these efforts in the cultural realm will be in vain, and King—as is explored elsewhere in the volume—sees no "separate black road to power and fulfillment" or "salvation for the Negro through isolation."[134] Indeed, as Robert Gooding-Williams argues, King devotes more attention to forms of black cultural reformation inspired by this end, than any expansive cultural nationalism.[135]

Political Revolution

Returning to the *structural* side of Carmichael and Hamilton's internal colonization analogy, we see that "institutional racism" is their attempt to meet the imaginative, analytical, and interpretive challenge posed by the limits of civil rights–era social theory. Institutional racism, as they describe it, does not operate primarily through overt acts of racial antipathy perpetrated by discrete individuals, but through the interpenetration of institutions whose resonant and reinforcing actions disproportionately disadvantage predominantly black communities and subject them to various forms of arbitrary power. The *racism*, of institutional racism, they contend, stems from the crucial role played by "the active and pervasive operation of anti-black attitudes and practices," including the creation of a normative order marked by a pervasive expectation of hierarchical group position that normalizes the sense that "blacks should be subordinated to whites."[136] Thus, the ostensibly normal or rational working of institutional logics, once bounded by an anti-black normative order, *produces* black disadvantage and *reproduces* the patterns and practices constitutive of "institutional racism." Chief among these are *epistemic ignorance* about the origins and character of black suffering; a perceptual orientation at *disquieting ease* with deprivation and subordination when it appears among blacks; psychic and material *interests* in reproducing advantages that accrue from group hierarchy; and *affective attachments and fears* that motivate aversive behaviors and anti-black forms of white political and social solidarity. The congealing of these phenomena help to create what they describe as an overarching relation of "colonial" domination, which can be broken into its component parts of political subordination, resource and opportunity hoarding, cultural stigma and social marginalization, and economic exploitation and expropriation.

As should be clear, this argument treats racism and capitalism as linked, arguing that expropriation, exploitation, and stigmatization of nonwhite peoples serve critical functions in the reproduction of capitalist and/or "imperialist" hegemony in the United States.[137] Different accounts are more or less idiosyncratic, but they share the contention that racial stigma legitimates the forced expropriation of wealth from nonwhite peoples, and sustains practices of "super-exploitation," which undermine resistance to downward pressure on wages for stigmatized populations (for instance, through labor market exclusions) and create pathways of least resistance for the elimination of labor through capital improvements (mechanization).[138] In addition, a handful of Black Power advocates argued that even the dynamics of "illicit capitalism," are heavily structured by race, with permanent unemployment and enduring social misery pushing black ghetto denizens disproportionately into the underground economy for subsistence while creating flourishing markets for cheap, escapist pleasures like narcotics.[139] That black communities are unable to disrupt these practices or confront the concentration of negative externalities (such as violence, disease, theft) that accompany them is a further artifact of powerlessness and isolation, borne of racial segregation, political disenfranchisement, and the power of racist ideology.[140]

In drawing these connections between racism and capitalism, some Black Power leaders, following Marcus Garvey, sought to seize the power of capital for "the race."[141] Rejecting the dream of interracial solidarity on the labor lines, they imagined a roughly parallel economy, structured by racial separatism and solidarity, where black communities could exclusively patronize ("Buy Black!") and collectively invest in black businesses. These businesses were expected to fulfill duties of hiring black workers, providing quality services to black communities, and helping insulate the race's institutions from the political, cultural, and social subordination that comes from accepting or needing funding from whites.[142]

On the Black Power left, however, paeans to "Black Capitalism" were met with scorn and ridicule.[143] These programs, they argued, indulged the fantasy that one could sustain a racially separate economy in defiance of the logics of capitalism, and sought to extract black consumer loyalty from exhortations to racial and cultural solidarity that were not, and could not, be reciprocal without running afoul of profit motives and capital reproduction.[144] The material wealth accrued by a small cohort of black capitalists in a segregated market, the Black Panther Party insisted, would do next to nothing to liberate black peoples from their structural unfreedom, which involves racialized and concentrated ownership of capital.[145] Nor could the workings of the market liberate blacks. Their centuries-long enslavement and expropriation had built insurmountable inequalities in capital ownership, and the flow of credit followed pathways strongly determined by racial stigma, compounding interest and insurance rates that were anathema to profit.

The Black Power left, instead, posited a real, vested, and collective material and psychic interest in the reproduction of these unjust distributive arrangements on behalf of capitalist elites and, to a lesser extent, white working classes. In doing so, it led them to argue that state protections like civil rights are likely to be constrained by entrenched elite interests, that moral suasion and rhetorical appeal are unlikely to be structurally transformative, and that class conflict, even *among* blacks, is likely to be intractable.[146] The combination of skepticism of moral appeal, government redress, and efficacious racial solidarity with a broader judgment that the modern, global order is fundamentally structured by dehumanizing forms of racism, capitalism, and imperialism, licensed a longing for total revolution that the Panthers rendered explicit and acted upon.[147] In the genealogy of revolutionary Marxism, however, the Panthers are relatively unique in that, given their lack of faith in white organized labor, radical intellectuals, and minority elites, they identified the so-called *lumpenproletariat* as the decisive class for revolutionary action and emancipatory hope.[148]

For Marx and Friedrich Engels, the lumpenproletariat was a pejorative characterization, meant to describe that group of persons characterized largely by their chronic unemployment, reliance on the underground/criminal economy for subsistence, and their social "degeneracy."[149] This class, according to Engels, was the "worst of all possible allies," as their desperation and dependency makes them vulnerable to recruitment by reactionary movements, and their various pathologies habituate them to predation, dissemblance, and parasitism.[150] Fanon, drawing from his experience in Algeria, was among those who broke with this Marxist consensus by suggesting that the lumpen, while undoubtedly flawed and vulnerable to counterrevolutionary recruitment, nonetheless had important revolutionary potential, particularly in their supposed spontaneity and intuitive recognition and acceptance of the need for violence.[151]

In the hands of the Panthers and the Black Power left, Fanon's tentative suggestions became a fully formed Marxist-Leninist vanguardism. Huey Newton, the co-founder of the BPP, suggested that the "intransigent hostility toward all those sources of authority that had a dehumanizing effect" that he discerned in "the brothers on the block," suggested deep alienation from the existing social order and few ideological illusions about its legitimacy, or foundations in anything other than theft or violence.[152] Inverting the traditional Marxist valuations, the Panthers suggested that certain forms of deviance and crime were, in truth, enactments of dissent that could, with the appropriate organizing, education, and program, be developed into a truly revolutionary movement. Newton saw the task of the BPP as mobilizing organically connected intellectuals and organizers to "awaken the people and teach them the strategic method [guerilla warfare] of resisting a power structure which is prepared not only to combat with massive brutality the people's resistance but to annihilate totally the black population."[153] The Panthers would then, on this account, galvanize revolutionary uprisings from other groups in society and across the globe. As Newton would put the point in a speech at Boston College, the aim is ultimately to "seize the means of production, [and] distribute the wealth and the technology in an egalitarian way to the many communities of the world."[154]

It is a measure of the seriousness with which he took Black Power that King responded thoughtfully and comprehensively to these visions of revolutionary overthrow, pressing a series of critically important objections that those who identify themselves with this legacy of revolutionary praxis would do well to consider. King agrees, in broad strokes, with the ideal—which he also acknowledges in communism—of "a world society transcending the superficialities of race and color, class and caste."[155] To achieve such a world, he argues, we must "take offensive action in behalf of justice and righteousness . . . [and] seek to remove those conditions of poverty, insecurity, injustice, and racial discrimination" through massive redistribution and new constitutional protections.[156] King's principal worry, however, is that in treating "Communism" as embodying the "only . . . revolutionary spirit," we obscure methods like mass civil disobedience, by which we might obtain morally similar ends (an end to "exploitation and oppression") without dissolving right and wrong in "the most expedient methods for dealing with a class war."[157]

Among these questions of right and responsibility is how we should think about the overwhelming asymmetry of violence that blacks would face. Leaders who call for it, he rightfully points out, would be partly responsible for the extraordinary casualties that would likely accrue.[158] Secondly, he reminds militants that public opinion suggests that blacks are overwhelmingly hostile to the idea of revolutionary uprisings, meaning that for all of their sound and fury, they lack a significant base to launch their efforts.[159] If they were to do so anyway, they would invite forms of intensive repression among a vulnerable population without their assent. Revolutions, King argues further, are doomed to failure unless they can capture the allegiance of a critical mass of the military and the broader public.[160] Such a feat was, and remains, impossible to imagine for Black Power in relation to the U.S. military. And, for those Black Power revolutionaries who suggested that a non-aligned Third World could be decisive allies to black revolutionary struggle, King is incredulous.[161] The state of economic and military development of these newly independent countries was so severely behind that of the United States, he contended, that not only would they surely meet military defeat, but their own most pressing social problems (poverty, education, neocolonialism) were more likely to be solved by the concerted effort of African Americans to reform civil government, foreign policy, and aid practices in the United States than efforts at transnational revolution.[162]

To their credit, BPP leaders like Newton and Cleaver were not unaware of these objections and attempted to meet them in various ways. The asymmetry of capacities for violence was conceded by nearly all Black Power militants, who sought therefore to elude the implications that King identifies by embracing two doctrines: asymmetric warfare (guerilla war/terrorism) and the idea of mutually assured destruction.[163] In an asymmetric paramilitary campaign, the social service programming of vanguard organizations like the BPP were supposed to build up enough goodwill in ghetto communities that when the violence began, BPP members could go underground and blend in with community support. To King's objection that this would visit violence upon the innocent, Newton agreed, and in fact welcomed it. He argued that the expected military and police reaction, in its violence and indiscriminate suppression, would reveal the racism of the state and further radicalize ghetto communities subject to violent repression in search of BPP militants, swelling the ranks of the BPP-led insurgency.[164]

Against the threat of extermination that King identifies, BPP leadership argued that such genocide could be eluded for two reasons. On one hand, the rebellion and vicious suppression of a large minority population, ostensibly in violation of its civil and human rights, would be an international scandal that diminished the global power and influence of the United States abroad, undermining international ambitions. Further, as the Panthers argued in their defense of interracial alliances from fellow Black Power critics who endorsed racial separatism, an illegitimate and brutal repression might inspire white youth to adopt more radical forms of dissent in solidarity. Indeed, according to Bryan Burroughs, a fundamental ideological commitment shared across primarily white New Left organizations that actually engaged in violence against the state was the belief that white radical violence would help precipitate a larger-scale black revolt.[165] Thus, while many Black Power militants accepted the premise that revolutionary violence, at least for its first wave, would be "suicidal," the longer-term hope was that repressive response would be constrained by geopolitics, constitutional norms, and white youth and liberal opinion, while perhaps setting the stage for forms of détente that would be the condition of possibility for the withdrawal of certain state functions (policing, judiciary, and so on) and the negotiation for forms of alternative, and mediated sovereignties ("community controlled" institutions) in black communities.[166]

In the fullest exposition of this alternative sovereignty, the BPP endorsed the idea of a United Nations sponsored plebiscite concerning black independence (and, implicitly, reparations). This *democratic* mechanism for ascertaining consent could have—the Panthers argued—further clarified the desires of the members of the "black colony," and also the scope of the right to revolution while allowing for a countervailing nonviolent power to American political elites through the newly "decolonized" United Nations.[167] There was never, however, a careful working through of the democratic dilemmas that come from designing such a plebiscite and the legitimacy of its various possible outcomes (who would participate, whether such a vote entails territorial separatism, what happens to blacks who want to stay, and so on).

King found the imagined scenarios of guerilla warfare exceedingly farfetched, naïve about the public reception of violence, and certainly not worth the blood that would be spilled in pursuit. Moreover, he thought that even a new society successfully *founded* on violence—particularly the kind of racially charged violence advocated by Black Power revolutionaries—would lodge the "evil" of such means in its notions of value, and likely reproduce forms of violence within its own governing logics.[168] In turning to the presumed expediency of violence, among the mistakes that revolutionaries make, King wants to suggest, is that they end up treating others with whom we share a society, a planet, and human dignity as unworthy of equal consideration or second-person respect. On this account, seeking to kill those we disagree with shows a dangerous disdain for their human capacities for conscientious action and communicative reason, not to mention the "sacredness of human personality." Moreover, it conveys a kind of unjustified arrogance in that it presumes, at fatal cost, "that it has everything to teach others and nothing to learn from them"—an attitude that King decries in other contexts.[169]

Even if the violence was simply rhetorical, and meant to secure self-determination, King's arguments about self-defense are applicable here again. To these he would add a critique of this sublimated separatism. "There is no theoretical or sociological divorce," he argued, "between liberation and integration." King's ultimate disavowal of the colonial analogy, one suspects, comes from the way that it emerged tightly tied to a politics of "national liberation" he found incompatible (ironically, as did Fanon) with the African American case. "I cannot see," he confessed, "how the Negro will be totally liberated from the crushing weight of poor education, squalid housing and economic strangulation until he is integrated, with power, into every level of American life."[170]

Nevertheless, this confrontation with Black Power revolutionaries had significant effects on King's thought. I have already discussed his turn toward a defense of mass, coercive civil disobedience, strident cultural particularity, and guaranteed basic minimum income, but one last development bears mentioning, namely, that in the wake of the riots and the emergence of Black Power, King devoted sustained time and attention to the same lumpenproletariat that so animated the Panthers. King spent much of 1966 in the slums of Chicago, attempting not only to galvanize a protest movement against ghetto conditions and the lack of education resources, but also taking up the charge of organizing and including gang members that many claimed could not be incorporated into politics, much less nonviolent politics. Transgressing all of the norms incumbent upon a southern Baptist preacher, King and his staff moved into the slums, recruiting gang members in pool halls, on street corners, and in his own home, engaging them in long debates about racial injustice, anger, poverty, and the politics of nonviolence.[171] These efforts were not always successful—a gang brawl shut down an SCLC meeting, and gang members were accused of inciting civil unrest in Lawndale—but King's efforts on this score were still notable.[172] Recruiting gang members from the Vice Lords, the Roman Saints, and the Blackstone Rangers, SCLC successfully deployed them in demonstrations in the 1966 Mississippi Freedom March and in open housing marches in Chicago later that Summer. This experience helped convince King that despite all of the neo-Fanonist prophesying about the inevitable violence of the so-called "lumpenproletariat," "nonviolence should not be written off for the future." Against arguments that saw violence as the only pathway for the expression of anger, King responded with genuine admiration: "We had some gang leaders and members marching with us. I remember walking with the Blackstone Rangers while bottles were flying from the sidelines, and I saw their noses being broken and blood flowing from their wounds; and I saw them continue and not retaliate, not one of them, with violence. I am convinced that even very violent temperaments can be channeled through nonviolent discipline, if the movement is moving, if they can act constructively and express through an effective channel their very legitimate anger."[173]

One of the most tragic losses of the fleeting problem-space of black politics that Black Power helped create is precisely this humane, receptive, and respectful engagement with those who, subject to accumulated disadvantage, subsist in the underground economy, belong to criminal organizations and gangs, and deviate from mainstream norms. Here, and in his more considered engagements with Black Power thought, King practices something akin to what Nikolas Kompridis describes as "intimate critique." Kompridis describes this as "a practice of critical dialogue that aims to preserve and renew trust, and to facilitate commitment to ongoing processes of cooperative problem solving." Its guiding *ethic* is one of *mutual recognition*, commensurate with a second person standpoint.[174] Its *performative* dimension entails *practical acknowledgment* of the fact that we are "the facilitators and guarantors of one another's fragile freedom."[175] Or, as King often put the point, "We are all caught in an inescapable network of mutuality, tied into a single garment of destiny ... made to live together."[176] This form of critique, therefore, entails careful listening and respectful, sympathetic dialogue that is less interested in the total demolishing and unmasking of the truth claims of one's interlocutors, than cultivating forms of critical reflection on our needs, interests, identities, and self-understandings that might open up new conceptual and practical possibilities on all sides for a future together. The aspiration that intimate critique embodies is the cultivation of novel forms of life, or the generation of social and political practices, that are capable of bearing emancipatory hopes and mutual trust shared between interlocutors, especially where these have broken down. Contemporary intellectuals and activists, and those who would seek to repair the intergenerational traumas bequeathed by mass incarceration and our failed policies toward the underground economy would do well to note that the character of King's engagement with Black Power, despite many profound disagreements, is in this vein. At the ethical and existential levels, we may have as much to learn from this *mode* of critical engagement, as we do politically from the *substance* of King's arguments. Indeed, the former may be the condition of possibility for the latter.

15

Hope and Despair: Past and Present

CORNEL WEST

> Hope encourages men to take risks; men in a strong position may follow her without ruin, if not without loss. But when they stake all that they have to the last coin (for she is a spendthrift), she reveals her real self in the hour of failure, and when her nature is known she leaves them without means of self-protection.
> —THUCYDIDES, The Melian Dialogue

> Life is a continual story of shattered dreams.
> —MARTIN LUTHER KING, JR., "Unfulfilled Dreams"

In the last days of his life, Martin Luther King, Jr., was haunted by the pervasive and poisonous threat of nihilism. King's best friend and lifelong comrade, Ralph Abernathy, noted, "He was just a different person. He was sad and depressed."[1] His close confidant Andrew Young reported, "In the later years he was given to a kind of depression that he had not had earlier. . . . He talked about death all the time. . . . He couldn't relax, he couldn't sleep. . . . He was spiritually exhausted."[2] And King's longtime friend Dorothy Cotton said that he "was just really *emotionally* weary, as well as physically tired. . . . That whole last year I felt his weariness, just weariness of the struggle, that he had done all that he could do."[3] Recently, in a heartfelt speech at the annual conference for the American Academy of Religion in San Antonio, Texas, Jesse Jackson talked about his last group meeting with King, in which King declared he was going to either leave the movement or fast unto death in order to unite the movement.[4]

By nihilism, I mean to denote a suffocating condition of spiritual blackout that shatters the human capacity to experience love, find meaning, and gain access to hope. Nihilism results from forms of soulcraft that put a premium on conquest and domination, mendacity and criminality. For King, nihilism is the ultimate nightmare—the stark opposite of his dream of the beloved community.[5]

This monumental wrestling with the nihilistic threat to King's life and witness had much to do with his deep sense of vocation and the immense weight of his increasing perception that America was a "sick, neurotic nation" unwilling to be truthful about itself.[6] King's profound embrace of responsibility for the morality and efficacy of nonviolent resistance and the intense entrenchment of the liberal status quo led him to say to Abernathy, "Maybe we just have to admit that the day of violence is here, and maybe we have to just give up and let violence take its course. The nation won't listen to our voice—maybe it'll heed the voice of violence."[7] King's devoted and brilliant wife Coretta Scott King wrote, "He was very depressed . . . and I kept trying to tell him, 'You mustn't hold yourself responsible, because you know you aren't.'"[8] And in an unusual tone and temperament King told his family friend Rev. D. E. King, "I have found out that all that I have been doing in trying to correct this system in America has been in vain. . . . The whole thing will have to be done away with."[9]

The last options seemed to be mass civil disobedience, widespread social disruption, or uncontrollable violent rebellion.[10] King stated, "The movement for social change has entered a time of temptation to despair, because it is clear now how deep and how systematic are the evils it confronts."[11] In short, King the exemplary dreamer was painfully coming closer to what both Malcolm X and W. E. B. Du Bois concluded before him—that America was a nightmare for the poor and the working-class black masses and that within America, oppressed black people would not win.[12] Hence, a move to the international stage was required for black sanity and possibility. In the U.S. context alone, massive melancholia and lacerating loneliness would prevail. This reality stands in stark contrast to King's popular image.

King's struggle with nihilism was threefold—*personal, political,* and *philosophical.* His Promethean effort to hold at bay his crisis of hope and overwhelming anguish was terminated by a violent act of hate—his ugly assassination—that plunged much of the country into a deep despair, and in some quarters, rage.[13] The very violence he hated and hoped to stop, put closure on his waning battle to see an alternative to violence, hatred, and hopelessness.

On the *personal* front, King's life was sheer chaos. Despite his deep love for his precious children and wife, his marriage was in serious trouble. In the words of some friends, "Coretta was the ideal wife for Martin," even as she "was most certainly a widow long before Dr. King died."[14] We can never fully grasp the inscrutable dynamics of a marriage, but it is undeniable that the stress and strain of the movement on the marriage and King's own choices of extramarital relationships—highlighted by FBI tapes sent to both of them along with a call for his suicide—left him in extreme emotional tatters.[15] Furthermore, King was devastated by betrayals from friends and movement comrades. Nearly all of his close confidants strongly objected to his Poor People's Campaign and his strident opposition to the Vietnam War, not to mention his commitment to the garbage workers' strike in Memphis, Tennessee.[16] They not only "were failing to stand by him in his hour of greatest need," but they also were loud and adamant in, according to Andrew Young, "telling him he was failing."[17] Besides the loyal Harry Belafonte and a few others, most of them abandoned him for lucrative careers, trashed him to gain mainstream acceptance, or dismissed him as an outdated leader. As his dear friend Deenie Drew put it, King was "very, very lonely . . . despite the fact that he was surrounded by people all the time. He was still alone—he was apart. . . . He had very few friends."[18]

Many, if not most, of his fellow Christian ministers closed their pulpits to him. King was already considered a kind of pariah by the black church establishment—as seen in the hostile treatment and explicit excommunication of King by Rev. J. H. Jackson, who led the massive and influential National Baptist Convention.[19] But now even King's earlier fellow travelers turned their backs on him. In addition to the more well-known attacks from the white power structure—such as President Lyndon Johnson (who called King a "nigger preacher") or J. Edgar Hoover (who viewed King as "the most dangerous man in America")—King had to bear the heavy cost of this lesser-known black church assault. Rabbi Abraham Joshua Heschel became one of his few and dearest friends among religious leaders.[20]

On the *political* front, the shrinkage of ideological space intensified. His nonviolent message was accepted by fewer people. Young revolutionaries dismissed and tried to humiliate King—subjecting him to a walkout during his address at the historic New Politics convention in Chicago in 1967 or loud booing and heckling (by Student Nonviolent Coordinating Committee activists) at King's address at Liberty Baptist Church in Chicago in 1966.[21] Professional opportunism among his colleagues, often draped in the veneer of "black empowerment," eclipsed his message of love-driven activism.[22] To black middle-class leaders hungering and angling for white mainstream approval, King angrily replied, "What you're saying may get you a foundation grant, but it won't get you into the kingdom of truth."[23] The white liberal establishment who had once heralded King as their select HNIC (Head Negro In Charge), with his *Time* magazine cover, now harshly rejected him. The *Washington Post* proclaimed that King's public opposition to the Vietnam War "has done a grave injury to those who are his natural allies . . . and . . . an even graver injury to himself. Many who have listened to him with respect will never again accord him the same confidence. He has diminished his usefulness to his cause, to his country and to his people."[24] Indicting King's anti-war politics, *Life* magazine wrote that King put forward "demagogic slander that sounded like a script for Radio Hanoi."[25]

Even the more progressive *New York Review of Books* declared that King "has been outstripped by his times, overtaken by the events which he may have obliquely helped to produce."[26] And to add insult to injury, the most influential liberal black journalist in America, Carl Rowan (the first to have his own TV show), angrily wrote in *Reader's Digest* that King's "exaggerated appraisal" of his own self-importance, and the communist influence on his thinking, made King "*persona non grata* to Lyndon Johnson" and "has alienated many of the Negro's friends and armed the Negro's foes."[27]

On the *philosophical* front, King was perplexed. Self-doubt became more pervasive and persuasive. Was he advocating integration into a burning house? What if nonviolent resistance simply didn't work in "sick America"? What if he—and Theodore Parker (the originator of the remark)—were wrong about the long arc of the universe bending toward justice?[28] What if his own version of American exceptionalism—America as the grand City on the Hill and moral exemplar of nations—was wrong? Was he deceived about the capacity of America to undergo a revolution in values and priorities that resulted in a redistribution of wealth and power downward and a new foreign policy that resulted in America no longer being "the greatest purveyor of violence in the world"?[29] And more pointedly, what if his Christian theology fell short in the face of stubborn Nietzschean realities of power and violence, envy and resentment, deception and illusion?[30]

We do know that the sermon King planned to deliver at Ebenezer Baptist Church—his home church—in Atlanta the Sunday he never lived to see—was entitled "Why America May Go to Hell." Was this what King saw on the mountaintop in his last speech in Memphis in Mason Temple? Did he foresee the decline and fall of the American empire—its military overreach, corrupted elites and decadent culture with its citizens eager for a strongman to restore law and order and make America "great again"? In a speech to the black D.C. Chamber of Commerce defending his Poor People's Campaign, King argued that his project was the last hope and best alternative to violent rebellion—a rebellion that would lead to a neo-fascist U.S. regime. "I don't have any faith in the whites in power responding in the right way. . . . They'll treat us like they did our Japanese brothers and sisters in World War II. They'll throw us into concentration camps. The Wallaces and the Birchites will take over. The sick people and the fascists will be strengthened. They'll cordon off the ghetto and issue passes for us to get in and out."[31]

In other words, was King's great rhetorical eloquence a desperate attempt to convince himself and others to hold on to a hope that was fading in the face of an avalanche of white backlash, class war from above, and imperial decay from without and within? The bleak prophetic words of Rabbi Heschel haunted King: "The whole future of America will depend upon the impact and influence of Dr. King."[32] In other words, the mighty American empire will collapse if we do not come to terms with our militarism, materialism, racism and poverty—the four catastrophic forces King warned were sucking the free and democratic spirit out of the U.S. experiment.

The arms industry linked to the military-industrial complex forged in the wake of World War II continues to have a stranglehold on the U.S. budget. Our military spending—more than that of the next twelve countries combined—in support of over 4,800 military facilities (with about 800 abroad) and potentially world-destructive weapons, makes the preparation for war our major priority—with less funding left for education, housing, or quality jobs. Our unacknowledged terrorism—invasions, occupations, drone strikes, house raids, and torture sites—breeds terrorism from others. Our domestic militarism—be it in hard power as in militarized police forces and criminalized poor youth of color or soft power as in militaristic narratives in film, TV, video, or Internet consumption—fuses massive weapons of destruction with massive weapons of distraction.

For King, a rejection of militarism is not an isolated criticism of a foreign policy but instead a full-fledged critique of the American empire *as a way of life*. King saw an intimate connection between guns and butter, strong U.S. militaristic policies, and weak anti-poverty programs.[33] He highlighted how imperial invasions and occupations devour the spirit of a country—especially the souls of its young soldiers, many of whom returned distraught and distrustful of their own government.[34] Bombs dropped abroad in unjust war have a boomerang effect in the form of spiritual blackout at home.

Similarly, an attenuation of materialism is an ecologically conscious critique of a highly commodified way of life that leads to the rule of Big Money—be it bribed politicians or avaricious bosses at the workplace—which reduces active citizens to passive consumers who feel politically powerless and culturally joyless. This market-driven soulcraft puts a premium on money, greed, and status and reinforces a fear and paranoia that results in a life-denying callousness toward others—especially those who are vulnerable. One of King's favorite statements—"I'd rather be dead than afraid"—should be understood, in part, as a stand against this ethos.[35]

For King the vicious legacy of white supremacy—be it directed toward indigenous peoples, Asians, Latinos or Black folk—is as American as cherry pie. Yet it has to be understood as inseparable from (though never reducible to) class inequalities and lived experiences of poverty. In regard to values and priorities, the U.S. government's militarism and close ties to Big Money (Wall Street and big business) leads to a "war against the poor."[36] And King's view of integration is not a class-neutral form of black faces in high places with no structural transformation of the system itself. Rather, as the brilliant and courageous Adolph Reed, Jr., has noted, liberal identity politics is a class politics that hides and conceals crucial dimensions of class inequality and poverty beneath the guise of "diversity."[37] King writes, "Integration . . . ended up as merely adding color to a still predominantly white power structure. What is necessary now is to see integration . . . where there is a sharing of power."[38]

The Poor People's Campaign was about this sharing of power—a radical democratizing of the power structure with a redistribution of wealth. In the press conference officially announcing the Poor People's Campaign, King proclaimed, "In this era of technological wizardry and political immorality, the poor are demanding that the basic need of people be met as the first priority of our domestic programs."[39] One of King's SCLC advisors, William A. Rutherford, reported that in this period, King confided to him that "obviously we've got to have some form of socialism, but America's not ready to hear it yet."[40] Further, as seen in Coretta Scott King's courageous stands against homophobia, ableism, and especially sexism and patriarchy, King's egalitarian stance carries a moral logic that rejects *any* form of xenophobia or racism—be it against Arabs, Jews, Palestinians, Dalits, or anyone else.[41]

The sum of King's four catastrophic forces—militarism, materialism, racism, and poverty—point to something larger in the American empire, namely, the spiritual blackout in the country. This spiritual blackout is the relative eclipse of integrity and honesty, trust and courage, in the dominant cultural life of the nation. We live in an age of impunity and mendacity—where fewer have responsibility for what they say and do and where the end justifies the means (success trumps character). King foresaw this deadly spiritual disease as a sign and symbol of the unraveling of the American empire.

One strong pillar of King's waning hope in the face of the escalating despair in the American empire was black spiritual integrity. His own work and witness exemplify the grand hope of King's own spiritual mentor, W. E. B. Du Bois, who wrote in *The Souls of Black Folk*: "We the darker ones come even now not altogether empty-handed: there are to-day no truer exponents of the pure human spirit of the Declaration of Independence than the American Negroes; . . . All in all, we black men seem the sole oasis of simple faith and reverence in a dusty desert of dollars and smartness."[42] For Du Bois and King, the black freedom struggle was the leaven in the American democratic loaf just as black spiritual integrity—in culture and especially music—was the antidote to psychic emptiness.[43] But what happens when the nihilistic threat pulls the rug from under any genuine quest for integrity and honesty in black America? What if a market-driven gangsterization of the country engulfs black culture and thereby renders all of us captive in a sunlit prison of hedonism and an iron cage of narcissism ruled by Big Money and distracted by cultural decadence? In this way, the worst of black culture—materialism, militarism, and xenophobia—undercut the black freedom struggle.

Du Bois acknowledged this possibility in his prophetic chapter "Of the Wings of Atalanta" in *The Souls of Black Folk*:

> In the Black world, the Preacher and Teacher embodied once the ideals of this people,—the strife for another and a juster world, the vague dream of righteousness, the mystery of knowing; but to-day the danger is that these ideals, with their simple beauty and weird inspiration, will suddenly sink to a question of cash and a lust for gold. Here stands this black young Atalanta, girding herself for the race that must be run; and if her eyes be still toward the hills and sky as in the days of old, then we may look for noble running; but what if some ruthless or wily or even thoughtless Hippomenes lay golden apples before her? What if the Negro people be wooed from

a strife for righteousness, from a love of knowing, to regard dollars as the be-all and end-all of life? . . . Whither, then, is the new-world quest of Goodness and Beauty and Truth gone glimmering? Must this, and that fair flower of Freedom which, despite the jeers of latter-day striplings, sprung from our fathers' blood, must that too degenerate into . . . lawless lust with Hippomenes?[44]

This profound and disturbing Du Boisian challenge horrifies King. The American democratic experiment goes under if its imperialist, materialist, racist, classist forces engulf black culture and community. To put it bluntly, for King the black freedom struggle requires a cross to bear, the dominant American way of life encourages a flag to wave.

King cried out loud alone after a four-hour ride in the pitch darkness of a police wagon with a vicious German shepherd dog threatening him on the way to Reidsville State Prison in Tattnall County, Georgia: "This is the cross that we must bear for the freedom of our people."[45] His cross—like Du Bois's ideals of his Black Preacher and Teacher—enacts and embodies unarmed truth and unconditional love. Both the cross and ideals may be trashed and crushed by the dominant American ways of life, but the integrity and courage they require are timeless—or at least precious, no matter the personal cost. King stated at Penn Community Center in Frogmore, South Carolina, "When I took up the cross, I recognized its meaning. . . . The cross is something that you bear and ultimately that you die on. The cross may mean the death of your popularity. It may mean the death of a foundation grant. It may cut down your budget a little, but take up your cross and just bear it. And that's the way I have decided to go."[46]

And in choosing to be faithful unto death to this bold and beautiful way of the cross, he adds, "I have decided that I will not be intimidated. . . . I will not be silent, and I will be heard."[47] This courageous form of black *parrhesia*—fearless speech, frank speech, plain speech, and unintimidated speech—will fuse eloquence with remembrance, reverence and resistance. His revolutionary piety will serve as a strong wind at his back even as the catastrophic forces bombard him. King is quite aware of what he is up against and what is required: "We must see now that the evils of racism, economic exploitation, and militarism are all tied together, and you really can't get rid of one without getting rid of the others. . . . The whole structure of American life must be changed. . . . America's problem in restructuring is that she is a conservative nation. . . . We in the civil rights movement must come all out now and make it clear that America is a hypocritical nation and that America must set her own house in order."[48]

For King, every flag is under the Cross. The American nation is to be judged in light of unarmed truth and unconditional love. Because a condition of truth is to allow suffering to speak, the voices of the vulnerable must be heard and their hurt attended to. Because justice is what love looks like in public, the basic security of everyone from domination must be established—freedom from fear and want and freedom of speech and worship, at the least. On a deeper spiritual level, "America First" must mean that America must first overcome its fear of the truth about itself—its past and present—and give up "its childish belief in the efficacy of lies as a method of human uplift."[49]

This means America must confront the barbaric nightside of its "nascent empire" (George Washington's term) or "Empire of liberty" (Thomas Jefferson's phrase)—from the land theft and genocidal assaults on indigenous peoples to bestial enslavement of Africans (whose labor would produce the economic foundations of early American democracy) to domination of white workers and marginalization of women and non-straights.[50] King's choice of the way of the cross—and its attendant sacrifices of reputation and resources—is exemplified by many other towering figures in the black freedom struggle. Gwendolyn Brooks, Paul Robeson, James Baldwin, Lorraine Hansberry, and Amiri Baraka all were darlings of the white liberal establishments early in their careers yet ended up dismissed by the mainstream—even as they now give us hope in these bleak times.

Yet for King the deepest sadness is the black spiritual captivity to American idolatry. This captivity not only tacitly encourages black people to consent to our own domination in the name of black elite representation. More pointedly, it also deploys blackness as a form of patriotic solidarity that renders class inequality, poverty, and U.S. war crimes abroad invisible. In short, black people become Barack Obama-like flag wavers rather than Martin King-like cross bearers. We become seduced by black faces in high places and mesmerized by black elite success—even as black social misery becomes more and more an afterthought in public discourse.

Does it surprise anyone that we get a powerful and prophetic Black Lives Matter movement under a black president, black attorney general, and black Homeland Security cabinet secretary? All the black elite power at the highest realms of government was still beholden to military interests and Wall Street interests, with hardly a substantive policy to target poverty or inequality.

The intense fight over the legacy of King was my fundamental motivation for my fierce criticisms of President Barack Obama's presidency as well as his uncritical supporters. In my first long phone call with him, my fundamental question was, "What is your campaign's relation to the precious legacy of Martin Luther King, Jr.?" Obama laid out his vision and argument and I pledged my critical support. After more than 65 events—from Iowa in December 2007 to Ohio in November 2008—I tried to remain true to King's legacy within the campaign. But after the links tightened between Wall Street and his personnel, and the imperial technocrats emerged as close advisors, I saw King's presence waning.

Unfortunately, these public matters of principle and integrity were tainted with personal matters regarding three tickets for my mother, brother, and myself to attend the inaugural events. In typical American fashion, the personal issues eclipsed the public ones, and my moral and political standards of critique and resistance to Obama's neoliberal and imperial rule were easily lost. Ironically, my critique and resistance were grounded in preserving the legacy of Martin Luther King, Jr., even as Obama was widely cast as the embodiment of this precious legacy.[51]

King would shed tears from the grave to see eight years of black symbolic celebration alongside concrete hibernation, of black break-dancing in the air and sleepwalking on the ground—as over one in three black children live in poverty.[52] Sixty-nine percent of blacks polled in a CNN/Opinion Research Corporation poll shortly before Barack Obama's inauguration believed Martin Luther King's dream had come true.[53] And Obama manipulated this false consciousness in many clever and misleading ways. King's sculptured face was placed in the Oval Office (even as he shed symbolic tears of sorrow over Wall Street bailouts, militarized police departments, drone strikes committing war crimes, and the top 1 percent reaping more than 95 percent of income gains during the first Obama term).[54] King's Bible was used at the swearing-in ceremony, and shirts were widely circulated with the faces of Martin, Malcolm, and Barack. Here, the cross was confused with the flag, moral greatness was conflated with political success, spiritual excellence was identified as presidential presence, and being a love warrior against the American empire was reduced to being a polished professional who headed the American empire. This massive spiritual blackout in black America was prefigured in Du Bois's sad words and King's melancholic witness.

Needless to say, the nearly wholesale capitulation of black intellectuals to the Obama celebration was a grand betrayal of Du Bois and King. It revealed the degree to which careerist carrots and opportunistic crumbs dangled in front of status-hungry academics and money-driven pundits rendered them conformist cheerleaders and complicit courtiers of our black imperial ruler—even as the poor and working classes were ignored, Palestinian occupation tightened, and U.S. terroristic attacks escalated.

For King, the Obama moment would represent not simply a political calculation or cost-benefit analysis. It is an issue of spiritual integrity and moral authority—of truth-telling and witness-bearing for justice. If the black freedom movement is reduced to just another American interest group with its middle-class elites primarily protecting their interests and careers in the name of the flag, then nihilism has triumphed in black America and the country as a whole.

As a revolutionary Christian, King understands the scandal of the Cross—the crushing of unarmed truth and unconditional love by empires and persons—as the dominant way of the world. Radical love in freedom and radical freedom in love is the absurd affirmation of life within the historical experience of relative impotence. The untenanted Cross—the imperial Roman removal of Jesus from Calvary—leads to either the perennial death of God or the resurrection of Christ, either the chronic crushing of truth and love or the feeble yet discernible evidences of truth and love generated by an Easter joy.[55] The revolutionary Christian—like King—lives in the dark shadows and bleak realities of lies and crimes with weak evidences of truth and love.

The Holy Saturday between Good Friday and Easter looms large in King's melancholic witness. Massive black conformity and complicity to American lies and crimes in the name of protecting a black president is not only a high form of idolatry but a collective forsaking of the spiritual integrity and moral authority that sustained King—and the sacred black freedom struggle that produced him. Lest we forget, when King died, many black Americans disapproved of him—as did 63 percent of all Americans.[56]

We enter this ugly Trump moment, this neo-fascist era, weak on habits of truth-telling and justice-bearing, and feeble on spiritual integrity and moral authority. The courageous and visionary Movement for Black Lives and the Moral Monday crusade constitute our major "evidence" of truth and love, our major efforts to have not sold our souls for a mess of pottage. Martin Luther King, Jr.'s nihilism would be the death of Aunt Esther—the symbol and flesh of black spiritual integrity and moral authority and the refusal to sell her soul to any power structure—in the grand August Wilson's ten-play cycle of black twentieth-century life. For Wilson, Aunt Esther was born in 1619 and died in the mid eighties, the Reagan era.

King's nihilistic threat was the death of black cross-bearers in a neoliberal or neo-fascist empire in which money and status would render the professionals complacent and police and prisons would keep the black poor and working class contained. And the comings and goings of black celebrities—the culture of superficial spectacle—would seduce the masses to live vicariously through them. This charade of spiritual obscenity, moral vacuity, and political impotence makes King turn over in his grave.

Yet in the face of overwhelming despair in his own life and time, King held on to what Du Bois called "a hope not hopeless but unhopeful . . . [in] a land whose freedom is to us a mockery and whose liberty a lie."[57] Or as James Weldon Johnson and Rosamond Johnson put it in The Negro National Anthem:

> Stony the road we trod,
> Bitter the chastening rod,
> Felt in the days when hope unborn had died[58]

In a certain sense, King, like Thucydides, gives up on hope as the sole comforter in the face of catastrophe. Yet he remains a Christian who chooses to *be a hope*. Like John Coltrane, he simply wants to be a force for good.[59] When King painfully declares, "I have no ambitions in life but to achieve excellence in the Christian ministry," he has been pushed against the wall or to the edge of life's abyss by personal chaos, betrayal, FBI surveillance, and national misunderstanding.[60] His uttered words constitute neither a theodicy nor a consistent Christian philosophy. It is not even clear whether he holds to the redemptive power of unearned suffering. But he does desperately hold on to his own soul and what sustains that soul, even if it is threatened to be devoured by the nihilism of his day.

In doing so, King echoes Du Bois's historic radio address on his ninety-first birthday, broadcast to Africa from Beijing University. Du Bois declared: "I speak with no authority; no assumption of age nor rank; I hold no position, I have no wealth. One thing alone I own and that is my own soul. Ownership of that I have even while in my own country for near a century, I have been nothing but a "nigger." On this basis and this alone I dare speak, I dare advise. . . . [F]or today Africa stands on new feet, with new eyesight, with new brains and asks: Where am I and why!"[61]

The late styles of Du Bois and King enact distinctive forms of spiritual fortitude (courage and greatness of character) or sheer existential resilience of remembrance, reverence and resistance. There is no guarantee of ultimate victory or grounds for progress. They view themselves as exemplary moments in long traditions of intellectual, moral, political, and spiritual struggles for freedom. Their lives and examples crystallize crucial features of these struggles—integrity, honesty, decency, courage, vision—even as they lay bare the wounds and bruises of the nihilistic threats of their day. Both reject any cheap optimism and opt for a costly hope—an enacted hope. King's Christian hope differs from Du Bois's more ecumenical spiritual hope—but both are groundless and soulful. Neither is rational or sterile. Their hope is closer to the songs of gospel singers or blues vocalists than the theories of systematic theologians or academic philosophers. And their examples are intended to keep alive traditions of resistance for the young in order to enact new revolutionary forms of soulcraft even as the world lurches toward neo-fascist versions of Babylon.

Both surmounted their despair with a deep sense of calling that yielded a tangible hope through courageous action, subtle reflection, and subversive memory. Both died after living lonely lives of monumental sacrifice and service. Du Bois and King are elevated and celebrated today though they are widely misunderstood. As King explicitly lamented, "I am nevertheless greatly saddened . . . that the inquirers have not really known me, my commitment or my calling."[62]

Afterword

Dignity as a Weapon of Love

JONATHAN L. WALTON

When Ieshia Evans left her home near Scranton, Pennsylvania, to head south to Baton Rouge during the summer of 2016, she did not plan to end up on news programs and mobile devices everywhere. The nurse and mother of a young son had a humbler agenda. As one of her friends posted to Facebook, Evans just wanted to "look her son in the eyes to tell him she fought for his freedom and rights." Like many in this nation, she was outraged over video footage of Baton Rouge police officers tackling and subsequently shooting Alton Sterling to death. So, without any claims to being an activist or a history of protest, Ms. Evans headed to Baton Rouge to stand alongside thousands of others in nonviolent protest. She had no idea that she would be arrested, and, in the process, arrest the world's attention.

As Baton Rouge police officers in full riot gear lined up along the street, they began to arrest one protester after another. Ieshia Evans felt strongly that the protesters were well within their constitutional rights. After witnessing two other protesters wrestled to the ground and carried away in handcuffs, Ms. Evans made her way into the street. A summer zephyr interrupted the heat and humidity just long enough to catch the bottom of her sundress. Her hands joined together in front of her svelte frame. Ms. Evans's eyes appeared to look beyond, if not right through, the two armor-clad police officers who clumsily descended upon her. This is when photographer Jonathan Bachman captured a moment that has come to define a movement.[1]

The visual contrasts are as instructive as they are arresting. The officers appear anxious, even defensive. Ieshia Evans looks still and serene. The officers represent the power and authority of the state. Ieshia Evans reflects another form of authority—power seemingly not derived from this world. The photograph also shows a crack in the asphalt that runs right between the arresting officers and Ms. Evans. The crack appears metaphorically placed. Ms. Evans and the arresting officers stand on two different planes of existence.

There is a reason I begin with this photograph. This iconic image of Ieshia Evans seems to answer two recurring questions that arise throughout this volume. First, what are the relationships between varying conceptions of dignity and nonviolent resistance as a form of mass protest? Second, how might these relationships be leveraged as a viable political philosophy within our current political context in the United States? In some ways, I suspect this now ubiquitous photograph linked to the current Black Lives Matter movement may elucidate a few of the major themes discussed in this volume.

By privileging these two questions, I realize that I am showing my intellectual cards. As a scholar of religion with strong normative commitments regarding the role of religion in public life, there are a few things that I take for granted when considering Martin Luther King, Jr. That Martin King was one of the most productive philosophers of the previous century is a given for me. My high regard for King as a deep and influential thinker is not a result of any hagiographic affinity born of my own Atlanta roots and Morehouse College education. But rather it is a result of how I view the philosopher's task. Philosophy at its core has two primary concerns: who we are and how we should live. Political philosophy, similarly, is concerned with attending to the central dimensions of government—laws, rights, liberty, justice—while considering what government owes its citizens, and vice versa.

Unfortunately, the purification of contemporary philosophy in the twentieth century has contributed to a circling of the wagons around research institutions. Ensconced within departments of research universities, philosophy is now the domain of professionally trained specialists who employ a guild-specific language. Such a self-reverential approach to the philosopher's task has led to what some now regard as a disciplinary pathology.[2] As a result, organic public intellectuals like Martin Luther King, Jr., are ignored at best, and viewed with supercilious disdain at worst. Political theorists measure activist intellectuals against their more "rigorous" and "original" academic counterparts. The former become less deserving of scholarly engagement. These sorts of professional developments say more about the academic discipline of philosophy and field of political theory than they do about Martin Luther King, Jr.'s philosophical and political import.

This is why I celebrate the editors and contributors to this volume. As the previous essays attest, Martin Luther King, Jr., possessed a mature philosophical framework that was neither theoretically derivative nor materially reductionist. He was an original thinker who championed grand ideals. Like those of the ancient Palestinian teacher Jesus, King's moral ideals and visions of a just society were often characterized as the kingdom of God. King was, first and foremost, a Christian preacher. Nevertheless, no one can ever accuse him of being so heavenly minded as to render his thoughts no earthly good.

Consider his dialectical approach to human suffering. His thesis often began with contrasting moral ideals and political approaches. King then moved toward a synthesis of new possibility. As one of King's former professors at Boston University, L. Harold DeWolf, said of his former student, "King never tired of moving from a one-sided thesis to a corrective, but also one-sided antithesis and finally to a more coherent synthesis beyond both."[3] For instance, in his final book, *Where Do We Go from Here*, King calls presciently and prophetically for a revolution of values that will run counter to the impending neoliberal turn of the final quarter of the twentieth century. "When machines and computers, profit motives and property rights are considered more important than people," King writes, "the giant triplets of racism, materialism, and militarism are incapable of being conquered."[4] Such a revolution will not emerge from the prevailing thesis of capitalism or its antithesis of communism, according to King. Each represented a partial truth. Both individualism and collectivism are important features of the moral life. Thus, we ought to neither privilege one nor be forced to choose between the two. King believed that the creative synthesis is found in "a socially conscious democracy which reconciles the truths of individualism and collectivism."[5]

Here we see that even King's economic critique was informed by his religious upbringing. Citing the biblical parable of the Good Samaritan, King concludes that a revolution of values will not look for the cheapest or easiest way to attend to human suffering. It is one thing to stop and assist those who fell among thieves along life's Jericho Road. Yet a reexamination of the infrastructure that contributes to the road being dangerous is a more appropriate task. Like the moral message found in the Good Samaritan parable, we are responsible for the well-being of our neighbors—particularly those neighbors who sit across lines of difference.

To be sure, King's deep religious commitment—what Cornel West refers to in his essay as a tradition of "black spiritual integrity"—may explain why King has not been vaulted to the heights of a W. E. B. Du Bois or Frantz Fanon within academia. Many political theorists advance the view that religious commitments are out of bounds when advancing political positions. They view religion as a "conversation stopper," to cite Richard Rorty's commonly evoked phrase.[6] Theological claims and appeals to metaphysical truths, some believe, do not fit within the discursive rubrics of modern democratic ideals.

When we consider the loudest religious voices attempting to influence public policy over the past few decades, this position is understandable. The exclusive, authoritarian, and anti-intellectual tendencies of the Religious Right and other white conservative Christian evangelicals belie the values of open debate and freedom of expression. With their claims of America as a "Christian nation," they offer a historically revised traditionalism that too often baptizes bigotry in the name of "religious freedom." Attempts to limit reproductive rights, deny labor protections to LGBTQ-identified citizens, and ban immigration from predominantly Muslim countries are just a few examples. Much of the publicized God-talk in American politics has left a lot to be desired.

The philosophical contributions of King, however, strike a valuable and viable contrast. King is valuable insofar as he demonstrates that religious commitments need not be inconsistent with the normative values of modern democracy. This is where those who oppose bringing normative religious commitments into the public sphere seem to overreach. It is not as if normative ideals and commitments do not undergird liberal democracy. The equality of humanity, checks and balances of governmental power, and equal treatment under the law are just a few such commitments. These values and ideals are even stated explicitly in the founding and governing documents of the United States. As the Declaration of Independence declares, "We hold these truths to be self-evident, that all men are created equal, that they are endowed by their Creator with certain unalienable Rights, that among these are Life, Liberty, and the Pursuit of Happiness." Thus, a normative commitment to the equality of humanity is what distinguishes current experiments in liberal democracy from our monarchical ancestors and autocratic contemporaries. This conception of equality lends itself to equal faith, equal voice, equal protections, and equal opportunity to hold government leaders responsible to their citizenry.[7]

As several of the chapters in this volume attest, King's deep theological reservoir impelled him to affirm the human dignity of all, regardless of race, class, or even religion. As he states so clearly in his "Letter from Birmingham City Jail," "Any law that uplifts human personality is just. Any law that degrades human personality is unjust."[8] This is what makes King's intellectual contributions particularly viable for the field of political theory. Even for those who do not hold King's theological commitments, his mature moral framework is transferable and intelligible to all radical democrats dedicated to promoting policies and political theories that advance the well-being of the most vulnerable among us.

For instance, recall King's own evangelical roots. He was a product of the Afro-Protestant tradition with its emphasis on the sovereignty of God and the radical equality of humanity. All are made in the *imago dei*. For King this had clear political consequences. In principle, this notion of the parenthood of God and siblinghood of humanity rejects any worldview or social structure that privileges any one group over another. Racism at the interpersonal level and segregation at the social level were equal sins. King believed that transformation of the individual and structural change must take place concurrently. Conversion of the heart divorced from a challenge to unjust structures was meaningless and immoral. Therefore, King had little tolerance for Christian preachers who called for immediate personal conversion from sin, yet cried, "Wait!" when it came to desegregation efforts in southern cities like Birmingham. As he states in "Pilgrimage to Nonviolence," "Any religion that professes to be concerned about the souls of men and is not concerned about the slums that damn them, the economic conditions that strangle them and the social conditions that cripple them is a spiritually moribund religion awaiting burial."[9]

From a political perspective, it may appear that King privileged structural change over individual conversion. The activist wing of Afro-Protestantism nurtured him. His grandfather the Reverend A. D. Williams was a founding member of the Atlanta Civic League, an alliance of African American clergy who organized in response to anti-black violence in the city in 1906. Daddy King helped secure positions with full arrest privileges for African American men within the Atlanta Police Department, and equal pay for African American teachers in relation to their white counterparts.[10] The express mission of King's Southern Christian Leadership Conference was "to redeem the soul of America." And to those who argued that legislation cannot really solve the nation's ills, because legislation cannot change the hearts of individuals, King was clear. "It may be true that the law cannot make a man love me but it can keep him from lynching me."[11]

To place too much emphasis on structural change at the expense of human personality, however, is to diminish King's religious commitments and distort his philosophical method. Justice will not emerge from a prevailing thesis of structural change or an antithesis of personal transformation. Again, *both* are important features of the moral life. King believed strongly the words of the children's Christian song, "Red and yellow, black and white, all are precious in God's sight." This explains, in part, why King gravitated toward the theological concept of personalism at Crozer and then Boston University. The belief that all individuals are endowed with ultimate intrinsic value was a consistent message at the Ebenezer Baptist Church of King's youth, and this belief had political corollaries for King's political philosophy. If every person is precious and full of dignity and worth, discrimination of any sort degrades God's unique creation. What is more, if every person is equal under the parenthood of God, then every person deserves equal protection under the law. One equal soul merits one equal vote. One soul replete with dignity and worth deserves equal opportunity regardless of the accidents of birth.

The creative synthesis that emerges out of King's theological commitments stands out for me as the overarching theme of this volume. The important place of human dignity in King's political thought and action seems to be the conceptual thread that runs through each of the essays. Robert Gooding-Williams, for instance, illumines the importance of dignity for King by identifying King's effort to frame *Stride toward Freedom* as an origin story. King, like Du Bois before him, understood the dehumanizing impact of slavery and segregation. Racial injustice and unjust segregation laws corrode the soul, just as poverty and slums, as Tommie Shelby's essay explains so convincingly, erode human beings' sense of self. In King's words, "segregation distorts the soul and damages the personality. It gives the segregator a false sense of superiority, and the segregated a false sense of inferiority."[12] This is why Gooding-Williams makes the compelling argument that King offers *Stride toward Freedom* as a counternarrative—an etiology of a "new Negro" born out of the crucible of protest.

Gooding-Williams's reading touches on another dimension of King's evangelical roots that is often overlooked—the exalted place of biblical narrative. Biblical stories provide communities the grist for sacred traditions of virtue. These shared narratives of faith provide the moral and intellectual resources to imagine concepts of redemption, forgiveness, and human potential for change.[13] This is where King as a public philosopher demonstrated so effectively his polyvalent political vocabulary. He could cite a range of shared narratives to underscore the normative ideals of a radically inclusive democracy.[14]

Recall in his "Letter from Birmingham City Jail" where King offers several prominent personalities whose lives are now legendary in the civic imaginary. They include biblical figures such as the Hebrew prophet Amos,

Jesus, and the apostle Paul. King also includes prominent political figures like Thomas Jefferson and Abraham Lincoln. King presents them as "creative extremists" who promoted the cause of justice and democracy. Whether from the biblical text or American history, these figures are central characters in narratives that extend the leitmotifs of freedom and equality. Civic narratives take on a sacred tone and texture insofar as they extend traditions of virtue and champion ultimate ideals. It makes sense, then, that King might view *Stride toward Freedom* as a potential moral resource for democracy. The Montgomery bus boycott was a narrative of American protest in which the otherwise oppressed might find pride and inspiration. In the valiant struggle for justice in Montgomery, African Americans everywhere might reimagine their inherent sacred worth and dignity that racial discrimination depletes. The fight for justice infused citizens with "a sense of somebodiness . . . a new determination to achieve freedom and human dignity."[15]

Similarly, just as a story is never just a story, mass protest is not just about a specific set of demands or intended political reform. Mass protest is performance art. It is akin to a religious ritual. It is the dramaturgical presentation and even theatrical representation of injustice and resistance. As King makes clear in his writings and sermons, protest is the performed narrative of a community's ideal. It is the sacred marking of memory, as well as casting a new vision. Protest is an important demonstration and marking of human dignity.

This explains why I began with the now iconic image of Ieshia Evans. Her photo now sits alongside other iconic images of protest and resistance that amplify the inherent value of the oppressed in the face of oppressive circumstances. These images provide an inspirational template and moral vision of virtuous action. Think of the images of student protesters at the Woolworth's lunch counter in Greensboro, North Carolina, in 1960. Consider images of anti-apartheid resistance in South Africa. Recall "Tank Man" in Tiananmen Square in 1989. There are reasons we continue to look to them for inspiration and motivation, even outside of their respective contexts. Memory and vision are at work. Models of dignity both as inherent and as a suitable moral posture for protest are on display.

Martha Nussbaum's essay in this volume captures King's concern for this sort of appropriate moral disposition. King sought to ensure that protesters developed a just response to injustice, the appropriate ethical means toward attaining moral ends. Influenced by Mohandas Gandhi and Bayard Rustin, King believed that protesters must overcome their natural affinity toward anger by a self-purification process. Anger toward others, though not toward injustice itself, was both impractical and immoral in regard to protest movements. Anger fuels a desire for retaliation. Retaliation leads to violence. And violence forecloses the human capacity toward reconciliation. For one can never seek structural transformation and not be concerned with how individuals engage one another on the other side of social change. In the struggle for justice, the aim of the oppressed is neither the defeat nor humiliation of the oppressor. Justice is sought to deliver all sides, the oppressed as well as the oppressor. King believed that only nonviolence could bring about this desired result.

Both Karuna Mantena and Ronald Sundstrom drive home this point. By linking King to intellectual interlocutors like Gandhi and Reinhold Niebuhr, they demonstrate how King saw the need for alternate forms of power in the fight for human rights. Too often the ruling elite are animated by subrational impulses like anxiety, fear, and pride. This translates into ideological and repressive violence to defend the unjust status quo. Hence, the oppressed need a different weapon that replaces brute force with moral suasion. Like Gandhi's *satyagraha*—truth or love force—and Niebuhr's use of *agape,* King saw nonviolent direct action as the appropriate moral weapon. Love is an appropriate form of moral power.

True to form, once again King refused to pit central concepts against one another. There is no need to place love and power within a false binary. Unlike his social gospel progenitors, King did not become intoxicated by Pollyannaish platitudes of love. Nor did he allow the allure of power to pull him from his moral commitments to justice. King situated love and power within a creative dialectical tension in his final presidential address to the Southern Christian Leadership Conference: "You see, what happened is that some of our philosophers got off base. And one of the great problems of history is that the concepts of love and power have usually been contrasted as opposites—polar opposites—so that love is identified with a resignation of power, and power with a denial of love. . . . What is needed is a realization that power without love is reckless and abusive, and love without power is sentimental and anemic. Power at its best is love implementing the demands of justice, and justice at its best is power correcting everything that stands against love."[16] Out of this emerges for King nonviolent civil disobedience as a corrective—an alternative form of moral power grounded in love toward the cause of justice. In other words, as Cornel West likes to put it, "justice is what love looks like in public."

Make no mistake. King has endured his fair share of criticism for his uncompromising philosophy of nonviolence. Many equate King's commitment to nonviolent direct action as a form of pacifism. Is it fair to expect people who already reside on the underside of oppression to further acquiesce to their oppressors? To ask victims of injustice to assume responsibility for the redemption of their victimizer is, for many, to put too high a price on a ticket for freedom. Others point to King's willingness to endure violence as the ultimate act of indignity and dehumanization. How can King call for people to maintain their dignity yet forgo their right to self-defense? This is particularly true among sectors of the African American community who define manhood narrowly according to the twin masculinist categories of "protector" and "provider."

Martha Nussbaum provides a subtle, though important, nuance of King's position that speaks directly to such critiques. First, there is nothing passive about nonviolent direct action. The goal is to uncover, and even unleash, structural violence that is inherent within unjust social systems. Asking protesters to purify themselves by adopting the right moral disposition—a moral disposition that conquers retaliatory anger—is hardly a form of acquiescence. To the contrary, as Nussbaum points out, it is a moral position that requires a considerable amount of courage. Second, to those who believe enduring abuse is an insult to human personality, we cannot separate King's varying conceptions of human dignity from acts of nonviolent demonstration. King never asked African Americans to give up their right to self-defense in their daily lives. He makes this clear in his discussion of Black Power in *Where Do We Go from Here*. "In a sense," King writes, "this is a false issue, for the right to defend one's home and one's person when attacked has been guaranteed through the ages by common law."[17] Yet in the next sentence he adds that the matter of nonviolent demonstration is a different matter altogether. This is why I liken mass protest to religious ritual above. King understood nonviolent demonstrations as public performances. They are dramaturgical representations of injustice and resistance. This is the context in which King asks that participants prepare themselves by vanquishing anger and embracing nonviolence—a form of human dignity.

In response to critiques that willingly submitting to violence is a form of self-disparagement, King was quick to note that structural violence and oppression are already present. The oppressed are besieged by violence daily in the form of economic, political, educational, and all other forms of injustice that are built into the structures of a given society. Rather than continuing to acquiesce to injustice, nonviolent protesters aim to dramatize this evil. In citing the evils of school segregation, for instance, King contends, "It is better to shed a little blood from a blow on the head or a rock thrown by an angry mob than to have children by the thousands finishing high school who can only read at a sixth grade level."[18]

King, then, has multiple conceptions of dignity operating at the same time. Dignity is the intrinsic value and moral worth of every individual. As Derrick Darby describes in his contribution to this volume, the right to vote and raise one's voice is recognition of that moral worth. Again, for King this is God-given. Dignity is also a disposition and demeanor that prepares one for the demands of mass protest. It is the moral posture that vanquishes anger, refuses to personalize injustice, and thus allows protesters to nonviolently dramatize evil and suffering in the public ritual of mass protest. Finally, dignity is also an orientation that ought to recognize itself in others. This is important on the other side of protest. By keeping one's focus on injustice and not personalizing evil, protesters can reconcile with those who previously oppressed. Acknowledging one's own self-worth along with the inherent dignity of others prepares one for the work of beloved community.

These are the reasons I believe Jonathan Bachman's photograph of Ieshia Evans has come to capture this particular historical moment. Whenever violence has erupted, whether in Baltimore, Ferguson, or Dallas, those who side with state power search out any excuse they can find to justify a militarized police presence. The evil of police brutality takes a backseat to property damage. Riots receive much more attention than the violence of repressive and ideological state apparatuses. And when those who are already overdetermined as inherently violent within the white supremacist imaginary participate in violence at any level, the evil forces of oppression are absolved of any responsibility. This is tragic and manipulative.

Bachman's image of Ms. Evans, however, disrupts any such narrative. The power of a repressive state was countered by a moral force for justice. The evil of a violent, militarized system was jarringly supplanted by a nonviolent, yet forceful presence. And when those who are otherwise framed as violent display their inherent dignity despite disquieting circumstances, evil is exposed and injustice is clearly identified. Arresting officers may have had the weapons, but Ieshia Evans had the power. This is the moral and strategic posture from which Black Lives Matter activists might consider combating militarized police forces, state sanctioned murder, and the prison industrial complex. Riots may be the language of the unheard. But nonviolence is the language of justice—a clear and coherent alliance of love and power speaking truth to injustice.

NOTES

ACKNOWLEDGMENTS

CONTRIBUTORS

INDEX

Notes

INTRODUCTION

1. James Baldwin, "The Dangerous Road before Martin Luther King," in *The Price of the Ticket: Collected Nonfiction, 1948–1985* (New York: St. Martin's Press/Marek, 1985), 245–304.

2. In 1999 in a special Gallup poll, King was rated the second most admired person of the twentieth century, falling short only of Mother Teresa. This is a far cry from Gallup polling data on King in the 1960s. Even at the height of his popularity, King was deeply polarizing, but by 1966 he garnered a 63 percent negative rating on Gallup's "scalometer." Frank Newport, "Martin Luther King Jr.: Revered More after Death than Before," Gallup.com (January 16, 2006), http://www.gallup.com/poll/20920/martin-luther-king-jr-revered-more-after-death-than-before.aspx.

3. Martin Luther King Jr. Day remains the only federal holiday established in honor of an individual American civilian, and only Columbus Day, named after the wayward Genoese explorer, and George Washington's Birthday, which is now known as the more inclusive "Presidents' Day," are officially named in honor of individuals at all. Matthew Spaulding, "It's George Washington's Birthday," *Features,* paper 116 (2005), http://scholarworks.gvsu.edu/features/116.

4. Derek H. Alderman, "Street Names as Memorial Arenas: The Reputational Politics of Commemorating Martin Luther King Jr. in a Georgia County" in *The Civil Rights Movement in American Memory,* ed. Renee C. Romano and Leigh Raiford (Athens: University of Georgia Press, 2006), 8–10, 73.

5. Martin Luther King, Jr., "I Have a Dream," in *A Testament of Hope: The Essential Writings and Speeches of Martin Luther King, Jr.,* edited by James M. Washington (New York: HarperCollins, 1986), 219.

6. Indeed, *The Liberatory Thought of Martin Luther King, Jr.: Critical Essays on the Philosopher King,* edited by Robert Birt (Lanham, MD: Lexington Books, 2012), is the only collection of essays on King's thought written by academic philosophers and political theorists. This is an important volume, to be sure. But it is, alas, just one.

7. The engagement with King in academic theology and the study of religion is far more developed. King himself was a scholar of systematic theology and received a doctorate from Boston University. His efforts in political theology, and his understanding of the significance of theological inquiry for black political life, inspired a

deluge of works in African American theology in the wake of his assassination and in the midst of the Black Power movement. The most influential of these texts was undoubtedly James H. Cone's *Black Theology and Black Power* (New York: Seabury, 1969). Cone's text inspired a vigorous debate over the possibility and substance of "Black Liberation Theology" and the extent to which such a project should be compatible with black nationalist themes. The masculinist and racialist excesses of black theology in the era of Black Power occasioned another critical movement in academic theology, "Womanism," which mounted a critique of patriarchal and heteronormative themes in Christianity and in Black Liberation Theology more specifically. On the development of African American theology in the wake of King's assassination, see Sylvester Johnson, "The African American Christian Tradition," in *The Oxford Handbook of African American Theology*, ed. Anthony B. Pinn and Katie G. Cannon (New York: Oxford University Press, 2014), 68–84.

8. By appealing to the genre of romance to describe a mode of historical narration, we underscore two contentions. The first is that understanding the meanings embedded in historical discourse often involves more than grasping particular explanatory claims or descriptions of events. Understanding also requires apprehending those formal and figurative qualities we usually associate with other forms of storytelling in historical discourse. The second, defended by a range of "narrativist" philosophers of history, literary critics, and political theorists, is that one may productively interrogate historical discourse with an eye toward the *meaning* produced by the use of various tropes, generic plot conventions, metaphors, and other figurative elements. The classic statement of this position, despite its excesses, is Hayden White, *Metahistory: The Historical Imagination in Nineteenth-Century Europe* (Baltimore: Johns Hopkins University Press, 1973). For an introduction to the broader debate, see the pieces collected in Geoffrey Roberts, ed., *The History and Narrative Reader* (New York: Routledge, 2001).

9. Martha C. Nussbaum, *Love's Knowledge: Essays on Philosophy and Literature* (New York: Oxford, 1990), 3–5.

10. For a comprehensive exposition of these claims, see Brandon M. Terry, "Which Way to Memphis? Political Theory, Narrative, and the Politics of Historical Imagination in the Civil Rights Movement" (PhD diss., Yale University, New Haven, CT, 2012).

11. Cass Sunstein, "What the Civil Rights Movement Was and Wasn't (with Notes on Martin Luther King, Jr. and Malcolm X)," *University of Illinois Law Review* 1 (1995): 193. Sunstein goes so far as to call the civil rights movement "Burkean," in reference to the eighteenth-century conservative thinker and British MP Edmund Burke, who extolled the virtues of tradition (specifically English common law, traditional mores, and constitutional monarchy) as repositories of genuine wisdom and warned against the revolutionary impulse to realize abstract ideals like liberty and equality at the expense of existing, historically evolved forms of government and social life. See Edmund Burke, *Reflections on the Revolution in France* (New York: Penguin, 1982).

12. For a similar critique of how the historical, political, and philosophical significance of the Haitian revolution is treated as a derivative fulfillment of European universalism in political theory, see Adom Getachew, "Universalism after the Post-Colonial Turn: Interpreting the Haitian Revolution," *Political Theory* 44, no. 6 (2016): 821–845.

13. Gunnar Myrdal, *An American Dilemma: The Negro Problem and Modern Democracy,* vol. 1 (New York: Harper and Bros., 1944), xlix.

14. Paul C. Taylor, "Taking Postracialism Seriously: From Movement Mythology to Racial Formation," *Du Bois Review* 11, no. 1 (2014): 9–25.

15. For more, see Chapter 10, by Shatema Threadcraft and Brandon M. Terry.

16. Although he frequently commented that he would have liked, one day, to become a university professor and did manage to co-teach a social philosophy course at Morehouse College.

17. In this regard, our efforts are similar to those undertaken by philosophers working on the thought of Frederick Douglass. See, for example, Bill Lawson and Frank Kirkland, eds., *Frederick Douglass: A Critical Reader* (Malden, MA: Blackwell, 1999).

18. Cornel West, "Black Culture and Postmodernism," in *Remaking History,* ed. Barbara Kruger and Phil Mariani (Seattle: Bay Press, 1989).

19. Jonathan Reider, who has produced the most comprehensive study of King's rhetorical performances in the broadest array of settings, writes that while King deploys a stunning range of rhetorical guises through "jokes, eulogies, sermons, speeches, chats, storytelling, exhortations, jeremiads, taunts, repartee, confessions, lamentation, complaints, and gallows humor," he nevertheless "exhibited a remarkable constancy" in the "rich complexities of his beliefs." Jonathan Reider, *The Word of the Lord Is Upon Me: The Righteous Performance of Martin Luther King, Jr.* (Cambridge, MA: Harvard University Press, 2008), 3.

20. Henry Louis Gates, Jr., "Literary Theory and the Black Tradition," in *Figures in Black: Words, Signs, and the "Racial" Self* (New York: Oxford University Press, 1989), 54.

21. Historians have long noted that, like many public figures, King wrote many of his texts in collaboration with his closest advisors, including, at different points, Stanley Levison, Clarence Jones, and Vincent Harding. While this fact is of historical interest, and worth noting, it is important that it does not obscure King's role as the primary organizer, author, and authorial voice behind these texts. Further, we think it appropriate to assume these texts, especially the published monographs, conveyed considered views that King endorsed at the time and assented to having his name and reputation singularly attached to. This form of collaboration, we think, does not raise the more complicated interpretive questions posed by, for example, the "group writing" that Danielle Allen meticulously unpacks in her study of the Declaration of Independence. See Danielle S. Allen, *Our Declaration: A Reading of the Declaration of Independence in Defense of Equality* (New York: Liveright, 2014), chaps. 5–13.

22. Robert Gooding-Williams, *In the Shadow of Du Bois* (Cambridge, MA: Harvard University Press, 2009), 2–3.

23. For two approaches to African American political thought that hew more closely to familiar categories in the history of political thought (for example, liberalism, Marxism, conservatism, feminism, and nationalism) while emphasizing African Americans' distinctive revisions, see Bernard Boxill, *Blacks and Social Justice*, rev. ed. (1984; Lanham, MD: Rowman and Littlefield, 1992); and Michael C. Dawson, *Black Visions: The Roots of Contemporary African American Political Ideologies* (Chicago: University of Chicago Press, 2001).

24. See, for example, Glenda Gilmore, *Defying Dixie* (New York: W. W. Norton, 2008); Thomas Sugrue, *Sweet Land of Liberty: The Forgotten Struggle for Civil Rights in the North* (New York: Random House, 2009); Jacqueline Dowd Hall, "The Long Civil Rights Movement and the Political Uses of the Past," *Journal of American History* 91, no. 4 (2005): 1233–1263; Nikhil Pal Singh, *Black Is a Country: The Unfinished Struggle for Race and Democracy* (Cambridge, MA: Harvard University Press, 2003); Risa Goluboff, *The Lost Promise of Civil Rights* (Cambridge, MA: Harvard University Press, 2007); Carol Anderson, *Eyes off the Prize: The United Nations and the African American Struggle for Human Rights* (New York: Cambridge University Press, 2003); Tomiko Brown-Nagin, *Courage to Dissent: Atlanta and the Long History of the Civil Rights Movement* (New York: Oxford University Press, 2011); Mary Dudziak, *Cold War Civil Rights: Race and the Image of American Democracy* (Princeton, NJ: Princeton University Press, 2000).

25. Vincent Harding, introduction, in Martin Luther King, Jr., *Where Do We Go from Here: Chaos or Community?* (Boston: Beacon Press, 2010), xi.

26. Boxill, *Blacks and Social Justice*.

27. It is often assumed, even by careful biographers, that King's quote is taken *directly* from the nineteenth-century abolitionist, but this is incorrect. The full Theodore Parker quote is as follows: "I do not pretend to understand the moral universe. The arc is a long one. My eye reaches but little ways. I cannot calculate the curve and complete the figure by experience of sight. I can divine it by conscience. And from what I see I am sure it bends toward justice." Theodore Parker, "Of Justice and the Conscience," in *Views of Religion* (Boston: American Unitarian Association, 1885), 151. King frequently paraphrased this section of Parker's sermon for dramatic effect, but his rendering often suggests a more assured grasp of transcendental ethical truth as well as the moral direction of "History."

28. For a similar effort, involving domestic concerns, see Tommie Shelby, "Justice and Racial Conciliation: Two Visions," *Daedalus* 140, no. 1 (Winter 2011): 95–107.

29. Christopher Lasch, *The True and Only Heaven: Progress and Its Critics* (New York: W. W. Norton, 1991), 407.

30. Cornel West, "The Making of an American Radical Democrat of African Descent," in *The Cornel West Reader* (New York: Basic Civitas, 1999), 3.

31. Martin Luther King, Jr. *A Trumpet of Conscience* (Boston: Beacon Press, 1968) 79; King, *Strength to Love* (Minneapolis: Fortress Press, 2010), 92.

1. The Afro-modern tradition of political thought is bound together by its thematic preoccupations (e.g., the political and social organization of white supremacy; the nature and effects of racial ideology; and the possibilities of black emancipation), and includes such figures Ottobah Cugoano, Martin Delany, Frederick Douglass, C. L. R. James, and Frantz Fanon. For a more detailed discussion of this tradition, as a tradition, see Robert Gooding-Williams, *In the Shadow of Du Bois: Afro-Modern Political Thought in America* (Cambridge, MA: Harvard University Press, 2009), 1–4.

2. Martin Luther King, Jr., *Where Do We Go from Here: Chaos or Community?* (Boston: Beacon Press, 2010), 3; King, *Stride toward Freedom: The Montgomery Story* (Boston: Beacon Press, 2010); King, *Why We Can't Wait* (Boston: Beacon Press, 2010).

3. King, *Where Do We Go from Here*, 3, 3–19.

4. W. E. B. Du Bois, "Of Mr. Booker T. Washington and Others," in Du Bois, *The Souls of Black Folk*, ed. David W. Blight and Robert Gooding-Williams (Boston: Bedford/St. Martin's Press, 1997), 62–72.

5. For a more detailed account of Du Bois's analysis of the Negro problem, see Gooding-Williams, *Shadow of Du Bois*, 58–65.

6. Du Bois, "Mr. Booker T. Washington," 65.

7. Ibid., 68.

8. Du Bois, "Of the Training of Black Men," in *Souls of Black Folk*, 101, 99; Du Bois, "Of the Faith of the Fathers," in *Souls of Black Folk*, 156–158.

9. Du Bois, "Mr. Booker T. Washington," 62–72; Du Bois, "Faith of the Fathers," 156–158.

10. Du Bois, "Mr. Booker T. Washington," 68.

11. For a more detailed account of the connection between Du Bois's social theory of the Negro problem and his critique of Washington, see Gooding-Williams, *Shadow of Du Bois*, 90–93.

12. King, *Stride toward Freedom*, 206, 208, 208–209.

13. Ibid., 215. Although King, echoing Du Bois, aspires to see the Negro integrated into the mainstream of American society, he also echoes Du Bois in likewise insisting that the Negro has a distinctive *gift* to give to American society and, more generally, to "Western civilization"—what he describes as a "new spiritual dynamic" (ibid., 220). For the centrality of the "gift thesis" to Du Bois's thought, throughout his career, and to the Africana tradition of political thought more generally, see Chike Jeffers, "The Black Gift: Cultural Nationalism and Cosmopolitanism in Africana Philosophy" (PhD diss., Northwestern University, 2010). For a more extended discussion of the role of the gift thesis in King's political thought, see Chapter 14, by Brandon Terry.

14. King, *Stride toward Freedom*, 221, 219, 218–220, 220.

15. Ibid.

16. Du Bois, "Mr. Booker T. Washington," 68.

17. For more on this point, see Gooding-Williams, *Shadow of Du Bois*, 147–150.

18. King, *Stride toward Freedom*, 54, 41.

19. Ibid., 182 ("bus struggle").

20. Arthur Danto, *Narration and Knowledge* (New York: Columbia University Press, 2007), 149.

21. Ibid., 151.

22. Ibid., 164.

23. This is one of Danto's examples. See ibid., 156.

24. King, *Stride toward Freedom*, 55. The first sentence is a "complex" narrative sentence that characterizes the movement in terms of four subsequent events, not just one. I read the second sentence as a characterizing the start of the movement ("that night") with reference to the larger impact of the movement described in the first sentence.

25. Ibid., 182.

26. Ibid., 48.

27. Ibid., 55.

28. Ibid., 50.

29. Ibid., 48.

30. Elsewhere in *Stride toward Freedom*, King states explicitly that this is a metaphysical premise, and a premise to which he is committed due to the influence of Edgar Brightman and L. Harold DeWolf, two of his teachers, on his thinking (88). For Brightman's idea that personality is "ultimately real," to which King alludes, see Edgar Sheffield Brightman, *Personality and Religion* (New York: Abingdon Press, 1934). For a helpful discussion of the idealist tendencies of the American personalist tradition to which King was heir, see https://plato.stanford.edu/entries/personalism/.

31. I'm thinking of the difference between *incipient* and *appropriate* self-respect as the difference between having a basic but somewhat inchoate sense of one's moral worth and holding one's moral worth in the high regard it is due.

32. In *The Second-Person Standpoint* (Cambridge, MA: Harvard University Press, 2006), esp. chap. 10, Stephen Darwall argues that having the authority to demand of another that she respect my dignity is essentially included in having that dignity. Consistent with Darwall's argument, King's position may have been that I can count as self-respecting (as respecting my own dignity) only if I respect my *own* authority to demand that others respect my dignity; and that I cannot count as respecting my *own* authority to demand that others respect my dignity unless I exercise that authority when others deny my dignity. (On my reading of his lecture "The Politics of Dignity," Michael Rosen attributes something like this view to King. See Rosen, "The Politics of Dignity," unpublished, Forschungskolleg Humanwissenschaften, Bad Homburg, Evening Lecture ms., July 2015, esp. 9.) For Darwall's brief remarks on King, see *The Second-Person Standpoint*, 83.

33. Frederick Douglass, *My Bondage and My Freedom*, ed. William L. Andrews (Urbana: University of Illinois Press, 1987), 151.

34. For an argument regarding the relation between self-respect and protest, with an affinity to King's views, see Bernard R. Boxill, "Self-Respect and Protest," in *Philosophy Born of Struggle*, ed. Leonard Harris, 2nd ed. (Dubuque, IA: Kendall/Hunt, 2000), 312–322. For a discussion of self-respect with regard to the charge that Booker T. Washington's politics expressed a lack of self-respect, see, in the same volume, Laurance M. Thomas, "Self-Respect: Theory and Practice," 324–339. For an insightful discussion of the social construction of self-respect, and of the ways that racism and discrimination can undermine self-respect, see Michele M. Moody-Adams, "Race, Class, and the Social Construction of Self-Respect," *Philosophical Forum* 24, nos. 1–3 (Fall–Spring 1992–1993): 251–266. Finally, for a general discussion of the centrality of the concept of dignity to the tradition of African American political thought, see Nick Bromell, *The Time Is Always Now: Black Thought and the Transformation of US Democracy* (New York: Oxford University Press, 2013), esp. chap. 1, "From Indignation to Dignity: What Anger Does for Democracy."

35. King, *Stride toward Freedom*, 51.

36. Ibid., 94.

37. See note 42.

38. Booker T. Washington, *Up from Slavery* (New York: Doubleday, Page and Co., 1904), 165.

39. King, *Stride toward Freedom*, 92–94. How does King conceptualize hate? King's references to the Holy Spirit and its work of creating community are clues, I think, to a plausible answer to this question. In opposing hate to the work of creating community, King suggests that what he has in mind is a rather broad spectrum of moral vices, ranging from ill will (hate in the narrow sense) to culpable failures to care (indifference), or to care enough, or to care in an appropriate way (hate in a broadly inclusive sense that extends to all forms of moral disregard for fellow human beings). For King, I am suggesting, a person who demonstrates any of these vices (1) lacks the sort of redemptive goodwill required to create community, (2) opposes herself, in effect, to the work of the Holy Spirit, and to that extent (3) is a *low-grade hater* at best. For insightful discussion of some of the distinctions I invoke here, see Jorge Garcia, "The Heart of Racism," in *Race and Racism*, ed. Bernard Boxill (New York: Oxford University Press, 2001), 257–296.

40. For the idea that we might think of certain rights as responsibilities—as "responsibility-rights"—and a defense of the related claim, which King endorses, that dignity, like a responsibility-right, can may make moral demands on us, see Jeremy Waldron, "Dignity, Rights, and Responsibilities," *Arizona State Law Journal* 43, no. 1107 (2011): esp. 1131. For a detailed treatment of the relation in King's thought between dignity and the right to vote (which some countries treat as a responsibility-right, Waldron notes), see Chapter 8, by Derrick Darby.

41. King, *Stride toward Freedom*, 94; King, *Why We Can't Wait*, 31.

42. In the second sentence of chapter 1 of *Stride toward Freedom*, King depicts himself as listening to the Metropolitan Opera broadcast of Donizetti's *Lucia di Lammermoor* as he set out to drive from Atlanta to Montgomery on a "cool Saturday afternoon in January 1954." Eric Sundquist suggests that, with this reference,

King means to establish "the credentials of his cultivation" (Sundquist, *King's Dream* [New Haven: Yale University Press, 2009], 199). It is also possible, however, that King may have intended his allusion to Donizetti's opera to foreshadow his worry that giving in to the temptation of hate and violence can cause one to lose one's soul—to go mad like Lucia. In this connection, we should note that King occasionally depicts *himself* as falling prey to the temptation of bitterness and hate along the way of the story he tells in *Stride toward Freedom* (see, e.g., chaps. 7 and 8).

43. King, *Stride toward Freedom*, 51–52.

44. Ibid., 182.

45. Ibid., 183. Italics mine.

46. Ibid., 183, 24.

47. See Hannah Arendt, *The Human Condition* (Chicago: University of Chicago Press, 1958), 188–192.

48. The literature on the long civil rights movement is now extensive. For a helpful discussion of key ideas and themes, see Jacquelyn Dowd Hall's groundbreaking "The Long Civil Rights Movement and the Political Uses of the Past," *Journal of American History* (March 2005): 1233–1263.

49. King, *Why We Can't Wait*, 17.

50. See King, *Where Do We Go from Here*, 92–93, 173. For more on this point, see Chapter 9, by Tommie Shelby.

51. King, *Why We Can't Wait*, 99.

52. Ibid., 98, 98–99; see also King, *Stride toward Freedom*, 22–24.

53. King, *Why We Can't Wait*, 99.

54. Ibid., 15–16, 159, 15–19.

55. Ibid., 28.

56. Ibid., 33.

57. Ibid., 36.

58. See, e.g., the discussion of political associations in the United States in Alexis de Tocqueville, *Democracy in America,* trans. George Lawrence (New York: Harper Collins, 2006), 189–195. See also Hannah Arendt, *The Human Condition*, passim, and Frederick Douglass, *My Bondage and My Freedom*, chaps. 18 and 19. For a discussion of Douglass in connection to Arendt, see Gooding-Williams, *Shadow of Du Bois*, chap. 5, and chaps. 1, 4, 5, and 6 for a critique of Du Bois that echoes King. Finally, I am grateful to Brandon Terry for pointing out to me that King begins *Stride toward Freedom* by acknowledging that his use of autobiography to tell the story of the bus struggle may obscure the fact that that struggle "was not a drama with only one actor," but an action-in-concert involving many actors. See King, *Stride toward Freedom*, xxix.

59. King, *Why We Can't Wait*, 28. Italics mine.

60. Ibid.

61. Ibid., 97–98.

62. Ibid., 96.

63. Ibid., 98.

64. Ibid.

65. Ibid., 96.

66. I suspect that King's treatment of the distinction between these opposed political stances—the detached observer and the engaged participant—expresses the existentialist roots of his political thought. See, e.g., Paul Tillich's discussion of the "existential attitude" in *The Courage to Be* (New Haven, CT: Yale University Press, 1952), 114–117. See also, in this connection, Simone de Beauvoir's critique of the "aesthetic attitude" in *The Ethics of Ambiguity*, trans. Bernard Frechtman (New York: Philosophical Library, 1948), 79–84; and Kierkegaard's treatment, in *Either/Or*, of the distinction between the aesthetic attitude and the ethical attitude (Søren Kierkegaard, *Either/Or*, pt. 2, trans. Howard V. Hong and Edna H. Hong [Princeton, NJ: Princeton University Press, 1987], 169–173 and passim).

67. Notwithstanding the deep moral and political differences separating King from the German political theorist Carl Schmitt, it is difficult not to hear an echo of Schmitt's depiction of the liberal's tendency to evade exacting moral decision in King's depiction of the white moderate who "constantly advises the Negro to wait for 'a more convenient season'" (see King, *Why We Can't Wait*, 97). For Schmitt's critique of liberalism, see his *Political Theology: Four Chapters on the Concept of Sovereignty*, trans. George Schwab (Chicago: University of Chicago Press, 2005). For helpful discussion of Schmitt's critique of liberalism, see John McCormick, "Irrational Choice and Moral Combat as Political Destiny: The Essential Carl Schmitt," *Annual Review of Political Science* 10 (2007): 315–339.

68. I say "largely," for *Where Do We Go from Here*, too, engages with the past, as well as the present, as when King famously writes, "We are now faced with the fact that tomorrow is today. We are confronted with the fierce urgency of *now*" (King, *Where Do We Go from Here*, 202). For a valuable discussion of the temporal sensibility animating *Where Do We Go from Here*, see Chapter 11, by Lawrie Balfour.

69. In Chapter 13, Michele M. Moody-Adams persuasively argues that, for King, conscientious citizenship requires that citizens acknowledge their accountability to several moral demands, including, above all, justice.

2. MORAL PERFECTIONISM

I'm grateful for the thoughtfulness and patience of this volume's editors, for the brilliance and collaborative spirit of the assembled contributors, for the firm but helpful guidance provided by Wendy Nelson's copyediting, and for the insightful suggestions provided—with considerable dispatch—by Dr. Stephanie Scott of Penn State's English Department.

1. King complains about "smooth patriotism" in "A Time to Break Silence," his address on Vietnam at Riverside Church on April 4, 1967. Martin Luther King, Jr., "A Time to Break Silence," in *A Testament of Hope: The Essential Writings and Speeches of Martin Luther King, Jr.*, ed. James M. Washington (New York: Harper Collins, 1991), 231.

2. Kipton E. Jensen, "Pedagogical Personalism at Morehouse College," *Studies in Philosophy and Education* 36, no. 2 (2017): 147–165. doi:10.1007/s11217-016-9510-y.

3. Ibid., 152, quoting Warren Steinkraus, "Martin Luther King's Personalism and Non-Violence," *Journal of the History of Ideas* 34, no. 1 (1973): 97–110, at 103.

4. Ibid., 152.

5. As quoted in ibid., 160.

6. Martin Luther King, Jr., *Stride toward Freedom: The Montgomery Story* (Boston: Beacon Press, 2010), 88.

7. Ibid.

8. Rufus Burrow, *God and Human Dignity: The Personalism, Theology, and Ethics of Martin Luther King, Jr.* (South Bend, IN: University of Notre Dame Press, 2006), 86.

9. Chris Lebron, *The Color of Our Shame* (New York: Oxford University Press, 2013), 126.

10. Ibid.

11. Ibid., 132.

12. Ibid., 138.

13. Stanley Cavell, "Moral Perfectionism," in *The Cavell Reader*, ed. Stephen Mulhall (Cambridge, MA: Blackwell, 1996), 355.

14. Richard Shusterman, "Putnam and Cavell on the Ethics of Democracy," in *Practicing Philosophy* (New York: Routledge, 1996), 89–110.

15. Ibid., 100–101.

16. Ibid., 101.

17. Ibid., citing Stanley Cavell, *Conditions Handsome and Unhandsome: The Constitution of Emersonian Perfectionism* (Chicago: University of Chicago Press, 1990, 12.

18. Ibid., citing Cavell, *Conditions*, 12, 16, 46.

19. I develop this conception of moral perfectionism somewhat more fully in Paul C. Taylor, "Making Niagara a Cataract: Cornel West, Greatness, and the Music of Ideas," *Contemporary Pragmatism* 4, no. 1 (June 2007): 91–115.

20. Martin Luther King, Jr., "Unfulfilled Dreams," *The King Encyclopedia*, http://kingencyclopedia.stanford.edu/encyclopedia/documentsentry/doc_unfulfilled_dreams.1.html.

21. Ibid.

22. Ibid.

23. King, "Our God Is Marching On!," in *A Testament of Hope*, 230.

24. King, "I See the Promised Land," in *A Testament of Hope*, 286.

25. King, "Unfulfilled Dreams."

26. Ibid.

27. Martin Luther King, Jr., *Where Do We Go from Here: Chaos or Community?* (Boston: Beacon Press, 2010).

28. Ibid., 180.

29. Ibid., 182.

30. Ibid., 61.

31. Ibid., 63, 17.

32. Ibid., 3.

33. Ibid., 3 ("first phase"), 4 ("presence of justice").

34. Ibid., 197.

35. See Jill Locke, *Democracy and the Death of Shame: Political Equality and Social Disturbance* (New York: Cambridge University Press, 2016).

36. King, "A Creative Protest" (February 16, 1960), Durham, NC, par. 8, in *The King Encyclopedia*, http://kingencyclopedia.stanford.edu/encyclopedia/documentsentry /a_creative_protest/. Also cited in David J. Garrow, *Bearing the Cross: Martin Luther King, Jr., and the Southern Christian Leadership Conference* (New York: Open Road Media, 2015), 290.

37. Garrow, *Bearing the Cross,* 56.

38. King, "Why Jesus Called a Man a Fool" (sermon delivered at Mount Pisgah Missionary Baptist Church, Chicago, on August 27, 1967), *The King Encyclopedia*, http://kingencyclopedia.stanford.edu/encyclopedia/documentsentry/doc_why_jesus _called_a_man_a_fool.1.html.

39. Ibid.

40. Ibid.

41. Ibid.

42. Theodore Parker, "Of Justice and the Conscience," in *Ten Sermons of Religion* (New York: Crosby, Nichols, and Co., 1852), 85.

43. King, "Love, Law, and Civil Disobedience," in *A Testament of Hope,* 46–47.

44. Ibid., 47.

45. King, "Unfulfilled Dreams."

46. Garrow, *Bearing the Cross,* 587–588.

3. The Roots of Civil Disobedience in Republicanism and Slavery

1. See, for example, Martin Luther King, Jr., "I Have a Dream" and "The American Dream," both in *A Testament of Hope: The Essential Writings and Speeches of Martin Luther King, Jr.,* ed. James M. Washington (New York: Harper Collins, 1991), 217, 208.

2. Hugo Adam Bedau, ed., *Civil Disobedience: Theory and Practice* (Indianapolis: Bobbs-Merrill, 1969), 5.

3. Martin Luther King, Jr., *Where Do We Go from Here: Chaos or Community?* (Boston: Beacon Press, 2010), 20. On the "Negro revolution," see, for example, Martin Luther King, Jr., *Why We Can't Wait* (Boston: Beacon Press, 2010), chap. 1.

4. Ibid., 41.

5. Frederick Douglass, "Inhumanity of Slavery," in *My Bondage and My Freedom,* ed. William L. Andrews (Urbana: University of Illinois Press, 1987), 279.

6. Thomas Jefferson, *Notes on the State of Virginia,* ed. William Peden (Chapel Hill: University of North Carolina Press, 1955), 138.

7. As quoted in Thomas G. West, *Vindicating the Founders: Race, Sex, Class, and Justice in the Origins of America* (New York: Rowman and Littlefield, 1997), 37.

8. Algernon Sidney, *Discourses concerning Government*, ed. Thomas G. West (Indianapolis: Liberty Fund 1996), 377, http://oll.libertyfund.org/titles/223.

9. W. E. B. Du Bois, "Of Our Spiritual Strivings," in *The Souls of Black Folk*, ed. David W. Blight and Robert Gooding-Williams (Boston: Bedford/St. Martin's Press, 1997), 43.

10. Martin R. Delany, *The Condition, Elevation, Emigration and Destiny of the Colored People of the United States* (Baltimore: Black Classic Press, 1993).

11. Jean-Jacques Rousseau, *The First and Second Discourses Together with Replies to Critics and Essay on the Origin of Languages*, ed., trans., ann. Victor Gourevitch (New York: Harper and Row, 1990), 187.

12. As quoted in Jack P. Greene, *Imperatives, Behaviors, and Identities: Essays in Early American Cultural History* (Charlottesville: University Press of Virginia, 1992), 270, 271.

13. Edmund Burke, "Speech on Conciliation with the Colonies," in *Select Works of Edmund Burke*, vol. 1 (Indianapolis: Liberty Fund, 1999), 237, http://oll.libertyfund.org/titles/796.

14. Burke, "Conciliation with the Colonies."

15. Ibid., 240.

16. Ibid.

17. Ibid.

18. Ibid.

19. Douglass, *My Bondage and My Freedom*, 152.

20. Ibid., 63.

21. Ibid., 78.

22. Ibid., 79.

23. Ibid., 152.

24. Martin Luther King, Jr., "Letter from Birmingham City Jail," in *A Testament of Hope*, 294.

25. Ibid., 293, 293–294, 294 (italics in original).

26. Ibid.

27. Ibid., 292.

28. Ibid., 290–291.

29. Ibid., 296.

30. John Rawls, *A Theory of Justice*, rev. ed. (Cambridge, MA: Belknap Press of Harvard University Press, 1999), 325–331, 335–343.

31. Douglass, *My Bondage and My Freedom*, 152.

4. Showdown for Nonviolence: The Theory and Practice of Nonviolent Politics

1. In 1945, when asked if he had a message for "the Negro people of America," Gandhi repeated an oft-quoted response, that his "life is its own message." M. K.

Gandhi, "Interview to Denton J. Brooks JR. (1945)," in *The Collected Works of Mahatma Gandhi* (Electronic Book: New Delhi, 1999), 87:8, http://www.gandhiserve .org/e/cwmg/cwmg.htm.

2. Martin Luther King, Jr., "Showdown for Nonviolence" in *A Testament of Hope: The Essential Writings and Speeches of Martin Luther King, Jr.*, ed. James M. Washington (New York: Harper Collins, 1991), 64–72. This is why King's assassination became a crucial moment of reckoning for nonviolent politics. See Eldridge Cleaver, "Requiem of Nonviolence," *Post-Prison Writings and Speeches* (New York: Ramparts, 1969), 74–75.

3. Sharon Erickson Nepstad, *Nonviolent Struggle: Theories, Strategies, and Dynamics* (New York: Oxford University Press, 2015); Mary King, *Mahatma Gandhi and Martin Luther King Jr: The Power of Nonviolent Action* (Paris: UNESCO, 1999); Mark Engler and Paul Engler, *This Is an Uprising: How Nonviolent Revolt Is Shaping the Twenty-First Century* (New York: Nation Books, 2016).

4. M. K. Gandhi, "Interview to American Negro Delegation (1936)," in *Collected Works*, 68:237–238.

5. For an account of this shift, see Sean Scalmer, *Gandhi in the West: The Mahatma and the Rise of Radical Protest* (New York: Cambridge University Press, 2011), 206–238.

6. Judith Stiehm, "Nonviolence Is Two," *Sociological Inquiry* 38, no. 1 (1968): 23–30. On this point, see also Stokely Carmichael with Ekwueme Michael Thelwell, *Ready for Revolution: The Life and Struggles of Stokely Carmichael (Kwame Ture)* (New York: Scribner's, 2003), 166.

7. Gene Sharp, *The Politics of Nonviolent Action* (Boston: Sargent, 1973). Recent uses and endorsements of this distinction can be found in Nepstad, *Nonviolent Struggle;* Kurt Schock, *Civil Resistance Today* (Cambridge: Polity Press, 2015); Erica Chenoweth and Maria J. Stephan, *Why Civil Resistance Works: The Strategic Logic of Nonviolent Conflict* (New York: Columbia University Press, 2011); and, from a more activist perspective, Engler and Engler, *This Is an Uprising.*

8. Engler and Engler, *This Is an Uprising.*

9. Martin Luther King, Jr., *Stride toward Freedom: The Montgomery Story* (Boston: Beacon Press, 2010), 72.

10. Ibid., 83.

11. Ibid. See also Taylor Branch, *Parting the Waters: America in the King Years, 1954–63* (New York: Simon and Schuster, 1988), chap. 3.

12. King, *Stride toward Freedom*, 84.

13. King, "Pilgrimage to Nonviolence," in *Testament of Hope*, 38.

14. Ibid.

15. Ibid.

16. More than other biographers, David Levering Lewis foregrounds nonviolence as one of King's intellectual commitments. Lewis, *King: A Biography*, 3rd ed. (Urbana: University of Illinois Press, 2013).

17. Branch, *Parting the Waters*, 87.

18. The classic account of these connections is Sudarshan Kapur, *Raising Up a Prophet: The African-American Encounter with Gandhi* (Boston: Beacon Press, 1992). See also Nico Slate, *Colored Cosmopolitanism: The Shared Struggle for Freedom in the United States and India* (Cambridge, MA: Harvard University Press, 2012); and, especially, Quinton H. Dixie and Peter Eisenstadt, *Visions of a Better World: Howard Thurman's Pilgrimage to India and the Origins of African American Nonviolence* (Boston: Beacon Press, 2011).

19. King, *Stride toward Freedom*, 89.

20. Two key, co-written pieces are "Nonviolence and Racial Justice" and "The Social Organization of Nonviolence," both in *Testament of Hope*, 5–9, 31–34.

21. See Charles M. Payne, *I've Got the Light of Freedom: The Organizing Tradition and the Mississippi Freedom Struggle*, 2nd ed. (Berkeley: University of California Press, 2007); and Aldon D. Morris, *The Origins of the Civil Rights Movement: Black Communities Organizing for Change* (New York: Free Press, 1984).

22. Scalmer, *Gandhi in the West*, 105–166; John D'Emilio, *Lost Prophet: The Life and Times of Bayard Rustin* (New York: Free Press, 2003).

23. Morris, *Civil Rights Movement*, 139–149.

24. Scalmer, *Gandhi in the West*, 144–166.

25. Peter Ackerman and Jack Duvall, *A Force More Powerful: A Century of Nonviolent Conflict* (New York: St. Martin's Press, 2000), 305–334.

26. Krishnalal Shridharani, *War without Violence: A Study of Gandhi's Method and Its Accomplishments* (New York: Harcourt, Brace, 1939) (key chapters of this work were republished as a pamphlet for CORE by FOR, and its influence on King can be seen in his summary of the steps involved in nonviolent resistance in his "Letter from Birmingham City Jail," in *A Testament of Hope*); Richard B. Gregg, *The Power of Non-Violence* (Philadelphia: J. B. Lippincott, 1934); Reinhold Niebuhr, *Moral Man and Immoral Society: A Study in Ethics and Politics* (New York: Charles Scribner's Sons, 1932).

27. This definition also undergirds the idea of principled nonviolence.

28. M. K. Gandhi, "The Doctrine of the Sword (1920)," in *Collected Works*, 21:133–136.

29. M. K. Gandhi, *Hind Swaraj*, chap. 16: "Brute Force," in *Collected Works*, 10:286–291.

30. King, "An Experiment in Love," in *Testament of Hope*, 17.

31. First in response to Robert Williams, in "Social Organization of Nonviolence," 31–34; and again in *Where Do We Go from Here: Chaos or Community?* (Boston: Beacon Press, 2010), 27.

32. King, "Social Organization of Nonviolence," 32.

33. "The basic question which confronts the world's oppressed is: How is the struggle against the forces of injustice to be waged?" King, "Nonviolence and Racial Justice," 7.

34. King, "The Rising Tide of Racial Consciousness," in *Testament of Hope*, 148.

35. King, "The Power of Nonviolence," in *Testament of Hope*, 12.

36. King, "The Case against 'Tokenism,'" in *Testament of Hope*, 108.

37. Ibid. See also King, *Stride toward Freedom,* 183 ("He has come to feel that he is somebody"); King, "Nonviolence and Racial Justice," 6 ("And so he came to feel that he was somebody"); and King, "An Address before the National Press Club," in *Testament of Hope,* 101 ("He has come to feel that he is somebody").

38. King, "Pilgrimage to Nonviolence," 39.

39. King, *Stride toward Freedom,* 48.

40. King, "Our Struggle," in *Testament of Hope,* 76.

41. Ibid.

42. King, *Stride toward Freedom,* 206.

43. Ibid., 71.

44. See Chapter 1, by Robert Gooding-Williams; and Chapter 8, by Derrick Darby.

45. King, "The Ethical Demands for Integration," in *Testament of Hope,* 120.

46. For example, in demands that the struggle "must always be on the highest level of dignity and discipline." King, "Rising Tide," 148.

47. King, "The Power of Nonviolence," 14.

48. King, "An Address," 102; and King, "The Case against 'Tokenism,'" 109.

49. King, *Stride toward Freedom,* 208.

50. King, "Showdown for Nonviolence," 69.

51. Frantz Fanon, *The Wretched of the Earth* (New York: Grove Press, 1963). See also H. Rap Brown, *Die Nigger Die!* (New York: Last Gasp Press, 1969); Eldridge Cleaver, "The Courage to Kill: Meeting the Panthers," in *Post-Prison Writings and Speeches,* 23–39; Bobby Seale, *Seize the Time: The Story of the Black Panther Party and Huey P. Newton* (New York: Random House, 1970). I thank Brandon Terry for pointing me to these references.

52. Leo Tolstoy, *"The Kingdom of God Is within You": Christianity Not as a Mystic Religion but as a New Theory of Life* (London: William Heinemann, 1894); Gandhi, *Hind Swaraj,* in *Collected Works,* 10:245–315; Karuna Mantena, "On Gandhi's Critique of the State: Sources, Contexts, Conjunctures," *Modern Intellectual History* 9, no. 3 (2012): 535–563.

53. King, "Ethical Demands for Integration," 118, 124.

54. Ibid., 124.

55. King, "An Address," 105.

56. King, "Ethical Demands for Integration," 117.

57. King, "Nonviolence: The Only Road," in *Testament of Hope,* 56.

58. Ibid.

59. King, *Where Do We Go from Here,* 60.

60. Ibid., 58.

61. King, "Nonviolence: The Only Road," 59; King, *Where Do We Go from Here,* 52.

62. King, "An Address," 99–105; King, "The American Dream," in *Testament of Hope,* 208–216; King, "Ethical Demands for Integration," 117–125; and King, *Where Do We Go from Here.*

63. King, *Stride toward Freedom,* 215.

64. Jonathan Schell, *The Unconquerable World: Power, Nonviolence, and the Will of the People* (New York: Metropolitan Books, 2003).

65. King, *Where Do We Go from Here*, 63–64.

66. Ibid., 64.

67. Ibid.

68. King, "Ethical Demands for Integration," 124, 121.

69. King, "Nonviolence: The Only Road," 58.

70. See Chenoweth and Stephan, *Why Civil Resistance Works*, esp. chap. 3.

71. Gandhi, "Interview to American Negro Delegation," 68:238.

72. King, *Stride toward Freedom*, 193.

73. Ibid., 211.

74. King, "If the Negro Wins, Labor Wins," in *Testament of Hope*, 201–207; and King, *Where Do We Go from Here*, 53–56.

75. King, *Where Do We Go from Here*, 26–34.

76. King, "Pilgrimage to Nonviolence," 36.

77. I take practical realism to be based on a pragmatic assessment of contingent political circumstances and constraints. By contrast, conceptual realism is a theoretical account of permanent features of political life that thwart rational progress in politics. This kind of realism can be utopian in goals and ends, but keeps an eye toward the recurring obstacles to social change.

78. Ibid., 39.

79. Niebuhr, *Moral Man and Immoral Society*, xxiii.

80. Patriotism was Niebuhr's most evocative example of this paradox. Ibid., chap. 4.

81. Ibid., 250.

82. Ibid., 232.

83. King, *Stride toward Freedom*, 208.

84. Niebuhr, *Moral Man and Immoral Society*, 238.

85. King, "A Time to Break Silence," in *Testament of Hope*, 243; King, *Where Do We Go from Here*, 61.

86. King, "Love, Law, and Civil Disobedience," in *Testament of Hope*, 47; see also, King, "An Experiment in Love," 18.

87. M. K. Gandhi, "Speech at Birmingham Meeting (1931)," in *Collected Works*, 54:48. Partially quoted by King in "An Experiment in Love," 18.

88. Terry captures this nicely in the idea of protest as offering a provocative pedagogy. Brandon Terry, "After Ferguson," *The Point* (2016), https://thepointmag.com/2015/politics/after-ferguson.

89. King, "The Case against 'Tokenism,'" 111.

90. King, "Nonviolence: The Only Road," 58 ("dramatize the evils of our society"), 60 ("dramatize an evil"); King, "Behind the Selma March," in *Testament of Hope*, 127 ("dramatize the existence of injustice"); King, "Letter from Birmingham City Jail," 291 ("dramatize the issue").

91. King, "Letter from Birmingham City Jail," 292, 295.

92. King, "Social Organization of Nonviolence," 33.

93. Ibid.; "Nonviolence: The Only Road," 57.

94. Niebuhr, *Moral Man and Immoral Society,* 250. King, "Letter from Birmingham City Jail," 289.

95. See Terry, "After Ferguson."

96. Niebuhr, *Moral Man and Immoral Society,* 248.

97. M. K. Gandhi, "Presidential Address at Belgaum Congress (1924)," in *Collected Works,* 29:497.

98. King, *Stride toward Freedom,* 210; King, *Where Do We Go from Here,* 62.

99. Ibid.

100. See, especially, William P. Jones, *The March on Washington: Jobs, Freedom, and the Forgotten History of Civil Rights* (New York: W. W. Norton, 2013).

101. Ibid.

102. D'Emilio, *Lost Prophet,* 345.

103. Ibid., 357.

104. King, "Kenneth B. Clarke Interview," in *Testament of Hope,* 337; and King, *Why We Can't Wait* (Boston: Beacon Press, 2010), 68.

105. King, *Why We Can't Wait,* 68–69.

106. King, "An Address," 102.

107. Gregg, *The Power of Non-Violence,* chap. 2.

108. King, "The Burning Truth in the South," in *Testament of Hope,* 97.

109. King, "The American Dream," 214.

110. For an insightful account of the innovation of this tactic amongst student protestors, see Erin Pineda, "The Awful Roar: Civil Disobedience, Civil Rights, and the Politics of Creative Disorder" (PhD diss., Yale University, 2015), chap. 2. See also Erin Pineda, "Civil Disobedience and Punishment: (Mis)reading Justification and Strategy from SNCC to Snowden," *History of the Present* 5, no. 1 (Spring 2015): 1–30.

111. King, "Facing the Challenge of a New Age," in *Testament of Hope,* 143; King, *Stride toward Freedom,* 212.

112. King, *Stride toward Freedom,* 210.

113. King, *Why We Can't Wait,* 117–118.

114. King, "The Case against 'Tokenism,'" 111.

115. King, "Facing the Challenge," 144.

116. In this vein, we might think of King's evocation of the idea of America and "the American Dream" as another example of an aspirational ideal that is meant to provoke critical self-evaluation through identification.

117. King, "Social Organization of Nonviolence," 33. See also King, "Address to the National Press Club," in *Testament of Hope,* 102.

118. Chenoweth and Stephan, *Why Civil Resistance Works,* 3–61.

5. FROM ANGER TO LOVE: SELF-PURIFICATION AND POLITICAL RESISTANCE

I would like to thank Tommie Shelby and Brandon Terry for extremely helpful comments on an earlier draft, and Scott Henney for valuable research assistance.

1. Martha Nussbaum, *Anger and Forgiveness: Resentment, Generosity, Justice* (New York: Oxford University Press, 2016).

2. For evidence that Gandhi did sometimes get angry, see Richard Sorabji, *Gandhi and the Stoics: Modern Experiments on Ancient Values* (Chicago: University of Chicago Press, 2012), 7, 24, 49.

3. See discussion in Nussbaum, *Anger and Forgiveness*, chap. 7.

4. See, e.g., Martin Luther King, Jr., "Nonviolence and Racial Justice," in *A Testament of Hope: The Essential Writings and Speeches of Martin Luther King, Jr.*, ed. James M. Washington (New York: Harper Collins, 1991), 8.

5. Ibid.

6. King, "The Most Durable Power," in *Testament of Hope*, 10.

7. King, "An Experiment in Love," in *Testament of Hope*, 17.

8. Ibid., 19.

9. Ibid.

10. King, "The Social Organization of Nonviolence," in *Testament of Hope*, 32.

11. Martin Luther King, Jr., *The Trumpet of Conscience* (Boston: Beacon Press, 2010), 60.

12. King, "Showdown for Nonviolence," in *Testament of Hope*, 69.

13. King, "Nonviolence and Racial Justice," 9.

14. King, "The Power of Nonviolence," in *Testament of Hope*, 13.

15. King, "An Experiment in Love," 18.

16. King, "Letter from Birmingham City Jail," in *Testament of Hope*, 290, 297.

17. Malcolm X, "Message to the Grassroots," in *Malcolm X Speaks: Selected Speeches and Statements*, ed. George Breitman (New York: Merit, 1965), 9.

18. Ibid., 12.

19. Obviously this is a bad metaphor—novocaine is in the person's own self-interest, and the dentist is helping the person achieve her ends.

20. Ibid., 16.

21. Winston Churchill, "Blood, Toil, Tears and Sweat," http://hansard.millbank-systems.com/commons/1940/may/13/his-majestys-government-1.

22. However, Gandhi did think that violence was a constant possibility among his followers, and it took tremendous preparation to hold a nonviolent protest. He also weeded out followers likely to get angry under attack. See Sorabji, *Gandhi and the Stoics*, 122.

23. M. K. Gandhi, *An Autobiography: The Story of My Experiments with Truth* (Boston: Beacon Press, 1993).

24. See Sorabji, *Gandhi and the Stoics*, 88–92. Human self-defense is not an exception, but there are a few cases where he did hold that violence is less bad than the alternative.

25. M. K. Gandhi, "How to Combat Hitlerism," in *The Gandhi Reader: A Source Book of His Life and Writings*, ed. Homer A. Jack (Bloomington: Indiana University Press, 1956), 337.

26. Gandhi, "Hitlerism and Aerial Warfare," in *The Gandhi Reader*, 340. Elsewhere, Gandhi also holds that hearts are changed by courageous self-sacrifice; see Sorabji, *Gandhi and the Stoics*, 83.

27. Gandhi, "How to Combat Hitlerism," 338.

28. King, "Social Organization of Nonviolence," 32.

29. King, "Nonviolence: The Only Road to Freedom," in *Testament of Hope*, 57.

30. King, "Pilgrimage to Nonviolence," in *Testament of Hope*, 39.

31. Ibid.

32. King, "Social Organization of Nonviolence," 34.

33. King, "Nobel Prize Acceptance Speech," in *Testament of Hope*, 224.

34. King, "Showdown for Nonviolence," 69.

35. King, "A Christmas Sermon on Peace," in *Testament of Hope*, 255.

36. King, "Love, Law, and Civil Disobedience," in *Testament of Hope*, 45.

37. Ibid., 50 ("aid and comfort"); King, "Letter from Birmingham City Jail," 295 ("aided and comforted"); King, "*Playboy* Interview: Martin Luther King, Jr.," in *Testament of Hope*, 356 ("aided and comforted").

38. Webb Miller, "Dharasana Salt Raid," in *The Gandhi Reader*, 250–251.

39. Nathuram Vinayak Godse, *May It Please Your Honour: Statement of Nathuram Godse* (Pune: Vitasta Prakashan, 1977).

40. See the excellent discussion in Dennis Dalton, *Mahatma Gandhi: Nonviolent Power in Action*, expanded ed. (New York: Columbia University Press, 2012), 12–16. As Dalton shows, Gandhi was also concerned not to use an English term for his idea; he even ran a contest for the Indian-language renaming of the central concept, insisting that it was "shameful" to permit the struggle to be known only by an English name.

41. King, "Nonviolence and Racial Justice," 7.

42. Gandhi, "The Satyagraha Ashram," in *The Gandhi Reader*, 138.

43. King, "Letter from Birmingham City Jail," 297.

44. King, "Nonviolence and Racial Justice," 7.

45. Ibid.

46. King, "Letter from Birmingham City Jail," 290–291.

47. Ibid., 292.

48. Ibid., 291, 294.

49. Gandhi, "A Puzzle and Its Solution," in *The Gandhi Reader*, 193.

50. Compare ancient Greek and Roman discussions of anger in armies. Both Philodemus and Seneca emphasize that the type of discipline required for successful military strategies is incompatible with giving personal anger a dominant role: see William Harris, *Restraining Rage: The Ideology of Anger Control in Classical Antiquity* (Cambridge, MA: Harvard University Press, 2001), 103, 105.

51. See Martha C. Nussbaum, *The Clash Within: Democracy, Religious Violence, and India's Future* (Cambridge, MA: Harvard University Press, 2007).

52. King, "An Experiment in Love," 19.

53. King, "Nonviolence: The Only Road," 61.

54. Ibid.

55. King, "Nonviolence and Racial Justice," 8.

56. King, "I Have a Dream," in *Testament of Hope*, 217–220. See the analysis of this speech in Nussbaum, *Political Emotions: Why Love Matters for Justice* (Cambridge, MA: Harvard University Press, 2013), chap. 9.

57. For just one example: "This sweltering summer of the Negro's legitimate discontent" in the "I Have a Dream" speech (218), refers to *Richard III,* Act I, scene 1, lines 1–2, "Now is the winter of our discontent/Made glorious summer by this son of York."

58. King, "Letter from Birmingham City Jail," 297.

59. Ibid.

60. He did attempt to impose this demand on his children, unsuccessfully; he was a very judgmental and punitive father, displaying Harilal attitudes that seem pretty close to anger. But he applauded Indira Nehru's wedding and wished her well (all the more because she married in a homespun sari woven by her father while in prison).

61. Dalton, *Mahatma Gandhi,* 66.

62. Jawaharlal Nehru, *The Discovery of India* (Delhi: Oxford University Press, 1989 [1946]), 274–275. See Dalton, *Mahatma Gandhi,* 66–67, 168–169. Nehru does not mention the connection between fear and violence, but this connection is surely salient for Gandhi.

63. King, "Eulogy for the Martyred Children," in *Testament of Hope,* 222.

64. See Nussbaum, *The Therapy of Desire: Theory and Practice in Hellenistic Ethics* (Princeton, NJ: Princeton University Press, 2013), 376.

65. Gandhi here is no Stoic. The Stoics were not ascetic. They thought bodily desire was fine; what was problematic was its association with personal love. The Greek Stoics valued consensual male-male and male-female relationships that served educational and friendly purposes, but that did not involve possessive personal love. (They opposed marriage when based on such love.) The Roman Stoic conception of marriage is that of a will-governed partnership for reproduction and other valuable ends.

66. As Sorabji shows in *Gandhi and the Stoics,* 32–42, Gandhi's attitude owes a good deal to Christian asceticism, sometimes filtered through Tolstoy.

67. See Martha C. Nussbaum, "The Morning and the Evening Star: Religion, Money, and Love in Sinclair Lewis's *Babbitt* and *Elmer Gantry,*" in *Power, Prose, Purse: Law, Literature, and Economic Transformations,* ed. Alison L. LaCroix, Saul Levmore, and Martha C. Nussbaum (New York: Oxford University Press, forthcoming 2018). The female evangelist is a different story, and Lewis's Sister Sharon Falconer, modeled on Aimee Semple McPherson, is careful to conceal evidence of her sexual life. The real-life McPherson was married three times, but apart from that the numerous allegations of love affairs have not been substantiated.

68. See Jonathan Rieder, *The Word of the Lord Is Upon Me: The Righteous Performance of Martin Luther King, Jr.* (Cambridge, MA: Belknap Press of Harvard University Press, 2010); and, more critical of King, Michael Eric Dyson, *I May Not Get There with You: The True Martin Luther King, Jr.* (New York: Free Press, 2001), chap. 8. On the miscegenation fear, see Justin Driver, "Of Big Black Bucks and Little Golden-Haired Girls: How Fear of Miscegenation Informed *Brown v. Board of Education* and Its Resistance," forthcoming in *The Empire of Disgust: Prejudice, Discrimination, and Policy in India and the U.S.,* ed. Zoya Hasan, Aziz Huq, Martha C. Nussbaum, and Vidhu Verma, under review by Oxford University Press, Delhi.

6. The Prophetic Tension between Race Consciousness and the Ideal of Color-Blindness

I would like to thank the participants at the workshop "The Philosophy and Political Thought of Martin Luther King, Jr." at the Radcliffe Institute for Advanced Study, Harvard University, in 2016, and Nathan L. Hobbs and William M. Sullivan for their comments on an earlier draft of this paper. I also owe a big debt of gratitude to my research assistant, Amy Dundon, for her research and editorial work.

1. Martin Luther King, Jr., "*Playboy* Interview: Martin Luther King, Jr.," in *A Testament of Hope: The Essential Writings and Speeches of Martin Luther King, Jr.,* ed. James M. Washington (New York: Harper Collins, 1991), 374. Outside of the *Playboy* interview, there is no other reference to the idea of color-blindness in *The Papers of Martin Luther King, Jr.,* 7 vols., ed. Ralph E. Luker et al. (Berkeley: University of California Press, 1992–2014). The paucity of references to color-blindness is confirmed by the lack of association between King and that idea in most of the major academic histories of the period—e.g., Taylor Branch, *Parting the Waters: America in the King Years, 1954–63* (New York: Simon and Schuster, 1988); Branch, *Pillar of Fire: America in the King Years, 1963–65* (New York: Simon and Schuster, 1998); Branch, *At Canaan's Edge: America in the King Years, 1965–68* (New York: Simon and Schuster, 2006); and David L. Lewis, *King: A Biography,* 3rd ed. (Urbana: University of Illinois Press, 2013).

2. See "Letter from Mrs. W. Brown to MLK," King Center Digital Archive, http://www.thekingcenter.org/archive/document/letter-mrs-w-brown-mlk. The date stamp on the document is obscured, but the letter refers to marches and might be a reaction to the demonstrations in Birmingham or Selma.

3. Andrew Kull, *The Color-Blind Constitution* (Cambridge, MA: Harvard University Press, 1992), 1–6.

4. *Plessy v. Ferguson,* 163 U.S. 537, 538, 16 S. Ct. 1138, 1138, 41 L. Ed. 256 (1896) overruled by *Brown v. Bd. of Ed. of Topeka, Shawnee Cty., Kan.,* 347 U.S. 483, 74 S. Ct. 686, 98 L. Ed. 873 (1954).

5. See Kull, *The Color-Blind Constitution,* 131–150 ("Separate but Equal"), 151–163 ("*Brown v. Board of Education*"); and Branch, *Parting the Waters,* 143–205 ("The Montgomery Bus Boycott").

6. Martin Luther King, Jr., "I Have a Dream," in *Testament of Hope,* 217–220.

7. Ibid., 219.

8. King, "The Rising Tide of Racial Consciousness," in *Testament of Hope,* 145–151.

9. Eric J. Sundquist, *King's Dream* (New Haven, CT: Yale University Press, 2009), 4–6.

10. Ronald R. Sundstrom, *The Browning of America and the Evasion of Social Justice* (Albany: SUNY Press, 2008), 37–64.

11. King, "Nonviolence and Racial Justice," in *Testament of Hope,* 8.

12. *Parents Involved in Cmty. Sch. v. Seattle Sch. Dist. No. 1,* 551 U.S. 701, 127 S. Ct. 2738, 168 L. Ed. 2d 508 (2007).

13. James Lindgren, "Seeing Colors," *California Law Review* 81 (1993): 1059–1088, at 1059–1060.

14. Mary Frances Berry, "vindicating Martin Luther King, Jr.: The Road to a Color-Blind Society," *Journal of Negro History* 81, no. 1/4 (1996): 137–144; Michael Eric Dyson, *I May Not Get There with You: The True Martin Luther King, Jr.* (New York: Free Press, 2000); Sundquist, *King's Dream*.

15. Martin Luther King, Jr., *Where Do We Go from Here: Chaos or Community?* (Boston: Beacon Press, 2010).

16. King, "Nobel Prize Acceptance Speech," in *Testament of Hope*, 224–226; King, "The World House," in *Where Do We Go from Here*, 177–202.

17. Sundquist, *King's Dream*, 4.

18. King, "*Playboy* Interview," 374 (emphasis added).

19. The iconic "mountaintop" phrase is drawn from King, "I See the Promised Land," in *Testament of Hope*, 286.

20. King, "Rising Tide," 145–151. A related parallel debate is whether King would have supported race-based policies created after his time, such as affirmative action in hiring and admissions. Clarence B. Jones, who was King's personal lawyer and assisted him in drafting "Letter from Birmingham City Jail," argued that King favored a reparations program and would have considered policies like affirmative action a "booby prize." See Clarence B. Jones and Joel Engel, *What Would Martin Say?* (New York: Harper, 2008), 69–100. Jones also claimed that King would agree with black public intellectuals who draw critical attention to the values and character of the young, black, and poor as well as to discriminatory social structures; see ibid., 81–91. For a rebuttal of Jones's reading of King, see Lewis V. Baldwin and Rufus Burrow Jr., eds., *The Domestication of Martin Luther King Jr.: Clarence B. Jones, Right-Wing Conservatism, and the Manipulation of the King Legacy* (Eugene, OR: Cascade Books, 2013).

21. King, "*Playboy* Interview," 375 (emphasis added).

22. Dyson, *I May Not Get There with You*, 3–4. For Dyson's analysis of why King should not be associated with the idea of color-blindness, see 11–29.

23. This follows the analysis of the idea of redemption and human life in Charles Taylor, "A Catholic Modernity?," in *Dilemmas and Connections: Selected Essays* (Cambridge, MA: Belknap Press of Harvard University Press, 2011), 167–187. Taylor explains the idea of the complementarity of human life and its relation to unity in God (or "unity-across-difference") thusly: "Redemption happens through Incarnation, the weaving of God's life into human lives, but these human lives are different, plural, irreducible to each other. Redemption-Incarnation brings reconciliation, a kind of oneness. This is the oneness of diverse beings who come to see that they cannot attain wholeness alone, that their complementarity is essential, rather than of beings who come to accept that they are ultimately identical. Or perhaps we might put it: complementarity and identity will both be part of our ultimate oneness" (168).

24. King, "The World House," 177–202.

25. There is a long tradition in black political thought that challenges false universals; see, for example, nearly every entry in *African-American Social and Political*

Thought, 1850–1920, ed. Howard Brotz (New Brunswick, NJ: Transaction, 1995). For a contemporary analysis of anti-black racism and false universals, see Charles Mills, *The Racial Contract* (Ithaca, NY: Cornell University Press, 1997); Mills, *Blackness Visible: Essays on Philosophy and Race* (Ithaca, NY: Cornell University Press, 1998).

26. On the challenging and expansion of universals as part of the continual grounding of normative theories, see Thomas McCarthy, *Race, Empire, and the Idea of Human Development* (New York: Cambridge University Press, 2009), 36–41. McCarthy's arguments about the recovery of a historically grounded version of the idea of human development provides an alternative to King's theologically based normative foundations. I am thankful to William M. Sullivan for pointing the connection between my analysis of King and McCarthy's argument.

27. Sundquist, *King's Dream,* 4.

28. *Plessy v. Ferguson.*

29. Gabriel Chin, "The Plessy Myth: Justice Harlan and the Chinese Cases," *Iowa Law Review* 82 (1996): 151–182; Frank Wu, *Yellow: Race in America beyond Black and White* (New York: Basic Books, 2002).

30. Sundstrom, *The Browning of America,* 40.

31. King, "*Playboy* Interview," 375.

32. Amy Gutmann, "Responding to Racial Injustice," in *Color Conscious: The Political Morality of Race,* ed. K. Anthony Appiah, Amy Gutmann, and David B. Wilkins (Princeton, NJ: Princeton University Press, 1998), 106–178.

33. Bernard R. Boxill, "The Color-Blind Principle," in *Blacks and Social Justice* (Lanham, MD: Rowman and Littlefield, 1992), 9–18; Ronald Dworkin, "Affirmative Action: Does It Work?" and "Affirmative Action: Is it Fair?," both in Dworkin, *Sovereign Virtue: The Theory and Practice of Equality* (Cambridge, MA: Harvard University Press, 2000), 386–408, 409–426.

34. King, "Rising Tide," 145–151.

35. Taylor's analysis of such absolutism parallels the common criticism of it as a false universality, but is especially relevant given the theological connections when this debate is applied to King. Taylor wrote about catholicity, by which he means catholicity in the broad sense and not in reference to the specific church. "Our great historical temptation has been to forget the complementarity, to go straight for the sameness, making as many people as possible into 'good Catholics'—and in the process failing of catholicity: failing of catholicity, because failing wholeness; unity bought at the price of suppressing something of the diversity in the humanity that God created; unity of the part masquerading as the whole. It is universality without wholeness, and so not true Catholicism" (Taylor, "A Catholic Modernity?," 168).

36. Derrick Bell, *Faces at the Bottom of the Well: The Permanence of Racism* (New York: Basic Books, 1992).

37. This has also affected its rebranded variant, "post-racialism." For my analysis of the idea and ideal of post-racialism, see Ronald R. Sundstrom, "On Post-Racialism: Or, How Color-Blindness Rebranded Is Still Vicious," in *The Routledge Companion*

to *Philosophy of Race,* ed. Paul C. Taylor, Linda Martín Alcoff, and Luvell Anderson (New York: Routledge, forthcoming).

38. See Taylor's analysis in "A Catholic Modernity?," 184. The realist rejection of color-blindness and other similar normative ideals, and even the absolutist or puritanical position toward them, reflects the range of reactions about normative ideals once those ideals face modern challenges. See also Taylor's *A Secular Age* (Cambridge, MA: Belknap Press of Harvard University Press, 2007).

39. John J. Ansbro, *Martin Luther King, Jr.: The Making of a Mind* (Maryknoll, NY: Orbis Books, 1982), 27–29, 163–197.

40. Howard Thurman, *Jesus and the Disinherited* (Boston: Beacon Press, 1996).

41. Ibid., 51.

42. King frequently referred to the philosophical-theological idea of "personalism." This idea stresses the dignity of the human person *qua* person, and has a long history in philosophical and theological debates, but King seems most influenced by Martin Buber's and Reinhold Niebuhr's versions. For more on King's personalism, see Ira G. Zepp, *The Social Vision of Martin Luther King, Jr.* (Brooklyn: Carlson, 1989). For more on personalism generally, see Thomas D. Williams and Jan Olof Bengtsson, "Personalism," in *The Stanford Encyclopedia of Philosophy,* ed. Edward N. Zalta, Summer 2016 ed., https://plato.stanford.edu/archives/sum2016/entries/personalism/.

43. Martin Luther King, Jr., *Stride toward Freedom* (Boston: Beacon Press, 2010), 88. This passage was quoted in Zepp, *Social Vision,* 173. For more on King's philosophical and theological formation and views, see Zepp, *Social Vision;* and Ansbro, *Martin Luther King, Jr.*

44. See Reinhold Niebuhr, *Moral Man and Immoral Society: A Study in Ethics and Politics* (Louisville, KY: Westminster John Knox Press, 2001); Niebuhr, *An Interpretation of Christian Ethics* (Louisville, KY: Westminster John Knox Press, 2013). For Niebuhr's influence on King, see King, *Stride toward Freedom;* King, *The Measure of a Man* (Minneapolis: Fortress Press, 1988); Ansbro, *Martin Luther King, Jr.;* and Zepp, *Social Vision.*

45. King, *Measure of a Man,* 9–10, 23.

46. Ibid., 18.

47. King is ambiguous on this point. In his *The Measure of a Man,* the distinction is blurred, if it is there at all: "This is man. He is God's marvelous creation. Through his mind he can leap oceans, break through walls, and transcend the categories of time and space. The stars maybe marvelous, but not so marvelous as the mind of man that comprehended them. . . . This is what the biblical writers mean when they say that man is made in the image of God. Man has rational capacity; he has the unique ability to have fellowship with God. Man is a being of spirit" (18). The relation of spirit to reason, their separation in the modern age, and the aftermath of that divorce is examined in Taylor, *A Secular Age.*

48. King, *Stride toward Freedom,* 88.

49. King, "The Theology of Reinhold Niebuhr," *The Martin Luther King, Jr. Papers Project,* 272–273, http://okra.stanford.edu/transcription/document_images

/Vol02Scans/269_Apr1953-June1954_The%20Theology%200f%20Reinhold%20
Niebuhr.pdf.

50. King, "The Ethical Demands for Integration," in *Testament of Hope*, 118–119 (emphasis in the original).

51. Ibid., 119 (emphasis in the original).

52. King, "Theology of Reinhold Niebuhr," 272–273.

53. King, "Letter from Birmingham City Jail," in *Testament of Hope*, 294.

54. King, *Stride toward Freedom*, 88.

55. Niebuhr, *Interpretation of Christian Ethics*, 8–9.

56. King, *Stride toward Freedom*, 88. The idea that Niebuhr neglected the idea of grace may be incorrect—Niebuhr states that the realization of love's triumph in the world depends on God's intervention; see Niebuhr, *Moral Man and Immoral Society*, 82. Niebuhr also thought that no society could ever be just, because society would always frustrate the moral ideals of humanity, which were more secure in the hearts and minds of individual persons.

57. King, "Our God Is Marching On!," in *Testament of Hope*, 230. Compare this with his statement in his "Nobel Prize Acceptance Speech" (225), wherein he stated that he accepted the award "with an abiding faith in America and an audacious faith in the future of mankind. I refuse to accept the idea that the 'isness' of man's present nature makes him morally incapable of reaching up for the eternal 'oughtness' that forever confronts him."

58. Niebuhr's *An Interpretation of Christian Ethics* included a chapter entitled "The Relevance of an Impossible Ethical Ideal" (103–135). King referred to this text in his essays on Niebuhr. According to Niebuhr, "Prophetic Christianity . . . demands the impossible; and by that very demand emphasizes the impotence and corruption of human nature, wresting from man the cry of distress and contrition, 'The good that I would, do I do not: but the evil that I would not, that I do . . . Woe is me . . . who will deliver me from the body of this death'" (103). See, as well, the conclusion to *Moral Man and Immoral Society*, where Niebuhr refers to the necessity for, yet vulnerability of, such ideals (277).

59. King, "Rising Tide," 150–151.

60. King, "Ethical Demands for Integration," 117–125.

61. James H. Cone, *A Black Theology of Liberation* (Maryknoll, NY: Orbis Books, 2010).

62. King, "The Bigness of God," *Martin Luther King, Jr. Papers Project*, 326–327, http://okra.stanford.edu/transcription/document_images/Vol02Scans/326_1951
-1955_The%20Bigness%200f%20God.pdf. See also, King, "Ethical Demands for Integration," 117–125; King, "Religion and Race," speech delivered to The Conference on Religion and Race, January 17, 1963, Martin Luther King Jr. Library and Archives, King Center for Nonviolence, Atlanta.

63. Cone, *Black Theology of Liberation*.

64. See "Guiding Principles," *Black Lives Matter*, http://blacklivesmatter.com
/guiding-principles/.

65. King, "Ethical Demands for Integration," 122.

66. Taylor, "A Catholic Modernity?," 168.

67. John Rawls, *Justice as Fairness: A Restatement*, ed. Erin Kelly (Cambridge, MA: Belknap Press of Harvard University Press, 2001), 4.

68. For examples of such political theories, see Christopher J. Lebron, *The Color of Our Shame: Race and Justice in Our Time* (New York: Oxford University Press, 2013); Sharon A. Stanley, *An Impossible Dream? Racial Integration in the United States* (New York: Oxford University Press, 2017).

69. King, *Where Do We Go from Here*, 56–69.

70. John Gray, *Black Mass: Apocalyptic Religion and the Death of Utopia* (New York: Farrar, Straus and Giroux, 2007).

71. Niebuhr, *Moral Man and Immoral Society*, 277.

72. King, "I Have a Dream," 218–219.

7. Integration, Freedom, and the Affirmation of Life

1. Martin Luther King, Jr., "The Ethical Demands for Integration," in *A Testament of Hope: The Essential Writings and Speeches of Martin Luther King, Jr.*, ed. James Melvin Washington (San Francisco: HarperCollins, 1990), 117–125.

2. I provide an extensive treatment of the sacrifice-ability of the positive liberties in the liberal tradition in Danielle Allen, "Difference without Domination," in *Difference without Domination: Justice and Democracy in Conditions of Diversity*, ed. D. Allen and R. Somanathan, under consideration, University of Chicago Press.

3. Melvin Rogers, "Race, Domination, and Republicanism," in Allen and Somanathan, *Difference without Domination*.

4. Ibid.

5. All parenthetical page references in this essay refer back to King's "Ethical Demands for Integration."

6. Allen, "Difference without Domination."

7. For a thorough treatment of the means–ends relationships required by Gandhian nonviolence, see Chapter 4, by Karuna Mantena; also Mantena, "Another Realism: The Politics of Gandhian Nonviolence," *American Political Science Review* 106 (2012): 455–470.

8. See Allen, "Difference without Domination," for a detailed account of where this position emerges in Rawls's landmark work, *A Theory of Justice*.

9. Heather Gerken has provided compelling arguments about how decentralized structures of political decision making can empower minorities within a democracy, with reference to gay rights movements (Heather Gerken, "The Loyal Opposition," *Yale Law Journal* 123 [2014]: 1958–1994) and with reference to race (Gerken, "Second-Order Diversity: An Exploration of Decentralization's Egalitarian Possibilities," in Allen and Somanathan, *Difference without Domination*).

10. For the categories "deliberative," "adversarial," and "prophetic" in political speech, see Danielle Allen, "Reconceiving Public Spheres," in *From Voice to Influence*, ed. Danielle Allen and Jennifer Light (Chicago: University of Chicago Press, 2015), 178–207.

11. Danielle Allen, *Talking to Strangers* (Chicago: University of Chicago Press, 2004), 17.

12. For a critique of *Talking to Strangers* that proceeds along this line, see Juliet Hooker, "Black Lives Matter and the Paradoxes of U.S. Black Politics: From Democratic Sacrifice to Democratic Repair," *Political Theory* 44, no. 4 (2016): 448–469.

13. This is Harvard, of course, but I name it here in the note rather than in the text because I think that, in the abstract, the points apply to any number of institutions.

14. Harvard University, "Statement of Values" (2002), http://www.harvard.edu/president/speeches/summers_2002/values.php.

8. A VINDICATION OF VOTING RIGHTS

I am grateful for discussion of this essay with audiences at Johns Hopkins University, Wayne State University, and New York University School of Law, and at a Harvard University workshop organized by the volume editors. This chapter draws on King's vast corpus of published writings. It also references unpublished material collected in my research at the King Library and Archive in Atlanta. I am grateful to Cynthia Lewis for the invitation. I am also indebted to Elaine Hall for superb research assistance during my visit; my research there would have been much less productive without her guidance in sorting through the massive volume of material. The epigraph is from Martin Luther King, Jr., "People in Action: Literacy Bill Dies," *New York Amsterdam News*, May 26, 1962.

1. For a canonical statement of the nature, scope, and importance of these institutions, see John Rawls, *A Theory of Justice* (Cambridge, MA: Belknap Press of Harvard University Press, 1971). For evidence of the impact of rights violations on societal stability and violence, see Oskar N. T. Thoms and James Ron, "Do Human Rights Violations Cause Internal Conflict?," *Human Rights Quarterly* 29 (2007): 674–705.

2. Keeanga-Yamahtta Taylor, *From #BlackLivesMatter to Black Liberation* (Chicago: Haymarket Books, 2016).

3. See, e.g., Penny M. Von Eschen, *Race against Empire: Black Americans and Anticolonialism, 1937–1957* (Ithaca, NY: Cornell University Press, 1997); Mary L. Dudziak, *Cold War Civil Rights: Race and the Image of American Democracy* (Princeton, NJ: Princeton University Press, 2000); Carol Anderson, *Eyes off the Prize: The United Nations and the African American Struggle for Human Rights, 1944–1955* (Cambridge: Cambridge University Press, 2003); Glenda Elizabeth Gilmore, *Defying Dixie: The Radical Roots of Civil Rights, 1919–1950* (New York: W. W. Norton, 2008).

4. Rex Martin, *A System of Rights* (New York: Oxford University Press, 1993).

5. Derrick Darby, *Rights, Race, and Recognition* (Cambridge: Cambridge University Press, 2009).

6. America arguably has several "fundamental" values. It would be illuminating to consider them one at a time and see what King has to say about them and how he

applies them in thinking about racial justice generally and voting rights in particular. For the sake of a manageable discussion, and because I am struck by how much King relies upon dignity, and also by the dignity renaissance in philosophy, law, and judicial reasoning, I have chosen to focus on this value. One concern about this might be that dignity cannot be understood as a fundamental "American" value that goes back to the founding era. Some might argue that it is a relatively recent twentieth-century invention, our current understanding of it having been developed during the World War II period on the international stage, or that it is a concept with origins in early Christian thought that predate the U.S. founding. I will leave this debate to those who study the history of ideas. Suffice it to say that King certainly believed that this was a prominent value in America's political morality. And he need not be read as claiming exclusive or even original American ownership of it. Here King was in good company with at least one U.S. Supreme Court Justice, William J. Brennan, Jr., who claimed that the U.S. Constitution and Bill of Rights were a "bold commitment by a people to the ideal of dignity protected through law." Cited in Leslie Meltzer Henry, "The Jurisprudence of Dignity," *University of Pennsylvania Law Review* 160 (2011): 169–233, at 171.

7. Jeremy Waldron, *Dignity, Rank, and Rights* (New York: Oxford University Press, 2012), 25.

8. Kant, *Anthropology from a Pragmatic Point of View,* 7:127. I will follow common practice of using the Academy volume and page numbers for references to Kant. My source for this work is Immanuel Kant, *Anthropology, History, and Education,* ed. Günter Zöller and Robert B. Louden (Cambridge: Cambridge University Press, 2007).

9. For an account of Kant's infamous contributions to these legacies, see Thomas McCarthy, *Race, Empire, and the Idea of Human Development* (Cambridge: Cambridge University Press, 2009), chap. 2.

10. Martin Luther King, Jr., *Strength to Love* (Minneapolis: Fortress Press, 2010), 29.

11. Waldron, *Dignity, Rank, and Rights,* 33.

12. To put this distinction another way, the former alternative suggests that specific rights can be inferred from a conception of dignity, whereas the latter alternative suggests that an existing system of rights tells us something about what we mean by dignity and how strongly we value it. I think that the latter alternative is a more modest position, but one that can also do some critical normative work.

13. Cornel West, *The Radical King: Martin Luther King, Jr.* (Boston: Beacon Press, 2015).

14. For criticism of the view that particular rights can be inferred from a particular conception of dignity, see Charles R. Beitz, "Human Dignity in the Theory of Human Rights: Nothing but a Phrase?," *Philosophy and Public Affairs* 41, no. 3 (2013): 259–290.

15. Gary May, *Bending toward Justice: The Voting Rights Act and the Transformation of American Democracy* (New York: Basic Books, 2013), xix.

16. Martin Luther King, Jr., *Where Do We Go from Here: Chaos or Community?* (Boston: Beacon Press, 2010), 145.

17. Martha C. Nussbaum, *Political Emotions: Why Love Matters for Justice* (Cambridge, MA: Belknap Press of Harvard University Press, 2013).

18. King, *Where Do We Go from Here*, 145.

19. A craving for normalcy arguably compelled Shelby County, Alabama, to appeal to the U.S. Supreme Court to lift the heavy burden placed on it and other jurisdictions for their shameful histories of voting rights abuses. They won their day in court in *Shelby County v. Holder* (2013). For discussion, see Derrick Darby, "Uncovering the Voting Rights Act: The Racial Progress Argument in *Shelby County*," *Kansas Journal of Law and Public Policy* 25 (2016): 329–346. As King might have predicted, the enactment, following *Shelby County*, of voter ID laws that made it harder for blacks and other citizens to vote suggests that some version of negative normalcy is what they were after all along. To be sure, it was not the kind of "normalcy in the state of Mississippi which made it possible for authorities to say that a Negro must starve if he wanted to vote" (Martin Luther King, Jr., "People to People: Civil Rights and Negative Normalcy," *New York Amsterdam News*, March 12, 1966). Nor was it the kind of normalcy they had in Alabama under Governor George Wallace, where blacks had to withstand the brutal force of Sheriff Jim Clark if they wanted to vote, and then pass a literary test if they made it to the ballot box. Nevertheless, it clearly is a kind of negative normalcy in which just being an American citizen of voting age is not enough. To procure the documents needed to vote, one must also have ample time and money, both of which are resources that are unequally distributed across the population of eligible voters and in disproportionately short supply for black Americans in particular.

20. King, "People to People." King uses the phrase "new birth of democracy" in letter to Laura R. Daly, April 19, 1966, thanking her for a financial contribution to the SCLC voting rights campaign.

21. King, "People to People."

22. As quoted in Martin Luther King, Jr., *"All Labor Has Dignity,"* ed. Michael K. Honey (Boston: Beacon Press, 1963), 97.

23. Ibid., 97–98.

24. King, "People to People."

25. King, *"All Labor Has Dignity,"* 98.

26. Ibid.

27. Ibid., 91.

28. Ibid., 90.

29. King, *Where Do We Go from Here*, 3–4. For a rich historical account of what was at stake in this phase of struggle, and how it advanced long-standing radical agendas, see Thomas F. Jackson, *From Civil Rights to Human Rights: Martin Luther King, Jr., and the Struggle for Economic Justice* (Philadelphia: University of Pennsylvania Press, 2007).

30. King, *Where Do We Go from Here*, 4.

31. Ibid., 5.

32. Elsewhere I propose how we might ground collective responsibility for addressing racial disparities if we follow King in taking seriously the psychology of white resistance. See Derrick Darby and Nyla R. Branscombe, "Beyond the Sins of the Fathers: Responsibility for Inequality," *Midwest Studies in Philosophy* 38 (2014): 121–137.

33. King, *Where Do We Go from Here*, 20.

34. Martin Luther King, Jr., "Draft of an Article on the Status of the Civil Rights Movement during 1965," 2, Martin Luther King, Jr., Papers, Speeches, Sermons, Etc., box 7, King Center Archive in Atlanta (hereafter cited as King Papers, King Center Archive).

35. In recent years there has been a steady flow of work by political philosophers and political theorists on the topic. See George Kateb, *Human Dignity* (Cambridge, MA: Harvard University Press, 2011); Michael Rosen, *Dignity: Its History and Meaning* (Cambridge, MA: Harvard University Press, 2012); and Waldron, *Dignity, Rank, and Rights*.

36. King, *Strength to Love*, 150.

37. Ibid.

38. Martin Luther King, Jr., *Stride toward Freedom: The Montgomery Story* (Boston: Beacon Press, 2010), 31.

39. See Bernard R. Boxill, *Blacks and Social Justice*, rev. ed. (Lanham, MD: Rowman and Littlefield, 1992), 193–194.

40. Ibid., 194.

41. Kant, *Groundwork of the Metaphysics of Morals*, 4:435. My source for his moral works is Immanuel Kant, *Practical Philosophy*, ed. Mary J. Gregor (Cambridge: Cambridge University Press, 1996).

42. In some cases the sanctions might be legal ones, imposed by laws that proscribe ways of acting or being treated that are deemed undignified. Laws against dwarf tossing, wearing a burqa, pornography, and prostitution can be located within this category. In these cases, a community conception of respect for the dignity, holiness, or sacredness of humanity is enshrined within a legal system of rights.

43. Kant, *The Metaphysics of Morals*, 6:436.

44. Martin Luther King, Jr., "Speech before the Youth March for Integrated Schools," in *A Testament of Hope: The Essential Writings and Speeches of Martin Luther King, Jr.*, ed. James M. Washington (New York: Harper Collins, 1991), 22.

45. King, *Where Do We Go from Here*, 103, 104.

46. Ibid., 102.

47. Ibid., 104.

48. Martin Luther King, Jr., "How Modern Christians Should Think of Man," 3, King Papers, box 1, King Center Archive.

49. King, *Where Do We Go from Here*, 102.

50. One philosopher puts the point this way: "The worst evil-doers have human dignity despite their atrocious acts, for this basic dignity is a moral status that is not earned and cannot be forfeited." See Thomas E. Hill, Jr., "Human Dignity and Tragic

Choices," *Proceedings and Addresses of the American Philosophical Association* 89 (2015): 74–97, at 86.

51. King credits his studies at Boston University for giving him "a metaphysical basis for the dignity and worth of all human personality" (King, *Stride toward Freedom,* 88). For a historical treatment of the philosophical influences on King's racial justice activism, see David Levering Lewis, *King: A Biography,* 3rd ed. (Urbana: University of Illinois Press, 2013).

52. It is commonly held that human beings are the only animals with dignity in this sense of inherent worth. But some philosophers have taken issue with this by offering a more inclusive reading of what makes a creature a Kantian end-in-itself. See, for instance, Christine M. Korsgaard, "Fellow Creatures: Kantian Ethics and Our Duties to Animals," in *The Tanner Lectures on Human Values,* vol. 5, ed. Grethe B. Peterson (Salt Lake City: Utah University Press, 2005).

53. King, *Strength to Love,* 29.

54. Ibid., 79.

55. King, "Draft of an Article," 12, 14.

56. Martin Luther King, Jr., "Press Statement 10/5/57 re Crusade for Citizenship SCLC Memphis, Tennessee," King Papers, box 1, ca. early 1950s, King Center Archive.

57. King, *"All Labor Has Dignity,"* 92.

58. Ibid., 93.

59. Ibid., 78.

60. Martin Luther King, Jr., *Why We Can't Wait* (Boston: Beacon Press, 2010), 93.

61. King, *"All Labor Has Dignity,"* 92. It is important to add, however, that blacks are not the only ones bound by chains here. In a draft of a speech on the passage of 1965 Voting Rights Act, King says: "For white people in our nation have been enslaved to the ideal of racial superiority and we cannot free ourselves without freeing them."

62. King's admonishment of rank, sorting persons into higher and lower rank, also shows up in his sharp criticism of churches that fail to "recognize that worship at its best is a social experience in which people from all levels of life come together to affirm their oneness and unity under God" (King, *Strength to Love,* 60).

63. King, *"All Labor Has Dignity,"* 129.

64. King, *Where Do We Go from Here,* 44.

65. My reading of King on honor, and on its bearing on yet another use of dignity in his work, is inspired and informed by Waldron's insightful treatment of dignity's relationship to honor and rank, though in this chapter I cannot give his views the careful attention they deserve. I am also struck by the many parallels between this approach to dignity and the one I take to rights in *Rights, Race, and Recognition.* There I treat being a bearer of rights as a social status rooted in practices of recognition, taking seriously the reality that this status is not guaranteed by the nature of our being but must be fought for and can be won or lost. I suspect that much of what I say there can be adapted to a socially grounded analysis of dignity.

66. Kant, *Anthropology from a Pragmatic Point of View,* 7:137.

67. Martin Luther King, Jr., "Address at Selma State Capitol in Montgomery, Alabama on 3/25/1965," 5, King Papers, box 8, King Center Archive.

68. King, *Why We Can't Wait*, 94, 99.

69. Public Statement at the Mississippi Freedom Democratic Party, July 22, 1964; Statement before the Credentials Committee, Democratic National Committee, August 22, 1964, King Papers, box 8, King Center Archive.

70. Martin Luther King, Jr., "The Right to Vote, the Quest for Jobs 3/65," 7, King Papers, box 8, King Center Archive. In the annotated copy, King crosses out this passage; however, his remark is insightful and a point worth making.

71. Keesha Gaskins and Sundeep Iver, "The Challenge of Obtaining Voter Identification," Brennan Center for Justice at New York University School of Law, July 29, 2012, available at http://www.brennancenter.org/publication/challenge-obtaining-voter-identification.

72. Martin Luther King, Jr., "Give Us the Ballot—We Will Transform the South," in *A Testament of Hope*, 197.

73. Ibid.

74. For an influential account of nondomination as a political ideal, see Philip Pettit, *Republicanism: A Theory of Freedom and Government* (New York: Oxford University Press, 1997), chap. 3.

75. King also discusses the consequences of the political domination involved in denying blacks the vote: such domination erodes democracy, and puts democracy on trial. No one can govern or respect people as well as they can represent or govern themselves, he argues, and therefore when they are subject to political domination, they face pressure to flee their circumstances if they cannot change them within the legal system of rights. They might flee the Iron Curtain from East to West, says King, or the Cotton Curtain from South to North. He laments how mass Northern migration, prompted partly by political domination, depleted the South of blacks and how it burdened Northern dark ghettos. He observes that it also depressed economic development in the South and left congressional power in the hands of the most reactionary bloc, which made national social welfare and education bills difficult to pass, and which put American democracy on trial on the global stage. See King, "Draft of an Article."

76. This argument can be generalized to cover many of the evil monsters or racial injustices that King highlights. Our national commitment to dignity can be enhanced by a legal system of rights that includes rights and duties that vanquish or guard against the ways in which evil monsters assail our dignity. But I shall keep the focus squarely on voting rights in expounding the argument.

77. Beitz, "Human Dignity," 288.

78. For a very insightful and detailed overview of the modern struggle for voting rights, see Ari Berman, *Give Us the Ballot: The Modern Struggle for Voting Rights in America* (New York: Farrar, Straus and Giroux, 2015).

79. Beitz, "Human Dignity," 288.

80. Waldron, *Dignity, Rank, and Rights*, 145.

9. Prisons of the Forgotten

Versions of this chapter were presented at a colloquium sponsored by the philosophy departments at Haverford College and Bryn Mawr College; the Inequality Seminar Series at the Harvard Kennedy School of Government; the Department of Philosophy at Pennsylvania State University; the Mershon Center at The Ohio State University; the Department of Philosophy at the University of Massachusetts at Amherst; the Institute of Ethics and Public Affairs at Old Dominion University; and as the Audi Lecture at Colgate University. I thank the audiences and participants at these venues for their questions and criticisms and Macalester Bell, Wendy Salkin, Jessie Scanlon, Mario Small, and Brandon Terry for helpful comments and discussion.

1. Martin Luther King, Jr., *Where Do We Go from Here: Community or Chaos?* (Boston: Beacon Press, 1968), 3; King, "Next Stop: The North," in *A Testament of Hope: The Essential Writings and Speeches of Martin Luther King Jr.,* ed. James M. Washington (New York: Harper Collins, 1986), 189–194.

2. King, *Where Do We Go from Here,* 19; King, "Next Stop," 192.

3. Clayborne Carson, ed., *The Autobiography of Martin Luther King, Jr.* (New York: Warner Books, 1998), 298–301.

4. King, *Where Do We Go from Here,* 3–4; Martin Luther King, Jr., *"All Labor Has Dignity,"* ed. Michael K. Honey (Boston: Beacon Press, 2011), 125–126, 128, 175–176.

5. Martin Luther King, Jr., *Stride toward Freedom: The Montgomery Story* (Boston: Beacon Press, 1958), 77.

6. King, *"All Labor Has Dignity,"* 128–129; Martin Luther King, Jr., "A Testament of Hope," in *A Testament of Hope,* 314–315; Martin Luther King, Jr., *The Trumpet of Conscience* (Boston: Beacon Press, 1967), 6.

7. King, *Where Do We Go from Here,* 5–6, 9–11; King, "A Testament of Hope," 321.

8. King, *Where Do We Go from Here,* 104–109.

9. Ibid., 105.

10. King, "Next Stop," 192.

11. King, *Where Do We Go from Here,* 114.

12. King, *"All Labor Has Dignity,"* 156; King, *Where Do We Go from Here,* 114.

13. King, *Where Do We Go from Here,* 115, 118–119.

14. Martin Luther King, Jr., *Why We Can't Wait* (Boston: Beacon Press, 2010), 164–166; King, "Next Stop," 191–192; King, "A Testament of Hope," 326.

15. King, *"All Labor Has Dignity,"* 26, 51.

16. Ibid., 39, 51, 96; King, *Why We Can't Wait,* 153.

17. King, *Why We Can't Wait,* 165.

18. King, *"All Labor Has Dignity,"* 105.

19. King, *Where Do We Go from Here,* 21; King, "Next Stop," 193.

20. King, *Trumpet of Conscience,* 10–13.

21. King, "A Testament of Hope," 321.

22. Ibid., 324–325.

23. King, *Trumpet of Conscience,* 14, 57–58.

24. Ibid., 58.

25. King, "Next Stop," 192.

26. King, *Trumpet of Conscience,* 58–59.

27. Martin Luther King, Jr., "A Time to Break Silence," in *A Testament of Hope,* 233.

28. King, *"All Labor Has Dignity,"* 159; King, *Where Do We Go from Here,* 112.

29. King, *Trumpet of Conscience,* 8.

30. King, *Where Do We Go from Here,* 21–22.

31. King, *"All Labor Has Dignity,"* 109.

32. King, "A Testament of Hope," 314.

33. I discuss King's vision of racial justice in "Justice and Racial Conciliation: Two Visions," *Daedalus* 140 (Winter 2011): 95–107.

34. King, *Why We Can't Wait,* 159–160, 162–164. Also see Chapter 11, by Lawrie Balfour.

35. Ibid., 159.

36. King, "A Testament of Hope," 317.

37. King, "I Have a Dream," in *A Testament of Hope,* 217.

38. Ibid., 218.

39. King, *Where Do We Go from Here,* 196–199.

40. King, *"All Labor Has Dignity,"* 28.

41. Ibid., 117, 131.

42. Ibid., 117.

43. King, *Trumpet of Conscience,* 15.

44. King, *"All Labor Has Dignity,"* 132–133; King, *Where Do We Go from Here,* 162.

45. King, *Where Do We Go from Here,* 130.

46. King, *Why We Can't Wait,* 163–166. See also King, *Where Do We Go from Here,* 81–82.

47. King, *"All Labor Has Dignity,"* 133.

48. King, *Where Do We Go from Here,* 164–165.

49. Ibid., 165.

50. King, "Nonviolence: The Only Road to Freedom," in *Testament of Hope,* 60; King, *Where Do We Go from Here,* 143–146; Martin Luther King, Jr., "I See the Promised Land," in *A Testament of Hope,* 282–283.

51. For a thorough discussion of King's philosophy of nonviolent direct action, see Greg Moses, *Revolution of Conscience: Martin Luther King, Jr., and the Philosophy of Nonviolence* (New York: Guilford Press, 1997), chap. 4. Also see Chapter, 4 by Karuna Mantena.

52. King, "Nonviolence," 60.

53. King, *"All Labor Has Dignity,"* 52; King, *Why We Can't Wait,* 168–169. Bayard Rustin, longtime advisor to King, strongly advocated an alliance between blacks, labor organizations, liberals, and progressive religious leaders. Only through

such a multiracial coalition, he argued, could racial and economic justice be secured in the United States. See Bayard Rustin, "From Protest to Politics: The Future of the Civil Rights Movement," *Commentary* 39 (1965), reprinted in *Time on Two Crosses: The Collected Writings of Bayard Rustin*, ed. Devon W. Carbado and Donald Weise (San Francisco: Cleis Press, 2003), 116–129.

54. King, *Stride toward Freedom*, 78.

55. King, "All Labor Has Dignity," 26, 38; King, *Where Do We Go from Here*, 141–143.

56. King, "All Labor Has Dignity," 39–43.

57. Ibid., 109.

58. Ibid., 115–116.

59. Ibid., 16, 59.

60. *Why We Can't Wait*, 151; King, *Where Do We Go from Here*, 165–166.

61. King, *Where Do We Go from Here*, 165.

62. Ibid., 186; King, "All Labor Has Dignity," 39; King, "A Time to Break Silence," 240–241.

63. King, "All Labor Has Dignity," 173–174.

64. King, *Where Do We Go from Here*, 176–181.

65. King, "Next Stop," 192.

66. King, *Where Do We Go from Here*, 111–112.

67. Ibid., 87, 164.

68. King, "All Labor Has Dignity," 175–176.

69. King, *Why We Can't Wait*, 161; also see King, *Where Do We Go from Here*, 79.

70. King, "All Labor Has Dignity," 36–37.

71. Ibid., 28.

72. Ibid., 37–38, 177–178.

73. Ibid., 39, 92.

74. King, *Where Do We Go from Here*, 163.

75. Ibid., 169.

76. King, "All Labor Has Dignity," 51–52.

77. King, *Where Do We Go from Here*, 186; King, "A Time to Break Silence," 240–241.

78. King, *Where Do We Go from Here*, 187; also see King, *Stride toward Freedom*, 82–83.

79. Martin Luther King, Jr., *Strength to Love* (Minneapolis: Fortress Press, 2010), 100.

80. King, "All Labor Has Dignity," 59; King, *Stride toward Freedom*, 79.

81. King, *Strength to Love*, 100–101.

82. King, "All Labor Has Dignity," 59; King, *Stride toward Freedom*, 79–80.

83. King, "All Labor Has Dignity," 59.

84. King, *Strength to Love*, 101.

85. King, *Where Do We Go from Here*, 186–187; King, "All Labor Has Dignity," 59; King, *Strength to Love*, 102.

86. King, *Stride toward Freedom*, 80.

87. Ibid., 81.

88. King, *Strength to Love*, 103–104.

89. King, *Where Do We Go from Here*, 189; King, "A Time to Break Silence," 241.

90. King, *Strength to Love*, 106–108.

91. King, *Stride toward Freedom*, 82.

92. King, "All Labor Has Dignity," 59.

93. King, *Strength to Love*, 106.

94. King, "All Labor Has Dignity," 59; also see King, *Strength to Love*, 105–106.

95. See, for example, Adam Fairclough, "Was Martin Luther King a Marxist?," *History Workshop* 15 (1983): 117–125; Douglass Sturm, "Martin Luther King, Jr., as Democratic Socialist," *Journal of Religious Ethics* 18 (1990): 79–105; Michael Eric Dyson, *I May Not Get There with You: The True Martin Luther King, Jr.* (New York: Touchstone, 2000), chap. 4; Paul Le Blanc, "The Radical Roots of Martin Luther King, Jr.: Christian Core, Socialist Bedrock," *Against the Current* 16 (2002); Thomas F. Jackson, *From Civil Rights to Human Rights: Martin Luther King, Jr. and the Struggle for Economic Justice* (Philadelphia: University of Pennsylvania Press, 2007); Richard A. Jones, "Martin Luther King Jr.'s *Agape* and World House," in *The Liberatory Thought of Martin Luther King Jr.*, ed. Robert E. Birt (Lanham, MD: Lexington Books, 2012), 135–155; and Cornel West, "Introduction: The Radical King We Don't Know," in Martin Luther King, Jr., *The Radical King*, ed. Cornel West (Boston: Beacon Press, 2015), ix–xvi.

96. King, *Where Do We Go from Here*, 187.

97. Ibid., 189.

98. I offer an interpretation of King's *public* philosophy—that is, one based on his published writings, speeches, sermons, and public statements. It is possible that he held, as a private conviction shared only with intimates, a more strongly socialist position than his public philosophy suggests. For example, Garrow reports that King privately told a confidant (William A. Rutherford) that "obviously we've got to have some form of socialism, but America's not ready to hear it yet." See David J. Garrow, *Bearing the Cross: Martin Luther King, Jr., and the Southern Christian Leadership Conference* (New York: William Morrow, 1986), 585. Just what this "form of socialism" comes to and whether it differs substantively from Scandinavian social democracy is never made clear.

99. I have attempted to develop a "black radical liberal" perspective on the black freedom struggle and ghetto poverty that takes these three developments into account in *We Who Are Dark: The Philosophical Foundations of Black Solidarity* (Cambridge, MA: Belknap Press of Harvard University Press, 2005) and in *Dark Ghettos: Injustice, Dissent, and Reform* (Cambridge, MA: Belknap Press of Harvard University Press, 2016).

100. For a nuanced discussion of this issue, see Jackson, *From Civil Rights to Human Rights*, 254–257. See also Chapter 10, by Shatema Threadcraft and Brandon Terry.

101. King, *Why We Can't Wait*, 87.

102. See Vincent Gordon Harding, "Beyond Amnesia: Martin Luther King, Jr. and the Future of America," *Journal of American History* 74 (1987): 468–476.

10. GENDER TROUBLE

1. Septima Clark, *Ready from Within: Septima Clark and the Civil Rights Movement,* ed. Cynthia Stokes Brown (Tremont, NJ: Africa World Press, 1990), 77. This does not mean that all ministers were equally abhorrent. Clark's interviews and recollection evince great esteem for King, but she is utterly disdainful of Ralph Abernathy, at one point describing him as "just a spoiled little boy" who needed to "grow up and be a real man" (Clark quoted in David J. Garrow, *Bearing the Cross: Martin Luther King, Jr. and the Southern Christian Leadership Conference* [New York: Vintage, 1988], 366).

2. Clark, *Ready from Within,* 77–78.

3. Ibid. 79. See also, for example, Clark's account of political differences with Ella Baker on the question of sexism in the movement: "Ella Baker sees things and gets very angry about them, and I see things and I want to work on them, but without the hostility. I see the same things that she saw, but I'm not going to be hostile. I'm not going to get mad with a man because he said I shouldn't be on the. . . . I just sit up there and listen to what he has to say, and then when I get a chance I let him know that I have made a contribution and that I can make a contribution." Oral History Interview with Septima Poinsette Clark, July 25, 1976, Interview G-0016, Southern Oral History Program Collection no. 4007, Southern Historical Collection, Wilson Library, University of North Carolina at Chapel Hill, published by Documenting the American South, May 16, 2017, http://docsouth.unc.edu/sohp/G -0016/G-0016.html.

4. bell hooks, *Ain't I a Woman: Black Women and Feminism* (New York: Routledge, 2015), 177, also see 94–95.

5. bell hooks, *We Real Cool: Black Men and Masculinity* (New York: Routledge, 2004), 10.

6. bell hooks, *Killing Rage: Ending Racism* (New York: Routledge, 1995), 263–272.

7. bell hooks, "The Beloved Community: A Conversation with bell hooks," *Appalachian Heritage* 40, no. 4 (Fall 2012): 76–86.

8. George Yancy and bell hooks, "bell hooks: Buddhism, the Beats and Loving Blackness," *New York Times: The Stone* (December 10, 2015), https://opinionator. blogs.nytimes.com/2015/12/10/bell-hooks-buddhism-the-beats-and-loving -blackness/?_r=0.

9. Thomas McCarthy, *Race, Empire, and the Idea of Human Development* (New York: Cambridge University Press, 2009), 36.

10. Susan Moller Okin, *Women in Western Political Thought* (Princeton, NJ: Princeton University Press, 1979), 4.

11. Charles Payne, a leading historian of this "view from the trenches," aptly characterizes these historiographical and critical accounts of the civil rights struggle as

shifting the analytical focus: instead of focusing on national political elites and events, they look at local conflict and community organizing; in place of unified accounts of black politics and identity, these newer accounts tend to emphasize fragmentation and difference; and they look back from the short period of intense contention in 1954–1968 to a longer tradition of activism and struggle within black communities. Charles Payne, "Debating the Civil Rights Movement: The View from the Trenches," in *Debating the Civil Rights Movement, 1945–1968*, 2nd ed., ed. Steven F. Lawson and Charles Payne (Oxford: Rowman and Littlefield, 2006), 125–126.

12. Barbara Ransby, *Ella Baker and the Black Freedom Movement: A Radical Democratic Vision* (Chapel Hill: University of North Carolina Press, 2003).

13. For Ransby, one way of describing this conflict is as a tension between the "missionary" tradition, which she associates with Baker and those women who have historically organized in more decentralized and democratic forms within the church, and the "messianic" or "ministerial" tradition, which she associates with King and other male ministers.

14. Oral History Interview with Ella Jo Baker, September 4, 1974, Interview G-0007, Southern Oral History Program Collection no. 4007, Southern Historical Collection, Wilson Library, University of North Carolina at Chapel Hill, published by Documenting the American South, May 16, 2017, http://docsouth.unc.edu/sohp /G-0007/menu.html (51 for Ella Baker interview with Walker).

15. Ransby, *Ella Baker*, 175–176.

16. Martin Luther King, Jr., "Recommendations to the Dexter Avenue Baptist Church for the Fiscal Year 1954–1955 (September 5, 1954)," in *The Papers of Martin Luther King, Jr.* (hereafter cited as *Papers*), ed. Clayborne Carson (Berkeley: University of California Press, 1994), 2:287.

17. For the classic statement on "the hermeneutics of suspicion," see Paul Ricouer, *Freud and Philosophy: An Essay on Interpretation* (New Haven, CT: Yale University Press, 1970). For a compelling, contemporary reconstruction, see Brian Leiter, "The Hermeneutics of Suspicion: Recovering Marx, Nietzsche, and Freud," in *The Future for Philosophy*, ed. Brian Leiter (New York: Oxford University Press, 2006), 74–106.

18. Erica Edwards, *Charisma and the Fictions of Black Leadership* (Minneapolis: University of Minnesota Press, 2012), 16, 13.

19. Ibid., 19.

20. Baker, quoted in Ransby, *Ella Baker*, 188.

21. In this sense Baker's conception of democracy is closer to that of someone like John Dewey rather than those who restrict the definition of democracy to decision-making procedures and political institutions. For Dewey, democracy refers to a broader cultural milieu that involves social inquiry, habits of citizenship, conceptions of the common good, and the cultivation of individuality. See, for example, John Dewey, *The Public and Its Problems*, ed. Melvin Rogers (Athens: Ohio State Press, 2016).

22. Baker, quoted in Ransby, *Ella Baker*, 369.

23. For an important attempt to restate Baker's scattered speeches and interviews, and accounts of her organizing presented in the idioms of democratic political theory, see Andrew Sabl, *Ruling Passions: Political Offices and Democratic Ethics* (Princeton, NJ: Princeton University Press, 2002), 280–288.

24. Ransby, *Ella Baker,* 191.

25. On King's personal donations to SNCC and CORE, see Garrow, *Bearing the Cross,* 368. This is beyond the scope of this paper, but the existing civil rights literature on leadership, power, hierarchy, and representation seems to suffer from two conceptual deficiencies. First, while the charismatic mode has been subjected, rightly, to trenchant critique on questions of marginalization, a similarly sophisticated level of analysis has not yet emerged to understand the forms of power, hierarchy, and influence that flourish in self-described "leaderless" or "leader-full" organizations in black communities. The touchstone for this sort of analysis remains Jo Freeman, "The Tyranny of Structurelessness," *Berkeley Journal of Sociology* 17 (1972–1973): 151–165. Second, this literature in African American Studies has largely ignored the recent renaissance in the study of representation in political theory, which in taking a supra-institutional and constructivist turn, offers other important terms of description and forms of evaluation for King's practice of leadership in a Jim Crow racial order. See, for example, Jane Mansbridge, "Rethinking Representation," *American Political Science Review* 97, no. 4 (2003): 515–528; Nadia Urbinati and Mark Warren, "The Concept of Representation in Contemporary Democratic Theory," *Annual Review of Political Science* 11 (2008): 387–412; Michael Saward, *The Representative Claim* (New York: Oxford University Press, 2010); and Lisa Disch, "The Constructivist Turn in Democratic Representation: A Normative Dead-End?," *Constellations* 22, no. 4 (2015): 487–499.

26. Seyla Benhabib, *The Reluctant Modernism of Hannah Arendt,* 2nd ed. (Lanham, MD: Rowan and Littlefield, 2003), 198.

27. Seyla Benhabib, "Feminist Theory and Hannah Arendt's Concept of Public Space," *History of the Human Sciences* 6, no. 2 (May 1993): 97–114.

28. Peter J. Ling, "Gender and Generation: Manhood at the Southern Christian Leadership Conference," in *Gender and the Civil Rights Movement,* ed. Peter J. Ling and Sharon Monteith (New York: Routledge, 1999), 108.

29. Martin Luther King, Jr., *Stride toward Freedom: The Montgomery Story* (Boston: Beacon Press, 2010), 48, 85 (emphasis added).

30. Wendy Brown, *Manhood and Politics: A Feminist Reading in Political Theory* (Lanham, MD: Rowman and Littlefield, 1988), 4.

31. Frederick Douglass, "The Do-Nothing Policy (9/12/1856)," in *Frederick Douglass: Selected Speeches and Writings,* ed. Philip Foner (Chicago: Lawrence Hill, 1999), 343 (emphasis added).

32. Frederick Douglass, *The Life and Times of Frederick Douglass* (Hartford, CT: Park, 1883), 177.

33. Frederick Douglass, "Is It Right and Wise to Kill a Kidnapper?," in Foner, *Frederick Douglass,* 279.

34. Robert F. Williams, quoted in Timothy Tyson, introduction to Robert F. Williams, *Negroes with Guns* (Detroit: Wayne State University Press, 1998), xxv.

35. Malcolm X, "With Mrs. Fannie Lou Hamer," *Malcolm X Speaks: Selected Speeches and Statements,* ed. George Breitman (New York: Grove, 1965), 107.

36. For a similar account, see Jacquelyn Dowd Hall, "The Mind That Burns in Each Body: Women, Rape, and Racial Violence," in *Powers of Desire,* ed. Ann Snitow, Christine Stansell, and Sharon Tompson (New York: Monthly Review Press, 1983), 335.

37. Partha Chatterjee, *The Nation and Its Fragments: Colonial and Postcolonial Histories* (Princeton, NJ: Princeton University Press, 1993), chap. 7.

38. Ling, "Gender and Generation," 112.

39. 2Pac, *2Pacalypse Now,* Interscope ntEastWest Records America, 1991. More recent echoes of this sentiment can be found in T. I., "Switchin' Lanes," *US or Else: Letter to the System,* Grand Hustle/RocNation. 2016; and Pusha T, "Sunshine," *King Push—Darkest Before the Dawn: The Prelude,* GOOD Music/Def Jam, 2015.

40. Lance Hill, *The Deacons for Defense: Armed Resistance and the Civil Rights Movement* (Chapel Hill: University of North Carolina Press, 2004), 27. It should be noted that while Coretta Scott King participated in many marches, SCLC studiously avoided situations where she was likely to be assaulted. One can only imagine how King's critics would have used such images to challenge his "manhood."

41. Richard Bak, *Joe Louis: The Great Black Hope* (Dallas: Da Capo Press, 1998); William Van Deburg, *Hoodlums: Black Villains and Social Bandits in American Life* (Chicago: University of Chicago Press, 2004); Cecil Brown, *Stagolee Shot Billy* (Cambridge, MA: Harvard University Press, 2004).

42. Saba Mahmood, *The Politics of Piety: The Islamic Revival and the Feminist Subject,* 2nd ed. (Princeton, NJ: Princeton University Press, 2011), 9.

43. Linda Zerilli, *Feminism and the Abyss of Freedom* (Chicago: University of Chicago Press, 2005), 60.

44. Martin Luther King, Jr., *Why We Can't Wait* (Boston: Beacon Press, 2011), 32.

45. Malcolm X, "Message to the Grassroots," in *Malcolm X Speaks,* 12.

46. King, *Why We Can't Wait,* 36–37. See also Martin Luther King, Jr., *Where Do We Go from Here: Chaos or Community?* (Boston: Beacon Press, 2010), 19.

47. For the classic statement on how the inversion of values can weaken the certainty of associations between valuations and social kinds or groups, see Friedrich Nietzsche, *On the Genealogy of Morality,* trans. Maudemarie Clark and Alan Swensen (Indianapolis: Hackett, 1998).

48. King, *Why We Can't Wait,* 31.

49. Ibid., 147.

50. King, *Where Do We Go from Here,* 66.

51. Martin Luther King, Jr., *Strength to Love* (Minneapolis: Fortress Press, 2010), 124.

52. Martin Luther King, "A Testament of Hope" (1968), in Martin Luther King, Jr., *A Testament of Hope,* ed. James Washington (New York: Harper Collins, 1991), 322–323.

53. Martin Luther King, Jr., "Nonviolence: The Only Road to Freedom," in *A Testament of Hope*, 57.

54. King, *Why We Can't Wait*, 129–130.

55. Ibid., 36–37.

56. Malcolm X, "The Ballot or the Bullet, Delivered at King Solomon Baptist Church (April 12, 1964)," available at *Say It Plain, Say It Loud: A Century of Great African American Speeches*, http://americanradioworks.publicradio.org/features /blackspeech/mx.html.

57. Erica Chenoweth and Maria J. Stephan, *Why Civil Resistance Works: The Strategic Logic of Nonviolent Conflict* (New York: Columbia University Press, 2011), 35.

58. Ibid.

59. Timothy Garton Ash, "A Century of Civil Resistance: Some Lessons and Questions," in *Civil Resistance and Power Politics*, ed. Adam Roberts and Timothy Garton Ash (New York: Oxford University Press, 2009), 379.

60. King, *Why We Can't Wait*, 117–118.

61. King, *Stride toward Freedom*, 54.

62. Robin D. G. Kelley, *Race Rebels: Culture, Politics, and the Black Working Class* (New York: Simon and Schuster, 1996), 8.

63. Edward Soja, *Seeking Spatial Justice* (Minneapolis: University of Minnesota Press, 2010).

64. Kelley, *Race Rebels*, 68. Gendered spatial occupational segregation was an important factor, but so were traditional gender relations, specifically traditional gender hierarchy. Even among working-class households with access to a car, men would be more likely to keep the car during the day and drop women off, either at work or at a nearby bus stop.

65. Ibid., 67–68.

66. Ibid.

67. Danielle L. McGuire, *At the Dark End of the Street: Black Women, Rape, and Resistance; A New History of the Civil Rights Movement from Rosa Parks to Black Power* (New York: Vintage, 2010), 59.

68. Ibid., 59–60.

69. Ibid. These were risks they faced simply getting to and from work, to say nothing of the workplace sexual harassment they faced in white homes.

70. Ibid., 13.

71. Ibid., 39.

72. Ranbsy, *Ella Baker*, 142.

73. McGuire, *Dark End of the Street*, 39.

74. Brooks Barnes, "From Footnote to Fame in Civil Rights History," *New York Times*, November 25, 2009.

75. King, *Stride toward Freedom*, 30.

76. Ibid., 31.

77. Ibid.

78. Mary Fair Burks, "Trailblazers: Women in the Montgomery Bus Boycott," in *Women in the Civil Rights Movement: Trailblazers and Torchbearers*, ed. Vicki L.

Crawford, Jacqueline Anne Rouse, and Barbara Woods (Bloomington: Indiana University Press, 1990), 71–72.

79. Kelley, *Race Rebels,* 8.

80. McGuire, *Dark End of the Street,* 62.

81. King, *Stride toward Freedom,* 31–32.

82. Ibid., 60.

83. Jo Anne Gibson Robinson, *The Montgomery Bus Boycott and the Women Who Started It: The Memoir of Jo Anne Gibson Robinson,* ed. David J. Garrow (Knoxville: University of Tennessee Press, 1987), 53.

84. King, *Stride toward Freedom,* 43.

85. Robinson, *Montgomery Bus Boycott,* 59.

86. King, *Stride toward Freedom,* 37.

87. Robinson, *Montgomery Bus Boycott,* 54. For sustained interrogations of the question of racial disloyalty, see Randall Kennedy, *Sellout: The Politics of Racial Betrayal* (New York: Vintage, 2009) and Brando Simeo Starkey, *In Defense of Uncle Tom: Why Blacks Must Police Racial Loyalty* (New York: Cambridge University Press, 2015)

88. King, *Stride Toward Freedom,* 64.

89. King, *Where Do We Go from Here,* 91–92.

90. Ibid., 119.

91. See Chapter 9, by Tommie Shelby.

92. Howard Brick, *Age of Contradiction: American Thought and Culture in the 1960s* (Ithaca, NY: Cornell University Press, 2000).

93. See, for example, the volume by Detroit-based Marxist intellectual and labor leader James Boggs: *The American Revolution: Pages from a Negro Worker's Notebook* (New York: Monthly Review, 1963), esp. chap. 4.

94. Indeed, by 1963, John F. Kennedy's advocacy for a civil rights bill included a sustained argument about how "unemployment falls with special cruelty on minority groups." Kennedy proposed a series of interventions meant specifically to reduce black unemployment and the negative externalities thought to accompany it ("delinquency, vandalism, gang warfare, disease, slums and the high cost of public welfare and crime"). See John F. Kennedy, "President Kennedy's Report to Congress Outlining a Civil Rights Bill," in *The Civil Rights Reader: Basic Documents of the Civil Rights Movement; Excerpts from Speeches and Reports,* ed. Leon Friedman (New York: Walker, 1967), 252–256.

95. Roy Wilkins, "At American Association of Advertising Agencies," in *Talking It Over with Roy Wilkins: Selected Speeches and Writings,* ed. Helen Soloman and Aminda Wilkins (Norwalk, CT: M & B, 1977), 23–24.

96. Daniel Patrick Moynihan, *The Negro Family: The Case for National Action* (Washington, DC: U.S. Government Printing Office, 1965), available at https://www.dol.gov/oasam/programs/history/webid-meynihan.htm.

97. Martin Luther King, quoted in Daniel Patrick Moynihan, *Family and Nation* (New York: Harcourt Brace Jovanovich, 1987), 39.

98. King, *Where Do We Go from Here,* 114, 133.

99. Ibid., 113–114, 123, 210–212.

100. Nancy Fraser, *Fortunes of Feminism: From State-Managed Capitalism to Neoliberal Crisis* (Brooklyn: Verso, 2013), 111–112.

101. King, *Why We Can't Wait,* 16.

102. Thomas F. Jackson, *From Civil Rights to Human Rights: Martin Luther King, Jr., and the Struggle for Economic Justice* (Philadelphia: University of Pennsylvania Press, 2013), 346.

103. Martin Luther King, Jr., "The Crisis in the Modern Family, Sermon at Dexter Avenue Baptist Church (May 8, 1955)," in *Papers,* 6:211–212.

104. Martin Luther King, Jr., "What Then Are Some of the Secrets of Happy Marriage," in *Papers,* 6:432.

105. King, "Crisis," 211.

106. For the classic account of theoretical issues raised by domestic violence against women of color, see Kimberle Crenshaw, "Mapping the Margins: Intersectionality, Identity Politics, and Violence against Women of Color," *Stanford Law Review* 43, no. 6 (July 1991): 1241–1299.

107. King's "Advice for Living" columns are collected in *Papers,* vol. 2.

108. King, "Crisis," 210–212.

109. For more on these as appropriate standards for gender justice, see Nancy Fraser, *Fortunes of Feminism,* 116–121.

110. For a similar argument, see Susan Moller Okin, *Justice, Gender, and the Family* (New York: Basic Books, 1989).

111. Jackson, *Civil Rights to Human Rights,* 205.

112. King, *Where Do We Go from Here,* 172.

113. Ibid., 171–175.

114. Ibid., 92.

115. Jackson, *Civil Rights to Human Rights,* 345. The NWRO also advocated for men's employment so that men could "assume normal roles as breadwinners and heads of families."

116. King, *Where Do We Go from Here,* 210–211.

117. Ibid., 210–212.

118. Ibid., 150.

119. Jackson, *Civil Rights to Human Rights,* 300.

120. King, "Crisis" and "Advice for Living."

121. David P. Stein, "'This Nation Has Never Honestly Dealt With the Question of a Peacetime Economy': Coretta Scott King and the Struggle for a Nonviolent Economy in the 1970s," *Souls* 18, no. 1 (January–March 2016): 80–105.

122. Coretta Scott King with Barbara Reynolds, *My Life, My Love, My Legacy* (New York: Henry Holt and Co., 2017), 189.

I am grateful for the incisive comments of Brandon Terry, Tommie Shelby, Justin Rose, Amy Hondo, and the seminar participants. Thanks to Daniel Henry for excellent research assistance.

1. Martin Luther King, Jr., *Where Do We Go from Here: Chaos or Community?* (Boston: Beacon Press, 2010), 5.

2. Martin Luther King, Jr., "I Have a Dream," in *A Testament of Hope: The Essential Writings and Speeches of Martin Luther King, Jr.*, ed. James M. Washington (New York: Harper Collins, 1991), 217.

3. Martin Luther King, Jr., *Stride toward Freedom: The Montgomery Story* (Boston: Beacon Press, 2010), 196–197.

4. Martin Luther King, Jr., "A Testament of Hope," in *A Testament of Hope*, 314.

5. Martin Luther King, Jr., *Why We Can't Wait* (Boston: Beacon Press, 2010), 151.

6. Alfred L. Brophy, *Reparations: Pro and Con* (Oxford: Oxford University Press, 2006), 36–37, n. 39, 224–225.

7. See Ta-Nehisi Coates, "Martin Luther King Makes the Case for Reparations," *The Atlantic*, June 12, 2014, http://www.theatlantic.com/business/archive/2014/06/martin-luther-king-makes-the-case-for-reparations/372696/.

8. Ta-Nehisi Coates, "Why Precisely Is Bernie Sanders against Reparations?," *The Atlantic*, January 19, 2016, http://www.theatlantic.com/politics/archive/2016/01/bernie-sanders-reparations/424602/.

9. King, *Why We Can't Wait*, 163.

10. Anthony E. Cook, "King and the Beloved Community: A Communitarian Defense of Black Reparations," *George Washington Law Review* 68 (July/September 2000): 959.

11. Preston N. Williams, "An Analysis of the Conception of Love and Its Influence on Justice in the Thought of Martin Luther King, Jr.," *Journal of Religious Ethics* 18 (Fall 1990): 27.

12. The phrase belongs to Clayborne Carson, who assembled a fourth text, *The Autobiography of Martin Luther King, Jr.*, from King's autobiographical writings after his death. Clayborne Carson, introduction, in King, *Stride toward Freedom*, xii.

13. I borrow this term from Robert Gooding-Williams, "Autobiography, Political Hope, Racial Justice," *Du Bois Review* 11, no. 1 (2014): 161.

14. King, *Stride toward Freedom*, xxix.

15. For an account of King's writing of the book and its reception, see David J. Garrow, "Where Martin Luther King, Jr., Was Going: *Where Do We Go from Here* and the Traumas of the Post-Selma Movement," *Georgia Historical Quarterly* 75, no. 4 (Winter 1991): 719–736.

16. All in-text page references are to *Where Do We Go from Here*.

17. Toni Morrison, *Beloved* (New York: Vintage, 1987), 148.

18. Darren Lenard Hutchinson, "Racial Exhaustion," *Washington University Law Review* 86 (2009): 917–974.

19. For an account of temporal inequalities as a fundamental element of racial oppression, see Michael Hanchard, "Afro-Modernity: Temporality, Politics, and the African Diaspora," *Public Culture* 11 (1999): 245–268. For a recent study of King's critique of patience as a political virtue, see Mario Feit, "Democratic Impatience: Martin Luther King, Jr. on Democratic Temporality," *Contemporary Political Theory* 16 (August 2017): 363–386.

20. Ian Haney-López, "Post-Racial Racism: Racial Stratification and Mass Incarceration in the Age of Obama," *California Law Review* 98 (June 2010): 1056.

21. Martin Luther King, Jr., *The Trumpet of Conscience* (Boston: Beacon Press, 2010), 10–13.

22. Ibid., 58–59.

23. Juliet Hooker, "Black Lives Matter and the Paradoxes of U.S. Black Politics: From Democratic Sacrifice to Democratic Repair," *Political Theory* 44, no. 4 (August 2016): 448–469.

24. Margaret Urban Walker, "Restorative Justice and Reparations," *Journal of Social Philosophy* 37, no. 3 (Fall 2006): 378 (emphasis in the original).

25. Iris Marion Young, *Responsibility for Justice* (Oxford: Oxford University Press, 2011), 108.

26. Ibid., 153, 179.

27. King, *Where Do We Go from Here,* 95 (emphasis in the original).

28. Martin Luther King, Jr., "Honoring Dr. Du Bois," in *Black Titan: W. E. B. Du Bois,* ed. John Henrik Clarke, Esther Jackson, Ernest Kaiser, and J. H. O'Dell (Boston: Beacon Press, 1970), 178–180.

29. King, *Where Do We Go from Here,* 71.

30. This is not to say that King abandons the phrase. In his last public address before his assassination, King reuses the wording from "Letter from Birmingham City Jail," in which he praises the student sit-in demonstrators for "carrying our whole nation back to those great wells of democracy which were dug deep by the Founding Fathers." My point, instead, is that the historical story he tells in *Where Do We Go from Here* fundamentally contests the veneration of the past and of the Founding Fathers. When he returns to the wells, then, it is less clear what they can provide. Compare "Letter from Birmingham City Jail" with "I See the Promised Land," in *Testament of Hope,* 302 and 286, respectively.

31. King, *Where Do We Go from Here,* 84.

32. Ibid., 83–84.

33. Saidiya V. Hartman, *Scenes of Subjection: Terror, Slavery, and Self-Making in Nineteenth-Century America* (Oxford: Oxford University Press, 1997), 119.

34. Compare King, "Letter from Birmingham City Jail," 297–298.

35. W. E. B. Du Bois, *The Suppression of the African Slave-Trade to the United States of America, 1638–1870* (Mineola, NY: Dover, 1970), 195.

36. Salamishah Tillet, *Sites of Slavery: Citizenship and Racial Democracy in the Post-Civil Rights Imagination* (Durham, NC: Duke University Press, 2012), 16.

37. King, *Stride toward Freedom,* 182.

38. Ibid., 221.

39. Ibid., 190, 220.

40. King, *Where Do We Go from Here*, 177.

41. David Scott, *Conscripts of Modernity: The Tragedy of Colonial Enlightenment* (Durham, NC: Duke University Press, 2004).

42. In the introduction to the Beacon Press edition of *Where Do We Go from Here* (p. xx), Vincent Harding notes that King asked him to write the first draft of that statement; but he does not indicate whether he drew on King's manuscript or supplied some of the language that appears in *Where Do We Go from Here*.

43. See also Nikhil Singh, *Black Is a Country: Race and the Unfinished Struggle for Democracy* (Cambridge, MA: Harvard University Press, 2004).

44. King, *Trumpet of Conscience*, 77–80.

12. The Costs of Violence: Militarism, Geopolitics, and Accountability

I would like to thank Tommie Shelby for helpful guidance and comments.

1. Barack Obama, "Remarks by the President at Acceptance of the Nobel Peace Prize," White House, December 10, 2009, https://geneva.usmission.gov/2009/12/11/nobel-peace-prize/.

2. Barack Obama, "Remarks by the President at the United States Military Academy Commencement Ceremony," White House, May 28, 2014, https://obamawhitehouse.archives.gov/the-press-office/2014/05/28/remarks-president-united-states-military-academy-commencement-ceremony. Contrary to the implied history, for instance, the United States obstructed UN intervention to stop the Rwandan genocide of 1994; see, e.g., Alison Des Forges, *"Leave None to Tell the Story": Genocide in Rwanda* (New York: Human Rights Watch, 1999).

3. Barack Obama, "Remarks by the President in Address to the Nation of Syria," White House, September 10, 2013, https://obamawhitehouse.archives.gov/the-press-office/2013/09/10/remarks-president-address-nation-syria.

4. Barack Obama and Shinzo Abe, "Remarks by President Obama and Prime Minister Abe of Japan at Hiroshima Peace Memorial," White House, May 27, 2016, https://obamawhitehouse.archives.gov/the-press-office/2016/05/27/remarks-president-obama-and-prime-minister-abe-japan-hiroshima-peace.

5. William J. Broad, "Reduction of Nuclear Arsenal Has Slowed under Obama, Report Finds," *New York Times*, May 26, 2016, http://www.nytimes.com/2016/05/27/science/nuclear-weapons-obama-united-states.html.

6. Martin Luther King, Jr., *Where Do We Go from Here: Chaos or Community?* (Boston: Beacon Press, 2010), 35.

7. Barack Obama, "Statement by the President on the Death of Taliban Leader Mansur," White House, May 23, 2016, https://obamawhitehouse.archives.gov/the-press-office/2016/05/23/statement-president-death-taliban-leader-mansur.

8. Barack Obama, "Remarks by the President on Osama Bin Laden," White House, May 2, 2011, https://obamawhitehouse.archives.gov/the-press-office/2011/05/02/remarks-president-osama-bin-laden.

9. Andrew J. Bacevich, "After 15 Years of 'Milestones,' War in the Middle East Still Has No End in Sight," *Nation,* May 31, 2016, http://www.thenation.com /article/after-15-years-of-milestones-war-in-the-middle-east-still-has-no-end-in-sight/.

10. See, e.g., Osama bin Laden, "The Towers of Lebanon," in *Messages to the World: The Statements of Osama Bin Laden,* ed. and intro. Bruce Lawrence, trans. James Howarth (London: Verso, 2005), 241.

11. Obama, "Military Academy Commencement Ceremony."

12. Jeremy Scahill, "The Assassination Complex: Secret Military Documents Expose the Inner Workings of Obama's Drone Wars," *Intercept,* October 15, 2015, https://theintercept.com/drone-papers/the-assassination-complex/.

13. "Dr. King's Error," *New York Times,* April 7, 1967, 36, http://kingencyclopedia. stanford.edu/kingweb/liberation_curriculum/pdfs/vietnameditorials.pdf.

14. See, e.g., Kimberly J. Morgan, "America's Misguided Approach to Social Welfare: How the Country Could Get More for Less," *Foreign Affairs,* January/February 2013, https://www.foreignaffairs.com/articles/united-states/2012-12-03/americas -misguided-approach-social-welfare; and Milton Friedman, "The Goldwater View of Economics," *New York Times Magazine,* October 11, 1964, http://0055d26.netsolhost .com/friedman/pdfs/nyt/NYT.10.11.1964.pdf.

15. Martin Luther King, Jr. "Beyond Vietnam: A Time to Break Silence," in *"In a Single Garment of Destiny": A Global Vision of Justice,* ed. and intro. Lewis V. Baldwin, foreword by Charlayne Hunter-Gault (Boston: Beacon Press, 2012), 166.

16. Dwight D. Eisenhower, "Farewell Address," White House, January 17, 1961, https://www.eisenhower.archives.gov/research/online_documents/farewell_address /1961_01_17_Press_Release.pdf.

17. *Credit Suisse Global Wealth Databook, 2015* (Zurich: Credit Suisse, 2015), 110, http://publications.credit-suisse.com/tasks/render/file/index.cfm?fileid=C26E3824 -E868-56E0-CCA04D4BB9B9ADD5 (accessed June 6, 2016).

18. Ibid., 38, 25, 27, https://publications.credit-suisse.com/tasks/render/file/?fileID =F2425415-DCA7-80B8-EAD989AF9341D47E (accessed June 6, 2016).

19. "Children of the Recession: The Impact of the Economic Crisis on Child Well-Being in Rich Countries," *UNICEF Innocenti Report Card 12* (Florence: UNICEF Office of Research, 2014), 12, https://www.unicef-irc.org/publications/pdf /rc12-eng-web.pdf (accessed June 6, 2016).

20. See Sam Perlo-Freeman et al., "Trends in World Military Expenditure, 2015," Stockholm International Peace Research Institute (SIPRI) Fact Sheet, April 2016, 2, http://books.sipri.org/files/FS/SIPRIFS1604.pdf (accessed June 6, 2016).

21. "Federal Spending: Where Does the Money Go," National Priorities Project, https://www.nationalpriorities.org/budget-basics/federal-budget-101/spending /(accessed June 2, 2016).

22. Brock Vergakis, "Navy Abandons 'Global Force for Good' to Broaden Appeal," *Salon,* January 31, 2015, http://www.salon.com/2015/01/31/navy_abandons _global_force_for_good_to_broaden_appeal/.

23. Obama, "Acceptance of the Nobel Peace Prize."

24. George W. Bush, "President Sworn-In to Second Term: Inauguration 2005," White House, January 20, 2005, https://georgewbush-whitehouse.archives.gov/news/releases/2005/01/20050120-1.html.

25. G. E. M. Anscombe, "War and Murder," in *Ethics, Religion, and Politics* (Minneapolis: University of Minnesota Press, 1981), 57.

26. Martin Luther King, Jr., "Racism and the World House," in *"Garment of Destiny,"* 48.

27. Ibid., 50.

28. See, e.g., Robert L. Holmes, "Pacifism for Nonpacifists," *Journal of Social Philosophy* 30, no. 3 (1999): 387–400.

29. Martin Luther King, Jr., "Address at the Thirty-Sixth Annual Dinner of the War Resisters League," in *"Garment of Destiny,"* 141–142.

30. Martin Luther King, Jr., "The Greatest Hope for World Peace," in *"Garment of Destiny,"* 146.

31. For a traditionalist treatment of just war theory, see, e.g., Michael Walzer, *Just and Unjust Wars: A Moral Argument with Historical Illustrations,* 3rd ed. (New York: Basic Books, 1977). The tradition defends a strict distinction between just cause and just means. Absolute pacifists recognize no such distinction: they rule out the use of violence, period.

32. King, "World Peace," 148. See also King, "War and the World House," in *"Garment of Destiny,"* 186.

33. King, "War Resisters League," 142–144.

34. Ibid., 141.

35. Judith M. Brown, introduction to *Mahatma Gandhi: The Essential Writings,* new ed., ed. and intro. Judith M. Brown (New York: Oxford University Press, 2008), xxxi.

36. Mahatma Gandhi, "Essentials of *Satyagraha,*" in ibid., 326.

37. Mahatma Gandhi, *"Satyagraha*—not 'passive resistance'" in Brown, *Mahatma Gandhi,* 315–316; also in that volume, Gandhi, "Instructions for *Satyagrahis,*" 331.

38. M. K. Gandhi, "The Doctrine of the Sword," in *Non-Violent Resistance (Satyagraha)* (New York: Schocken Books, 1961; repr., Mineola, NY: Dover, 2001), 132–133.

39. Nelson Mandela, "I Am Prepared to Die," in *Mandela, Tambo, and the African National Congress: The Struggle against Apartheid, 1948–1990; A Documentary Survey,* ed. Sheridan Johns and R. Hunt Davis, Jr. (New York: Oxford University Press, 1991), 120.

40. Ibid.

41. Mahatma Gandhi, "Timing and Tactics," in Brown, *Mahatma Gandhi,* 342.

42. See Tom Lodge, *Sharpeville: An Apartheid Massacre and Its Consequences* (New York: Oxford University Press, 2011).

43. Mahatma Gandhi, "Looking Back on the Indian Struggle in South Africa," in Brown, *Mahatma Gandhi,* 310.

44. King, "Beyond Vietnam," 169.

45. *Congressional Record,* 89th Cong., 2nd sess., 1966, 112, pt. 20, 27523–27525.

46. See, e.g., Daniel Ellsberg, "Lying about Vietnam," *New York Times,* June 29, 2001, http://www.nytimes.com/2001/06/29/opinion/lying-about-vietnam.html.

47. On the U.S. military's attachment to the use of "night raids" in Afghanistan, see Paul Joseph, *"Soft" Counterinsurgency: Human Terrain Teams and US Military Strategy in Iraq and Afghanistan* (New York: Palgrave Macmillan, 2014), 88–89.

48. "In 1966 . . . four-in-ten (41.8%) of African-Americans were poor; blacks constituted nearly a third (31.1%) of all poor Americans. By 2012, poverty among African-Americans had fallen to 27.2%—still more than double the rate among whites (12.7%, 1.4 percentage points higher than in 1966)." Drew DeSilver, "Who's Poor in America? 50 Years into the 'War on Poverty,' a Data Portrait," *Fact Tank,* Pew Research Center, January 13, 2014, http://www.pewresearch.org/fact-tank/2014 /01/13/whos-poor-in-america-50-years-into-the-war-on-poverty-a-data-portrait /(accessed June 15, 2016).

49. "Blacks suffered . . . 12.6% of the total deaths of U.S. military personnel. . . . Since African Americans comprised, on average, about 9.3 percent of the total active duty personnel assigned to Vietnam, the death rate for blacks was roughly 30 percent higher than the death rate for U.S. forces. . . . The problem was that African Americans tended to be concentrated in combat, as opposed to support, units and thus were far more likely to see fighting." James E. Westheider, *Fighting on Two Fronts: African Americans and the Vietnam War* (New York: NYU Press, 1977), 13.

50. King, "Beyond Vietnam," 166.

51. Ibid., 177.

52. King, "The Middle East Question," in *"Garment of Destiny,"* 182 (italics in the original).

53. King, "The Casualties of the War in Vietnam," in *"Garment of Destiny,"* 155.

13. THE PATH OF CONSCIENTIOUS CITIZENSHIP

1. Martin Luther King, Jr., "A Time to Break Silence" (1967), in *A Testament of Hope: The Essential Writings and Speeches of Martin Luther King, Jr.,* ed. James M. Washington (New York: Harper Collins, 1991), 231–244.

2. Ibid., 232.

3. Ibid.

4. King, "Letter from Birmingham City Jail," in *A Testament of Hope,* 290.

5. Martin Luther King, Jr., *Stride toward Freedom: The Montgomery Story* (Boston: Beacon Press, 2010), 184.

6. King, "A Time to Break Silence," 232.

7. Ibid., 242.

8. For the connections between King's and Royce's views, see Gary Herstein, "The Roycean Roots of the Beloved Community," *Pluralist* 4, no. 2 (2009): 91–107. See also Rufus Burrow, Jr., "The Beloved Community: Martin Luther King, Jr. and Josiah Royce," *Encounter* 73, no. 1 (2012): 37–64.

9. To the extent that King came to describe himself as a "citizen of the world" (as he did in "A Time to Break Silence," 238), we might see his stance on such issues as nuclear nonproliferation as evidence that thought he had an absolute duty to resist injustice anywhere in the world. Yet he did not seem to think that this concept of world citizenship had much moral or political purchase more broadly.

10. King, "The Birth of a New Nation," sermon delivered at Dexter Avenue Baptist Church (April 7, 1957), 162–163, available at http://okra.stanford.edu /transcription/document_images/Vol04Scans/155_7-Apr-1957_THhe%20Birth%20 of%20a%20New%20Nation.pdf.

11. Martin Luther King, Jr., *The Trumpet of Conscience* (Boston: Beacon Press, 2010), 47–48.

12. Herbert J. Storing, "The Case Against Civil Disobedience," in *Civil Disobedience in Focus,* ed. Hugo Adam Bedau (New York: Routledge, 1991), 85–102, esp. 86, 87. In fairness, it must be noted that Storing's essay was published before John Rawls's account of civil disobedience as a potentially justifiable corrective for injustice in conditions of "partial compliance" in a liberal democracy.

13. Martin Luther King, Jr., *Why We Can't Wait* (Boston: Beacon Press, 2010), 156.

14. John Rawls, *A Theory of Justice* (Cambridge, MA: Belknap Press of Harvard University Press, 1971), 335–337.

15. King writes of "the true meaning of the Montgomery story" in *Stride toward Freedom,* 190; and "the true meaning of the struggle" in "Address before the National Press Club," in *A Testament of Hope,* 101.

16. King, *Stride toward Freedom,* 190.

17. King, "A Time to Break Silence," 241.

18. Cornel West has offered an especially rich account of King's status as an organic intellectual in his essay "Martin Luther King, Jr.: Prophetic Christian as Organic Intellectual," in *Prophetic Fragments: Illumination of the Crises in American Religion and Culture* (Grand Rapids, MI: Eerdmans, 1988), 3.

19. King, *Stride toward Freedom,* 84.

20. Ibid., chaps. 3, 9, and 11, esp. 212–214.

21. Ibid., 212.

22. Ibid., 214.

23. One notable passage says "ultimate" rather than "beloved" (ibid., 214).

24. Ibid., 199.

25. This is a consistent challenge of King interpretation across a range of topics.

26. I have benefited from reading Robert Michael Franklin, "In Pursuit of a Just Society: Martin Luther King, Jr., and John Rawls," *Journal of Religious Ethics* (1990): 57–77.

27. King, "Letter from Birmingham City Jail," 294.

28. Franklin, "In Pursuit," 60.

29. Martin Luther King, Jr., *Where Do We Go from Here: Chaos or Community?* (Boston: Beacon Press, 2010), 197.

30. Ibid., 198.

31. King, "Pilgrimage to Nonviolence," in *A Testament of Hope,* 36.

32. Ibid., 38.

33. See Mahatma Gandhi and Dennis Dalto, *Gandhi: Selected Political Writings* (Cambridge, MA: Hackett, 1996), 50–57, 122, 143.

34. See King, *Strength to Love* (Minneapolis: Fortress Press, 2010).

35. King, "Suffering and Faith," in *A Testament of Hope,* 41; see also *Stride toward Freedom,* 179.

36. King, "Birth of a New Nation," 165.

37. See esp. King, *Strength to Love,* 92; but see also "A Testament of Hope," in *A Testament of Hope,* 327–328.

38. King, "The Power of Nonviolence," in *A Testament of Hope,* 13–14.

39. Frantz Fanon, The *Wretched of the Earth,* trans. Richard Philcox (New York: Grove Press, 2004), 23. See also Kathryn T. Gines, "Martin Luther King Jr. and Frantz Fanon: Reflections on the Politics and Ethics of Violence and Nonviolence," in *The Liberatory Thought of Martin Luther King Jr.: Critical Essays on the Philosopher King,* ed. Robert E. Birt (Lanham, MD: Lexington Books, 2012), 249–250.

40. King, *Stride toward Freedom,* 86.

41. This quote is attributed to Carmichael in Karen Grigsby Bates, "Stokely Carmichael: A Philosopher behind the Black Power Movement," *NPR,* March 10, 2014, http://www.npr.org/sections/codeswitch/2014/03/10/287320160/stokely-carmichael -a-philosopher-behind-the-black-power-movement.

42. King, "My Trip to the Land of Gandhi," in *A Testament of Hope,* 26.

43. King, *Where Do We Go from Here,* 33–36.

44. King, *Stride toward Freedom,* 39.

45. Ibid.

46. The view to which I refer is set forth in Iris Marion Young, *Responsibility for Justice* (Oxford: Oxford University Press, 2010).

47. See, for instance, Frederick Douglass, "Why Should a Colored Man Enlist?," *Douglass' Monthly,* April 1863, http://www.frederick-douglass-heritage.org/why -should-a-colored-man-enlist/.

48. King, *Stride toward Freedom,* 212.

49. Ibid., 213, 215, 220.

50. I discuss this fiction, and the way in which Homer Plessy's lawyer sought to combat that fiction during his arguments before the Supreme Court, in Michele Moody-Adams, "The Legacy of *Plessy v. Ferguson*" in *A Companion to African-American Philosophy,* ed. Tommy L. Lott and John P. Pittman (Malden, MA: Blackwell, 2006). For an especially detailed account of the nature of the opposition to crafting the Civil Rights Act of 1964, see Todd S. Purdum, *An Idea Whose Time Has Come: Two Presidents, Two Parties, and the Battle for the Civil Rights Act of 1964* (New York: Henry Holt, 2014).

51. King, "Letter from Birmingham City Jail," 292–293.

52. See Michele Moody-Adams, "Culture, Responsibility, and Affected Ignorance," *Ethics* 104, no. 2 (1994): 291–309.

53. Bruce Ackerman, *We the People*, vol. 3, *The Civil Rights Revolution* (Cambridge, MA: Harvard University Press, 2014), 79–89.

54. John Dewey, *Art as Experience* (New York: Penguin, 2005). See also Michele Moody-Adams, "Moral Progress and Human Agency," *Ethical Theory and Moral Practice* (2016): 1–16.

55. See Sharon Ann Musher, *Democratic Art: The New Deal's Influence on American Culture* (Chicago: University of Chicago Press, 2015), 130–145, for an especially enlightening account of the New Deal photography project.

56. See Greg Moses, *Revolution of Conscience: Martin Luther King, Jr., and the Philosophy of Nonviolence* (New York: Guilford Press, 1998).

57. King's willingness to articulate this overlap in values anticipates Rawls's demand (in, for instance, *Political Liberalism*) that arguments drawing on the values of a "comprehensive conception" must be capable of eventually being stated in terms of publicly accessible reasons. See John Rawls, *Political Liberalism* (New York: Columbia University Press, 2005).

58. Aldon D. Morris, *The Origins of the Civil Rights Movement: Black Communities Organizing for Change* (New York: Simon and Schuster, 1986); see also Aldon Morris, "Reflections on Social Movement Theory: Criticisms and Proposals," *Contemporary Sociology* 29, no. 3 (2000): 445–454.

59. Rawls, *A Theory of Justice*, 335–337.

60. King, *Stride toward Freedom*, 190.

61. James Q. Wilson, "The Strategy of Protest: Problems of Negro Civic Action," *Journal of Conflict Resolution* 5, no. 3 (1961): 291–292.

62. Michael Lipsky, "Protest as a Political Resource," *American Political Science Review* 62, no. 4 (1968): 1144–1158.

63. It also failed to provide a framework for thinking about the successes of the civil rights movement, successes that would later come to be seen by social movement theory in several disciplines as a virtual blueprint for activism by other social groups—from the women's movement to the movements for gay and lesbian rights. See Morris, *The Origins of the Civil Rights Movement*, 288–289.

64. Bayard Rustin, "From Protest to Politics: The Future of the Civil Rights Movement," *Commentary* 39, no. 2 (1965): 62.

65. Ibid., 61.

66. King, "Showdown for Nonviolence," in *A Testament of Hope*, 69.

67. Stokely Carmichael, "Toward Black Liberation," *Massachusetts Review* 7, no. 4 (1966): 646.

68. King, *Where Do We Go from Here*, 44–45, 133.

69. Ibid., 45.

70. King, "Showdown for Nonviolence," 69, 72.

71. King, *Where Do We Go from Here*, 19.

72. See King's last SCLC Presidential Address (1968), "Where Do We Go from Here?," in *A Testament of Hope*, esp. 247.

73. See King, "The American Dream," in *A Testament of Hope*, 208–216.

74. John Dewey, "Creative Democracy: The Task before Us," in *The Later Works of John Dewey*, ed. J. A. Boydston, vol. 14 (Carbondale: Southern Illinois University Press, 2008).

14. REQUIEM FOR A DREAM

I would like to thank Alex Gourevitch, Destin Jenkins, John Marshall, Aziz Rana, Tyler Jankauskas, Tommie Shelby, Jovanna Jones, Forrest Hylton, Jaime Cobham, and the participants at the Radcliffe Institute Seminar on the Political Philosophy of Martin Luther King, Jr., the Johns Hopkins Political and Moral Thought Seminar, and the Washington University in St. Louis Political Theory Workshop for their comments and suggestions.

1. James Meredith, quoted in "Mississippi Story," *New York Times*, June 12, 1966. This account of the March Against Fear draws primarily from Taylor Branch, *At Canaan's Edge: America in the King Years, 1965–1968* (New York: Simon and Schuster, 2006), chaps. 28–29; David J. Garrow, *Bearing the Cross: Martin Luther King, Jr. and the Southern Christian Leadership Conference* (New York: William Morrow, 1986), chaps. 8–9; Stokely Carmichael with Ekwueme Michael Thelwell, *Ready for Revolution: The Life and Struggles of Stokely Carmichael (Kwame Ture)* (New York: Scribner, 2003), chaps. 21–22; and Peniel Joseph, *Stokely: A Life* (New York: Basic Civitas, 2014), chap. 8.

2. As the march neared its completion in Jackson, these organizations would offer more qualified support, but the 1966 civil rights bill would be successfully defeated by filibuster in Congress. Particularly fatal was the opposition to its open housing and fair jury selection provisions. See Nick Kotz, *Judgment Days: Lyndon Johnson, Martin Luther King, Jr., and the Laws That Changed America* (New York: Houghton Mifflin Harcourt, 2006), 368.

3. "Mississippi Story." It is important to note, however, that disagreement does not equal enmity. As Carmichael would later reflect, "The fondest memories I have of Dr. King came from that march. . . . During those sweltering Delta days Dr. King became to many of us no longer a symbol or an icon, but a warm, funny, likable, unpretentious human being who shared many of our values." Carmichael and Thelwell, *Ready for Revolution*, 505, 509–510.

4. As quoted in Branch, *At Canaan's Edge*, 486.

5. Joseph, *Stokely*, 115.

6. Carmichael did not invent the phrase "Black Power," although he did popularize its use. Occasionally it is argued that its earliest use comes from Frederick Douglass, in an 1855 speech entitled "The Doom of the Black Power." Douglass did deploy the phrase, but his meaning was essentially the opposite of its present connotations. For him it was a synonym for "The Slave Power," that alliance of political interests aligned with the maintenance of slavery, and he used the latter term more regularly. The earliest use of any kind that I have been able to find is not Douglass, but an invidious description of postrevolutionary Haiti in a screed against West

Indian emancipation by the British polemicist and publisher William Cobbett in his weekly *Political Register*. Most accounts of its origin highlight the famed novelist Richard Wright's use of the term to describe the early phase of African independence in 1954 and its mention by the controversial Harlem politician Adam Clayton Powell in early 1966 to describe black political demands. Lost in this familiar genealogy is arguably the more directly influential use by Carmichael ally and journalist Lerone Bennett, Jr., who used the phrase "Black Power" as the title for a series of 1965 essays, published in *Ebony*, on black political empowerment during Reconstruction. See Frederick Douglass, "The Doom of the Black Power," in *The Portable Frederick Douglass*, ed. Henry Louis Gates, Jr., and John Stauffer (New York: Penguin, 2016), 441–447; "Mentor, on the Slave Trade (January 31, 1807)," *Cobbett's Political Register* 11 (January–June 1807): 187; Richard Wright, *Black Power: Three Books from Exile: Black Power, The Color Curtain, and White Man Listen!* (New York: Harper-Collins, 2010); on Powell, see Cedric Johnson, *Revolutionaries to Race Leaders* (Minneapolis: University of Minnesota Press, 2007), 57–58. For Lerone Bennett, Jr., see his "Black Power, Part One," *Ebony*, November 1965, 28–48.

7. Kenneth B. Clark, "Social Power and Social Change in America: An Address," in *Social Power and Social Change in Contemporary America* (Washington, DC: Equal Employment Opportunity Program, 1966), 8. On the concept of a black counterpublic, and historical accounts that elaborate upon this judgment, see Michael C. Dawson, *Black Visions: The Roots of Contemporary African-American Political Ideologies* (Chicago: University of Chicago Press, 2001), esp. chaps. 1, 3, and 5; and Michael C. Dawson, *Blacks In and Out of the Left* (Cambridge, MA: Harvard University Press, 2013), chap. 2.

8. Johnson, *Revolutionaries to Race Leaders*, xxxiv. For representative narratives, see Todd Gitlin, *The Twilight of Common Dreams: Why America Is Wracked by Culture Wars* (New York: Henry Holt, 1996); Richard Rorty, *Achieving Our Country: Leftist Thought in Twentieth-Century America* (Cambridge, MA: Harvard University Press, 1999); for critiques of this account, see Dawson, *Blacks In and Out of the Left*, esp. chap. 3.

9. For criticisms of attempts to treat Black Power as a *northern* phenomenon alone, see Hasan Kwame Jeffries, *Bloody Lowndes: Civil Rights and Black Power in Alabama's Black Belt* (New York: NYU Press, 2010); for a critique of attempts to treat black militancy as psychopathology, see Jonathan M. Metzl, *The Protest Psychosis: How Schizophrenia Became a Black Disease* (Boston: Beacon Press, 2010); and for a critique of attempts to obscure the overlapping generations involved in the movement, see Peniel E. Joseph, *Waiting 'til the Midnight Hour: A Narrative History of Black Power in America* (New York: Henry Holt, 2007).

10. Martin Luther King, Jr., *Where Do We Go from Here: Chaos or Community?* (Boston: Beacon Press, 2010), 33.

11. For critical, thoughtful accounts of this legacy, see Tommie Shelby, *We Who Are Dark: The Philosophical Foundations of Black Solidarity* (Cambridge, MA: Belknap Press of Harvard University Press, 2005); Adolph Reed, Jr., *Stirrings in the Jug: Black Politics in the Post-Segregation Era* (Minneapolis: University of Minne-

sota Press, 1999); Johnson, *Revolutionaries to Race Leaders;* and the essays in Eddie Glaude, Jr., ed., *It's Nation Time: Contemporary Essays on Black Power and Black Nationalism* (Chicago: University of Chicago Press, 2002).

12. John Rawls, *Lectures on the History of Political Philosophy,* ed. Samuel Freeman (Cambridge, MA: Harvard University Press, 2009), 11; Gareth Steadman Jones, *Greatness and Illusion* (Cambridge, MA: Harvard University Press, 2016), esp. chaps. 5–9.

13. Nikolas Kompridis, *Critique and Disclosure: Critical Theory between Past and Future* (Cambridge, MA: MIT Press, 2006), chaps. 1, 5.

14. See, for example, Karl Marx, "On the Jewish Question," in *Selected Writings,* 2nd ed., ed. David McLellan (New York: Oxford University Press, 2000), 46–70; Philip Pettit, *Just Freedom: A Moral Compass for a Complex World* (New York: Norton, 2014); Axel Honneth, *The Struggle for Recognition: The Moral Grammar of Social Conflicts* (Cambridge, MA: MIT Press, 1996); and Carl Schmitt, *The Concept of the Political,* trans. George Schwab (Chicago: University of Chicago Press, 2007).

15. David Scott, *Conscripts of Modernity: The Tragedy of Colonial Enlightenment* (New York: Columbia University Press, 2004), 4 (emphasis added).

16. I think properly understood, Scott—in following Quentin Skinner—is ultimately committed to the notion that it is reckless to think that we can expect particular beliefs, judgments, or claims to flow inexorably from the inspection of purportedly brute facts. These are always mediated through the concepts, vocabularies, theories, and purposes that we have available—making, of course, sufficient allowances for semantic, conceptual, and theoretical innovation and imagination. It strikes me that a logical consequence of Scott's formulation is that even *claiming* that there exists a division between the "colonial" and "postcolonial" is a result of an entire scaffolding of interpretative judgments and conceptual commitments that could be (and often are) challenged *precisely through the sort of competing narratives he is most invested in reconstructing.* This is not to say that we have no evaluative criteria by which to judge interpretations of evidence and experience (perspicacity, purposefulness, ethics, politics, truth value). Nor is it to deny that mind-independent reality can resist our judgments and theories, and the purposes that underlie them, and compel us in frustration to rethink their content. It is simply to insist on the much more prosaic point that the semantic/discursive shifts that Scott aims to track with the notion of "problem-space" cannot be so tightly tethered to changes in historical "facticity" that we inevitably expect particular formulations to emerge from particular events or processes. After all, such happenings themselves must be described and narrated through contentious practices. For Skinner's endorsement of the position above, see Quentin Skinner, *Visons of Politics,* vol. 1, *Regarding Method* (New York: Cambridge University Press, 2002), 8–57.

17. See, for example, Martin Luther King, Jr., *Stride toward Freedom: The Montgomery Story* (Boston: Beacon Press, 2010), 184, 220. On "creative minorities" as a source of redemption and rejuvenation in declining societies generally, and African Americans as possibly becoming such a group through the achievements of African

American Christianity, see Arnold J. Toynbee, *A Study of History: Abridged Edition of Volumes 1–6,* ed. D. C. Somerwell (New York: Oxford University Press, 1947), 129, 230–240. Despite the resonance of Toynbee's remarks on African Americans with Du Bois's early work on the spiritual "gifts" of black folk, Du Bois did not think very highly of Toynbee's work, charging him with "naïve, religious bias" that prevented him "from being a real scientist," and a myopic race prejudice that led him to deny the cultural achievements of Africans. W. E. B. Du Bois, "Letter to Isabel Aiken, March 21, 1949," W. E. B. Du Bois Papers (MS 312), Special Collections and University Archives, University of Massachusetts Amherst Libraries. Also see W. E. B. Du Bois, *The World and Africa/Color and Democracy* (New York: Oxford University Press, 2007), 63, 116.

18. Martin Luther King, Jr., "*Playboy* Interview" (1965), in *A Testament of Hope: The Essential Writings and Speeches of Martin Luther King, Jr.,* ed. James Washington (New York: HarperCollins, 1991), 364 (emphasis added). The Hegelian resonances of these passages are clear. On King's self-identification with Hegelian themes, see Martin Luther King, Jr., *Strength to Love* (Minneapolis: Fortress Press, 2010), 1.

19. I have in mind two sets of texts. First, the texts that precede the Black Power era, but that are tremendously influential: Robert F. Williams, *Negroes with Guns* (Detroit: Wayne State University Press, 1998); Malcolm X with Alex Haley, *The Autobiography of Malcolm X* (New York: Grove Press, 1965); Malcolm X, *Malcolm X Speaks: Selected Speeches and Statements,* ed. George Breitman (New York: Grove Press, 1965); Frantz Fanon, *The Wretched of the Earth,* trans. Richard Philcox (New York: Grove Press, 2007); Fanon, *Black Skin/White Masks,* ed. Richard Philcox (New York: Grove Press, 2008); Harold Cruse, *The Crisis of the Negro Intellectual: A Historical Analysis of the Failure of Black Leadership* (New York: Morrow, 1967); and Mao Zedong, *Quotations from Chairman Mao Tse-Tung* (repr., San Francisco: China Books, 1990). Second, those that are the most influential and/or important distillations of Black Power militants from the late 1960s and early 1970s, including, but not limited to, Stokely Carmichael (Kwame Ture) and Charles Hamilton, *Black Power: The Politics of Liberation* (New York: Vintage, 1992); Eldridge Cleaver, *Soul on Ice* (New York: McGraw Hill, 1967); Huey Newton's writings and speeches collected in *The Huey P. Newton Reader,* ed. David Hilliard and Donald Weise (New York: Seven Stories Press, 2002); Floyd Barbour, ed., *The Black Power Revolt* (Boston: Extending Horizons Books, 1968); Amiri Baraka, *Raise Race Rays Raze: Essays since 1965* (New York: Random House, 1971); and Angela Y. Davis, ed., *If They Come in the Morning: Voices of Resistance* (New York: Third Press, 1971).

20. Given the expansive literature on the emergence of "black theology" as, in part, a critical response to King's interpretation of African American Christianity, I do not broach this particular topic here.

21. In drawing these distinctions, I take inspiration from Cruse, *The Crisis of the Negro Intellectual,* 347–381.

22. Williams, *Negroes with Guns,* 14.

23. Robert F. Williams, quoted in Timothy B. Tyson, introduction, in Williams, *Negroes with Guns,* xv.

24. See King's essay "Pilgrimage to Nonviolence" in *Strength to Love.*

25. King, "The Social Organization of Nonviolence" (1958), in *A Testament of Hope,* 33.

26. Williams, *Negroes with Guns,* 50–51.

27. Ibid., 3–4.

28. King, "Social Organization of Nonviolence," 32.

29. King, *Where Do We Go from Here,* 27.

30. Lance Hill, *The Deacons for Defense: Armed Resistance and the Civil Rights Movement* (Chapel Hill: University of North Carolina Press, 2004), 58.

31. King, *Where Do We Go from Here,* 27 (emphasis added).

32. Shatema Threadcraft and I address this problem of manhood and self-defense in Chapter 10.

33. Williams, *Negroes with Guns,* 26, 31, 4.

34. Ibid., 5, 70–71.

35. Ibid., 5.

36. Ibid.

37. King, *Strength to Love,* 7, 47.

38. Ibid., 124–125. See E. Franklin Frazier, "The Pathology of Race Prejudice," *Forum,* June 1927, 856–861.

39. King, *Where Do We Go from Here,* 62; King, *Strength to Love,* 125.

40. For a similar view, see Danielle S. Allen, *Talking to Strangers: Anxieties of Citizenship Since Brown v. Board of Education* (Chicago: University of Chicago Press, 2004).

41. King, *Where Do We Go from Here,* 57–58.

42. Williams, *Negroes with Guns,* 44–45, 50–51.

43. Ibid., 51–53.

44. Timothy Tyson, *Radio Free Dixie: Robert F. Williams and the Roots of Black Power* (Chapel Hill: University of North Carolina Press, 2009), 299–304.

45. King, *Strength to Love,* 7.

46. James Boggs, "Foreword to Monroe, North Carolina . . . Turning Point in American History," in *Pages from a Black Radical's Notebook: A James Boggs Reader,* ed. Stephen M. Ward (Detroit: Wayne State University Press, 2011), 72. For King on states' rights, see his "Speech to the Freedom Riders (May 21, 1961)," King Center Digital Archive, http://www.thekingcenter.org/archive/document/speech-freedom-riders.

47. Hill, *Deacons for Defense,* 75, 124, 157, 195.

48. Martin Luther King, Jr., "Address at the Fiftieth Annual NAACP Convention (July 17, 1959)," in *The Papers of Martin Luther King, Jr.,* vol. 5, *Threshold of a New Decade,* ed. Clayborne Carson (Berkeley: University of California Press, 2005), 248.

49. King, *Strength to Love,* 21–52.

50. Ibid., 1, 4–5, also 108.

51. See Mary Dudziak, *Cold War Civil Rights: Race and the Image of American Democracy* (Princeton, NJ: Princeton University Press, 2000); Thomas Borstelmann,

The Cold War and the Color Line: American Race Relations in the Global Arena (Cambridge, MA: Harvard University Press, 2001); Derrick Bell, Jr., *Silent Covenants: Brown v. Board of Education and the Unfulfilled Hopes for Racial Reform* (New York: Oxford University, 2004), chap. 6.

52. King, *Where Do We Go from Here*, 200–201 (emphasis added).

53. K. Anthony Appiah, *The Honor Code: How Moral Revolutions Happen* (New York: Norton, 2010).

54. King, *Stride toward Freedom*, 212.

55. Although he does not draw out this connection, Christopher J. Lebron approaches the question of racial injustice in a similar fashion in *The Color of Our Shame: Race and Justice in Our Time* (New York: Oxford University Press, 2013).

56. Martin Luther King, Jr., "The Unresolved Race Question," in *"All Labor Has Dignity,"* ed. Michael K. Honey (Boston: Beacon Press, 2011), 95.

57. This account is indebted to Michael E. Latham, "The Cold War in the Third World, 1963–1975," in *The Cambridge History of the Cold War*, vol. 2, *Crises and Détente*, ed. Melvyn P. Leffler and Odd Arne Westad (New York: Cambridge University Press, 2010), 258–280.

58. J. Dana Stuster, "Mapped: The 7 Governments the U.S. Has Overthrown," *Foreign Policy*, August 20, 2013, http://foreignpolicy.com/2013/08/20/mapped-the-7-governments-the-u-s-has-overthrown/.

59. See, for example, the nearly uniformly disparaging coverage of American foreign policy in the newspaper *The Black Panther*.

60. Carmichael and Hamilton, *Black Power*, xvii, xix. On political peoplehood as entailing competing conceptions of political and ethical obligation, see Rogers Smith, *Stories of Peoplehood: The Politics and Morals of Political Membership* (New York: Cambridge University Press, 2003). Toward the end of his life, King would more forthrightly foreground his critique of neo-imperialism and militarism abroad, explicitly tying it to the failure of social justice at home. See Chapter 12, by Lionel McPherson.

61. Taylor Branch, *At Canaan's Edge*, 767; *Report of the National Advisory Commission on Civil Disorders* (New York: Bantam Books, 1968), 6.

62. Martin Luther King, Jr., *The Autobiography of Martin Luther King, Jr.*, ed. Clayborne Carson (New York: Grand Central, 2001), 296.

63. The Kerner Commission report, for example, has a section titled "Revolution of Rising Expectations," where nonviolent direct action figures largely; see *Report of the National Advisory Commission*, 226–227.

64. Martin Luther King, Jr., *The Trumpet of Conscience* (Boston: Beacon Press, 1968), 6.

65. Stokely Carmichael, "Power and Racism," in *Stokely Speaks: From Black Power to Pan-Africanism* (Chicago: Lawrence Hill Books, 2007), 18. For a sympathetic but conservative critique of King's theory and practice of civil disobedience that suggests his complicity in undermining respect for the law, see Herbert J. Storing, "Against Civil Disobedience," in *Toward a More Perfect Union*, ed. Joseph M. Bessette (Washington, DC: AEI Press, 1995), 236–258.

66. Amiri Baraka, "What Does Non-Violence Mean?," in *Home: Social Essays* (New York: Morrow, 1966), 133–154.

67. Carmichael, "Power and Racism," 17.

68. Bertrand Russell, *Autobiography* (London: Routledge, 1998), 635. Rustin recounts his debates with Watts militants who endorse this view, in Bayard Rustin, "The Watts 'Manifesto' and the McCone Report," in *Down the Line: The Collected Writings of Bayard Rustin* (Chicago: Quadrangle Books, 1971), 142.

69. See, for example, H. Rap Brown, *Die Nigger Die! A Political Autobiography* (New York: Last Gasp Books, 1969), 38, 144.

70. See, for example, Amiri Baraka, "Black People!," in *The LeRoi Jones/Amiri Baraka Reader,* ed. William J. Harris (New York: Thunder's Mouth Press, 1991). This description draws upon Jason Frank, "'Delightful Horror': Edmund Burke and the Aesthetics of Democratic Revolution," in *The Aesthetic Turn in Political Thought,* ed. Nikolas Kompridis (New York: Bloomsbury, 2014), 3–28.

71. King, "Showdown for Nonviolence," 69; King, "Testament of Hope," 322.

72. Frantz Fanon, *Wretched of the Earth,* 23–29. See also Malcolm X's purported account of the parasitic relation between nonviolence and the threat of violence, in Coretta Scott King, *My Life with Martin Luther King, Jr.* (New York: Henry Holt, 1993), 256.

73. Reinhold Niebuhr, "Moral Man and Immoral Society," in *Major Works on Religion and Politics,* ed. Elizabeth Sifton (New York: Library of America, 2015), 323.

74. Martin Luther King, "Interview by Lester Margolies (March 22, 1961)," in *The Papers of Martin Luther King, Jr.*, vol. 7, *To Save the Soul of America, January 1961–August 1962,* ed. Clayborne Carson and Tenisha Hart Armstrong (Oakland: University of California Press, 2014), 187.

75. King, "My Trip to the Land of Gandhi," in *A Testament of Hope,* 39. For Gandhian elements of King's thought, see Chapter 4, by Karuna Mantena.

76. King, *Why We Can't Wait,* 90.

77. King, *Trumpet of Conscience,* 14–16.

78. Ibid., 16.

79. Niebuhr, "Moral Man and Immoral Society," 330.

80. King, *Trumpet of Conscience,* 7.

81. King, *Where Do We Go from Here,* 21.

82. King, "Conversation with Martin Luther King," in *A Testament of Hope,* 675.

83. Gerald D. McKnight, *The Last Crusade: Martin Luther King, Jr., the FBI, and the Poor People's Campaign* (Boulder, CO: Westview Press, 1998).

84. See King, "*Playboy* Interview," 344. On the evolution of government repression, see McKnight, *The Last Crusade.*

85. Sheldon Wolin, "What Revolutionary Action Means Today," in *Fugitive Democracy and Other Essays,* ed. Nicholas Xenos (Princeton, NJ: Princeton University Press, 2016), 368.

86. King, *Trumpet of Conscience,* 52.

87. Sacvan Bercovitch, *The American Jeremiad* (Madison: University of Wisconsin Press, 1978).

88. King, "Showdown for Nonviolence," 69.

89. King, *Where Do We Go from Here*, 22.

90. Openly, lovingly, and with a willingness to accept the penalty is, of course, the famed formulation for civil disobedience from "Letter from Birmingham Jail." See King, *Why We Can't Wait*, 95.

91. Charles V. Hamilton, "Riots, Revolts, and Relevant Response," in Barbour, *The Black Power Revolt*, esp. 174–177. See also, for example, Eldridge Cleaver, *Credo for Rioters and Looters* (San Francisco: Black Panther Party, 1969); and Cleaver, "*Playboy* Interview," in *Post-Prison Writings and Speeches*, ed. Robert Scheer (London: Panther Books, 1969). In the latter, Cleaver expounds at length on the BPP's demand that all black prisoners be freed. Instead of advancing their original platform's argument, which was about the unfairness of jury trials in white supremacist society, Cleaver advances his contention that a society characterized by this level of basic structural injustice does not have the legitimacy to punish its oppressed minority groups. Further, his argument entails the existence of a fundamental hermeneutical injustice with regard to crime, because many crimes that are forms of rebellion and resistance against oppression are interpreted as morally disgraceful deviance, further underscoring the lack of legitimacy to punishment. A similar argument is found in Angela Davis, *If They Come*, 19–36.

92. Eldridge Cleaver, "Domestic Law and International Order," in *Soul on Ice*, 134.

93. Ibid., 135.

94. Ibid., 133.

95. See, for example, Amiri Baraka's 1973 poem "Afrikan Revolution," in *LeRoi Jones/Amiri Baraka Reader*, 243–247. The "Uncle Tom" point was not merely rhetorical for all parties. In 1968 two members of the Revolutionary Action Movement were convicted of plotting to assassinate Whitney Young, the executive director of the National Urban League. See Nancy Joan Weiss, *Whitney Young, Jr. and the Struggle for Civil Rights* (Princeton, NJ: Princeton University Press, 2014), 223.

96. Cleaver, *Credo*, 1. Cleaver signifies upon former U.S. Supreme Court Chief Justice Roger B. Taney's infamous defense of white supremacist constitutionalism in *Dred Scott v. Sanford* (1857) with bitter irony.

97. Cleaver, "Psychology: The Black Bible," in *Post-Prison Writings*, 44.

98. Fanon, *Wretched of the Earth*, 4–6.

99. On a metalanguage of race, see Evelyn Brooks Higginbotham, "African-American Women's History and the Metalanguage of Race," *Signs* 17, no. 2 (Winter, 1992): 251–274. On habits of domination and acquiescence, see Allen, *Talking to Strangers*, 5–12, 35–49.

100. Fanon, *Wretched of the Earth*, 11–14.

101. Ibid., 6–8.

102. Malcolm X, "With Mrs. Fannie Lou Hamer," in *Malcolm X Speaks*, 108.

103. H. Rap Brown, *Die Nigger Die!*, 107.

104. Amiri Baraka, *The Autobiography of LeRoi Jones/Amiri Baraka* (New York: Freundlich Books, 1984), 266.

105. Fanon, *Wretched of the Earth*, 9.

106. Ibid., 1.

107. Malcolm X, "With Mrs. Fannie Lou Hamer," 107.

108. King, *Trumpet of Conscience*, 8.

109. Ibid., 22.

110. Ibid., 59.

111. King "A Testament of Hope," 322.

112. King, *Trumpet of Conscience*, 74.

113. King, *Where Do We Go from Here*, 18.

114. King, *Strength to Love*, 48.

115. King, *Where Do We Go from Here*, 47.

116. King, *Trumpet of Conscience*, 16.

117. Reed, *Stirrings in the Jug*, 16–17.

118. Joshua Bloom and Waldo Martin, *Black against Empire: The History and Politics of the Black Panther Party* (Berkeley: University of California Press, 2013), 2–3; Bryan Burroughs, *Days of Rage: America's Radical Underground, the FBI, and the Forgotten Age of Revolutionary Violence* (New York: Penguin, 2015).

119. Marx, "On the Jewish Question." See, for example, Amiri Baraka, "The Last Days of the American Empire (Including Some Instructions for Black People)," in *Home*, 205–209.

120. Kathleen Cleaver, "Looking Back through the Heart of Dixie," in *The Promise of Multi-Culturalism: Education and Autonomy in the 21st Century* (London: Routledge, 1998), 26.

121. See, for example, Cleaver, "*Playboy* Interview"; Huey Newton, "In Defense of Self-Defense," *Black Panther*, July 3, 1967, 3, 7.

122. Lewis Gordon, *What Fanon Said: A Philosophical Introduction to His Life and Thought* (New York: Fordham University Press, 2015), 87.

123. Fanon, *Wretched of the Earth*, 15–21.

124. Carmichael, "Free Huey," in *Stokely Speaks*, 120.

125. Baraka, *Raise Race Rays Raze*, 47.

126. Ibid., 29–48; Carmichael and Hamilton, *Black Power*, 34–35.

127. Baraka, *Raise Race Rays Raze*, 133–146.

128. King, *Where Do We Go from Here*, 54–55.

129. Ibid., 41–42, 54–55, 130–131.

130. Ibid., 130–131.

131. Ibid., 59. See also King, "*Playboy* Interview," 364; King, "'Let My People Go': South Africa Benefit Speech (December 10, 1965)," in "*In a Single Garment of Destiny*": *A Global Vision of Justice*, ed. and intro. Lewis V. Baldwin, foreword by Charlayne Hunter-Gault (Boston: Beacon Press, 2012), 39–44.

132. For an elaboration of this point, see Nick Bromell, *The Time Is Always Now: Black Thought and the Transformation of US Democracy* (New York: Oxford University Press, 2013), 13–36. King defended temporary forms of political separatism as "waystations" on the path to integration without domination. See King, "Conversation with Martin Luther King," 666.

133. King, *Where Do We Go from Here,* 53.

134. Ibid., 49.

135. See Chapter 1, by Robert Gooding-Williams.

136. Carmichael and Hamilton, *Black Power,* 5.

137. See, for example, Angela Y. Davis and Elaine Brown, "Welcome Home, Angela Davis," *Black Panther,* March 4, 1972, p. H; Stokely Carmichael, "The Dialectics of Liberation," in *Stokely Speaks,* 87.

138. For relatively clear statements, see Eldridge Cleaver, "The Land Question and Black Liberation," in *Post-Prison Writings,* 80–88; Cleaver, "On Lumpen Ideology," *Black Scholar* 4, no. 3 (November–December 1972): 2–10.

139. Michael Cetewayo Tabor, *Capitalism plus Dope Equals Genocide* (New York: Ministry of Information, Black Panther Party, 1970), available at https://www.marxists.org/history/usa/workers/black-panthers/1970/dope.htm.

140. Davis and Brown, "Welcome Home, Angela Davis," pp. C–D; Huey P. Newton, "Affirmative Action in Theory and Practice: Letters on the *Bakke* Case, September 22, 1977," in *The Huey Newton Reader,* 331–336.

141. Marcus Garvey, *The Philosophy and Opinions of Marcus Garvey,* vol. 1, ed. Amy Jacques Garvey (Paterson, NJ: Frank Cass and Co., 1923), 36–37, 41.

142. Carl Stokes, *The Promises of Power: A Political Autobiography* (New York: Simon and Schuster, 1973), 108–130.

143. See, for example, Landon Williams, "Black Capitalism and What It Means," *Black Panther,* March 16, 1969, 4–5.

144. "The Roots of the Party," *Black Panther,* May 25, 1969, 4.

145. King did not share this contempt for black business, and acknowledged the important role played by business persons in Montgomery.

146. Amiri Baraka, "Clout: What It Is?" (1977), in *Daggers and Javelins: Essays, 1974–1979* (New York: William Morrow, 1984), 70–80.

147. Bernard Yack, *The Longing for Total Revolution: Philosophic Sources of Social Discontent from Rousseau to Marx and Nietzsche* (Berkeley: University of California Press, 1992), 3–27.

148. Eldridge Cleaver, *On the Ideology of the Black Panther Party* (San Francisco: Black Panther Party, 1970).

149. Karl Marx, "The Eighteenth Brumaire of Louis Bonaparte" (1852), Marx/Engels Internet Archive, https://www.marxists.org/archive/marx/works/1852/18th-brumaire/cho5.htm.

150. Friedrich Engels, "The Peasant War in Germany" (1850), 8, Marx/Engels Internet Archive, https://www.marxists.org/archive/marx/works/1850/peasant-war-germany/index.htm. Amiri Baraka, once he moved toward more traditional Marxism-Leninism, argued a similar position in Baraka, "Black Solidarity," in *Daggers and Javelins,* 289.

151. Fanon, *Wretched of the Earth,* 81–82, 87.

152. Huey P. Newton with J. Herman Blake, *Revolutionary Suicide* (New York: Penguin, 2009), chap. 11.

153. Huey P. Newton, "The Correct Handling of a Revolution (July 20, 1967)," in *The Huey Newton Reader,* 143.

154. Huey P. Newton, "Speech Delivered at Boston College (November 18, 1970)," in *The Huey Newton Reader,* 170.

155. King, *Strength to Love,* 103.

156. Ibid., 108.

157. Ibid., 101; King, *Trumpet of Conscience,* 34.

158. King, *Where Do We Go from Here,* 58.

159. King, "Conversation with Martin Luther King, Jr.," 663.

160. King, *Where Do We Go from Here,* 60.

161. Malcolm X, for example, absurdly claimed that African Americans had as allies "700 million Chinese who are ready to die for human rights." Malcolm X, "Interview by A. B. Spellman (March 19, 1964)," in Malcolm X, *By Any Means Necessary,* ed. George Breitman (New York: Pathfinder, 1970), 29. For a critique of contemporary scholarship that does not subject Third World solidarities to appropriate realist skepticism, see Brandon M. Terry, "Book Review: Saladin Ambar, *Malcolm X at Oxford Union," Perspectives on Politics* 14, no. 1 (March 2016): 207–208.

162. King, *Where Do We Go from Here,* 59.

163. The following discussion relies primarily on Newton, "Correct Handling of a Revolution"; and Cleaver, "Ideology."

164. They do not seem to have predicted what actually happened, which is that the police repression of these communities turned many ghetto denizens against the black militants.

165. Burroughs, *Days of Rage,* chaps. 1 and 2.

166. I argue that the ideological core of the Newton/Cleaver split in the Black Panther Party runs along this axis (setting aside FBI infiltration). Cleaver appealed especially to the small cadre who actually wanted to pursue revolutionary/anarchic violence against police and precipitate larger revolt. Their imagined paradigm was their knowledge of Castro's rebellion in Cuba and the mythos that had grown up around his small band of followers in the Sierra Maestra mountains. Newton's wing, which noncoincidentally claimed a larger group of black women, tended to treat revolutionary violence as either a long-term goal or a rhetorical invocation meant to challenge the sovereignties of the state and create space for the BPP to assume those functions (schooling, medical service provision, policing, diplomacy, etc.). See Huey P. Newton, "On the Defection of Eldridge Cleaver," in *Huey P. Newton Reader,* esp. 200–206. On Castro and the Black Panther imagination, see Michael L. Clemons and Charles E. Jones, "Global Solidarity: The Black Panther Party in the International Arena," in *Liberation, Imagination and the Black Panther Party,* ed. Kathleen Cleaver and George Katsiaficas (New York: Routledge, 2001), 31. King explicitly criticizes the Castro comparison in *Where Do We Go from Here,* 60.

167. Cleaver, "Black Liberation and the Land Question," in *Post-Prison Writings,*

168. King, *Where Do We Go from Here,* 65.

169. King, *Trumpet of Conscience*, 32–33, 74.

170. Ibid., 63–64.

171. James R. Ralph, Jr., *Northern Protest: Martin Luther King, Jr., Chicago, and the Civil Rights Movement* (Cambridge, MA: Harvard University Press, 1993), 56.

172. Ibid., 92, 111.

173. King, *Trumpet of Conscience*, 60.

174. "Second-personal address commits us, quite generally, to an authority that anyone has just by virtue of second-personal competence. Briefly: addressing second-personal reasons always presupposes not just the addresser's authority and competence to hold the addressee responsible for compliance, but also the addressee's authority and competence to hold himself responsible. It is committed, therefore, to the authority of a perspective that addresser and addressee can occupy in common: the second-person standpoint of mutually accountable persons." Stephen Darwall, *The Second Person Standpoint* (Cambridge, MA: Harvard University Press, 2006), 138.

175. Kompridis, *Critique and Disclosure*, 270.

176. King, *Trumpet of Conscience*, 71.

15. HOPE AND DESPAIR

1. David J. Garrow, *Bearing the Cross: Martin Luther King, Jr., and the Southern Christian Leadership Conference* (New York: William Morrow, 1986), 599.

2. Ibid., 602. King's early suicide attempt at age twelve, upon the death of his grandmother, complicated any talk of death in his short life.

3. Ibid.

4. Jesse Jackson, "Reclaiming the Radical Revolutionary: Celebrating the Ten-Year Anniversary of Obery Hendricks's *The Politics of Jesus*," presentation at the Annual Meeting of the American Academy of Religion, November 19, 2016, https://youtu.be/pxqDefOECxQ.

5. For more extended treatments of nihilism, as concept and lived reality, see Cornel West, *Race Matters* (Boston: Beacon Press, 1994), 15–33; West, *Democracy Matters: Winning the Fight against Imperialism* (New York: Penguin, 2004), 25–62.

6. As quoted in Garrow, *Bearing the Cross*, 594.

7. As quoted in ibid., 611–612. For more on King's complex relationship to violence and the Black Power movement, see Chapter 14, by Brandon M. Terry.

8. As quoted in Garrow, *Bearing the Cross*, 612.

9. Ibid., 580.

10. Martin Luther King, Jr., "A Testament of Hope," in *A Testament of Hope: The Essential Writings and Speeches of Martin Luther King, Jr.*, ed. James M. Washington (New York: Harper Collins, 1986), 313–328.

11. As quoted in Garrow, *Bearing the Cross*, 581.

12. W. E. B. Du Bois, for example, proclaimed in 1961, "I just cannot take any more of this country's treatment. We leave for Ghana October 5th and I set no date for return. . . . Chin up, and fight on, but realize that American Negroes can't win." As quoted in Gerald Horne, *Black and Red: W. E. B. Du Bois and the Afro-American*

Response to the Cold War, 1944–1963 (Albany: SUNY Press, 1986), 345. In 1964 Malcolm X was exhorting African Americans to appeal to the United Nations: "When you expand the civil-rights struggle to the level of human rights, you can then take the case of the black man in this country before the nations in the UN. . . . You can take Uncle Sam before a world court. . . . Civil rights keeps you under his restrictions, under his jurisdiction." Malcolm X, "The Ballot or the Bullet," in *Malcolm X Speaks: Selected Speeches and Statements,* ed. George Breitman (New York: Merit, 1965), 34–35.

13. See, for example, Eldridge Cleaver, "The Death of Martin Luther King: Requiem for Nonviolence," in *Eldridge Cleaver: Post-Prison Writings and Speeches,* ed. Robert Scheer (New York: Random House, 1969).

14. As quoted in Garrow, *Bearing the Cross,* 617.

15. David J. Garrow, *The FBI and Martin Luther King, Jr.: From "Solo" to Memphis* (New York: Penguin, 1983), chap. 3.

16. See, for example, Bayard Rustin, "Guns, Bread, and Butter" and "Dr. King's Painful Dilemma," both in *Down the Line: The Collected Writings of Bayard Rustin* (Chicago: Quadrangle Books, 1971), 166–168, 169–170.

17. Garrow, *Bearing the Cross,* 616.

18. Ibid., 603.

19. "Dr. King Is Accused in Baptist Dispute," *New York Times,* September 10, 1961, 35.

20. See, for example, King's interview with Heschel in "Conversation with Martin Luther King," in *Testament of Hope,* 657–679.

21. Garrow, *Bearing the Cross,* 577, 527.

22. For an expanded argument, see Cornel West, "The Paradox of the African American Rebellion," in *Keeping Faith: Philosophy and Race in America* (New York: Routledge, 1993), 241–259.

23. As quoted in Garrow, *Bearing the Cross,* 546.

24. Ibid., 553.

25. Ibid., 554.

26. Ibid., 568.

27. Ibid., 576–577.

28. Theodore Parker, "Of Justice and the Conscience," in *The Collected Works of Theodore Parker,* vol. 2, *Sermons and Prayers* (London: Trubner and Co., 1879), 48.

29. King, "A Time to Break Silence," in *Testament of Hope,* 233.

30. See, for example, King, "Showdown for Nonviolence," in *Testament of Hope,* 64–72.

31. As quoted in Garrow, *Bearing the Cross,* 596.

32. King, "Conversation with Martin Luther King," 658.

33. See also Chapter 12, by Lionel McPherson.

34. See King, *Trumpet of Conscience* (Boston: Beacon Press, 2010), esp. chaps. 2 and 3.

35. As quoted in Garrow, *Bearing the Cross,* 622.

36. Ibid., 562.

37. See, for example, Adolph Reed, Jr., "The Limits of Anti-Racism," *Left Business Observer*, no. 121, September 2009, http://www.leftbusinessobserver.com/Antiracism .html; Adolph Reed, Jr., "From Jenner to Dolezal: One Trans Good, the Other Not So Much," Commondreams.org, June 15, 2015, http://www.commondreams.org/views /2015/06/15/jenner-dolezal-one-trans-good-other-not-so-much.

38. As quoted in Garrow, *Bearing the Cross*, 608. See also King, "A Testament of Hope," esp. 317, where King writes, "When I speak of integration, I don't mean a romantic mixing of colors, I mean a real sharing of power and responsibility."

39. Martin Luther King, Jr., "Public Statement on the Poor People's Campaign" (December 4, 1967), King Center Online Archive, http://www.thekingcenter.org /archive/document/mlk-public-statement-poor-peoples-campaign.

40. As quoted in Garrow, *Bearing the Cross*, 585.

41. See, for example, the speeches and essays collected in Martin Luther King, Jr., *"In a Single Garment of Destiny": A Global Vision of Justice*, ed. Lewis V. Baldwin (Boston: Beacon Press, 2012, esp. §§1, 5, 6.

42. W. E. B. Du Bois, "Of Our Spiritual Strivings," in *The Souls of Black Folk*, ed. David W. Blight and Robert Gooding-Williams (Boston: Bedford/St. Martin's Press, 1997), 43. For King's fascinating reflections on Du Bois, see Martin Luther King, Jr., "Honoring Dr. Du Bois," in *The Radical King*, ed. Cornel West (Boston: Beacon Press, 2015), 113–121.

43. See, for example, King on the psychic (and political) power of the "freedom songs" once sung by slaves, in King, *Why We Can't Wait* (Boston: Beacon Press, 2011), 65–66.

44. Du Bois, "Of the Wings of Atalanta," in *The Souls of Black Folk*, 85. See also Du Bois, *The Autobiography of W. E. B. DuBois: A Soliloquy on Viewing My Life from the Last Decade of Its First Century* (New York: International, 1968), 418.

45. "Martin Luther King, Jr., "[*26 October 1960*] To Coretta Scott King, Reidsville, Ga.," in *The King Encyclopedia*, http://kingencyclopedia.stanford.edu/encyclopedia /documentsentry/to_coretta_scott_king.1.html.

46. As quoted in Garrow, *Bearing the Cross*, 564.

47. Ibid.

48. Ibid.

49. W. E. B. Du Bois, "The White World," in *Dusk of Dawn: An Essay toward an Autobiography of a Race Concept* (New York: Harcourt Brace, 1940), 151.

50. George Washington, "From George Washington to Edward Newenham, 29 August 1788," *National Archives Founders Online*, https://founders.archives.gov /GEWN-04-06-02-0436; and Thomas Jefferson, "From Thomas Jefferson to George Rogers Clark, 25 December 1780," *National Archives Founders Online*, https:// founders.archives.gov/documents/Jefferson/01-04-02-0295.

51. For a critique of the Obama–King comparison, see Tommie Shelby, "Justice and Racial Conciliation: Two Visions," *Daedalus* 140 (Winter 2011): 95–107.

52. Eileen Patten and Jens Manuel Krogstad, "Black Child Poverty Rate Holds Steady, Even as Other Groups See Declines," *Fact Tank: News in the Numbers, Pew*

Research Center, July 14, 2015, http://www.pewresearch.org/fact-tank/2015/07/14/black-child-poverty-rate-holds-steady-even-as-other-groups-see-declines/.

53. "Most Blacks Say MLK's Vision Fulfilled, Poll Finds," *CNN,* January 19, 2009, http://www.cnn.com/2009/POLITICS/01/19/king.poll/.

54. Regarding the top 1 percent and income growth, see economist Emmanuel Saez, "Striking It Richer: The Evolution of Top Incomes in the United States," September 3, 2013, https://eml.berkeley.edu//~saez/saez-UStopincomes-2012.pdf.

55. For more on the philosophical significance of Easter and Christian joy, see my "A Philosophical View of Easter" and "Subversive Joy and Revolutionary Patience in Black Christianity," both in West, *The Cornel West Reader* (New York: Basic Books, 2000), 415–420, 435–440.

56. Frank Newport, "Martin Luther King, Jr.: Revered More after Death than Before," Gallup News Service, January 16, 2006, http://www.gallup.com/poll/20920/martin-luther-king-jr-revered-more-after-death-than-before.aspx.

57. Du Bois, "Of the Passing of the First-Born," in *The Souls of Black Folk,* 160.

58. James Weldon Johnson (lyrics) and Rosamond Johnson (music), "Lift Every Voice and Sing," PBS Black Culture Connection, http://www.pbs.org/black-culture/explore/black-authors-spoken-word-poetry/lift-every-voice-and-sing/.

59. John Coltrane, interview with Frank Kofsky (1966), https://soundcloud.com/pacificaradioarchives/bc1266-an-interview-with-john-coltrane-by-frank-kofsky.

60. As quoted in Garrow, *Bearing the Cross,* 576.

61. Du Bois, *Autobiography,* 405.

62. King, "A Time to Break Silence," 232. Note also Du Bois's sad words about the great Alexander Crummell, who "worked alone, with so little human sympathy. His name to-day, in this broad land, means little, and comes to fifty million ears laden with no incense of memory or emulation." Du Bois, "Of Alexander Crummell," in *The Souls of Black Folk,* 170–171. Lastly Du Bois writes just prior to his own death about his own "bitter experience." "I bowed before the storm. But I did not break. . . . The color line was beginning to break. Negroes were getting recognition as never before. Was not the sacrifice of one man, small payment for this? Even those who disagreed with this judgment at least kept quiet. The colored children ceased to hear my name." Du Bois, *Autobiography,* 395.

AFTERWORD

1. "Taking a Stand in Baton Rouge," Reuters Wider Image, https://widerimage.reuters.com/story/taking-a-stand-in-baton-rouge.

2. Robert Frodeman and Adam Briggle, *Socrates Tenured: The Institutions of Twenty-First-Century Philosophy* (London: Rowman and Littlefield, 2016), 20.

3. David J. Garrow, *Bearing the Cross: Martin Luther King, Jr., and the Southern Christian Leadership Conference* (New York: Morrow, 1986), 46.

4. Martin Luther King, Jr., *Where Do We Go from Here: Community or Chaos?* (Boston: Beacon Press, 1968), 186.

5. Ibid., 187.

6. Richard Rorty, "Religion as Conversation-Stopper," *Common Knowledge* 3, no. 1 (1994).

7. For a great treatment of this topic, see Jeffrey Stout, "Religious Reasons in Political Arguments," in *Democracy and Tradition* (Princeton, NJ: Princeton University Press, 2004).

8. Martin Luther King, Jr., "Letter from Birmingham City Jail," in *A Testament of Hope: The Essential Writings and Speeches of Martin Luther King, Jr.*, ed. James M. Washington (New York: Harper Collins, 1991), 293.

9. Martin Luther King, Jr., "Pilgrimage to Nonviolence" in *Testament of Hope*, 38.

10. Martin Luther King, Sr., and Clayton Riley, *Daddy King: An Autobiography* (New York: Morrow, 1980), 84–87.

11. Martin Luther King, Jr., "The American Dream," in *Testament of Hope*, 213.

12. King, "Letter from Birmingham City Jail," 293.

13. This is why I would acknowledge and underscore Paul Taylor's admission that reading King into a tradition of moral perfectionism without recourse to King's deeply held religious commitments is a dangerous strategy.

14. King, "Letter from Birmingham City Jail," 297–298.

15. Martin Luther King, Jr., "The Case against Tokenism," in *Testament of Hope*, 108.

16. Ibid., 247. It must also be noted that King's quote here is also informed by the other leading neo-orthodox theologian and philosopher of the era, Paul Tillich; see Tillich, *Love, Power, and Justice: Ontological Analyses and Ethical Applications* (New York: Oxford University Press, 1960).

17. King, *Where Do We Go from Here*, 55.

18. Ibid.

Acknowledgments

Our biggest debt is to our wonderful and brilliant contributors. This effort, in which we take tremendous pride, was a collective labor of love but also an immeasurably rewarding intellectual experience made possible by the commitment, wisdom, and professionalism of its multiple authors. We learned a great deal from reading drafts of your papers, grappling with your arguments, and discussing King's ideas with you. We are especially grateful for your willingness to prioritize this work amid your busy schedules and for meeting our various deadlines.

This volume is a testament to the generosity and labors of our own small, beloved community. This project would not have been possible without the generous financial and logistical support of Harvard's Office of the Dean of Arts and Humanities and, especially, the Radcliffe Institute for Advanced Study at Harvard University, where this book began as an exploratory seminar. We are especially thankful to Radcliffe's incredible staff, including Paul Beran, Ellen Setser, Maura Madden, and Kristen Osborne, for their assistance. In addition, we want to thank our colleague Lizabeth Cohen for her visionary leadership as dean of the Radcliffe Institute. In addition to the contributors, we want to thank the other participants and students who generously attended the seminars in which we discussed the essays in this collection, including Jorge Garcia, Ronni Gura Sadovsky, Jason Lee, Bréond Durr, Lidal Dror, and Laurie Shrage. We also thank the students who enrolled in the various courses we have taught on black political thought. These were invaluable opportunities for us to try out and refine our approach to King's political philosophy.

We are immensely grateful to Lindsay Waters, executive editor for the humanities at Harvard University Press, for his steadfast support and enthusiasm for this project. Joy Deng offered excellent editorial advice and guidance. Louise Robbins and Kimberly Giambattisto were thoughtful, meticulous, and patient editors. Wendy Nelson copyedited the manuscript with the thoroughness and professionalism we have come to expect and continue to admire. Tim Jones and his staff designed a beautiful cover and welcomed and were responsive to our feedback. An anonymous reviewer for the Press offered helpful comments and suggestions.

Wendy Salkin, an outstanding philosopher and serious student of King's writings, tracked down elusive bibliographic information, edited the notes, and drafted the index. We are enormously thankful for her hard and conscientious work. Special thanks also to Myisha Cherry for last-minute help proofreading.

Our spouses, Sheggai and Jessie, provided helpful feedback on the introduction and general encouragement throughout the project. But more than that their invaluable partnership and love make almost all of what we do possible and worthwhile.

We dedicate this book to our beloved children—Ayana, Christopher, and Ella. We hope you will get to see the just and peaceful world that King envisioned and sacrificed so much to help build.

Contributors

DANIELLE ALLEN is Director of the Edmond J. Safra Center for Ethics and James Bryant Conant University Professor at Harvard University. She is the author of *The World of Prometheus: The Politics of Punishing in Democratic Athens* (2000), *Talking to Strangers: Anxieties of Citizenship since Brown vs. the Board of Education* (2004), *Why Plato Wrote* (2010), *Our Declaration: A Reading of the Declaration of Independence in Defense of Equality* (2014), *Education and Equality* (2016), and *Cuz: The Life and Times of Michael A.* (2017). She is the coeditor of *Education, Justice, and Democracy* (2013, with Rob Reich) and *From Voice to Influence: Understanding Citizenship in the Digital Age* (2015, with Jennifer Light).

LAWRIE BALFOUR teaches political theory and American studies at the University of Virginia. The author of *Democracy's Reconstruction: Thinking Politically with W. E. B. Du Bois* (2011) and *The Evidence of Things Not Said: James Baldwin and the Promise of American Democracy* (2001), she has published numerous articles and book chapters on race, gender, literature, and democracy. Currently she is working on two projects: one on reparations for slavery, Jim Crow, and their legacies; and another on the meanings of freedom in Toni Morrison's novels and essays. She also serves as editor of *Political Theory*.

BERNARD R. BOXILL is Professor of Philosophy (Emeritus) at the University of North Carolina, Chapel Hill. He is the author of *Blacks and Social Justice* (1984, 1992) and the editor of *Race and Racism* (2001), and he is currently completing *A History of African American Political Thought: From Martin Delany to the Present*.

DERRICK DARBY is Professor of Philosophy at the University of Michigan, Ann Arbor. He is the coauthor (with John L. Rury) of *The Color of Mind: Why the Origins of the Achievement Gap Matter for Justice* (2018), author of *Rights, Race, and Recognition* (2009), and coeditor (with Tommie Shelby) of *Hip Hop and Philosophy: Rhyme 2 Reason* (2005).

ROBERT GOODING-WILLIAMS is the M. Moran Weston/Black Alumni Council Professor of African-American Studies and Professor of Philosophy at Columbia University. He is the author of *In the Shadow of Du Bois: Afro-Modern Political Thought in America* (2009), *Look, a Negro!: Philosophical Essays on Race, Culture, and Politics* (2006), and *Zarathustra's Dionysian Modernism* (2001), and the editor of *Reading Rodney King/Reading Urban Uprising* (1993).

KARUNA MANTENA is Associate Professor of Political Science at Yale University and co-director of the International Conference for the Study of Political Thought (CSPT). Her first book, *Alibis of Empire: Henry Maine and the Ends of Liberal Imperialism* (2010), analyzed the transformation of nineteenth-century British imperial ideology. She is currently working on a book project on M. K. Gandhi and the politics of nonviolence.

LIONEL K. MCPHERSON is Associate Professor of Philosophy at Tufts University. He has written numerous articles in moral and political philosophy and is currently completing the book *The Afterlife of Race.*

MICHELE MOODY-ADAMS is Joseph Straus Professor of Political Philosophy and Legal Theory at Columbia University and a former Dean of Columbia College and Vice President for Undergraduate Education. She is the author of numerous articles and *Fieldwork in Familiar Places: Morality, Culture and Philosophy* (1997).

MARTHA C. NUSSBAUM is Ernst Freund Distinguished Service Professor of Law and Ethics at the University of Chicago, appointed in the Philosophy Department and the Law School. She is the winner of the 2016 Kyoto Prize in Philosophy. Her most recent books are *Anger and Forgiveness* (2016) and (with Saul Levmore) *Aging Thoughtfully* (2017). Her book *The Monarchy of Fear: A Philosopher Looks at Our Political Crisis* will be published by Simon and Schuster in 2018.

TOMMIE SHELBY is the Caldwell Titcomb Professor of African and African American Studies and Professor of Philosophy at Harvard University. He is the author of *Dark Ghettos: Injustice, Dissent, and Reform*

(2016), *We Who Are Dark: The Philosophical Foundations of Black Solidarity* (2005), and coeditor (with Derrick Darby) of *Hip Hop and Philosophy: Rhyme 2 Reason* (2005). He is also a former editor of the magazine *Transition*.

RONALD R. SUNDSTROM is a Professor and former Chair of the Philosophy Department, member of the African American Studies and Critical Diversity Studies programs, and former Faculty Director of the Core Curriculum at the University of San Francisco. His areas of research include race theory, political and social theory, and African American philosophy. He published several essays and a book in these areas, including *The Browning of America and The Evasion of Social Justice* (SUNY 2008). His current book project is on inequality, segregation, gentrification, and America's housing crisis.

PAUL C. TAYLOR is Professor of Philosophy and African American Studies at the Pennsylvania State University, where he also serves as the Associate Dean for Undergraduate Studies. He is the author of *Race: A Philosophical Introduction* (2004), *On Obama* (2015), and *Black Is Beautiful: A Philosophy of Black Aesthetics* (2016). He is one of the founding editors of the journal *Critical Philosophy of Race*.

BRANDON M. TERRY is Assistant Professor of African and African American Studies and Social Studies at Harvard University. His current book project sits at the intersection of political theory, philosophy of history, and African American Studies and is titled *The Tragic Vision of the Civil Rights Movement*.

SHATEMA THREADCRAFT is Associate Professor of Government at Dartmouth College. She is the author of *Intimate Justice: The Black Female Body and the Body Politic* (2016).

JONATHAN L. WALTON is the Plummer Professor of Christian Morals and Professor of Religion and Society at Harvard University. He is the author of *Watch This! The Ethics and Aesthetics of Black Televangelism* (2009).

CORNEL WEST is Professor of the Practice of Public Philosophy at Harvard University, appointed in the Department of African and African American Studies and the School of Divinity. Among his many books are *Prophesy*

Deliverance! An Afro-American Revolutionary Christianity (1982), *Prophetic Fragments* (1988), *The American Evasion of Philosophy: A Genealogy of Pragmatism* (1989), *The Ethical Dimensions of Marxist Thought* (1991), *Race Matters* (1993), *Keeping Faith: Philosophy and Race in America* (1993), *Democracy Matters: Winning the Fight against Imperialism* (2004), and *The Radical King* (2015).

Index

Abernathy, Ralph, 325, 326
Abolitionist movement, 12, 50, 53, 130, 202, 250, 354
Acquiescence, 22, 25, 29, 34, 81, 87, 105, 110–112, 121–122, 207, 210–211, 214, 233, 314, 347; acquiescent submission, 21–26; Du Bois's and King's criticisms of, 22–27
Aesthetics, 123, 208–209, 216, 218, 243, 291, 306, 309, 315; of riots, 302, 304
Afghanistan, war in, 254, 257, 264
Africa, 63, 65, 89, 175, 179, 195, 250, 258, 262, 266, 297, 315, 316, 333, 336. See also South Africa
African American / Black / Afro-Modern political thought and philosophy, 3–10, 19, 26, 31, 128, 133, 142, 144, 147, 157, 212, 247
African National Congress (ANC), 112, 117, 262
Agape (love), 27, 55, 56, 86, 113, 122, 123, 125, 132, 144, 276, 281, 283, 346. See also Goodwill; Love
Agency (human), 20, 30–32, 34, 39, 41, 87, 99; moral, 302; women's, 218, 220, 223–227. See also Political agency; Time
Alliances, 89, 92, 233, 234, 283, 286, 304, 343, 348; black-white, 169, 271; civil rights–labor, 194, 202; military, 258; multiracial, 278, 283, 321
American Civil War, 167, 188, 237, 248, 303; Civil War Amendments, 248; King's civil war analogy, 44, 55, 56; post–Civil War labor conditions, 239
Anarchy, 96, 310, 312, 313
Androcentrism, 206, 219, 227, 232
Anger, 11, 87, 93, 105–136, 217, 288, 307, 310, 311, 321, 322, 323, 345, 346, 347, 348; nonanger, 11, 111–112, 117, 118, 120, 124, 126; Transition-Anger, 109, 111, 112, 113, 115, 116, 123
Anticolonialism: anticolonial movement, 90; anticolonial self-assertion, 46; anticolonial struggle, 250, 309; global anticolonial revolt, 294
Antidiscrimination: law, 311; legislation, 165, 169; measures, 191. See also Discrimination
Antiwar: activism, 82, 265; King's positions on, 119, 328. See also War
Apartheid, 111, 258, 259, 262, 303, 345. See also Mandela, Nelson; South Africa
Arendt, Hannah, 29, 31, 210
Aristotle, 106, 108, 114
Asia, 175, 179, 195, 250, 294, 297; Asian people, 89, 294, 330; Southeast Asia, 265
Assassination of Martin Luther King, Jr., 1, 78, 79, 101, 152, 202, 235, 246, 265, 271, 303, 308, 326
Atlanta, Georgia, 193, 222, 328, 340, 343
Authenticity, 80, 211, 312, 316

Authoritarianism, 91, 100, 208, 303, 342

Authority, 5, 19, 23, 208, 209, 213, 224, 264, 294, 319, 336, 340; absolute, 208; antidemocratic and repressive, 209; charismatic, 209, 210; government, 308; interpretive, 312; legal, 161; moral, 49, 161, 179, 183, 298, 306, 335; natural, 196; normative, 52; political, 209, 340; unjust, 122; white, 58. *See also* Morality

Automation, 190, 228–229, 233, 316

Autonomy, 90, 148, 151, 173, 199, 294

Baker, Ella, 207–209, 211, 222

Baldwin, James, 1, 142, 333

Baptist Church, 163, 213, 235, 282, 322; address at Liberty Baptist Church in Chicago (1966), 327; American Baptist Church, 140; Dexter Avenue Baptist Church, 208, 224, 269; Ebenezer Baptist Church, 42, 328, 344; eulogy for victims of 16th Street Baptist Church bombing, 125; First Baptist Church in Montgomery, 299; National Baptist Convention, 327. *See also* Holt Street Baptist Church speech ("Day of Days" speech)

Baraka, Amiri, 310, 314, 333. *See also* Black Arts Movement (BAM)

Belief, 51, 52, 99, 121, 122, 243, 255, 282, 321, 333; in principles, 207, 223, 270, 273, 276, 277, 280, 282, 284, 285, 288, 315, 344; and relation to faith, 54, 264; religious, 194; theological, 129

Bell, Derrick, 135

Beloved community, 11, 122, 129, 135, 139, 141, 144, 206, 239, 270, 271, 273, 275, 278, 280, 316, 326, 348. *See also* Community

Berlin, Isaiah, 146, 147, 151. *See also* Liberty

"Beyond Vietnam." *See* "Time to Break Silence, A"

Bill of Rights for the Disadvantaged, 193, 237, 238

Birmingham, Alabama, 31, 166, 168, 218, 221, 271, 302, 343; 1963 SCLC Birmingham campaign, 83, 97, 98, 165, 168, 219, 305. *See also* "Letter from a Birmingham City Jail"

Black Arts Movement (BAM), 291, 310. *See also* Baraka, Amiri

Black freedom movement, 9, 12, 24, 25, 29, 45, 46, 47, 58, 119, 187, 191, 194, 203, 204, 271, 272, 291, 296, 331, 332, 333, 335. *See also* Civil Rights Movement

Black Lives Matter movement, 144, 165, 252, 333, 340, 348

Black Nationalism, 8, 30, 31, 89, 290, 293, 315; as emigration, 21–23, 65, 294. *See also* Black Power movement

Black Panther Party (BPP), 291, 308, 313, 318, 319, 320, 321, 322

Black politics, 3, 4, 5, 30, 31, 32, 208–209, 212, 304, 315, 323; black political action, 296; black political agency, 33; black political culture, 5, 14; black political hope, 218; black political life, 292, 293, 313; black political options, 30; black political organizing, 209; black political power, 47; black political spokespersons, 303; black political strivings, 212; black political struggle, 20, 33, 85. *See also* African American/Black/Afro-modern political thought and philosophy

Black Power movement, 14, 46, 47, 58, 59, 64, 79, 87, 89, 143, 144, 165, 194, 217, 240, 243, 278, 286, 290–324; King's views of, 240, 243, 244, 278, 286, 347; and masculinity, 13, 210, 211–214, 235; studies on, 292

Black youth, 190, 214

Blame, 68, 77, 95, 110, 191, 246, 249, 279

Bloody Sunday, 165, 170. *See also* Marches; Selma, Alabama

Boston University, 137, 139, 341

Boxill, Bernard, 10, 171

Boycotts, 90, 283, 305; economic, 193, 284. *See also* Montgomery bus boycott

Branch, Taylor, 61

Brightman, Edgar S., 27, 137

Brooks, Gwendolyn, 333

Brotherhood, 33, 122, 150, 166, 178

Brown, H. "Rap," 309–310

Brown, Wendy, 212

Brown v. Board of Education, 243, 248, 281, 292, 301

Burke, Edmund, 68

Burks, Mary Fair, 223–224

Capital, 152, 197, 198, 228, 255, 263, 317, 318; capitalists, 197, 198, 201, 206, 232, 317, 318; capital-labor relations, 12; capital owner-ship, 318

Capitalism, 47, 84, 188, 198–201, 233, 250, 274–275, 295, 317–318, 341

Carmichael, Stokely, 92, 243, 278, 286, 290–291, 303, 310, 314, 316

Categorical imperative, 138, 139, 172, 181, 182. *See also* Means-Ends

Cavell, Stanley: account of perfec-tionism, 9, 39–41, 46; as Emersonian, 39–41

Character, 11, 39, 40, 42, 44, 45, 55, 56, 128, 129, 134, 135, 136, 139, 140, 142, 172, 223, 300, 331, 336; character-based criticisms of the poor, 142

Charisma, 5, 208, 209, 210; and leader-ship, 207, 208, 209, 218, 234

Chicago, Illinois, 82, 187, 193, 222, 240, 322, 323, 327

Christianity, 25, 32, 125, 138, 302; African American Christianity, 5, 9, 207, 283, 295, 315; asceticism in Christianity, 125; Christian *agape*, 276, 281, 283; Christian conception of suffering, 94; Christian ethics, 136, 137, 304; Christian faith, 52, 194; Christian health, 141; Chris-tian liberal egalitarianism, 45, 133; Christian love, 28, 81, 139, 170, 171, 276, 304; Christian moral worldview, 51; Christian norms, 53; Christian rhetoric, 45; Christian roots of re-tributive anger, 111; Christian tropes, 85; Christocentric idioms of ethical discourse, 56; Christ's teachings, 32, 33, 53, 80, 214; Communism as antithetical to Christianity, 198; Gandhi as Christian figure, 49; King's Christian commitments and influ-ences, 47, 49, 51, 52, 53, 54, 81, 121, 130, 214, 280, 282, 283, 328, 337, 344; nonviolent reconciliation as Christian imperative, 94; resurrection of Christ, 335; un-Christian, 195. *See also* Christian Realism; Christians; Personalism; Social gospel

Christian Realism, 11, 127, 132, 136, 137, 138, 139, 140. *See also* Chris-tianity; Niebuhr, Reinhold

Christians, 32, 53; America as a "Christian nation," 342; Christian preachers and desegregation, 343; Christians in the book of Revelation, 111; King as Christian, 130, 199, 336; King as Christian minister, 5, 53, 163, 194, 336, 341; King as revolu-tionary Christian, 335; King's appeals to fellow Christians, 170; King's fellow Christian ministers, 327; and Stoicism, 125; white conservative Christian evangelicals, 342

"Christmas Sermon on Peace," 119, 137, 252

Church, 142, 250; African American churches, 125; bombings of black Christian churches, 175, 310; Emanuel African Methodist Episcopal Church in Charleston, South Carolina, 166; King as pariah of black church establishment, 327; King's criticisms of U.S. churches, 53; King's view of the leadership role of the pastor, 208; northern black church, 21, 23; Protestant churches, 125; role of women in the southern church, 207; southern black church, 21. *See also* Baptist Church; Christianity

Citizenship, 2; active, 243; American, 294; civil disobedience and, 271–272, 283–284; democratic, 41; equal, 135, 196, 197, 202, 280; first-class, 28, 272, 279, 284; rights of, 284, 313; second-class, 197, 314; separate-but-equal, 280, 281; voting as badge of full, 175. *See also* Conscientious citizenship

Civil disobedience, 2, 10, 13, 58–77, 128, 211, 235, 271, 280, 282, 283, 304, 305, 306, 307, 308, 320, 322, 326, 346. *See also* Disobedience; Nonviolence

Civil rights, 11, 134, 211, 237, 271, 301, 318; African American civil rights, 161, 296, 300; armed self-defense in African American civil rights activism, 296, 297; civil rights advocacy, 127, 128; civil rights agenda, 274; civil rights era antidiscrimination legislation, 169; civil rights-labor alliance, 194, 202; color-conscious civil rights remedies, 127; historiography of, 8, 82; King as civil rights activist, 163, 256; King's civil rights organizing, 242; laws, 243; legislation, 78, 96, 269, 292; liberalism, 292; limits of civil rights-era social theory, 316; "peace and civil rights don't mix," 269; progress in, 229; United States' failure to secure, 301; unpunished murders of civil rights workers, 243. *See also* Black freedom movement; Civil Rights Act of 1964; Civil Rights Bill of 1966; Civil Rights Movement

Civil Rights Act of 1964, 130, 133, 165, 168, 271, 285, 313

Civil Rights Bill of 1966, 290

Civil Rights Movement, 2, 3, 4, 8, 9, 10, 12, 14, 19, 24, 25, 29, 34, 50, 53, 58, 79, 82, 86, 90, 91, 95, 96, 99, 100, 111, 130–133, 137, 165, 168, 169, 187, 207, 218, 219, 222, 239–242, 271–275, 277, 280, 281, 283–286, 291, 304, 332; activists, 3, 10, 163, 290, 296, 303; civil rights revolution, 9, 19, 29, 34, 272, 282, 283; civil rights struggle, 9, 137, 286, 287; demonstrations and protests, 165, 297, 298, 302; leaders of, 206, 290. *See also* Black freedom movement; Civil rights; Civil Rights Act of 1964

Civil War. *See* American Civil War

Clark, Septima, 205

Class, 4, 93, 132, 187–188, 202, 220–225, 285, 318–320; class conflict, 318; class inequality, 166, 330, 333; class interests, 6, 304, 335; classless society, 199–200; class war, 320, 329

Cleaver, Eldridge, 308, 309, 313, 320

Coates, Ta-Nehisi, 237, 238

Coercion, 93, 97, 230, 233, 282, 304, 305, 306, 307, 308, 322

Cold War, 301, 303, 304; geopolitics of, 294, 295

Collectivism, 47, 198, 275, 341. *See also* Individualism

Colonialism, 175, 270, 276, 309, 314, 315, 322; colonial arrogance, 250; colonial bourgeoisie, 277; colonial domination, 317; colonial power, 90; colonial problem, 277; colonial situation, 277; colonial subjection, 175; colonial world, 309; European, 162, 309

Colonization, 316; the colonized, 251, 277, 310, 313, 314; colonizer, 309. *See also* Decolonization

Color-blindness, 128, 130–136. *See also* Color-consciousness

Color-consciousness, 127, 129, 132, 133, 134, 135, 141. *See also* Color-blindness; Race consciousness; "Rising Tide of Racial Consciousness, The"

Communism, 47, 119, 188, 198–200, 258, 274, 275, 301, 303, 319, 341. *See also* Communists; Marx, Karl

Communists, 199, 200, 263, 301; anticommunist policymakers, 301; communist agitation, 95; communist influence on King's thinking, 328; communist propaganda, 301

Community, 27, 35, 45, 75, 77, 142, 146, 148, 300, 345; African American, 233, 272, 287, 299, 332, 347; broken, 279; "community controlled" institutions, 321; concern for, 200; conscience of the, 74, 75, 76; creation of, 15, 27, 122; ethos of, 299; intellectual, 38; intracommunity violence, 314; membership in, 158, 159, 299; organizing by, 210, 291; political, 99; protection of, 214, 218; redemptive, 88; sense of, 285; ultimate, 273, 280; white, 286. *See also* Beloved community; *Where Do We Go from Here: Chaos or Community?*

Compassion, 35, 93, 140, 200, 275, 288; compassionate grief, 106

Compensation, 13, 191, 197, 201, 230, 237, 238

Congress on Racial Equality (CORE), 82, 92, 291

Conscience, 13, 46, 67, 74–77, 86, 88, 92, 94, 97–99, 267, 278, 279, 283, 285–287. *See also* Conscientious citizenship; *Trumpet of Conscience* (1968)

Conscientious citizenship, 13, 269–282, 287–289

Conservatism, 8, 89, 142, 249, 294, 305; American, 294; gender, 249; reactionary, 305

Constant, Benjamin, 146, 147, 151

Constitution: constitutional constraints against arbitrary power, 146; constitutional democracy, 271, 283; constitutional interpretation, 128; constitutional norms, 321; constitutional order, 147, 300; constitutional protections, 319; constitutional rights, 76, 173, 193, 233, 251, 271, 299, 339; separate but equal as substitute, 280; Thirteenth, Fourteenth, and Fifteenth Amendments, 167, 280, 283; U.S. Constitution, 128, 129, 130, 131, 134, 240, 242

Consumerism, 244, 315, 318

Cooperation, 105, 123, 135, 208, 279, 283, 284, 293, 298, 323; cooperative disagreement, 159; cooperative self-defense, 297, 301; cooperative social goods, 209; economic, 197, 198; egalitarian, 316; with good, 273; with the oppressor, 279; passive cooperation with evil, 279. *See also* Noncooperation

Courage, 11, 25, 28, 36, 40, 41, 43, 72, 87, 98, 112, 121, 122, 125, 171, 205, 217, 218, 224, 225, 254, 260, 264, 276, 278, 279, 283, 292, 296, 297, 330–333, 335–337, 347

Covey, Edward, 26, 71, 72, 73, 77, 212

Cowardice, 84, 121, 214, 219, 260, 261, 297

Crime, 108, 110, 188, 189, 191, 213, 230, 237, 238, 243, 248, 251, 252, 281, 310, 311, 319, 335; criminality, 95, 154, 326; war crimes, 333, 334

Cruelty, 58, 60, 61, 98, 280, 281, 315

Danto, Arthur, 23–24. *See also* Narrative

David, King (biblical), 43, 44, 55

Death, 9, 43, 59, 63, 64, 65, 71, 72, 73, 76, 107, 152, 190, 213, 218, 309, 325, 332; of black Americans in combat, 242, 265; of black cross-bearers, 336; civilian, 255; death is not the end, 125; of Aunt Esther, 335; of evil, 175; fear of, 217; "Give me liberty or give me death," 59, 65, 152; King's, 1, 8, 201, 202, 236; King's discussions of, 325, 332; of martyrs, 125; perennial death of God, 335; of reasonable utopias, 144; scared to death, 221; of Alton Sterling, 339; threats, 52; tragic deaths, 125

Debt, 236–241, 246, 247, 250, 252; debt of justice, 250, 252; to future generations, 252; Kant on, 172; King's intellectual debt to Du Bois, 30; King's intellectual debt to Kant, 173; King's intellectual debt to Niebuhr, 81; moral, 13

Declaration of Independence, 58, 59, 64, 138, 167, 237, 240, 242, 251, 313, 331, 342

Decolonization, 301, 321

Delany, Martin, 64–65, 294

Democracy, 3, 4, 7, 11, 15, 31, 33, 39, 41, 47, 50, 88, 90, 91, 100, 101, 141, 149, 152, 156, 157, 160, 161, 165, 175, 198, 200, 209, 233, 236, 237, 243, 244, 247, 250, 271, 275, 284, 288, 293, 294, 301, 307, 331–333, 341, 342, 344, 345; abolition democracy, 250; achieving ends democratically, 209; antidemocratic authority, 209; antidemocratic political action and organization, 207, 208; constitutional, 271, 283; democracy and nonviolent persuasion, 92–101; democratic accountability, 288; democratic aims, 208; democratic arguments, 249; democratic citizens, 39, 41, 45, 155, 159, 180; democratic culture, 39; democratic dilemmas, 321; democratic dream, 88; democratic elements in King's political thought, 10; democratic government, 228, 308; democratic greatness, 248; democratic hope of social equality, 92; democratic ideals, 239, 247, 342; democratic institutions, 41; democratic liberalism, 134; democratic life, 36, 38, 83, 88, 101, 157, 288; democratic participation, 130; democratic political process, 180; democratic politics, 31, 83, 91, 92, 100, 101, 156; democratic practice, 42; democratic principles, 247, 301; democratic public, 91, 100, 101; democratic repair, 245; democratic sacrifice, 292; democratic self-governance, 201; democratic society, 10, 13, 57, 144, 149, 232, 241, 298, 301; democratic spirit, 41, 329; democratic states, 39, 161; democratic values, 197; democratic will, 198; egalitarian, 181; liberal, 293, 342; multiracial, 47, 301; nondemocratic regimes, 91; nonviolent reconciliation as democratic imperative, 91; pluralist, 194; radically democratic form of political struggle, 207; radically inclusive, 344; representative, 168; social, 234; undemocratic practices, 179; United Nations democratic mechanism, 321; workplace, 201. *See also* Democratic theory; Democrats

Democratic theory, 146, 147, 151.
See also Democracy; Democrats
Democrats: Great Society Democrats,
304; race-conscious radical democrats, 150; radical democrats, 250,
343; social democrat, 201. *See also*
Democracy; Democratic theory
Demonstrations, 29, 91, 96, 97, 122,
123, 131, 165, 193, 217, 219, 292,
295–299, 302, 306, 312, 323, 345,
347. *See also* Protest
Desegregation, 11, 82, 88, 129, 147,
148, 149, 154, 187, 188, 301, 343.
See also Segregation
Despair, 2, 9, 42, 43, 44, 45, 68, 87,
109, 115, 125, 145, 190, 218, 276,
278, 286, 287, 288, 292, 307, 325,
326, 331, 336, 337
Destiny, 6, 28, 88, 203, 223, 284, 286,
313, 323
Deterrence: armed, 299; expected, 298;
general, 107; justified, against excessive brutality, 297, 298; self-defense
as, 303; specific, 107, 117; welfare-
oriented, 107. *See also* Punishment
de Tocqueville, Alexis, 31
Detroit Revolutionary Union Movement (DRUM), 291
Dewey, John, 282, 288, 388n21
DeWolf, L. Harold, 27, 137, 341
Dialectical approach, 45, 46, 47, 294,
303, 310, 341, 346
Dignity, 9, 11, 19, 21, 30, 31, 33, 34,
37, 39, 73, 85, 86, 87, 88, 90, 94, 95,
111, 133, 137–139, 159, 161–183,
199, 202, 212, 214, 216, 218, 220,
222, 223, 224, 227, 232, 233, 244,
291, 297, 314, 316, 339–348; as
equal moral standing, 30, 170–174,
175–176, 195–196, 202, 228, 316;
and hate, 21, 26–28; as inherent
moral worth, 12, 26, 34, 37, 133,
137–139, 162, 167–168, 173–174;
and poverty, 192, 195–196; and

protest, 26–29, 86, 94, 168, 170–172,
211–214, 284, 339–340; and the
right to vote, 10, 12, 161–183; as
self-respecting conduct, 12, 22–26,
28–29, 84–88, 94–95, 99–100, 162,
170–174, 305–306; as social rank,
162–163, 175–179. *See also* Indignity; Self-respect
Disadvantage, 13, 130, 189, 191, 192,
193, 201, 202, 203, 237, 238, 244,
316, 317, 323
Disappointment, 44, 52, 55, 144, 158,
198, 243, 244, 278, 292
Discipline, 10, 56, 80, 86, 87, 88,
94, 95, 96, 97, 100, 296, 306, 312,
313; disciplined protest, 97; disciplined suffering, 84, 85; discipline
of nonviolence, 101, 149, 155, 159;
nonviolent, 94, 95, 98, 101, 323; self-
discipline, 94, 124, 277; tactical, 97
Discrimination, 313, 344; color, 31;
de jure, 168; employment, 190,
193, 194, 201; housing, 130, 189,
201, 254; labor, 233; lending, 166;
racial, 11, 129, 130, 131, 135, 141,
142, 166, 172, 174, 177, 178, 189,
190–194, 228, 229, 242, 243, 244,
319, 345
Disobedience, 60, 64, 69, 70, 74, 76.
See also Civil disobedience
Disrespect, 125, 190, 221, 235, 315
Dissent, 35, 80, 99, 101, 193, 211,
224, 304, 306, 307, 310, 319, 321
Distrust, 315, 330; civic, 15, 298;
racial, 301. *See also* Trust
Divine: the divine, 133, 208, 253;
divine force, 220, 224; divine gift,
311; divine justice, 106–107, 113;
divine law, 52, 178; divine love, 129;
divine mission, 266; divine nature,
139; divine order, 51; divine plan, 43;
divine presence, 277; divine reassurance, 50; divine voice, 49; divinity,
138; near-divine wisdom, 6

Domination, 26, 60, 63, 67, 68, 100, 152, 154, 155, 159, 160, 180, 230, 232, 297, 300, 309, 310, 313, 326, 333; arbitrary, 209, 233; class, 93; "colonial," 317; extreme, 309; imperial, 93; political, 175, 177, 182; racial, 11, 80, 85, 86, 92, 93, 95, 96, 98, 99, 101, 116, 149, 152, 229, 298, 316; sociopolitical, 314; white, 116, 219; of white workers, 333. *See also* Nondomination; Subordination

Doubt, 68, 81, 181, 224, 259, 281; self-doubt, 328

Douglass, Frederick, 26, 31, 60, 64, 70, 71, 72, 73, 74, 77, 138, 167, 182, 212, 213, 247, 248, 279

Du Bois, W. E. B., 5, 9, 14, 19–34, 64, 73, 142, 225, 239, 246, 247, 248, 250, 294, 315, 326, 331, 332, 334, 336, 337, 342, 344

Due process, 166, 191

Duty, 12, 34, 40, 86, 97, 120, 130, 131, 148, 149, 172, 173, 174, 211, 213, 232, 249, 261, 262, 270–273, 279, 280, 284, 288, 308, 311, 312, 315, 317. *See also* Obligation; Responsibility

Economic injustice. *See* Injustice

Economy, 46, 194, 202, 236, 343; agrarian, 248; American, 233; capitalist, 198; exploitative, 238; full employment, 190, 192; licit, 203; mixed, 201; separate, 317, 318; underground, 317, 318, 323, 324; unreconstructed, 237

Edmund Pettus Bridge, 12, 170

Education, 37, 66, 67, 93, 94, 110, 129, 143, 157, 158, 168, 176, 180, 188–193, 202, 225, 228, 243, 250, 257, 277, 281, 301, 319, 320, 322, 329, 340, 347

Egalitarianism, 151, 205, 310; Christian liberal, 133

Elites, 5, 31; aristocratic, 31; black, and middle class, 31, 202, 304, 318, 333; black spiritual, 220; capitalist, 318; colonized, 277; corrupted, 329; entrenched interests of, 318; hegemony of, 209; media, 210; middle-class, 335; minority, 318; political, 228, 321; resistance by, 209; ruling, 346; white, 206, 297

Ellison, Ralph, 315

Elmer Gantry, 125. *See also* Lewis, Sinclair

Emancipation, 7, 14, 61, 88, 167, 197, 237, 247, 248, 313

"Emancipation Proclamation," 167. *See also* Lincoln, Abraham

Embodiment, 11, 128, 133, 138, 142, 143, 334

Emerson, Ralph Waldo, 11, 128, 133, 138, 141, 142, 143, 334. *See also* Moral Perfectionism

Emotion, 5, 11, 42, 95, 97, 106, 108, 109, 113–117, 123–126, 138, 152, 164, 217, 226, 231, 292, 303, 314, 325, 327. *See also* Feelings

Employment, 110, 189, 190, 192, 228, 250, 281; black, 193; compensation, 197; guaranteed, 235; insecure, 198; laws, 191; private sector, 198; racial discrimination in, 193, 194, 201; secure, 233; underemployment, 190, 193, 198, 287; unemployment, 130, 188, 189, 190, 192, 193, 198, 201, 203, 228, 229, 230, 242, 244, 254, 317, 318; and working-class women's transportation needs, 221

Engels, Friedrich, 318

Envy, 68, 195, 314, 328

Epistemic: epistemic borders, 38; epistemic insight, 311; epistemic violence, 309; epistemology, 51, 309; faith as a non-epistemic condition, 51, 52; King's epistemic critique of beliefs about masculinity, 216

Equality, 19, 30, 88, 90, 141, 149, 161, 162, 167–170, 176, 197, 206, 209, 227, 235, 241, 242, 246, 275, 280, 297, 301, 305, 345; civic, 228, 233; economic, 19, 30, 193, 194–198, 229, 293; equal rights, 32; and equals, 31, 176, 181, 196, 199, 226, 297, 298; equal standing, 196, 311, 316; fair equality of opportunity, 134, 166, 298; gendered, 232; of humanity, 342; legal, 129, 131, 134; moral, 300; Negro, 33, 256; political, 30, 128, 129, 131, 228; racial, 2, 129, 132, 133, 141, 190, 212, 229, 239, 240, 248, 251; radical equality of humanity, 343; social, 90, 92; society of equals, 196, 298; socioeconomic, 285, 286; substantive, 187, 193; treatment with equality, 169, 241. *See also* Inequality

Equal opportunity, 134, 141, 281, 342, 344; fair, 134, 166, 298; obstacles to, 191

Equal protection, 166, 175, 176, 180, 192, 281, 310, 342, 344

Eros, 113, 125

"Ethical Demands for Integration, The," 11, 138, 142, 146, 156–60

Ethics, 3, 49, 148, 300; appeal to others' moral or ethical sense, 305; ceaseless ethical transformation, 51; Christian ethics, 136, 137, 304; colorblindness as ethical ideal, 128; democracy as broad ethical ideal, 209; ethical-aesthetic force, 216, 302; ethical agent, 56; ethical commitments, 37, 39; ethical decision making, 127, 137; ethical demands, 11, 14, 138, 142, 146, 148, 149, 153, 156, 157, 158, 159, 160, 212; ethical demands for integration, 92; ethical depth, 36; ethical depth of King's commitment to critical self-reflection and self-improvement,
9; ethical dilemmas of coercion, 305; ethical dimensions of democratic life, 36; ethical discourse, 56; ethical experimentation, 45; ethical force of black dissent, 310; ethical framework, 149; ethical judgments, 53; ethical life, 43, 44, 49, 52, 138; ethically motivated sense of shame, 302; ethically permissible modes of dissent, 35; ethical political struggle, 300; ethical practice, 56; ethical purity, 305; ethical response to racial oppression, 137; ethical significance of American citizenship, 294; ethical significance of collective, armed self-defense, 297; ethical standards, 39; ethical traditions, 38; ethical vision, 38; ethical work, 150; ethic of abstract altruism, 35; ethic of community protection, 218; ethic of love, 10, 11; ethics in welfare politics, 211; ethics of nondomination, 155; ethics of political friendship, 156; ethics of racial solidarity, 291; ethics of rhetorically calling for the oppressed to use violence, 295; ethics of war and political violence, 13; Fanon on ethics, 309; guiding ethic of intimate critique, 323; King's love ethic, 307; King's theological ethics, 143; love ethic, 55, 56; Niebuhr's *An Interpretation of Christian Ethics,* 137; Niebuhr's notion of impossible ethical ideals, 144, 145; nonviolent political and ethical thought, 10; normative ethical theory, 105; perfectionist ethic, 52, 53, 54; political ethics, 7, 8; rationalistic ethical and political theories, 145; religious ethics, 37, 38; renunciation as central ethical goal, 125; social ethics, 36; transformation in ethical self-conception, 301; virtue ethics, 2, 40

Europe, 118, 162, 192, 248, 266, 292, 309

Evangelism, 133; American evangelism, 125, 126; King's evangelical roots, 343, 344; white conservative Christian evangelicals, 342

Evil, 3, 12, 85, 326, 332; absence of not equivalent to justice, 46; coercion and man's capacity for, 305; dignified protest as exposing, 94, 171, 322, 347–348; King on wars to prevent, 259; noncooperation and, 193, 259–260, 273, 275–276, 278; nuclear war as the "most colossal of," 119; Obama on, 255; on oppression and injustice as "evil monsters," 174–182; retaliation and, 114; segregation as, 281–282; the self as divided between good and, 55; St. Paul on, 44, 561

Exceptionalism, 145; American, 140, 254, 255, 264, 266, 328

Exclusion, 3, 20, 24, 133, 136, 218, 277, 282, 283, 313, 317

Exemplarity, 44, 79, 207, 239, 251, 326, 328, 336; exemplary unfreedom of slavery, 11

Existential: existential burden, 42; existential Christian commitments, 51; existential considerations, 51; existential costs, 43; existential demand, 14; existential effects, 51; existential element of action, 87; existential expression, 139; existential framework King applies to his definition of "freedom," 147; existential level, 324; existential-phenomenological analysis of the "lived experience of the Black," 142; existential power, 150; existential resilience of remembrance, reverence, and resistance, 336; existential resource, 53; existential sustenance, 52; existential threat, 229, 306; existential toll, 36; King's existentialist

approach, 51; King's reliance on the existential, 53

Experiment: America's democratic experiment, 161, 168, 284, 329, 332; ethical experimentation, 42, 45; experimentalism, 42, 44; experimental striving, 36; experiments in liberal democracy, 342; experiment with nonviolence, 78, 80, 82, 91; formal experimentation, 8; King as experimentalist, 54; life as experiment, 43

Exploitation, 88, 168, 228, 237, 238, 311, 317, 320, 332; of black Americans, 237, 238, 239, 240, 258; economic, 31, 175, 189, 249, 258, 317; the exploited, 200; exploiting convictions and sentiments, 4; Fanon on colonialism as, 309; global exploitation of colored peoples, 265; labor, 187, 192, 197, 201, 230; nonexploitative capital-labor relations, 12; of poor whites, 194, 238; racialized, 239; racist, 258; symbols of, 311; of women, 230, 232, 233

Expropriation, 309, 317, 318

Extramarital affairs of King, 44, 56, 126

Failure: of American attempts to redress injustice, 247, 287; of love for fellow citizens, 110; of recognition, and microaggressions, 155; to resist evil, 279, 281, 301, 310; role of, in family, 231; sense of black masculinity as, 213; Thucydides on, 320; tragic sensibility and, 42–44, 54; voting right denial as failures concerning dignity, 163

Fairness, 135, 259; civic, 197; and competition for jobs and promotions, 188; and distribution of wealth, 200; economic, 12, 187; and employment compensation, 197, 201; and equality of opportunity, 134, 166, 298; fair play, 169; fair rents, 194; fair terms in a market society, 191; fair treatment, 225; fair wage or profit margin, 197; and housing protections, 130; and obstacles to well-paying jobs, 190; realization of, 135

Faith: bad faith, 169, 263, 303; blind faith in American military power, 254, 258; Christian faith and communism, 198; distinction between faith and belief, 54; faith in redemption of American political order, 300–301; good faith, 158; in integration, 132; King's crises of faith, 329, 332; in metaphysical and existential philosophy, 51–53; narratives of faith, 344; Niebuhr on, 145; in political institutions, 15; practical faith, 206; in public reason, 49–50, 194; purifying power of faith, 276

Family, 12, 56, 142, 175, 187, 188, 189, 201, 203, 207, 210, 213, 214, 219, 227, 229–235, 240, 249, 295, 296, 326

Fanon, Frantz, 5, 87, 89, 142, 144, 277, 309, 310, 311, 314, 319, 322, 323, 342

Farmer, James, 82

Fear, 46, 58, 61, 68, 69, 70, 85, 87, 92, 93, 96, 98, 124, 125, 149, 152, 176, 188, 189, 217, 245, 254, 260, 290, 298, 301, 304, 306, 310, 314, 316, 317, 330, 333, 346; fearless speech, 332

Feelings, 21, 52, 58, 66, 72, 94, 99, 111, 115, 195, 205, 228, 244, 259, 306, 312; of inferiority, 31. *See also* Emotion

Feminism, 13, 232, 233, 234; black feminists, 203; feminist historians, 225; feminist interpretations and assessments of King, 205, 207, 211, 227; post-feminist, 132; spatial feminists, 221

Ferguson, Missouri, 348

Force, 26, 85, 98, 212, 304; aesthetic, 209, 218, 306; brute, 100, 346; creative, 115, 282, 284; divine, 220, 224; ethical-aesthetic, 216; ethical-aesthetic force of violence, 302; ethical force of black dissent, 310; forced obedience, 61, 63; forceful resistance, 71; forcing negotiation, 122, 131; futility of, 98; government use of, 262; infinite hope as a, 287; of labor discrimination, 233; legal, 283; love, 276, 346; moral, 216, 306; moral, for justice, 348; of nonviolent resistance, 284; normative, 128; Obama on necessity of, 255; obligatory force of duty to obey the law, 308; physical, 261; public, 177; purest-soul, 263; social, 94, 280, 284; spectacular, 302, 307; superior, 306; technology as tyrannical and frightening, 198; truth, 121, 276, 346; use of, 83, 93, 95, 120

Forgiveness, 105, 106, 140, 283, 298, 301, 305, 344

Fraser, Nancy, 230

Frazier, E. Franklin, 229, 298

Freedom, 10, 25, 32, 33, 59, 63, 65–68, 70, 71, 73, 74, 76, 81, 85–89, 91, 112, 122, 124, 138, 141, 146, 147, 148, 152, 153, 155, 156, 157, 160, 161, 166, 169, 171, 192, 199, 212, 237, 248, 257, 270, 275, 276, 293, 304, 323, 332, 336, 339, 345, 347; abstract, 248; African American, 280; of association, 187; as capacity for rational choice, 199; comparative, 72; complete, 74; conventional liberal view of, 151; eliminative, 147, 148; of expression, 342; from fear, 333; formal, 196; full, 148; illusory, 248; life-quality, 147, 151, 152; love of, 47, 59, 65, 66, 67, 68, 143; moral, 86; more than half, 70, 73, 74, 76, 77;

Freedom (*continued*)
negative, 67, 68, 73, 148; as non-domination, 11; as noninterference, 11, 146, 147; positive, 152, 153; from prohibition, 147; quality-life, 153; racial, 262; radical, in love, 335; real, 196, 250; religious, 342; republican, 65, 67, 73; of speech, 333; struggle for, 81, 212, 276, 277, 296, 337; to do, 147, 152; unfreedom, 10, 68, 69, 70, 318; of worship, 333. *See also* Black freedom movement; Liberty; *Stride Toward Freedom: The Montgomery Story*

Freedom rides, 82, 283, 296; Freedom Riders, 299. *See also* Monroe, North Carolina

Friendship, 117, 124, 260, 300, 305; civic friendship, 301; fair-weather white friends, 47; political friendship, 11, 156

Gandhi, Mohandis K., 9, 10, 49, 78–88, 90, 91, 94, 96, 97, 98, 100, 105, 106, 107, 111, 112, 113, 117–126, 155, 171, 255, 258, 260–263, 276, 280, 281, 282, 286, 289, 345, 346; Gandhian movement, 82

Gangs, 323. *See also* Lumpenproletariat

Garrow, David, 51, 56

Gay marriage, 174

Gender, 4, 12, 100, 163, 210, 218, 221, 224, 234, 295; gender analysis, 222; gender complementarity, 231; gender composition of southern congregations, 213; gender conservatism, 249; gendered distinctions between activity and passivity, 215; gendered division of labor, 207, 234; gendered pattern in Montgomery, 221; gender equality, 232; gender equity, 225; gender hierarchies, 207, 228; gender identity, 232, 234; gender inequality, 202, 203; gender justice, 13, 205, 210, 232; gender norms, 207, 228, 235; gender presentation, 223; gender privilege, 232; gender relations, 222; gender-specific abuses faced by black women, 221; gender stereotypes, 231; intersections of gender, 223; intraracial gender hierarchy, 222; King's conception of, 228, 230, 232; King's gender ideology, 235; King's ontology of, 210, 227, 234; SCLC gender ideology, 211; significance of gender in King's understanding of the boycott, 220, 223, 224; spatialized gendered occupational problem, 220; traditional gender roles, 220

Geopolitics, 253, 294, 295, 302, 321

George III, King, 64

Georgia, 150, 166, 265, 307, 332

Ghettos, 130, 187, 189, 228, 382; black ghetto culture, 58, 115, 188, 189; housing in, 189; poverty in, 12, 14, 130, 166, 187, 188, 192, 194, 195, 305; riots in, 187, 190–191, 303–313; social problems of, 188–204, 228–229, 317

God, 26, 28, 33, 34, 38, 43, 44, 48, 49, 50, 54, 55, 74, 86, 99, 119, 125, 128, 129, 132, 133, 136–143, 148, 166, 167, 173, 176, 178, 199, 200, 211, 232, 252, 302, 308, 311, 335, 341, 342, 343, 344, 348

Godse, Nathuram, 120, 121, 122

Gooding-Williams, Robert, 7

Goods, 39, 64; basic goods of material significance, 153; cooperative social goods, 209; "inward-facing" goods and political protests, 284; material goods, 152; psychosocial goods, 281

Goodwill, 27, 55, 57, 86, 95, 114, 122, 164, 197, 231, 241, 306, 320, 357. See also *Agape* (love)

Grace, 128, 132, 136, 139, 140, 299

Harding, Vincent, 9

Harper, Frances Ellen Watkins, 167

Hartmann, Heidi, 232

Hate, 21, 22, 23, 25, 27, 55, 64, 70, 85, 113, 114, 117, 122, 123, 217, 255, 260, 286, 326

Hatred, 21, 22, 23, 24, 25, 26, 27, 28, 29, 30, 34, 55, 67, 119, 122, 136, 217, 271, 278, 305, 312, 326

Hegel, Georg Wilhelm Friedrich, 46, 47, 293, 310

Henry, Patrick, 59, 65

Heschel, Rabbi Abraham Joshua, 327, 329

Hierarchy, 310; antihierarchical forums for political speech and action, 209; gender, 207, 218; group, 317; hierarchical account of the body, 217; hierarchical politics, 31; hierarchical social relations, 163; hierarchical tendencies, 88; hierarchy of ends, 40; hierarchy-sustaining injustices, 163; hierarchy-sustaining social relations, 162; intraracial gender, 222; King's hierarchical and antidemocratic modes of political action, 207; non-hierarhical form of political struggle, 207; objectionable forms of, 214; patriarchal, 209; racial, 221, 224, 304, 316; stratified social hierarchy of persons, 177, 178, 179, 182

Hinduism, tradition, 106, 120–122

Historical materialism, 199. *See also* Marxism; Materialism

Holt Street Baptist Church speech ("Day of Days" speech), 23–25, 28–29, 86

Holy Spirit, 27, 143

Honor, 1, 26, 68, 167, 177, 178, 212, 213, 302; dishonor, 168, 261, 302; honorific social status, 162, 163, 178, 179, 181, 182; national honor, 301, 302

Hooker, Juliet, 245

hooks, bell, 206

Hope, 14, 287, 295; aesthetic means of arousing, 123; and black celebrity icons, 218; black cultural and spiritual practices as source of, 331; for civil rights movement, 275, 277; colorblindness as King's, 132–134, 140; democratic hope of social equality, 92; Du Bois on, 336; and economic progress/security, 190; and fear, 125; Gandhi and King on hope for cooperative future, 105; as generative of sublime madness, 144–145; and God's grace, 136, 139, 252; hopelessness, 286, 293, 326; and internationalism, 251; King on "infinite hope," 277, 280, 287; King's hope for world peace, 258–259; lumpenproletariat as source of hope, 318; Montgomery as occasion for, 24–25; nihilism and, 326; and revolution, 286; of slaves, 59, 64, 70–71, 73–74; "stone of hope," 1–2; *Testament of Hope*, 7; Thucydides on, 325; and "Transition-anger," 108, 115, 122

Housing, 130, 168, 188, 189, 190, 193, 201, 234, 250, 254, 257, 281, 322, 323, 329

Humanity, 13, 26, 48, 128, 129, 138, 139, 140, 141, 142, 144, 148, 149, 168, 172, 173, 176, 182, 212, 224, 239, 253, 257, 259, 270, 273, 310, 342, 343

Human nature, 26, 44, 55, 61, 71, 93, 118, 138, 139, 162, 212; essential natures and relation to dignity, 174, 178, 182; nature of a person's life, 154; nature of a woman, 231; nature of a man, 68, 86, 231; nature of persons, 162. *See also* Personhood

Human rights, 53, 181, 199, 259, 310, 321, 346

Humiliation, 71, 87, 92, 108, 155, 175, 187, 189, 195, 211, 213, 214, 218, 221, 228, 230, 231, 233, 238, 260, 274, 300, 314, 327, 346

Ideal Chronicler, 23–24. *See also* Narrative
Idealism, 137, 255, 258; personal, 37, 38
Ideals, 10, 11, 13, 99, 127, 166, 180, 182, 199, 206, 235, 239, 270, 300, 301, 340; American, 3–4, 254, 257, 342; of armed self-defense, 95; of colorblindness, 128–145; of Communists, 199, 319; of conscientious citizenship, 269–289; contradiction between practices and, 179, 182, 302; in democracy, 180, 209, 239, 247, 342, 344, 345; of Du Bois, 331–332; of family, 231–232, 234; of Gandhi, 86; gendered, 211–212, 230, 232; idolization of, 136; of integration, 88–89, 148, 151, 156–157; legal 135–136; of love and nonviolence, 211; of participatory parity, 227; prophetic dimensions of, 127–128, 140, 144; religion as source of, 139; of self-transformation, 40, 48
Ideal witness, 23–24. *See also* Narrative
Identity, 135, 210, 239, 295, 314; African American, 314–315; black, 35, 294; gender, 232, 234; identity politics, 292, 330; masculine, 212; national, 3, 302; racial, 134, 295; shared, 294, 314; social, 302; unity-through-identity, 143
"I Have a Dream," 1, 108, 122, 128, 129, 133, 150, 192, 237, 247, 283
Imperialism, 2, 8, 57, 175, 270, 276, 314, 318
Inclusion, 143, 154, 155, 157, 158, 205, 207, 218, 219, 294, 313

Income, 72, 77, 202; guaranteed annual income (GAI), 232, 233, 235; guaranteed basic minimum income, 13, 193, 196, 198, 201, 203, 210, 211, 232, 233, 235, 250, 274, 322; high-income countries, 257; income gains of wealthy during first Obama term, 334; income inequality, 175, 176, 232, 233; income support for poor families, 202; loss of income during imprisonment, 203. *See also* Wages
Independence, 58, 90, 175, 208, 263, 316; black, 321; Ghanaian, 271, 277; Indian, 78; movements for, 175. *See also* Declaration of Independence
India, 78, 79, 82, 83, 91, 118, 120, 121, 124, 247, 261, 277, 278
Indigenous peoples, 216, 263, 330, 333
Indignity, 163, 171, 174, 175, 177, 182, 280, 281, 291, 347
Individualism, 47, 198, 231, 275, 310, 341. *See also* Collectivism
Individuality, 138, 234, 275
Inequality, 13, 15, 78, 176, 193, 281, 333; class, 166, 333; economic, 2, 193, 200, 202, 227, 228, 274, 287, 298; gender, 202, 203; of humankind, 167; income, 232; material, 281; racial, 191, 202, 212, 248; substantive, 175; unequal distribution of resources, 180; unequal military conscription, 244; unequal protection of law, 175; unequal shares of income, 175; unequal social relations, 176. *See also* Equality
Inferiority, 28, 31, 58, 74, 85, 87, 171, 176, 209, 213, 239, 242, 298, 310, 314, 344
Injury, 55, 61, 67, 106, 108, 109, 114, 328; noninjury, 155, 156, 157, 158, 159; status-injury, 106
Injustice, 4, 108, 111, 136, 163, 216, 223–224, 276, 281, 288, 301, 303,

304, 319; awakening awareness of, 110, 345; civil disobedience and, 74, 77, 95, 99, 131; duties to protest, 25–26, 76, 86, 171–174, 211, 270–271, 273, 275, 279; economic, 12, 187–204, 244, 307, 347; educational, 347; gender, 228, 230, 295; historic, 229, 238, 241, 245, 249, 308; past, 191, 241; political, 182, 347; racial, 12, 20–22, 33, 162, 164–179, 187, 189, 191, 201, 230, 242, 247, 248, 295, 308, 322, 344; structural, 245–246; violent retaliation or deterrence against, 216, 245, 299; voter suppression as, 162

Institutions, 15, 36–37, 38, 40, 41, 45, 82, 89, 90, 101, 118, 136, 142, 146, 150, 154, 157, 159, 161, 182, 193, 235, 244, 275, 282, 285, 286, 294, 314, 316, 317, 318, 321, 340

Integration, 10, 11, 20–22, 47, 79, 85–92, 114, 129, 132, 134, 138, 142, 146–160, 196, 206, 225, 240, 243, 244, 283, 295, 298, 304, 322, 328, 330; fantastical ideals of, 151; integrationism, 294; and racial demographics, 151. *See also* "Ethical Demands for Integration, The"

Integrity, 156, 302, 331, 332, 334, 337; black spiritual, 331, 335, 341; family, 231; intellectual, 2

Interpretation, 7, 9, 10, 50, 128, 137, 164, 167, 205, 209, 210, 219, 240, 261, 263, 274, 286

Interracial: interracial alliances, 321; interracial audience, 241; interracial coalitions, 92, 291; interracial freedom rides, 82; interracial group, 55; interracial moral appeal, 92; interracial reconciliation, 79; interracial solidarity, 317; Rosa Parks's anti-interracial sexual violence work, 222

Iraq War, 219, 257, 264

Jackson, Jesse, 193
Jackson, Rev. J. H., 327
James, William, 49
Jefferson, Thomas, 61, 63, 166, 247, 248, 251, 333, 345
Jensen, Kipton, 36
Jim Crow, 2, 3, 4, 12, 20, 33, 187, 189, 229, 242, 292, 297, 301, 315
Joblessness, 192, 196, 198, 201, 230
Johnson, James Weldon, 336
Johnson, Lyndon B., 164, 165, 168, 169, 187, 229, 241, 256, 264, 269, 290, 303, 327, 328
Johnson, Mordecai, 81
Joy, 68, 226, 231; Easter joy, 335; joylessness, 330; religious joy, 126; subversive joy, 226
Judgment, 1, 3, 14, 15, 36, 49, 53, 132, 136, 140, 145, 179, 206, 207, 210, 212, 227, 283, 298, 300, 301, 304, 310, 311, 312, 315, 318
Justice: compensatory and reparative, 13, 129, 191, 247, 306; criminal, 154, 202, 203; distributive, 129, 153, 197, 198, 244; economic, 12, 13, 14, 57, 169, 188, 192, 194–198, 200, 201, 202, 204, 228, 232, 235; just society, 11, 47, 132, 135, 172, 198, 274, 275, 312, 341; racial, 7, 133, 136, 164, 167, 168, 169, 173, 174, 179, 248, 294; revolutionary, 105, 110, 111; social, 2, 11, 28, 128, 191, 197, 200, 229, 282, 295, 298, 311, 316; unjust society, 172
Justification, 84, 119, 206, 259, 279, 295, 299, 305

Kant, Immanuel, 138, 139, 140, 147, 162, 170, 172, 173, 174, 177, 182, 199; Kantianism, 40, 147, 148
Kierkegaard, Søren, 51, 54
King, Coretta Scott, 56, 234, 326, 327, 330

Knowledge, 23, 24, 33, 51, 53, 54, 81, 142, 157, 158, 195, 209, 312
Korean War, 231. *See also* War

Labor, 2, 8, 176, 198, 304, 342; capital-labor relations, 12; civil rights-labor alliance, 194, 202; gendered division of labor, 207, 234; labor exploitation, 187, 197, 230, 238; labor leaders, 82, 96, 197; labor movement, 194; labor organizations, 194, 197, 201; menial, 189; organized, 194, 198, 232, 234, 286, 318; uncompensated domestic, 230
Lasch, Christopher, 14
Latin America, 179, 297
Latinos, 136, 202, 330
Lawson, James, 82, 83, 96
Leadership, 23, 78, 82, 83, 120, 157, 158, 193, 202, 205, 208, 226, 227, 243; charismatic, 207, 208, 209, 218, 234; Ella Baker's conferences on, 222; pulpit-to-pew conception of, 208, 225
Lebron, Chris, 39, 41, 45, 46
Legitimacy, 12, 84, 90, 156, 291, 296, 308, 311, 319, 321; illegitimacy, 230
"Letter from a Birmingham City Jail," 2, 30, 32, 34, 95, 137, 139, 176, 270, 273, 276, 280, 281, 283, 342, 344
Lewis, Sinclair, 125
Liberalism, 8, 9, 14, 39, 49, 50, 81, 134, 139, 144, 146, 147, 188, 199, 292, 293, 308
Liberation, 89, 90, 91, 175, 240, 248, 286, 310, 322; *Black Theology of Liberation, A* (James Cone), 143; "Toward Black Liberation" (Stokely Carmichael), 286
Liberty, 59, 65, 67, 68, 71, 151, 152, 167, 192, 197, 199, 208, 265, 336, 340, 342; basic, 151, 192, 199, 228; equal, 152, 274; love of, 59, 65, 68; negative, 146, 147, 148, 151, 153;

positive, 146, 147, 151, 152, 153, 154, 157
Lincoln, Abraham, 167, 237, 248, 251, 345
Locke, John, 5, 63
Louis, Joe, 214, 218
Louisiana, 166, 300
Love: Christian, 28, 171, 304; disinterested, 277, 280; erotic, 123, 125; love ethic, 11, 55, 56, 304, 307; love force (satyagraha), 276, 346; personal, 124; unconditional, 13, 270, 332, 333, 335
Lumpenproletariat, 318, 322, 323
Lunch counter sit-ins, 82, 283, 345

MacIntyre, Alasdair, 40
Malcolm X, 14, 92, 111, 116, 121, 122, 175, 213, 214, 215, 218, 219, 309, 310, 311, 326, 334
Mandela, Nelson, 106, 112, 117, 118, 119, 253, 262
Manhood, 12, 205, 211–218, 227–230, 242, 244, 249, 297, 347
Manliness, 22, 211, 214; unmanliness, 120, 126, 214, 219
Marches, 31, 100, 122, 165, 166, 168, 193, 215, 242, 283, 306; in Birmingham, 97, 98; at Dharasana Salt Works, 120; from Selma to Montgomery, 165, 170, 178, 219; housing marches in Chicago, 323; March Against Fear / James Meredith March, 290–291; March on Washington, 43, 96, 116, 128, 130, 192, 208; 1966 Mississippi Freedom March, 323
Marriage, 107, 231, 232, 234, 327; gay marriage, 174
Martin Luther King Jr. Day, 1, 35, 36
Marx, Karl, 5, 27, 199, 200, 232, 318; Marxism, 8, 188, 199, 292, 293, 313, 318, 319
Masculinity, 13, 14, 122, 126, 206, 207, 209, 211–217, 230–231, 235;

Black Power's masculinist politics,
210; masculinist categories of protector and provider, 347; masculinist
conflation of dignity, manhood, and
violence, 214, 227
Masses, 100, 226, 277, 336; black, 31,
326; Negro, 20
Mass incarceration, 203, 252, 324
Materialism, 47, 288, 331, 341;
American, 287, 329; attenuation
of, 330; and conceptions of human
personhood, 137, 138, 139. *See also*
Historical materialism
Mays, Benjamin, 81
Means-Ends, 36, 96, 129, 133, 199,
234, 264, 345; color-conscious
means, 133, 134, 135; effective
means, 100, 197, 272; ends justify
means, 119, 331; improved means to
an unimproved end, 45; nonviolent
action as means, 85, 87, 92; scrutiny
of means, 95; seizing power by any
means, 47; treating men as ends, not
means (categorical imperative), 139,
148, 154, 160, 172, 199; violence as
a means, 261, 262, 322
Memphis, Tennessee, 97, 175, 290,
327, 329
Middle East, 254, 265, 266
Militancy, 24–27, 92, 115, 116, 213,
215, 217, 221, 234, 290; black
militancy, 213, 217, 304; Black
Power militants, 302, 303, 308, 312,
313, 320, 321; Du Bois on militant,
self-respecting self-assertion, 21, 22;
militant nonviolence, 88, 115, 215,
245, 306; militant self-defense, 84
Militarism, 14, 47, 53, 57, 88, 166,
215, 243, 253, 255, 266, 288, 301,
329, 330, 331, 332, 341; militarized
police forces, 329, 334, 348; militarized responses to ghetto riots, 310
Military, 90, 98, 177, 190, 201, 245,
253, 256, 303, 320, 329; military-
industrial complex, 256, 264, 329;
military power, 255, 257, 264, 265;
military spending, 256, 257, 329;
Obama administration's foreign
policy and military endeavors, 13
Miller, Webb, 120, 121, 122
Ministry, 53, 211, 336
Mississippi, 166, 179, 290, 291, 300,
302
Modi, Narendra, 125
Monroe, North Carolina, 295, 296,
299
Montgomery bus boycott, 9, 21, 23,
24, 25, 26, 27, 28, 29, 30, 52, 79,
80–83, 86, 97, 130, 168, 170, 171,
208, 211, 219–227, 236, 250, 260,
269, 271, 276, 278, 284, 299, 345;
meaning of, 25, 28, 29, 272, 284,
345
Montgomery Improvement Association, 283
Morality, 1, 15, 68, 79, 93, 114, 147,
164, 166, 172, 188, 252, 259, 269,
309, 326; political, 1, 15, 166, 188,
283
Moral Man and Immoral Society
(Reinhold Niebuhr), 83, 93, 137
Moral perfectionism, 35–57; Cavell on
perfectionism, 39–40, 46; Emer-
sonian perfectionism, 39–40, 46;
Lebron on perfectionism, 39, 41, 46;
tragic perfectionism, 45
Moral suasion, 2, 75, 318, 346
Moral universe (the arc of), 12, 44, 54,
140, 167, 172, 179, 182
Morehouse College, 36, 37, 82, 340
Moynihan, Daniel Patrick, 188, 202,
229, 249
Moynihan Report. See *The Negro
Family: The Case for National Action*
(Daniel Patrick Moynihan)
Muhammad, Elijah, 31
Murray, Albert, 315
Myrdal, Gunnar, 3

Narrative, 23–25, 29, 34; narrative sentences, 23–25; romantic historical narratives, 2–3, 8, 14

National Association for the Advancement of Colored People (NAACP), 128, 129, 207, 222, 223, 229, 283, 290, 295, 296

National Black Political Convention, 291

National Urban League (NUL), 290

Nazi Germany, 259, 260

Negro Family in the United States, The (E. Franklin Frazier), 229. *See also* Frazier, E. Franklin

Negro Family: The Case for National Action, The (Daniel Patrick Moynihan), 188, 202, 229, 249

Negro revolution, 58, 85

Neocolonialism, 250, 303, 320

Newton, Huey P., 175, 319, 320

Niebuhr, Reinhold, 11, 27, 53, 81, 83, 93, 95, 127, 131, 132, 135, 136, 137, 138, 139, 140, 144, 145, 305, 306, 307, 346

Nietzsche, Friedrich, 27, 328

Nihilism, 14, 312, 325, 326, 335, 336

Nixon, E. D., 82, 222, 225

Nixon, Richard (presidential administration), 299

Nkrumah, Kwame, 277

"Nobel Prize Acceptance Speech," 131, 137

Noncooperation, 90, 122, 193; Gandhian, 90, 111, 281; Khilafat movement, 78; noncooperation as *satyagraha*, 280; noncooperation with evil, 193, 273, 275, 276; nonviolent, 80, 276, 281

Nondomination, 10, 11, 151, 153, 154, 155, 156, 157, 160, 180, 181

Nonviolence, 2, 9, 26–28, 47, 78–101, 111, 113, 117–120, 139, 149, 153, 155, 159, 170, 172, 193, 227, 251, 273, 274–279, 285, 288, 304, 322, 323, 346, 347, 348; in African American life, 85, 91; and anger, 115, 117, 120–126; critics of, 79–80, 84, 91, 113, 116, 118, 120–121, 211–214, 240, 243–244, 278, 295–324; and democracy, 91–101, 270–271; distinction between principled and strategic, 80; in global affairs, 251, 253–266; history of, in political thought, 78–83; and inclusivity, 100, 149, 214–216; and masculinity, 216–219, 277; nonviolent direct action, 14, 46, 58, 73–75, 78, 82–83, 86, 91, 92, 94, 97, 100, 121, 123, 193, 218, 270, 278, 297, 301, 304, 305, 307, 346, 347; nonviolent politics, 22, 78, 80, 85, 87–88, 91, 92, 96, 101, 292, 322; nonviolent protest, 10, 31, 79, 83, 86, 87, 91, 94–97, 100, 105, 115, 116, 120, 124, 156, 171, 214, 217, 302, 305, 308, 339, 347; nonviolent resistance, 77, 115, 124, 149, 155–156, 159, 190, 193, 219, 258–262, 270, 273, 278, 280, 284–285, 305, 326, 328, 340; and pacifism, 119–120, 139, 257–261, 265–266; and self-defense, 295–303; of spirit, 55; and suffering, 87, 279; tactical advantages of, 87–89; training in, 83

Nuclear: nuclear age, 259; nuclear annihilation, 294; nuclear modernizations, 254; nuclear war, 119, 254, 260; nuclear weapons, 119, 254, 259, 260

Nussbaum, Martha, 3

Obama, Barack, 13, 14, 253, 254, 255, 256, 257, 258, 259, 266, 333, 334, 335

Obligation, 40, 130, 140, 226; of black Americans to behave with dignity, 162, 179; of conscientious citizens to resist and redress injustice, 270–271, 272, 279, 289; of non-cooperation with evil and cooperation with good, 273, 275, 279; unenforceable, 149

Ontology: Benhabib's reconstruction of Arendt's ontological categories, 210; freedom as ontologically tied to the nature of man, 86; King's ontological-theological conception of personhood, 130, 133; King's ontology of gender, 227, 234; King's social ontology, 210, 230; ontological foregrounding of God and the universal, 143; prioritizing ethics over ontology, 49

Operation Breadbasket, 193

Oppression, 29, 99, 115, 120, 136, 158, 171, 175, 206, 274, 279, 294, 297, 305, 308, 311, 313, 320, 347, 348; formerly oppressed, 122, 160, 270, 273; former oppressors, 90, 122, 270, 273, 348; moral psychology of oppression, 87; the oppressed, 21, 22, 23, 24, 26, 81, 85, 86, 90, 111, 155, 159, 212, 224, 274, 276, 295, 309, 314, 345, 346, 347; oppressed black Americans, 89, 133, 326; the oppressor, 24, 90, 92, 99, 111, 155, 171, 279, 297, 302, 309, 346; racial oppression, 3, 47, 135, 137, 171, 224, 239, 244, 249, 269, 278, 279, 298, 315; resisting oppression, 21, 26, 29, 155, 227

Optimism, 43, 93, 138, 139, 165, 258, 292, 293, 337

Organizing, 208, 291, 300, 319; black political, 209; civil rights, 242; community, 210, 291; of gang members, 322; grassroots, 4, 82, 207, 222; labor, 82, 198; for the NWRO, 235; of the poor, 234

Pacificism, 83, 119, 139, 214, 256–263, 265, 266, 346

Paine, Thomas, 247

Parker, Theodore, 12, 54, 328

Parks, Rosa, 82, 171, 208, 221, 222, 223, 225, 260

Patriarchy, 12, 227, 232, 330; black support for, 206; patriarchal attitudes prevalent within a larger black church culture, 207; patriarchal families, 249; patriarchal lens, 203; patriarchal role of familial protector of women and children, 213; reinforcement of patriarchal hierarchies, 209; white male patriarchs, 206; white supremacist capitalist, 206

Patriotism, 14, 35, 121, 333

Paul, Saint, 34, 44, 56

Peace, 13, 43, 90, 117, 199, 252, 254, 256, 264, 266, 269, 306; peaceful nonviolent movement, 165; peaceful protest, 99, 168, 262, 274, 296; peaceful revolution, 116, 265; permanent peace, 299; world peace, 1, 251, 258

Personalism, 27, 36–39, 48, 136, 137, 140, 142, 344; Christian, 9

Personality (human), 26, 27, 30, 34, 37, 39, 126, 137, 138, 139, 141, 155, 167, 173, 176, 178, 179, 223, 274, 311, 322, 342, 343, 344, 347

Personhood, 130, 132, 133, 136, 137, 139, 142, 143, 154, 155

Pessimism, 11, 128, 136, 139, 142, 145, 293, 295, 315

Philia, 113, 125

"Pilgrimage to Nonviolence," 227, 276, 343

Plato, 217, 276, 280; Apology, 276

Plessy v. Ferguson, 128, 134, 280, 281

Pluralism, 7, 144; pluralist democracy, 50, 194; reasonable, 144; value, 206

Police, 76, 96, 98, 120, 135, 190, 219, 220, 226, 245, 281, 291, 296, 299, 300, 308, 320, 336, 339, 343; global leadership as policing foreign nations, 254, 266; militarized police forces, 329, 334, 348; police brutality, 98, 176, 189, 308, 310, 332, 348; resistance to police repression, 310

Political agency, 13, 33, 86, 218, 219, 234, 284, 295

Political power, 47, 233, 285, 286, 293

Poor People's Campaign, 83, 86, 233, 287, 306, 327, 329, 330

Poverty, 78, 142, 168, 169, 178, 187–188, 238, 240, 252, 256, 265–266, 282, 287–288, 301, 307, 329–334, 344; and capitalism, 200–201; child poverty, 257, 334; culture of poverty, 31, 58; and dignity, 196, 232–233; and family life, 188–189, 229–233, 249; and gender, 228, 234–235; and guaranteed basic income, 13, 193, 196, 198, 201, 203, 210, 211, 232, 233, 235, 250, 274, 322; and inequality, 195–196, 275, 330, 334; and unemployment, 192–193; War on Poverty, 193, 202, 256, 263, 265; and welfare policy, 202

Power of Non-Violence, The (Richard Gregg), 83, 97, 98

Pragmatism, 46, 254, 266; pragmatic, 46, 80, 254, 255, 258, 264, 304, 306, 308; pragmatic militarism, 255, 266; pragmatic skepticism, 254, 266

Praxis, 4, 205, 207, 209, 211, 212, 214, 216, 309, 319

Prejudice, 5, 20, 21, 46, 93, 149, 282, 311, 313

Pride, 68, 92, 93, 149, 244, 294, 345, 346

Promised land, 44, 55, 132, 252, 294

Property, 26, 36, 70, 116, 130, 141, 151, 175, 190, 191, 195, 197, 224, 245, 296, 304, 306, 308, 311, 341, 348

Prophetic, 5, 9, 11, 123, 127, 129, 140, 143, 144, 145, 156, 211, 273, 285, 312, 329, 331, 333, 341

Protest, 25, 43, 63, 86–88, 91, 111–116, 120–124, 200, 215, 262, 285, 296, 307; and anger, 107–112; as boycott, 90, 193, 283–284, 305; and

discipline, 80, 86, 94, 96–98, 101, 149, 155, 159, 217, 296, 306, 323; as disruption, 95, 306; and gender, 211–214, 218–227; and nonviolence, 31, 78–80, 83, 86, 87, 91, 94–97, 100, 105, 115, 116, 120, 124, 156, 171, 214, 217, 302, 305, 308, 339, 347; and riots, 115–116, 190–191, 244–245, 303–305; and self-respect (dignity), 26–29, 86, 94, 168, 170–172, 211–214, 284, 339–340

Public sphere, 49, 50, 312, 313, 342

Punishment, 60, 70, 107, 110, 117

Race consciousness, 127–130, 132, 135, 150, 192

Racial ideology, 7, 355

Racism, 47, 57, 108, 130, 140, 142, 192, 200, 276, 297–298, 304, 310, 320, 330, 332, 343; and capitalism, 317–318; and color-blindness, 129–136; institutional, 316–317; and personhood, 132–133, 143, 178; and poverty, 142; racist ideology, 306, 310, 317; reverse, 243; and white backlash, 190, 246–247, 287, 329

Radicalism, 79, 305, 307, 308, 316, 321; the radical King, 57

Rage, 115, 120, 190, 191, 310–312, 326

Randolph, A. Philip, 82, 96, 192, 243

Ransby, Barbara, 207, 208, 209, 211, 222

Rauschenbusch, Walter, 53, 136

Rawls, John, 10, 40, 49, 76, 144, 146, 148, 151, 271, 283

Realism, 80, 87–101, 135–136, 164, 301, 304, 305

Rebellion, 65, 87, 261, 292, 306, 308, 310, 321, 326, 329; obligation to rebel, 63; slave rebellion, 21, 65

Reconciliation, 10, 82, 89–92, 113, 117, 270, 271, 273, 293, 298, 303, 346; Fellowship of Reconciliation

(FOR), 82; Journey of Reconciliation, 82; racial reconciliation, 14, 22, 79

Reconstruction, 32, 250; post-reconstruction, 133; Thirteenth, Fourteenth, and Fifteenth Amendments to the U.S. Constitution, 167, 280, 283

Redemption, 3, 14, 55, 88, 114, 115, 132, 136, 144, 212, 261, 271, 307, 343, 344, 347; redemptive suffering, 94, 125, 277, 280, 282, 336

Reed, Adolph, Jr., 330

Reform, 41, 75–77, 88, 107, 130, 158, 168, 200, 203, 231, 263, 314, 316, 320, 345

Religion, 9, 14, 28, 50, 138, 139, 140, 144, 147, 194, 199, 208, 295, 314, 325, 340, 342, 343; King's religious commitments, 49, 51, 53, 54, 341, 342, 343; religious discourse, 50; religious values, 50

Reparations, 2, 13, 237–239, 250, 321; reparative justice, 13, 129, 247, 306

Representation, 162, 177, 180, 210, 234, 242, 278, 299, 314, 345, 347; black elite, 333; political, 180, 242; racial, 210, 314

Representatives, 63, 150; representative democracy, 168; representatives of black communities, 297; union representatives, 197

Republicanism, 9, 10, 58, 59, 76, 77, 147, 293; republican freedom, 11, 67, 73, 146; republicans, 63, 64, 65, 152

Resentment, 14, 25, 61, 86, 87, 93, 95, 101, 105, 113, 119, 123, 152, 190, 191, 195, 305, 328

Resignation, 19, 20, 22, 30, 32, 92, 308, 346

Resistance, 22, 90, 218, 221, 227, 258–259, 260–262, 276–281, 300, 305, 308, 316, 319, 326, 328, 332, 336, 337, 340, 345, 347; vs. acquiescence (nonresistance), 22, 120–121, 258;

as infrapolitics, 220; passive, 121, 261, 263, 296; and riots, 115–116, 190–191, 244–245, 303–305; slave, 71–72, 212–213;

Respect, 6, 26, 32, 33, 34, 90, 94, 119, 122, 137, 141, 153, 155, 159, 162, 164, 167, 172, 174, 178, 181, 182, 200, 209, 212, 213, 216, 223, 270, 275, 308, 309, 311, 328; politics of respectability, 223; recognition-respect, 302; second-person respect, 322

Responsibility, 12, 13, 28, 86, 137, 149, 153, 154, 158, 159, 191, 198, 202, 233, 237, 246, 279, 320, 326, 331, 347, 348

Retaliation, 61–62, 85, 87, 89, 114–116, 216, 244, 260, 298, 299, 303, 323, 346, 347

Retribution, 11, 105–110, 116, 117, 245; retributive aggression, 116, 122; retributive anger, 111–114, 116; retributive emotions, 117; retributive punishment, 117; retributive violence, 124; retributive wish, 111, 115, 117, 123; retributivism, 107, 115

Revenge, 21, 22, 87, 96, 106, 218, 298

Revolt, 14, 21, 22, 244, 294, 303, 304, 321

Revolutionary justice, 105, 110, 111

Righteousness, 36, 48, 52, 145, 167, 170, 242, 245, 258, 262, 279, 301, 331, 332

Riots, 14, 15, 87, 115–116, 187, 190–191, 202, 244–245, 287, 290, 294, 295, 303–312, 322, 339, 348

"Rising Tide of Racial Consciousness, The," 128, 132, 135, 137, 141

Robeson, Paul, 333

Robinson, Amelia Boynton, 170, 172, 173

Robinson, Jackie, 214

Robinson, Jo Ann, 208, 221, 225, 226, 227

Rogers, Melvin, 147

Rousseau, Jean-Jacques, 5, 65, 66, 67

Royce, Josiah, 270

Rule of law, 270, 293, 297, 299, 300, 301, 304

Russell, Bertrand, 304

Rustin, Bayard, 82, 83, 96, 110, 127, 192, 285, 345

Rutherford, William A., 330, 386

Sacrifice, 1, 14, 28, 62, 84, 86, 117, 151, 158, 159, 178, 196, 207, 208, 209, 241, 251, 253, 270, 277, 279, 282, 284, 304, 333, 337; democratic, 292; ethos of, 298; nonsacrifice-ability, 146, 147, 151, 152, 153; self-sacrifice, 149, 271

Salt Satyagraha, 34, 44, 56

Santideva, 106

Satyagraha (truth force), 78, 98, 105, 121, 124, 261–263, 276, 280, 346

Schmitt, Carl, 293, 359n67

Secularity, 37, 38, 277; King's secular arguments, 147, 194, 199, 283; sacred and secular narrative impulses, 208; secular age, 282; secular formu-lation of the value of humanity, 173; secular moral views, 283; secular political philosophers, 38

Security, 96, 146, 252, 253, 258, 266, 298, 301, 302, 333

Segregation, 74–75, 88, 129, 134, 139, 140, 149, 152, 162, 166, 213, 240, 274, 280–284; and dignity, 174; and domination, 153–156; housing, 130; school, 130, 165. See also Desegregation

Self-defense, 14, 46, 71, 84, 95, 111, 117–121, 212, 213, 214, 240, 259, 260, 291, 294–301, 303, 311, 322, 347

Self-determination, 90, 263, 294, 295, 303, 322

Self-loathing, 41, 42, 45, 47, 55, 56

Self-purification, 11, 105, 121, 277

Self-respect, 19, 21, 22–31, 34, 73, 85–87, 94, 120, 121, 137, 171, 172, 211, 223, 272, 281, 297, 302, 310, 311, 314–316

Self-transformation, 36, 40, 41, 42, 48, 51, 53, 56, 301, 330

Selma, Alabama, 12, 19, 165, 168, 170, 172, 178, 271, 278

Separatism, 244; black, 315; cultural, 315; political, 322; racial, 89, 317, 321; sublimated, 322; territorial, 321

Servility, 11, 111, 171, 172, 214

Sexism, 12, 211, 232, 295; Coretta Scott King's stand against, 330; King's and SCLC's sexist practices, 227; King's, 205, 206, 211, 219; post-sexism, 132; SCLC's, 207, 208; sexist forms of inequality and leisure time distribution, 232; sexist ideology, 227; sexist occupational segregation, 232

Sexual harassment, 221, 391

Sexual renunciation (Brahmacharya), 125, 126

Shakur, Tupac, 214

Shame, 27, 39, 41, 42, 46, 48, 61, 88, 94, 99, 144, 165, 260, 261, 276, 278, 291, 302, 303, 305, 314, 315; civic shame, 45; unashamed, 143

Sharp, Gene, 80

Shusterman, Richard, 40

Six-Day War, 266

Slavery, 19, 13, 20, 27, 28, 53, 58–72, 85, 140, 162, 163, 182, 188, 189, 212, 229, 237–240, 242, 247–250, 274, 318, 333, 344; slave rebellion, 21, 65

Smiley, Glenn, 82

Social contract, 8, 156, 292, 293

Social gospel, 9, 45, 81, 93, 136, 137, 346

Socialism, 12, 188, 199, 200, 201, 330

Social movement, 1, 15, 195, 202, 208, 209, 210, 271, 272, 282, 291

Solidarity, 14, 86, 88, 97, 129, 179, 202, 206, 218, 230, 288, 291, 294, 303, 304, 315, 317, 318, 321, 333

Solomon, 43

Somebodiness, 28, 86, 119, 143, 177, 249, 315, 345

South Africa, 78, 111, 258, 259, 261, 262, 263, 276, 303, 345

South America, 65, 195, 250, 294

Southern Christian Leadership Conference (SCLC), 46, 83, 205, 207, 208, 210, 211, 227, 234, 235, 265, 283, 304, 323, 330, 343, 346

Spirituality, 199, 257, 261, 312; black spiritual integrity, 331, 335, 341; King's spiritual hopes, 9; spiritual affinity, 151, 156, 157, 160; spiritual apartness, 149; spiritual awakening, 149; spiritual blackout, 326, 330, 331, 334; spiritual exhaustion, 325; spiritual hope, 337; spiritual ills, 215; spiritual inadequacy, 105; spiritual life of the northern Negro church, 23; spiritual redemption, 307; spiritual struggles for freedom, 337; spiritual togetherness, 148, 149; spiritual wickedness, 145

Spokespersons, 10, 79, 83, 210, 303, 305

Stoicism, 125, 126; Gandhi as Stoic, 124; Stoic detachment, 123, 124; Stoics, 106, 110, 113

Storing, Herbert, 271, 280, 283

Stout, Jeffrey, 50

Strength to Love, 6, 276–277

Stride toward Freedom: The Montgomery Story, 6, 9, 19, 21, 22, 23, 24, 27, 28, 30, 31, 34, 80, 82, 86, 194, 211, 237, 239, 250, 251, 270, 272, 273, 277, 279, 284, 344, 345

Strikes, 97, 175, 193, 305, 327

Student Nonviolent Coordinating Committee (SNCC), 47, 82, 92, 207, 210, 283, 290, 291, 309, 327

Submission, 58, 85, 120, 122, 180, 182, 213, 219, 278, 296; acquiescent, 21, 22, 23, 24, 25, 26

Subordination, 49, 93, 100, 198, 203, 224, 249, 309, 314, 316, 317, 318

Suicide, 64, 65, 76, 219, 327

Sundquist, Eric J., 128, 131, 133, 134, 142

Sunstein, Cass, 3

Sympathy, 59, 87, 89, 95, 99, 120, 122, 206, 257, 300; sympathetic critics, 10, 285; sympathetic dialogue, 323

Taylor, Charles, 143

Taylor, Recy, 222

Technology, 195, 198, 200, 201, 228, 319, 330

Terrorism, 166, 176, 253, 264, 295, 320, 329; counterterrorism, 255, 266

Theology, 2, 4, 10, 37, 49, 54, 81, 82, 85, 129, 130, 132, 133, 136, 137, 138, 140–145, 147, 194, 252, 305, 328, 337, 342–344; King's theological commitments, 37, 49, 141, 194, 252, 343, 344

Thoreau, Henry David, 45

Thurman, Howard, 37, 79, 81, 82, 136, 137

Tillich, Paul, 139

Time, 20, 30, 32, 33, 34, 35, 236–252; leisure time, 198, 232; relationship to human agency, 20, 30, 33, 34; revolutionary times, 45; temporality, 19, 20, 34, 90, 129, 242, 246; vista of time, 43, 49

"Time to Break Silence, A" ("Beyond Vietnam"), 251, 256, 262, 265, 269–270, 272, 287–288

Tolstoy, Leo, 86, 88, 98

Torture, 60, 70, 77, 249, 253, 329

Tragedy, 45, 52, 139, 252, 348; man's tragic separation, 139; tragic, earthly striving, 44; tragic complexity of human motivation, 81; tragic decision, 263; tragic discipline of continual self-criticism, 52; tragic experimentalism, 44; tragic perfectionism, 42, 45; tragic recognition of reality, 265; tragic sense of inferiority, 28, 85; tragic sensibility, 42; tragic themes in King's works, 9, 36, 285, 301

Transportation, 96, 220, 221

Trumpet of Conscience (1968), 6, 115, 190, 271, 273, 285

Trust, 110, 127, 158, 323, 324, 331

Truth, 3, 46, 47, 52, 58, 121, 166, 198, 200, 220, 246, 247, 254, 261, 274, 275, 276, 278, 280, 283, 319, 323, 326, 328, 332, 333, 335, 341, 342, 346, 348

"Unfulfilled Dreams," 42–45, 47, 54, 55, 56, 325

Unions, 82, 130, 193, 194, 197, 201, 233, 234, 291

Utilitarianism, 40, 136, 147

Utopia, 144, 151, 157, 169, 199

Vietnam War, 13, 90, 119, 164, 190, 240, 244, 251, 254, 255, 256, 262–265, 269, 270, 278, 287, 288, 290, 303, 305, 327, 328

Violence, 22, 23, 25, 30, 55, 87–89, 112, 113, 117–120, 166, 190, 209, 214–219, 253, 258–263, 266, 311, 319–324; asymmetric, 295, 320; defensive, 84, 118, 212, 295–303; domestic, 231, 303; epistemic, 309; and hatred, 2–23, 26–28, 34; internal, 115, 260; interpersonal, 308, 311; intimate, 230; and masculinity, 212–214, 227; police, 76, 189–190, 308, 310, 339; political, 22, 89, 191,

199, 253, 254, 255, 257, 258, 259, 262, 263, 266, 295, 307; racial, 301, 322; racialized sexual, 222; retaliatory, 75, 115, 303; revolutionary, 199, 295, 313, 316–322; symbolic, 314; tactical, 89, 254, 259; white mob, 296, 299; white radical, 321

Virtue, 2, 40, 48, 49, 52, 66, 68, 136, 140, 162, 163, 172, 178, 216, 226, 232, 262, 280, 282, 283, 306, 344, 345

Voice, 43, 49, 52, 94, 97, 130, 180, 190, 230, 311, 326, 333, 342, 348

Voter registration, 225, 291

Voter suppression, 12, 163

Voting rights, 2, 12, 89, 161, 163–165, 170, 172, 179; right to vote, 10, 12, 74, 161, 162, 163, 164, 168–170, 173, 175, 179–183, 187, 193, 274, 348

Voting Rights Act of 1965, 12, 19, 164, 168, 169, 172, 182, 187, 241, 271, 285, 286, 313

Wages, 168, 180, 189, 194, 197, 201, 232, 233, 238, 317; paycheck, 30

Waldron, Jeremy, 167, 182

Walker, David, 64

Walker, Margaret Urban, 245

War, 8, 12, 13, 43, 63, 78, 84, 94, 117, 119, 198, 200, 217, 251–255, 258, 263, 265, 266, 279, 296; asymmetric warfare, 320; conventional warfare, 260; drone warfare, 255; English civil wars, 292; Gandhi on war, 118; global war on terrorism, 264; guerilla warfare, 295, 307, 319, 320, 321; just war, 2, 117, 119, 199, 259, 262, 329; mutually assured destruction, 320; nuclear war, 119, 254, 259, 260; race wars, 61; revolutionary war, 89; unjust war, 263, 264, 330; war crimes, 333, 334; warfare, 119; war's costs, 258

War in Afghanistan, 254, 257, 264

War on Drugs, 203

War on Poverty, 193, 202, 256, 263, 265

"War Resisters League" address, 258, 260, 261

War without Violence (Krishnalal Shridharani), 83

Washington, Booker T., 9, 19–22, 26, 27, 30–33; *Up from Slavery*, 27

Washington, George, 251, 333

Watts uprising, 87, 187, 190, 202, 240, 292, 306, 308

Wealth, 68, 89, 140, 176, 177, 191, 195, 196, 200, 201, 228, 233, 237, 238, 239, 247, 250, 252, 254, 275, 317, 318, 319, 328, 330, 336

Welfare, 2, 13, 107, 109, 110, 130, 131, 152, 191, 198, 202, 211, 229, 230, 233, 234, 300, 311

West, Cornel, 7, 51, 272, 341, 346

Where Do We Go from Here: Chaos or Community?, 6, 30, 34, 42, 45–47, 48, 130, 131, 137, 144, 192, 236, 239, 240, 241, 244, 246, 247, 248, 249, 251, 252, 273, 274, 285, 287, 341, 347

White supremacy, 7, 20, 21, 23, 93, 132, 206, 217, 238, 239, 241, 243, 249, 250, 290, 301, 309, 314, 330, 348

"Why Jesus Called a Man a Fool," 51, 52, 53

Why We Can't Wait, 6, 9, 19, 27, 30, 31, 32, 237, 247, 251

Williams, Bernard, 40

Williams, Preston, 239

Williams, Robert F., 213, 295, 296

Wilson, August, 335

Wilson, James Q., 284

Wisdom, 5, 6, 63, 207, 214, 253, 264, 281, 288, 297

Wolin, Sheldon, 41, 307

Women's Political Council of Montgomery, 223, 224, 225

Workers, 175, 176, 190, 192, 194, 196–198, 201, 202, 203, 226, 232, 243, 250, 277, 285, 310, 317, 327, 333

World War I, 24

World War II, 117, 119, 231, 258, 329